Lecture Notes in Computer Science 8352

Commenced Publication in 1973
Founding and Former Series Editors:
Gerhard Goos, Juris Hartmanis, and Jan van Lee

For further volumes:
http://www.springer.com/series/7410

Jean-Luc Danger · Mourad Debbabi
Jean-Yves Marion · Joaquin Garcia-Alfaro
Nur Zincir Heywood (Eds.)

Foundations and Practice of Security

6th International Symposium, FPS 2013
La Rochelle, France, October 21–22, 2013
Revised Selected Papers

 Springer

Editors
Jean-Luc Danger
Télécom ParisTech
Paris
France

Mourad Debbabi
Concordia University
Montreal, QC
Canada

Jean-Yves Marion
École des Mines
Nancy
France

Joaquin Garcia-Alfaro
Télécom SudParis
Evry
France

Nur Zincir Heywood
Dalhousie University
Halifax, NS
Canada

ISSN 0302-9743
ISBN 978-3-319-05301-1
DOI 10.1007/978-3-319-05302-8
Springer Cham Heidelberg New York Dordrecht London

ISSN 1611-3349 (electronic)
ISBN 978-3-319-05302-8 (eBook)

Library of Congress Control Number: 2014933577

LNCS Sublibrary: SL4 – Security and Cryptology

Printed on acid-free paper

Springer is part of Springer Science+Business Media (www.springer.com)

Preface

The 6th International Symposium on Foundations and Practice of Security (FPS 2013) was held at the Hotel Mercure, La Rochelle, France, during October 21–22, 2013. The symposium was organized by the Institut Mines-Télécom and sponsored by Télécom Bretagne and LabSTICC. FPS 2013 received 65 submissions, from countries all over the world. Each paper was reviewed by at least three committee members. The Program Committee selected 25 papers for presentation. The program was completed with two excellent invited talks given by Jean Goubault-Larrecq (LSV, ENS Cachan) and Bruno Crispo (DISI, University of Trento).

Many people contributed to the success of FPS 2013. First we would like to thank all the authors who submitted their research results. The selection was a challenging task and we sincerely thank all the Program Committee members, as well as the external reviewers, who volunteered to read and discuss the papers. We greatly thank the two general chairs, Frédéric Cuppens (Télécom Bretagne) and Ali A. Ghorbani (University of New Brunswick), for steering FPS 2013 and choosing the magnificent place of La Rochelle. We are also indebted to the two organizing committee chairs, Nora Cuppens-Boulahia (Télécom Bretagne) and Ghislaine Le Gall (Télécom Bretagne), for their great efforts with the symposium logistics, including the nice restaurant and the visit to La Rochelle. Finally, we also want to express our gratitude to the two publication chairs, Joaquin Garcia-Alfaro (Télécom SudParis) and Nur Zincir Heywood (Dalhousie University), and the webmaster Said Oulmakhzoune (Télécom Bretagne), for the great work they provided in programming, editing the proceedings, and managing the informations on the website.

As security becomes an essential issue in information and communication technologies, there is a growing need to develop efficient methods to analyze and design systems providing a high level of security and privacy. We hope the articles in this proceedings volume will be valuable for your professional activities in this area.

December 2013

Jean-Luc Danger
Mourad Debbabi
Jean-Yves Marion

Organization

General Chairs

Frédéric Cuppens   Telecom Bretagne, France
Ali A. Ghorbani   University of New Brunswick, Canada

Program Chairs

Jean-Luc Danger   Telecom Paristech, France
Mourad Debbabi   Concordia University, Canada
Jean-Yves Marion   Mines de Nancy, France

Organizing Chairs

Nora Cuppens-Boulahia   Telecom Bretagne, France
Ghislaine Le Gall   Telecom Bretagne, France

Publication Chairs

Joaquin Garcia-Alfaro   Telecom SudParis, France
Nur Zincir Heywood   Dalhousie University, Canada

Webmaster

Said Oulmakhzoune   Telecom Bretagne, France

Program Committee

Diala Abihaidar   Dar Al Hekma College, Saudi Arabia
Carlisle Adams   Ottawa University, Canada
Kamel Adi   Université du Quebec en Outaouais, Canada
Gildas Avoine   Catholic University of Louvain, Belgium
Michel Barbeau   Carleton University, Canada
Guillaume Bonfante   Université de Lorraine, France
Jordi Castella-Roca   Rovira i Virgili University, Spain
Ana Cavalli   Telecom SudParis, France
Frédéric Cuppens   Telecom Bretagne, France

Lena Wiese   University of Göttingen, Germany
Nicola Zannone   Eindhoven University of Technology, The Netherlands
Mohammad Zulkernine   Queen's University, Canada

Additional Reviewers

Alessio Di Mauro
Tongjie Zhang
Mahavir Jhawar
Yang Li
Shivam Bhasin
Asem Kitana
Elli Androulaki
Samiha Ayed
Mohammad Hajiabadi
Benedikt Schmidt
Liangfeng Zhang
Fatih Turkmen

Sherif Saad
Cedric Lauradoux
Anil Kurmus
Laurent Mounier
Yosr Jarraya
Isabella Mastroeni
Eugenia Papagiannakopoulou
Samir Ouchani
Maria Koukovini
Clara Bertolissi
Martin Gagne

Contents

Resilience

Intrusion Detection

Keynote Address

On the Efficiency of Mathematics
in Intrusion Detection: The NetEntropy Case

Jean Goubault-Larrecq[1][✉] and Julien Olivain[1,2]

[1] ENS Cachan, Cachan, France
[2] INRIA, Valbonne, France
{goubault,olivain}@lsv.ens-cachan.fr

Abstract. NetEntropy is a plugin to the Orchids intrusion detection tool that is originally meant to detect some subtle attacks on implementations of cryptographic protocols such as SSL/TLS. Netentropy compares the sample entropy of a data stream to a known profile, and flags any significant variation. Our point is to stress the *mathematics* behind Netentropy: the reason of the rather incredible precision of Netentropy is to be found in *theorems* due to Paninski and Moddemeijer.

Keywords: Sample entropy · Paninski estimator · Malware · Intrusion detection

1 Introduction

In 2006, we described a tool, NetEntropy, whose goal is to detect subverted cryptographic network flows [16]. We had initially developed it as a plugin to the Orchids intrusion detection tool [8] to help detect attacks such as [11] or [22] where network traffic is encrypted and therefore cannot be inspected—unless we rely on key escrows [12, Sect. 13.8.3], but NetEntropy is much easier to install and use.

What NetEntropy does is estimate whether a source of bytes is sufficiently close to a random, uniformly distributed source of bytes. Encrypted data, random keys and nonces, compressed data should qualify as close. Plain text, but also shellcodes, viruses and even polymorphic viruses should not.

To this end, NetEntropy computes the sample entropy H_N of the source, and compares it to an estimator $\hat{H}_N$—a good enough approximation of what the average value of H_N should be if the source were indeed drawn at random, uniformly. We use the *Paninski estimator* (to be introduced later), and show that it gives an extraordinarily precise statistical test of non-randomness.

The purpose of this paper is to stress the mathematics behind this extraordinary precision. Before we had researched the mathematics, the best we could say was that NetEntropy worked well in practice, and this was supported by experiments. How well it fared was beyond us: it was only when we discovered the theorems in the literature that we realized that our entropy estimation technique was in fact precise up to levels we had never even dreamed of.

J.-L. Danger et al. (Eds.): FPS 2013, LNCS 8352, pp. 3–16, 2014.
DOI: 10.1007/978-3-319-05302-8_1, © Springer International Publishing Switzerland 2014

Outline. We start by reviewing the attack that led us into inventing NetEntropy in Sect. 2. As we said, NetEntropy evaluates the sample entropy of a flow of bytes. We review the known estimators of sample entropy in Sect. 3, and justify our choice of the Paninski estimator. In Sect. 4, we attack the central twin questions of this paper: how do we compute the value $H_N(\mathcal{U})$ the sample entropy should have on a uniformly distributed random N-byte flow? (Sect. 4.1) and how far away from $H_N(\mathcal{U})$ should the sample entropy be for us to conclude that the flow is not random? (Sect. 4.2) We shall see that entropy-based detection is extremely precise, already for small values of N (Sect. 4.3). We conclude in Sect. 5.

2   The mod_ssl Attack

Our primary example will be the mod_ssl attack [11]. Similar attacks include the SSH CRC32 attack [22].

The mod_ssl attack uses a heap overflow vulnerability during the key exchange (handshake) phase of SSL v2 to execute arbitrary code on the target machine. A normal (simplified) execution of this protocol is tentatively pictured in Fig. 1, left. Flow direction is pictured by arrows, from left (client) to right (server) or conversely. The order of messages is from top to bottom. The handshake phase consists of the top six messages. Encrypted traffic then follows. We have given an indication of the relative level of entropy by levels of shading, from light (clear text, low entropy) to dark gray (encrypted traffic, random numbers, high entropy).

Encrypted traffic is (using state-of-the-art cryptographic algorithms) indistinguishable from random traffic. The byte entropy of a random sequence of characters is 8 bits per byte, at least in the limit $N \to +\infty$. On the other hand, the byte entropy of a non-encrypted sequence of characters is much lower.

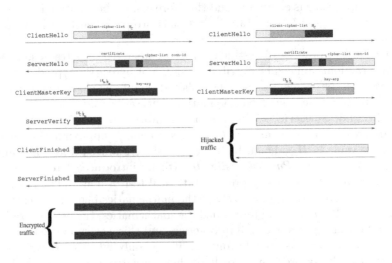

Fig. 1. Normal SSL v2 session (*left*), hijacked (*right*)

According to [4, Sect. 6.4], the byte entropy of English text is no greater than 2.8, and even 0-order approximations do not exceed 4.26.

Shellcodes that are generally used with the mod_ssl attack hijack one session, and reuse the https connection to offer basic terminal facilities to the remote attacker. We detect this by realizing that the byte entropy of the flow on this connection, which should tend to 8, remains low. We can therefore detect the attack when we see the final payload in clear. Since the shellcode itself, whose entropy is low, is sent in lieu of a session key, the entropy is already low in some parts of the key exchange. This can be used to detect the attack even if the shellcode does not communicate over the https channel, which is also common.

While NetEntropy was meant to detect attacks, it can also be used, and has been used, for other purposes, typically network policy enforcement: Skype detection [5], detecting encrypted botnet traffic or encrypted malwares themselves [10,19,23]. Entropy checking had already been used for traffic analysis before [7], and our contribution is to show how extraordinarily precise this technique is even in undersampled situations. In particular it is much more precise than distribution identification tools such as PAYL [21]: we only seek to compare a byte stream to *uniform* random byte streams, and this is a setting where a mathematical miracle happens (Moddemeijer's Theorem in the so-called degenerate case, see Sect. 4.2).

Entropy checking can also be used as a randomness test, e.g., in checking the adequacy of pseudo-random number generators to cryptographic applications [20, 2.12]. In this setting as well as in ours, it has a number of advantages over other approaches. First, it is *fast* and requires *little memory*: we do not need to store the data to test for randomness, only the current distribution (256 integer registers). Second, it is extremely *precise*, as we shall show and demonstrate. Finally, it can be computed *online*, that is, as the input data come in, which makes it ideal in our network-sniffing situation. In cryptographic applications, it would still be fair to complement entropy-checking with other tests: see [9] for a theory of statistical tests suited to the domain.

3 Sample Entropy and Estimators

First, a note on notation. We take log to denote base 2 logarithms. Entropies will be computed using log, and will be measured in *bits*. The notation ln is reserved for natural logarithms.

Let w be a word of length N, over an alphabet $\Sigma = \{0, 1, \ldots, m-1\}$. We may count the number n_i of occurrences of each letter $i \in \Sigma$. The *frequency* f_i of i in w is then n_i/N. The *sample entropy* of w is:

$$\hat{H}_N^{MLE}(w) = -\sum_{i=0}^{m-1} f_i \log f_i$$

(The superscript MLE is for *maximum likelihood estimator*.) The formula is close to the notion of entropy of a random source, but the two should not be confused. Given a probability distribution $p = (p_i)_{i \in \Sigma}$ over Σ, the *entropy* of p is

$$H(p) = -\sum_{i=0}^{m-1} p_i \log p_i$$

In the case where each character is drawn uniformly and independently, $p_i = 1/m$ for every i, and $H(p) = \log m$.

It is hard not to confuse H and $\hat{H}_N^{MLE}$, in particular because a property known as the asymptotic equipartition property (AEP, [4, Chap. 3]) states that, indeed, $\hat{H}_N^{MLE}(w)$ converges in probability to $H(p)$ when the length N of w tends to $+\infty$, as soon as each character of w is drawn independently according to the distribution p. In the case of the uniform distribution, this means that $\hat{H}_N^{MLE}(w)$ tends to $\log m$ (= 8, for bytes).

However, we are *not* interested in the limit of $\hat{H}_N^{MLE}(w)$ when N tends to infinity, essentially because we would like to flag an anomalous value of the sample entropy as soon as possible, and also because the actual messages we monitor may be short: the encrypted payload is only a few dozen bytes long in short-lived SSH connections, for example. In practice, we only compute the sample entropy for words w of length $N \leq N_{\max}$. $N_{\max} = 65\,536$ is sufficient in the intended intrusion detection applications.

Let us plot the average $\hat{H}_N^{MLE}$ of $\hat{H}_N^{MLE}(w)$ when w is drawn uniformly among words of size N, for $m = 256$, and N ranging from 1 to 4 096 (Fig. 2). The x-axis has logarithmic, not linear scale. ($\hat{H}_N^{MLE}$ was evaluated by sampling over words generated using the `/dev/urandom` source.) The value of $H(p)$ is shown as the horizontal line $y = 8$. As theory predicts, when $N \gg m$, typically when N is of the order of roughly at least 10 times as large as m, then $\hat{H}_N^{MLE} \sim H(p)$.

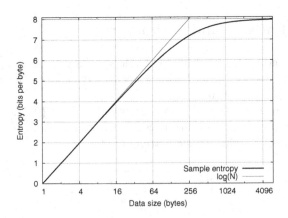

Fig. 2. Average sample entropy $\hat{H}_N^{MLE}(w)$ of words w of size N

On the other hand, when N is small (roughly at least 10 times as small as m), then $\hat{H}_N^{MLE} \sim \log N$. Considering the orders of magnitude of N and m cited above, clearly we are interested in the regions where $N \sim m$... precisely where $\hat{H}_N^{MLE}$ is far from $H(p)$.

Let us turn to the mathematical literature. The field of research most connected to this work is called *entropy estimation* [2], and the fact that $N \sim m$ or $N < m$ is often characterized as the fact that the probability p is *undersampled*. Note that for, say, $N = 32$ and $m = 256$, there is absolutely no chance we may have seen all bytes! This is as far as we can imagine to classical statistical experiments, with large sample sets. Despite this, we shall still be able to obtain informative statistical results.

In classical statistics, our problem is often described as follows. Take objects that can be classified into m *bins* (our bins are just bytes) according to some probability distribution p. Now take N *samples*, and try to decide whether the entropy of p is $\log m$ (or, in general, the entropy of a given, fixed probability distribution) just by looking at the samples. The papers [1,17,18] are particularly relevant to our work, since they attempt to achieve this precisely when the probability is undersampled, as in our case.

The problem that Paninski tries to solve [17,18] is finding an *estimator* $\hat{H}_N$ of $H(p)$, that is, a statistical quantity, computed over randomly generated N-character words, which gives some information about the value of $H(p)$. Particularly interesting estimators are the *unbiased estimators*, that is those such that $E(\hat{H}_N) = H(p)$, where E denotes mathematical expectation (i.e., the average of all $\hat{H}_N(w)$ over all N-character words w).

Our task is:

- first, find an unbiased estimator $\hat{H}_N$ (or one with a small bias): we shall do this in Sect. 4.1;
- second, evaluate the confidence intervals (how close to $\hat{H}_N$ should $H_N(w)$ be for w be to be classified as random with, say, 95 % confidence?); we shall do this in Sect. 4.2.

The sample entropy $\hat{H}_N^{MLE}$, introduced above, is an estimator, sometimes called the *plug-in estimate*, or *maximum likelihood estimator* [17]. As Fig. 2 demonstrates, it is biased, and the bias can in fact be rather large. So $\hat{H}_N^{MLE}$ does not fit our requirements for $\hat{H}_N$.

Comparing $\hat{H}_N^{MLE}$ to the entropy at the limit, $\log m$, is wrong, because $\hat{H}_N^{MLE}$ is biased for any fixed N. Nonetheless, we may introduce a correction to the estimator $\hat{H}_N^{MLE}$. To this end, we must estimate the bias. Historically, the first estimation of the bias is the Miller-Madow bias correction [13] $(\hat{m} - 1)/(2N \ln 2)$, where $\hat{m} = |\{i \mid f_i \neq 0\}|$ is the number of characters that do appear at all in our N-character string w, yielding the *Miller-Madow estimator*:

$$\hat{H}_N^{MM}(w) = \hat{H}_N^{MLE}(w) + \frac{\hat{m} - 1}{2N \ln 2} = -\sum_{i=0}^{m-1} f_i \log f_i + \frac{\hat{m} - 1}{2N \ln 2}.$$

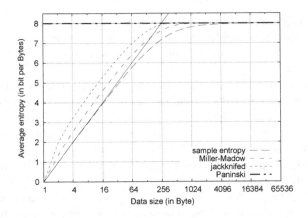

Fig. 3. Sample entropy estimators

Another one is the *jackknifed MLE* [6]:

$$\hat{H}_N^{JK}(w) = N\,\hat{H}_N^{MLE}(w) - \frac{N-1}{N}\sum_{j=1}^{N}\hat{H}_N^{MLE}(w_{-j})$$

where w_{-j} denotes the $(N-1)$-character word obtained from w by removing the jth character. While all these corrected estimators indeed correct the $1/N$ term from biases at the limit $N \to +\infty$, they are still far from being unbiased when N is small: see Fig. 3, where the closer to the constant curve with y value $\log m = 8$ the better.

In the case that interests us here, i.e., when p is the uniform distribution over m characters, an exact asymptotic formula for the bias is known as a function of $c > 0$ when N and m both tend to infinity and N/m tends to c: the result is due to Liam Paninski [17, Theorem 3]. The corrected estimator is:

$$\hat{H}_N^P(w) = \hat{H}_N^{MLE}(w) - \log c + e^{-c}\sum_{j=1}^{+\infty}\frac{c^{j-1}}{(j-1)!}\log j \qquad (1)$$

where the correction $-\log c + e^{-c}\sum_{j=1}^{+\infty}\frac{c^{j-1}}{(j-1)!}\log j$ is the *Paninski bias*.

While the formula is exact only when N and m both grow to infinity, in practice $m = 256$ is large enough for this formula to be relevant. On our experiments, the difference between the average of $\hat{H}_N^P(w)$ over random experiments and $\log m = 8$ is between -0.0002 and 0.0051 for $N \leq 100\ 000$, and tends to 0 as N tends to infinity. (On Fig. 3, it is impossible to distinguish $\hat{H}_N^P$—the "Paninski" curve—from the constant curve with y-value $\log m = 8$.) $\hat{H}_N^P$ is an estimator of $H(p)$ with a very small bias, when p is the uniform distribution.

4 Evaluating the Average Sample Entropy

Instead of trying to compute a correct estimator of the actual entropy $H(p)$, which is, as we have seen, a rather difficult problem, we turn the problem around.

Let $H_N(p)$ be the N-*truncated entropy* of the distribution $p = (p_i)_{i \in \Sigma}$. This is defined as the average of the sample entropy $\hat{H}_N^{MLE}(w)$ over all words w *of length N*, drawn at random according to p. In other words, this is what we plotted in Fig. 2. A direct summation shows that

$$H_N(p) = \sum_{\substack{n_0,\ldots,n_{m-1} \in \mathbb{N} \\ n_0 + \cdots + n_{m-1} = N}} \left[\binom{N}{n_0, \ldots, n_{m-1}} p_0^{n_0} \cdots p_{m-1}^{n_{m-1}} \times \left(\sum_{i=0}^{m-1} -\frac{n_i}{N} \log \frac{n_i}{N} \right) \right]$$

where $\binom{N}{n_0,\ldots,n_{m-1}} = \frac{N!}{n_0!\ldots n_{m-1}!}$ is the multinomial coefficient.

When p is the uniform distribution $\mathcal{U}$ (where $p_i = 1/m$ for all i), we obtain the formula

$$H_N(\mathcal{U}) = \frac{1}{m^N} \sum_{\substack{n_0,\ldots,n_{m-1} \in \mathbb{N} \\ n_0 + \cdots + n_{m-1} = N}} \left[\binom{N}{n_0, \ldots, n_{m-1}} \times \left(\sum_{i=0}^{m-1} -\frac{n_i}{N} \log \frac{n_i}{N} \right) \right] \quad (2)$$

By construction, $\hat{H}_N^{MLE}$ is then an unbiased estimator of H_N. Our strategy to detect non-random text is then to take the flow w, of length N, to compute $\hat{H}_N^{MLE}(w)$, and to compare it to $H_N(\mathcal{U})$. If the two quantities are significantly apart, then w is not random.

Not only is this easier to achieve than estimating the actual entropy $H(p)$, we shall see (Sect. 4.2) that this provides us much narrower confidence intervals, that is, much more precise estimates of non-randomness.

For example, if w is the word

```
0x55 0x89 0xe5 0x83 0xec 0x58 0x83 0xe4
0xf0 0xb8 0x00 0x00 0x00 0x00 0x29 0xc4
0xc7 0x45 0xf4 0x00 0x00 0x00 0x00 0x83
0xec 0x04 0xff 0x35 0x60 0x99 0x04 0x08
```

of length $N = 32$ (so $N \ll m = 256$, a very much undersampled situation), then $H_N(\mathcal{U}) = 4.87816$, to 5 decimal places. Since 3.97641 is significantly less than 4.87816 (about 1 bit less information), one is tempted to conclude that w above is *not* random. (This is indeed true: this w is the first 32 bytes of the code of the **main()** function of an ELF executable, compiled under **gcc**. However, we cannot yet conclude, until we compute confidence intervals, see Sect. 4.2.)

Consider, on the other hand, the word

```
0x85 0x01 0x0e 0x03 0xe9 0x48 0x33 0xdf
0xb8 0xad 0x52 0x64 0x10 0x03 0xfe 0x21
0xb0 0xdd 0x30 0xeb 0x5c 0x1b 0x25 0xe7
0x35 0x4e 0x05 0x11 0xc7 0x24 0x88 0x4a
```

This has sample entropy $\hat{H}_N(w) = 4.93750$. This is close enough to $H_N(\mathcal{U}) = 4.87816$ that we may want to conclude that this w is close to random. And indeed, this w is the first 32 bytes of a text message encrypted with **gpg**. Comparatively, the entropy of the first 32 bytes of the corresponding plaintext is only 3.96814.

Note that, provided a deviation of roughly 1 bit from the predicted value $H_N(\mathcal{U})$ is significant, the $\hat{H}_N^{MLE}$ estimator allows us to detect deviations from random-looking messages extremely quickly: using just 32 characters in the examples above. Actual message sizes in SSL or SSH vary from a few dozen bytes (usually for small control messages) to a few kilobytes (user data), with a maximum of 64 KB.

4.1   Computing $H_N(\mathcal{U})$

There are basically three ways to compute $H_N(\mathcal{U})$. (Recall that we need this quantity to compare $\hat{H}_N^{MLE}(w)$ to.) The first is to use Eq. (2). However, this quickly becomes unmanageable as m and N grow.

A much better solution is to recall Eq. (1). Another way of reading it is to say that, for each constant c, when N and m tend to infinity in such a way that N/m is about c, then $H_N(\mathcal{U})$ is equal to $\log m$ minus the Paninski bias, namely:

$$H_N(\mathcal{U}) = \log m + \log c - e^{-c} \sum_{j=1}^{+\infty} \frac{c^{j-1}}{(j-1)!} \log j + o(1). \qquad (3)$$

As we have seen, when $m = 256$, this approximation should give a good approximation of $H_N(\mathcal{U})$. In fact, this approximation is surprisingly close to the actual value of $H_N(\mathcal{U})$. The $o(1)$ error term is plotted in Fig. 4. It is never more than 0.004 bit, and decreases quickly as N grows. The series (3) converges quickly, too: the sum stabilizes after a number of iterations that is roughly linear in c. We implemented this using 64-bit IEEE floating-point numbers, and never

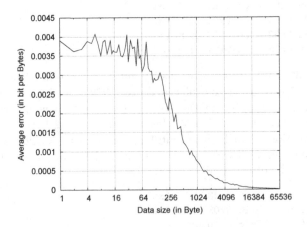

Fig. 4. Error term in (3)

needed more than 398 iterations for $N \leq 65\ 536$ ($c = 256$). This grew to 415 iterations with 96-bit IEEE floating-point numbers, and to 786 iterations with 512-bit floating-point numbers using the arbitrary precision floating-point arithmetic library MPFR [15]. Comparing the values of the Paninski bias computed with 64-bit and 512-bit numbers reveals a relative difference that never exceeds $1.1\ 10^{-11}$, which is negligible: 64-bit computations are enough.

The third method to evaluate $H_N(\mathcal{U})$ is the standard Monte-Carlo method consisting in drawing enough words w of length N at random, and taking the average of $\hat{H}_N(w)$ over all these words w. This is how we evaluated $H_N(\mathcal{U})$ in Fig. 2, and how we defined the reference value of $H_N(\mathcal{U})$ which we compared to (3) in Fig. 4. To be precise, we took the average over 100 000 samples for $N < 65\ 536$, taking all values of N below 16, taking one value in 2 below 32, one value in 4 below 64, ..., and one value in 4 096 below 65 536. The spikes are statistical variations that one may attribute to randomness in the source. Note that they are in general smaller than the error term $o(1)$ in (3).

In the end, the fastest implementation is just by using a pre-filled table of values of $H_N(\mathcal{U})$ for values of $c = N/m = N/256$, with N ranging from 0 to $N_{\max}$. One can then use any of the above three methods to fill the table. With $N_{\max} = 65\ 536$, this requires a table that takes less than one megabyte. We can also save some memory by exploiting the fact that $H_N(\mathcal{U})$ is a smooth and increasing [17, Proposition 3] function of c, storing only a few well-chosen points and extrapolating; and by using the fact that values of N that are not multiples of 4 or even 8 are hardly ever needed.

4.2   Confidence Intervals

Evaluating $\hat{H}_N^{MLE}(w)$ only gives a statistical indication of how close we are to $H_N(\mathcal{U})$. Recall our first example, where w was the first 32 bytes of the code of the `main()` function of some ELF executable. We found $\hat{H}_N^{MLE}(w) = 3.97641$, while $H_N(\mathcal{U}) = 4.87816$. What is the actual probability that w of length $N = 32$ is non-random when $\hat{H}_N^{MLE}(w) = 3.97641$ and $H_N(\mathcal{U}) = 4.87816$?

It is again time to turn to the literature. According to [1, Sect. 4.1], when N tends to $+\infty$, $\hat{H}_N^{MLE}$ is asymptotically Gaussian, in the sense that $\sqrt{N} \ln 2 (\hat{H}_N^{MLE} - H)$ tends to a Gaussian distribution with mean 0 and variance $\sigma_N^2 = Var\{-\log p(X)\}$. In non-degenerate cases (i.e., when $\sigma_N^2 > 0$), the expectation of $(\hat{H}_N^{MLE} - H)^2$ is $\Theta(1/N)$, so the standard deviation will be proportional to $1/\sqrt{N}$... but precisely, the $p = \mathcal{U}$ case *is* degenerate.

As we shall see below, this is actually good news! In the degenerate case, the standard deviation will be proportional to $1/N$ indeed, which goes to zero much faster than $1/\sqrt{N}$.

This means that the confidence intervals will be remarkably small, of the order of $1/N$. Said differently, this means that to reach small confidence intervals, we shall only need very few bytes. Let us see how much. Much less is known about the variance of $\hat{H}_N^{MLE} = \hat{H}_N^{MLE}$ when $N \sim m$ or $N < m$ than about its bias. One useful inequality is that the variance of $\hat{H}_N^{MLE}$ is bounded from

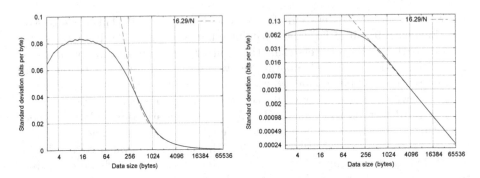

Fig. 5. Standard deviation of $\hat{H}_N^{MLE}(w)$ (linear scale left, log scale right)

above by $\log^2 N/N$ [1, Remark (iv)], but this is extremely conservative. An improved bound is due to Moddemeijer [14, Eq. (12)]: the variance of $\hat{H}_N^{MLE}$ evolves as $\sigma_N^2 + \frac{m-1}{2N^2 \ln^2 2}$ when $N \to +\infty$. In degenerate cases, where $\sigma_N = 0$, this means that the statistical standard deviation $SD(\hat{H}_N^{MLE})$ of $\hat{H}_N^{MLE}(w)$, on random words w of length N, is asymptotically equal to $\sqrt{\frac{m-1}{2}} \frac{1}{\ln 2}$ times $1/N$. With $m = 256$, this is about $16.29/N$. To confirm this, we have estimated the standard deviation of $\hat{H}_N$ by a Monte-Carlo method, see Fig. 5. The curve on the right is the same as the one on the left, except the y-axis is in log scale, showing the relation between $SD(\hat{H}_N^{MLE})$ and $16.29/N$ more clearly.

For typical sizes of 1, 2, 4, and 8 KB, the standard deviation $SD(\hat{H}_N^{MLE})$ is 0.016, 0.008, 0.004, and 0.002 bit respectively. This is extremely small.

Let us estimate percentiles, again by a Monte-Carlo method, see Fig. 6: the y values are given so that a proportion of all words w tested falls within $y \times SD(\hat{H}_N^{MLE})$ of the average value of $\hat{H}_N^{MLE}$. The proportions go from 50 %

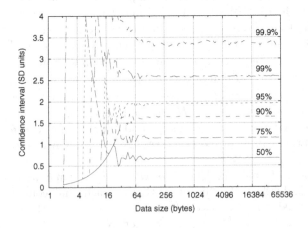

Fig. 6. Percentiles

(bottom) to 99.9 % (top). Unless $N \leq 16$ (which is unrealistic), our estimate of $\hat{H}_N^{MLE}$ is exact with an error of at most $4 \times SD(\hat{H}_N^{MLE})$, with probability 99.9 %. $4SD(\hat{H}_N)$ is at most $64/N$, and in any case no larger than 0.32 bit (for words of about 16 characters).

Let's return to our introductory question: What is the actual probability that w of length $N = 32$ is non-random when $\hat{H}_N^{MLE}(w) = 3.97641$ and $H_N(\mathcal{U}) = 4.87816$? For $N = 32$, $SD(\hat{H}_N^{MLE})$ is about maximal, and equal to 0.081156. So we are at least 99.9 % sure that the entropy of a 32-byte word with characters drawn uniformly is $4.87816 \pm 4 \times 0.081156$, i.e., between 4.55353 and 5.20279: if $\hat{H}_N^{MLE}(w) = 3.97641$, we can safely bet that w is *not* random.

Note that $N = 32$ is not only a terribly undersampled case, but is also close to the worst possible case we could dream of (see Fig. 5). Still, $\hat{H}_N^{MLE}$ is already a reliable estimator of randomness here.

For sizes 1, 2, 4, and 8 KB, and a confidence level of 99.9 % again, $\hat{H}_N^{MLE}$ is precise up to ± 0.0625, ± 0.0313, ± 0.0156, and ± 0.0078 bit respectively. These are remarkably small values.

4.3   Practical Experiments

We report some practical experiments in Fig. 7, on non-cryptographic sources. This gives an idea of the amount of redundancy in common data sources. The entropy of binary executables (ELF format, i386 architecture) was evaluated under Linux and FreeBSD by collecting all .text sections of all files in /bin and /usr/bin. Similarly, the entropy of shell scripts was computed by collecting all shell scripts on the root volume of Linux and FreeBSD machines (detected by the file command). Terminal activity was collected by monitoring a dozen telnet connections (port 23) on tcp from a given machine with various activity, such as text editing, manual reading, program compilation and execution (about 1 MB of data). As far as e-mail is concerned, the measured entropy corresponds

Data source	Entropy (bits/byte)	
	$\hat{H}_N^{MLE}$	H_N
Binary executable (elf-i386)	6.35	8.00
Shell scripts	5.54	8.00
Terminal activity	4.98	8.00
1 Gbyte e-mail	6.12	8.00
1KB X.509 certificate (PEM)	5.81	7.80 ± 0.061
700B X.509 certificate (DER)	6.89	7.70 ± 0.089
130B bind shellcode	5.07	6.56 ± 0.24
38B standard shellcode	4.78	5.10 ± 0.28
73B polymorphic shellcode	5.69	5.92 ± 0.27
Random 1 byte NOPs (i386)	5.71	7.99

Fig. 7. Sample entropy of some common non-random sources

to 3 years of e-mail on the second author's account. These correspond to large volumes of data (large N), so that H_N is 8 to 2 decimal places, and confidence intervals are ridiculously small.

The next experiments were made on smaller pieces of data. Accordingly, we have given H_N in the form $H \pm \delta$, where δ is the 99.9 % confidence interval. Note that X.509 certificates are definitely classified as non-random. We have also tested a few shellcodes, because, first, as we have seen in Fig. 1, it is interesting to detect when some random piece of data is replaced by a shellcode, and second, because detecting shellcodes this way is challenging. Indeed, shellcodes are typically short, so that H_N is significantly different from 8. More importantly, modern polymorphic and metamorphic virus technologies, adapted to shellcodes, make them look more random. (In fact, the one we use *is* encrypted, except for a very short prolog.) While the first two shellcodes in Fig. 7 are correctly classified as non-random (even a very short 38 byte non-polymorphic shellcode), the last, polymorphic shellcode is harder to detect. The 99.9 % confidence interval for being random is $[5.65, 6.19]$: the sample entropy of the 73 byte polymorphic shellcode is at the left end of this interval. The 99 % confidence interval is 5.92 ± 0.19, i.e., $[5.73, 6.11]$: with 99 % confidence, this shellcode is correctly classified as non-random. In practice, shellcodes are usually preceded with padding, typically long sequences of the letter A or the hexadecimal value 0x90 (the No-OPeration i386 instruction), which makes the entropy decrease drastically, so the examples above are a worst-case scenario. Detecting that the random key-arg field of Fig. 1 (left) was replaced by a shellcode (right) is therefore feasible.

Another worst-case scenario in polymorphic viruses and shellcodes is given by mutation, whereby some specific instructions, such as nop, are replaced with other instructions with the same effect, at random. This fools pattern-matching detection engines, and also increases entropy. However, as the last line shows on a large amount of random substitutes for nop on the i386 architecture, this makes the sample entropy culminate at a rather low value compared to 8.

All in all, $\hat{H}_N^{MLE}$ is an extraordinarily precise estimator of $H_N(\mathcal{U})$, even in very undersampled cases. If you didn't believe the mathematics, we hope that these experimental data have convinced you. However, in the end, it is the mathematics which give you the right estimator (the Paninski estimator) and the bounds to expect of confidence intervals (Moddemeijer's theorem).

5   Conclusion

We have described the basic principles behind NetEntropy, a tool that we originally designed so as to detect attacks against cryptographic network flows, but can also be used for traffic analysis and malware detection. NetEntropy compares the sample entropy of the flow to an estimator $\hat{H}_N^{MLE}$ with a very small bias, and signals any deviation above some threshold of the order of $16.29/N$.

The bias of the Paninski estimator $\hat{H}_N^{MLE}$ is extremely small, and the threshold $16.29N$ is minute, which allows us to correctly conclude that certain hard-to-qualify sources such as some polymorphic shellcodes are definitely non-random, even after having read only a few bytes (73 in our example). This is extraordinary: statistically, we are *undersampling* a probability distribution, to the point that we cannot have possibly seen all possible bytes; still, we can conclude.

The key to the miracle is *mathematics*: here, Paninski's estimator and Moddemeijer's theorem. In practical security, mathematics is often seen as an intellectual's game, which the rest of us don't need. We hope to have made a convincing statement that mathematics, as in most sciences, is essential.

Acknowledgments. Thanks to Mathieu Baudet, Elie Bursztein and Stéphane Boucheron for judicious advice. This work was partially supported by the RNTL Project DICO, and the ACI jeunes chercheurs "Sécurité informatique, protocoles cryptographiques et détection d'intrusions".

Availability

NetEntropy is a free open source project. It is available under the CeCILL2 license [3]. The project homepage can be found at http://www.lsv.ens-cachan.fr/net-entropy/.

References

1. Antos, A., Kontoyiannis, I.: Convergence properties of functional estimates for discrete distributions. Random Struct. Algorithm. **19**, 163–193 (2001)
2. Bialek, W., Nemenman, I. (eds.): Estimation of entropy and information of undersampled probability distributions-theory, algorithms, and applications to the neural code. In: Satellite of the Neural Information Processing Systems Conference (NIPS'03), Whistler, Canada (2003). http://www.menem.com/ilya/pages/NIPS03/
3. CEA, CNRS, INRIA: Cecill free software license agreement (2005). http://www.cecill.info/licences/Licence_CeCILL_V2-en.html
4. Cover, T.M., Thomas, J.A.: Elements of Information Theory. Wiley, New York (1991)
5. Dorfinger, P., Panholzer, G., Trammell, B., Pepe, T.: Entropy-based traffic filtering to support real-time skype detection. In: Proceedings of the 6th International Wireless Communications and Mobile Computing Conference (IWCMC'10), pp. 747–751. ACM, New York (2010)
6. Efron, B., Stein, C.: The jackknife estimate of variance. Ann. Stat. **9**, 586–596 (1981)
7. Fu, X., Graham, B., Bettati, R., Zhao, W.: Active traffic analysis attacks and countermeasures. In: Proceedings of the 2nd IEEE International Conference Computer Networks and Mobile Computing, pp. 31–39 (2003)
8. Goubault-Larrecq, J., Olivain, J.: A smell of Orchids. In: Leucker, M. (ed.) RV 2008. LNCS, vol. 5289, pp. 1–20. Springer, Heidelberg (2008)
9. Lubicz, D.: On a classification of finite statistical tests. Adv. Math. Commun. **1**(4), 509–524 (2007)
10. Lyda, R., Hamrock, J.: Using entropy analysis to find encrypted and packed malware. IEEE Secur. Priv. **5**(2), 40–45 (2007)

11. McDonald, J.: OpenSSL SSLv2 malformed client key remote buffer overflow vulnerability (2003). http://www.securityfocus.com/bid/5363 (BugTraq Id 5363)
12. Menezes, A.J., Vanstone, S.A., Oorschot, P.C.V.: Handbook of Applied Cryptography. CRC Press, Boca Raton (1996)
13. Miller, G.A.: Note on the bias of information estimates. In: Quastler, H. (ed.) Information Theory in Psychology: Problems and Methods II-B, pp. 95–100. Free Press, Glencoe (1955)
14. Moddemeijer, R.: The distribution of entropy estimators based on maximum mean log-likelihood. In: Biemond, J. (ed.) Proceedings of the 21st Symposium on Information Theory in the Benelux, Wassenaar, The Netherlands, pp. 231–238 (2000)
15. The GNU MPFR library: Consulted December 02 (2013). http://www.mpfr.org/
16. Olivain, J., Goubault-Larrecq, J.: Detecting subverted cryptographic protocols by entropy checking. Research Report LSV-06-13, Laboratoire Spécification et Vérification, p. 19. ENS Cachan, France, June 2006
17. Paninski, L.: Estimation of entropy and mutual information. Neural Comput. **15**, 1191–1253 (2003)
18. Paninski, L.: Estimating entropy on m bins given fewer than m samples. IEEE Trans. Inf. Theor. **50**(9), 2200–2203 (2004)
19. Rossow, C., Dietrich, C.J.: Provex: Detecting botnets with encrypted command and control channels. In: Rieck, K., Stewin, P., Seifert, J.P. (eds.) DIMVA 2013. LNCS, vol. 7967, pp. 21–40. Springer, Heidelberg (2013)
20. Rukhin, A., Soto, J., Nechvatal, J., Smid, M., Barker, E., Leigh, S., Levenson, M., Vangel, M., Alan Heckert, D.B., Dray, J., Vo, S.: A statistical test suite for random and pseudorandom number generators for cryptographic applications. In: Bassham III, L.E. (ed.) NIST (Revised) (2010)
21. Wang, K., Cretu, G.F., Stolfo, S.J.: Anomalous payload-based worm detection and signature generation. In: Valdes, A., Zamboni, D. (eds.) RAID'2005. LNCS, vol. 3858, pp. 227–246. Springer, Heidelberg (2006)
22. Zalewski, M.: SSH CRC-32 compensation attack detector vulnerability (2001). http://www.securityfocus.com/bid/2347 (BugTraq Id 2347)
23. Zhang, H., Papadopoulos, C., Massey, D.: Detecting encrypted botnet traffic. In: IEEE Conference on Computer Communications Workshops (INFOCOM WKSHPS), pp. 163–168 (2013)

Security Protocols

On the Feasibility of a Censorship Resistant Decentralized Name System

Matthias Wachs$^{(\boxtimes)}$, Martin Schanzenbach, and Christian Grothoff

Technische Universität München, München, Germany
{wachs,schanzen,grothoff}@in.tum.de

Abstract. A central problem on the Internet today is that key infrastructure for security is concentrated in a few places. This is particularly true in the areas of naming and public key infrastructure. Secret services and other government organizations can use this fact to block access to information or monitor communications. One of the most popular and easy to perform techniques is to make information on the Web inaccessible by censoring or manipulating the Domain Name System (DNS). With the introduction of DNSSEC, the DNS is furthermore posed to become an alternative PKI to the failing X.509 CA system, further cementing the power of those in charge of operating DNS.

This paper maps the design space and gives design requirements for censorship resistant name systems. We survey the existing range of ideas for the realization of such a system and discuss the challenges these systems have to overcome in practice. Finally, we present the results from a survey on browser usage, which supports the idea that delegation should be a key ingredient in any censorship resistant name system.

1 Introduction

> "The Domain Name System is the Achilles heel of the Web. The important thing is that it
> is managed responsibly." – Tim Berners-Lee

Recent global news [1] on extensive espionage and cyberwar efforts by the US government and its "second class" allies, in particular the UK, have been met by some with calls to "encrypt everything" [2]. While this is hardly a solution for governments monitoring communication patterns (meta-data) and accessing data stored in plaintext at major service providers, encryption is clearly the baseline defense against government intrusions and industrial espionage [3]. However, encryption is useless without a secure public key infrastructure, and existing PKIs (DNSSEC, X.509 or the German ePa) are easily controlled and bypassed by major intelligence agencies. To realize the vision of an Internet where dissent is possible, we thus need to create an alternative, decentralized method for secure name resolution. Given a secure decentralized name system, we can then begin to build secure decentralized solutions for communication (e-mail, voice) and social networking applications and liberate the network from comprehensive government surveillance.

J.-L. Danger et al. (Eds.): FPS 2013, LNCS 8352, pp. 19–30, 2014.
DOI: 10.1007/978-3-319-05302-8_2, © Springer International Publishing Switzerland 2014

Today, the Domain Name System (DNS) is a key service for the Internet. DNS is primarily used to map names to IP addresses. Names are easier to remember for humans than IP addresses, which are used for routing but generally not meaningful for humans. DNS thus plays a central rôle for access to information on the Web; consequently, various institutions are using their power — including legal means — to censor or modify DNS information. These attacks on the DNS are sufficient to threaten the availability and integrity of information on the Web [4]. Furthermore, tampering with the DNS can have dramatic side effects, as a recent study about the worldwide effects of China's DNS censorship in China shows [5]: Chinese censorship of DNS can result in invalid results for parties that are far away from China. Many institutions like the European Parliament [6] or the OpenNet initiative [7] realize the dangers arising from DNS censorship, especially with respect to the importance that obtaining free information on the Web had in recent events as the Arab Spring or the Green Revolution in Iran.

Significant efforts have been made to harden DNS against attacks with DNSSEC providing data integrity and authenticity. These efforts are limited in their effect against institutional attackers performing censorship using their oppressive or legal powers to modify the results of an DNS request; even if end-to-end security between authoritative DNS servers and DNS clients were deployed, legal attacks coercing DNS authorities to hand over control of names would still be possible. A hypothetical mandatory DNSSEC deployment with end-to-end security providing integrity and authenticity cannot prevent or even detect such attacks, as the censored results would still be signed by a valid (albeit coerced) authority.

To prevent such attacks, we need a censorship resistant name system ensuring availability and resilience of names. For such a censorship resistant name systems, this paper advocates a solution in line with the ideas of the GNU project. Richard Stallman, founder of the GNU project, writes [8]: "When a program has an owner, the users lose freedom to control part of their own lives." Similarly, ownership of a name implies the existence of some authority to exercise control over the property, and thus implies the possibility of coercion of that authority. Cryptographic identifiers can be created without the need for an authority; similarly, when users locally assign values to private labels, as done in *petname* systems, such personal labels also cannot be owned or confiscated.

Based on these two central concepts, this paper discusses the design space and requirements for the "GNU Name System", which would be a fully-decentralized, ownership-less name system that provides censorship-resistance, privacy and security against a wide range of attacks by strong adversaries. We also discuss challenges alternative name systems face in practice and present the results of a survey characterizing common usage patterns of name systems on the Web.

2   Requirements Analysis

To analyze the requirements a censorship resistant name system has to fulfill, we start with a practical adversary model and the attacks a system has to withstand. Based on these, we then develop functional requirements for a censorship resistant name system.

2.1 Adversary Model

The adversary used in this paper is modeled after nation state trying to limit access to information on the Internet. Our adversary can participate in any role in the system and can also assume multiple identities (Sybils) without an upper bound in relation to the total number of participants. The adversary can take over control of names using judicial or executive powers and is allowed to have more computational power then all benign users. This model excludes the use of a trusted third party.

On the other hand, the adversary cannot break cryptographic primitives and not prevent the usage of cryptography or encrypted communication. The adversary is also not able to take direct control of the systems of individual users, or at least if he does so, the system does not have to protect the users that are directly affected by such actions. As far as network communication is concerned, we assume that the adversary cannot generally prevent communication between benign participants.

Our adversary's goal is to prevent access to information on the Web by affecting the name resolution process, either by making it fail or by changing the value associated with an existing name. He can do so by influencing or controlling parties participating in the name system.

Some name systems were designed with a weaker adversary model in mind; in particular, the assumption that the adversary does not control the majority of the nodes or the majority of the computing power is a popular model in computer security in general. However, censorship resistance is typically an issue for activists, and thus hardly a topic for the majority of Internet users. As a result, it is unlikely that any censorship resistant name system is going to be used widely enough to compete with the computational power available to major governments. Thus, we advocate using the assumption that the adversary might have more computational power than all other participants combined.

2.2 Functional Requirements

The basic functionality of a name system for the Internet is to map memorable names to correct values. After all, name resolution provides names for systems such that human beings can easily remember them, instead of having to remember the more complicated (and possibly frequently changing) address values used by the network.

One of the most important Internet services is the Web, and a fundamental building block for Web services is the ability to link to information hosted on different systems; as humans often manually create these links, links are specified using names. Thus, a name system should be designed to support link resolution: a service provider must be able to link to a foreign resource, and the users of the service must then be able to resolve the name to an address for the intended destination.

3   Design Space for Name Systems

This section explores the theoretical design space for name systems; we will structure our discussion on how a name system can be realized using Zooko's triangle [9], an insightful conjecture on the design space for name systems (Fig. 1).

Definition 1 (Memorable). *A name is memorable if it is feasible for an attacker in our adversary model to obtain it by enumerating names (bit strings). In other words, the number of bits of entropy in a memorable name is insufficient against enumeration attacks.*

Definition 2 (Secure). *A secure name system must enable benign participants to register and retrieve correct name-value mappings while experiencing active, malicious participants (which are assumed to follow the adversary model described in Sect. 2.1).*

Definition 3 (Global). *The system supports an unlimited number of participants without prior coordination or certification of participants. All benign participants receive the same (global) values for the same names.*

Theorem 1 (Zooko's Triangle). *It is impossible to have a name system that achieves* **memorable**, **secure** *and* **global** *names at the same time.*

We confirmed with Zooko Wilcox-O'Hearn that these definitions represent the intended interpretation of his formulation. We show now that Zooko's triangle is a valid conjecture *in our adversary model*:

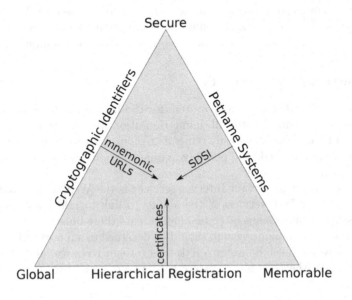

Fig. 1. Illustration of Zooko's triangle and key approaches to name systems.

Proof. All participants, including the adversary, are supposed to be able to register names under the "secure" property of the name system. As names are memorable, an adversary can enumerate all possible names. Thus, the adversary can perform a squatting attack by (if necessary) assuming the identities of name system components that restrict registration and performing the necessary computations (we assumed he is able to do those faster than the rest of the network combined). The adversary can use this attack to register *all* memorable names. As names are global, once the adversary has registered a name, that name can no longer be registered by anyone else.

Thus, the squatting attack can prevent the registration of memorable names by normal participants. Thus, in our security model, it is impossible to create a secure, global name system where memorable names are guaranteed to be available for registration by normal users.

A trusted authority in control of name assignments would easily prevent such an attacker from being successful; however, the existence of such an authority is outside of our security model. We would like to point out that the proof given above is controversial in the research community. We have had comments from reviewers ranging from assertions that the theorem is a trivial (or at least well-known) fact that does not require proof, to those questioning its veracity. We believe that this is the first formalization of Zooko's hypothesis and that the theorem holds in our security model — and that it is false under weaker assumptions. Thus, any name system *in our security model* must deemphasize one of the properties from Definitions 1–3. Figure 1 describes the three major design approaches in this context. The edges of the triangle represent the three simple designs, and the arrows towards the middle represent the three main designs which move toward satisfying all three properties.

3.1 Hierarchical Registration

In Zooko's triangle, a name system using hierarchical registration is a name system providing global and memorable names; however, in the hierarchical structure names are owned by organizations. These organizations receive the power to manage a subspace of the namespace by delegation from an organization ranked higher in the tree, which enables censorship. The well-known DNS is a distributed database realizing access to a name system with such a hierarchical structure.

In the original DNS, globally unique memorable names are managed by a handful of organizations with no security guarantees [10]. DNSSEC improves security by providing authenticity and integrity protection using cryptographic certificates; however, DNSSEC still requires trusted authorities and is thus open to certain types of attacks in our adversary model, as governments can typically easily compel a limited number of easily identified service providers. In particular, given the delegation hierarchy, an adversary can put pressure on organization to obtain control over all subdomains. As a result, top-level domain providers are both extremely powerful and extremely high-value targets, as is the control over the root zone itself.

3.2   Cryptographic IDs and Mnemonics

A name system that can securely map globally unique identifiers to values can be achieved using cryptographic identifiers as names. In such a system security is achieved by certifying values using the private key associated with the cryptographic identifier. Names are with high probability globally unique. However, as cryptographic identifiers are long random bitstrings, they are not memorable. An example for a deployed name system with cryptographic identifiers is Tor's ".onion" namespace [11].

The proposed Tor mnemonic URL system [12] aims to make the ".onion" names more memorable by encoding the hashes names into "human-meaningful" sentences. However, the resulting names will not be memorable by our Definition 1 as the high entropy of the original cryptographic identifiers remains. As (assuming sufficiently strong cryptographic primitives are used) an adversary would not be able to enumerate all cryptographic identifiers, Tor's mnemonic URL system would not result in memorable names as those names correspond to cryptographic identifiers and thus could also not be enumerated. Finally, it is important to note that Tor's mnemonic URLs are still work in progress; it is thus difficult to assess the usability of this approach.

3.3   Petnames and SDSI

A secure name system with memorable names can be created using so called *petnames*. In a petname system, each user establishes names of his choice for other entities [13]. Each user or service would be identified using a cryptographic identifier based on a public key; the service provider can then sign mapping information to certify integrity and authenticity of the data. Memorable names are achieved by mapping petnames to cryptographic identifiers. While such a system can provide security and memorability, the mappings are only local and petnames are meaningless (or have a different meaning) for other users. A simple example of a petname system is the /etc/hosts file that allows administrators to create a mapping from hostnames to addresses for the local system.

Extending petname systems with ideas from Rivest's Simple Distributed Security Infrastructure (SDSI) [14] adds the possibility of (secure) *delegation*, allowing users to reference the petnames of other users. SDSI based delegation enables users to resolve other participant's names and thus enables linking to external resources. Delegation essentially adds another user's namespace in a subtree under a specific name. This creates an hierarchical namespace from the point of view of each user; globally, the resulting structure is simply a directed graph. While delegation broadens the accessibility of mappings, it does not achieve global names.

3.4   Timeline-Based Name Systems

Timeline-based name systems, such as the Namecoin system [15], manage to combine global names, memorable names and security. In these systems, a global timeline with the domain registrations is secured by users performing proof-of-work computations, which in turn are used as "payment" for name registration.

Their existence does not contradict Zooko's triangle as their security depends on the adversary not having more computational power than the honest nodes; an adversary with sufficient computational power can create an alternative timeline with different domain registrations and a stronger proof-of-work, which would ultimately result in the system switching to the adversarial timeline. Thus, timeline-based systems do not fit the realistic adversary model we assumed for this paper (Sect. 2.1).

4   Practical Considerations

The previous section has outlined the design space for censorship resistant name systems. However, implementations of these alternatives will have to address a range of technical and practical concerns which be will discussed here.

4.1   Interoperability with DNS

To be accepted by users, a censorship resistant name system should respect user's usage patterns and integrate with existing technologies. Users should not have to manually switch between alternative name systems and DNS. Syntax and semantics of the different name systems should also be similar to not confuse the user about the meaning of names.

Thus a central requirement for any alternative name system will be interoperability with DNS. Users are used to DNS names and virtually all network applications today use DNS for name resolution. Thus, being interoperable with DNS will allow censorship-resistant alternatives to be used with a large body of legacy applications and facilitate adoption by end users.

Interoperability with DNS largely implies that alternative name systems should follow DNS restrictions on names, such as limiting names to 253 ASCII characters, limiting labels to 63 characters and using Internationalizing Domain Names in Applications (IDNA) [16] for internationalization. Furthermore, the name system should be prepared to return standard DNS records (such as "A" and "AAAA") to typical applications.

Interoperability with DNS should also include accessing the information of DNS from within the namespace of the censorship resistant name system. For example, it is conceivable that a censor might block access to `www.example.com` by removing the nameserver information for `example.com` in the `.com` TLD, without blocking access to the nameserver of `example.com`. In this case, a censorship resistant name system only needs to provide an alternative way to learn the nameserver for `example.com` — the lookup of `www` can then still be transmitted directly to the authoritative nameserver. In an alternative name system supporting delegation, this simply requires support for delegating subdomains back to DNS. This allows users to bypass censorship closer to the root of the

DNS hierarchy even if the operators of the censored service do not explicitly support the censorship resistant name system.

Finally, for good interoperability users must not be required to exclusively use an alternative domain name system — alternating between accessing DNS for domain names that are not censored and using the censorship resistant name system should not require the user to reconfigure his system each time!

Interoperability and using multiple name systems with the same configuration can be easily achieved using pseudo-TLDs. A pseudo-TLD is a top level domain that is not actually participating in the official DNS. For example, using the pseudo-TLD ".key", a user might specify "ID.key" to access a name system based on cryptographic identifiers, or "NICK.pet" to access a pseudo-TLD ".pet" for petnames. Naturally, this only works as long as the names chosen for the pseudo-TLDs are not used by the global DNS.

Once pseudo-TLDs have been selected, the local DNS stub resolver can be configured (for example, using the Name Service Switch [17]) to apply special resolution logic for names in the pseudo-TLDs. The special logic can then use alternative means to obtain and validate mappings, which will work as long as the final results returned can be again expressed as a DNS response.

4.2 End-to-End Security and Errors

Today, client systems typically only include a DNS stub resolver, delegating the name resolution process to a DNS resolver operated by their Internet Service Provider (ISP). As ISPs might be involved in censorship, they cannot be trusted to perform proper name resolution. Thus, secure name systems (including DNSSEC) must be deployed end-to-end to achieve the desired security.

This may not only require updating operating system resolvers. Existing applications sometimes implement their own DNS clients, and typical DNS APIs (such as POSIX's name resolution functions) do not include error reporting that incorporates security attributes. Browsers will thus be unable to benefit from TLSA records [18] until they either implement full DNSSEC resolver functions, or until operating system APIs are enhanced to allow returning additional information. A particularly critical example is the possibility to return unsigned records even within a DNSSEC deployment. As a result, DNSSEC protections can easily be disabled by replacing signed valid records with a set of invalid records without signature information.

4.3 Petnames and Legacy Applications

In addition to integration with existing systems an alternative name system also has to consider assumptions made by applications in higher layers, for example existing applications assuming globally unique names. Existing support for virtual hosting of websites in HTTP-based applications and TLS/SSL certificate validation both assume that the names given by the client match exactly the (DNS) name of the respective server. Links to external websites are typically specified using (globally unique) DNS names; as a result, relative names involving delegation from a SDSI-based name system would not be properly understood by today's browsers.

In lieu of directly modifying legacy applications, it might be possible to perform the necessary adaptations using proxies. Proxies might be used to translate hostnames from websites using delegation, and to perform SSL certificate validation (for example, by looking at TLSA [18] records from the secure name system instead of hostnames). Reverse proxies could be used to generate the virtual host names expected by the server, and to translate links with absolute links to those using the delegation chains provided by a SDSI-based name system. Additional records in the name system might be used to aid the conversion between relative names and legacy names by the proxies. In order to achieve end-to-end security, these proxies would naturally have to be operated within the trusted zone of the respective endpoints in the system.

4.4   Censorship-Resistant Lookup

Censorship resistant distributed name systems need to consult name information from other participants and thus require a network protocol to perform censorship resistant lookups. The most common method for implementing key-based searches in decentralized overlay networks is the use of a *distributed hash table* (DHT).

Typical attacks on DHTs include poisoning and eclipse attacks. In a poisoning attack, the adversary attempts to make interesting mappings hard to find by placing many invalid mappings into the DHT. A censorship-resistant DHT for a name system that uses public keys to lookup values signed by the respective private key can easily defeat this type of attack by checking signatures. In an eclipse attack, the adversary tries to isolate particular key-value mappings from the rest of the network. Modern DHTs defend against this type of attack by replicating values at multiple locations [19].

Some censorship resistant DHTs such as X-Vine [20] and R^5N [21] additionally accept limited connectivity between the peers in the DHT, making it harder for the adversary to disrupt DHT operations in the IP layer. Furthermore, this also allows peers to restrict connections to known friends, making the DHTs more robust against Sybil attacks [22] by building the overlay topology using existing social relationships.

One important property in this context will be query privacy. In existing centralized name systems, infrastructure providers can easily observe which names are used by which users. When the database is decentralized in a DHT, these central observation points are eliminated; however, now ordinary users can observe other user's queries, which maybe even more problematic for some applications. Thus, it is desirable to have encryption for queries and responses in the DHT. The encryption could be based on secrets only known to the user performing the resolution (such as the label and the zone); as a result, other users could only decrypt the resolution traffic with a confirmation attack where they would have to guess the label and zone of a query (or response). This would strengthen censorship-resistance as participants would typically not know which requests they are routing. Additional query privacy might be achieved by anonymizing the source of the request, for example by using onion routing [11]. Naturally, using such anonymization techniques increases latency.

4.5   Case Study: Usability

Unlike DNS, the user's experience when using a name system based on SDSI depends on high-level user behavior: following a link corresponds to traversing the delegation graph and resolution is fully automatic. However, when users want to visit a fresh domain that is not discovered via a link, SDSI requires a trust anchor to be supplied via a registrar or out-of-band mechanisms, such as QR codes. This raises the question: how often are these inconvenient methods needed in practice?

To answer this question, we did a survey on surfing behavior. Specifically, we wanted to find out how often users would typically type in a new domain name for a site. A domain name is "new" if the user has never visited it before, and if the user is typing it in the name is also not easily available via some link. Typed in new domain names are thus the case where a SDSI-based name system (or PKI) would need to use some external mechanism to obtain the public key of the zone.

Based on a limited and most likely biased survey where users volunteered the output of a simple shell script that inspected their browsers history database, we determined that given current Internet behavior, approximately 8 % of domain names would require introduction via some out-of-band exchange. A key limitation of the survey's methodology was that we did not attempt to control who submitted results; we simply used the data of anyone who was willing and able to download and run the shell script that performed the analysis. This limited the sample to somewhat more technologically sophisticated users. The complete results from our survey and details on the methodology can be found in [23]. Our conclusion is that a name system based on petnames and SDSI-style delegation stands a chance of being an acceptable choice if communication is hindered by censorship or strong security assurances (beyond those offered by the X.509 PKI or DNSSEC) are required.

5   Censorship in Other Layers

Censorship does not stop with the name system. For example, censors can also attempt to block information by destination IP address. Blocking IP addresses is actually easier than censoring DNS; however, there is an increased chance of collateral damage as with virtual hosting, a single IP address can host many sites and services. Tools that help users circumvent IP-level censorship can also benefit from censorship resistant name systems.

For example, the Tor network [11] is an anonymizing public virtual network for tunneling TCP connections over the P2P overlay network. While Tor is often associated with the goal of providing anonymity for HTTP clients, it can also be used to circumvent censorship by tunneling (the Tor overlay) traffic in other protocols, such as TLS. Tor also offers the possibility of hosting services within the Tor network, here with the primary goal of providing anonymity to the operators of the servers. Accessing these "hidden services" using cryptographic identifiers is not particularly user-friendly.

Given a decentralized censorship resistant name system, it should be easy to provide names for services offered within such P2P overlays. The name system would map names to a new record type that identifies the respective service and peer (instead of using "A" or "AAAA" records to reference a host on the Internet). Such service endpoint addresses can then again be translated to IP addresses in the entry node's private address range to enable communication of legacy applications with the P2P service. The result would be still close to hidden services in Tor, though it would not necessarily have to also provide support for anonymity.

6 Conclusion

We have outlined the limitations of censorship resistant name systems and shown that it is not possible to achieve memorable, secure and global names in a unified name system. However, it is possible to use pseudo-TLDs to allow users to cherry-pick between multiple name systems, offering combinations of two of the three desirable properties. Among the theoretical ideas, the SDSI-design using delegation is the only which has so far not been attempted in practice. Here, the lack of globally unique names creates additional issues for legacy applications that need to be mitigated. Focusing on Web applications, we have performed a survey which shows that a delegation-based name system would offer significant benefits over simpler petname systems, as most name resolutions in practice arise from users following links. As each design offers unique advantages, developers of censorship circumvention tools should consider the integration or interoperability of their systems with *multiple* secure name systems via pseudo-TLDs, including DNS/DNSSEC, cryptographic identifiers and petnames with delegation.

Acknowledgments. This work was funded by the Deutsche Forschungsgemeinschaft (DFG) under ENP GR 3688/1-1. We thank everyone who submitted information about their browser history for our study of surfing behavior. We thank Jacob Appelbaum, Daniel Bernstein, Ludovic Courtès, Ralph Holz, Luke Leighton, Simon Josefsson, Nikos Mavrogiannopoulos, Ondrej Mikle, Stefan Monnier, Niels Möller, Chris Palmer, Martin Pool, Richard Stallman, Neal Walfield and Zooko Wilcox-O'Hearn and the anonymous reviewers for FPS'2013 for insightful comments and discussions on an earlier draft of the paper. We thank Krista Grothoff for editing the paper.

References

1. Greenwald, G., MacAskill, E.: NSA prism program taps in to user data of apple. Google and others, The Guardian, June 2013

2. Times, R.: Post PRISM: encrypted communications boom after NSA leaks. http:// www.youtube.com/watch?v=JJY3EXVdyiM (2013)
3. Schmid, G.: Report on the existence of a global system for the interception of private and commercial communications (ECHELON interception system). European Parliament Session Document 2001/2098(INI), July 2001
4. http://politi.dk/: Fejl blokerede internetsider kortvarigt. http://goo.gl/beQFm (2012)
5. Anonymous, : The collateral damage of internet censorship by dns injection. ACM SIGCOMM Comp. Comm. Rev. **42**(3), 22–27 (2012)
6. European parliament: resolution on the EU-US summit of 28 November 2011 P7-RC-2011-0577, November 2011
7. The OpenNet initiative. http://opennet.net/ (2013)
8. Stallman, R.: Why software should not have owners. http://www.gnu.org/ philosophy/why-free.html (2012)
9. Wilcox-O'Hearn, Z.: Names: decentralized, secure, human-meaningful: choose two. http://zooko.com/distnames.html (2006)
10. Mockapetris, P.: Rfc 1035: domain names - implementation and specification. Technical report, Network Working Group, November 1987)
11. Dingledine, R., Mathewson, N., Syverson, P.: Tor: The second-generation onion router. In: Proceedings of 13th USENIX Security Symposium, August 2004
12. Sai, A.F.: Mnemonic.onion urls. http://goo.gl/aOpKo (2012)
13. Stiegler, M.: An introduction to petname systems. http://www.skyhunter.com/ marcs/petnames/IntroPetNames.html (2005)
14. Rivest, R.L., Lampson, B.: SDSI – a simple distributed security infrastructure. http://groups.csail.mit.edu/cis/sdsi.html (1996)
15. http://dot-bit.org/: The Dot-BIT project, A decentralized, open DNS system based on the bitcoin technology. http://dot-bit.org/ (2013)
16. Faltstrom, P., Hoffman, P., Costello, A.: RFC 3490: internationalizing domain names in applications (IDNA). Technical report, Network Working Group, March 2003
17. Foundation, F.S.: The GNU C library - system databases and name service switch. http://goo.gl/gQY0w
18. Hoffman, P., Schlyter, J.: The DNS-Based authentication of named entities (DANE) transport layer security (TLS) protocol: TLSA. IETF RFC 6698, August 2012
19. Polot, B.: Adapting blackhat approaches to increase the resilience of whitehat application scenarios. Master's thesis, Technische Universität München (2010)
20. Mittal, P., Caesar, M., Borisov, N.: X-vine: secure and pseudonymous routing using social networks. CoRR abs/1109.0971 (2011)
21. Evans, N., Grothoff, C.: R^5N: randomized recursive routing for restricted-route networks. In: 5th International Conference on Network and System Security, pp. 316–321 (2011)
22. Douceur, J.R.: The Sybil attack. In: Druschel, P., Kaashoek, M.F., Rowstron, A. (eds.) IPTPS 2002. LNCS, vol. 2429, pp. 251–260. Springer, Heidelberg (2002)
23. Schanzenbach, M.: A censorship resistant and fully decentralized replacement for DNS. Master's thesis, Technische Universität München (2012)

A General Framework for Group Authentication and Key Exchange Protocols

Huihui Yang$^{(\boxtimes)}$, Lei Jiao, and Vladimir A. Oleshchuk

Department of Information and Communication Technology, University of Agder,
Kristiansand, Norway
{huihui.yang,LeiJiao,vladimir.oleshchuk}@uia.no

Abstract. In this paper, we propose a novel framework for group authentication and key exchange protocols. There are three main advantages of our framework. First, it is a general one, where different cryptographic primitives can be used for different applications. Second, it works in a one-to-multiple mode, where a party can authenticate several parties mutually. Last, it can provide several security features, such as protection against passive adversaries and impersonate attacks, implicit key authentication, forward and backward security. There are two types of protocols in our framework. The main difference between them is that the authenticator in Type II has a certificate while in Type I does not. Under the general framework, we also give the details of protocols based on Diffie-Hellman key exchange system, and discrete logarithm problem (DLP) or elliptic curve discrete logarithm problem (ECDLP) based ElGamal encryption respectively. Session keys will be established at the end of each session and they can be utilized later to protect messages transmitted on the communication channel.

Keywords: Group authentication · Diffie-Hellman key exchange · Discrete logarithm problem · Elliptic curve discrete logarithm problem

1 Introduction

Online social networks (OSNs) are platforms offering social services in an online format, and they became very popular during recent years. OSNs can be used in many ways, such as news sharing, group chatting and video conferences and so on. For all these applications, authentication is of great importance. Consider the example of group chatting. All group members should be whom one expects to communicate with, and messages delivered between them should also be protected. It is also very important for servers to authenticate their clients. However, due to the large number of clients for most OSNs, the time spent by servers to authenticate clients may become a bottleneck of the whole service if it is done in the traditional one-to-one mode. Therefore, an efficient and secure protocol for authenticating and key exchanges is needed.

J.-L. Danger et al. (Eds.): FPS 2013, LNCS 8352, pp. 31–45, 2014.
DOI: 10.1007/978-3-319-05302-8_3, © Springer International Publishing Switzerland 2014

Authentication can be achieved by usernames and passwords [1,2] or public certificates [3]. Password based approach is usually selected for the authentication in a client and server mode, where usernames and passwords are required. For certificate based authentication, however, a public key infrastructure is needed to be built first and then an initiation phase for key distribution is required. Besides, key based authentication works in a one-to-one mode, so only one user or client can be authenticated each time. To save both time and bandwidth, group authentication [4] is proposed in this paper. Under most circumstances, group authentication is related to group key management in multimedia or wireless network and etc. It is mainly used to prove that a member belongs to a certain group without revealing its identity. However, we give a new definition of group authentication in this paper, where all members in a group can be authenticated at one time. The main difference between the traditional definition and ours is that the former aims at authentication without revealing anonymity while ours is to save time and increase authentication efficiency. This new definition of group authentication has already been proposed in [2], which is password based authentication and can be used to verify multiple users' identities at the same time. We will adopt this new definition in our paper.

Compared with existing work, our paper mainly has three contributions. First of all, the authentication in all our protocols is group based, and thus it is more effective and can save both bandwidth and time. Secondly, our framework is a general one and can be based on different cryptographic primitives. Meanwhile, we give two detailed applications using DLP [5] and ECDLP [6] based ElGamal encryption [7]. Finally, our protocols can satisfy security requirements such as mutual and implicit key authentication, protection against passive adversaries and impersonation attacks and forward and backward secrecy. Later, we will give detailed proofs for each of these security requirements.

2   Related Work

A lot of research has already been done in the area of authentication and key exchanges [8,9]. We will mainly discuss those related to group authentication rather than authentication in the one-to-one mode. As mentioned in Sect. 1, the traditional group authentication is to prove that a member belongs to a certain group. Among all approaches to achieve it, group signatures [10] and ring signatures [11] are often used. In group signatures, a member of a group or the signer generates a signature, a verifier can check whether the signer belongs to this group or not, without knowing the singer's identity. However, the manager of this group can "open" the signature and thus the identity of the signer will be revealed if necessary. Ring signature is based on public key system. There is no group manager, and a signer can choose anyone whose public key is registered in a trusted authority to create a random group. The signer uses its own secret key and other members' public keys to generate a signature. The other members can deny that the signature is created by them and the real identity of the signer can be revealed in this way.

There are also some other researches based on group or ring signatures. The protocol in [12] is based on digital signature algorithm (DSA) [13] and is designed to authenticate vehicles. However, the sender or authenticator deals with the received responses from each vehicle separately because each vehicle encrypts its response by the authenticator's public key. As a result, this protocol does not contribute much to saving computational cost. In [14], the protocol is DSA and DLP based. It can be used to authenticate a group member, subgroups or all members in a group, but it differs from our protocols in several ways. First of all, in their protocol there should be a group leader or a trusted party, who signs the message first and checks whether other users' signatures are valid or not. Secondly, it is designed for an outsider to authenticate a group who shares a public key, while the outsider does not need to know any of the group members. Similarly, the model proposed in [15] is also designed for an outsider to verify the signature of a group, so theoretically it can be used to authenticate a group of members. However, the group should be stable and every member should have a certificate. In [16], a series of protocols are designed for batch or group authentication in a one-to-multiple mode. They can be applied to a scenario where strangers are to be authenticated by a party under the help of a trusted friend in a P2P based decentralized social network. They propose protocols based on one-way hash function [17], ElGamal signature [7,18] and certificates respectively. However, even though their one-way hash function based protocol in [16] can be utilized to authenticate a group of members, the computational cost does not decrease compared with that in a one-to-one mode, so it does not benefit much in time saving on the authenticator's side. Their work differs from ours in several ways. The most significant difference is that we emphasis on a general framework where several cryptographic primitives can be used to it, rather than specific primitives. Besides, the protocols in [14,15] do not provide key exchange functionality, and they are not fit for the authentication inside a group. In this paper, we propose a framework for the mutual authentication within a group and it also provides key exchanges.

The rest of the paper is organized as follows. In Sect. 3, two usage scenarios are introduced first. Then the main notations and parameters that will be used later in our framework are explained and the framework for both types of protocols is described. Next, two examples are given to demonstrate how our framework works. Finally, a formal description of what cryptographic primitives can be used to our framework is presented. The correctness and security analysis are presented in Sects. 4, 5 respectively. In Sect. 6, we will give some comparisons of the computation and communication costs of our protocols and the traditional one-to-one mode ones. Finally, we conclude this paper in the last section and give some suggestions about how to apply our framework.

3   The General Framework

In this section, we firstly explain two typical usage scenarios where our framework can be applied, and then the general parameters, notations, message flows of our

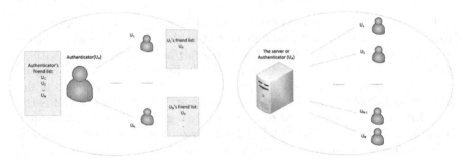

(a) Relations between the Authenticator and his or her Friends

(b) Relations between the Server and its Clients

Fig. 1. Relations of two parties in two scenarios. **a** Relations between the authenticator and his or her friends. **b** Relations between the server and its clients

general framework are presented. Next, we implement some specific primitives of our framework to demonstrate how it works. Finally, we describe which kinds of cryptographic primitives can be applied to our framework.

3.1   Two Usage Scenarios

All protocols in our framework are suitable for two scenarios, illustrated in Fig. 1. In scenario 1(a), an ordinary user temporarily creates a group with his or her friends and authenticates each of them. Scenario 1(b) is for a server to authenticate several of its clients. Both the group initiator and the server shares some secrets with his or her friends or its clients, and it will use these secrets for mutual authentication later. Our protocols have two goals: mutual authentication and session key agreement. At the end of each session, session keys are established. The group session key is generated by the authenticator and distributed to each group member, while the other session keys are computed according to Diffie-Hellman [19] key exchange. In scenario 1(b), however, only session keys between the server and its clients are established. Our protocols can be divided into two types. The main difference between them is that the authenticator in Type I does not have a certificate while a certification is needed in Type II, and thus the authenticator is authenticated differently in protocols of Type I and Type II.

3.2   Parameters and Notations

The parameters and notations for all protocols are listed in Table 1. Among them, we will only give some explanations to k_i. For both scenarios mentioned in Sect. 3.1, k_i is a long time shared secret, generated by U_A and has been delivered to U_i via a safe channel in advance. For the first scenario, since we assume that the number of U_A's friends is not big, it is practical to generate enough pairwise

Table 1. Parameters and notations

Symbol	Description
U_A	The authenticator to authenticate a group of users or clients denoted by $\mathbb{U}$
$\mathbb{U}$	A user group to be authenticated, $\mathbb{U} = \{U_1, U_2, \ldots, U_N\}$
N	The number of members in group $\mathbb{U}$
ID_A	The identity of U_A
ID_i	The identity of U_i, $i \in \{1, \ldots, N\}$
UID	Identities of all members in $\mathbb{U}$, $UID = \{ID_1, ID_2, \ldots, ID_N\}$
$H()$	One-way hash function with the output of length l, $H() : \{0,1\}^* \rightarrow \{0,1\}^l$
MAC	The message authentication code generated by a keyed hash function
ξ	$\xi = \{ID_A, UID\}$, message used for group authentication
K_G	Group session key, generated by U_A during a specified session, one time use
SK_{Ai}	Session key between U_A and U_i in a specified session, one time use
SK_{ij}	Session key between U_i and U_j in a specified session, one time use
SK_A	U_A's private key
$SIGN_K(m)$	The signature of message m with private key K
KP_A	Key parameters generated by U_A, $KP_A = \{g^{m_1}, \ldots, g^{m_N}\}$ in DLP based protocols and $KP_A = \{m_1 G, \ldots, m_N G\}$ in ECDLP based protocols
KP_U	Key parameters generated by members in $\mathbb{U}$, $KP_U = \{g^{n_1}, \ldots, g^{n_N}\}$ in the DLP based protocol and $KP_U = \{n_1 G, \ldots, n_N G\}$ in the ECDLP based protocol
k_i	$k_i \in \mathbb{K} = \{k_1, k_2, \ldots, k_N\}$. It is a long time shared secret between U_A and U_i. k_i, k_j $(1 \leq i, j \leq N, i \neq j)$ are pairwise prime
t_i	One-time nonce, used to make sure of the freshness of a session
q, p	Large prime numbers, and $q = 2p + 1$
g	The generator of the cyclic multiplicative group G_q
y_A	A secret shared between U_A and members in $\mathbb{U}$
y_i	$y_i = g^{x_i}/x_i G$ in the DLP and ECDLP based protocols respectively It is a secret shared between U_A and U_i
G	Base point of the selected elliptic curve

prime numbers k_i. In the second scenario, there can be a huge number of users per server. In this case, U_A can generate several groups of different k_i, where they are pairwise prime within the same group. As a result, U_A can authenticate clients with k_i within the same group at one time. However, this mechanism is needed only when the number of clients exceeds the threshold that the server can deal with.

3.3 Message Flows

There are four steps in our framework and the message flows are illustrated in Fig. 2. During the message flows, C_i, V_i and W_i all depends on different

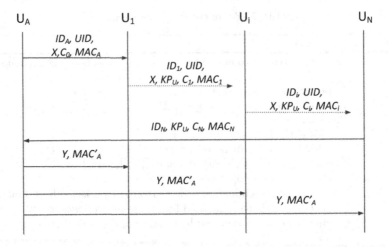

Fig. 2. Message flows of the general framework

cryptographic primitives and will be explained later. The details of the four steps of message flows are as follows:

(1) $U_A \rightarrow U_1 : ID_A, UID, X, C_0, MAC_A$.

(2) $U_i \rightarrow U_{i+1} : ID_i, UID, X, KP_U, C_i, MAC_i$, where $1 \leq i \leq N - 1$.

(3) $U_N \rightarrow U_A : ID_N, KP_U, C_N, MAC_N$.

(4) $U_A \rightarrow \mathbb{U} : Y, MAC'_A$.

(1) U_A initiates a new session in this step. It calculates X by formula (1) using the Chinese remainder theorem (CRT) [20], but it has to be sure that $V_i \oplus k_i < k_i$ $(1 \leq i \leq N)$ (The details will be explained later in Sect. 3.4.).

$$X \equiv V_i \oplus k_i \pmod{k_i}, \text{where } 1 \leq i \leq N. \tag{1}$$

Here, V_i should contain the identity information of both U_A and U_i, group session key K_G, session key parameters and a cryptographic primitive h_i for U_A's authentication. We use one-way hash functions to compute h_i in this paper for simplicity. Then U_A generates C_0 which will be used by U_i to compute C_i. Finally, U_A computes MAC_A and sends it to U_1. After U_1 receives the message, it gets V_1 by $X(\bmod\, k_i) \oplus k_1$, extracts parameters in it and checks MAC_A. If MAC_A is valid, it continues and the authentication for U_A by U_1 is achieved or else it aborts the session. Next it calculates the session key with U_A.

(2) U_i randomly generates its key parameter, appends it to KP_U and computes C_i. Finally, it calculates MAC_i and then sends the message to the next user. After U_{i+1} receives the message, what it does is the same as U_1 in step (1).

(3) The behavior of U_N is the same as U_1. After U_A receives the message from U_N, it checks the validity of MAC_N first. If it is valid, it computes C'_N and checks whether $C'_N = C_N$ holds. If it does, the group authentication is achieved.

(4) U_A generates Y by formula (2) and $W_i \oplus k_i < k_i$ must hold.

$$Y \equiv W_i \oplus k_i \pmod{k_i}, \text{ where } 1 \leq i \leq N. \tag{2}$$

When U_i receives message as step (4), it proceeds as follows.

(a) Check MAC'_A to make sure that the message is not tampered.

(b) Get W_i by $Y(\bmod k_i) \oplus k_i$.

(c) Retrieve parameters from W_i. If it contains $\{ID_A, ID_i\}$, U_i is successfully authenticated. Then it calculates session keys with U_j ($1 \leq j \leq N, i \neq j$) and erase its key parameter.

3.4 DLP Based Protocols

The same as the message flows described in Sect. 3.3, the DLP based protocols include four steps and the following are the details.

(1) Let $C_0 = \xi(r) = \xi(g^{r_A})$, where $r_A \in [1, p-1]$ is randomly generated. V_i is derived from V'_i. In the protocol of Type I, $V'_i = \{y_i \oplus K_G, y_i \oplus t_i, g^{m_i}, h_i\}$, where $h_i = H(ID_A \oplus ID_i \oplus y_A \oplus t_i)$, while in Type II, $V'_i = SIGN_{SK_A}\{ID_A, ID_i, K_G, g^{m_i}, t_i\}$. As mentioned in Sect. 3.3, we should make sure that $X_i \oplus k_i < k_i$ and $W_i \oplus k_i < k_i$. Suppose the security parameters of k_i and also the length of V'_i is $sl(k_i)$, then the length of k_i should be $l(k_i) > sl(k_i)$ and the highest $l(k_i) - sl(k_i)$ bits are used for the purpose of CRT. When k_i is generated, the highest $l(k_i) - sl(k_i)$ bits are initiated as 1. The highest $l(k_i) - sl(k_i)$ bits of V_i are also initiated as 1 and the rest bits are the same as V'_i, so we can be sure that $V_i \oplus k_i < k_i$ holds. The same approach will be applied to generate W_i.

(2) In protocols of Type I, the authentication of U_A by U_i is obtained by checking h_i. After U_i gets V_i, it extracts t_i, computes $h'_t = H(ID_A \oplus ID_i \oplus y_A \oplus t_i)$ and checks whether $h'_i = h_i$ holds. If it does, U_A is successfully authenticated. Furthermore, $C_1 = \xi(r^{x_1})$ and $C_i = C_{i-1} \times r^{x_i} = \xi(r^{\sum_{t=1}^{i} x_t})$ ($2 \leq i \leq N$). The session keys SK_{Ai} and SK_{ij} are calculated as $g^{m_i n_i}$ and $g^{n_i n_j}$ respectively.

(3) U_A authenticates the whole user group by checking whether $C'_N = C_N$ holds, where $C'_N = \xi(\prod_{t=1}^{N} y_t^{r_A})$.

(4) Let $W'_i = \{ID_A, ID_i, KP_i\}$ and $KP_i = KP_U - \{g^{n_i}\}$.

3.5 ECDLP Based Protocols

The same as the DLP based protocols, the authentication of U_A by U_i of ECDLP based protocols also depends on the one-way hash function. Parameters and users' behaviors about ECDLP based protocols are listed as follows.

(1) Let $C_0 = G_r = r_A G$, where $r_A \in [1, n-1]$ is randomly selected. In the protocol of Type I, $V_i' = \{y_i \oplus K_G, m_i G, y_i \oplus t_i, h_i\}$, where $h_i = H(ID_A \oplus ID_i \oplus y_A \oplus t_i)$. For the protocol of Type II, however, $V_i' = SIGN_{SK_A}\{ID_A, ID_i, K_G, m_i G, t_i\}$.

(2) In the protocol of Type I, the authentication of U_A by U_i is also obtained by checking h_i. Furthermore, $C_1 = \xi(x_1 G_r)$ and $C_i = C_{i-1} + \xi(x_i G_r) = \xi(r_A \sum_{t=1}^{i} x_t G)$ $(2 \le i \le N-1)$. The session keys SK_{Ai} and SK_{ij} are computed as $m_i n_i G$ and $n_i n_j G$ $(1 \le i, j \le N, i \ne j)$.

(3) U_A authenticates the whole user group by checking whether $C_N' = C_N$ holds, where $C_N' = \xi(\sum_{t=1}^{N} r_A y_i)$.

(4) Let $W_i' = \{ID_A, ID_i, KP_i\}$ and $KP_i = KP_U - \{n_i G\}$.

3.6   Requirements of Cryptographic Primitives

The DLP and ECDLP based protocols described above are only two specific examples and other cryptographic primitives can also be implemented to our framework. Suppose the underlying cryptographic scheme we use is F, $*$ is the operation that joins the results of U_i and U_{i+1} $(1 \le i \le N-1)$ and $\circ$ is the operation that U_A uses for the shared secrets. Let $f_i = F(\xi, k_i)$, where ξ is the message as illustrated in Table 1, f_i is the result of what U_i calculates and k_i is the secret parameter shared between U_A and U_i. If Eq. (3) holds, then it can be applied to our framework.

$$f_1 * \cdots * f_N = F(\xi, k_1 \circ \cdots \circ k_N) \tag{3}$$

The left side of Eq. (3) means that it needs N times operation of F to authenticate all members in $\mathbb{U}$ in the traditional one-to-one mode. However, the same goal can be achieved by only performing F once and $\circ$ N times, where $\circ$ is supposed to be much more time saving compared with F.

In our DLP and ECDLP based protocols, we use one-way hash functions to authenticate U_A, however, many other cryptographic primitives can be used, such as ElGamal signature, DSA and so on, depending on different user scenarios or devices etc.

4   Correctness Analysis

Since our framework does not include specific cryptographic primitives for mutual authentication, we will only give the correctness analysis to DLP and ECDLP based protocols.

4.1   Correctness of DLP Based Protocols

In the protocol of Type I, the authentication for U_A by U_i is promised by checking whether h_i' is equal to h_i, where h_i' is the hash value calculated by U_i. After deriving V_i by $X \oplus k_i$, U_i calculates t_i by $y_i \oplus t_i \oplus y_i$. Besides, y_A is shared between

U_A and U_i, so if U_A is not impersonated or compromised by an adversary, $h'_i = h_i$ will hold. However, the authentication of U_A in Type II is achieved by public key signature system.

Next, we will discuss the correctness of group authentication by U_A. U_1 calculates C_1 by $C_1 = r^{x_1} = \xi(g^{r_A x_1})$. After U_i $(2 \le i \le N)$ receives C_{i-1}, it calculates C_i according to $C_i = C_{i-1} \times r^{x_i} = \xi(g^{r_A \sum_{t=1}^{i} x_t})$. Therefore, $C_N = \xi(g^{r_A \sum_{t=1}^{N} x_t})$ and when U_A receives C_N, it calculates C'_N as $C'_N = \xi((g^{x_1} \times \cdots \times g^{x_N})^{r_A}) = \xi(g^{r_A \sum_{t=1}^{N} x_t})$. We can see that $C_N = C'_N$ holds. Thus, the mutual authentication is correct for protocols of both types.

4.2   Correctness of ECDLP Based Protocols

The authentication of U_A in Type I and Type II are promised by one-way hash function and public key signature system respectively, the same as illustrated in Sect. 4.1, but the authentication of $\mathbb{U}$ relies on C_N. $C_1 = \xi(x_1 G_r) = \xi(r_A x_1 G)$ and $C_i = C_{i-1} + \xi(x_i G_r) = \xi(r_A \sum_{t=1}^{i} x_t G)$ $(2 \le i \le N)$. Thus, $C_N = \xi(r_A \sum_{t=1}^{N} x_t G)$. So after U_A receives the message from U_N, it calculates C'_N as $C'_N = \xi(r_A(G_1 + G_2 + \cdots + G_N)) = \xi(r_A \sum_{t=1}^{N} G_t)$. It is straightforward that C_N equals to C'_N.

5   Security Analysis

In this section, we analyze the security requirements of both DLP and ECDLP based protocols. In this paper, we only consider passive adversaries denoted by E, who can only receive messages on the communication channel and then analyzing them acting as a probabilistic polynomial time Turing machine.

5.1   Security Requirements

Both types of our protocols provide mutual and group authentication, protection against passive adversaries and impersonation attacks. They also satisfy implicit key authentication, forward and backward secrecy. We will use the theory of random oracle (RO) [21] and decisional Diffie-Hellman (DDH) [22] assumption to prove these security requirements. First of all, we will introduce the following two assumptions based on which our security proofs are derived.

Assumption 1 *DLP based DDH Assumption. Suppose G_p is a cyclic group of order p with generator g. $a, b, c \in [1, |G_p|]$ are randomly generated. Given g^a, g^b and g^c, it is supposed that there is no probabilistic polynomial time algorithm to distinguish g^{ab} and g^c.*

Assumption 2 *ECDLP based DDH Assumption. Suppose E_G is a secure non-singular elliptic curve with G as its base point and n its order, $a, b, c \in [1, n-1]$ are randomly generated. Given aG, bG and cG, it is supposed that there is no probabilistic polynomial time algorithm to distinguish abG and cG.*

Group authentication. It means that U_A can authenticate all members in user group $\mathbb{U}$ at one time. From the correctness analysis in Sect. 4, it is obvious that both the DLP and ECDLP based protocols can provide group authentication.

Mutual authentication. At the end of each protocol, U_A can authenticate each member U_i in $\mathbb{U}$, and U_i can also authenticate U_A. From both Sect. 4 and the message flows in Sect. 3, we can see that the authentication of $\mathbb{U}$ and U_A can be achieved in step (3) and (4) respectively if the protocol is successfully executed.

Theorem 1. *Based on Assumption 1 and 2, both the DLP and ECDLP based protocols are against passive adversaries, which means:*

(1) E cannot derive any information about y_A from h_i;
(2) E cannot derive any information about ξ from C_i.

Proof. In the first step, we will prove that h_i is secure against passive adversaries. Since y_A is protected by the one-away hash function H, based on the theory of RO in [21], the probability that E derives any useful information about y_i from $H(ID_A \oplus ID_i \oplus y_A \oplus t_i)$ is negligible.

In the second step, we prove that E cannot obtain any information about ξ. In DLP and ECDLP based protocols, C_N is computed by $C_i = \xi(g^{r_A \sum_{t=1}^{i} x_t})$ and $C_i = \xi(r_A \sum_{t=1}^{i} x_t G)$, where C_0 is $\xi(g^{r_A})$ and $\xi(r_A G)$ respectively. Obviously, they are DLP and ECDLP based ElGamal encryption. According to the results in [18], ElGamal encryption is as hard as DDH problem. Thus, based on Assumption 1 and 2, C_i is secure against passive adversaries. □

Theorem 2. *Based on Assumption 1 and 2, and the difficulties of DLP and ECDLP, both the DLP and ECDLP based protocols are against impersonation attacks, which means:*

(1) E cannot forge h_i to impersonate U_A;
(2) E cannot forge C_i to impersonate U_i.

Proof. According to (1) of Theorem 1, we know that E cannot derive any information about y_A. And then based on the robustness of one-way hash function [17,23], it is impossible for E to forge h_i without the knowledge of y_A or t_i.

Next, we will demonstrate that it is impossible for E to forge C_i. According to difficulties of DLP and ECDLP, E cannot derive x_i without compromising U_i. Thus, it generates l_i instead and computes $C_i' = \xi(g^{r_A \sum_{i=1}^{i} l_i})/C_i' = \xi(r_A \sum_{i=1}^{i} l_i G)$ (To simplify our presentation, we will use the symbol "/" to represent "or".). Since r_A is only known to U_A, E needs to successfully generate $\sum_{i=1}^{i} l_i$ such that $\xi(g^{r_A \sum_{i=1}^{i} l_i})/\xi(r_A \sum_{i=1}^{i} l_i G)$ equals to $\xi(g^{r_A \sum_{i=1}^{i} x_i})/\xi(r_A \sum_{i=1}^{i} x_i G)$. Again, according to the difficulties of DLP and ECDLP, E cannot deduce $\sum_{i=1}^{N} x_i$. However, it can compute the right value of $\xi(g^{r_A \sum_{i=1}^{i} x_i})/\xi(r_A \sum_{i=1}^{i} x_i G)$, which is contradictory to Assumption 1 and 2. As a result, both the DLP and ECDLP based protocols are against impersonate attacks. □

Theorem 3. *Based on the difficulties of DLP and ECDLP, Assumption 1 and 2, and the security of CRT, both the DLP and ECDLP based protocols can provide implicit key authentication, which means:*

(1) Only U_A and U_i can access to the group session key K_G;
(2) Only U_A and U_i can compute the right session key SK_{Ai};
(3) Only U_i and U_j can compute the right session key SK_{ij}, where $1 \leq i, j \leq N$ and $i \neq j$.

Proof. From the formats of V_i and message flows, we know that K_G is protected by CRT. Therefore, E cannot get K_G without knowing k_i.

As for the session key SK_{Ai}, it is computed by parameters g^{m_i}/m_iG and g^{n_i}/n_iG based Diffie-Hellman key exchange system. g^{n_i}/n_iG is transmitted in plaintext, however, E cannot derive n_i by the difficulties of DLP and ECDLP. So the only way for E to obtain SK_{Ai} is to compute it by both key parameters, but this is contradict to Assumption 1 and 2.

The security of session key SK_{ij} is almost the same as SK_{Ai}, with the exception that both g^{n_i}/n_iG and g^{n_j}/n_jG are exposed to the adversaries. For the same reason as mentioned above, E cannot derive session key SK_{ij}.

As a result, both DLP and ECDLP based protocols are proved to provide implicit key authentication. $\square$

Theorem 4. *Based on the difficulties of DLP and ECDLP, Assumption 1 and 2, both the DLP and ECDLP based protocols can provide forward secrecy, which means: the exposure of session key $SK_{Ai,r}$ or $SK_{ij,r}$ in session s_r will not lead to the exposure of session key $SK_{Ai,t}$ or $SK_{ij,t}$ in session s_t, where $1 \leq t < r$.*

Proof. Suppose that all parameters specified to session s_r have been exposed to an adversary E. Here, parameters specified to a session refer to those newly generated in this session, and will be expired when this session finishes, not including those shared in all sessions. Let $g^{m_{i,r}}/m_{i,r}G$ and $g^{n_{i,r}}/n_{i,r}G$ be the key parameters in session s_r, $g^{m_{i,t}}/m_{i,t}G$ and $g^{n_{i,t}}/n_{i,t}G$ be the key parameters in session s_t. Session keys $SK_{Ai,r} = g^{m_{i,r}n_{i,r}}/m_{i,r}n_{i,r}G$ and $SK_{ij,r} = g^{n_{i,r}n_{j,r}}/n_{i,r}n_{j,r}G$ are exposed to E. Since m_i and n_i for each session are randomly generated, and those in a different session cannot be deduced by them. Consequently, even though $SK_{Ai,r}$ and $SK_{ij,r}$ are exposed, $m_{i,t}$, $n_{i,t}$ and $n_{j,t}$ are still unknown to E, and only $g^{m_{i,t}}$, $g^{n_{i,t}}$ and $g^{n_{j,t}}$ are known. Based on the difficulties of DLP and ECDLP, E cannot get $m_{i,t}$, $n_{i,t}$ or $n_{j,t}$ from them. And also by Assumption 1 and 2, we know E cannot compute either $g^{m_{i,t}n_{i,t}}/m_{i,t}n_{i,t}G$ or $g^{n_{i,t}n_{j,t}}/n_{i,t}n_{j,t}G$. As a result,both the DLP and ECDLP based protocols can provide forward secrecy. $\square$

Theorem 5. *Based on the difficulties of DLP and ECDLP, Assumption 1 and 2, both the DLP and ECDLP based protocols can provide backward secrecy, which means: the exposure of session key $SK_{Ai,t}$ or $SK_{ij,t}$ in session s_t will not lead to the exposure of session key $SK_{Ai,r}$ or $SK_{ij,r}$ in session s_r, where $1 \leq t < r$.*

Proof. The proof of Theorem 5 is similar to that of Theorem 4. The only difference is that parameters specified to a session s_t cannot be utilized to deduce those in a later session s_r.   □

Except all these security requirements discussed on the above, there is one issue worthy explaining. When U_A and all members in $\mathbb{U}$ calculate MAC, the key they utilize is K_G. Thus there is a possibility that any user who has obtained K_G can tamper another user's message and then calculate the right MAC. However, since the purpose of any user in $\mathbb{U}$ is to get authenticated by U_A, we assume that they will not carry out this kind of inside attacks.

6   Comparisons

Except for authentication and key exchanges, another two purposes we want to achieve in our framework are to save both computation and communication costs. According to Eq. (3), we know that the computation cost mainly depends on operation F and $\circ$, denoted by C_F and $C_\circ$ respectively. There are three possibilities. First, if $C_\circ$ is negligible compared with C_F, the computation cost of our framework is $O(1)$ rather than $O(N)$ in the one-to-one mode with respect to C_F. Second, if $C_\circ$ is almost the same as C_F, the computation cost will be $O(N)$ in both modes. The last possibility is the opposite to the first one, and then our framework becomes more time consuming instead of time saving.

Unlike the complexity of computation cost, our protocol can save some communication cost in general. However, the extent to which it can save depends on many factors, such as which cryptographic primitives are chosen, the length of security parameters and so on. To better compare the communication cost, the general message flows of the traditional one-to-one mode protocol can be simply described as follows.

(1) $U_A \rightarrow U_i$: $ID_A, ID_i, y_i \oplus K_G, y_i \oplus t_i, g^{m_i}/m_iG, h_i, C_0, MAC_A$.

　　or: $ID_A, SIGN_{SK_A}\{ID_i, y_i \oplus K_G, y_i \oplus t_i, g^{m_i}/m_iG\}, C_0, MAC_A$.

(2) $U_i \rightarrow U_A$: $ID_i, ID_A, t_i', g^{n_i}/n_iG, C_i, MAC_i$.

(3) $U_A \rightarrow \mathbb{U}$: ID_A, ID_i, KP_i, MAC_A'.

Here, all the parameters have the same meaning as explained in Table 1. Since the possibility of a bottleneck in communication can mostly happen at U_A, we will only compute the communication cost of U_A. Then in the following,

Table 2. Lengths of parameters (Bits)

	ID	K_G	t_i/t_i'	g^{m_i}/m_iG	h_i	C_N	MAC
DLP based	32	128	128	1,024	160	1,024	160
ECDLP based	32	128	128	160	160	160	160

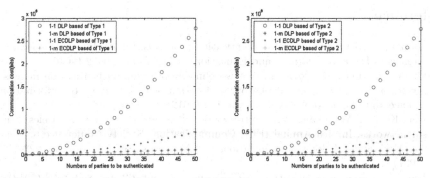

(a) Communication Cost Comparisons Of (b) Communication Cost Comparisons Of
Protocols of Type I   Protocols of Type II

Fig. 3. Communication cost comparisons.

we will show the experiments results about our DLP and ECDLP based protocols in Fig. 3, and the lengths of parameters we use are listed in Table 2. From
the figures, we can see that there are big differences between one-to-one (1-1)
and one-to-multiple (1-m) modes, and also some differences between DLP and
$ECDLP$ based protocols. Suppose the number of user group is N as stated in
Table 1, and then the communication cost for protocols in one-to-one mode is
$O(N^2)$ but $O(N)$ for one-to-multiple mode protocols. When the number of parties to be authenticated is small, there is not much difference. However, when N
increases, the differences will grow fast. Therefore, for systems that have large
numbers of users to be authenticated frequently or the computation or communication resources are limited, our framework can gain an obvious advantage.

7   Conclusions

In this paper, we propose a general framework where different cryptographic
primitives can be applied to authenticate several users or clients at one time in
two scenarios, where authenticators are with or without certificates. In our protocols, mutual authentication can be achieved at the third step. The fourth step for
protocols of Type I is optional, since it aims at establishing session keys between
different members in group 𝕌. By applying our framework, the authenticator
can authenticates users or clients in a one-to-multiple mode, which is more effective and thus less time consuming. To demonstrate how our framework works,
we give two example, i.e., DLP and ECDLP based protocols. Based on these
two examples, we prove that our protocols satisfy certain security requirements,
such as against passive and impersonation attacks, and providing implicit key
authentication, forward and backward secrecy. In applications of our framework,
it is suggested that the certificate-based systems should be the same as the cryptographic primitives to simplify the calculations and also save resources.

References

1. Huiping, J.: Strong password authentication protocols. In: 4th International Conference on Distance Learning and Education (ICDLE), pp. 50–52 (2010)
2. Ghanbarimaman, R., Pour, A.: A new definition of group authentication increasing performance of server calculation. In: International Conference on Information Science and Applications (ICISA), pp. 1–6 (2012)
3. Ren, K., Lou, W., Zhang, Y.: Multi-user broadcast authentication in wireless sensor networks. In: 4th Annual IEEE Communications Society Conference on Sensor, Mesh and Ad Hoc Communications and Networks (SECON '07), pp. 223–232 (2007)
4. Harn, L.: Group authentication. IEEE Trans. Comput. **62**(9), 1893–1898 (2013)
5. Blake, I., Gao, X., Mullin, R., Vanstone, S., Yaghoobian, T.: The discrete logarithm problem. In: Menezes, A. (ed.) Applications of Finite Fields. The Springer International Series in Engineering and Computer Science, vol. 199, pp. 115–138. Springer, New York (1993)
6. Hankerson, D., Menezes, A.: Elliptic curve discrete logarithm problem. In: Tilborg, H. (ed.) Encyclopedia of Cryptography and Security, pp. 186–189. Springer, New York (2005)
7. Elgamal, T.: A public key cryptosystem and a signature scheme based on discrete logarithms. IEEE Trans. Inf. Theor **31**(4), 469–472 (1985)
8. Zhao, J., Gu, D.: A security patch for a three-party key exchange protocol. Wuhan Univ. J. Nat. Sci. **15**(3), 242–246 (2010)
9. Zhang, X.L.: Authenticated key exchange protocol in one-round. In: Hua, A., Chang, S.L. (eds.) Algorithms and Architectures for Parallel Processing. LNCS, vol. 5574, pp. 226–233. Springer, Heidelberg (2009)
10. Chaum, D., Van Heyst, E.: Group signatures. In: Proceedings of the 10th Annual International Conference on Theory and Application of Cryptographic Techniques (EUROCRYPT'91), pp. 257–265. Springer, Heidelberg (1991)
11. Rivest, R., Shamir, A., Tauman, Y.: How to leak a secret: theory and applications of ring signatures. In: Goldreich, O., Rosenberg, A., Selman, A. (eds.) Theoretical Computer Science. LNCS, vol. 3895, pp. 164–186. Springer, Heidelberg (2006)
12. Guo, H., Wu, Y., Chen, H., Ma, M.: A batch authentication protocol for v2g communications. In: 4th IFIP International Conference on New Technologies, Mobility and Security (NTMS), pp. 1–5 (2011)
13. Johnson, D., Menezes, A., Vanstone, S.: The elliptic curve digital signature algorithm (ecdsa). Int. J. Inf. Sec. **1**(1), 36–63 (2001)
14. Farah, A., Khali, H.: Joint multiple signature scheme for group-oriented authentication and non-repudiation. In: IEEE GCC Conference, pp. 1–5 (2006)
15. Bellare, M., Neven, G.: Multi-signatures in the plain public-key model and a general forking lemma. In: Proceedings of the 13th ACM conference on Computer and communications security (CCS '06), pp. 390–399. ACM, New York (2006)
16. Yeh, L.Y., Huang, Y.L., Joseph, A., Shieh, S., Tsaur, W.: A batch-authenticated and key agreement framework for p2p-based online social networks. IEEE Trans. Veh. Technol. **61**(4), 1907–1924 (2012)
17. Merkle, Ralph C.: One way hash functions and DES. In: Brassard, G. (ed.) CRYPTO 1989. LNCS, vol. 435, pp. 428–446. Springer, Heidelberg (1990)
18. Tsiounis, Y., Yung, M.: On the security of elgamal based encryption. In: Imai, H., Zheng, Y. (eds.) Public Key Cryptography. LNCS, vol. 1431, pp. 117–134. Springer, Heidelberg (1998)

19. Boneh, D.: The decision Diffie-Hellman problem. In: Buhler, J. (ed.) Algorithmic Number Theory. LNCS, vol. 1423, pp. 48–63. Springer, Heidelberg (1998)
20. Chiou, G.H., Chen, W.T.: Secure broadcasting using the secure lock. IEEE Trans. Softw. Eng. **15**(8), 929–934 (1989)
21. Bellare, M., Rogaway, P.: Random oracles are practical: a paradigm for designing efficient protocols. In: Proceedings of the 1st ACM conference on Computer and communications security. CCS '93, pp. 62–73. ACM, New York (1993)
22. Boneh, Dan: The decision Diffie-Hellman problem. In: Buhler, Jeremy P. (ed.) ANTS 1998. LNCS, vol. 1423, pp. 48–63. Springer, Heidelberg (1998)
23. Fridrich, J., Goljan, M.: Robust hash functions for digital watermarking. In: Proceedings on the International Conference on Information Technology: Coding and Computing, pp. 178–183 (2000)

Modelling Simultaneous Mutual Authentication for Authenticated Key Exchange

Zheng Yang[(✉)]

Horst Görtz Institute for IT Security, Chair for Network- and Data Security,
Ruhr-University, Bochum, Germany
zheng.yang@rub.de

Abstract. Most recent security models for authenticated key exchange (AKE) do not explicitly model the entity authentication, which enables a party to identify its communication peer in specific session. However, it is quite necessary in many real-world applications and is a general way to enhance the security of AKE protocols. Despite much work on AKE, we notice that there is no good definition of entity authentication security involving simultaneous protocol execution that would improve the bandwidth efficiency in practice. Based on eCK model, we define a security model called eCK-A that deals with simultaneous mutual authentication. Besides the eCK-A model particularly formulates the security properties regarding resilience to the leakage of various combinations of long-term key and ephemeral session state, and provision of perfect forward secrecy in a single model. We present a generic protocol compiler to achieve the eCK-A security based on any eCK secure protocols.

Keywords: Authentication · Authenticated key exchange · Protocol compiler · Security model · Perfect forward secrecy

1 Introduction

Authenticated key exchange (AKE) is one of the most important public key primitives that form a fundamental building block for creating confidential or integrity-protected communication channel. Cryptographically game-based modelling for AKE protocols was initiated by the seminal work of Bellare and Rogaway [2] (which we refer to as the BR93 model). Since then, there has been continuing trends to strengthen adversary powers or add required security properties in the newly proposed models in this tradition. However, along with development of formal AKE security models, some important security goal of AKE is obsolete in recent models [7,9,15,16], i.e. entity authentication. One of the reasons is that those models are mainly used to provide security argument for two-message key exchange protocols where only implicit key authentication was satisfied. Since, it is impossible to achieve mutual entity authentication within only two protocol moves.

J.-L. Danger et al. (Eds.): FPS 2013, LNCS 8352, pp. 46–62, 2014.
DOI: 10.1007/978-3-319-05302-8_4, © Springer International Publishing Switzerland 2014

However, entity authentication is one of the most important security methods in cryptography that assures one party Alice of the identity of its communication partner Bob within specific session via some kind of corroborative evidence (this implies Alice is also assured that Bob was active at the time the evidence was created or acquired). The entity authentication techniques also lay the foundation for other security topics such as access control that is related to real-world applications (e.g. online banking). On the other hand, some security attributes of key exchange might be realized with the aid of entity authentication, like the perfect forward secrecy (PFS). Although in literatures [5,9] the authors introduced models and solutions to achieve PFS for two-message protocols without entity authentication, their security results have not truly overthrown the argument of Krawczyk [15] that no two-move protocol can achieve full PFS in presence of adversary who can reveal critical session states. Consider the PFS attack scenario against any two-message protocol, the adversary can compromise the secret session states (used to compute the session key) and replay the message (e.g. ephemeral key) generated involving such session states, to target session on behalf of the sender; to this end, the adversary can corrupt sender after the session key is established. Then such adversary can compute the session key of target session with both ephemeral and long-term secrets used to compute the session key of target session. It is obvious that PFS security is broken in this way. This kind of ephemeral key compromise and replay (ECR) attacks might be very harmful, if the honest party uses the session key determined by adversary to encrypt some critical information that would be later exposed to adversary. Surprisingly, the eCK-PFS model [9] allows adversary to learn session states of sessions, but the above practical ECR attack scenario is never covered. Thus, it is questionable about the PFS property achieved by the solution introduced in [9] in a model where the revelation of ephemeral secret information is allowed. On the other side all replay attacks can be circumvented via entity authentication techniques. Because, for any secure AKE protocol with entity authentication, an active adversary should be unable to impersonate any uncorrupted honest party to establish a session key with another honest party.

With respect to modelling entity authentication for key exchange, certain partnership must be formulated first to cover the situation that two parties are involved in one on-line (real-time) communication. While examining the definitions of partnership, the most prominent general approach is 'matching conversations (MC) introduced by Bellare and Rogaway [2]. Roughly speaking, a conversation is identified via a transcript of protocol messages sent and received by a session in a *time sequence* (which emulates a session). Then two sessions are matched if theirs transcripts are identical or the transcript of a session *correctly* covers the transcript of another session (except for the last protocol message). However, a drawback of this approach is that it cannot model the simultaneous protocol execution which allows very low latency mutual authentication and key agreement. In this case, the transcripts recorded by two sessions are totally different that would lead to the MC approach fail. So far we are not aware any *general* approach based on message transcript that can formalize the simultaneous mutual authentication. However such simultaneous protocol execution is very likely existence in the real world protocols. It is still an open question on how to model mutual authentication involving simultaneous protocol execution.

Contributions. In this paper we solve the above open problem, to push forward the theoretical barrier of authenticated key exchange security notions. In order to bridge the gap between practical protocol execution and theoretical security notions, we introduce a new concept of matching sessions for modelling simultaneous mutual authentication, which relaxes (and implies) the notion of matching conversations. We incorporate our new notion into the eCK model that yields a new security model called eCK-A, in which two main security goals are formalized: entity authentication and key distribution. Besides the eCK-A captures almost all desirable security attributes identified so far that include: resistance to key compromise impersonation (KCI) attacks, chosen identity and public key attacks (CIDPK) and leakage of session states (LSS), and provision of perfect forward secrecy (PFS) in a single model. Thus the resulting model is strictly stronger than the eCK-PFS model in [9]. One of the reasons is that new proposed model capture a stronger notion of PFS that is resilience of ephemeral key compromise and replay attacks other than the eCK-PFS model.

On the second, we present a generic compiler for modular design of AKE protocols that contributes towards strengthening the overall system security by integrating more security attributes. On input any two-message AKE protocol which is secure in the eCK model [16] (or its variants), the generic compiler yields a two round AKE protocol which is secure in the eCK-A model. Our compiler doesn't require extra long-term key pair, which is built based on a pseudorandom function family and message authentication code schemes. Although our compiler introduces one more communication round to exchange authentication evidence, those authentication messages can be generated independently and sent simultaneously. Of course one could also integrate those authentication messages within the subsequent application data transmission. In this way multiround AKE may also provide very bandwidth efficient key agreement comparing to two-message AKE. The security proof of our transformation is given without random oracles in the eCK-A security model. In other word, if the original protocol is eCK-secure without random oracles (e.g. the protocols introduced in [22]) then the resultant protocol is eCK-A-secure in the standard model.

Related Works. In BR93 model, security goals are formalized by requiring the protocol to provide security of not only key distribution but also entity authentication. Partnership in BR93 is defined using the notion of matching conversations. However, the notion of matching conversations does not capture the real world situations then the protocol instances executed simultaneously by two session participants.

A revision to the BR93 model was proposed in 2000 by Bellare et al. [1] hereafter referred to as the BPR2000 model, which also formulated the mutual authentication. Unlike the BR93 model, the partnership notion in BPR2000 is defined based on session identifier which is required to be a unique string generated during the execution of each protocol instance. However such session identifier is less generic. Since each protocol analyzed in the BPR2000 model has to define a session identifier itself that might be error prone. On the other hand, an existing protocol without defining a session identifier cannot be analysed in the BPR2000 model. In contrast, our goal is to seek more general approach to formalize the partnership in order to model simultaneous mutual authentication.

In 2007 LaMacchia et al. [16] proposed an extended Canetti-Krawczyk (eCK) model, to capture almost all desirable security attributes for two-message AKE. Since then many AKE protocols e.g. [10,11,14,18–22], have been proposed to capture eCK security. However the eCK model does not capture security goal of mutual authentication and perfect forward secrecy property. In Section 4, we are going to show how to transform those eCK-secure protocols to be eCK-A secure protocols.

Meanwhile both famous two-message protocols HMQV and NAXOS have three pass version with key confirmation, i.e. HMQV-C [15] and NAXOS-C [17], but they are never 'completely' analyzed due to lack of explicit authentication related definition in underlying security models. Krawczyk claims that the security of HMQV-C holds in Universal Composability (UC) model [6] of key-exchange protocols. But it is better first thoroughly analyze the security of a protocol in the standard model to avoid missing important security aspects of AKE.

2   Preliminaries

Notations. We let $\kappa \in \mathbb{N}$ denote the security parameter and 1^κ the string that consists of κ ones. Let a 'hat' on top of a capital letter denote an identity; without the hat the letter denotes the public key of that party. Let $\emptyset$ denote the empty string. Let $[n] = \{1, \ldots, n\} \subset \mathbb{N}$ be the set of integers between 1 and n. If S is a set, then $a \xleftarrow{\$} S$ denotes the action of sampling a uniformly random element from S. Let $\mathcal{IDS}$ be an identity space. Let $\mathcal{K}_{\mathsf{AKE}}$ be the key space of session key, and $\{\mathcal{PK}, \mathcal{SK}\}$ be key spaces for long-term public/private key respectively. Those spaces are associated with security parameter κ.

2.1   Notations for Two-Message AKE

In a two-message AKE protocol (TMAKE), each party may send a single message'. The key exchange procedure is done within two pass and a common shared session key is generated to be known only by session participants, which is shown in Fig. 1.

A general TMAKE protocol may consist of four polynomial time algorithms (TMAKE.Setup, TMAKE.KGen, TMAKE.MF, TMAKE.KF) with following semantics:

- $pms \leftarrow$ TMAKE.Setup(1^κ): On input 1^κ, outputs pms, a set of system parameters.

- $(sk_{\mathsf{ID}}, pk_{\mathsf{ID}}) \xleftarrow{\$} \mathsf{TMAKE.KGen}(pms, \mathsf{ID})$: This algorithm takes as input system parameters pms and a party's identity $\mathsf{ID} \in \mathcal{IDS}$, and outputs a pair of long-term private/public key $(sk_{\mathsf{ID}}, pk_{\mathsf{ID}}) \in \{\mathcal{PK}, \mathcal{SK}\}$ for party ID.
- $m_{\mathsf{ID}_1} \xleftarrow{\$} \mathsf{TMAKE.MF}(pms, sk_{\mathsf{ID}_1}, \mathsf{ID}_2, pk_{\mathsf{ID}_2}, r_{\mathsf{ID}_1}, m_{\mathsf{ID}_2})$: This algorithm takes as input system parameters pms and the sender ID_1's secret key sk_{ID_1}, the intended receiver ID_2's public key pk_{ID_2}, a randomness $r_{\mathsf{ID}_1} \xleftarrow{\$} \mathcal{R}_{\mathsf{TMAKE}}$ and a message $m_{\mathsf{ID}_2} \in \mathcal{M}_{\mathsf{TMAKE}}$ from party ID_2, and outputs a message $m_{\mathsf{ID}_1} \in \mathcal{M}_{\mathsf{TMAKE}}$ to be sent, where $\mathcal{R}_{\mathsf{TMAKE}}$ is the randomness space and $\mathcal{M}_{\mathsf{TMAKE}}$ is message space. We remark that the secret key sk_{ID_1} of sender, the identity ID_2 and public key pk_{ID_2} of receiver are only optional for generating the message.
- $K \leftarrow \mathsf{TMAKE.KF}(pms, sk_{\mathsf{ID}_1}, \mathsf{ID}_2, pk_{\mathsf{ID}_2}, r_{\mathsf{ID}_1}, m_{\mathsf{ID}_2})$: This algorithm take as the input system parameters pms and ID_1's secret key sk_{ID_1}, a public key pk_{ID_2} of ID_2, a randomness $r_{\mathsf{ID}_1} \xleftarrow{\$} \mathcal{R}_{\mathsf{TMAKE}}$ and a received message m_{ID_2} from party ID_2, and outputs session key $K \in \mathcal{K}_{\mathsf{TMAKE}}$, where $\mathcal{K}_{\mathsf{TMAKE}}$ is the session key space of TMAKE.

We say that the $\mathsf{TMAKE.KF}$ algorithm is correct, if for all $(sk_{\mathsf{ID}_1}, pk_{\mathsf{ID}_1}) \xleftarrow{\$} \mathsf{TMAKE.KGen}(pms, \mathsf{ID}_1)$ and $(sk_{\mathsf{ID}_2}, pk_{\mathsf{ID}_2}) \xleftarrow{\$} \mathsf{TMAKE.KGen}(pms, \mathsf{ID}_2)$, for all $r_{\mathsf{ID}_1}, r_{\mathsf{ID}_2} \xleftarrow{\$} \mathcal{R}_{\mathsf{TMAKE}}$ and for all messages $m_{\mathsf{ID}_1} \xleftarrow{\$} \mathsf{TMAKE.MF}(pms, sk_{\mathsf{ID}_1}, \mathsf{ID}_2, pk_{\mathsf{ID}_2}, r_{\mathsf{ID}_1}, \emptyset)$ and $m_{\mathsf{ID}_2} \xleftarrow{\$} \mathsf{TMAKE.MF}(pms, sk_{\mathsf{ID}_2}, \mathsf{ID}_1, pk_{\mathsf{ID}_1}, r_{\mathsf{ID}_2}, m_{\mathsf{ID}_1})$, it holds that $\mathsf{TMAKE.KF}(pms, sk_{\mathsf{ID}_1}, \mathsf{ID}_2, pk_{\mathsf{ID}_2}, r_{\mathsf{ID}_1}, m_{\mathsf{ID}_2}) = \mathsf{TMAKE.KF}(pms, sk_{\mathsf{ID}_2}, \mathsf{ID}_1, pk_{\mathsf{ID}_1}, r_{\mathsf{ID}_2}, m_{\mathsf{ID}_1})$

A the system initiation phase, the parameters would be generated as $pms \leftarrow \mathsf{TMAKE.Setup}(1^\kappa)$. Figure 1 briefly illustrates the generic protocol execution of TMAKE on input pms.

Please note that if in the above execution, if the party ID_2's message m_{ID_2} is generated to be independent of m_{ID_1} then the TMAKE is a one-round AKE pro-

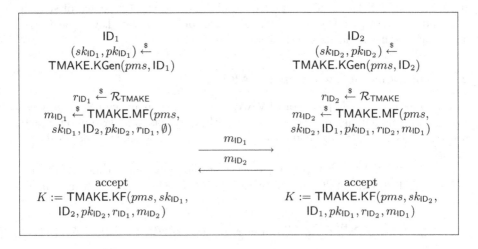

Fig. 1. General TMAKE protocol

tocol, i.e. $m_{\mathsf{ID}_2} \xleftarrow{\$} \mathsf{TMAKE.MF}(pms, sk_{\mathsf{ID}_2}, \mathsf{ID}_1, pk_{\mathsf{ID}_1}, r_{\mathsf{ID}_2}, \emptyset)$. The independence property of one-round AKE enables parties to run protocol instances simultaneously (which is a key feature of one-round protocol). Moreover, in the paper, we only consider the TMAKE to be stateless that no state is pre-shared by two parties before session initiation.

2.2   Other Definitions

In addition, we need standard security notions of pseudo-random functions PRF and message authentication code MAC (which should be EUF-CMA secure). Those detail definitions can be found in literature [12], which are omitted here due to lack of space. Generally speaking, both PRF and MAC are required to be deterministic algorithms (in this paper) which takes as the key in corresponding key space and some bit string in corresponding message space, and return a string in corresponding range space. One of those primitives (PRF and MAC) is said to be (t, ϵ)-secure, if there is no t-time adversary which can break corresponding security with advantage that is larger than ϵ.

3   Security Model

The security goals and attributes are normally formulated in some security model for proving security of considered authenticated key-exchange (AKE) protocol. In this section we present the formal security model for two party AKE. Generally speaking, the adversary is able to take full control over the communication network (e.g., alter or inject messages as she wishes). In particular she may compromise the long-term keys of parties or the secret states of protocol instances at any time. To capture those adversarial capabilities, an active adversary is provided with an 'execution environment' following an important research line research [3,7,13,15,16] which is initiated by Bellare and Rogaway [2]. In the sequel, we will use the similar frameworks as [13].

Execution Environment. In the execution environment, we fix a set of honest parties $\{\mathsf{ID}_1, \ldots, \mathsf{ID}_\ell\}$ for $\ell \in \mathbb{N}$, where ID_i $(i \in [\ell])$ is the identity of a party which is chosen uniquely from space $\mathcal{IDS}$. Each identity is associated with a long-term key pair $(sk_{\mathsf{ID}_i}, pk_{\mathsf{ID}_i}) \in (\mathcal{SK}, \mathcal{PK})$ for authentication.[1] Each honest party ID_i can sequentially and concurrently execute the protocol multiple times with different intended partners, this is characterized by a collection of oracles $\{\pi_i^s : i \in [\ell], s \in [d]\}$ for $d \in \mathbb{N}$.[2] Oracle π_i^s behaves as party ID_i carrying out

---

[1] For simplicity, we consider the security of one selective public key pair of each honest party. Of course one my apply the much more complicated certificate authority setting in [4] that each party may possess multiple public keys. But in this case, in the security proof, the adversary still has to choose one uncompromised public key of honest party to attack. On the other hand, we have to consider the model that is compatible to previous model for our upcoming generic protocol transformation.

[2] An oracle in this paper might be alternatively written as $\pi_{\mathsf{ID}_i}^s$ which is conceptually equivalent to π_i^s.

Table 1. Internal states of oracles

Variable	Decryption
Ψ_i^s	Storing the identity and public key of its intended communication partner, e.g. $(\mathsf{ID}_j, pk_{\mathsf{ID}_j})$
Φ_i^s	Denoting the decision $\Phi_i^s \in \{\texttt{accept}, \texttt{reject}\}$
ρ_i^s	Denoting the role $\rho_i^s \in \{Initiator(I), Responder(R)\}$
K_i^s	Recording the session key $K_i^s \in \mathcal{K}_{\mathsf{AKE}}$
st_i^s	Storing the ephemeral keys that allows to be revealed by adversary, e.g. the randomness used to generate ephemeral public key
sT_i^s	Recording the transcript of messages sent by oracle π_i^s
rT_j^t	Recording the transcript of messages received by oracle π_i^s

a process to execute the s-th protocol instance (session), which has access to the long-term key pair $(sk_{\mathsf{ID}_i}, pk_{\mathsf{ID}_i})$ and to all other public keys. Moreover, we assume each oracle π_i^s maintains a list of independent internal state variables with semantics listed in Table 1.

All those variables of each oracle are initialized with empty string which is denoted by the symbol $\emptyset$ in the following. At some point, each oracle π_i^s may complete the execution always with a decision state $\Phi_i^s \in \{\texttt{accept}, \texttt{reject}\}$. Furthermore, we assume that the session key is assigned to the variable K_i^s (such that $K_i^s \neq \emptyset$) iff oracle π_i^s has reached an internal state $\Phi_i^s = \texttt{accept}$.

Adversarial Model. An adversary $\mathcal{A}$ in our model is a PPT Turing Machine taking as input the security parameter 1^κ and the public information (e.g. generic description of above environment), which may interact with these oracles by issuing the following queries.

- $\mathsf{Send}(\pi_i^s, m)$: The adversary can use this query to send any message m of his own choice to oracle π_i^s. The oracle will respond the next message m^* (if any) to be sent according to the protocol specification and its internal states. Oracle π_i^s would be initiated as *initiator* via sending the oracle the first message $m = (\top, \widetilde{\mathsf{ID}}_j)$ consisting of a special initialization symbol $\top$ and a value $\widetilde{\mathsf{ID}}_j$. The $\widetilde{\mathsf{ID}}_j$ is either the identity ID_j of intended partner or empty string $\emptyset$. After answering a Send query, the variables $(\Psi_i^s, \Phi_i^s, K_i^s, st_i^s, sT_i^s, rT_i^s)$ will be updated depending on the specific protocol.[3]
- $\mathsf{RevealKey}(\pi_i^s)$: Oracle π_i^s responds with the contents of variable K_i^s.
- $\mathsf{RevealState}(\pi_i^s)$: Oracle π_i^s responds with the ephemeral keys stored in variable st_i^s, i.e. the random coins generated by π_i^s.

---

[3] For example, the variable Ψ_i^s might be set as identity ID_j and public key pk_{ID_j} at some point when the oracle receives a message containing identity related information of its partner; the messages m and m^* will be appended to transcript rT_i^s and sT_i^s respectively. A protocol here might be either run in pre- or post-specified peer setting [8, 17]. As for a protocol running under post-specified peer setting, we always have that $\widetilde{\mathsf{ID}}_j = \emptyset$.

- Corrupt(ID_i): Oracle π_i^1 responds with the long-term secret key sk_{ID_i} of party ID_i if $i \in [\ell]$.
- RegisterDishonest($\mathsf{ID}_\tau, pk_{\mathsf{ID}_\tau}$): This query allows the adversary to register an identity ID_τ ($\ell < \tau$ and $\tau \in \mathbb{N}$) and a static public key pk_{ID_τ} on behalf of a party ID_τ, if $\mathsf{ID}_\tau \neq \mathsf{ID}_i$ for all $i \in [\ell]$. Parties established by this query are called dishonest.
- Test(π_i^s): If the oracle has state $\Omega = \mathtt{reject}$ nor $K_i^s = \emptyset$, then the oracle π_i^s returns some failure symbol $\bot$. Otherwise it flips a fair coin b, samples a random element K_0 from key space $\mathcal{K}_{\mathsf{AKE}}$, and sets $K_1 = K_i^s$. Finally the key K_b is returned. This query is allowed to be asked at most once during the following security game.

Secure AKE Protocols. In order to formulate the security, we define the partnership via following new type of *matching sessions*. Matching sessions are used in this models in three distinct ways. First, they are used to define a minimal form of protocol correctness. Second, they are used to define the adversary capabilities (e.g., the adversary can reveal the session key of non-matching sessions). Third, we need to model the mutual authentication based on matching sessions.

Assume there are two transcripts $T_i^s \in \{sT_i^s, rT_i^s\}$ and $T_j^t \in \{sT_j^t, rT_j^t\}$. We say that T_i^s is a prefix of T_j^t if $|T_i^s| > 0$ and the first $|T_i^s|$ messages in transcripts T_i^s and T_j^t are pairwise equivalent as binary strings.

Definition 1 (Matching sessions (MS)). *We say that an oracle π_i^s has a matching session to oracle π_j^t, if π_i^s accepts and all the following conditions hold:*

- $\rho_i^s \neq \rho_j^t$, $\Psi_i^s = (\mathsf{ID}_j, pk_{\mathsf{ID}_j})$, $\Psi_j^t = (\mathsf{ID}_i, pk_{\mathsf{ID}_i})$, *and*
- rT_j^t *is a prefix of* sT_i^s *and* $rT_i^s = sT_j^t$.

We call the oracle π_i^s to be the partner-oracle of π_j^t.

Remark 1 In contrast to the definition of matching conversations [1], we define the matching session via two separate transcripts of protocol messages. This enables us to model the relative simultaneous protocol execution. In real world protocols, the messages within each transcript would have also internal order. For example, message authentication key is generated if and only if the ephemeral key is received. Then the received ephemeral key will be recorded in front of the subsequent confirmation message (as in Fig. 2) generated using session key, that is why we require $rT_i^s = sT_j^t$. In particular, the sender of last protocol message has to 'accept' without knowing whether its last message was received by the client correctly. We have to take this into account in the definition of matching sessions, since an active adversary may simply drops the last protocol message.

On the other hand, our matching sessions notion implies the notion of matching conversations, when those protocol messages are exchanged dependently according to the time sequence. In this case, one could only somehow combine two transcript sT and rT (in order of priority) to yield a uniform transcript to model a conversation.

CORRECTNESS. We say an AKE protocol Π is correct, if two oracles π_i^s and π_j^t accept such that π_i^s has a matching session to π_j^t, then both oracles hold the same session key, i.e. $K_i^s = K_j^t$.

Before introducing the security definition, we need the notion of *freshness* of oracles to exclude trivial attacks.

Freshness Definitions. In the following, we review the freshness definitions with (weak) perfect forward secrecy. Let π_i^s be an accepted oracle with intended partner ID_j. Meanwhile, let π_j^t be an oracle (if it exists) with intended partner ID_i, such that π_i^s has a matching session to π_j^t.

Definition 2 (eCK-fresh). *The oracle π_i^s is said to be eCK-fresh if none of the following conditions holds: (i)$\mathcal{A}$ queried* RegisterDishonest$(\mathsf{ID}_j, pk_{\mathsf{ID}_j})$; *(ii) $\mathcal{A}$ queried* RevealKey(π_i^s); *(iii) if π_j^t exists, $\mathcal{A}$ queried* RevealKey(π_j^t); *(iv) $\mathcal{A}$ queried both* Corrupt(ID_i) *and* RevealState(π_i^s); *(v) if π_j^t exists, $\mathcal{A}$ queried both* Corrupt(ID_j) *and* RevealState(π_j^t); *(vi)if π_j^t does not exist, $\mathcal{A}$ queried* Corrupt(ID_j).

Definition 3 (eCK-A-fresh). *The oracle π_i^s is said to be eCK-A-fresh if none of the following conditions holds: (i) $\mathcal{A}$ queried* RegisterDishonest$(\mathsf{ID}_j, pk_{\mathsf{ID}_j})$; *(ii) $\mathcal{A}$ queried* RevealKey(π_i^s); *(iii) if π_j^t exists, $\mathcal{A}$ queried* RevealKey(π_j^t); *(iv) $\mathcal{A}$ queried both* Corrupt(ID_i) *and* RevealState(π_i^s); *(v) If π_j^t exists, $\mathcal{A}$ queried both* Corrupt(ID_j) *and* RevealState(π_j^t); *(vi) if π_j^t does not exist, $\mathcal{A}$ queried* Corrupt(ID_j) *prior to $\Phi_i^s = $ accept.*

In the sequel, we let Fresh be a variable indicating the freshness notion defined above, i.e. Fresh $\in \{$eCK-fresh, eCK-A-fresh$\}$.

Definition 4 (Session Key Security). *A correct key exchange protocol Π is called $(t, \epsilon, $Fresh$)$-session-key-secure if for all adversaries $\mathcal{A}$ running within time t in the above security game and for some negligible probability $\epsilon = \epsilon(\kappa)$ in the security parameter κ, it holds that:*

– *When $\mathcal{A}$ returns b' such that*
  - *$\mathcal{A}$ has issued a* Test *query to an oracle π_i^s without failure,*
  - *π_i^s is Fresh-fresh throughout the security experiment,*
  *then the probability that b' equals the bit b sampled by the **Test**-query is bounded by*

$$|\Pr[b = b'] - 1/2| \leq \epsilon.$$

Definition 5 (Secure Authenticated Key Exchange). *We say that a correct two-party AKE protocol Π is (t, ϵ)-secure, if for all adversaries $\mathcal{A}$ running the AKE security game within time t while having some negligible probability $\epsilon = \epsilon(\kappa)$, it holds that:*

1. *When $\mathcal{A}$ terminates, there exists no oracle π_i^s with internal states $\Phi_i^s = $ accept and $\Psi_i^s = \mathsf{ID}_j$, such that*
   – *π_i^s is Fresh-fresh, and*
   – *there is no unique oracle π_j^t such that π_i^s has a matching session to π_j^t.*
2. *The protocol Π is $(t, \epsilon, $eCK-A-fresh$)$-session-key-secure.*

Table 2. Summary on models used in this thesis.

	Security goals		Security attributes						
	EAuth	KD	KSK	KCI	CIDPK	PFS	wPFS	Target LSS	Other LSS
eCK	×	√	√	√	√	×	√	√	√
eCK-A	√	√	√	√	√	√	√	√	√

We summarize the security goals and attributes that are covered by the models mentioned above in Table 2. The eCK and eCK-A securities are different from the aspects regarding security goal and freshness definition (in particular for Corrupt query).

The terms 'EAuth' and 'KD' are abbreviations of entity authentication and key distribution. The term 'Target LSS' denotes the leakage of session states from target session and its partner session, and the term 'Other LSS' denote the leakage of session states from sessions other than test session and its partner session. The symbols '√/×' means that the model does/doesn't capture the attack.

4 A Generic Transformation

In this following, we show the generic compiler $\mathsf{MAC}(\Pi)$ based on message authentication code scheme MAC. By applying the $\mathsf{MAC}(\Pi)$ compiler, we show the resultant protocol is secure in the eCK-A model as long as the original protocol Π is eCK secure. The generic transformation is generalized from the HMQV-C [15] protocol.

Protocol Description. The proposed protocol between two parties ID_1 and ID_2 is shown in the Fig. 2. This protocol consists of two parts: the original TMAKE and the protocol transformation.

Remark 2. We highlight that the transformation part in the generic compiler $\mathsf{MAC}(\Pi)$ can be executed simultaneously and independently by two session participants. Moreover, if the original TMAKE protocol Π is a one-round protocol then the whole resultant protocol can be simultaneously executed. This would improve the efficiency of bandwidth usage. Meanwhile, the concrete eCK-secure one-round AKE protocols in the standard model under standard assumptions can be found in [22].

Security Analysis. We are going to show the protocols obtained from the above generic transformation are secure in the eCK-A model via the following theorem.

Theorem 1. *For any* TMAKE *protocol Π, if Π is $(t, \epsilon_{\mathsf{eCK}}, \mathsf{eCK}\text{-}\mathsf{fresh})$-session-key-secure in the sense of Definition 4, the pseudo-random function family* PRF

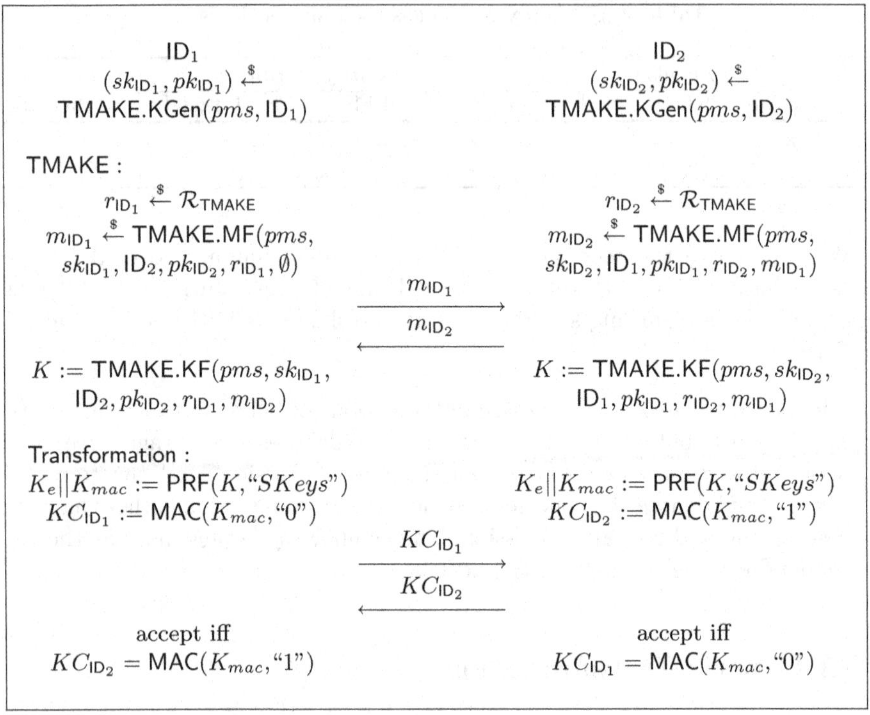

$$
\begin{array}{ll}
\text{ID}_1 & \text{ID}_2 \\
(sk_{\text{ID}_1}, pk_{\text{ID}_1}) \xleftarrow{\$} & (sk_{\text{ID}_2}, pk_{\text{ID}_2}) \xleftarrow{\$} \\
\text{TMAKE.KGen}(pms, \text{ID}_1) & \text{TMAKE.KGen}(pms, \text{ID}_2)
\end{array}
$$

TMAKE :

$$
\begin{array}{ll}
r_{\text{ID}_1} \xleftarrow{\$} \mathcal{R}_{\text{TMAKE}} & r_{\text{ID}_2} \xleftarrow{\$} \mathcal{R}_{\text{TMAKE}} \\
m_{\text{ID}_1} \xleftarrow{\$} \text{TMAKE.MF}(pms, & m_{\text{ID}_2} \xleftarrow{\$} \text{TMAKE.MF}(pms, \\
\quad sk_{\text{ID}_1}, \text{ID}_2, pk_{\text{ID}_2}, r_{\text{ID}_1}, \emptyset) & \quad sk_{\text{ID}_2}, \text{ID}_1, pk_{\text{ID}_1}, r_{\text{ID}_2}, m_{\text{ID}_1})
\end{array}
$$

$$
\xrightarrow{\quad m_{\text{ID}_1} \quad}
$$
$$
\xleftarrow{\quad m_{\text{ID}_2} \quad}
$$

$$
\begin{array}{ll}
K := \text{TMAKE.KF}(pms, sk_{\text{ID}_1}, & K := \text{TMAKE.KF}(pms, sk_{\text{ID}_2}, \\
\quad \text{ID}_2, pk_{\text{ID}_2}, r_{\text{ID}_1}, m_{\text{ID}_2}) & \quad \text{ID}_1, pk_{\text{ID}_1}, r_{\text{ID}_2}, m_{\text{ID}_1})
\end{array}
$$

Transformation :

$$
\begin{array}{ll}
K_e \| K_{mac} := \text{PRF}(K, \text{``SKeys''}) & K_e \| K_{mac} := \text{PRF}(K, \text{``SKeys''}) \\
KC_{\text{ID}_1} := \text{MAC}(K_{mac}, \text{``0''}) & KC_{\text{ID}_2} := \text{MAC}(K_{mac}, \text{``1''})
\end{array}
$$

$$
\xrightarrow{\quad KC_{\text{ID}_1} \quad}
$$
$$
\xleftarrow{\quad KC_{\text{ID}_2} \quad}
$$

$$
\begin{array}{ll}
\text{accept iff} & \text{accept iff} \\
KC_{\text{ID}_2} = \text{MAC}(K_{mac}, \text{``1''}) & KC_{\text{ID}_1} = \text{MAC}(K_{mac}, \text{``0''})
\end{array}
$$

Fig. 2. Generic compiler MAC(Π)

is $(q_{prf}, t, \epsilon_{\text{PRF}})$-*secure and the message authentication scheme* MAC *is deterministic and* $(q_{mac}, t, \epsilon_{\text{MAC}})$-*secure, then the protocol* MAC(Π) *is* $(t', \epsilon_{\text{eCK-A}})$-*secure in the sense of Definition 5, such that* $t \approx t'$, $q_{prf} \geq 2$, $q_{mac} \geq 2$ *and*

$$
\epsilon_{\text{eCK-A}} \leq 3 \cdot \epsilon_{\text{eCK}} + 2d\ell \cdot (\epsilon_{\text{eCK}} + \epsilon_{\text{PRF}} + \epsilon_{\text{MAC}}).
$$

The proof of Theorem 1 is given in Appendix A.

5   Conclusions

We have introduced a new eCK-A security notion which particularly formulate the security goal of simultaneous mutual authentication for AKE protocols. Besides the eCK-A model capture almost all desirable security attributes in a single model. We presented a generic compiler for security-strengthening that is able to transform any two-message eCK-secure into protocol secure in eCK-A. This allows for very general module approach to construct eCK-A secure AKE protocol. Namely one could first propose a protocol secure in the eCK model (that would be much simpler) and then apply our generic transformation to obtain a eCK-A secure protocol. It might be an interesting open question whether there exists more efficient or succinct (with less assumptions) transformations that yield AKE protocols secure in the eCK-A model, e.g. two parties proceed mutual authentication based on the confidential channel established via the symmetric encryption primitives.

A Proof of Theorem 1

We prove Theorem 1 in two stages. First, we show that the AKE protocol is a secure authentication protocol except for probability ϵ_{auth}, that is, the protocol fulfils security property 1.) of the AKE definition. In the next step, we show that the session key of the AKE protocol is secure except for probability ϵ_{ind} in the sense of the Property 2.) of the AKE definition. Then we have the overall probability ϵ that adversary breaking the protocol is at most $\epsilon \leq \epsilon_{auth} + \epsilon_{ind}$.

Lemma 1. *If the protocol Π is (t, ϵ_{eCK})-eCK-secure, the pseudo-random function family* PRF *is $(q_{prf}, t, \epsilon_{PRF})$-secure and the MAC scheme is $(q_{mac}, t, \epsilon_{MAC})$-secure, then the above protocol meets the security Property 1.) of the eCK-A security definition except for probability with*

$$\epsilon_{auth} \leq \epsilon_{eCK} + d\ell \cdot (\epsilon_{eCK} + \epsilon_{MAC}),$$

where all quantities are as the same as stated in the Theorem 1.

Proof. Let S^1_δ be the event that (i) there exists oracle $\pi_i^{s^*}$ reaches internal state $\Phi_i^{s^*} = \texttt{accept}$ with intended communication partner ID_j, but (ii) there is no oracle π_j^t such that $\pi_i^{s^*}$ has a matching session to π_j^t, in Game δ.

Game 0. This is the original security game. We have that

$$\Pr[\mathsf{S}^1_0] = \epsilon_{auth}.$$

Game 1. In this game, the challenger proceeds exactly like previous game, except that we add a abortion rule. The challenger raises event $\mathsf{abort}_{\mathsf{trans}}$ and aborts, if during the simulation either the message m_{ID} replied by an oracle π_i^s but it has been sample by another oracle π_u^w or sent by adversary before. Since there are $d\ell$ such values would be sampled randomly. We claim that the event $\mathsf{abort}_{\mathsf{trans}}$ occurs with probability $\Pr[\mathsf{abort}_{\mathsf{trans}}] \leq \epsilon_{eCK}$. We elaborate the proof as follows. Please first recall that if the under-attacked oracle $\pi_i^{s^*}$ (generating message $m_{\mathsf{ID}_i}^{s^*}$) is fresh then the adversary is not allowed to issue both $\mathsf{Corrupt}(\mathsf{ID}_i)$ and $\mathsf{RevealState}(\pi_i^{s^*})$, as otherwise the security is trivially broken. However, consider the case that there is another oracle π_w^v generate the same message as $\pi_i^{s^*}$ then the adversary can issue $\mathsf{RevealState}(\pi_w^v)$ to learn the states of $\pi_i^{s^*}$. At the same time that the adversary can ask $\mathsf{Corrupt}(\mathsf{ID}_i)$ to learn sk_{ID_i}. Then the adversary to compute the session key of $\pi_i^{s^*}$ with both ephemeral and long-term secrets of test session. Furthermore, the probability that the collisions among the messages generated by TMAKE.MF in either protocol Π or MAC(Π) is the same. The security of Π

in the eCK model, implies the collision probability among outgoing messages is negligible. We therefore have that

$$\mathsf{Adv}_0 \leq \mathsf{Adv}_1 + \epsilon_{\mathsf{eCK}}.$$

Game 2. This game proceeds exactly as the previous game but the challenger aborts if it fails to guess the under attacked oracle $\pi_i^{s^*}$. Since there are ℓ honest parties and d oracles for each party, the probability that the adversary guesses correctly is at least $1/(d\ell)$. Thus we have that

$$\mathsf{Adv}_1 \leq d\ell \cdot \mathsf{Adv}_2.$$

Game 3. In this game, the challenger proceeds exactly like previous game, except that we replace the intermediate key K^* of oracle $\pi_i^{s^*}$ with a random value $\widetilde{K}^*$. If the adversary can distinguish this game from previous game, then it must be able to break the eCK security of protocol Π. We therefore have that

$$\mathsf{Adv}_2 \leq \mathsf{Adv}_3 + \epsilon_{\mathsf{eCK}}.$$

Game 4. In this game, we change function $\mathsf{PRF}(K^*, \text{``SKeys''})$ for the test oracle and its partner oracle with a truly random function. We make use of the fact, that the secret seed of the PRFs of test oracle is a truly random value due to the modification in previous game. If there exists a polynomial time adversary $\mathcal{A}$ can distinguish the Game 4 from Game 3. Then we can construct an algorithm $\mathcal{B}$ using $\mathcal{A}$ to break the security of PRF. Exploiting the security of PRF, we have that

$$\mathsf{Adv}_3 \leq \mathsf{Adv}_4 + \epsilon_{\mathsf{PRF}}.$$

Game 5. This game proceeds exactly like the previous game except that the challenger aborts if the eCK-A-fresh oracle $\pi_i^{s^*}$ accepts a confirmation message $KC_j^{s^*}$ but it has not been sent by any oracle of its intended partner ID_j. In this game, the eCK-A-fresh $\pi_i^{s^*}$ accepts if and only if it has a unique partner oracle. Thus no adversary can break authentication property, and we have $\Pr[\mathsf{S}_5^1] = 0$. Applying the security of MAC we have that

$$\Pr[\mathsf{S}_4^1] \leq \Pr[\mathsf{S}_5^1] + \epsilon_{\mathsf{MAC}}.$$

Put altogether advantages of adversary in each game, we proved this lemma.

Lemma 2. *If the protocol Π is $(t, \epsilon_{\mathsf{eCK}})$-eCK-secure, the pseudo-random function family PRF is $(q_{prf}, t, \epsilon_{\mathsf{PRF}})$-secure and the MAC scheme is $(q_{mac}, t, \epsilon_{\mathsf{MAC}})$-secure, then the above protocol meets the security Property 2.) of the eCK-A security definition except for probability with*

$$\epsilon_{ke} \leq 2 \cdot \epsilon_{\mathsf{eCK}} + d\ell \cdot (\epsilon_{\mathsf{eCK}} + \epsilon_{\mathsf{PRF}} + \epsilon_{\mathsf{MAC}}),$$

where all quantities are as the same as stated in the Theorem 1.

Proof. It is straightforward to verify that two accepted oracles (of considered protocol) having matching sessions would generate the same session key. Since a correct eCK protocol must also be eCK-A protocol. In the sequel, we wish to show that the adversary is unable to distinguish random value from the session key of any eCK-A-fresh oracle. In the following, we use the superscript '*' to highlight corresponding values processed in test oracle π_i^{s*} which has intended communication partner ID_j.

Let π_i^s be an accepted oracle with intended partner ID_j. Let π_j^t be an oracle (if it exists) with intended partner ID_i, such that π_i^s has a matching session to π_j^t. Let π_j^t be an oracle (if it exists), such that π_j^t has a origin session to π_i^s. Besides the freshness restrictions of test oracle concerning RevealKey and RegisterDishonest queries, if the adversary breaks the indistinguishability security property of considered protocol, then at least one of the fresh cases related to RevealState query and Corrupt query in the following might occur in terms of the Definition 3: (i) if π_j^t exists, $\mathcal{A}$ did not query RevealState(π_i^s) nor RevealState(π_j^t); (ii) if π_j^t exists, $\mathcal{A}$ did not query Corrupt(ID_i) nor RevealState(π_j^t); (iii) if π_j^t exists, $\mathcal{A}$ did not query Corrupt(ID_i) nor Corrupt(ID_j); (iv) if π_j^t exists, $\mathcal{A}$ did not query RevealState(π_i^s) nor Corrupt(ID_j); (v) if π_j^t does not exist, $\mathcal{A}$ did not query Corrupt(ID_i) nor Corrupt(ID_j) prior to $\Phi_i^s = \mathtt{accept}$; (vi) if π_j^t does not exist, $\mathcal{A}$ did not query RevealState(π_i^s) nor Corrupt(ID_j) prior to $\Phi_i^s = \mathtt{accept}$.

Let S_δ be the event that the adversary wins the security experiment under the Game δ and one of the above freshness cases. Let $\mathsf{Adv}_\delta := \Pr[\mathsf{S}_\delta] - 1/2$ denote the advantage of $\mathcal{A}$ in Game δ. We consider the following sequence of games.

Game 0. This is the original eCK-A security game with adversary $\mathcal{A}$. Thus we have that
$$\Pr[S_0] = 1/2 + \epsilon_{ke} = 1/2 + \mathsf{Adv}_0.$$

Game 1. The challenger in this game proceeds as before, but it aborts if the test oracle accepts without unique partner oracle. Thus we have
$$\mathsf{Adv}_0 \leq \mathsf{Adv}_1 + \epsilon_{\mathsf{auth}} \leq \epsilon_{\mathsf{eCK}} + d\ell \cdot (\epsilon_{\mathsf{eCK}} + \epsilon_{\mathsf{PRF}} + \epsilon_{\mathsf{MAC}}),$$

where ϵ_{auth} is an upper bound on the probability that there exists an oracle that accepts without unique partner oracle in the sense of Definition 4 (cf. Lemma 1). We have now excluded active adversaries between test oracle and its partner oracle.

Game 2. This game is similar to the previous game. However, the challenger $\mathcal{C}$ now guesses the test oracle π_i^{s*}. $\mathcal{C}$ aborts if its guess is not correct. Thus we have that
$$\mathsf{Adv}_1 \leq d\ell \cdot \mathsf{Adv}_2.$$

We are now in a game where both oracles accept and the adversary cannot make active attacks.

Game 3. This game is proceeded as previous game, but the challenger $\mathcal{C}$ replaces the session key of test oracle and its partner oracle with a uniform random value.

If there exists an adversary $\mathcal{A}$ can distinguish the Game 3 from Game 2 then we can use it to construct an adversary $\mathcal{B}$ to break the eCK-security of Π.

Intuitively, the security reduction from eCK-A to eCK is possible in this game, since both eCK-A-fresh and eCK-fresh encompass freshness cases when the test oracle has matching session. Let $\mathcal{B}$ be an adversary which interacts with an eCK-challenger $\mathcal{C}$ and tries to breaks the eCK security of Π in the eCK security game. $\mathcal{B}$ runs $\mathcal{A}$ (who is a successful eCK-A attacker) as subroutine and simulates the challenger for $\mathcal{A}$ as previous game. For every oracle $\{\pi_i^s : i \in [\ell], s \in [d]\}$ simulated by $\mathcal{C}$, $\mathcal{B}$ keeps a corresponding dummy oracle $\pi_i^{s'}$ and the adversary $\mathcal{A}$ is able to interacts with those dummy oracles simulated by $\mathcal{B}$. Specifically, a dummy oracle proceeds as following:

- For any $\mathsf{Send}(\pi_i^{s'}, m)$ query from $\mathcal{A}$, if m belongs to original Π then $\mathcal{B}$ then $\mathcal{B}$ just issues $m^* \leftarrow \mathsf{Send}(\pi_i^s, m)$ and return m^* to $\mathcal{A}$. Meanwhile if π_i^s terminate with acceptance and π_i^s is not guessed as under attacked oracle or its partner oracle, then $\mathcal{B}$ asks $\mathsf{RevealKey}(\pi_i^s)$ to learn corresponding key material to generate the MAC key and corresponding key confirmation message. If π_i^s is guessed under attacked oracle or its partner oracle, then $\mathcal{B}$ just uses a random key material to compute MAC key and corresponding key confirmation message. All generated key confirmation messages are returned to adversary.
- For any $\mathsf{Corrupt}(\mathsf{ID}_i)$ ($i \in [\ell]$) query, $\mathcal{B}$ asks $\mathsf{Corrupt}(\mathsf{ID}_i)$ to $\mathcal{C}$ to obtain sk_{ID_i} and returns it to $\mathcal{A}$.
- For any other oracles queries on $\pi_i^{s'}$ (including Test query), $\mathcal{B}$ just asks corresponding oracles queries on π_i^s to $\mathcal{C}$ and returns the results to $\mathcal{A}$.

So that $\mathcal{B}$ is able to perfectly simulate the environment for $\mathcal{A}$. If the session key returned by Test query is a true key, then the simulation is exactly the same as previous game, otherwise it is equivalent to this game. Finally, $\mathcal{B}$ returns what $\mathcal{A}$ returns to $\mathcal{C}$. If $\mathcal{A}$ wins the game with non-negligible probability, so does $\mathcal{B}$. Thus we have that

$$\Pr[\mathsf{S}_2^1] \leq \Pr[\mathsf{S}_3^1] + \epsilon_{\mathsf{eCK}}.$$

Game 4. In this game, we change function $\mathsf{PRF}(K^*, \text{"SKeys"})$ for the test oracle and its partner oracle with a truly random function. We make use of the fact, that the secret seed of the PRFs of test oracle is a truly random value due to the modification in previous game. So the security of PRF ensures that

$$\mathsf{Adv}_3 \leq \mathsf{Adv}_4 + \epsilon_{\mathsf{PRF}}.$$

Note that in this game the session key returned by Test-query is totally a truly random value which is independent to the bit b and any messages. Thus the advantage that the adversary wins this game is $\mathsf{Adv}_4 = 0$.

In this game, the session key given to adversary is independent of the bit b of Test query, thus $\Pr[\mathsf{S}_4^1] = 0$. Sum up the probabilities from Game 0 to Game 4, we proved this lemma.

References

1. Bellare, M., Pointcheval, D., Rogaway, P.: Authenticated key exchange secure against dictionary attacks. In: Preneel, B. (ed.) EUROCRYPT 2000. LNCS, vol. 1807, p. 139. Springer, Heidelberg (2000)
2. Bellare, M., Rogaway, P.: Entity authentication and key distribution. In: Stinson, D.R. (ed.) CRYPTO 1993. LNCS, vol. 773, pp. 232–249. Springer, Heidelberg (1994)
3. Blake-Wilson, S., Johnson, D., Menezes, A.: Key agreement protocols and their security analysis. In: Darnell, M. (ed.) 6th IMA International Conference on Cryptography and Coding. LNCS, vol. 1355, pp. 30–45. Springer, Berlin (1997)
4. Boyd, C., Cremers, C., Feltz, M., Paterson, K.G., Poettering, B., Stebila, D.: Asics: authenticated key exchange security incorporating certification systems. IACR Cryptol. ePrint Arch. **2013**, 398 (2013)
5. Boyd, C., González Nieto, J.: On forward secrecy in one-round key exchange. In: Chen, L. (ed.) IMACC 2011. LNCS, vol. 7089, pp. 451–468. Springer, Heidelberg (2011)
6. Canetti, R.: Universally composable security: a new paradigm for cryptographic protocols. In: 42nd Annual Symposium on Foundations of Computer Science, pp. 136–145. IEEE Computer Society Press, October 2001
7. Canetti, R., Krawczyk, H.: Analysis of key-exchange protocols and their use for building secure channels. In: Pfitzmann, B. (ed.) EUROCRYPT 2001. LNCS, vol. 2045, pp. 453–474. Springer, Heidelberg (2001)
8. Canetti, R., Krawczyk, H.: Security analysis of IKE's signature-based key-exchange protocol. In: Yung, M. (ed.) CRYPTO 2002. LNCS, vol. 2442, pp. 143–161. Springer, Heidelberg (2002). http://eprint.iacr.org/2002/120/
9. Cremers, C., Feltz, M.: Beyond eCK: perfect forward secrecy under actor compromise and ephemeral-key reveal. In: Foresti, S., Yung, M., Martinelli, F. (eds.) ESORICS 2012. LNCS, vol. 7459, pp. 734–751. Springer, Heidelberg (2012)
10. Fujioka, A., Suzuki, K.: Designing efficient authenticated key exchange resilient to leakage of ephemeral secret keys. In: Kiayias, A. (ed.) CT-RSA 2011. LNCS, vol. 6558, pp. 121–141. Springer, Heidelberg (2011)
11. Fujioka, A., Suzuki, K., Xagawa, K., Yoneyama, K.: Strongly secure authenticated key exchange from factoring, codes, and lattices. In: Fischlin, M., Buchmann, J., Manulis, M. (eds.) PKC 2012. LNCS, vol. 7293, pp. 467–484. Springer, Heidelberg (2012)
12. Jager, T., Kohlar, F., Schäge, S., Schwenk, J.: Generic compilers for authenticated key exchange. In: Abe, M. (ed.) ASIACRYPT 2010. LNCS, vol. 6477, pp. 232–249. Springer, Heidelberg (2010)
13. Jager, T., Kohlar, F., Schäge, S., Schwenk, J.: On the security of TLS-DHE in the standard model. In: Safavi-Naini, R., Canetti, R. (eds.) CRYPTO 2012. LNCS, vol. 7417, pp. 273–293. Springer, Heidelberg (2012)
14. Kim, M., Fujioka, A., Ustaoğlu, B.: Strongly secure authenticated key exchange without NAXOS' approach. In: Takagi, T., Mambo, M. (eds.) IWSEC 2009. LNCS, vol. 5824, pp. 174–191. Springer, Heidelberg (2009)
15. Krawczyk, H.: HMQV: a high-performance secure Diffie-Hellman protocol. In: Shoup, V. (ed.) CRYPTO 2005. LNCS, vol. 3621, pp. 546–566. Springer, Heidelberg (2005)
16. LaMacchia, B.A., Lauter, K., Mityagin, A.: Stronger security of authenticated key exchange. In: Susilo, W., Liu, J.K., Mu, Y. (eds.) ProvSec 2007. LNCS, vol. 4784, pp. 1–16. Springer, Heidelberg (2007)

17. Menezes, A., Ustaoglu, B.: Comparing the pre- and post-specified peer models for key agreement. In: Mu, Y., Susilo, W., Seberry, J. (eds.) ACISP 2008. LNCS, vol. 5107, pp. 53–68. Springer, Heidelberg (2008)
18. Sarr, A.P., Elbaz-Vincent, P., Bajard, J.-C.: A new security model for authenticated key agreement. In: Garay, J.A., De Prisco, R. (eds.) SCN 2010. LNCS, vol. 6280, pp. 219–234. Springer, Heidelberg (2010)
19. Sarr, A.P., Elbaz-Vincent, P., Bajard, J.-C.: A secure and efficient authenticated Diffie-Hellman protocol. In: Proceedings of the 6th European Conference on Public Key Infrastructures, Services and Applications, EuroPKI'09, pp. 83–98. Springer, Heidelberg (2010)
20. Ustaoglu, B.: Obtaining a secure and efficient key agreement protocol from (h)mqv and naxos. Des. Codes Crypt. **46**(3), 329–342 (2008)
21. Ustaoglu, B.: Comparing SessionStateReveal and EphemeralKeyReveal for Diffie-Hellmanp protocols. In: Pieprzyk, J., Zhang, F. (eds.) ProvSec 2009. LNCS, vol. 5848, pp. 183–197. Springer, Heidelberg (2009)
22. Yang, Z.: Efficient eCK-secure authenticated key exchange protocols in the standard model. In: Qing, S., Zhou, J., Liu, D. (eds.) ICICS 2013. LNCS, vol. 8233, pp. 185–193. Springer, Heidelberg (2013)

Formal Methods

Model-Based Specification and Validation of Security and Dependability Patterns

Brahim Hamid$^{(\boxtimes)}$ and Christian Percebois

IRIT, University of Toulouse, 118 Route de Narbonne,
31062 Toulouse Cedex 9, France
{hamid,percebois}@irit.fr

Abstract. The requirement for higher Security and Dependability (S&D) of systems is continuously increasing, even in domains traditionally not deeply involved in such issues. In our work, we propose a modeling environment for pattern-based secure and dependable embedded system development by design. Here we study a general scheme for representing security and dependability (S&D) design patterns whose intention specification can be defined using a set of local properties. We propose an approach that associates Model Driven Engineering (MDE) and formal validation to get a common representation to specify patterns for several domains. The contribution of this work is twofold. On the one hand, we use model-based techniques to capture a set of artifacts to specify patterns. On the other hand, we introduce a set of artifacts for the formal validation of these patterns in order to guarantee their correctness. As an illustration of the approach, we study the authorization pattern.

Keywords: Pattern · Meta-model · Domain · Formalization · Model driven engineering · Security and Dependability

1 Introduction

Extra-functional concerns have become a strong requirement on one hand, and on the other hand more and more difficult to achieve, even in safety critical systems. They can be found in many application sectors such as automotive, aerospace and home control. Such systems come with a large number of common characteristics, including real-time, temperature, computational processing and power constraints and/or limited energy and common extra-functional characteristics such as dependability and security [1] as well as efficiency.

The integration of such concerns, for instance security, safety and dependability, requires the availability of both application development and concerns expertise at the same time. Therefore, the development of such systems involves specific software building processes. These processes are often error-prone because not fully automated, even if some level of automatic code generation or even

J.-L. Danger et al. (Eds.): FPS 2013, LNCS 8352, pp. 65–82, 2014.
DOI: 10.1007/978-3-319-05302-8_5, © Springer International Publishing Switzerland 2014

model driven engineering support is applied. Furthermore, many critical systems also have assurance requirements, ranging from very strong levels, involving certification (e.g., DO178 and IEC-61508 for safety relevant embedded systems development), to lighter levels based on industry practices.

Over the last two decades, the need for a formally defined safety lifecycle process has emerged. Model-Driven Engineering (MDE) [17] provides a very useful contribution for the design of these systems, since it bridges the gap between design issues and implementation concerns. It helps the designer to specify in a separate way extra-functional requirements at a higher level which are important to guide the implementation process. Of course, an MDE approach is not sufficient but offers an ideal development context. Hence capturing and providing this expertise by the way of specific *patterns* can enhance safety critical systems development. While using an MDE framework, it is possible to help concerns specialists in their task.

In this paper, we investigate the design process of Security and Dependability (S&D) patterns. The main goal of this work is to define a modeling and development framework to support the specifications and the validation of S&D patterns and to assist the developers of trusted applications for resource constrained embedded systems. The solution envisaged here is based on combining metamodeling techniques and formal methods to represent S&D pattern at two levels of abstraction fostering reuse during the process of pattern development and during the process of pattern-based development. The contribution of this work is twofold: (1) An S&D pattern modeling language to get a common representation of S&D patterns for several domains in the context of embedded systems using model driven software engineering, (2) Formal specification and validation of a pattern in order to guarantee its correctness during the pattern integration. Therefore, patterns can be stored in a repository and can be loaded in function of their desired properties. As a result, patterns will be used as bricks to build applications through a model driven engineering approach.

The rest of this paper is organized as follows. An overview of the modeling approach we proposed including a set of definitions is presented in Sect. 2. Then, Sect. 3 presents in detail the pattern modeling language. Section 4 illustrates the pattern modeling process in practice. Section 5 presents the validation process through the example of the authorization pattern. In Sect. 6, we review most related works addressing pattern specification and validation. Finally, Sect. 7 concludes this paper with a short discussion on future works.

2   Conceptual Framework

We promote the separation of general-purpose parts of the pattern from its required mechanisms. This is an important issue to understand the use of patterns to embed solutions targeting extra-functional concerns. This section is dedicated to present the pattern modeling framework. We begin with a set of definitions and concepts that will prove useful in understanding our approach.

2.1 Definitions and Concepts

In [5], a design pattern abstracts the key artifacts of a common design structure that make it useful for creating a reusable object-oriented design. They proposed a set of design patterns for several object-oriented design problems. Several generalizations on this basis to describe software design patterns in general are proposed in literature. Adapting the definition of security patterns given in [18], we propose the following:

Definition 1 (Security and Dependability Pattern). *A security and dependability pattern describes a particular recurring security/and or dependability problem that arises in specific contexts and presents a well-proven generic scheme for its solution.*

Unfortunately, most of S&D patterns are expressed, as informal indications on how to solve some security problems, using identical template to traditional patterns. These patterns do not include sufficient semantic descriptions, including those of security and dependability concepts, for automated processing within a tool-supported development and to extend their use. Furthermore, due to manual pattern implementation use, the problem of incorrect implementation (the most important source of security problems) remains unsolved. For that, model driven software engineering can provide a solid basis for formulating design patterns that can incorporate security and dependability aspects and offering such patterns at several layers of abstraction. We will use metamodeling techniques for representing and reasoning about S&D patterns in model-based development. Note, however, that our proposition is based on the previous definition and on the classical GoF [5] specification, and we deeply refined it in order to fit with the S&D needs.

To foster reuse of patterns in the development of critical systems with S&D requirements, we are building on a metamodel for representing S&D pattern in the form of a subsystem providing appropriate interfaces and targeting S&D properties to enforce the S&D system requirements. Interfaces will be used to exhibit pattern functionality in order to manage its application. In addition, interfaces supports interactions with security primitives and protocols, such as encryption, and specialization for specific underlying software and/or hardware platforms, mainly during the deployment activity. As we shall see, S&D and resource models are used as model libraries to define the S&D and resource properties of the pattern (see part *B* of Fig. 2).

Security and Dependability patterns are not only defined from a platform independent viewpoint (i.e. they are independent from the implementation), they are also expressed in a consistent way with domain specific models. Consequently, they will be much easier to understand and validate by application designers in a specific area. To capture this vision, we introduced the concept of *domain view*. Particularly an S&D pattern at domain independent level exhibits an abstract solution without specific knowledge on how the solution is implemented with regard to the application domain.

Definition 2 (Domain). *A domain is a field or a scope of knowledge or activity that is characterized by the concerns, methods, mechanisms, ... employed in the development of a system. The actual clustering into domains depends on the given group/community implementing the target methodology.*

In our context, a domain represents all the knowledge including protocols, processes, methods, techniques, practices, OS, HW systems, measurement and certification related to the specific domain. With regard to the artifacts used in the system under development, we will identify the first classes of the domain to specialize such artifacts. For instance, the specification of a pattern at domain independent point of view is based on the software design constructs. The specialization of such a pattern for a domain uses a domain protocol to implement the pattern solution (see example of authorization pattern given in Sects. 4.1 and 4.2).

The objective is to reuse the domain independent model S&D patterns for several industrial application domain sectors and also let them be able to customize those domain independent patterns with their domain knowledge and/or requirements to produce their own domain specific artifacts. Thus, the 'how' to support these concepts should be captured in the specification languages.

2.2   Motivational Example: Authorization Pattern

As example of a common and widely used pattern, we choose the *Authorization Pattern* [19]. For instance, in a distributed environment in which users or processes make requests for data or resources, this pattern describes who is authorized to access specific resources in a system, in an environment in which we have resources whose access needs to be controlled. As depicted in the left part of Fig. 1, it indicates how to describe allowable types of accesses (authorizations) by active computational entities (subjects) to passive resources (protection objects).

However, these authorization patterns are slightly different with regard to the application domain. For instance, a system domain has its own mechanisms and means to serve the implementation of this pattern using a set of protocols ranging from RBAC (Role Based Access Control), Firewall, ACLs (Access Control Lists), Capabilities, and so on. For more breadth and depth, the reader is

Fig. 1. Authorization pattern/protecting resources using capabilities

referred to [21]. To summarize, they are similar in their goal, but different in the implementation issues. The motivation is to handle the modeling of patterns following different abstraction levels. In the followings, we propose to use *Capabilities* [21] to specialize the implementation of the authorization pattern. This solution is already used at hardware and operating system level to control resources.

More particular, the access rights of subjects with respect to objects are stored in an *access control matrix* M. Each subject is represented by a row and each object is represented by a column. An entry in such a matrix $M[s, o]$ contains precisely the list of operations subject s is allowed to request on object o. A more efficient way to store the matrix is to distribute the matrix row-wise by giving each subject a list of capabilities it has for each object. Without such a capability for a specific object means that the subject has no access rights for that object. Then, requests for resources are intercepted and validated with the information in the capabilities. The interception and the validation are achieved by a special program usually referred to as *reference monitor*. For instance, whenever a subject s requests for the resource r of object o, it sends such a request passing its capability. The reference monitor will check whether it knows the subject s and if that subject is allowed to have the requested operation r, as depicted in the right part of Fig. 1. Otherwise the request fails. It remains the problem of how to protect a capability against modification by its holder. One way is to protect such a capability (or a list of them) with a signature handed out by special certification authorities named *attribute certification authorities*.

2.3   Pattern DSL Building Process and Artifacts

A Domain Specific Language (DSL) typically defines concepts and rules of the domain using a metamodel for the abstract syntax, and a (graphical or textual) concrete syntax that resembles the way the domain tasks usually are depicted. As we shall see, such a process reuses a lot of practices from Model-Driven Engineering (MDE), for instance, metamodeling and transformation techniques. There are several DSML (Domain Specific Modeling Language) environments available. In our context, we use the Eclipse Modeling Framework (EMF) [20] open-source platform. Note, however, that our vision is not limited to the EMF platform.

In Fig. 2, we illustrate the usage of a DSL process based on MDE technology to define the modeling framework to design a pattern on one hand and the use of such a framework on the other hand. As shown in part A of Fig. 2, a DSL process is divided into several kinds of activities: DSL definition, transformation, coherency and relationships rules, designing with DSLs and qualification. The first three activities are achieved by the DSL designer and last two are used by the DSL end-user. In the following we detail the following artifacts and their related processes:

- *Pattern Metamodel:* Sect. 3 (see part A of Fig. 2).
- *Pattern Modeling.* Section 4 (see part A of Fig. 2).
- *Pattern Formalization.* Section 5 (see part C of Fig. 2).

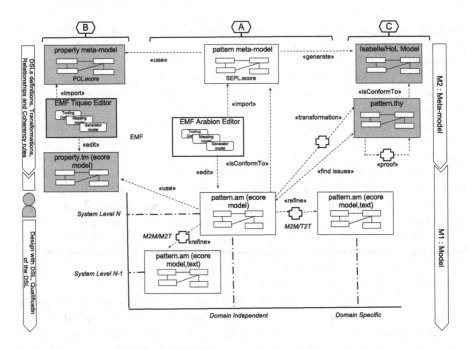

Fig. 2. Overview of the pattern DSL building process and artifacts

3 Pattern Specification Metamodel (SEPM)

The System and Software Engineering Pattern Metamodel (SEPM), as depicted in Fig. 3, is a metamodel which defines a new formalism for describing patterns and which constitutes the base of our pattern modeling language. Such a formalism describes all the concepts (and their relations) required to capture all the facets of patterns. These patterns are specified by means of a domain-independent generic representation and a domain-specific representation.

The principal classes of the metamodel are described with Ecore notations in Fig. 3 and their meanings are more detailed in the following paragraph.

– This block represents a modular part of a system that encapsulates a solution of a recurrent problem. A *DIPattern* defines its behavior in terms of provided and required interfaces. Larger pieces of a system's functionality may be assembled by reusing patterns as parts in an encompassing pattern or assembly of patterns, and wiring together their required and provided interfaces. A *DIPattern* may be manifested by one or more artifacts. This is the key entry artifact to model patterns at domain independent level (DIPM).

– *Interface.* A *DIPattern* interacts with its environment with *Interfaces* which are composed of *Operations*. A *DIPattern* owns provided and required interfaces. A provided interface is implemented by the *DIPattern* and highlights the services exposed to the environment. A required interface corresponds

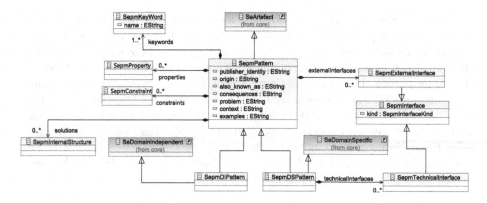

Fig. 3. The SEPM metamodel- overview

to services needed by the pattern to work properly. Finally, we consider two kinds of interface:

- *External interface.* Allows implementing interaction with regard to the integration of a pattern into an application model or to compose patterns.
- *Technical interface.* Allows implementing interaction with the platform. For instance, at a low level, it is possible to define links with software or hardware module for the cryptographic key management. Please note, a *DIPattern* does not have *TechnicalInterfaces*.

- *Property.* Is a particular characteristic of a pattern related to the concern it is dealing with and dedicated to capture its intent in a certain way. Each property of a pattern will be validated at the time of the pattern validating process and the assumptions used, will be compiled as a set of constraints which will have to be satisfied by the domain application.
- *Constraint.* Is a requisite of the pattern. If the constraints are not met, the pattern will not be able to deliver its properties.
- *InternalStructure.* Constitutes the implementation of the solution proposed by the pattern. Thus the *InternalStructure* can be considered as a white box which exposes the details of the *IPatterns*. In order to capture all the key elements of the solution, the *InternalStructure* is composed of two kinds of *Structure*: *static* and *dynamic*. Please, note that the same pattern could have several possible implementations
- *DSPattern.* Is a refinement of a *DIPattern*. It is used to build a pattern at DSPM. Furthermore a *DSPattern* has *TechnicalInterfaces* in order to interact with the platform. This is the key entry artifact to model pattern at domain specific level (DSPM).

3.1 Generic Property Modeling Language (GPRM)

The metamodel of property [23] captures the common concepts of the two main concerns of trusted RCES (Resources-Constrained Embedded Systems) applications: *Security*, *Dependability* and *Resource* on the one hand and *Constraints* on these properties on the other hand. The libraries of properties and constraints includes units, types, categories and operators. For example, security attributes such as authenticity, confidentiality and availability [1] are categories of S&D properties. The reader is referred to [23] for a full description of the properties metamodel. These models are used as external model libraries to type the properties of patterns. Especially during the design and later on for the selection of the pattern (see next sections), we define the properties and the constraints using these libraries. Note, however, that modeling languages such as MARTE (Modeling and Analysis of Real-Time and Embedded systems) [16] may be used as well for depicting these properties.

4   Pattern Modeling Process

We now present an overview of our pattern modeling process. Along this description, we will give the main keys to understand why our process is based on a general and a constructive approach. It consists of the following phases: (1) the specification of the pattern at domain independent level (DIPM), (2) the refinement of DIPM pattern to specify one of its representations at domain specific level (DSPM). These two levels of the Authorization pattern presented in Sect. 2.2 are illustrated. For the sake of simplicity, many functions and artifacts of this pattern have been omitted. We only detail the properties and interfaces that we need to describe the validation process. Note that the document representing the formalization and the proof are detailed in Sect. 5.

4.1   Domain Independent Pattern Model (DIPM)

This level is intended to generically represent patterns independently from the application domain. This is an instance of the SEPM. As we shall see, we introduce new concepts through instantiation of existing concepts of the SEPM metamodel in order to cover most existing patterns in safety critical applications. In our example, the DIPM of the authorization pattern consists of:

- *Properties*. At this level, we identify one property: *confidentiality*.
- *External Interfaces*. The authorization pattern exposes its functionalities through function calls:
  - $req(S, AT, PR)$: the subject S sends request about access type AT concerning the protected resource or data PR.

4.2   Domain Specific Pattern Model (DSPM)

The objective of the specific design level is to specify the patterns for a specific application domain. This level offers artifacts at down level of abstraction with more precise *information* and *constraints* about the target domain. This modeling level is a refinement of the DIPM, where the specific characteristics and dependencies of the application domain are considered. Different DSPM would refine a same DIPM for all needed domain. For instance, when using *Capabilities* as a mechanism related to the application domain to refine the authorization pattern at DSPM, we identify the following artifacts:

- *Properties.* In addition to the refinement of the property of confidentiality identified in the DIPM, at this level, one can consider: *deny unauthorized access*, *permit authorized access*, and *efficiency* properties.
- *External Interfaces.* This is a refinement of the DIPM external interface: $req(S, AT, PR, C)$: the subject S sends request about access type AT concerning the protected resource PR passing its capability C.
- *Technical Interfaces.* Let the subset of functions related to the use of capabilities to refine the authorization pattern:
  - $sign(C)$: the certification authority signs the capability C,
  - $verifyCert()$: the attribute capability certificate is verified,
  - $extractCap()$: the capability is extracted from the certificate,
  - $checkRight(S, AT, PR, C)$: the reference monitor verifies, using the capability, whether PR appears in the C.

5   Pattern Validation Process

We propose to use theorem proving techniques to formalize patterns and to prove their properties. This part completes the framework as depicted in Fig. 2 (see Part C). In our work, we used the interactive Isabelle/HOL proof assistant [15] to do so. First we model the pattern as a data type. Then we define and prove a set of properties and constraints that it meets. These two steps are applied successively to DIPM and DSPM levels. Finally, we deal with the correspondence between the DIPM and DSPM formal models.

5.1   Pattern Formalization

Before coding the pattern and its properties in Isabelle/HOL, one has to define what are an agent and an action. Both are records i.e. tuples, with a name attached to each component. We note *i_action* the record for an action defined at the DIPM level, and we will talk about *s_action* when dealing with the specific level. The right part of the action data type with "..." refers to specific actions defined at the DSPM model.

Definitions mainly concern the refinement process of pattern from the DIPM model to the DSPM model. We formalize this refinement by adding to the definitions of DIPM a subset of functions related to the mechanisms employed in the application domain. Compared to independent actions embodied by the *i_action* records at the DIPM level of the pattern, records of type *s_action* devoted to DSPM may have additional fields. This is easily done by the *s_action* definition of which extends the first specification by the keyword + (see left part of Table 1). We so consider that the DSPM formal model contains the same set

Table 1. Data types for the authorization pattern

DIPM	DSPM
`datatype agentType = S`	
`datatype actionType = req	...`	
`datatype accessType = at`	
`datatype dataType = PR`	
	`datatype capabilityType = C`
`record i_action =`	`datatype actionType = req	...	checkRight`
`agent : : "agentType"`	
`access : : "accessType"`	`record s_action = i_action +`
`data : : "dataType"`	
	`capability : : "capabilityType"`
`record agent =`	
`name : : "agentType"`	
`i_actions : : "i_action set"`	
`s_actions : : "s_action set"`	

of agents as the DIPM one. Its actions correspond to the external and internal domain specific interface function calls.

For our case, we introduce how to specify the confidentiality property. Let G be a set of agents, D be the critical data and A be the actual set of actions that use D. Then, the confidentiality property on D, denoted by $conf(A, D, G)$, means that only agents in G are allowed to know the value of D. All others, when looking at actions in A shall not be able to derive its value.

The definitions and the proofs used in this section are extracted from the code of our experiment applied to the authorization pattern and its related mechanism from the application domain: capabilities. Table 1 defines these artifacts in Isabelle.

Domain Independent Pattern Model (DIPM). As previously defined in Sect. 4.1, the authorization pattern exposes its functionalities through the function calls $req(S, AT, PR)$. In this formula, the subject S sends requests about access type AT concerning the protected data PR. Applying the previous definition $conf$, we get $A = req(S, at, PR)$ where $at \in AT$, $D = PR$ and $G = S$.

Function calls $req(S, at, PR)$ are independent requests of the authorization pattern formalized in Isabelle as shown in the left part of Table 2 owing to the *create_i_Action* definition and the *req* constant. In the same way, an agent is introduced by the *createAgent* definition and the subject constant nominates the active computational entity of the pattern.

Domain Specific Pattern Model (DSPM). The DSPM model of the authorization pattern introduces a capability C as mechanism to ensure the communication between the subject and the passive resources. Consequently, the DSPM $req(S, AT, PR, C)$ external interface is a refinement of the DIPM one where

Table 2. Definitions of the authorization pattern

DIPM	DSPM
definition create_i_Action : : "agentType ==> accessType ==> dataType ==> i_action" where "create_i_Action ag a d == (agent=ag, access=a, data=d)"	definition create_s_Action : : "agentType ==> accessType ==> dataType ==> capabilityType ==> s_action" where "create_s_Action ag a d c == (agent=ag, access=a, data=d,
definition req : : "i_action" where "req == create_i_Action S at PR"	capability=c)"
definition createAgent : : "agentType ==> (i_action set) ==> (s_action set) ==> agent" where "createAgent ag i_as s_as == (name=ag, i_actions=i_as, s_actions=s_as)"	definition checkRight : : "s_action" where "checkRight == create_s_Action S at PR C"
definition subject : : "agent" where "subject == createAgent S req checkRight, ..."	

the subject S sends requests about access type AT concerning the protected resource PR passing its capability C. We formalize this refinement by the code in the right part of Table 1 which adds to the definitions of the DIPM part the subset of functions *sign*, *verifyCert*, *extractCap* and *checkRight* related to capabilities. This code also defines the counterpart *s_action* of an independent action *i_action*. For sake of clarity, we only give the code of the *checkRight* constant defined as an *s_action*.

Following the definition of Sect. 4.1 and applying the previous definition *conf*, we get the confidentiality property $conf(checkRight(S, at, PR, C), PR, S)$.

5.2 Pattern Validation

The goal now is to identify the set of assumptions required to prove the properties. Then, the proof consists to find a scheduling of valid steps using Isabelle's tactics such as applying (*command apply*) a simplification considering that each step corresponds to a sub-goal to resolve. Our proof only uses simplification rules (*command simp*) which consist in rewriting specified equations from left to right in the current goal. Correctness of the proof is guaranteed by construction from the first goal to resolve (a lemma or a theorem) until the message *"no sub-goals"* is produced by the framework which confirms that the proof is finished (*command done*).

Domain Independent Pattern Model (DIPM). For our case, we have to find the assumptions for the $conf(req(S, at, PR), PR, G)$ property to hold, supposing $S \in G$ and $at \in AT$. Informally, to achieve such a property, we need to demonstrate that G is the only set of agents that can access to PR using an action $req(S, at, PR)$ and that such an action doesn't provide any information to an agent outside of G in order to derive the value of the protected data. The pattern describes in fact who is authorized to access specific resources in a system and whose accesses need to be controlled.

By definition, as presented in Sect. 2.2, we have a vector $M[s1..sn][PR]$ to denote the access rights. An entry in such a matrix $M[si, PR]$ contains precisely the list of operations of AT subject si that are allowed to request on the object PR. At this level, it's obvious that the only agents allowed to use the protected data are those listed in the defined matrix. For the second concern, we have to assume that the matrix is protected itself and that agents outside of G looking at actions in $req(S, at, PR)$ shall not be able to derive the value of PR.

Table 3. Proving the conf property

DIPM	DSPM
definition isAllowed : :	
"i_action ==> dataType ==> agent	
==> bool" where	
"isAllowed a d ag == a in (i_actions ag)	
and data a = d"	
definition isAllowedSubject : : "bool"	
where	
"isAllowedSubject == isAllowed req	
PR subject"	
	definition conf_s_action : :
definition conf_i_action : :	"s_action ==> dataType ==> agent
"i_action ==> dataType ==> agent	==> bool"
==> bool" where	where
"conf_i_action a d ag ==	"conf_s_action a d ag == a
isAllowed a d ag and isProtected a d ag"	in (s_actions ag)
	and data a = d"
lemma confReq : "conf_i_action req	
PR subject"	lemma confCheckRight :
apply (simp only : conf_i_Action_def)	"conf_s_action checkRight
apply (simp only : isAllowed_def	PR subject"
isProtected_def)	
apply (simp only : req_def)	
apply (simp only : create_i_Action_def)	
apply (simp only : subject_def)	
apply (simp only : createAgent_def)	
apply (simp add : req_def)	
apply (simp only : create_i_Action_def)	
done	

In our Isabelle experiment, we have weakened these constraints assuming two predicates *isAllowed* for authorized accesses to a specific resource and *isProtected* related to its encapsulated access. We simulate the matrix by a set of actions. We also ensure that the term $req(S, at, PR)$ verifies these preconditions. With these assumptions, the relation $conf(req(S, at, PR), PR, S)$ holds as proved by the *lemma confReq* (confidentiality of the req request) of the left part of Table 3.

In the next section, using a specific mechanism, namely *Capabilities*, to implement such a pattern, we will refine these assumptions.

Domain Specific Pattern Model (DSPM). As an example, the confidentiality property $conf(checkRight(S, at, PR, C), PR, S)$ is then established by the *confCheckRight lemma* (confidentiality of the checkRight request) given in the right part of Table 3, with similar simplification tactics when proving the *confReq* lemma of the left part of Table 3.

For our experiment, no assumptions have been introduced for this proof, but we can easily extend our formalization by considering for instance a precedence order between the calls *sign*, *verifyCert*, *extractCap* and *checkRight* related to capabilities.

5.3   Correspondence between DIPM and DSPM

Correspondence between the DIPM and DSPM formal models is assumed when proving that the property introduced at the DIPM model is transferred to the DSPM model. More precisely, this means that the DIPM model is an abstraction of the DSPM model. In particular, we must show that using a specific mechanism for verifying the property together with function calls of the specific domain is a specific case of proving the upper-level property.

We so have to map actions of the DSPM model onto the actions of the DIPM model by an appropriate homomorphism h and then prove that this homomorphism preserves the property. As a property is proved both for the DIPM and DSPM models, h validates the refinement of the proof. In practice, h is required to preserve each operation or a pseudo-operation which summarizes the behavior of a set of operations.

In our case, we must show that using *capabilities* for verifying the property $conf(checkRight(S, at, PR, C), PR, S)$ together with function calls of the specific domain is a specific case of proving the upper-level property $conf(req(S, at, PR), PR, S)$. Fig. 4 specifies h and the resulting *confReqH theorem* (confidentiality of the *req* request using h). In this code, for simplicity of illustration, we only map *checkRight* to *req*, and we introduce a null action for all other mappings.

Hence h preserves confidentiality into the DIPM request access to the protected data. The $conf(req(S, at, PR), PR, S)$ relation transferred to the DSPM model is identical to $conf(checkRight(S, at, PR, C), PR, S)$. We can formally verify this assumption according to the Isabelle's framework which displays the same sub-goals to resolve as soon as the DSPM current goal of Fig. 4 has been split by a case distinction on a Boolean condition (*command simp* with *if_def*).

```
definition h :: "s_action ==> i_action" where
"h a == if a = checkRight then req else null"

theorem confReqH :
"conf_i_action (h checkRight) PR subject"
apply (simp only : conf_i_action_def)
apply (simp only : h_def)
apply (simp only : if_def)
apply (simp)
apply (simp only : req_def)
apply (simp only : create_i_Action_def)
apply (simp only : subject_def)
apply (simp only : createAgent_def)
apply (simp add : req_def)
apply (simp only : isAllowed_def isProtected_def)
apply (simp only : create_i_Action_def)
apply (simp)
done
```

Fig. 4. Proving the correspondence between DIPM and DPSM models

6 Related Works

Design patterns are a solution model to generic design problems, applicable in specific contexts. Supporting research tackles the presented challenges includes domain patterns, pattern languages and recently formalisms and modeling languages to foster their application in practice. To give an idea of the improvement achievable by using specific languages for the specification of patterns, we look at pattern formalization and modeling problems targeting the integration of the pattern specification and validation steps into a broader MDE process.

Several tentatives exist in the literature to deal with patterns for specific concern [7,22]. They allow to solve very general problems that appear frequently as sub-tasks in the design of systems with security and dependability requirements. These elementary tasks include secure communication, fault tolerance, etc. The pattern specification consists of a service-based architectural design and deployment restrictions in form of UML deployment diagrams for the different architectural services.

To give a overview of the improvement achievable by using specific languages, we look at the pattern specification and formalization problems. *UMLAUT* [8] is an approach that aims to formally model design patterns by proposing extensions to the UML metamodel 1.3. They used OCL language to describe constraints (structural and behavioral) in the form of meta-collaboration diagrams. In the same way, *RBML(Role-Based Metamodeling Language)* [12] is able to capture various design perspectives of patterns such as static structure, interactions, and state-based behavior.

While many patterns for specific concern have been designed, still few works propose general techniques for patterns. For the first kind of approaches [5], design patterns are usually represented by diagrams with notations such as UML object, annotated with textual descriptions and examples of code. There are some well-proven approaches [3] based on Gamma et al. However, this kind of technique does not allow to reach the high degree of pattern structure flexibility which is required to reach our target.

Formal specification has also been introduced in [14] in order to give rigorous reasoning of behavioral features of a design pattern in terms of high-level abstractions of communication. In this paper, the author considers an object-oriented formalism for reactive system (DisCo) [11] based on TLA (Temporal Logic of Actions) to express high-level abstractions of cooperation between objects involved in a design pattern. However, patterns are directly formalized at the pattern level including its classes, its relations and its actions, without defining a metamodel.

[6] presents a formal and visual language for specifying design patterns called LePUS. It defines a pattern in an accurate and complete form of formula in Z, with a graphical representation. With regard to the integration of patterns in software systems, the DPML (Design Pattern Modeling Language) [13] allows the incorporation of patterns in UML class models. However, this kind of techniques does not allow to achieve the high degree of pattern structure flexibility which is required to reach our target, and offered by the proposed pattern modeling language. The framework promoted by LePUS is interesting but the degree of expressiveness proposed to design a pattern is too restrictive.

Regarding the analysis aspects, [10] used the concept of security problem frames as analysis patterns for security problems and associated solution approaches. They are also grouped in a pattern system with a list of their dependencies. The analysis activities using these patterns are described with a highlight of how the solution may be set, with a focus on the privacy requirement anonymity. For software architecture, [9] presented an evaluation of security patterns in the context of secure software architectures. The evaluation is based on the existing methods for secure software development, such as guidelines as well as on threat categories.

Another important issue is the identification of security patterns. [2] proposed a new specification template inspired on secure system development needs. The template is augmented with UML notations for the solution and with formal artifacts for the requirement properties. Recently [4] presented an overview and new directions on how security patterns are used in the whole aspects of software systems from domain analysis to the infrastructures.

To summarize, in software engineering, design patterns are considered effective tools for the reuse of specific knowledge. However, a gap between the development of systems using patterns and the pattern information still exists. This becomes even more visible when dealing with specific concerns namely security and dependability for several application sectors.

- From the pattern methodological point of view: The techniques presented above do not allow to reach the high degree of pattern structure flexibility. The framework promoted by LePUS is interesting but the degree of expressiveness proposed to design a pattern is too restrictive. The main critic of these modeling languages is that no variability support of the pattern specification, because a pattern by nature covers not only one solution, but describes a set of solutions for a recurring design problem. Furthermore there are no elements in existing modeling languages to model appropriate architectural concepts and properties provided by patterns and even more security and dependability aspects. The problem is obvious in UML and ADLs. The main shortcoming of the UML collaboration approach stems from the non-support of variability. However, we do believe that the advantages of using UML for engineering software outweigh these disadvantages.

- From the pattern-based software engineering methodological point of view: Few works are devoted to this concern. They are in line for the promotion of the use of patterns in each system/software development stage. However, existing approaches using patterns often target one stage of development (architecture, design or implementation) due to the lack of formalisms ensuring both (1) the specification of these artifacts at different levels of abstraction, (2) the specification of relationships that govern their interactions and complementarity and (3) the specification of the relationship between patterns and other artifacts manipulated during the development lifecycle and those related to the assessment of critical systems.
- From the pattern validation process point of view: There are mainly two approaches when dealing with formal reasoning: model-checking and interactive theorem proving. Model-checking is attractive because it offers a high degree of automation and is therefore accessible to uninitiated users. However, model checkers have to provide an intuitive operational understanding of a model under properties they have to verify. In contrast theorem proving focuses on abstract properties on a model and not on its behavior. This is the case for our pattern validation process with Isabelle/HOL: proof obligations introduce formulas that are so many assumptions to validate, and DSPM actions mapped on to DIPM actions must normally encompass the same subset of proof obligations.
- From the tool support point of view: Existing tools support the specification of patterns and their application in the design of software systems, notably Netbeans, StarUML, Sparx systems. In these tools, patterns are provided as UML libraries and usually embedded in the tool without extension support. The integration of pattern in these tools result merely in copying a solution into a model.

7   Conclusion and Future Work

We present an approach for the design and verification of patterns to provide practical solutions to meet security and dependability (S&D) requirements. As it follows the MDE paradigm for system's design, using patterns on different levels of abstraction, it allows for integration into the system's design process, hence supports this process. To this end, the proposed representation takes into account the simplification and the enhancement of such activities, namely : selection/search based on the properties, and integration based on interfaces. Yet the system development process is not the topic we focus on in our paper.

Indeed, a classical form of pattern is not sufficient to tame the complexity of safety critical systems – complexity occurs because of both the concerns and the domain management. To reach this objective and to foster reuse, we introduced the specification at domain independent and domain specific levels. The former exhibits an abstract solution without specific knowledge on how the solution is implemented with regard to the application domain. Following the MDE process, the domain independent model of patterns is then refined towards a domain specific level, taking into account domain artifacts, concrete elements such as mechanisms to use, devices that are available, etc.

We also provide an accompanying formalization and validation framework to help precise specification of patterns based on the interactive Isabelle/HOL proof assistant. The resulting validation artefacts may mainly (1) complete the definitions, and (2) provide semantics for the interfaces and the properties in the context of S&D. Like this, validation artefacts may be added to the pattern for traceability concerns. In the same way, the domain refinement is applied during the formal validation process for the specification and validation of patterns.

Furthermore, we walk through a prototype of EMF tree-based editors supporting the approach. Currently the tool suite named *Semcomdt*[1] is provided as Eclipse plugins. The approach presented here has been evaluated on two case studies from TERESA's project[2] resulting in the development of a repository of S&D patterns with more than 30 S&D patterns. By this illustration, we can validate the feasibility and effectiveness of the proposed specification and design framework.

The next step of this work consists in implementing other patterns including those for security, safety, reconfiguration and dependability to build a repository of multi-concerns patterns. Another objective for the near future is to provide guidelines and tool-chain supporting the whole pattern life cycle (i.e., create, store patterns, retrieve) and the integration of pattern in an application. All patterns are stored in a repository. Thanks to this, it is possible to find a pattern regarding to concern criteria. At last, guidelines will be provided during the pattern development and the application development (i.e., help to choose the appropriate pattern and its usage).

References

1. Avizienis, A., Laprie, J.C., Randell, B., Landwehr, C.: Basic concepts and taxonomy of dependable and secure computing. IEEE Trans. Dependable Secure Comput. **1**, 11–33 (2004)
2. Cheng, B., Cheng, B.H.C., Konrad, S., Campbell, L.A., Wassermann, R.: Using security patterns to model and analyze security. In: IEEE Workshop on Requirements for High Assurance Systems, pp. 13–22 (2003)
3. Douglass, B.P.: Real-time UML: Developing Efficient Objects for Embedded Systems. Addison-Wesley, Reading (1998)
4. Fernandez, E.B., Yoshioka, N., Washizaki, H., Jürjens, J., VanHilst, M., Pernul, G.: Using security patterns to develop secure systems. In: Mouratidis, H. (ed.) Software Engineering for Secure Systems: Industrial and Research Perspectives, pp. 16–31. IGI Global (2010)

---

[1] http://www.semcomdt.org
[2] http://www.teresa-project.org/

5. Gamma, E., Helm, R., Johnson, R.E., Vlissides, J.: Design Patterns: Elements of Reusable Object-Oriented Software. Addison-Wesley, Reading (1995)
6. Gasparis, E., Nicholson, J., Eden, A.H.: LePUS3: an object-oriented design description language. In: Stapleton, G., Howse, J., Lee, J. (eds.) Diagrams 2008. LNCS (LNAI), vol. 5223, pp. 364–367. Springer, Heidelberg (2008)
7. Di Giacomo, V., et al.: Using security and dependability patterns for reaction processes. In: Proceedings of the 19th International Conference on Database and Expert Systems Application, pp. 315–319. IEEE Computer Society (2008)
8. Le Guennec, A., Sunyé, G., Jézéquel, J.-M.: Precise modeling of design patterns. In: Evans, A., Caskurlu, B., Selic, B. (eds.) UML 2000. LNCS, vol. 1939, pp. 482–496. Springer, Heidelberg (2000)
9. Halkidis, S.T., Chatzigeorgiou, A., Stephanides, G.: A qualitative analysis of software security patterns. Comput. Secur. **25**(5), 379–392 (2006)
10. Hatebur, D., Heisel, M., Schmidt, H.: A security engineering process based on patterns. In: Proceedings of the 18th International Conference on Database and Expert Systems Applications, DEXA '07, pp. 734–738. IEEE Computer Society, Washington (2007)
11. Jarvinen, H.M., Kurki-Suonio, R.: Disco specification language: marriage of actions and objects. In: 11th International Conference on Distributed Computing Systems, pp. 142–151. IEEE Press (1991)
12. Kim, D.K., France, R., Ghosh, S., Song, E.: A UML-based metamodeling language to specify design patterns. In: Patterns, Proceedings Workshop Software Model Engineering (WiSME) with Unified Modeling Language Conference 2004, pp. 1–9 (2004)
13. Mapelsden, D., Hosking, J., Grundy, J.: Design pattern modelling and instantiation using dpml. In: CRPIT '02: Proceedings of the Fourteenth International Conference on Tools Pacific, pp. 3–11. Australian Computer Society Inc. (2002)
14. Mikkonen, T.E.: Formalizing design patterns. In: Proceeding ICSE '98 Proceedings of the 20th International Conference on Software Engineering. IEEE Press (1998)
15. Nipkow, T., Paulson, L.C., Wenzel, M.: Isabelle/HOL – A Proof Assistant for Higher-Order Logic. LNCS, vol. 2283. Springer, Heidelberg (2002)
16. OMG. OMG. A UML profile for MARTE: modeling and analysis of real-time embedded systems, beta 2. (June 2008). http://www.omgmarte.org/Documents/Specifications/08-06-09.pdf
17. Schmidt, D.: Model-driven engineering. IEEE Comput. **39**(2), 41–47 (2006)
18. Schumacher, M.: Security Engineering with Patterns - Origins, Theoretical Models, and New Applications. LNCS, vol. 2754. Springer, Heidelberg (2003)
19. Schumacher, M., Fernandez, E., Hybertson, D., Buschmann, F.: Security Patterns: Integrating Security and Systems Engineering. Wiley, Chicester (2005)
20. Steinberg, D., Budinsky, F., Paternostro, M., Merks, E.: EMF: Eclipse Modeling Framework 2.0., 2nd edn. Addison-Wesley Professional, Reading (2009)
21. Tanenbaum, A.S., Steen, M.: Distributed systems, principles and paradigms, 2/E. Prentice-Hall Inc., Upper Saddle River (2007)
22. Yoshioka, N., Washizaki, H., Maruyama, K.: A survey of security patterns. Prog. Inform. **(5)**, 35–47 (2008)
23. Ziani, A., Hamid, B., Trujillo, S.: Towards a unified meta-model for resources-constrained embedded systems. In: 37th EUROMICRO Conference on Software Engineering and Advanced Applications, pp. 485–492. IEEE (2011)

Enforcing Information Flow by Combining Static and Dynamic Analysis

Andrew Bedford, Josée Desharnais,
Théophane G. Godonou, and Nadia Tawbi[(✉)]

Université Laval, Qubec, Canada
{andrew.bedford.1,theophane-gloria.godonou.1}@ulaval.ca
{josee.desharnais,nadia.tawbi}@ift.ulaval.ca

Abstract. This paper presents an approach to enforce information flow policies using a multi-valued type-based analysis followed by an instrumentation when needed. The target is a core imperative language. Our approach aims at reducing false positives generated by static analysis, and at reducing execution overhead by instrumenting only when needed. False positives arise in the analysis of real computing systems when some information is missing at compile time, for example the name of a file, and consequently, its security level. The key idea of our approach is to distinguish between negative and may responses. Instead of rejecting the possibly faulty commands, they are identified and annotated for the second step of the analysis; the positive and negative responses are treated as is usually done. This work is a hybrid security enforcement mechanism: the *maybe-secure* points of the program detected by our type based analysis are instrumented with dynamic tests. The basic type based analysis has been reported in [6], this paper presents the modification of the type system and the newly presented instrumentation step. The novelty of our approach is the handling of four security types, but we also treat variables and channels in a special way. Programs interact via communication channels. Secrecy levels are associated to channels rather than to variables whose security levels change according to the information they store. Thus the analysis is flow-sensitive.

1 Introduction

In today's world, we depend on information systems in many aspects of our lives. Those systems are interconnected, rely on mobile components and are more and more complex. Security issues in this context are a major concern, especially when it comes to securing information flow. How can we be sure that a program using a credit card number will not leak this information to an unauthorized person? Or that one that verifies a secret password to authenticate a user will not write it in a file with public access? Those are examples of information flow breaches in a program that should be controlled. Secure information flow analysis is a technique used to prevent misuse of data. This is done by restricting how data are transmitted among variables or other entities in a program, according to their security classes.

J.-L. Danger et al. (Eds.): FPS 2013, LNCS 8352, pp. 83–101, 2014.
DOI: 10.1007/978-3-319-05302-8_6, © Springer International Publishing Switzerland 2014

Our objective is to take advantage of the combination of static and dynamic analysis. We design a multi-valued type system to statically check non-interference for a simple imperative programming language. To the usual two main security levels, public (or *Low*) and private (or *High*), we add two values, *Unknown* and *Blocked*. The former was introduced in [6] and captures the possibility that we may not know, before execution, whether some information is public or private. Standard two-valued analysis has no choice but to be pessimistic with uncertainty and hence generate false positive alarms. If uncertainty arises during the analysis, we tag the instruction in cause: in a second step, instrumentation at every such point together with dynamic analysis will allow us to head to a more precise result than purely static approaches. We get reduced false alarms, while introducing a light runtime overhead by instrumenting only when there is a need for it. In this paper, we add a fourth security type, *Blocked*, which is used to tag a public channel variable that must not receive any information, even public, because its value (the name of the channel) depends on private information. As long as no information is sent over such a channel, the program is considered secure.

The program on the left of Fig. 1 shows how the blocking type results in fewer false positive alarms. The figure also exhibit our analysis of the program (which we will explain later) as well as the output given by our implementation. The identifiers *privateChannel*, *publicChannel*, *highValue* and *lowValue* in all the examples are predefined constants. The security types L, H, U, B represent *Low*, *High*, *Unknown* and *Blocked*, respectively, *pc* is the security type of the context, and $\_instr = L$ to tell that there is no need for instrumentation. The first four lines of the program would be rejected by other analyses, including [6], because channel c is assigned a *Low* channel in the **then** branch, which depends on a private condition, *highValue*. In our work, c is just marked as blocked ("$c \mapsto B\,chan$") when it is assigned a public channel in a private context. However, in the last line, an information of low content is sent to c, which cannot be allowed, as it would reveal information on our confidential condition *highValue*. It is because of this last line that the program is rejected by our analysis: without it, c is just typed as B.

The goal of our security analysis is to ensure non-interference, that is, to prevent inadvertent information leaks from private channels to public channels. More precisely, in our case, the goal is to ensure that (1) a well-typed program satisfies non-interference, (2) a program not satisfying non-interference is rejected (3) a program that may satisfy non-interference is detected and sent

Input to analyzer	Inference analysis		
	Environment	*pc*	*i*
if *highValue*		$pc_{if} = H$	2
then $c := publicChannel$	$G(2) = \lfloor\_instr \mapsto L, c \mapsto B\,chan\rfloor$	H	3
else $c := privateChannel$	$G(3) = \lfloor\_instr \mapsto L, c \mapsto H\,chan\rfloor$	H	4
end;	$G(1) = \lfloor\_instr \mapsto L, c \mapsto B\,chan\rfloor$	H	4
send *lowValue* **to** c	**fail** since $c \mapsto B\,chan$		
Output :	Error (Send) : Cannot send *lowValue* to channel c because it is blocked.		

Fig. 1. Analysis of a program where an implicit flow may lead to a leak of information

to the instrumentation step. Furthermore, we consider that programs interact with an external environment through communication *channels*, i.e., objects through which a program can exchange information with users (printing screen, file, network, etc.). In contrast with the work of Volpano et al. [21], variables are not necessarily channels, they are local and hence their security type is allowed to change throughout the program. This is similar to flow-sensitive typing approaches like the one of Hunt and Sands, or Russo and Sabelfeld [10,17]. Our approach distinguishes clearly communication channels, through which the program interacts and which have a priori security levels, from variables, used locally.Therefore, our definition of non-interference applies to communication channels: someone observing the final information contained in communication channels cannot deduce anything about the initial content of the channels of higher security level.

We aim at protecting against two types of flows, as explained in [4]: *explicit flow* occurs when the content of a variable is directly transferred to another variable, whereas *implicit flow* happens when the content assigned to a variable depends on another variable, i.e., the guard of a conditional structure. Thus, the security requirements are:

- explicit flows from a variable to a channel of lower security are forbidden;
- implicit flows where the guard contains a variable of higher security than the variables assigned are forbidden.

Our static analysis is based on the typing system of [6]; our contributions are an improvement of the type system to allow fewer false positive, by the introduction of the blocked type, and the instrumentation algorithm that we have developed and implemented [3].

The rest of this paper is organized as follows. After describing in Sect. 2 the programming language used, we present the type system ensuring that information will not be leaked improperly in Sect. 3. The inference algorithm is presented in Sect. 4. The instrumentation algorithm is presented in Sect. 5. Section 6 is dedicated to related work. We conclude in Sect. 7.

2   Programming Language

We illustrate our approach on a simple imperative programming language, introduced in [6], a variant of the one in [19], which was adapted to deal with the communication via channels.

2.1   Syntax

Let Var be a set of identifiers for variables, and C a set of communication channel names. Throughout the paper, we use generically the following notation: variables are $x \in Var$, and there are two types of constants: $n \in \mathbb{N}$ and $nch \in C$. The syntax is as follows:

(phrases) $p ::= e \mid c$
(expressions) $e ::= x \mid n \mid nch \mid e_1 \text{ op } e_2$
(commands) $c ::= \textbf{skip} \mid x := e \mid c_1; c_2$
　　　　　　　　if e **then** c_1 **else** c_2 **end** $\mid$ **while** e **do** c **end** $\mid$
　　　　　　　　receive$_c$ x_1 **from** x_2 $\mid$
　　　　　　　　receive$_n$ x_1 **from** x_2 $\mid$
　　　　　　　　send x_1 **to** x_2

Values are integers (we use zero for false and nonzero for true), or channel names. The symbol **op** stands for arithmetic or logic binary operators on integers and comparison operators on channel names. Commands are mostly the standard instructions of imperative programs.

We suppose that two programs can only communicate through channels (which can be, for example, files, network channels, keyboards, computer screens, etc.). We assume that the program has access to a pointer indicating the next element to be read in a channel and that the send to a channel would append an information in order for it to be read in a first-in-first-out order. When an information is read in a channel it does not disappear, only the read pointer is updated, the observable content of a channel remains as it was before. Our programming language is sequential; we do not claim to treat concurrency and communicating processes as it is treated in [12,15]. We consider that external processes can only read and write to public channels. The instructions related to accessing channels deserve further explanations.

Table 1. A few rules of the structural operational semantics

(ASSIGN)	$\dfrac{\langle e, \mu \rangle \rightarrow_e v}{\langle \mathbf{x} := \mathbf{e}, \mu \rangle \rightarrow \mu[x \mapsto v]}$
(RECEIVE-CONTENT)	$\dfrac{x_2 \in \mathrm{dom}(\mu) \qquad read(\mu(x_2)) = n}{\langle \textbf{receive}_c \ x_1 \ \textbf{from} \ x_2, \mu \rangle \rightarrow \mu[x_1 \mapsto n]}$
(RECEIVE-NAME)	$\dfrac{x_2 \in \mathrm{dom}(\mu) \qquad read(\mu(x_2)) = nch}{\langle \textbf{receive}_n \ x_1 \ \textbf{from} \ x_2, \mu \rangle \rightarrow \mu[x_1 \mapsto nch]}$
(SEND)	$\dfrac{x_1 \in \mathrm{dom}(\mu)}{\langle \textbf{send} \ x_1 \ \textbf{to} \ x_2, \mu \rangle \rightarrow \mu, update(\mu(x_2), \mu(x_1))}$
(CONDITIONAL)	$\dfrac{\langle e, \mu \rangle \rightarrow_e n \qquad n \neq 0}{\langle \textbf{if } e \textbf{ then } c_1 \textbf{ else } c_2 \textbf{ end}, \mu \rangle \rightarrow \langle c_1, \mu \rangle}$
	$\dfrac{\langle e, \mu \rangle \rightarrow_e n \qquad n = 0}{\langle \textbf{if } e \textbf{ then } c_1 \textbf{ else } c_2 \textbf{ end}, \mu \rangle \rightarrow \langle c_2, \mu \rangle}$

The instruction **receive$_c$** x_1 **from** x_2 stands for "receive content". It represents an instruction that reads a value from a channel with name x_2 and assigns its content to x_1. The instruction **receive$_n$** x_1 **from** x_2 stands for "receive name". Instead of getting data from the channel, we receive another channel name, which might be used further in the program. This variable has to be treated like a channel. The instruction **send** x_1 **to** x_2 is used to output on a channel with name x_2 the content of the variable x_1. The need for two different receive commands is a direct consequence of our choice to distinguish variables from channels. It will be clearer when we explain the typing of commands, but observe that this allows, for example, to receive a private name of channel through a public channel[1]: the information can have a security level different from its origin's. This is not possible when variables are observable.

2.2 Semantics

The behavior of programs follows a commonly used operational semantics [6]; we present a few rules in Table 1. An instruction p is executed under a memory map $\mu : \mathit{Var} \to \mathbb{N} \cup \mathcal{C}$. Hence the semantics specifies how *configurations* $\langle p, \mu \rangle$ evolve, either to a value, another configuration, or a memory. Evaluation of expressions under a memory involves no "side effects" that would change the state of memory. In contrast, the role of commands is to be executed and change the state. Thus we have two evaluation rules: $\langle e, \mu \rangle$ leads to a value resulting from the evaluation of expression e on memory μ; this transition is designated by $\to_e$. Finally, $\langle c, \mu \rangle$ leads to a memory produced by the execution of command c on memory μ; this transition is designated by $\to$.

We explain the rules that manipulate channels. The instructions **receive$_c$** x_1 **from** x_2 and **receive$_n$** x_1 **from** x_2 are semantically evaluated similarly. Information from the channel x_2 is read and assigned to the variable x_1. The distinctive feature of the rule RECEIVE-CONTENT is that the result of evaluation is an integer variable, while for the rule RECEIVE-NAME, the result is a channel name. Here, we introduce a generic function *read(channel)* that represents the action of getting information from a channel (eg. get a line from a file, input from the keyboard, etc.). The content of a channel remains the same after both kinds of receive.

The instruction **send** x_1 **to** x_2 updates the channel x_2 with the value of the variable x_1. This is done by the generic function *update(channel, information)*, which represents the action of updating the channel with some information. Note that the content of the variable x_2, that is, the name of the channel, does not change; hence μ stays the same. The content of the channel is updated after a **send**.

3 Security Type System

We now present the security type system that we use to check whether a program of the language described above, either satisfies non-interference, may satisfy it

---

[1] But not the converse, to avoid implicit flow leaks

or does not satisfy it. It is an improvement of the one introduced in [6]: we add a security level, B, to tag a channel that should be blocked.

The security types are defined as follows:

$$\begin{aligned}
&\textit{(data types)} \quad \tau :: = \; L \mid U \mid H \mid B \\
&\textit{(phrase types)} \; \rho :: = \; \tau \; val \mid \tau \; chan \mid \tau \; cmd
\end{aligned}$$

We consider a set of four security levels $SL = \{L, U, H, B\}$. This set is extended to a lattice $(SL, \sqsubseteq)$ using the following order: $L \sqsubseteq U \sqsubseteq H \sqsubseteq B$ (we use freely the usual symbols $\sqsupseteq$ and $\sqsupset$). It is with respect to this order that the supremum $\sqcup$ and infimum $\sqcap$ over security types are defined. We lift this order to phrase types in the trivial way, and assume this returns $\bot$ when applied to phrases of different types, e.g., $H \; chan \sqcup H \; val = \bot$.

When typing a program, security types are assigned to variables, channels and commands, hence phrase types – and to the context of execution. The meaning of types is as follows. A variable of type $\tau \; val$ has a content of security type τ; a channel of type $\tau \; chan$ can store information of type τ or lower (indeed, a private channel must have the possibility to contain or receive both private and public information). The security typing of commands is standard, but has a slightly different meaning: a command of type $\tau \; cmd$ is guaranteed to only allow flows into channels whose security types are τ or higher. Hence, if a command is of type $L \; cmd$ then it may contain a flow to a channel of type $L \; chan$. Type B will only be assigned to channels, to indicate that they were of type $L \; chan$ but must be blocked, to avoid an implicit flow. The context type pc represents the type of the surrounding conditionals and helps in indicating implicit flows.

Our type system satisfies two natural properties: *simple security*, applying to expressions and *confinement*, applying to commands [19]. *Simple security* says that an expression e of type $\tau \; val$ or $\tau \; chan$ contains only variables of level τ or lower. Simple security ensures that the type of a variable is consistent with the principle stated in the precedent paragraph. *Confinement* says that a command c of type $\tau \; cmd$ executed under a context of type pc allows flows only to channels of level $\tau \sqcup pc$ or higher, in order to avoid a flow from a channel to another of lower security (H to L for example). Those two properties are used to prove non-interference. The complete soundness proof of this algorithm is similar to the one presented in [7].

Our typing rules are shown in Table 2. They are the same as in [6] except for the three rules that deal with channels. A *typing judgment* has the form $\Gamma, pc \vdash p : \rho, \Gamma'$, where Γ and Γ' are typing environments, mapping variables to a type of the form $\tau \; val$ or $\tau \; chan$ that represents their security level; pc is the security type of the context. The program is typed with a context of type L; according to the security types of conditions, some blocks of instructions are typed with a higher context, as will be explained later. The typing judgment can be read as: within an initial typing environment Γ and a security type context pc, the command p has type ρ, yielding a final environment Γ'. When the typing environment stays unchanged, Γ' is omitted. Since the type of channels is constant, there is a particular typing environment for channel constants, named

Table 2. Typing rules

(CHAN_S)	$\dfrac{TypeOf\_Channel(nch) = \tau}{\Gamma, pc \vdash nch : \tau\ chan}$ $\qquad$ (INT_S) $\quad \Gamma, pc \vdash n : L\ val$
(OP_S)	$\dfrac{\Gamma, pc \vdash e_1 : \tau_1\ \alpha, \qquad \Gamma, pc \vdash e_2 : \tau_2\ \alpha}{\Gamma, pc \vdash e_1\ \textbf{op}\ e_2 : (\tau_1 \sqcup \tau_2)val}$ $\quad$ (VAR_S) $\quad \dfrac{\Gamma(x) = \tau\ \alpha}{\Gamma, pc \vdash x : \tau\ \alpha}$
(SKIP_S)	$\Gamma, pc \vdash \textbf{skip}\ :\ H\ cmd$
(ASSIGN-VAL_S)	$\dfrac{\Gamma, pc \vdash e : \tau\ val}{\Gamma, pc \vdash x := e : (\tau \sqcup pc)\ cmd, \Gamma \dagger [x \mapsto (\tau \sqcup pc)val]}$
(ASSIGN-CHAN_S)	$\dfrac{\Gamma, pc \vdash e : \tau\ chan}{\Gamma, pc \vdash x := e : \tau\ cmd, \Gamma \sqcup [\_instr \mapsto HL_L^L(pc, \tau)] \dagger [x \mapsto HL_\tau^B(pc, \tau)chan]}$
(RECEIVE-CONTENT_S)	$\dfrac{\Gamma(x_2) = \tau\ chan}{\Gamma, pc \vdash \textbf{receive}_c\ x_1\ \textbf{from}\ x_2 : (\tau \sqcup pc)\ cmd, \Gamma \dagger [x_1 \mapsto (\tau \sqcup pc)val]}$
(RECEIVE-NAME_S)	$\dfrac{\Gamma(x_2) = \tau\ chan}{\substack{\Gamma, pc \vdash \textbf{receive}_n\ x_1\ \textbf{from}\ x_2 : \tau\ cmd, \\ \Gamma \sqcup [\_instr \mapsto HL_\tau^L(pc, \tau)] \dagger [x_1 \mapsto HL_{U \sqcup \tau}^B(pc, \tau)chan]}}$
(SEND_S)	$\dfrac{\Gamma(x_1) = \tau_1\ \alpha \qquad \Gamma(x_2) = \tau\ chan \qquad \neg((\tau_1 \sqcup pc) = H \wedge \tau = L) \qquad \tau \neq B}{\Gamma, pc \vdash \textbf{send}\ x_1\ \textbf{to}\ x_2 : \tau\ cmd, \Gamma \sqcup [\_instr \mapsto HL_L^U(\tau_1 \sqcup pc, \tau)]}$
(CONDITIONAL_S)	$\dfrac{\Gamma, (pc \sqcup \tau_0) \vdash c_1 : \tau_1\ cmd, \Gamma' \qquad \Gamma, pc \vdash e : \tau_0\ val \qquad \Gamma, (pc \sqcup \tau_0) \vdash c_2 : \tau_2\ cmd, \Gamma'' \qquad \Gamma' \sqcup \Gamma'' \sqsupset \bot}{\Gamma, pc \vdash \textbf{if}\ e\ \textbf{then}\ c_1\ \textbf{else}\ c_2\ \textbf{end} : (\tau_1 \sqcap \tau_2)\ cmd, \Gamma' \sqcup \Gamma''}$
(LOOP1_S)	$\dfrac{\Gamma, pc \vdash e : \tau_0\ val \qquad \Gamma, (pc \sqcup \tau_0) \vdash c : \tau\ cmd, \Gamma' \qquad \Gamma = \Gamma \sqcup \Gamma' \sqsupset \bot}{\Gamma, pc \vdash \textbf{while}\ e\ \textbf{do}\ c\ \textbf{end} : \tau\ cmd, \Gamma \sqcup \Gamma'}$
(LOOP2_S)	$\dfrac{\Gamma, pc \vdash e : \tau_0\ val \quad \Gamma, (pc \sqcup \tau_0) \vdash c : \tau\ cmd, \Gamma' \quad \Gamma \neq \Gamma \sqcup \Gamma' \sqsupset \bot \quad \Gamma \sqcup \Gamma', (pc \sqcup \tau_0) \vdash \textbf{while}\ e\ \textbf{do}\ c\ \textbf{end} : \tau'\ cmd, \Gamma''}{\Gamma, pc \vdash \textbf{while}\ e\ \textbf{do}\ c\ \textbf{end} : \tau'\ cmd, \Gamma''}$
(SEQUENCE_S)	$\dfrac{\Gamma, pc \vdash c_1 : \tau_1\ cmd, \Gamma' \qquad \Gamma', pc \vdash c_2 : \tau_2\ cmd, \Gamma''}{\Gamma, pc \vdash c_1; c_2 : (\tau_1 \sqcap \tau_2)\ cmd, \Gamma''}$

TypeOf_Channel that is given before the analysis. In the rules, α stands for either the label *val* or *chan*, depending on the context.

We use, as in [6], a special variable *_instr*, whose type (maintained in the typing environment map according to the typing rules) tells whether or not the program needs instrumentation. The initial value of *_instr* is L; if the inference algorithm detects a need for instrumentation, its value is changed to U, H or B, depending on the rule applied, most of the time depending on the type of a channel. When it is updated, the supremum operator is always involved to make sure that the need for instrumentation is recorded until the end.

We need to define three operators, two of which on typing environments: $\Gamma\dagger[x\mapsto\rho]$ and $\Gamma\sqcup\Gamma'$. The former is a standard update, where the image of x is set to ρ, no matter if x is in the original domain of Γ or not. For the conditional rule in particular, we need a union of environments where common value variables must be given, as security type, the supremum of the two types, and where channel variables are given type U if they differ and none of them is blocked.

Definition 1. *The supremum of two environments is given as* $dom(\Gamma\sqcup\Gamma') = dom(\Gamma)\cup dom(\Gamma')$, *and*

$$\Gamma\sqcup\Gamma'(x)=\begin{cases} \Gamma(x) & \text{if } x\in dom(\Gamma)\setminus dom(\Gamma') \\ \Gamma'(x) & \text{if } x\in dom(\Gamma')\setminus dom(\Gamma) \\ U\,chan & \text{if } B\,chan\neq\Gamma(x)=\tau\,chan\neq\tau'\,chan=\Gamma'(x)\neq B\,chan \\ \Gamma(x)\sqcup\Gamma'(x) & \text{otherwise.} \end{cases}$$

Note that $\Gamma\sqcup\Gamma'(x)$ can return $\bot$ if Γ and Γ' are incompatible on variable x, for example if $\Gamma(x)$ is a value, and $\Gamma'(x)$ is a channel (this can only happen if Γ and Γ' come from different branches of an **if** command).

In the three rules that modify a channel, ASSIGN-CHAN_S, RECEIVE-NAME_S et SEND_S, the following operator is also used.

Definition 2. *The function HL computes the security level of _instr and channel variables in the three typing rules where a channel is modified.*

$$HL_\nu^\psi(pc,\tau)=\begin{cases} \psi \text{ if } (pc,\tau)=(H,L) \\ U \text{ if } (pc,\tau)\in\{(U,L),(U,U),(H,U)\} \\ \nu \text{ otherwise.} \end{cases} \quad \text{where } \psi,\nu,pc,\tau\in SL.$$

The notation *HL* refers to a downward flow "H to L" because this (handy and maybe tricky) function encodes (with ψ and ν), in particular, how such a flow from pc to τ should be handled. When it is clear that there is a downward flow, from H to L, then *HL* returns type ψ. When we are considering the security type of a channel variable, ψ is either U or B. Such a flow may not lead to a rejection of the program, nor to an instrumentation: when a variable is blocked, there is no need to instrument. For other flows, the analysis distinguishes between safe flows and uncertain ones. For example, flows from U to H are secure, no matter what the types of uncertain variables actually are at runtime (L or H). In these cases, $HL_\nu^\psi(pc,\tau)$ returns ν. However, depending on the actual type of the U variable at runtime, a flow U to L, from U to U or from H to U may be secure or not. A conservative analysis would reject a program with such flows but ours will tag the program as needing instrumentation and will carry on the type analysis. Hence, in these cases, *HL* will return U.

In related work, there are *subtyping judgements* of the form $\rho_1\subseteq\rho_2$ or $\rho_1\leq\rho_2$ [19,21]. For instance, given two security types τ and τ', if $\tau\subseteq\tau'$ then any data of type τ can be treated as data of type τ'. Similarly, if a command assigns contents only to variables of level H or higher then, *a fortiori*, it assigns only to variables L or higher; thus we would have $H\,cmd\subseteq L\,cmd$. In our work, we integrated those requirements directly in the typing rules. Instead of using type coercions, we assign a fixed type to the instruction according to the more general type. For two expressions e_1 and e_2 of type τ_1 and τ_2 respectively, $e_1 \textbf{ op } e_2$ is typed with $\tau_1 \sqcup \tau_2$. For two commands c and c' typed τ and τ', the composition through sequencing or conditionals is typed with $\tau \sqcap \tau'$.

We now comment the typing rules that are modified with respect to [6]. ASSIGN-CHAN_S and RECEIVE-NAME_S both modify a channel variable and they make use of the function HL_ν^ψ. The usual condition for the modification of a channel would be to avoid downward flow by imposing $pc \sqsubseteq \tau$ or, as in [6], $pc \preceq \tau$; the latter is a weakening of the former, that returns false only if $pc = H$ and $\tau = L$. In this paper, we chose to only reject a program if an unauthorized **send** is performed. If we detect an implicit flow in ASSIGN-CHAN_S or RECEIVE-NAME_S, that is, $pc = H$ and $\tau = L$, we rather block the assigned channel (by $\psi = B$ in HL_-^B), as in the program of Fig. 1; if the channel is never used, a false positive has been avoided. If the channel is blocked, there is no need for instrumentation, hence $\psi = L$ in HL_-^L for both rules. In RECEIVE-NAME_S, we must call instrumentation when τ is U or H to prevent a downward flow from x_2 to x_1. In that case, the channel variable obtains security type $U \sqcup \tau$ because its type is unknown: we could receive the name of a private channel on a public one (but could not read on in). In ASSIGN-CHAN_S, this type is τ, the type of the assigned expression.

The rule for SEND_S states that the typing fails in two situations where the leak of information is clear: either the channel to which x_1 is sent is blocked ($\tau = B$), or it is of type L and either the context or the variable sent has type H ($(\tau_1 \sqcup pc) = H$). An example where $\tau = B$ was just discussed above. If the typing does not fail, the instrumentation will be called in each case where there is a possibility, at runtime, that $\tau_1 \sqcup pc$ be H while the channel has type L; those are the cases $(\tau_1 \sqcup pc, \tau) \in \{((U, L), (U, U), (H, U)\}$. The "$\psi$ branch" in the definition of HL_-^ψ is useless, as it is a case where the typing rejects the program.

The rule CONDITIONAL_S requires to type the branches c_1 and c_2 under the type context $pc \sqcup \tau_0$, to prevent downward flows from the guard to the branches.

We now explain why $\sqcup$ is defined differently on channel variables and value variables. If Γ and Γ', the environments associated to the two branches of the **if** command, differ on a value variable, we choose to be pessimistic, and assign the supremum of the two security types. A user who prefers to obtain fewer false positive could assign type U to this variable, and leave the final decision to dynamic analysis. In the case of channel variables, we do not have the choice: different unblocked channels must obtain the type $U\,chan$. The program on the left of Fig. 3 illustrates why. The last line of the program would require that c be typed as $L\,chan$ so that the program be rejected. However, since the **else** branch makes c a private information, a command like **send** c **to** *publicChannel* should also be rejected, and hence in this case we would like that c had been typed $H\,chan$. Hence we must type c as $U\,chan$, justifying the definition of $\sqcup$. Interestingly, this also shows that in our setting, the uncertain typing is necessary.

We conclude this section by discussing occurrences of false positive alarms. A rejection can only happen from the application of the rule SEND_S: either the channel to which x_1 is sent is blocked, or it is of type L and the context, or the variable sent, is of type H. According to our rules, type L can only be assigned if it is the true type of the variable, but H can be the result of a supremum taken in rule CONDITIONAL_S or LOOP_S. False positive can consequently occur from typing an **if** or **while** command whose guard always prevent a "bad" branch to be taken. This is unavoidable in static analysis, unless we want to instrument any uncertainty arising from the values of guards. Nevertheless, our inference typing rules prevent more false positives than previous work through the blocking of channels and the unknown types U.

4   Inference Algorithm

The inference algorithm implements the specification given by the type system together with some refinements we adopted in order to prepare for the instrumentation step. The refinements consist in keeping track of the command line number and of the generated environment for this command. Although it may seem overloading, this strategy lightens the dynamic step since it avoids type inference computation whenever it is already done. The algorithm is implemented as the function `Infer` which is applied to the current typing environment, $g_e : Var \rightarrow \{L, H, U, B\}$, a number identifying the current command to be analyzed, the command line i, the security level of the current context, pc, and the actual command to be analyzed, c . Along the way, `Infer` returns a typing environment representing the environment valid after the execution of the command c and an integer representing the number identifying the next command to be analyzed. `Infer` updates $G : int \rightarrow (Var \rightarrow \{L, H, U, B\})$ as a side effect; G associates to each command number a typing environment valid after its execution. Recall that the environment associates to a specific variable _instr a security level. After the application of the inference algorithm, if the program is not rejected and the resulting environment associates U, H or B to _instr then the program needs instrumentation, otherwise it is safe w.r.t. non-interference.

To analyze a program P, `Infer` is invoked with $g_e = [\_instr \mapsto L]$, $i = 0$, $pc = L$ and $c = P$. The inference algorithm uses a set of utility functions that implement some operators, functions and definitions appearing in the typing system. Their meaning and their implementation are straightforward. Here is the list of these functions. The set $SecType$ stands for $\{\tau \quad v : \tau \in \{L, U, H, B\}, v \in \{val, chan\}\}$, t and t_i ranges over $SecType$, and g_i ranges over Env, `lessOrEqual` implements $\sqsubseteq$, `inf` and `sup` implement respectively the infimum and the supremum of two security levels. `supEnv` implements the supremum of two environments, as in Definition 1. `infV` : $SecType \times SecType \rightarrow SecType \cup \{\bot_T\}$ returns $\bot_T$ if the two security types do not have the same nature. If the nature is the same, then it returns a security type where the security level is the infimum of the two security types given as argument, `supV` : $SecType \times SecType \rightarrow SecType \cup \{\bot_T\}$ behaves the same way as `infV` except that it returns a security type where the security level is the supremum of the two security types given as argument, `incBottomEnv` : $Env \rightarrow bool$ returns true if at least one variable is associated to $\bot_T$ in its parameter, `updateEnv` : $Env \times Var \times SecType \rightarrow Env$ implements $\Gamma \dagger [x \mapsto \rho]$, `eqEnv` : $Env \times Env \rightarrow bool$ checks if two environments are equal. It returns true if the two environments have the same domain and all their variables have the same security type. It returns false otherwise, `evalN` : $SecType \rightarrow \{val, chan\}$, extracts the nature of a security type (val or $chan$), `evalT` : $SecType \rightarrow \{L, U, H, B\}$, extracts the level of a security type, `inferE` : $Env \times Exp \rightarrow SecType$ returns the highest security type of the variables present in the expression to which it is applied, and `HL` : $\{L, U, H, B\}^4 \rightarrow \{L, U, H, B\}$ implements the function HL as in Definition 2.

The inference algorithm `Infer` is presented in Table 3. Some examples of its output are presented in the following section.

Correctness Proof. To guarantee the correction of the algorithm we have to prove its soundness and its completeness w.r.t. the type system.

Theorem 1 *(Correctness of* `Infer` *algorithm). Let P be a program in our target language, G a typing environment, and pc a security level,* $\text{Infer}(G, 0, pc, P) = (G', j) \Longleftrightarrow G, pc \vdash P : rho, G'$, *and* `Infer` *rejects P if and only if the typing system leads to a similar conclusion.*

5   Instrumentation

Our instrumentation is based on the inference algorithm. It is a new contribution w.r.t. [6]. It inserts commands in the program so that, during execution, the program will update the security level of variables which were unknown (U) statically. Each instruction is treated with its corresponding line number and its context security level. Instructions may be inserted to prevent unsecure executions. The instrumentation algorithm is shown in Table 4; it is given a command cmd to instrument and the number of this command. The algorithm updates IC : $String$ as a side effect, which is the instrumented program; it uses the matrix of typing environments G produced by the inference algorithm, which is a global variable. $G(i)$ refers to the typing environment of instruction i, and hence $G(i)(x)$ is the security type of variable x at instruction i.

Commands are inserted so that the instrumented program will keep a table g_M of the security levels of variables, picking the already known types in G. This table is also a global variable. g_M offers two advantages, it keeps track of the most recent values of the variables. No further analysis is necessary to find which instruction was the last to modify the variables. It is also easier to read the value from a table than from the matrix G. The usefulness of g_M can be shown with the following example.

receive$_n$ c **from** *publicChannel*;
receive$_c$ a **from** *publicChannel*;
if $(a \bmod 2 \neq 0)$ **then**
    receive$_c$ a **from** c
end;
send a **to** *publicChannel*

Table 3. Inference algorithm

Infer: $Env \times int \times Sec \times cmd \rightarrow Env \times int$

$Infer(g_e, i, pc, c) =$
    case c of
        skip : $G(i) = g_e$
            return $(G(i), i + 1)$
        x := e :
            $\tau = \texttt{evalT}(\texttt{inferE}(g_e, e))$
            case $\texttt{evalN}(\texttt{inferE}(g_e, e)$) of
                val: $G(i) = \texttt{updateEnv}(g_e, x, \texttt{sup}(pc, \tau) \ \ val)$
                    return $(G(i), i + 1)$
                $chan$: $\_instr_t = \texttt{HL}(L, L, pc, \tau)$
                    $x_t = \texttt{HL}(B, \tau, pc, \tau)$
                    $\_instr_{t2} = g_e(\_instr)$
                    $G(i) = \texttt{updateEnv}(\texttt{updateEnv}(g_e, \_instr, \texttt{sup}(\_instr_t, \_instr_{t2})), x, x_t \ \ chan)$
                    return $(G(i), i + 1)$
        receive$_c$ x_1 from x_2 :
            $\tau = \texttt{evalT}(g_e(x_2))$
            $G(i) = \texttt{updateEnv}(g_e, x_1, \texttt{sup}(pc, \tau) \ \ val)$
                return $(G(i), i + 1)$
        receive$_n$ x_1 from x_2 :
            $\tau = \texttt{evalT}(g_e(x_2))$
            $\_instr_t = \texttt{HL}(L, \tau, pc, \tau)$
            $\_instr_{t2} = g_e(\_instr)$
            $x1_t = \texttt{HL}(B, \texttt{sup}(U, \tau), pc, \tau)$
            $G(i) = \texttt{updateEnv}(\texttt{updateEnv}(g_e, \_instr, \texttt{sup}(\_instr_t, \_instr_{t2})), x_1, x1_t \ \ chan)$
            return $(G(i), i + 1)$
        send x_1 to x_2 :
            $\tau_1 = \texttt{evalT}(g_e(x_1))$
            $\tau = \texttt{evalT}(g_e(x_2))$
            $\_instr_t = \texttt{HL}(U, L, \texttt{sup}(\tau_1, pc), \tau)$
            $\_instr_{t2} = g_e(\_instr)$
            if$((\tau \neq B) \ and \ \neg(\texttt{sup}(\tau_1, pc) = H \ and \ \tau = L)))$
                then $G(i) = \texttt{updateEnv}(g_e, \_instr, \texttt{sup}(\_instr_t, \_instr_{t2}))$
                else **fail**
            return $(G(i), i + 1)$
        c$_1$; c$_2$:
            $(g_1, j) = \texttt{Infer}(g_e, i, pc, c_1)$
            $(g_2, k) = \texttt{Infer}(g_1, j, pc, c_2)$
            return (g_2, k)
        if e then c_1 else c_2 end:
            $t = \texttt{evalT}(\texttt{inferE}(g_e, e))$
            $pc_{if} = \texttt{sup}(pc, t)$
            $(g_1, j) = \texttt{Infer}(g_e, i + 1, pc_{if}, c_1)$
            $(g_2, k) = \texttt{Infer}(g_e, j, pc_{if}, c_2)$
            if$(\neg\texttt{incBottomEnv}(\texttt{supEnv}(g_1, g_2)))$ then $G(i) = \texttt{supEnv}(g_1, g_2)$
                else **fail**
            return $(G(i), k)$
        while e do c end:
            $t = \texttt{evalT}(\ \texttt{inferE}(g_e, e))$
            $pc_{while} = \texttt{sup}(pc, t)$
            $(g_{e'}, j) = \texttt{Infer}(g_e, i + 1, pc_{while}, c)$
            if $(\texttt{eqEnv}(g_e, \texttt{supEnv}(g_e, g_{e'}))$ and $(\neg\texttt{incBottomEnv}(\texttt{supEnv}(g_e, g_{e'}))))$
                then $g_{res} = \texttt{supEnv}(g_e, g_{e'})$
                else if $(\neg\texttt{eqEnv}(g_e, \texttt{supEnv}(g_e, g_{e'}))$ and $(\neg\texttt{incBottomEnv}(\texttt{supEnv}(g_e, g_{e'}))))$
                    then $(g_{res}, j) = \texttt{Infer}(\texttt{supEnv}(g_e, g_{e'}), i, pc_{while}, \textbf{while } e \textbf{ do } c \textbf{ end})$
                  else **fail**
            $G(i) = \texttt{supEnv}(G(i), gres)$
            return (g_{res}, j)

Table 4. Instrumentation algorithm

Instrument: cmd * int → int

Instrument$(c, i) =$ case c of
   skip : $IC \wedge$ " **skip;** "
   return $(i + 1)$
   x := e :
      $\tau = $ evalT(inferE$(G(i), e)$))
      case evalN(inferE$(G(i), e)$) of
        val: $IC = IC \wedge$ "**x := e** ; "
            if $(\tau = U)$ then
                $IC = IC \wedge$"updateEnv$(G(i), x, $sup(evalT(TypeOf_Expression(e)), top$(pc))val)$; "
            end ;
            $IC = IC \wedge$ " updateEnv$(g\_M, x, G(i)(x))$; "
        return $(i + 1)$
        chan: $IC = IC \wedge$ "**x := e** ; "
             if $(\tau = U)$ then
                $IC = IC \wedge$" updateEnv$(G(i), x, $TypeOf_Channel$(e)$); "
            end
            $IC = IC \wedge$ " updateEnv$(g\_M, x, G(i)(x))$; "
        return $(i + 1)$
   receive$_c$ x_1 from x_2 :
      $IC = IC \wedge$ "**receive$_c$ x_1 from x_2;** "
      if $(G(i)(x_1) = Uval)$ then
         $IC = IC \wedge$ " updateEnv$(G(i), x_1, $sup(evalT(TypeOf_Expression(x_2)), top$(pc))val)$; "
      end
      $IC = IC \wedge$ "updateEnv$(g\_M, x_1, G(i)(x_1))$; "
      return $(i + 1)$
   receive$_n$ x_1 from x_2 :
      $IC = IC \wedge$ "**receive$_n$ x_1 from x_2** ";
      if $(G(i)(x_2) \mathrel{!=} L\ chan)$ then
        then $IC = IC \wedge$ " if TypeOf_Channel$(x_1) = L\ chan$ and TypeOf_Channel$(x_2) = H\ chan$
          then updateEnv$(G(i), x_1, B\ chan)$
          else updateEnv$(G(i), x_1, $TypeOf_Channel$(x_1))$
          end "
        else $IC = IC \wedge$ "updateEnv$(G(i), x_1, $TypeOf_Channel$(x_1))$"
      end
      $IC = IC \wedge$ " updateEnv$(g\_M, x_1, G(i)(x_1))$; "
   return $(i + 1)$
   $c_1 ; c_2$:
      $j = $ Instrument$(c_1, i); k = $ Instrument(c_2, j)
      return k
   send x_1 to x_2 :
      $IC = IC \wedge$ " $tau = $ TypeOf_Expression(x_2) ; $tau_1 = $ TypeOf_Expression(x_1);
      if$(((tau = L\ chan)$ and (sup(evalT(tau_1), top$(pc)) = H))$ or $(tau = B\ chan))$
      then fail else send x_1 to x_2 end; "
   return $(i + 1)$
   if e then c_1 else c_2 end :
      $IC = IC \wedge$ "push(sup(top(pc), evalT(TypeOf_Expression(e))), $pc)$;
      if e then "
      $j = $ Instrument$(c_1, i + 1)$
      $IC = IC \wedge$ "else "
      $k = $ Instrument(c_2, j)
      $IC = IC \wedge$ "end;
      pop (pc); "
   return k
   while e to c end:
   $IC = IC \wedge$
      "push(sup$(top(pc)$, evalT(TypeOf_Expression(e))), $pc)$;
      while e do "
   $j = $ Instrument$(c, i + 1)$
   $IC = IC \wedge$ "end ;
      pop (pc) ; "
   return j

The inference algorithm determines after the first instruction that the type of c is U *chan*. Variable a, before the **if** command, has the type L *val*. The static analysis will conclude that the type of a after executing the **if** command is U *val*. If the instrumented program updates the variables immediately in G, the type of a would be H *val*. The following **send** would be considered unsecure no matter what the dynamic value of a is. Our instrumentation will insert instructions that put in g_M the last type of a when it was read. So depending on whether the execution of the instrumented program enters the **then** branch or not, a will take either the security level of c, or it will keep the security level of *publicChannel*. This will allow the instrumented program to be rejected during execution only if it is actually unsecure.

A set of utility functions are predefined in the target language and used by the instrumented programs. Function TypeOf_Channel serves as a register for the constant channels defined prior to the execution. Function TypeOf_Expression returns the actual type of an expression: it uses the information of g_M for variables, TypeOf_Channel for actual channels and takes the supV of these values when the expression is $e_1 \text{op} \ e_2$. TypeOf_Expression and TypeOf_Channel are commands executed by the instrumented program. To prevent implicit flows, commands are inserted so that the instrumented program will keep a stack of contexts pc. Each time the execution branches on an expression, whether it is in an **if** or a **while** command, the context is pushed onto the stack. The context is the supremum of the type of expression e and the context in which the actual command is executed. The last context is popped from the stack everytime the execution of a branching command finishes. The stack pc is initially empty and the result of reading an empty stack is always L. The functions push and pop are used to manipulate the stack of contexts during the execution of the instrumented program. The remaining functions are an implementation of their counter part in the algorithm Infer.

The analysis and the instrumentation has been implemented. The interested reader can find a link to the implemented code in [3]. The implementation is divided into two parts : an analyzer and an interface. The analyzer is written in OCaml. It uses OCamllex and OCamlyacc to generate the lexer and parser. In order to maximize the portability of our application, we use OCaml-Java to compile our OCaml code into bytecode so that it may run on a Java Virtual Machine. As for the interface, it is written in Java and uses the standard Swing library. If an error is detected while analyzing, whether it is a lexical, syntactic, semantic or flow error, the analyzer stops and displays a message explaining the cause of the error. If the analyzer infers that the code needs to be instrumented, it automatically generates and displays the instrumented code. If no error occurs and there is no need for instrumentation, then a message of correctness is displayed.

Examples. A few examples of the whole approach are presented in the following figures. The figures show the returned environment G, the returned command number i as well as the input pc, the security level of the context. Recall that the identifiers *privateChannel*, *publicChannel*, *highValue* and *lowValue* are

Input to analyzer	Inference analysis		
	Environment	pc	i
if $highValue$		$pc_{if} = H$	2
then x := $lowValue$	$G(2) = \lfloor\_instr \mapsto L, x \mapsto H\,val\rfloor$	H	3
else skip	$G(3) = \lfloor\_instr \mapsto L\rfloor$	H	4
end;	$G(1) = \lfloor\_instr \mapsto L, x \mapsto H\,val\rfloor$	H	4
send x **to** $publicChannel$	**fail** since $H \not\sqsubseteq L$		
Output : Error (Send) : Cannot send x (H) to publicChannel (L).			

Fig. 2. Implicit flow

Input to analyzer	Inference analysis		
	Environment	pc	i
if $lowValue$	$G(1) = \lfloor\_instr \mapsto L\rfloor$	$pc_{if} = L$	2
then $c := publicChannel$	$G(2) = \lfloor\_instr \mapsto L, c \mapsto L\,chan\rfloor$	L	3
else $c := privateChannel$	$G(3) = \lfloor\_instr \mapsto L, c \mapsto H\,chan\rfloor$	L	4
end;	$G(1) = \lfloor\_instr \mapsto L, c \mapsto U\,chan\rfloor$	L	4
send $highValue$ **to** c	$G(4) = \lfloor\_instr \mapsto U, c \mapsto U\,chan\rfloor$	L	5
Output : push(sup(top(pc), evalT(TypeOf_Expression($lowValue$))), pc);			
if $lowValue$ **then**			
$c := publicChannel$;			
updateEnv($g\_M, c, G(2)(c)$);			
else			
$c := privateChannel$;			
updateEnv($g\_M, c, G(3)(c)$);			
end;			
pop(pc);			
$tau =$ TypeOf_Expression(c);			
$tau1 =$ TypeOf_Expression($highValue$);			
if$(((tau = L\,chan)$ and (sup(evalT($tau1$), top(pc)) $= H))$ or ($tau = B\,chan$))			
then fail;			
else send $highValue$ **to** c;			

Fig. 3. The send of a high value on an unknown channel calls for instrumentation

predefined constants. The result of the analysis, including instrumentation when necessary, is shown in the lower part of the figures.

The program of Fig. 2 is rejected. The security level of the value variable x is H because its value is assigned inside the context of $highValue$, which is of type H. There is an attempt to send x on a public channel, which make the program be rejected.

The program in Fig. 3 is similar to the one in Fig. 1 except that the context in which c is defined is now L instead of H. For this reason, it is not necessary to block channel c. Since c can either be a public or private channel (depending on the value of $lowValue$), it is marked as unknown. A call for instrumentation results from the first send, to ensure that $highValue$ is only sent to a private channel.

The example presented in Fig. 4 shows how the instrumentation algorithm works. The inference algorithm determines that the program needs instrumentation. The program is shown on the upper left corner of the figure. The instrumentation result is shown in the lower part of the figure. The third instruction receives a channel name on another one. The instrumentation is necessary to obtain the real type of this channel. In the sixth instruction of the instrumented program, the update of $G(3)$ is due to the fact that the inference algorithm

Input to analyzer	Inference analysis		
	Environment	pc	i
receive$_c$ v **from** *privateChannel*;	$G(1) = [\_instr \mapsto L, v \mapsto H\ val]$	L	2
if *lowValue* **then**		$pc_{if} = L$	3
receive$_n$ c **from** *publicChannel*;	$G(3) = [\_instr \mapsto L, v \mapsto H\ val, c \mapsto U\ chan]$	L	4
send v **to** c	$G(4) = [\_instr \mapsto U, v \mapsto H\ val, c \mapsto U\ chan]$	L	5
else skip	$G(5) = [\_instr \mapsto L, v \mapsto H\ val]$	L	6
end	$G(2) = [\_instr \mapsto U, v \mapsto H\ val, c \mapsto U\ chan]$	L	6

Output : **receive$_c$** v **from** *privateChannel*;
           updateEnv($g\_M, v, G(1)(v)$);
           push(sup(top(pc), evalT(TypeOf_Expression(*lowValue*))), pc);
           if *lowValue* **then**
              receive$_n$ c **from** *publicChannel*;
              updateEnv($G(3), c$, TypeOf_Channel(c));
              updateEnv($g\_M, c, G(3)(c)$);
              tau = TypeOf_Expression(c);
              $tau1$ = TypeOf_Expression(v);
              if$(((tau = L\ chan)$ *and* (sup(evalT($tau1$), top(pc)) = H))
               or $(tau = B\ chan))$
                then fail;
                else send v **to** c;
           else skip;
           end;
           pop(pc);

Fig. 4. The **send** of a high value on an unknown channel calls for instrumentation

Input	**receive$_c$** *stockMarketReports* **from** *internet*; **send** *stockMarketReports* **to** *screen*; **receive$_c$** *creditCardNumber* **from** *settings*; **send** *creditCardNumber* **to** *secureLinkToBank*; **receive$_c$** *latestTransactions* **from** *secureLinkToBank*; **send** *latestTransactions* **to** *screen*; *cleverlyEncodedCreditCardNumber* := *creditCardNumber* $* 3 + 2121311611218191$; **send** *cleverlyEncodedCreditCardNumber* **to** *internet*
Output	Error (Send) : Cannot send *cleverlyEncodedCreditCardNumber* (H) to *internet* (L).

Fig. 5. Example from [22]

marks the channel c as unknown on that line. The fourth instruction is a **send** command. A check is inserted in the instrumented code to ensure that a secret information is neither sent on a public channel (the type of c being unknown statically) nor on a blocked one (B).

A more "realistic" example is described in [22]: one may want to "prohibit a personal finance program from transmitting credit card information over the Internet even though the program needs Internet access to download stock market reports. To prevent the finance program from illicitly transmitting the private information (perhaps cleverly encoded), the compiler checks that the information flows in the program are admissible." This could be translated into the code of Fig. 5 where all the channels, except *internet*, are private.

6   Related Work

Securing flow information has been the focus of active research since the seventies. Dynamic techniques were the first methods as in [8]. Some of those techniques try to prevent explicit flows as well as implicit flows in program runs. Those techniques are given with no soundness proof. Denning and Denning [5] introduce for the first time, secure information-flow by static analysis, based on control and data flow analysis. Subsequently, many approaches have been devised using type systems. They vary in the type of language, its expressivness and the property being enforced. Volpano and Smith in [21] introduce a type based analysis for an imperative language. Pottier and Simonet in [16] analyse the functional language ML, with references, exceptions and polymorphism. Banerjee and Naumann devise a type based analysis for a Java-like language. Their analysis however has some trade-offs like low security guards for conditionals that involve recursive calls. In [14], Myers statically enforces information policies in JFlow, an extension of Java that adds security levels annotations to variables. Barthe et al. in [2], investigate logical-formulation of non-interference, enabling the use of theorem proving or model-checking techniques. Nevertheless, purely static approaches are too conservative and suffer from a large number of false positive. In fact some information need to take an accurate decision are often only available during execution. This has cause a revival of interest for dynamic analysis. Russo and Sabelfeld in [18], prove that dynamic analyses could enforce the same security policy enforced by most static analyses, termination-insensitive non-interference and even be more permissive (with less false-positive). This is true for flow insensitive analyses but not for flow sensitive ones. In [17], Russo and Sabelfeld show the impossibility for a sound purely dynamic monitor to accept the same set of programs accepted by the classic flow sensitive analysis [11] of Hunt and Sands. Russo and Sabelfeld in [17] present a monitor that uses static analysis during execution. In [9], the authors present an interesting approach to non-interference based on abstract interpretation.

Our approach is flow sensitive, similarly to [11]. However, it distinguishes between variables in live memory and channels. We argue that our approach lead to less false positive and to lighter executions than existing approaches.

7 Conclusion

Ensuring secure information flow within sensitive systems has been studied extensively. In general, the key idea in type-based approaches is that if a program is well typed, then it is secure according to the given security properties.

We define a sound type system that captures lack of information in a program at compile-time. Our type system is flow sensitive, variables are assigned the security levels of their stored values. We clearly distinguish between variables and channels through which the program communicates, which is more realistic.

Our main contribution is the handling of a multi-valued security typing. The program is considered well typed, ill typed or uncertain. In the first case, the program can safely be executed, in the second case the program is rejected and need modifications, while in the third case instrumentation is to be used in order to guarantee the satisfaction of non-interference. This approach allows to eliminate false positives due to conservative static analysis approximations and to introduce run-time overhead only when it is necessary. We obtain fewer false positives than purely static approaches because we send some usually rejected programs to instrumentation. Future work includes extensions to take into account concurrency, declassification and information leakage due to termination [1,13,20]. We would like to scale up the approach to deal with real world languages and to test it on elaborate programs. The use of abstract interpretation to prove the correctness is also to be considered in a future work.

References

1. Askarov, A., Chong, S.: Learning is change in knowledge: knowledge-based security for dynamic policies. In: Proceedings of the 25th IEEE Computer Security Foundations Symposium, pp. 308–322. IEEE Press, Piscataway, June 2012
2. Barthe, G., D'Argenio, P.R., Rezk, T.: Secure information flow by self-composition. In: Proceedings of the IEEE Workshop on Computer Security Foundations (2004)
3. Bedford, A., Desharnais, J., Godonou, T. G., Tawbi, N.: Hybrid flow analysis implementation. http://lsfm.ift.ulaval.ca/Recherche/Hybrid_analysis (2013)
4. Denning, D.E.: A lattice model of secure information flow. Commun. ACM **19**, 236–243 (1976)
5. Denning, D.E., Denning, P.J.: Certification of programs for secure information flow. Commun. ACM **20**, 504–513 (1977)
6. Desharnais, J., Kanyabwero, E.P., Tawbi, N.: Enforcing information flow policies by a three-valued analysis. In: Kotenko, I., Skormin, V. (eds.) MMM-ACNS 2012. LNCS, vol. 7531, pp. 114–129. Springer, Heidelberg (2012)
7. Desharnais, J., Kanyabwero, E.P., Tawbi, N.: Enforcing information flow policies by a three-valued analysis, long version. http://www.ift.ulaval.ca/departement/professeurs/tawbi_nadia/ (2012)
8. Fenton, J.S.: Memoryless subsystems. Comput. J. **17**(2), 143–147 (1974)
9. Giacobbazzi, R., Mastroeni, I.: Abstract non-interference: parameterizing non-interference by abstract interpretation. SIGPLAN Not. **39**(1), 186–197 (2004)
10. Hunt, S., Sands, D.: On flow-sensitive security types. In: Conference Record of the 33rd ACM SIGPLAN-SIGACT Symposium on Principles of Programming Languages, POPL '06, pp. 79–90. ACM, New York (2006)
11. Hunt, S., Sands, D.: On flow-sensitive security types. SIGPLAN Not. **41**(1), 79–90 (2006)
12. Kobayashi, N.: Type-based information flow analysis for the pi-calculus. Acta Informatica **42**(4–5), 291–347 (2005)
13. Moore, S., Askarov, A., Chong, S.: Precise enforcement of progress-sensitive security. In: Proceedings of the 19th ACM Conference on Computer and Communications Security, pp. 881–893. ACM Press, New York, October 2012
14. Myers, A.C.: Jflow: practical mostly-static information flow control. In: Proceedings of the ACM Symposium on Principles of Programming Languages (1999)
15. O'Neill, K.R., Clarkson, M.R., Chong,S.: Information-flow security for interactive programs. In: Proceedings of the IEEE Computer Security Foundations Workshop, July 2006
16. Pottier, F., Simonet, V.: Information flow inference for ML. In: Proceedings of the ACM Symposium on Principles of Programming Languages (2002)

17. Russo, A., Sabelfeld, A.: Dynamic vs. static flow-sensitive security analysis. In: Proceedings of the IEEE Computer Security Foundations Symposium (2010)
18. Sabelfeld, A., Russo, A.: From dynamic to static and back: riding the roller coaster of information-flow control research (2009)
19. Smith, G.: Principles of secure information flow analysis. In: Christodorescu, M., Jha, S., Maughan, D., Song, D., Wang, C. (eds.) Malware Detection, vol. 27, pp. 291–307. Springer, Heidelberg (2007)
20. Thomas, J., Cuppens-Boulahia, N., Cuppens, F.: Declassification policy management in dynamic information systems. In: ARES 2011: 6th International Conference on Availability, Reliability and Security (2011)
21. Volpano, D., Irvine, C., Smith, G.: A sound type system for secure flow analysis. J. Comput. Secur. 4(2–3), 167–187 (1996)
22. Zdancewic, S., Myers, A.C.: Secure information flow via linear continuations. High. Order Symbolic Comput. 15, 209–234 (2002)

Physical Security

Fault Injection to Reverse Engineer DES-Like Cryptosystems

Hélène Le Bouder[1,2]($\boxtimes$), Sylvain Guilley[3]($\boxtimes$), Bruno Robisson[1,4], and Assia Tria[1,4]

[1] Département Systèmes et Architectures Sécurisés (SAS), Gardanne, France
lebouder@emse.fr
[2] Institut Mines-Télécom, École des Mines de Saint-Étienne (EMSE), Gardanne, France
[3] Institut Mines-Télécom, TELECOM-ParisTech, Paris, France
sylvain.guilley@telecom-paristech.fr
[4] Commissariat à l'énergie atomique et aux énergies alternatives (CEA), Institut CEA-Tech en Régions, DPACA/LSAS, 13770 Gardanne, France

Abstract. This paper presents a fault injection attack in order to reverse engineer unknown s-boxes of a DES-like cryptosystem. It is a significant improvement of the FIRE attack presented by San Pedro *et al.* which uses differentials between s-boxes outputs. Since injecting faults on a cryptographic circuit may irreversibly damage the device, our aim has been to minimise the number of faults needed. We show that by considering faults in the penultimate round instead of last round, twice less faults are needed to reverse the s-boxes. Our attack requires no a priori knowledge on the s-boxes. However, if we assume that s-boxes satisfy some selected properties, then our attack can be made even more efficient, by a factor of two. Finally our attack needs four times less faults.

Keywords: Physical attacks · Fault injection attacks · Reverse engineering · FIRE · DES-like cryptosystem · S-boxes

1 Introduction

Although Kerckhoffs' principle [1] enunciates that a cryptosystem should be secure even if its algorithm is public knowledge, private algorithms are still used. For instance, Cryptomeria Cipher (C2) is a proprietary block cipher used to protect DVDs. An other example is the suite of A3/A5/A8 algorithms used for authentication/confidentiality/key agreement in GSM applications, that are designed to contain some secret customization. However, creating a strong new cryptosystem from scratch is not easy. It is better to use an algorithm which has gained one's spurs, therefore private algorithms are often derived from well-known algorithms. These algorithms respect some properties identical to their model.

J.-L. Danger et al. (Eds.): FPS 2013, LNCS 8352, pp. 105–121, 2014.
DOI: 10.1007/978-3-319-05302-8_7, © Springer International Publishing Switzerland 2014

A DES-like cryptosystem or pseudo-DES is an algorithm based on DES [2], but which slightly differs. For example in [3], DES was obfuscated by secret external encoding. In this article, we study a pseudo-DES whose s-boxes differ.

When the goal of an attacker is to retrieve information on a private algorithm, his attack is termed "reverse-engineering". One has to remark that the cipher key is often considered known in a reverse engineering attack.

Algorithms can be secured against algorithmic attacks for reverse engineering. In the case of DES, Luby and Rackoff demonstrated in [4] the following result: no efficient algorithm exists to determine the round function of a more than 3-rounds Feistel, with only observation of couples (plain-text, cipher-text). Despite this security, an algorithm may be vulnerable to physical cryptanalysis for reverse engineering. There are two family of physical cryptanalysis for reverse engineering: SCARE (Side Channels for Reverse Engineering) attacks as in [5–9]; and FIRE (Fault Injection for Reverse Engineering) attacks.

In this paper we have chosen to speak about FIRE. Fault injection attacks consist in disrupting the circuit's behaviour in order to alter the correct progress of the algorithm. Biham and Shamir studied fault injection attacks on DES, in [10,11] in order to recover the key. The first time that fault injection attacks were used to reverse engineer a DES-like cryptosystem was described by Clavier *et al.* in [3]. But this pseudo-DES was different than the one studied here. Our attack studies a DES-like where s-boxes are customised. Indeed, there is an extremely large choice of s-boxes, whereas the other parts of a Feistel network have less degrees of freedom to be varied. FIRE attacks against secret s-boxes were presented in [12] by San Pedro *et al.* on DES-like and AES-like cryptosystems, and in [13] by Ming *et al.* on substitution-permutation networks and Feistel structures. These state-of-the-art reverse-engineering attacks focus in a generic way on relations in the last round of the Feistel cipher. A feature of our paper is that results are obtained with differentials between s-boxes outputs as in [12,13]. But, our approach is different: we fully exploit the knowledge of the cipher structure to design an adapted attack. The main idea is injecting faults in register $R14$ instead of $R15$ as in [12]. The second idea is to consider some properties of DES s-boxes described in [14].

The paper is organised as follows. The Sect. 2 describes the DES. The Sect. 3 presents previous works. Our proposed improvement of FIRE is described in 4. The Sect. 5 presents the algorithm for cryptanalysis and our results. The conclusion is drawn in Sect. 6.

2   Description of DES

Data Encryption Standard (DES) was developed by the National Bureau of Standards [2]. Even if Advanced Encryption Standard (AES [15]) is the new cipher block standard, the DES is not outdated. DES and 3DES are still in use in many devices. Figure 1 presents DES. DES is a symmetric cryptosystem, specifically a 16-round Feistel cipher. DES starts by IP, a permutation of 64 bits and finishes by its inverse IP^{-1}.

The round function F on 32 bits consists in 4 steps.

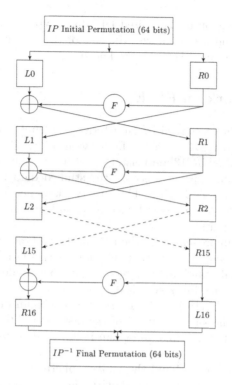

Fig. 1. Scheme of data encryption standard

- Expansion E which maps 32 bits in 48 bits by duplicating half of the bits. One can note that two bits are used only once in each s-box. And an s-box has two bits in common with the next s-box and two bits in common with the previous s-box; we consider that s-box 1 follows s-box 8.
- Xor with the 48 bits of round key K_j, $j \in [\![1, 16]\!]$.
- S-boxes S_i, $i \in [\![1, 8]\!]$, which substitute a 6-bits input m_i for a 4-bits output y_i We note:

$$S_i(m_i) = y_i \tag{1}$$

In the standard, s-boxes are represented with a table of 4 lines and 16 columns. Let m_i be one input, the first and the last bit establish the line number. The bits in the middle establish the column number[1]. To sum up m_i defines the position in the s-box of a cell and y_i defines the value in the same cell. For example, if $m_i = (25)_{10} = (011001)_2$, the number of line is $(01)_2 = (1)_{10}$ and that of column is $(1100)_2 = (12)_{10}$. The output y_i is equal to the value in the cell of the table associated with S_i, at line 1, column 12.
- Permutation P of 32 bits.

---

[1] The columns and lines numbering starts at 0.

In this paper, we focus on a customised DES-like cryptosystem, whose s-boxes have been changed and are unknown, the rest of the algorithm being genuine, i.e. P, E, IP and the round keys K_j are known.

3   Previous Work on FIRE

In this article, a variable marked by an asterisk (*) denotes a data modified by a fault injection; for example x^* is the faulty value of x.

The attack described in [13] on Feistel structures is generic in the size of the s-boxes and of the linear parts. Because the studied data path is different, it cannot be applied to a pseudo-DES. They use two keys per round instead of one for DES. Their results are presented on a Twofish-like cryptosystem, and they need in average 234 faults.

Our attack is an improvement of the FIRE attack of San Pedro et al. [12] on a DES-like cryptosystem. This section summarizes this last one. Unlike in [13] which applies an 8-bits random fault model, the fault model of [12] is a single bit fault: the value of one bit is switched.

The fault occurs in $R15$ in [12]. There is a maximum of two different bits between m^* and m the s-boxes inputs of the last round. To ascertain whether the collected information is exploitable, San Pedro et al. focus on the last round as illustrated in Fig. 2.

Knowing the ciphertext C and the faulty ciphertext C^*, the values of $L16$, $R16$, $L16^*$ and $R16^*$ can be obtained with the permutation IP the inverse function of IP^{-1}. From the description of DES, $L16 = R15$. The round key

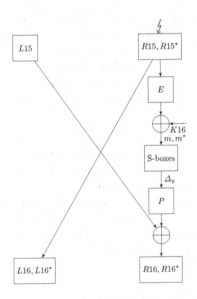

Fig. 2. Attack path of the FIRE attack [12]

$K16$ and the expansion E are known. Thus the s-boxes inputs m and m^* can be retrieved with Eq. (2):

$$m = E(R15) \oplus K16 = E(L16) \oplus K16$$
$$m^* = E(R15^*) \oplus K16 = E(L16^*) \oplus K16 \qquad (2)$$

Because $L15$ is unknown, the s-boxes outputs y and y^* cannot be retrieved;

$$y = P^{-1}(R16 \oplus L15)$$
$$y^* = P^{-1}(R16^* \oplus L15)$$

However the differential between the s-boxes outputs: $\Delta_y = y \oplus y^*$ can be computed as follows:

$$\Delta_y = P^{-1}(R16 \oplus R16^* \oplus L15 \oplus L15)$$

Thus:

$$\Delta_y = P^{-1}(R16 \oplus R16^*) \qquad (3)$$

Thereby in FIRE attack, only the inputs m, m^* and the differential Δ_y, can be computed and split. So for $i \in [\![1,8]\!]$ we have: $S_i(m_i) \oplus S_i(m_i^*) = \Delta_{y_i}$.

From now on, for an s-box S_i we call a relation (4) the link between any two inputs m_{i_0}, m_{i_1} and a differential output Δ_{y_i}.

$$S_i(m_{i_0}) \oplus S_i(m_{i_1}) = \Delta_{y_i} \qquad (4)$$

One has to remark that the transitive relation of the xor operator, is used to perform the FIRE attack. It can be applied for relations (4) in the same s-box to obtain more relations (4). Let m_{i_0}, m_{i_1} and m_{i_2} be any three inputs, we have:

$$\left. \begin{array}{l} S_i(m_{i_0}) \oplus S_i(m_{i_1}) = \Delta_{y_i} \\ S_i(m_{i_0}) \oplus S_i(m_{i_2}) = \Delta'_{y_i} \end{array} \right\} \Rightarrow S_i(m_{i_1}) \oplus S_i(m_{i_2}) = \Delta_{y_i} \oplus \Delta'_{y_i} \qquad (5)$$

Because only relations (4) are known but not equalities (1), y_i and y_i^* are unknown and the s-boxes cannot be obtained directly. We say that each s-box is "defined up to a translation". Knowing all relations (4) of one s-box S_i, only one couple (m_i, y_i) which satisfies (1) is needed to fully define S_i. For this reason, FIRE attack must finish with an exhaustive search. The attacker must test the 16 values for a cell (an output y_i associated with an input m_i) of each s-box. There are $16^8 = 2^{32}$ guesses to fully define all 8 s-boxes.

In attack [12], 130 faults are needed in average to define one s-box up to a translation. In total, $130 \cdot 8 = 1040$ faults are needed to find all 8 s-boxes.

4   Proposed Improvements

This section presents the two improvements of our FIRE attack.

4.1   The Attack Path

Fault Model. Unfortunately, in fault injection attacks the circuit can be damaged. Sakiyama *et al.* in [16] emphasizes the importance of limiting the number of fault injections. So, our attack is conducted with this goal in mind.

In our attack, the fault attack randomly changes one and only one bit of register $R14$, at the end of the fourteenth round. The fault model is a single bit fault as in [12], but the location of the injection differs.

Biham and Shamir showed the relevance of using injected faults in the penultimate rounds of DES to discover the cipher key. They studied the reverse engineering of s-boxes on DES-like. However they did not use injected faults in the penultimate rounds to discover DES-like s-boxes. Based on these seminal works [10,11], we improved their s-boxes recovery attack, by applying faults in the last but one round. A fault in $R14$ is more propagated than a fault in $R15$, i.e. more bits in the s-boxes inputs of the last round are faulted. We note e the fault on $R14^*$, so $e = R14 \oplus R14^*$.

Expansion E duplicates half of the bits of the previous R ($R14$ or $R15$). A faulty bit at an s-box input can change the 4 bits at the output. Thus the combination of expansion and s-boxes can fault 8 bits in $R15^*$. With the expansion on last round, 16 bits of m^* can differ with m. Thanks to this propagation which is illustrated in the Fig. 3, many s-boxes can be attacked at the same time. The injection of one faulty bit is rarely uniform, thus with a single-bit fault injected in $R15$ as in [12], some s-boxes may be difficult to reach. This problem does not exist in our attack.

One might argue that targeting precisely $R14$ might seem tough; but in practice, it is possible to know if a fault occurred in the last or the last but one round. If $L16$ has more than 8 faulty bits, then the fault occurred earlier than $R14$, and shall be discarded since not usable by our attack. Otherwise if $L16$ contains less than 9 faulty bits, the fault occurs in $R14$. One has to remark that if $L16$ contains only one faulty bit the fault can have occurred in $R15$. Although such a fault conveys less information than one in $R14$, it can nonetheless be exploited.

As explained in Sect. 3, we focus on the last round as explained in Sect. 3, knowing only $R16$, $L16$, $R16^*$ and $L16^*$. The inputs m and m^* can be computed with Eq. (2). Since the fault is injected in $R14$ instead of $R15$: $R14^* = L15^* \neq L15$. So :

$$\Delta_y = P^{-1}(R16 \oplus R16^* \oplus L15 \oplus L15^*) = P^{-1}(R16 \oplus R16^* \oplus e)$$

Thus, Δ_y cannot be computed as in [12]. In our attack we compute instead:

$$\Delta_z = P^{-1}(R16 \oplus R16^*) \tag{6}$$

One has to remark that $\Delta_z \neq \Delta_y$. It comes from the fact that, $L15^* = L15 \oplus e$, so:

$$\Delta_y = \Delta_z \oplus P^{-1}(e) \tag{7}$$

Δ_z and Δ_y differs only by one bit. We must find the value of e in order to get Δ_y. The steps to retrieve e are described in the next paragraph 4.1.

An Unknown Differential. We are now interested in finding e. For that purpose we study Δ_m. Let Δ_m be the differential between s-boxes inputs in the last round.

$$\Delta_m = m \oplus m^*$$

Δ_m can be computed and then split in eight Δ_{m_i}, one for each s-box.

Case where e is discovered $\Delta_{m_i} = 0 \Rightarrow \Delta_{y_i} = 0$. Indeed for a given s-box S_i if inputs m_i and m_i^* are equal, output y_i equals y_i^*. If $\Delta_{m_i} = 0$ and $\Delta_{z_i} \neq 0$ the fault is found; the faulty bit is the bit of Δ_{z_i} which equals 1 up to the permutation P^{-1}. We have found e thus Δ_y can be computed with (7). For all s-boxes we have relations (4). In practice for 10000 faults, this case occurs with a probability equals to 0.56.

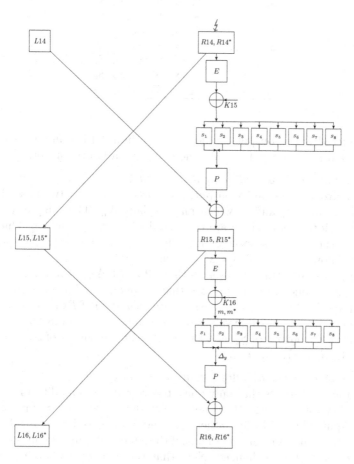

Fig. 3. Propagation of the fault on $R14$ in the round 15 and 16.

Case where e stays unknown. In this paragraph we list the different values of e which may explain our experiment. We note e_b the guessed fault for e such that all bits of e_b are equal to zero except the bits b.

If there are no $\Delta_{m_i} = 0$ with $\Delta_{z_i} \neq 0$, input differentials Δ_{m_i} must be examined in more details. The differentials $\Delta_{m_i} \neq 0$ indicate s-boxes which have a faulty output in round 15. Table 1 indicates the s-box in round 15 from which each bit of m_i comes from.

Table 1. Origin of the 6 bits of Δ_{m_i} in the last round from the s-boxes in round 15.

round 16\bits	1	2	3	4	5	6
Δ_{m_1}	S_7	S_4	S_2	S_5	S_6	S_8
Δ_{m_2}	S_6	S_8	S_3	S_7	S_5	S_1
Δ_{m_3}	S_5	S_1	S_4	S_6	S_7	S_2
Δ_{m_4}	S_7	S_2	S_5	S_8	S_3	S_1
Δ_{m_5}	S_3	S_1	S_2	S_6	S_4	S_8
Δ_{m_6}	S_4	S_8	S_7	S_1	S_3	S_5
Δ_{m_7}	S_3	S_5	S_4	S_8	S_2	S_6
Δ_{m_8}	S_2	S_6	S_3	S_1	S_7	S_4

An observed faulty output implies a faulty input. In round 15, either two s-boxes have a faulty output or only one s-box has a faulty output.

- *Two s-boxes have a faulty output in round* 15.

If two s-boxes have a faulty output, there are always only two possible faulty bits in $R14^*$, noted b_1 and b_2 which may explain Δ_m. The table of expansion is used to retrieve them. There are two possible values e_{b_1} and e_{b_2}. One has to remark that there are 6 s-boxes S_i for which $(P^{-1}(e_{b_1}))_i = (P^{-1}(e_{b_2}))_i = 0$; thus Δ_{y_i} is known and equals to Δ_{z_i}. We have 6 relations (4).

Suppose that the attacker observes that bits 6 of Δ_{m_1}, 4 of Δ_{m_2}, 1 and 4 of Δ_{m_4} are equal to one. Table 1 indicates that in round 15 s-boxes S_7 and S_8 have faulty outputs. In the table of expansion, bits 28 and 29 of $R14$ are shared on S_7 and S_8. There are two possible values of e: e_{28} and e_{29}. $P^{-1}(\{28, 29\}) = \{6, 22\}$. The bit 6 is at the output of S_2, and the bit 22 is at the output of S_6. For s-boxes S_i, $i \in \{1, 3, 4, 5, 7, 8\}$, $\Delta_{y_i} = \Delta_{z_i}$.

- *Only one s-box has a faulty output in round* 15.

The attacker observes that only one s-box S_i output is modified in round 15 and the faulty bit does not affect necessarily only one s-box S_i input. It may affect the inputs of two s-boxes, either S_{i-1} and S_i or S_i and S_{i+1}. In s-boxes two inputs may have the same output. Thus, if the single bit fault modifies the input, the output could stay unchanged. Note that the case where only one s-box is affected is more likely. As a consequence, six single bit faults $R14^*$ are possible. They can be retrieved with the expansion E. There are six possible values e_{b_1}, e_{b_2}, e_{b_3}, e_{b_4}, e_{b_5} and e_{b_6}. One has to remark that there are 2 s-boxes S_i for which $(P^{-1}(e_{b_j}))_i = 0$; thus Δ_{y_i} is known and equals to Δ_{z_i}. We have 2 relations (4).

For example, the attacker observes that bits 6 of Δ_{m_4}, 2 of Δ_{m_5} and 3 of Δ_{m_7} are not equal to zero. Table 1 indicates that in round 15 only S_1 has faulty outputs. The set of bits $\{32, 1, 2, 3, 4, 5\}$ of $R14$ determines the input of S_1. There are six possible values of e: $e_{32}, e_1, e_2, e_3, e_4$ and e_5 $P^{-1}(\{32, 1, 2, 3, 4, 5\}) = \{25, 16, 7, 20, 21, 29\}$. The bit 25 respectively $16, 7, 20, 21$ and 29 is at the output of S_7, S_4, S_2, S_5, S_6 and S_8. For s-boxes S_i, $i \in \{1, 3\}$, $\Delta_{y_i} = \Delta_{z_i}$.

In conclusion for any Δ_m we have a set of possible fault values in $R14^*$. More precisely there are one, two or six possible fault values, noted e_{b_j}. Each e_{b_j} gives an Eq. (8).

$$S(m) \oplus S(m^*) = \Delta_z \oplus P^{-1}(e_{b_j}) \tag{8}$$

We call I this set of equations, where only one of these equations is correct.

This set can be split in eight subsets I_i, one for each s-box. If $|I| = 1$, we have Δ_y thus we have 8 relations (4). If $|I| = 2$, we have 6 relations (4). And if $|I| = 6$, we have 2 relations (4).

It may be noted that many simplifications appear in the sub-sets I_i. The b_j are always next to each other. When going through P^{-1} these bits are dispatched to different s-boxes. Thus an s-box S_i is concerned by only one b_j. As a consequence, for $l \neq j$, $(P^{-1}(e_{b_l}))_i = 0$ and:

$$\Delta_{y_i} = \Delta_{z_i} \text{ or } \Delta_{z_i} \oplus (P^{-1}(e_{b_j}))_i$$

Thus a fault e gives, for each s-box such that $m_i \neq m_i^*$, a maximum of two possible differentials Δ_{y_i}.

Even if the fault value e is unknown when it is injected, the set of possibilities is very small. We have a lot of information on Δ_y, which in the end lead us to define the s-boxes up to a translation.

4.2 S-Box Properties

S-boxes of a DES-like cryptosystem can be a priori any $\{0, 1\}^6 \to \{0, 1\}^4$ function. Obviously such functions are not invertible, but this is anyway not a requirement since the DES-like decipherment also uses the direct s-boxes. However, to resist cryptanalytic attacks, it is highly recommended that the s-boxes respect some properties. Some desired properties of s-boxes are described and justified by Brickell in [14].

We decided to take into account only the two following properties, which are used in many pseudo-DES ciphers, as for example in DESL [17][2].

Of course, different or additional constraints could be assumed as well, without fundamentally changing our conclusions.

Property P1. *Changing 1 input bit of an s-box results in changing at least 2 output bits.*

---

[2] Let us notice that DESL is *not* primarily intended to resist reverse-engineering attacks, but to be more lightweight [18] than the genuine DES. Still, it is an illustration that trading s-boxes for others can done safely

P1 implies that a faulty bit at the input of one s-box changes its output. Thus the case where the output of one s-box affected by a single bit fault e is unchanged is excluded. So, P1 reduces the number of possible single bit faults b_j from six to two. With this property and the paragraph 4.1, there are a maximum of only two possible faults in $R14^*$, noted e_{b_1} and e_{b_2}.

Let's use the example of the paragraph 4.1. Only the bits 2 and 3 are only at the input of S_1, the other bits are also at the input of S_8 and S_2. There are two possible error values e_2 and e_3.

Property P2. *Each line of an s-box is a permutation of the integers 0 to 15.*

Property P2 implies that a line contains 16 different values. If the values of 15 cells on the same line are known; by elimination, the last cell is equal to the missing integer in interval $[\![0, 15]\!]$. The number of possible s-boxes is $(16!)^{4 \cdot 8} \approx 2^{1376}$. It would be natural to think that $4 \cdot 16 - 1 = 63$ relations are needed to define an s-box up to a translation. But, P2 implies that with 14 adequate relations we can find all the relations on this line. Thus to define an s-box up to a translation, $4 \cdot 14 = 56$ relations are sufficient.

Property P2 allows to eliminate wrong hypotheses for differentials Δ_{y_i}. Indeed, let m_{i_0}, m_{i_1} be any two inputs which are associated with the same line; $S_i(m_{i_0}) = y_{i_0} \neq y_{i_1} = S(m_{i_1})$. Thus, $\forall m_{i_2}$, an input such that $S_i(m_{i_2}) = y_{i_2}$, we have:

$$S_i(m_{i_0}) \oplus S_i(m_{i_2}) = y_{i_0} \oplus y_{i_2} \neq y_{i_1} \oplus y_{i_2} = S_i(m_{i_1}) \oplus S_i(m_{i_2})$$

In practice, for a relation (4) with $m_{i_0} \neq m_{i_1}$ we have one of the following properties: either (9) or (10).

- m_{i_0}, m_{i_1} belong to the same line. Let m_{i_2} be any input, different from m_{i_0} and m_{i_1}:

$$S_i(m_{i_0}) \oplus S_i(m_{i_1}) = \Delta_{y_i} \Rightarrow \begin{cases} S_i(m_{i_0}) \oplus S_i(m_{i_2}) \neq \Delta_{y_i} \\ S_i(m_{i_1}) \oplus S_i(m_{i_2}) \neq \Delta_{y_i} \end{cases} \qquad (9)$$

- m_{i_0} and m_{i_1} are associated with two different lines l and l'. Let $m_{i_2} \neq m_{i_0}$ be an input associated with l. Let $m_{i_3} \neq m_{i_1}$ be an input associated with l':

$$S_i(m_{i_0}) \oplus S_i(m_{i_1}) = \Delta_{y_i} \Rightarrow \begin{cases} S_i(m_{i_0}) \oplus S_i(m_{i_3}) \neq \Delta_{y_i} \\ S_i(m_{i_1}) \oplus S_i(m_{i_2}) \neq \Delta_{y_i} \end{cases} \qquad (10)$$

In FIRE attack [12], property P2 is not fully exploited. Thereby properties (9) and (10) are not used.

5   Implementation and Results

5.1   Experimental Validation

In order to validate the fault model, we conducted an experimental campaign of faults against a smart-card that embeds a hardware DES accelerator. Of course, the DES module in this smart-card is genuine (i.e. the s-boxes are original), but the kind of faults that will appear is likely to be representative of a DES despite its s-boxes are customized.

The smart-card is fabricated in CMOS 130 nm technology. Internally, the DES runs at 66 MHz under a voltage supply of 1.3 V. The DES co-processor computes one round per clock cycle. Its s-boxes are implemented in logic gates, and not in ROM. It is known that in such designs, the critical path goes through the s-boxes, because they are made up of several layers of gates.

The experiment consisted in reducing the power supply and to check for the integrity of the DES computation. For each voltage value, the DES module was submitted 1000 single-block encryptions in ECB (Electronic Code Book) mode of operation (i.e. without initial vector nor chaining).

The produced cipher-texts were processed with two metrics. The first one is simply the *proportion of incorrect encryptions*. Intuitively, the smaller the supplied voltage, the more incorrect encryptions are obtained. The second metric is the *proportion of incorrect encryptions caused by a bit-flip*. To compute this metric, a software version of the DES has been programmed, in which any intermediate bit can be flipped: thus, there are 64×16 possible locations, corresponding to the 64 bits of the LR register and to the 16 rounds. If for one of these positions, the software yields the same erroneous cipher-text as obtained experimentally, then it is confirmed that this a bit-flip indeed occurred in the circuit. Of course, the proportion of incorrect encryptions is greater than proportion of incorrect encryptions caused by a bit-flip. The difference is labeled "multiple faults".

The results are shown in Fig. 4. It can be seen that the DES starts to produce erroneous encryptions at a relatively low voltage. Nonetheless, the chip remains functional, and so the voltage can be lowered even more. We can see that there

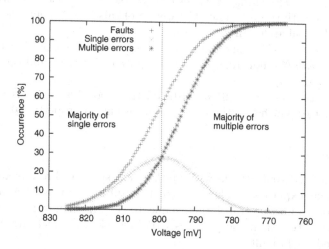

Fig. 4. Proportion of incorrect encryptions, and proportion of incorrect encryptions due to bit-flips, as obtained from a hardware DES module.

is a range, between 0.825 and .820, where all the faults are bit-flips. Below this interval, a bit-flip cannot explain the fault found in the ciphertext. This is due to the fact many bit-flips occur, which hinders our reverse-engineering attack. Nonetheless, our attack perfectly works in the identified voltage range $[0.825, 0.820]$.

5.2   Implementation

Graphs. The relations in s-boxes can be represented with eight disjoint graphs G_i, one for each s-box. The nodes of a graph represent the 64 different input values of an s-box S_i. Two nodes are linked by one edge, such that its weight is equal to the number of possible Δ_{y_i} for these inputs. At the beginning all possible differentials are possible. The weight of an edge is equal to 16, or 15 if the edge connects two inputs of a same line. The attack ends when all the weights are equal to one. Eventually, the total weight is equal to $\sum_{i=1}^{63} i = 2016$.

Algorithms. In A, Algorithm 1 *Attack* keeps running until s-boxes are retrieved, i.e. all G_i, $i \in [\![1,8]\!]$ have not a total weight of 2016. A fault injection e gives a set I of Eq. (8) as explained in 4.1 . It is stored in a list L. It is split in eight, and each part is exploited by the sub-function Algorithm 2 *Update_graph* which updates graphs G_i, $i \in [\![1,8]\!]$.

More precisely Algorithm 2 in A uses relations r associated with an s-box S_i. A relation r contains two inputs m_i and m_i' and a list of possible Δ_{y_i} extracted from I_i or from properties propagation. If there is only one Δ_{y_i}, r is a relation (4). In this case properties (5) and (9) or (10) can be applied.

- *Simplify r*: if the number of Δ_{y_i} can be reduced, i.e. there are some e_{b_j} such that $(P^{-1}(e_{b_j}))_i = 0$.
- *Update G_i with r*: the Δ_{y_i} listed in r stays assigned to the edge which links the m_i node with the m_i^* node. The weight of this edge becomes equal to the number of possible Δ_{y_i} in r.
- *Update L_i with r*: if it can eliminate some e_{b_j} in a set of equation I.
- *Update G_i with* (5): new relations are computed with r, G_i and the transitive property of xor (5).
- *Update G_i with property* (9) *or* (10): on the s-box lines: Δ_{y_i} is withdrawn from the edges which link the node m_i, according to property (9) or (10).

5.3   Results

We have simulated 1000 attacks with Matlab. The statistical results are detailed in Table 2. Our experiments showed that 423 faults were needed in average to define all s-boxes up to a translation thanks to the injection of faults in $R14$. It is 2.45 times better than the previous FIRE attack [12] which inject faults in $R15$ and needs 1040 faults.

Furthermore taking into account P1 and P2 improves again our attack. Property P2 decreases greatly the needed number of faults. Property P1 simplifies

Table 2. Statistics about the number of faults necessary to succeed an attack (estimated from 1000 attacks)

Statistic tool	Without P1 and P2	With P1 and P2
Mean	423.07	234.76
Standard Deviation	63.30	34.08
Median	413	231
Minimum	313	168
Maximum	654	394

the algorithm, since it reduces the size of the set I. Indeed, only 234 faults were needed in average. Finally our attack is 4.44 times better than the previous FIRE attack [12].

We study an example of attack, illustrated in Fig. 5. This attack needed 352 faults to define s-boxes up to a translation. Compared to the mean this case is deliberately chosen bad in order to observe the attack behaviour. The number of new relations obtained at each fault is given in Fig. 5.

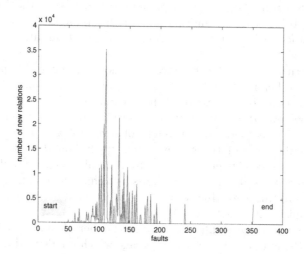

Fig. 5. Number of new relations obtained at each fault for an instance of an attack which needs 352 faults

At the start, a fault gives between 2 and 8 relations. It is expected since at the beginning we have only few relations in graphs. Starting from approximately 50 faults, the algorithm obtains a lot of relations. The different properties allow to bring out many relations. The number of new relations (4) discovered at each fault injection, starts by increasing at the beginning of the attack and then decreases to zero. Starting from approximately 250 faults to the last one, faults bring almost no new relations.

Table 3. Results for 100 attacks with different numbers of faults

Number of faults	Average of number of s-boxes which are retrieved up to a translation	Median of maximal number of guesses to define s-boxes up to a translation	Maximum number of guesses to totally define s-boxes
120	0.04	$4.549 \cdot 10^{42}$	2^{174}
140	0.89	$9.5105 \cdot 10^{14}$	2^{82}
160	2.76	62208	2^{47}
180	4.53	16	2^{36}
200	6.06	8	2^{35}
220	6.93	4	2^{33}
240	7,5	0	2^{32}

Due to the randomness of faults, at the end of an attack, Algorithm 1 *Attack* waits for an adequate fault to be injected. The other faults do not give any new relations. Algorithm 1 eliminates all relations obtained by these faults, because there are already known. Algorithm 2 *Update_graph* is not called any more.

Exhaustive Search. The previous paragraph shows that the last faults in attack do not bring a lot of information. In this paragraph, the new idea is to stop the attack before s-boxes are defined up to a translation and finish in exhaustive search.

When Algorithm 1 *Attack* is stopped at a chosen number of faults, the total graph weight is different than 2016. There are edges with a weight not equal to 1. Relations (4) have to be guessed to find the s-boxes.

Using properties (5), (9) and (10), each new guess eliminates some possible relations (4) and thus modifies the weight of several edges. The weight of the minimum spanning tree of the graph is the upper bound on the number of guesses. Indeed this weight represents the total number of guesses if guesses are independent. Kruskal's algorithm [19] allows us to find the spanning tree and its weight. Thanks to this algorithm we have a correct maximization of the number of guesses to finish our attack.

Table 3 presents three results for a given number of faults on 100 attacks. First, it gives the number of s-boxes in average which are defined up to a translation. The second column indicates the maximum number of guesses which are used to retrieve s-boxes up to a translation. We prefer to use the median rather than the mean because of the presence of sparse extreme values which alter the representative power of the mean number. The last column gives a rough estimate of the number of guesses needed to define fully the s-boxes. It takes into account the 2^{32} guesses on s-boxes when there are defined up to a translation.

According to his computational power, an attacker can stop the attack at the number of fault given in Table 3. For example, with a computational power of 2^{47}, we need only 160 faults to retrieve fully the 8 s-boxes by an achievable exhaustive search. Recall that the exhaustive search of the s-boxes (without FIRE) would require an infeasible amount of $2^{4 \times 2^6 \times 8} = 2^{2048}$ hypotheses.

We have briefly studied a single bit fault attack on $R13$. But a single bit fault affects too many bits in Δ_z. The guesses on the injected fault are too numerous to be operated.

6   Conclusion

In this paper we have presented a FIRE attack on a pseudo-DES which has unknown s-boxes. Our attack is inspired by [12] and decreases the required number of faults. Our improvement is based on the innovative idea to exploit faults striking the penultimate round ($R14$) instead of the last one ($R15$). Although the differential equations are more complicated, they are also more rich in that they allow a parallel attack on a large number of s-boxes. This cuts the number of faults to succeed the attack by a factor of two. Furthermore, our attack has the remarkable property that it can easily be educated with a priori information about the s-boxes. Typically, by considering basic properties of balancedness and propagation criteria, the attack's convergence can be sped up by an additional factor two.

Concretely, we show that by considering this fault injection, 423 faults were needed in average to define all s-boxes up to a translation. It is 2.45 times better than the previous FIRE attack [12] which injects faults in $R15$. Our attack requires no a priori knowledge on the s-boxes. However, in practice, it is desirable that Feistel schemes' s-boxes have some properties. We show that if we assume that s-boxes have some selected properties, then our attack can be made even faster. Indeed, this strategy is winning since it converges to the correct solution in about 4.44 times fewer faults than the FIRE attack [12]. Finally we need 234 faults in average to define 8 s-boxes up to a translation. The attack limits the number of fault injections which can damage the circuit.

Furthermore we show that a trade-off between the number of injected faults and the final exhaustive search can be tuned. For example, with a computational power of 2^{47}, we need only 160 faults to retrieve fully the 8 s-boxes by an achievable exhaustive search.

Acknowledgements. The authors would like to thank Ronan Lashermes, Manuel San Pedro, Guillaume Reymond and Loc Zussa for their valuable contributions to the development and understanding of the issues discussed in the paper.

This work was partially funded by the French DGCIS (Direction Générale de la Compétitivité de l'Industrie et des Services) through the CALISSON 2 project. Parts of this research has been founded by the **MARSHAL+** project, *"Mechanisms Against Reverse-engineering for Secure Hardware and Algorithms"*, from call FUI 12, co-labellized by the competitivity clusters System@tic et SCS.

Sylvain Guilley is also scientific advisor of Secure-IC S.A.S., 80 avenue des Buttes de Coësmes, 35700 Rennes, France.

A Appendix

Algorithm 1. *Attack* : inject faults until s-boxes are defined up to a translation.

Output : 8 graphs G_i, $i \in [\![1,8]\!]$ of total weight 2016 for 8 s-boxes.

Initialization of 8 graphs G_i
Create an empty list L of sets I associated with e
while All G_i have not a total weight of 2016 **do**
    Generate a new couple ciphertext, faulty ciphertext (C, C^*)
    Compute m, m^* with equation (2) and Δ_z with (6)
    Write I (the size of I depends on the use P1 or not)
    $L = [L, I]$
    Split I in sub-sets I_i
    for $i = 1$ to 8 **do**
        $Update\_graph(I_i, G_i, L)$
    end for
end while
Return the 8 graphs G_i

Algorithm 2. *Update_graph* : Store and process relations (4) and (8) for a given s-box

---

Input : one graph G_i, $i \in [\![1,8]\!]$
L list of sets I (8)
I_i a sub-set of equations on S_i
Output : a graph G_i, a list L

$l = r$ obtained from I_i
while l is not empty **do**
    Take the first relation r in l
    Simplify r if it is possible
    if r is new relation in G_i **then**
        Update G_i with r
        Update L with r
        if r is a relation (4) **then**
            Update G_i with property (5)
            if m_i and m'_i are on same line **then**
                Update G_i with property (9) (Only if P2)
            else
                Update G_i with property (10) (Only if P2)
            end if
        end if
        Store new relations in l
    end if
    Remove r from l
end while

References

1. Kerckhoffs, A.: La cryptographie militaire. J. des Sci. Militaires **9**(1), 5–38 (1883)
2. NIST: data encryption Standard. FIPS PUB 46–3 (1977)
3. Clavier, C.: Secret external encodings do not prevent transient fault analysis. In: Paillier, P., Verbauwhede, I. (eds.) CHES 2007. LNCS, vol. 4727, pp. 181–194. Springer, Heidelberg (2007)
4. Luby, M., Rackoff, C.: How to construct pseudo-random permutations from pseudo-random functions. In: Williams, H.C. (ed.) CRYPTO 1985. LNCS, vol. 218, p. 447. Springer, Heidelberg (1986)
5. Daudigny, R., Ledig, H., Muller, F., Valette, F.: SCARE of the DES. In: Ioannidis, J., Keromytis, A.D., Yung, M. (eds.) ACNS 2005. LNCS, vol. 3531, pp. 393–406. Springer, Heidelberg (2005)
6. Guilley, S., Sauvage, L., Micolod, J., Réal, D., Valette, F.: Defeating any secret cryptography with SCARE attacks. In: Abdalla, M., Barreto, P.S.L.M. (eds.) LAT-INCRYPT 2010. LNCS, vol. 6212, pp. 273–293. Springer, Heidelberg (2010)
7. Clavier, C.: An improved SCARE cryptanalysis against a secret A3/A8 GSM algorithm. In: McDaniel, P., Gupta, S.K. (eds.) ICISS 2007. LNCS, vol. 4812, pp. 143–155. Springer, Heidelberg (2007)
8. Clavier, C., Isorez, Q., Wurcker, A.: Complete SCARE of AES-like block ciphers by chosen plaintext collision power analysis. In: Paul, G., Vaudenay, S. (eds.) INDOCRYPT 2013. LNCS, vol. 8250, pp. 116–135. Springer, Heidelberg (2013)
9. Rivain, M., Roche, T.: SCARE of secret ciphers with SPN structures. In: Sako, K., Sarkar, P. (eds.) ASIACRYPT 2013, Part I. LNCS, vol. 8269, pp. 526–544. Springer, Heidelberg (2013)
10. Biham, E., Shamir, A.: Differential fault analysis of secret key cryptosystems. In: Kaliski Jr, B.S. (ed.) CRYPTO 1997. LNCS, vol. 1294, pp. 513–525. Springer, Heidelberg (1997)
11. Biham, E., Shamir, A.: Differential cryptanalysis of DES-like cryptosystems. J. Cryptology **4**(1), 3–72 (1991)
12. San Pedro, M., Soos, M., Guilley, S.: FIRE: fault injection for reverse engineering. In: Ardagna, C.A., Zhou, J. (eds.) WISTP 2011. LNCS, vol. 6633, pp. 280–293. Springer, Heidelberg (2011)
13. Ming, T., Zhenlong, Q., Hui, D., Shubo, L., Huanguo, Z.: Reverse engineering analysis based on differential fault analysis against secret S-boxes. China Commun. **9**(10), 10–22 (2012)
14. Brickell, E.F., Moore, J.H., Purtill, M.R.: Structure in the S-boxes of the DES. In: Odlyzko, A.M. (ed.) CRYPTO 1986. LNCS, vol. 263, pp. 3–8. Springer, Heidelberg (1987)
15. NIST: specification for the advanced encryption standard. FIPS PUB 197 **197** (November 2001)
16. Sakiyama, K., Li, Y., Iwamoto, M., Ohta, K.: Information-theoretic approach to optimal differential fault analysis. IEEE Trans. Inf. Forensics Secur. **7**(1), 109–120 (2012)
17. Leander, G., Paar, C., Poschmann, A., Schramm, K.: New lightweight DES variants. In: Biryukov, A. (ed.) FSE 2007. LNCS, vol. 4593, pp. 196–210. Springer, Heidelberg (2007)
18. Poschmann, A., Leander, G., Schramm, K., Paar, C.: New light-weight crypto algorithms for RFID. In: ISCAS, pp. 1843–1846 (2007)
19. Kruskal, J.B.: On the shortest spanning subtree of a graph and the traveling salesman problem. Proc. Am. Math. Soc. **7**, 48–48 (1956)

Software Camouflage

Sylvain Guilley[1,2]($\boxtimes$), Damien Marion[3], Zakaria Najm[1], Youssef Souissi[2], and Antoine Wurcker[3]

[1] TELECOM-ParisTech, COMELEC dpt — UMR CNRS 5141, 39 rue Dareau, 75014 Paris, France
[2] Secure-IC S.A.S., 80 avenue des Buttes de Coësmes, 35700 Rennes, France
[3] XLIM — UMR CNRS 7252, 123, avenue Albert Thomas, 87060 Limoges Cedex, France
`sylvain.guilley@enst.fr`

Abstract. Obfuscation is a software technique aimed at protecting high-value programs against reverse-engineering. In embedded devices, it is harder for an attacker to gain access to the program machine code; of course, the program can still be very valuable, as for instance when it consists in a secret algorithm. In this paper, we investigate how obscurity techniques can be used to protect a secret customization of substitution boxes in symmetric ciphers, when the sole information available by the attacker is a side-channel. The approach relies on a combination of a universal evaluation algorithm for vectorial Boolean functions with indistinguishable opcodes that are randomly shuffled. The promoted solution is based on the noting that different logic opcodes, such as AND/OR or AND/XOR, happen to be very close one from each other from a side-channel leakage point of view. Moreover, our solution is very amenable to masking owing to the fact the substitution boxes are computed (combinationally).

Keywords: Side-channel analysis · Reverse-engineering · Cryptography · substitution boxes (sboxes) · CNF · ANF · Masking · Camouflage · Obscurity

1 Introduction

Side-channel analysis is a well-known technique to extract keys from secure devices. It can be adapted to recover secret algorithms. In this case, it takes on the name of side-channel analysis for reverse-engineering (SCARE). Several scholar papers describe use-cases how SCARE can work in various contexts. For example, Novak shows in [1–3] how to attack GSM algorithms. Such attacks are later improved by Clavier [4]. Some other papers analyse general methods to attack software implementations (references are [5–9]).

To combat SCARE, protections shall be implemented. Usually proposed solutions to prevent SCARE attacks consist in applying standard side-channel countermeasures (as described for instance in the "Differential Power Analysis"

J.-L. Danger et al. (Eds.): FPS 2013, LNCS 8352, pp. 122–139, 2014.
DOI: 10.1007/978-3-319-05302-8_8, © Springer International Publishing Switzerland 2014

book [10]). Now, robust side-channel countermeasures are costly. For instance, a provable first-order masking scheme for the AES [11] makes its cost increase from 3 kcycles to 129 kcycles.

It is noteworthy that lowest-level solutions exist to prevent embedded information stealth. For instance, at silicon-level, they consist in shaping standard cells in such a way that different functions appear alike. This is illustrated on the example displayed in Fig. 1. Thus, an attacker that wishes to recover the circuit's functionality by its destratification will eventually be deceived when attempting to recognize gates. This is why this technique is termed *hardware camouflage*[1]. However, this technological option is low-level, namely circuit layout level, and thus might not be applicable to all business models (especially *fabless* models).

In this article, we place ourselves in a context where the secret application (or data) to be protected against SCARE is a code executed by a processor. For this purpose, we explore a software solution based on *camouflaged instructions*[2]. The idea is to take advantage of indistinguishable instructions, from a side-channel point of view, to deceive an attacker eager to uncover the secret running code.

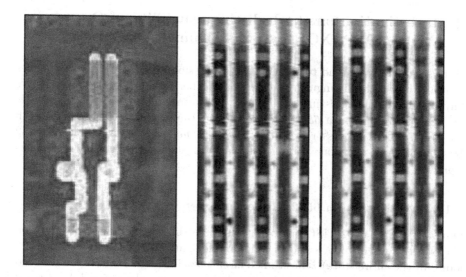

Fig. 1. Hardware-level camouflage of gates. <u>Left</u>: an unprotected gate, whose function is easy to identify. <u>Center, right</u>: *almost* indistinguishable AND/OR camouflaged gates. *[courtesy of SMI / SypherMedia Library]*

---

[1] This is colloquially known as *hardware "camo"*; there are many such examples of technologies, such as this patent [12] by IBM and the tens of patents cited by this patent.

[2] We notice that the paper [13] also tackles a similar issue, but requires to process simultaneously a *decoil* value, like in *dual-rail with precharge logics* [14]. In our *software camouflage* technique, the opcodes are balanced natively *per se*, without any *deus ex machina* support.

The rest of the paper is organized as follows. In Sect. 2 we show that some classes of instructions are delicate to recognize using side-channel leakage (which will be all the more true as the data processed by the instruction is unknown). These conclusions are derived from real-world side-channel studies on representative embedded devices. In Sect. 3 we provide a software camouflage based on the use of AND and OR, or AND and XOR (shown as hardly distinguishable), and compare the cost of our countermeasure to alternative protections against SCA or SCARE. This section considers the case-study of the secret customization of substitution boxes (sboxes) in some block cipher. The remarkable compatibility of our software camouflage method with masking is also explained. The Sect. 4 discusses further considerations, such as the possibility to use cryptographically strong sboxes that are parametrized in a more lightweight way than the generic sboxes computations, or the resistance of software camouflage to fault injection attacks. Eventually, the conclusions are given in Sect. 5. Source codes for the most important algorithms are given in Appendix A. The source code for the truth table to ANF conversion algorithm is given in Appendix A.

2   Investigation on the Indistinguishability of Opcodes AND / OR / XOR by Side-Channel Analysis

In this section, we intend to show that it is possible to choose a set of opcodes that are difficult to distinguish one from each other by side-channel analysis. We have conducted three distinct studies on two distinct platforms. The first one is an ASIC that contains a *6502 microcontroller*; the second one is an AT91 with an ARM7-TDMI processor executing a *virtual machine* JAVA simple RTJ (32 bits); finally, the third one is the same platform, but executing *native code* this time.

2.1   Investigation on 6502 Microcontroller

Our work on the 6502 CISC microcontroller is realized with power consumption traces of the execution of a known code sample of an AES SubBytes function (16 loops for the entire state). The studied circuit has been synthesized and founded in STMicroelectronics CMOS 130 nm technology, from a behavioral description in VHDL of the 6502 processor [15]. Thanks to MODELSIM[3] simulations of the 6502 VHDL code, we know the values of several internals (registers, flags, signals, ...) at each clock cycle of the execution. The best linear model of the consumption by a pair of internals using the *least-squares* method (also known as "stochastic method" [16]) reveals that more than 98 % of the consumption is explained by the values of the Rd (Read data) and We (Write enable) signals [17]. These signals are generated by the 6502 CPU to control the RAM memory; they can take three values:

---

[3] MODELSIM is a commercial tool, sold by Mentor Graphics, capable of simulating a behavioral event-based HDL codes (*e.g.* VHDL or Verilog codes).

1. Rd/We = 0/0, noted O, when the memory is not accessed,
2. Rd/We = 1/0, noted R, when the memory is read, and
3. Rd/We = 0/1, noted W, when the memory is written to.

Of course, the last case (Rd/We = 1/1) never happens in practice. Using MOD-ELSIM we observed that the sequence of values of the Rd/We signals during the execution of a given opcode is always the same.

Table 1. Rd/We signature for a set of opcodes and for all addressing modes of the 6502

	AND (AND)	OR (AOR)	XOR (EOR)	ADD (ADC)	SUB (SBC)
IMM	ORR	ORR	ORR	ORR	ORR
Z-PAGE	ORR	ORR	ORR	ORR	ORR
Z-PAGE, X	ORR	ORR	ORR	ORR	ORR
ABS	RORRR	RORRR	RORRR	RORRR	RORRR
ABS, X	RORRR	RORRR	RORRR	RORRR	RORRR
ABS, Y	RORRR	RORRR	RORRR	RORRR	RORRR
(IND, X)	ORRORRR	ORRORRR	ORRORRR	ORRORRR	ORRORRR
(IND), Y	ORRORRR	ORRORRR	ORRORRR	ORRORRR	ORRORRR

Calling *signature* of an opcode its sequence of Rd/We signals, we interestingly noticed that, for any given addressing mode, some sets of distinct opcodes share the same signature. This is illustrated in Table 1 for the following set of opcodes: AND, AOR, EOR (*logic AND, OR, XOR operations*), and ADC and SBC (*arithmetic addition and subtraction*). Given the tight relation between the power consumption and the Rd and We signals, such set of opcodes which share the same signature are virtually indistinguishable by side-channel analysis. The interpretation of this interesting remark is that signals that are driving the RAM are heavily loaded and thus have a strong leakage, whereas which operation is executed by the ALU (arithmetic and logic unit) is selected by a local signal that leaks little. This motivates the assumptions made in the sequel that, in particular, AND, OR and XOR, cannot be distinguished.

2.2   Investigation on ARM7 Java

The goal of our work done with the ARM7 and the virtual machine is the same as in the previous section with the 6502: find whether there are sets of bytecodes that are hard to distinguish by side-channel analysis. For this purpose, we choose a set of bytecodes (ADDV1, DUP, ICONST0, ...) executed on our platform and record their electromagnetic emission (average of 50 traces for each bytecode). Next we compute the cross-correlation between each pair of traces. Figure 2 shows the results we have obtained. The fact that we get a high level of cross-correlation (always beyond 0.86) is due to the common part of each trace which

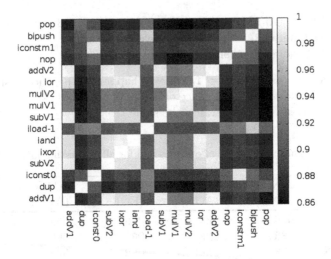

Fig. 2. Representation of the cross-correlation between each opcodes' traces

is related to the instruction fetch at the Java level. We can identify groups of bytecodes that have really similar electromagnetic leakages: *e.g.* (MULV1, MULV2) or (IXOR, IAND, IOR, SUBV1, SUBV2, ADDV1, ADDV2).

2.3   Investigation on ARM7 Native Machine Code

We have practiced another experience on our ARM7 platform: this time, it is profiled at the assembly level. This practice follows the same protocol that we have used for our study at the Java level. The traces of the electromagnetic leakage during the execution of an opcode are captured and analyzed. The result

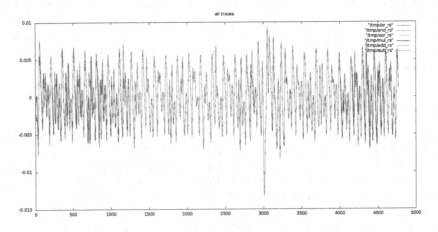

Fig. 3. Traces of the electromagnetic leakage of all the opcodes

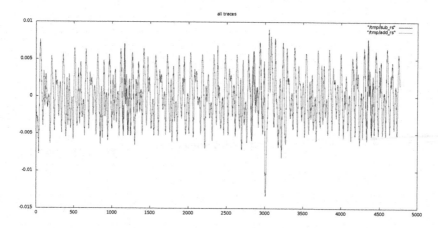

Fig. 4. Traces of the electromagnetic leakage of the ADD and SUB

of this work is plotted on the three Figs. 3, 4 and 5. The first one, namely Fig. 3, shows all the traces obtained after the execution of all the chosen opcodes (SUB, ADD, OR, AND, XOR and MUL). The second one, namely Fig. 4 shows the electromagnetic leakage obtained with the execution of a ADD and a SUB; this graphic reveals that it is possible to distinguish these two opcodes. The last one, namely Fig. 5, concerns the execution of the opcodes AND, OR and XOR; these traces show that it is difficult to distinguish between this three opcodes using side-channel analysis. The same arguments as given for the 6502 apply to account for this noting: the only difference while executing a logic bitwise operation is a selection in the ALU block within the CPU core.

3 Universal Computation Schemes for Substitution Boxes Based on AND, OR & XOR

This section shows how the indistinguishability of AND, OR & XOR opcodes can be taken advantage of to dissimulate the functionality of an sbox from a side-channel attacker. We assume the context in which a block cipher, such as AES, is customized, so as to make its attack still more complex. This secret cryptography practice is common in some market verticals, such as the conditional access (Pay-TV smartcards) or the telecom protocols (encryption algorithms between the terminal and the base station). Instead of redesigning a completely new block cipher, which is error-prone, it is often observed that a standardized algorithm, trustworthy since well analyzed by crytanalysts, is slightly customized. One classical customization is the replacement of the sboxes by others that have similar properties in terms of linear and differential characteristics. We thus assume in this section that the goal of the designer is to compute a secret sbox in such a way it cannot be uncovered even in the presence of side-channel leakage.

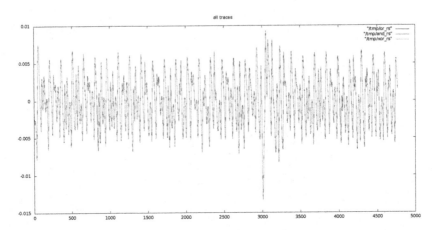

Fig. 5. Traces of the electromagnetic leakage of the AND, XOR and OR

3.1 Tabulated *versus* Computed Substitution Boxes

The sboxes implemented in memories (look-up-tables) have been shown to be attackable thanks to a divide-and-conquer approach in [18]. The reason is that every coordinate of the sbox can be guessed independently. Thus, a leakage model can be determined by selecting some sub-functions, for example $2 \to 1$ functions (there are 16 of them) and attempting to correlate with them. Therefore, it is advised to use standard countermeasures against side-channel attacks to prevent those exploits. They are usually classified in two categories:

1. **hiding** [10, Chap. 7], that consists in balancing the leakage *statically* (*e.g.* thanks to dual-rail with precharge logic), and
2. **masking** [10, Chap. 9], that consists in balancing the leakage *statistically* (*e.g.* thanks to a secret sharing representation of the intermediate variables).

Direct application of masked logic or dual-rail logic is awkward, due to the huge overhead in terms of area it requires. Indeed, the memory size, initially $n \to m$, becomes in both cases $2n \to 2m$ (with the notation: number of input bits $\to$ number of output bits). Let us call $f : \mathbb{F}_2^n \to \mathbb{F}_2^m$ the unprotected sbox, and $\tilde{f} : \mathbb{F}_2^{2n} \to \mathbb{F}_2^{2m}$ the protected sbox.

Regarding first-order masking, the equation of the masked table can for instance write as:

$$Y = \tilde{f}(X) = (f(X_{\text{mask}}), f(X_{\text{mask}} \oplus X_{\text{masked\_data}}) \oplus f(X_{\text{mask}})) \ , \qquad (1)$$

where $X = (X_{\text{mask}}, X_{\text{masked\_data}}) \in \mathbb{F}_2^{2n}$ and $Y = (Y_{\text{mask}}, Y_{\text{masked\_data}}) \in \mathbb{F}_2^{2m}$. The two items in X and Y are called the *shares*. The Eq. (1) satisfies the masking property that $X_{\text{mask}} \oplus X_{\text{masked\_data}}$ is actually the unmasked sensitive variable; the same holds at the output of the sbox for $Y_{\text{mask}} \oplus Y_{\text{masked\_data}}$, because $Y_{\text{mask}} \oplus Y_{\text{masked\_data}} = f(X_{\text{mask}} \oplus X_{\text{masked\_data}})$. The masking is first-order only because it makes use of only one mask per sensitive variable to protect, and because the mask used at the input of the sbox is reused to mask its output.

For dual-rail logic, the new sbox has this equation:

$$Y = \tilde{f}(X) = \begin{cases} (\neg f(\neg X_{\text{true}}), f(X_{\text{true}})) & \text{if } \neg X_{\text{false}} = X_{\text{true}}, \\ (0,0) & \text{otherwise, } i.e. X_{\text{false}} = X_{\text{true}} = 0, \end{cases}$$

where $X = (X_{\text{false}}, X_{\text{true}}) \in \mathbb{F}_2^{2n}$ and $Y = (Y_{\text{false}}, Y_{\text{true}}) \in \mathbb{F}_2^{2m}$. The property satisfied by this redundant representation of the sbox is that the number of transitions of variables in $\mathbb{F}_2^{2n}$ (or $\mathbb{F}_2^{2m}$) is constant if they are operated through the precharge-evaluation protocol: X is equal to $(0,0)$ in precharge phase, and then takes the valid value $X = (\neg X_{\text{true}}, X_{\text{true}})$ at evaluation phase.

So, to summarize with a typical example, when $n = m = 8$, the number of memory points in the memory is raised from $2\,048$ (8×2^8) for f to $1,048,576$ (16×2^{16}) for $\tilde{f}$, i.e. an about $500\times$ increase in size. This is considered unaffordable for many applications.

Therefore, other protections shall be envisioned. Concerning masking, the alternative of the *global look-up table* (Eq. (1)) is the *table recomputation*. This terminology stems from this paper [19] by Prouff et al.

The recomputation in "masking" is actually also prohibitive. For instance, the execution time of an AES secured at first order is multiplied by 43 while at the same time its implementation size is multiplied by 3 [11]. However, this masking protects the data but not the operations. Thus, the cost to mask both the data and the operations is expected to still be greater (*cf.* Sect. 4.1 for a quantitative analysis).

We therefore explore the possibility to use the "hiding" paradigm applied to sbox recomputation. This has been first mentioned in asymmetric cryptography, to protect against simple power attacks, *i.e.* against attacks that attempt to break the key with one sole trace. The idea is to make two operations (in asymmetric cryptography, it is the squaring and the multiplication) indistinguishable. To that end, each time the algorithm involves a key dependent choice, the two branches are coded in such a way they look alike when analyzed from a side-channel perspective. This approach is called the *atomicity countermeasure* [20]. We leverage on this idea to protect not only two portions of codes, but any of the 2^n executions of an $n \rightarrow m$ sbox.

Our solution against the SCARE attack of the sbox relies on two features:

1. The opcodes used for the sbox computation leak, irrespective of the data they process. It is thus important to already provide a regular sbox evaluation that does not leak the computation in simple power analysis. This aspect requires universal regular sbox evaluation algorithms, that are able to compute any sbox in an identical way (from a side-channel analysis standpoint). This is covered in Sect. 3.2.
2. Second, even if a *horizontal* analysis of the leakage is not possible owing to the indistinguishability countermeasure, the implementation shall all the same resist *vertical* attacks that aim at recovering the computed function based

on the possibility (or not) to correlate with a guessed leakage. The solutions described in Sect. 3.2 are amendable to *shuffling* [21], *i.e.* a countermeasure that consists in executing the code in a random order. This aspect is the subject of Sect. 3.3.

3.2   Universal and Regular Sbox Evaluation

In this section, we present several ways to compute a secret substitution box $\mathbb{F}_2^n \to \mathbb{F}_2^m$ using only AND & XOR instructions.

Conjunctive Normal Form (CNF). Each component $j \in [\![1, m]\!]$ of the sbox is written as:

$$f_j(x) = \bigvee_{y \in \mathbb{F}_2^n} f_j(y) \wedge \bigwedge_{i=1}^{n} (1 \oplus x_i \oplus y_i) \ . \tag{2}$$

As each term $\bigwedge_{i=1}^{n}(1 \oplus x_i \oplus y_i)$ (also known as *minterm*, that is equal to 1 if and only if x is equal to y) differs for different x, the CNF can be written alternatively only with AND & XOR operations:

$$f_j(x) = \bigoplus_{y \in \mathbb{F}_2^n} f_j(y) \wedge \bigwedge_{i=1}^{n} (1 \oplus x_i \oplus y_i) \ . \tag{3}$$

The overall cost is $m \times (2^n - 1) \times (2n+1)$ bitwise operations. If the bitwidths are $n = m = 8$ and if the CPU registers are at least bytes, then the m coordinates can be computed in parallel, resulting in $(2^n - 1) \times (2n + 1)$ byte operations.

Algebraic Normal Form (ANF). Each component can also be written in a unique way [22, Sec. 2.1.] as:

$$f_j(x) = \bigoplus_{y \in \mathbb{F}_2^n} a_y \wedge \bigwedge_{i=1}^{n} x_i^{y_i} \ , \tag{4}$$

where for any $x_i, y_i \in \mathbb{F}_2, x_i^{y_i}$ is equal to x_i if $y_i = 1$, or 1 otherwise. The constant a_y is equal to $\bigoplus_{z \in \mathbb{F}_2^n / z \preceq y} f_j(z)$, where $(z \preceq y) = 1 \iff (z \wedge y) = z$, *i.e.* z has 1s at coordinates where y also has. We also say that z is *covered* by y. In particular, the a_y of Eq. (4) are not connected to the $f_j(y)$ of Eq. (3). A fast algorithm to compute all the a_y is given in the code listing 1.1 in Appendix A. The monomial $\bigwedge_{i=1}^{n} x_i^{y_i}$ is also noted x^y. It needs not be computed in a *bitslice* manner; indeed, all the $1 \leq j \leq m$ computations in Eq. (4) can be handled *in parallel*, as illustrated in the code listing 1.2 in Appendix A. The overall cost is $m \times (2^n - 1) \times (n+1)$ bitwise operations. Indeed, in average on y, the computation of x^y requires only $n/2$ AND. Therefore, ANF is computed about *twice faster* than CNF.

As noted for the CNF, an 8-bit CPU can evaluate the $m = 8$ coordinates at once, and thus a $8 \rightarrow 8$ function can be computed in $(2^n - 1) \times (n + 1)$ byte operations.

Finally, it must be underlined that ANF and CNF can execute truly in *constant time*; indeed, the sboxes are fully computed is a thorough method to prevent timing attacks (refer for instance to the notice by Bernstein *et al.* [23]). Even proven masking schemes (such as [11,24]) are prone to timing attacks if the Galois field multiplication is not implemented as a computation but as a look-up table.

3.3   Secure Sbox Evaluation

Additional caution must be taken to prevent an attacker from correlating with intermediate data that appears while Eq. (4) is computed. This computation can be executed whichever the order of the y value. Therefore, there are $(2^n)!$ different permutations possible to shuffle the monomials x^y. In particular, the first operation realized is (almost) never the same, and thus a correlation power analysis is doomed to failure. The standard method to extract information from shuffled or disaligned instructions consists in averaging the side-channel trace over a window large enough to certainly contain the sensitive variable leakage. In the scientific literature, it is referred to as an *integrated DPA attack* [25]. Numerically, the expected correlation coefficient in an integrated DPA attack is divided by the square root of $(2^n)!$ [26, Sect. 3.2], *i.e.* divided by 2.9×10^{253}; this justifies why a correlation power analysis is considered impossible. Notice that this is an *intra-sbox* shuffling; it can also be combined with an *inter-sbox* shuffling, *i.e.* a shuffling between the 16 sboxes used by AES during each round.

A new attack on secret executed code consists in uncovering a hidden Markov chain, as used for instance in the removal of a random delay countermeasure [27]. The similarity of the AND/XOR guarantees that such an attack is infeasible in practice.

The AES block cipher calls the sbox, called SubBytes, 16 times per round, and those are all identical. But that could be made different in the customized version of the algorithm. One advantage of the *computation* over the *tabular* of the sbox is that the 16 sboxes can be made unique at the cost of a limited overhead. The reason is that the code for the sbox evaluation can be shared, and that only the constants (that is, either $f(y)$ in CNF or the a_y in ANF) change.

3.4   Software Camouflage Masking

It must be noted that despite the random shuffling of the sbox inner computations with ANF, at the end of evaluation, the result shall be stored; such operation might leak unless care is taken. This side effect can be devastating if the sbox computation is stored in memory: the leak is expected to be of similar amplitude to that of the direct sbox evaluation as a table in RAM! This should not happen in practice, when the sbox ANF formula is computed in registers. But let us assume that the code is written in a high-level language such as C (instead of an assembly language). It thus happens that a leakage exists in the likely case the compiled program ends with a memory transfer. To point this out, two actual implementations of the sbox using a regular look-up-table and the ANF formula (obtained from a C program) have been evaluated in practice, using a setup identical to that of the DPA contest version 4 [28]. The C code is given in source listing 1.2; it has been compiled without optimizations (-O0 flag in avg-gcc). The C code has been compiled without optimizations (-O0 flag in avg-gcc). The code is loaded into an ATMega163 8-bit smartcard, and evaluated on a SASEBO-W platform [29], which is well-designed for side-channel attacks experiments. The measurements are done with a LeCroy wave-runner 6100A oscilloscope by mean of a Langer EMV 3 GHz electromagnetic probe. The smartcard is clocked at 3.57 MHz. Exemplary traces are shown for both ways of evaluating the sbox in Fig. 6. The result of a correlation power analysis (CPA [30]) on 200 traces is represented in Fig. 7. The window corresponds to the sbox evaluation; the horizontal units are samples, knowing that the sampling rate is 500 Msample/s. Clearly, when addressing a look-up-table, the leakage is *evident*. When the implementation is an ANF computation, the CPA profile is *flat*: there is no leakage during the computation, as expected. However, after the computation, when the result is saved in RAM, it leaks[4].

In order to prevent such problem, an option consists in masking the sbox. This operation is trivial with the ANF formula, as it costs only one operation. In the Eq. (4), if the constant $a_{(0\ldots0)_2}$ is toggled, then the whole sbox is turned into the complementary sbox. Such computation makes it possible to defeat *first degree* attacks (refer for instance to [31]), at a virtually free overhead. This means that the peaks occurring at the end of Fig. 7(b) disappear.

4   Discussion

4.1   Comparison with an Approach Based on Masking the Data and the Code

As already mentioned, masking is costly when it comes to compute nonlinear operations. To solve our problem, namely computing a secret sbox with masked data, the cost of the masking will still be higher. In this section, we estimate the cost of masking at order one the data and the code of an sbox written in a generic way.

As argued by Rivain and Prouff in their seminal paper about hi-order masking on CPUs [11], the masking of nonlinear functions are done more efficiently at the word level rather than at the bit level[5].

---

[4] Notice that the storage of the sbox result is *one option* when computed in ANF, whereas it is *inherent* (i.e. unavoidable) to the computation with a Look-up-Table.

[5] The work by Kim *et al.* [24] has shown that for some specific problems, *e.g.* when the sbox has a given structure (which is the case of the AES), minor improvements can be got by computing on half-words, *e.g.* on nibble instead of bytes. But this result does not negate the noting by Rivain and Prouff that computing masking schemes on larger bitwidths is faster than computing at the bit level.

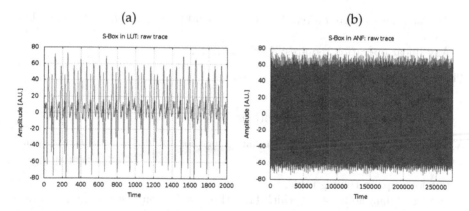

Fig. 6. Example of traces for the (a) *regular* LUT and the (b) *new* ANF implementation of SubBytes

Therefore, the masking schemes are the most efficient when operating on the Galois field $(\mathbb{F}_{2^n}, \oplus, \odot)$. In this notation, $\oplus$ is the additive law (the XOR), and $\odot$ the multiplicative law. Using the Lagrange interpolation polynomial, any function $f : \mathbb{F}_{2^n} \to \mathbb{F}_{2^m}$ can write:

$$f(x) = \bigoplus_{i=0}^{2^n-2} b_i \odot x^i \ , \tag{5}$$

where, here, x^i is the ith power of $x \in \mathbb{F}_{2^n}$, and where $b_i \in \mathbb{F}_{2^m} \sim \mathbb{F}_2^m$ are constants.

The cost is $2^n - 2$ multiplications and $2^n - 1$ additions. When applying dth-order masking, the overhead is given below [11]:

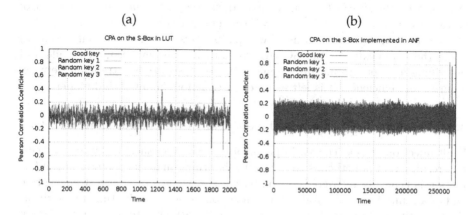

Fig. 7. Correlation Power Analysis of the Sbox (a) in a table, i.e., an array stored in a RAM, and (b) computed using the ANF formula

- Any nonlinear operation requires: $(d+1)^2$ field products, $2d(d+1)$ field additions:
- Any linear operation requires: d field additions.

Thus, Eq. (5) masked at order $d = 1$ requires:

- $(2^n - 2) \times 4$ field products, and
- $(2^n - 2) \times 4 + (2^n - 1)$ field additions.

A field product can be computed thanks to log-alog tables [32], which represents 6 clock cycles:

- two look-ups in the log table,
- one (modular) addition — which lasts three cycles, one for the addition, one to test the carry flag, and a last conditional reduction (always done to prevent from timing attacks),
- and one look-up in the alog table.

So, if $n = m = 8$, the cost of the computing Eq. (5) masked at first order is: $254 \times 4 \times 6 + 254 \times 4 + 255 = 7,367$ cycles.

This is more than 3 times more than the shuffled ANF, which requires only $(2^n - 1) \times (n + 1) = 2,295$ byte operations, $i.e.$ $2,295$ cycles.

However, it is expected that the proposed scheme is more efficient than masking, because it exploits a property of the hardware (namely the indistinguishability of the AND / OR or AND / XOR opcodes).

4.2   Strong Sboxes with a Compact Encoding

There are $2^{m \times 2^n}$ different sbox $\mathbb{F}_2^n \to \mathbb{F}_2^m$, hence $m \times 2^n$ bits of data is required to parametrize them. This number applies to general block ciphers, such as Feistel networks, that do not require the sboxes to be invertible. Some other generic constructions of block ciphers, such as the substitution-permutation networks (SPN), need the sboxes to be invertible. In this case, $n = m$ and the number of sboxes is equal to $(2^n)! < 2^{n \times 2^n}$. Still, this number is very large.

It is certainly possible to use fewer parameters ($e.g.$ 128 bits only, so as to make the complexity of the SCARE as hard as the key recovery) while still describing a cryptographically strong sbox. As this work is a trade-off between security and efficiency, it is left as an open issue for the interested reader.

4.3   Vulnerability of Secret Sboxes against Fault Injection Attacks

Fault injection attacks consist in perturbing a device in such a way to get incorrect results, that nonetheless contain some information on the secrets. This information is typically recovered by comparing the outputs of a correct encryption and of a faulted one. Naturally, fault injection attacks can be tuned to serve as the recognition of secret sboxes. In this case, the attack is termed fault injection for reverse-engineering (FIRE). Clearly, unless actions are taken, our countermeasure is vulnerable to FIRE attacks.

However, there exist simple ways to make those attacks inefficient. First of all, the randomization of operations within an sbox computation (as promoted in Sect. 3.3), as well as the possible randomization of sboxes evaluation order in an AES round, significantly complexifies fault injection attacks, as the position and the reproducibility of faults cannot be ascertained. Another option is to check the computation based on the assertion of an invariant. For example, the computation can be carried out nominally, which turns a plaintext into a ciphertext. Then, before outputting this ciphertext, the latter is injected in the decryption cipher. If the encryption and the decryption were successful, then the decrypted cipher shall match with the plaintext. Now, it is very unlikely that a fault during decryption manages to cancel the effect of a fault in encryption mode. The reason is that fault injection is usually modelled as a probabilistic effect, and that encryption is different from decryption. A third option consists to deny the possibility for the attacker to submit twice the same plaintext. This can be done easily simply by enforcing a mode of operation that makes use of a random initialization vector.

The existence of these simple practices justifies that FIRE is not considered a plausible threat.

5   Conclusions

It is discovered in this paper that logical operations of a CPU are almost indistinguishable using side-channel analysis. Therefore, generic constructions of functions computations can be devised. We jointly refer to them as *software camouflage*. We show that secret (customized) substitution boxes can be computed without simple side-channel leakage (since all opcodes used in the computation are alike), and without vulnerability against differential side-channel leakage (by a shuffling of the operations). In addition, the computation result of this software camouflage can be masked at virtual no cost, which secures the leakage that can happen when moving this value (e.g., by a transfer from a register to a RAM). The resulting construction is shown to be more than three times faster than the state-of-the-art solution, namely the masking of the sbox computation on masked data. This result shows that the *a priori* knowledge of a device leakage can be constructively exploited to reduce the overhead of protections against side-channel analyses.

Acknowledgments. Parts of this work have been funded by the MARSHAL+ (*Mechanisms Against Reverse-engineering for Secure Hardware and Algorithms*) FUI #12 project, co-labellized by competitivity clusters System@tic and SCS.

We also thank the audience from PHISIC '13 for a positive feedback on this research.

A   Algorithms Source Code

It is shown by Carlet in [22, page 11] that there exists a simple divide-and-conquer butterfly algorithm to compute the ANF from the truth-table (or vice-versa). It is called the "Fast Möbius Transform". An implementation in python is given in code listing 1.1, for $n \rightarrow 1$ Boolean functions. As already underlined in Sect. 3.2, the very same code also works for $n \rightarrow n$ vectorial Boolean functions.

Code Listing 1.1. Truth table to ANF table transformation

```
1   from operator import xor
2
3   n = 8 # Problem's size (we handle bytes, i.e., 8-bit words)
4
5   def tt2anf( S ):
6       """Truth table to ANF"""
7       # S is an array of 256 bits or bytes
8       # (depending the function is Boolean or vectorial Boolean)
9       h = {}
10      h[0] = {}
11      for a in range( 1<<n ):
12          h[0][a] = [S[a]]
13      for k in range( n ):
14          h[k+1] = {}
15          for b in range( 1<<(n-k-1) ):
16              #                the "+" expresses the concatenation
17              h[k+1][b] = h[k][2*b] + map( xor, h[k][2*b], h[k][2*b+1] )
18      return h[n][0]
```

The application of the code listing 1.1 to $f = \texttt{SubBytes}$ (array noted S_TT) is given as S_AND in the code listing 1.2. The values in the array S_TT are $\{f(y), y \in \mathbb{F}_2^8\}$, in this order, whereas the values in the array S_ANF are $\{a_y, y \in \mathbb{F}_2^8\}$ (recall Eq. (4)). In the same code listing, the function `anti_scare_eval` applies SubBytes on a byte x, with the formula of Eq. (4). Furthermore, in this code, the y's are shuffled (See Sect. 3.3) by a simple XOR with a random byte r.

Code Listing 1.2. Shuffled evaluation of `SubBytes` with the ANF computation

```
1   /** Portable C types. We use uint8_t */
2   #include <stdint.h>
3
4   /** Original SubBytes [provided for self-containedness] */
5   static uint8_t S_TT[] = {
6       0x63, 0x7c, 0x77, 0x7b, 0xf2, 0x6b, 0x6f, 0xc5, 0x30, 0x01, 0x67, 0x2b, 0xfe, 0xd7, 0xab, 0x76,
7       0xca, 0x82, 0xc9, 0x7d, 0xfa, 0x59, 0x47, 0xf0, 0xad, 0xd4, 0xa2, 0xaf, 0x9c, 0xa4, 0x72, 0xc0,
8       0xb7, 0xfd, 0x93, 0x26, 0x36, 0x3f, 0xf7, 0xcc, 0x34, 0xa5, 0xe5, 0xf1, 0x71, 0xd8, 0x31, 0x15,
9       0x04, 0xc7, 0x23, 0xc3, 0x18, 0x96, 0x05, 0x9a, 0x07, 0x12, 0x80, 0xe2, 0xeb, 0x27, 0xb2, 0x75,
10      0x09, 0x83, 0x2c, 0x1a, 0x1b, 0x6e, 0x5a, 0xa0, 0x52, 0x3b, 0xd6, 0xb3, 0x29, 0xe3, 0x2f, 0x84,
11      0x53, 0xd1, 0x00, 0xed, 0x20, 0xfc, 0xb1, 0x5b, 0x6a, 0xcb, 0xbe, 0x39, 0x4a, 0x4c, 0x58, 0xcf,
12      0xd0, 0xef, 0xaa, 0xfb, 0x43, 0x4d, 0x33, 0x85, 0x45, 0xf9, 0x02, 0x7f, 0x50, 0x3c, 0x9f, 0xa8,
13      0x51, 0xa3, 0x40, 0x8f, 0x92, 0x9d, 0x38, 0xf5, 0xbc, 0xb6, 0xda, 0x21, 0x10, 0xff, 0xf3, 0xd2,
14      0xcd, 0x0c, 0x13, 0xec, 0x5f, 0x97, 0x44, 0x17, 0xc4, 0xa7, 0x7e, 0x3d, 0x64, 0x5d, 0x19, 0x73,
15      0x60, 0x81, 0x4f, 0xdc, 0x22, 0x2a, 0x90, 0x88, 0x46, 0xee, 0xb8, 0x14, 0xde, 0x5e, 0x0b, 0xdb,
16      0xe0, 0x32, 0x3a, 0x0a, 0x49, 0x06, 0x24, 0x5c, 0xc2, 0xd3, 0xac, 0x62, 0x91, 0x95, 0xe4, 0x79,
17      0xe7, 0xc8, 0x37, 0x6d, 0x8d, 0xd5, 0x4e, 0xa9, 0x6c, 0x56, 0xf4, 0xea, 0x65, 0x7a, 0xae, 0x08,
18      0xba, 0x78, 0x25, 0x2e, 0x1c, 0xa6, 0xb4, 0xc6, 0xe8, 0xdd, 0x74, 0x1f, 0x4b, 0xbd, 0x8b, 0x8a,
19      0x70, 0x3e, 0xb5, 0x66, 0x48, 0x03, 0xf6, 0x0e, 0x61, 0x35, 0x57, 0xb9, 0x86, 0xc1, 0x1d, 0x9e,
20      0xe1, 0xf8, 0x98, 0x11, 0x69, 0xd9, 0x8e, 0x94, 0x9b, 0x1e, 0x87, 0xe9, 0xce, 0x55, 0x28, 0xdf,
21      0x8c, 0xa1, 0x89, 0x0d, 0xbf, 0xe6, 0x42, 0x68, 0x41, 0x99, 0x2d, 0x0f, 0xb0, 0x54, 0xbb, 0x16 };
22
23  /** SubBytes under ANF form [obtained by the python script tt2anf] */
24  static uint8_t S_ANF[] = {
25      0x63, 0x1f, 0x14, 0x13, 0x91, 0x86, 0x89, 0x20, 0x53, 0x2e, 0x43, 0x6e, 0x5f, 0x9e, 0x8b, 0xa9,
26      0xa9, 0x57, 0x17, 0xef, 0xa1, 0x6d, 0x37, 0xc8, 0x34, 0x1f, 0x4f, 0xe6, 0x5e, 0x34, 0xd4, 0xbf,
27      0xd4, 0x55, 0x30, 0xec, 0x10, 0xc5, 0x6c, 0xed, 0xd0, 0xf5, 0xb6, 0x14, 0x9b, 0xe5, 0xff, 0x6c,
28      0x1a, 0xde, 0x14, 0x33, 0x3c, 0x63, 0xe8, 0x37, 0xb4, 0x12, 0x1a, 0xc8, 0x6a, 0xdb, 0x44, 0x34,
29      0x6a, 0x95, 0x31, 0xaf, 0x83, 0x79, 0xed, 0x13, 0x08, 0xcd, 0xe2, 0xde, 0x36, 0xc2, 0x6d, 0xf7,
30      0xf3, 0x5f, 0x61, 0x3c, 0xc0, 0xcc, 0x91, 0xa2, 0x56, 0xdf, 0x69, 0x1f, 0x64, 0x91, 0x36, 0x0f,
31      0x0d, 0xe0, 0x6f, 0x3e, 0x91, 0x0b, 0x02, 0x08, 0x1e, 0x95, 0x2a, 0x0b, 0x74, 0x58, 0x9b, 0x7e,
32      0xc1, 0x1b, 0x09, 0xb3, 0x0d, 0x0e, 0xff, 0x74, 0xae, 0xa9, 0x76, 0x52, 0xb9, 0x87, 0x1a, 0x08,
33      0xae, 0xde, 0xca, 0x2d, 0x03, 0x8f, 0x4c, 0x85, 0x6a, 0x8c, 0x27, 0x70, 0x6d, 0xcd, 0x89, 0x7f,
34      0x04, 0x77, 0xe6, 0xa3, 0x71, 0x8d, 0x6f, 0x0f, 0x1b, 0xf4, 0xfa, 0x8e, 0xb6, 0xa6, 0x60, 0x5f,
35      0xf9, 0x46, 0x34, 0x30, 0x2b, 0x51, 0x1e, 0x9d, 0xfb, 0x94, 0x66, 0x37, 0x53, 0x3e, 0x51, 0x29,
36      0xb0, 0x03, 0xef, 0xe8, 0x2f, 0x69, 0x14, 0xef, 0x32, 0x2f, 0x53, 0xcc, 0x1b, 0x93, 0x1c, 0x10,
37      0x1d, 0x96, 0x70, 0x58, 0xb7, 0x08, 0x1f, 0xd7, 0x53, 0x98, 0x85, 0x57, 0x01, 0x2a, 0x04, 0x89,
38      0x94, 0xf3, 0xca, 0x24, 0x8e, 0x51, 0x85, 0x4a, 0x3a, 0xd9, 0x2c, 0xc7, 0x56, 0xae, 0x3f, 0x17,
39      0x7b, 0x28, 0x8d, 0xbb, 0x84, 0x4e, 0xd9, 0x43, 0x1d, 0x9f, 0x9c, 0xc4, 0x64, 0x8f, 0x3a, 0x2e,
40      0xcc, 0x7e, 0xd4, 0x05, 0x3b, 0xa4, 0x29, 0x63, 0xdc, 0x10, 0xc3, 0xce, 0x0d, 0x9d, 0x04, 0x00 };
```

```
41
42    /**
43     * Application of S_TT on input "x" via the ANF table (S_ANF),
44     * with a random ordering equal to "yr" (yr = y XOR r),
45     * where "r" is a uniformly distributed byte
46     */
47    uint8_t anti_scare_eval( uint8_t* S_ANF, uint8_t x, uint8_t r )
48    {
49        uint8_t result = 0x00u;
50        uint8_t y = 0x00u, yr;
51
52        do
53        {
54            yr = y^r;
55            result ^= S_ANF[yr] & ((( x | ( 0xffu^yr )) == 0xffu ) ? 0xffu : 0x00u );
56        }
57        while( y++ != 0xffu );
58
59        /* At this stage, the variable "result" is equal to S_TT[x], no matter the value of the shuffling
                random parameter "r" */
60        return result;
61    }
```

References

1. Novak, R.: Side-channel attack on substitution blocks. In: Zhou, J., Yung, M., Han, Y. (eds.) ACNS 2003. LNCS, vol. 2846, pp. 307–318. Springer, Heidelberg (2003)
2. Novak, R.: Sign-based differential power analysis. In: Chae, K.-J., Yung, M. (eds.) WISA 2003. LNCS, vol. 2908, pp. 203–216. Springer, Heidelberg (2004)
3. Novak, R.: Side-Channel Based Reverse Engineering of Secret Algorithms. In: Zajc, B. (ed.) Proceedings of the Twelfth International Electrotechnical and Computer Science Conference (ERK 2003), pp. 445–448. Ljubljana, Slovenia, Slovenska sekcija IEEE (2003)
4. Clavier, Ch.: An improved SCARE cryptanalysis against a secret A3/A8 GSM algorithm. In: McDaniel, P., Gupta, S.K. (eds.) ICISS 2007. LNCS, vol. 4812, pp. 143–155. Springer, Heidelberg (2007)
5. Daudigny, R., Ledig, H., Muller, F., Valette, F.: SCARE of the DES. In: Ioannidis, J., Keromytis, A.D., Yung, M. (eds.) ACNS 2005. LNCS, vol. 3531, pp. 393–406. Springer, Heidelberg (2005)
6. Fournigault, M., Liardet, P.-Y., Teglia, Y., Trémeau, A., Robert-Inacio, F.: Reverse engineering of embedded software using syntactic pattern recognition. In: Meersman, R., Tari, Z., Herrero, P. (eds.) OTM 2006 Workshops. LNCS, vol. 4277, pp. 527–536. Springer, Heidelberg (2006)
7. Vermoen, D., Witteman, M., Gaydadjiev, G.N.: Reverse engineering java card applets using power analysis. In: Sauveron, D., Markantonakis, K., Bilas, A., Quisquater, J.-J. (eds.) WISTP 2007. LNCS, vol. 4462, pp. 138–149. Springer, Heidelberg (2007)
8. Amiel, F., Feix, B., Villegas, K.: Power analysis for secret recovering and reverse engineering of public key algorithms. In: Adams, C., Miri, A., Wiener, M. (eds.) SAC 2007. LNCS, vol. 4876, pp. 110–125. Springer, Heidelberg (2007)
9. Réal, D., Dubois, V., Guilloux, A.-M., Valette, F., Drissi, M.: SCARE of an unknown hardware feistel implementation. In: Grimaud, G., Standaert, F.-X. (eds.) CARDIS 2008. LNCS, vol. 5189, pp. 218–227. Springer, Heidelberg (2008)
10. Mangard, S., Oswald, E., Popp, T.: Power Analysis Attacks: Revealing the Secrets of Smart Cards. http://www.springer.com/ Springer, Heidelberg (2006). ISBN 0-387-30857-1
11. Rivain, M., Prouff, E.: Provably secure higher-order masking of AES. In: Mangard, S., Standaert, F.-X. (eds.) CHES 2010. LNCS, vol. 6225, pp. 413–427. Springer, Heidelberg (2010)

12. Hsu, L.L., Joshi, R.V., Kruger, D.W.: Techniques for impeding reverse engineering (2011) IBM. Patent US 7994042 B2
13. Brier, E., Fortier, Q., Korkikian, R., Magld, K.W., Naccache, D., de Almeida, G.O., Pommellet, A., Ragab, A.H., Vuillemin, J.: Defensive Leakage Camouflage. In: [33], pp. 277–295
14. Guilley, S., Sauvage, L., Flament, F., Hoogvorst, P., Pacalet, R.: Evaluation of power-constant dual-rail logics counter-measures against DPA with design-time security metrics. IEEE Trans. Comput. **9**, 1250–1263 (2010). doi:10.1109/TC.2010. 104
15. Kessner, D.: Free VHDL 6502 core (2000) http://www.free-ip.com/ is no longer available, but http://web.archive.org/web/20040603222048/ http://www.free-ip. com/6502/index.html is
16. Schindler, W., Lemke, K., Paar, Ch.: A stochastic model for differential side channel cryptanalysis. In: Rao, J.R., Sunar, B. (eds.) CHES 2005. LNCS, vol. 3659, pp. 30–46. Springer, Heidelberg (2005)
17. Marion, D.,Wurcker, A.: Read, Write Signals Reconstruction Using Side Channel Analysis for Reverse Engineering, : COSADE, 2013. Short talk, TELECOM-ParisTech, Paris, France (2013)
18. Guilley, S., Sauvage, L., Micolod, J., Réal, D., Valette, F.: Defeating any secret cryptography with SCARE attacks. In: Abdalla, M., Barreto, P.S.L.M. (eds.) LAT-INCRYPT 2010. LNCS, vol. 6212, pp. 273–293. Springer, Heidelberg (2010)
19. Prouff, E., Rivain, M.: A generic method for secure SBox implementation. In: Kim, S., Yung, M., Lee, H.-W. (eds.) WISA 2007. LNCS, vol. 4867, pp. 227–244. Springer, Heidelberg (2008)
20. Chevallier-Mames, B., Ciet, M., Joye, M.: Low-cost solutions for preventing simple side-channel analysis: side-channel atomicity. IEEE Trans. Comput. **53**, 760–768 (2004)
21. Veyrat-Charvillon, N., Medwed, M., Kerckhof, S., Standaert, F.-X.: Shuffling against side-channel attacks: a comprehensive study with cautionary note. In: Wang, X., Sako, K. (eds.) ASIACRYPT 2012. LNCS, vol. 7658, pp. 740–757. Springer, Heidelberg (2012)
22. Carlet, C.: Boolean functions for cryptography and error correcting codes. In: Crama, Y., Hammer, P. (eds.) Chapter of the Monography Boolean Models and Methods in Mathematics, Computer Science, and Engineering. cambridge University Press, Cambridge (2010). http://www.math.univ-paris13.fr/carlet/chap-fcts-Bool-corr.pdf
23. Bernstein, D.J., Chou, T., Schwabe, P.: McBits: fast constant-time code-based cryptography. In: Bertoni, G., Coron, J.-S. (eds.) CHES 2013. LNCS, vol. 8086, pp. 250–272. Springer, Heidelberg (2013)
24. Kim, H.S., Hong, S., Lim, J.: A fast and provably secure higher-order masking of AES S-Box. In: Preneel, B., Takagi, T. (eds.) CHES 2011. LNCS, vol. 6917, pp. 95–107. Springer, Heidelberg (2011)
25. Clavier, C., Coron, J.-S., Dabbous, N.: Differential power analysis in the presence of hardware countermeasures. In: Paar, C., Koç, C. (eds.) CHES 2000. LNCS, vol. 1965, pp. 252–263. Springer, Heidelberg (2000)
26. Rivain, M., Prouff, E., Doget, J.: Higher-order masking and shuffling for software implementations of block ciphers. In: Clavier, C., Gaj, K. (eds.) CHES 2009. LNCS, vol. 5747, pp. 171–188. Springer, Heidelberg (2009)
27. Durvaux, F., Renauld, M., Standaert, F.X., van Oldeneel tot Oldenzeel, L., Veyrat-Charvillon, N.: Efficient removal of random delays from embedded software implementations using hidden markov models. In: [33], pp. 123–140

28. TELECOM ParisTech SEN research group: DPA Contest (4th edn.) (2013–2014). http://www.DPAcontest.org/v4/
29. RCIS-AIST, J.: SASEBO (Side-channel Attack Standard Evaluation Board, Akashi Satoh) development board: http://www.risec.aist.go.jp/project/sasebo/ (2013)
30. Brier, E., Clavier, C., Olivier, F.: Correlation power analysis with a leakage model. In: Joye, M., Quisquater, J.-J. (eds.) CHES 2004. LNCS, vol. 3156, pp. 16–29. Springer, Heidelberg (2004)
31. Bhasin, S., Danger, J.L., Guilley, S., Najm, Z.: A low-entropy first-degree secure provable masking scheme for resource-constrained devices. In: Proceedings of the Workshop on Embedded Systems Security, WESS '13. ACM, New York (2013)
32. Daemen, J., Rijmen, V.: The Design of Rijndael: AES - The Advanced Encryption Standard. Springer (2002)
33. Mangard, S. (ed.): CARDIS 2012. LNCS, vol. 7771. Springer, Heidelberg (2013)

Investigation of Parameters Influencing the Success of Optical Fault Attacks

Thomas Korak[✉]

Institute for Applied Information Processing and Communications (IAIK),
Graz University of Technology, Inffeldgasse 16a, 8010 Graz, Austria
thomas.korak@iaik.tugraz.at

Abstract. Fault attacks are a very powerful class of attacks targeting cryptographic primitives implemented on e.g., microcontrollers. These attacks are used to uncover some secret information by analysing the results of faulty computations. The faulty computations can be caused by intentional irradiation of parts of the chip with a laser beam. In order to succeed in inducing faults with a laser beam a reliable optical fault-injection environment is required and several parameters need to be chosen carefully. The main goal of this work is to show how to set up a reliable optical fault-injection environment. Therefore we examine the influence of laser beams on different microcontroller platforms in detail. We have performed several experiments like single and multiple fault injections in SRAM registers from the front side and the rear side of the chip using different laser sources. Furthermore several parameters influencing the success in order to induce optical faults are examined in detail and an approach to find laser-sensitive spots on the chip is presented. This approach increases the efficiency of optical fault attacks significantly.

Keywords: Laser beam · Optical fault injection · Microcontroller · SRAM

1 Introduction

A huge number of electronic devices nowadays have some cryptographic algorithm implemented in order to achieve confidentiality, authenticity or integrity of processed data. Also the privacy of the user has to be protected in many use cases which is also achieved by cryptography. One example where cryptography plays an important role are sensor nodes. Sensor nodes typically consist of a low-power microcontroller together with several sensors in order to record environmental data. The data is sent to a base station for further processing. The channel between sensor node and base station is insecure and might be eavesdropped by an attacker. Therefore the transmitted data is typically encrypted. An attacker might furthermore gain physical access to sensor nodes quite easy as sensor nodes are often used in environments not observed by human beings.

J.-L. Danger et al. (Eds.): FPS 2013, LNCS 8352, pp. 140–157, 2014.
DOI: 10.1007/978-3-319-05302-8_9, © Springer International Publishing Switzerland 2014

This physical access enables to carry out several attacks that can be classified into three classes: non-invasive attacks, semi-invasive attacks and invasive attacks (c.f. [12]). Non-invasive attacks do not require any modification of the device (e.g., power-analysis attacks), invasive attacks require access to the chip surface (e.g., microprobing). Semi-invasive attacks also require access to the chip surface but the passivation layer stays intact. Optical fault attacks are classified as semi-invasive attacks.

Optical fault attacks can be used to corrupt memory content of microcontrollers. Secret information like encryption keys are often stored in non-volatile memory like EEPROM or Flash while critical data processed during calculations is typically stored in volatile memory, e.g., SRAM. Corrupting this data stored in non-volatile and/or volatile memory can lead to an exposure of secret information, e.g., leakage of the secret key. This threat was already uncovered in the late nineties by Anderson et al. [3] as well as Boneh et al. [6]. In [2] it is shown how to block the EEPROM write operation. In [10] the authors use ultraviolet (UV) irradiation in order to modify memory content and in [14] a laser beam is used to flip single bits in registers. A laser beam with a certain power can also be used to disable the write operation on memory cells in an SRAM. By disabling the write operation the content of the cells always stays the same. This fact is used in order to perform optically enhanced power analysis attacks, introduced in [13]. Optical fault attacks on an CRT-based RSA implementation are reported in the work of Schmidt et al. [9]. Memory write and erase operations are the target of the attacks presented in [11]. A detailed overview of different types of fault attacks can be found in the work of Bar-El et al. [5]. Summing up the optical fault attacks reported in literature in the last years it is obvious that the memory (volatile and non-volatile) of microcontrollers is the preferred target for that class of attacks.

All the attacks mentioned above assume that a working optical fault injection-environment is available. In this work we want to give some detailed information on the main parts which need to be included in such an environment. Furthermore some important parameters which influence the effectiveness of optical fault attacks are examined in detail. We repeat several experiments already documented in literature targeting two different microcontrollers, one PIC 16F84 and one ATMEGA 162/v. The objective of repeating this experiments is to prove the proper function of the environment as well as to evaluate the influence of selected parameters in an efficient way. We are sure that the results of these experiments can also be used for evaluating other devices. An approach in order to find laser sensitive spots on the chip surface based on light-induced voltage alteration (LIVA, [1]) is also presented in this work and performed on the two microcontroller platforms. By identifying laser sensitive spots on the chip the efficiency of optical fault attacks can be increased significantly. Even from the rear side, where no chip structure is visible, e.g., the location of the SRAM can be found. The optical fault injection setup does not need to be modified for subsequent attacks taking advantage of the gathered location information.

The rest of the paper is organized as follows. A general introduction on optical fault-injection attacks is given in Sect. 2. Section 3 describes the main parts included in our optical fault-injection environment as well as the used microcontrollers. The conducted experiments are introduced in Sect. 4 and the corresponding results are summarized in Sect. 5. Section 6 concludes the paper.

2   Optical Fault-Injection Attacks

In this section general information about optical fault attacks is given. Optical fault attacks can be performed e.g., with flash lights or laser beams. The advantage of using a laser beam is that it can be focused to a small spot, so the targeted spot on the chip surface can be selected with high accuracy. In order to enable optical fault attacks the chip has to be exposed in a first step. Exposing means gaining access to the chip surface by removing the package. Two possibilities exist, opening the chip from the front side or from the rear side. Gaining access to the front side of the chip requires the usage of toxic acids (as presented in e.g., [12]) in order to remove the package material. This technique should only be applied by chemists in an adequate environment. Rear side opening can be performed using a mill in order to remove the package and then removing the heat-sink metal plate e.g., with small pliers. As opening a chip from the rear side does not require any expensive or dangerous equipment it can be conducted with small effort. Figure 1 depicts the exposed microcontroller chips we have used for our experiments. The pictures on top correspond to the PIC 16F84 microcontroller (left: front side, right: rear side) and the pictures at the bottom correspond to the ATMEGA 162/v microcontroller (left: front side, right: rear side). Potential targets of optical fault attacks on microcontrollers are the SRAM or the EEPROM memory. The reason for the sensitivity of these parts on laser irradiation is outlined in the following. Furthermore an introduction and explanation of the proposed method for finding optical sensitive spots on the chip surface is given in this section. This method is based on light-induced voltage alteration (LIVA, [1]).

Fig. 1. Exposed microcontrollers. From left to right: PIC 16F84 front side (circle indicates the location of the SRAM); PIC 16F84 rear side; ATMEGA 162/v front side; ATMEGA 162/v rear side.

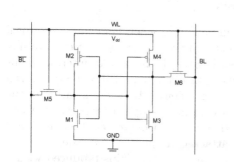

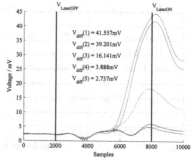

Fig. 2. Architecture of an SRAM cell.

Fig. 3. Voltage drop across the resistor in the ground line while irradiating different spots on the chip (laser active from 5 000 to 10 000 samples).

2.1 Influence of Light Irradiation on Memory Cells

A detailed description on how light irradiation can be used to manipulate EEP-ROM or Flash memory on microcontrollers as well as on dedicated storage chips can be found in [11]. As we do not target EEPROM nor Flash memory in this work no detailed description is given here.

The main target of the optical fault attacks carried out in this work is the SRAM of microcontrollers. A detailed description of the functionality of SRAM is following. SRAM is the short form for *static random-access memory* and it is a volatile memory. Volatile memories loose their stored value when the supply voltage is switched off. The architecture of an SRAM cell is depicted in Fig. 2. The cell typically consists of six transistors overall where four transistors form a flip-flop (M1 ... M4) and the remaining two (M5, M6) are used for write and read access. When a cell stores a logical zero M2 and M3 are conducting and M1 and M4 are non-conducting. On the other hand, when the cell stores a logical one M2 and M3 are non-conducting and M1 and M4 are conducting. A laser beam with sufficient power targeting one specific transistor can force this transistor to change the state from non-conducting to conducting. If e.g., the targeted cell stores a logical one and the laser beam is focused on M3 the state of M3 changes from non-conducting to conducting if the power of the laser beam is sufficient. As a result the flip-flop changes the state then from logical one to logical zero. The same effect can also be achieved if a cell stores a logical zero and M1 is targeted with the laser beam. Then the stored value of the cell is flipped to logical zero. The newer the production technology of the attacked chip is the more difficult is it to target a single transistor with the laser beam. The size of the transistors decreases on the one hand but the minimum size of the laser spot is limited on the other hand. So newer technologies make it harder to induce predictable faults as the laser beam influences several transistors at the same time.

2.2   Finding Optical Sensitive Spots

One of the first steps (after the decapsulation step) when launching an optical
fault attack is to identify the area of interest. If the attack e.g., targets intermediate values during a computation stored in SRAM, the area of interest equals
the location of the SRAM. For older microcontrollers (e.g., PIC 16F84) this is a
quite easy task if the front side of the chip is opened. Here the location of the
SRAM can be found by visual inspection with a microscope. Things change when
the attack is performed from the rear side or when a microcontroller produced
with a newer fabrication technology is attacked. From the rear side no structure is visible with the human eye using a microscope. Chips produced with a
newer fabrication technology also have several metal layers on top. This metal
layers make front-side attacks very difficult because the metal layers shield the
underlying transistors from the laser irradiation. In the following a method is
presented which should assist in finding such sensitive spots. The method works
for front-side attacks and rear-side attacks the same way. In order to conduct
the method only the power (V_{dd}) and ground (GND) pins of the analysed chip
need to be connected to a power supply. The chip has to be powered with a
constant voltage and a resistor has to be added into the ground line just like in
a standard power-analysis scenario. The voltage drop across the resistor is measured using an oscilloscope. Several spots on the chip surface are illuminated by
short laser pulses and the voltage drop across the resistor is measured shortly
before and during the laser pulse. Each recorded trace is stored together with
some location information corresponding to the illuminated spot on the chip.
In an analysis step the difference of the voltage values during the laser pulse
($V_{LaserON}$) and before the laser pulse ($V_{LaserOFF}$) for every spot is calculated:
$V_{diff} = V_{LaserON} - V_{LaserOFF}$. If the analysed spot is not sensitive to laser
irradiation $V_{diff} \approx 0$. On the other hand $V_{diff} > 0$ if the spot is sensitive to
laser irradiation. The reason for that difference, especially when the laser beam
hits a transistor of an SRAM cell can be described the following: If only V_{dd}
and GND are connected, each SRAM cell has a random state. If the state of
the cell illuminated by the laser beam equals logical one (M2 and M3 are non-
conducting) and the laser beam hits M3, the state of M3 changes to conducting
for the duration of the laser irradiation. So M3 and M4 generate a short circuit
between V_{dd} and GND what can be detected by an increasing voltage across the
transistor in the ground line. Figure 3 shows the recorded traces for five different
spots of the ATMEGA 162/v microcontroller. The laser was active between 5 000
and 10 000 samples. It can be clearly observed that two spots are highly sensitive
to the laser irradiation ($V_{diff}(1), V_{diff}(2)$), one is medium sensitive ($V_{diff}(3)$)
and two spots are less sensitive ($V_{diff}(4), V_{diff}(5)$). Combining the V_{diff} values
and the corresponding location information a sensitivity plot of the chip can be
created. In the result section sensitivity plots of the PIC 16F84 microcontroller
as well as the ATMEGA 162/v microcontroller are presented.

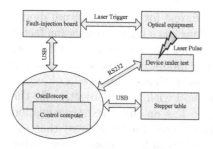

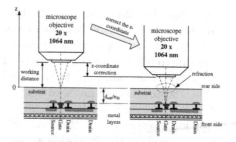

Fig. 4. The interaction of the different part of the optical fault-injection environment. The used oscilloscope also acts as the control computer so it is drawn as a single device.

Fig. 5. When irradiating the gate of a CMOS transistor from the rear side using a focused laser beam a correction of the z coordinate is necessary. If the initial distance between chip surface and objective equals the working distance of the objective the distance has to be decreased according to the thickness of the substrate d_{sub}.

3   Optical Fault-Injection Environment

In this section the optical fault-injection environment used to perform the optical fault attacks is presented. This optical fault-injection environment can be split into several components which are discussed in the following: the optical equipment, the stepper table, the oscilloscope, the control computer and the FPGA-based fault-injection board (FIB). Figure 4 depicts the interaction between all the mentioned components. In the end of this section also some information about the devices under test (DUT) used for the experiments, namely the PIC 16F84 and the ATMEGA 162/v microcontrollers, can be found.

3.1   Optical Equipment

In order to enable front-side attacks as well as rear-side attacks different types of laser diodes are used. First front-side attacks were conducted using a laser diode with a wavelength of 780 nm and an optical output power of 90 mW cw (continuous wave) and 200 mW pulsed (max. pulse length: 500 ns, duty cycle: 50 %) respectively. In order to increase the pool of attackable devices using front-side attacks another laser diode with a higher output power was used. The latter laser diode has a wavelength of 808 nm and a maximum optical output power of 16 W. This diode can only be operated in pulsed mode with a maximum pulse length of 200 ns and a duty cycle of 0.1 %. For rear-side attacks a laser diode with a wave length of 1064 nm and a maximum optical output power of 16 W was used. Also this diode can only be operated in pulsed mode with a maximum pulse length of 200 ns and a duty cycle of 0.1 %. The diodes are mounted in a laser mount with an integrated collimation lens in order to collimate the laser beam.

Two different collimation lenses had to be used, one for the 780/808 nm diodes and the other one for the 1064 nm diode. Each lens has a high transmission factor for the specific wavelength range. So a well-collimated laser beam as well as low losses due to reflection are guaranteed. The laser mount is attached on top of the microscope. The collimated laser beam is focused with a standard 50 x objective for the 780 nm and 808 nm wavelength diodes and with a 20 x objective for the 1064 nm wavelength diode. The 20 x objective has an improved transmission factor for wavelengths in the range of 1064 nm. Experiments showed that the objective used for the front-side attacks does not work for rear-side attacks due to the higher wavelength of the laser source required for the rear side.

3.2   Stepper Table

In order to enable automated scanning of the chip surface a stepper table which can be controlled via MATLAB commands is used. The stepper table can be moved in x, y and z direction with an accuracy of $0.1\,\mu$m. With the x and y coordinate the spot where the laser beam hits the chip is selected and with the z coordinate the focus of the laser beam is set. Our results show that the z coordinate is a crucial factor when performing optical fault attacks.

3.3   Oscilloscope and Control Computer

A WavePro 725 Zi oscilloscope from LeCroy is used in order to record the required signals. These signals involve trigger signals from the device under test for the laser pulse on the one hand and power traces on the other hand. Power traces were recorded in order to measure the influence of the laser beam on the power consumption of the device. The oscilloscope has a bandwidth of 2.5 GHz, 4 input channels and a maximum sampling rate of 20 GS/s (4 active channels) and 40 GS/s (2 active channels) respectively. We have used a sampling rate of 10 GS/s in order to record the power traces. Furthermore we have activated the build-in 20 MHz lowpass filter in order to cut off high-frequency noise.

The WavePro 725 Zi oscilloscope is also capable of running MATLAB scripts and so it was also used as the control computer. Communication with the device under test, the FPGA-based fault-injection board as well as with the stepper table can be realized with this oscilloscope.

3.4   FPGA-Based Fault-Injection Board (FIB)

A self-build fault-injection board (FIB) based on an FPGA is used in order to generate the laser pulses. Laser pulses generated by the FIB can be triggered by two events. The first event for triggering a laser pulse is a MATLAB command (*shoot_laser_man*), so the laser pulse is triggered manually. The second event is an external trigger event occurring at the trigger input pin of the FPGA (e.g., by a trigger pin of the device under test). The length of the laser pulse as well as the delay after the trigger event (for the latter case) can be set on the FIB.

The clock signal and the power supply for the DUT are also provided by the FIB. The clock signal can be stopped manually in order to pause the DUT for a specific time interval.

3.5 Devices Under Test (DUT)

For the performed experiments two different 8 bit microcontrollers were used, one PIC 16F84 [8] (1.2 μm process technology) and one ATMEGA 162/v [4] (0.8 μm process technology). Several optical fault attacks on the PIC 16F84 microcontroller have been reported in literature so far (e.g., [11,14]) mainly targeting the SRAM. We were able to repeat the reported experiments successfully with our optical fault-injection environment and these results serve as the base for our work. For the ATMEGA 162/v microcontroller on the other hand hardly any reported practical optical fault attacks could be found in literature. We used this type of microcontroller to confirm that the results achieved with the PIC 16F84 can be transformed on other microcontroller platforms.

4 Performed Experiments

In this section the conducted optical experiments are introduced. For the experiments, one PIC 16F84 microcontroller and one ATMEGA 162/v microcontroller serve as DUT. The reason for that choice is that several attacks on the PIC 16F84 microcontroller have been reported in literature. Parts of these attacks have been repeated with our optical fault-injection environment and serve as a base for further analyses. The ATMEGA 162/v microcontroller has been chosen in order to show that the achieved results targeting the PIC 16F84 can be transformed on other platforms.

The experiments are divided into two main parts. In the first part the experiments targeting the front side of the microcontrollers are discussed. The second part focuses on the experiments targeting the rear side of the microcontrollers.

4.1 Front Side Experiments

The first experiment was an optical fault injection attack targeting the SRAM of a PIC 16F84 microcontroller similar to the one presented in [14]. A simple test program was executed on the DUT for that purpose. This test program first initializes the SRAM with known values, verifies the SRAM content in a next step and reports if faults were introduced due to laser irradiation (c.f. Algorithm 1). An I/O pin of the microcontroller is set after the initialization is finished in order to trigger the laser pulse. The area where the SRAM is located on the PIC 16F84 micrcontroller can be found by optical inspection using a microscope. Having a focused picture of the chip surface is also an indicator for the correct distance between objective and chip surface. This distance equals the working distance of the objective which is given in it's specification. The stepper table was used to step over the whole SRAM area and the z-coordinate

```
while true do
    WaitForTrigger();
    InitSRAM();
    SetTriggerInitDone();
    faults = VerifySRAM();
    if faults == 1 then
        ReportFaults();
    end
end
```

Algorithm 1: PIC 16F84 program for SRAM fault verification.

was modified for each spot in the range of $70\,\mu m$. The modification of the z-coordinate had to be done in order to find the best focus for the laser spot. Early experiments figured out that the approach with the working distance is not that accurate. A detailed explanation about the influence of the distance between objective and chip surface is given in Sect. 4.2. The length of the laser pulse for that experiment was 200 ns and the laser pulse was triggered by setting one pin of the DUT using the method *SetTriggerInitDone()*.

In the next experiment the influence of the following parameters on the ability to induce the faults was examined: *laser pulse length, laser power, z-coordinate (focus)*. Therefore one location of the chip was targeted where a fault can be induced (known because of the previous experiment). Then the three parameters were varied one after the other until the fault did not happen any more.

The fact that our FIB allows us to stop the clock for a defined period of time, the goal of the next experiment was to induce more than one fault at the same time. In order to induce more faults we stopped the clock after *SetTriggerInitDone()*. While the clock was stopped we moved the laser to several spots in order to corrupt the value of several SRAM cells. The spots where faults can be induced are known because of the first experiment.

In the last performed front side experiment we applied the method to find laser sensitive spots on the chip. This experiment was performed for both DUT, the PIC 16F84 microcontroller and the ATMEGA 162/v microcontroller. For that purpose only the V_{dd} and GND pins of the devices were connected to a power supply providing a constant supply voltage of 3.3 V. In the GND line a $47\,\Omega$ resistor was inserted and the voltage drop was measured with an oscilloscope. Using the stepper table different spots of a predefined area were selected and illuminated with the laser beam. The power trace including voltage values shortly before and during the laser pulse together with the location information (x and y coordinates) were stored for further analyses.

No further experiments targeting the ATMEGA 162/v microcontroller were performed because the success rate for finding the SRAM area on the one hand and inducing faults in that area on the other hand seemed to be too low due to the metal layers on top. So we decided to immediately switch to experiments targeting the rear side.

4.2   Rear-Side Experiments

As the first experiment targeting the rear side the method to find laser sensitive spots was chosen. We have changed the order of the experiments because the exact location of the SRAM from the rear side was not known. The PIC 16F84 microcontroller was used as DUT for the first experiment. The location of the SRAM from the front side is known so we could approximately assume the location of the SRAM at the rear side opened chip. This fact enabled us to narrow down the search area for the SRAM and increase the speed of the evaluation. After setting the search area the evaluation worked similar as in the equivalent front-side experiment. Now the 1064 nm laser diode was used together with the optimized 20 x objective. The distance between the objective and the chip die surface was set to approximately 6 mm which equals the working distance of the objective. This data can be found in the specification of the objective. It figured out that the approach using the working distance is not that accurate. In order to enhance the efficiency a correction of the z coordinate is necessary. Figure 5 depicts the reason why this correction of the z coordinate has to be performed. The main target of the laser beam (the transistor) is located a specific distance d_{sub} below the substrate. So the initially set working distance has to be decreased by d_{sub}/n_{Si}. n_{Si} equals the refractive index of silicone ($n_{Si} \approx 3.5$, [7]). That means the objective moves closer to the chip surface. With the microscope and the objective optimized for 1064 nm no visible picture for an observation with the human eye can be created. That makes finding the correct distance even more complicated as a focused picture is an indicator for the correct working distance which can be used as a starting point. Further experiments show how to find the optimal distance between objective and chip-die surface taking the mentioned points into account.

The second experiment uses the location information of the laser sensitive spots on the chip obtained by the previous experiment. First the optimal distance between the objective and the chip surface needs to be found. Therefore the laser was moved to a sensitive spot and power measurements were performed while modifying the z coordinate in the range of 6 mm $\pm$ 2 mm. The highest V_{diff} is an indicator for the optimal distance. After the optimal distance was found Algorithm 1 was executed on the DUT. The laser sensitive spots were irradiated with short laser pulses with a length of 200 ns and the occurring faults were recorded.

In a third experiment the influence of the parameters *laser pulse length, laser power and z-coordinate (focus)* on the ability to induce faults was examined. For that purpose the laser was positioned to a spot where a fault could be induced. At this spot the three parameters were modified one after the other until the fault could not be induced any more.

The same experiments were performed with the ATMEGA 162/v microcontroller as DUT. As no location information of the SRAM was available, we had to analyse the whole chip area in order to find laser sensitive spots. So the evaluation time for that DUT was significantly larger.

5   Results

In this section the results of the conducted optical fault-injection experiments are presented. First the results targeting the front-side opened chips are presented followed by the results achieved with the rear-side opened chips. Attacks targeting the rear side have several advantages. First, the decapsulation process is not that critical as no toxic acids have to be used. Second, there are no metal layers which shield the transistors from the laser beam. One disadvantage of the rear-side approach is that no chip structure is visible with e.g., a microscope. So it is difficult to find the correct area where to induce a fault. The results of our method to find laser sensitive spots show that this method is well suited to assist in finding the correct areas for an attack from the rear side.

5.1   Results of Front-Side Experiments

The first experiment targets the SRAM of the PIC 16F84 microcontroller. The whole SRAM area was analysed and the distance between the spots illuminated with the laser beam was 10 μm in x and y direction. The 50 x objective was used in order to focus the laser beam and the initial distance between chip die surface and objective was set according to the working distance of the objective (9 mm). At each spot the z coordinate was varied in a range of 70 μm in order to find the best focus for the laser beam. The length of the laser pulse was set to 200 ns. With that setup it was possible to influence the state of each single SRAM cell similar to the results presented in [14]. This results show that the used optical fault-injection environment works properly. The laser diode with a wavelength of 780 nm and a maximum optical output power of 200 mW was sufficient in order to achieve this results. The same results were also achieved with the high-power 808 nm diode. The aim of using this diode was to verify the proper operation for further experiments. A second important observation during this experiment was that the variation of the z coordinate is inevitable. Only for some values of the z coordinate the faults could be induced. In order to get a better understanding of the influence of the z coordinate together with the parameters pulse length and laser power we examined their influence in the second experiment.

The location of the spots where faults can be induced serve as the base for the second experiment where the influence of the *z coordinate, the laser pulse length and the laser power* are examined in detail. As we are not able to measure the optical laser power the electrical power at the laser diode is used instead. Therefore we measure the current through the laser diode I_{diode} and the voltage drop across the laser diode U_{diode}. With these values the electrical power $P_{diode,el} = U_{diode} \cdot I_{diode}$ can be calculated. Because of several losses it can be assumed that $P_{diode,el} > P_{diode,opt}$. The results of the evaluation are summarized in Fig. 12 and can be described the following: Increasing the *laser output power* as well as increasing the *laser pulse length* make the setup less sensitive on the z coordinate. A one in the graphs indicates that the fault for the current setting (*pulse length, laser power, z coordinate*) could be induced where a zero means

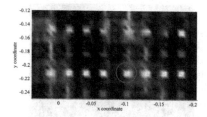

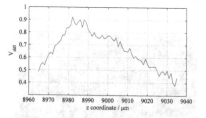

Fig. 6. The plot is showing the result of a laser sensitivity evaluation of one part of the SRAM of the PIC 16F84 from the front side. The area inside the circle was used for further evaluating the influence of the z coordinate.

Fig. 7. The influence of the z coordinate on V_{diff} for one specific spot on the PIC 16F84 (front side).

that no fault could be induced. The *electrical laser power* has been increased in five steps (150 mW, 170 mW, 190 mW, 200 mW, 220 mW) and four different *pulse length values* have been examined (100 ns, 200 ns, 500 ns, 1000 ns). 150 mW *electrical laser power* is not sufficient in order to induce a fault even with the largest *pulse length* of 1000 ns.

From the previous experiments targeting the PIC 16F84 microcotroller several locations on the chip where single bits of the SRAM registers can be modified are known. This location information together with the clock-stop feature of the FIB allowed us to manipulate several bits of the same register as well as bits in different registers in any combination. The clock was stopped after the initialization of the SRAM was finished. Stopping the clock allows to target several spots on the chip by moving the stepper table. Each spot was illuminated with a short laser pulse of 200 ns. Then the clock was started again and the verification routine reported several faults. This approach equals an attack using N laser beams in parallel, where N is the number of faults which should be induced at the same time. The higher N is the more difficult is the attack with N laser beams. Each beam needs to be put in place with a high accuracy an the size of the objectives focusing the beams does not allow targeting spots close together. This problems can be solved by stopping the clock and relocating a single laser source. Of course this only works if the attacked device supports external clocks and does not detect the corruption of the clock. Many laser diodes need a specific cool-down time. This cool-down time equals an interval between two consecutive laser pulses which must not be undercut. The clock can be stopped if the fault attack targets two consecutive register values and the time in between is not sufficient in order to cool down the laser diode. One attack targeting consecutive register values is shown in [15]. In this work the authors present a multi fault laser attack targeting a protected CRT-RSA implementation.

Next the results of the application of the method to find laser sensitive spots on the chip is presented. Figure 6 depicts the result of a scan of one part of the SRAM area of the PIC 16F84 microcontroller. Laser-sensitive spots are bright

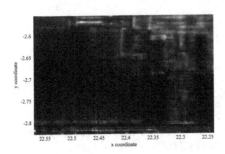

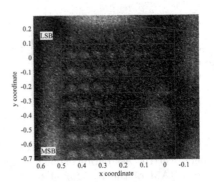

Fig. 8. The plot is showing the result of a laser sensitivity evaluation of one part of the chip area of the ATMEGA 162/v from the front side.

Fig. 9. The plot is showing the result of a laser sensitivity evaluation of the whole SRAM area of the PIC 16F84 from the rear side. The spots in the lowermost square influence the MSB of the SRAM registers while the spots in the uppermost square influence the LSB of the SRAM registers.

while spots which did not show sensitivity on laser irradiation are dark. The bright locations correlate with the locations where fault injections were successful in the first experiment. Figure 7 depicts the result of the evaluation focusing on the influence of the z coordinate. The spot with a high sensitivity with the x coordinate -0.10 and the y coordinate -0.21 (marked with the circle in Fig. 6) has been selected for that purpose and V_{diff} has been calculated for different z coordinates. The z coordinate (equals the distance between objective and chip surface) has been modified in the range of $9000\,\mu m \pm 35\mu m$ with a step size of $1\,\mu m$. $9000\,\mu m$ equals the specified working distance of the used objective. As a result of this evaluation the optimal distance for conducting optical fault attacks is between $8980\,\mu m$ and $8990\,\mu m$ because the maximum V_{diff} values are achieved in that interval.

Figure 8 depicts the result of a scan of a randomly chosen area of the ATMEGA 162/v microcontroller. Only a small number of laser-sensitive spots in the upper part of the plot can be observed. Further analyses of these spots did not yield any results, i.e. laser irradiation targeting these spots during the execution of a program did not produce any faults. As rear-side attacks seemed to be more promising we decided to switch to rear-side evaluations instead of performing further evaluations targeting the front side of the ATMEGA 162/v.

5.2   Results of Rear-Side Experiments

The first experiment targeting the rear side was finding laser sensitive spots on the PIC 16F84 microcontroller. The main focus of the experiments is put on the

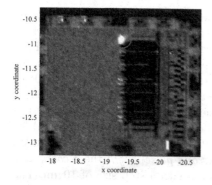

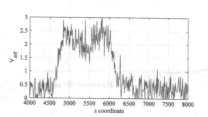

Fig. 10. The plot is showing the result of a laser sensitivity evaluation of the whole chip area of the ATMEGA 162/v from the rear side. Irradiating the area inside the circle with the laser beam influences the program execution.

Fig. 11. The influence of the z coordinate on V_{diff} for one specific spot on the PIC 16F84 (rear side).

SRAM so the goal was to create a rear-side sensibility plot of the SRAM. The result of this experiment is depicted in Fig. 9. The location of the SRAM on the front-side opened chip is known. This information was used in order to decrease the search area on the rear-side opened chip. The area inside the box in the figure equals the whole SRAM of the PIC 16F84 microcontroller. Due to the fact that we used a 20 x objective for the rear-side evaluations compared to a 50 x objective for the front-side evaluations the achieved resolution compared to the front-side evaluations is significantly lower. In order to show the influence of the z coordinate for rear-side evaluations we have chosen one spot with a high sensitivity on the laser irradiation. At this spot the z coordinate was modified in the range of $6000\,\mu m \pm 2000\mu m$ with a step size of $10\,\mu m$. For every step V_{diff} was calculated and the result is plotted in Fig. 11. The result is comparable to the result achieved during the front-side evaluation (Fig. 7). Again decreasing the distance between objective and chip surface increases the sensibility to laser irradiation.

In the second experiment we used the location information of the laser sensitive spots from the previous experiment. Each spot with a V_{diff} above a given threshold was illuminated with a laser pulse with a length of 200 ns. The DUT was executing Algorithm 1 during that evaluation. The analysis of the results showed that with the given setup it is possible to influence each single bit of every SRAM register similar to the corresponding front-side experiment. Targeting the lower part of the SRAM area influences the *most significant bit (MSB)* while targeting the upper part influences the *least significant bit (LSB)*. Some spots lead to bit faults in more than one register. This is due to the fact that the achievable spot size with the 20 x objective is limited. So the laser spot on the chip influences neighbouring transistors at the same time.

The next experiment focused on the influence of the parameters *laser pulse length, laser power and z coordinate*. We targeted on spot on the chip where a single bit of the SRAM could be influenced. This information was available because of the previous experiment. Then we varied the three parameters one after the other and verified if the current parameter setting leads to a fault or not. The following *laser pulse lengths* were verified: 75 ns, 100 ns, 125 ns, 150 ns, 175 ns and 200 ns. In order to give values for the *laser power* we used the electrical power ($P_{diode,el} = U_{diode} \cdot I_{diode}$) and the following *power values* were used for the experiment: 140 mW, 280 mW, 450 mW, 670 mW, 760 mW, 780 mW, 900 mW, 975 mW. For each combination of *laser power and pulse length* the *z coordinate* was varied in the range of 6000 μm $\pm$ 2000 mum with a step size of 10 μm. The result of this experiment is depicted in Fig. 13. A one indicates that for the current setting a fault could be induced. It can be observed that the *pulse length* needs to be at least 100 ns in order to induce a fault. The larger the *pulse length* and the higher the *laser power* are the smaller is the influence of the *z coordinate*. Another observation is that the *z coordinate* where faults can be induced is significantly smaller than the working distance of the objective. That is due to the fact depicted in Fig. 5 and correlates well with the result depicted in Fig. 11.

Figure 10 depicts the result of a sensitivity scan of the whole chip area of the ATMEGA 162/v microcontroller from the rear side. The size of the whole scan area is 3 mm $\times$ 3 mm and the step size was 30 μm. Brighter spots indicate a higher sensitivity to laser irradiation and darker spots are less sensitive on laser irradiation. The area inside the circle is most sensitive to laser irradiation so we examined this area in further experiments.

For the investigation of the area marked with the circle on the chip Algorithm 1 was executed on the DUT. After the initialization of the SRAM the spots inside the mentioned area were irradiated with laser pulses with a length of 200 ns. For several spots inside this area the execution of the program stopped and a reset of the DUT was required. One explanation for that behaviour is that the SRAM is located in this area and the laser pulse influences several registers. Some of the influenced registers might hold some information required for the RS 232 communication between control computer and DUT. By modifying these values no proper communication can be achieved any more. One of these values could e.g., be a timer reload value which is required to achieve the correct baud rate. If this value is corrupted the communication does not work properly any more. Investigations of sensitive spots outside of the circle did not produce any faulty behaviour. This results shows that the method for finding laser sensitive spots on the chip works also for the ATMEGA 162/v microcontroller very well. The main limiting factor is the 20 x objective that limits the minimum size of the laser spot.

6   Conclusion and Future Work

The aim of this work is to cover several aspects which influence the success of optical fault attacks using laser beams. Front-side evaluations as well as rear-side evaluations were performed on two microcontrollers, one PIC 16F84 and one ATMEGA 162/v. Rear-side attacks are the preferred choice because of the easier decapsulation process and the missing metal layers. These metal layers shield the targeted transistors when performing a front-side attack. The disadvantage of a rear-side attack is that the chip structure is not visible using a microscope. In order to circumvent this disadvantage we present a method to find laser sensitive spots on the chip which uses the effect of light induced voltage alteration (LIVA, [1]). The location of laser sensitive spots can be used to speed-up further attacks as the area to analyse can be narrowed down. The rather old microcontrollers were used in order to achieve comprehensible results which prove the proper operation of the optical fault-injection environment. So we were able to repeat the attacks on the PIC 16F84 microcontroller reported in [14] and these results are the basis for our further investigations. These investigations mainly include the influence of *laser pulse length, laser power and laser focus* on the fault injection success.

Future work includes the usage of an objective with 50 x magnification optimized for the 1065 nm wavelength. With this step it should be possible to increase the resolution of rear-side scanning. We are also going to investigate techniques to make the substrate thinner in order to decrease the loss of laser power when performing rear-side attacks. Furthermore we are going to repeat the experiments on a current microcontroller in order to increase the comparability.

Acknowledgments. The work presented in this article has been supported by the European Commission through the ICT program TAMPRES (Tamper Resistant Sensor Node) under contract ICT-SEC-2009-5-258754.

A   Appendix

Figures 12 and 13 depict the influence of several parameters on the ability to induce faults on the PIC 16F84 from the front side and from the rear side, respectively.

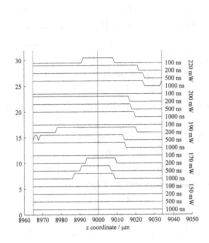 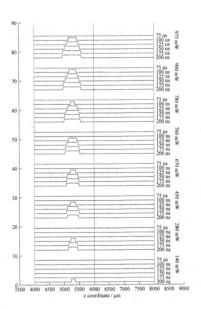

Fig. 12. Influence of the parameters (*laser pulse length, laser power, z coordinate*) on the ability to induce a fault at a specific position at the front side of the PIC 16F84.

Fig. 13. Influence of the parameters (*laser pulse length, laser power, z coordinate*) on the ability to induce a fault at a specific position at the rear side of the PIC 16F84.

References

1. Ajluni, C.: Two new imaging techniques promise to improve IC defect identification. Electronic Des. **43**(14), 37–38 (1995)
2. Anderson, R.J., Kuhn, M.G.: Tamper resistance - a cautionary note. In: Proceedings of the 2nd USENIX Workshop on Electronic Commerce, Oakland, California, November 18–21, pp. 1–11. USENIX Association, November 1996. ISBN 1-880446-83-9
3. Anderson, R.J., Kuhn, M.G.: Low cost attacks on tamper resistant devices. In: Christianson, B., Crispo, B., Lomas, M., Roe, M. (eds.) Security Protocols. LNCS, vol. 1361, pp. 125–136. Springer, Heidelberg (1997)
4. Atmel Corporation. ATmega 162/v Datasheet (2003)
5. Bar-El, H., Choukri, H., Naccache, D., Tunstall, M., Whelan, C.: The sorcerer's apprentice guide to fault attacks. Cryptology ePrint Archive. http://eprint.iacr.org/, Report 2004/100 (2004)
6. Boneh, D., DeMillo, R.A., Lipton, R.J.: On the importance of checking cryptographic protocols for faults. In: Fumy, W. (ed.) EUROCRYPT 1997. LNCS, vol. 1233, pp. 37–51. Springer, Heidelberg (1997)
7. Li, H.: Refractive index of silicon and germanium and its wavelength and temperature derivatives. ICON **5**, 9 (1979)
8. Microchip Technology Inc. PIC16F84 Data Sheet (2001)

9. Schmidt, J.-M., Hutter, M.: Optical and EM fault-attacks on CRT-based RSA: concrete results. In: Posch, K.C., Wolkerstorfer, J. (eds.) Proceedings of Austrochip 2007, October 11, Graz, Austria, pp. 61–67. Verlag der Technischen Universität Graz, October 2007. ISBN 978-3-902465-87-0

10. Schmidt, J.-M., Hutter, M., Plos, T.: Optical fault attacks on AES: a threat in violet. In: Naccache, D., Oswald, E. (eds.) Fault Diagnosis and Tolerance in Cryptography, Procceedings of Sixth International Workshop, FDTC 2009, Lausanne, Switzerland, 6 September, pp. 13–22. IEEE-CS Press, (2009)

11. Skorobogatov, S.: Optical fault masking attacks. In: Fault Diagnosis and Tolerance in Cryptography (2010)

12. Skorobogatov, S.P.: Semi-invasive attacks - a new approach to hardware security analysis. Ph.D. thesis, University of Cambridge - Computer Laboratory (2005). http://www.cl.cam.ac.uk/TechReports/

13. Skorobogatov, S.Y.: Optically enhanced position-locked power analysis. In: Goubin, L., Matsui, M. (eds.) CHES 2006. LNCS, vol. 4249, pp. 61–75. Springer, Heidelberg (2006)

14. Skorobogatov, S.P., Anderson, R.J.: Optical fault induction attacks. In: Kaliski Jr, B.S., Koç, Ç., Paar, C. (eds.) CHES 2002. LNCS, vol. 2523, pp. 2–12. Springer, Heidelberg (2003)

15. Trichina, E.: Multi-fault laser attacks on protected CRT RSA. Invited Talk - FDTC 2010 (2010)

Attack Classification
and Assessment

ONTIDS: A Highly Flexible Context-Aware and Ontology-Based Alert Correlation Framework

Alireza Sadighian[1(✉)], José M. Fernandez[1], Antoine Lemay[1],
and Saman T. Zargar[2]

[1] Department of Computer and Software Engineering,
École Polytechnique de Montréal, Montréal, Canada
{alireza.sadighian,antoine.lemay,jose.fernandez}@polymtl.ca
[2] School of Information Sciences, University of Pittsburgh, Pittsburgh, PA, USA
stzargar@sis.pitt.edu

Abstract. Several alert correlation approaches have been proposed to date to reduce the number of non-relevant alerts and false positives typically generated by Intrusion Detection Systems (IDS). Inspired by the mental process of the contextualisation used by security analysts to weed out less relevant alerts, some of these approaches have tried to incorporate contextual information such as: type of systems, applications, users, and networks into the correlation process. However, these approaches are not flexible as they only perform correlation based on the narrowly defined contexts. information resources available to the security analysts while preserving the maximum flexibility and the power of abstraction in both the definition and the usage of such concepts, we propose ONTIDS, a context-aware and ontology-based alert correlation framework that uses ontologies to represent and store the alerts information, alerts context, vulnerability information, and the attack scenarios. ONTIDS employs simple ontology logic rules written in Semantic Query-enhance Web Rule Language (SQWRL) to correlate and filter out non-relevant alerts. We illustrate the potential usefulness and the flexibility of ONTIDS by employing its reference implementation on two separate case studies, inspired from the DARPA 2000 and UNB ISCX IDS evaluation datasets.

Keywords: Intrusion detection · Alert correlation · Ontology · Context-aware

1 Introduction

IDS collect data from the IT infrastructure and analyse it to identify ongoing attacks. Various IDS types have been proposed in the past two decades and commercial off-the-shelf (COTS) IDS products have found their way into Security Operations Centres (SOC) of many large organisations. Nonetheless, the usefulness of the single-source IDS has remained relatively limited due to two main factors: their inability to detect new types of attacks (for which new detection rules or training data are unavailable) and their often very high false positive rates.

J.-L. Danger et al. (Eds.): FPS 2013, LNCS 8352, pp. 161–177, 2014.
DOI: 10.1007/978-3-319-05302-8_10, © Springer International Publishing Switzerland 2014

One of the approaches that has been suggested to address these challenges is the *alert correlation*, where the alert streams from several different IDS or more generally various alert sensors are jointly considered and analysed to provide a more accurate picture of the threats. When individual IDS examine the same type of data, their alert correlations is called the *homogeneous IDS correlation*. In fact, the majority of the research projects and real-world deployments of the correlation approaches involve the analysis of the alerts generated by different network IDS (NIDS), such as: SNORT or Bro, examining network traffic streams at different network locations.

Nonetheless, most of the attacks, whether automated malware infections or manual network intrusions, do not leave traces only on the captured network traffic but also on the host-based IDS (HIDS), on other security products, and sometimes even on non security-related logs of commodity or corporate applications. This fact has been successfully exploited by security analysts worldwide to detect sophisticated attacks by automatically or manually correlating these versatile information and alert sources. Since various sensors examine different types of events and raw data sources, their alert correlations is called the *heterogeneous alert correlation*.

One of the main challenges for heterogeneous correlation is the integration of data from various alert sources with potentially different formats and semantics. At the same time, sensor-specific attributes must also be retained in order to preserve the ability for the security analyst to *drill down* and refine his analysis. For instance, for finding root causes, determining attack type, attack objectives, and *etc.*

Moreover, one of the fundamental alert management principles is that the security analysts must be able to understand the alerts and the *context* they are generated in. This is what allows one to consider the relevance and relative importance of the alerts. Unfortunately, security analysts often need to manually gather such information from multiple systems to feed the correlation process in order to integrate and validate the alerts and identify the consequences of any intrusion. This is why certain researchers have proposed approaches to automatically include such contextual information into the alert correlation process, approaches that are referred to as the *context-aware* alert correlation approaches. The simple and intuitive idea here to reduce the false positive is that the alerts that are related to a certain type of attack are only relevant if the context in which they happen is indeed vulnerable to that type of attack. Hence, the context aware alert correlation must consider the vulnerability information, and potentially the attack models in order to be useful.

The difficulty in implementing the aforementioned approaches resides in integrating the information into a data model that is generic enough to allow the global view of the data while retaining maximum data granularity for drill-down analysis. The flexibility and extensibility of the data model is thus a key requirement of any such approaches. Finally, the method by which security analysts extract information and intelligence from such data stores must itself also be flexible and extensible. It must support generic simple queries and detailed analysis.

To this purpose, in this paper, we present ONTIDS that relies heavily on the ontologies and the ontology description logic to accomplish these goals. We mainly describe how ONTIDS addresses the high positive rate problem of the existing IDS. ONTIDS has the following characteristics:

1. It performs heterogeneous alert correlation to detect complex attacks that might leave traces in different types of sensors.
2. It includes a set of comprehensive but extensible ontologies, allowing correlation and reasoning with information collected from various resources, including context information, vulnerability databases and assessments, and attack models.
3. It can be used to seamlessly and automatically implement various alert correlation approaches on the same data model.
4. It can be applied in different deployment and analysis contexts, from simple to complex IT infrastructures, generic threat detection to complex attack forensics analysis.

The rest of this paper is organized as follows. In Sect. 2, we discuss the related work. In Sect. 3, we present our framework in detail. In Sect. 4, we demonstrate the flexibility of our framework by describing a reference implementation and applying it to the analysis of two different case studies. We conclude, in Sect. 5, by describing the limitations of these case studies to conclusively demonstrate the reduction of the non-relevant alerts and the false positives.

2   Related Work

In a keynote publication, *Valeur et al.* propose a correlation approach consisting of ten steps, which we will use later to exemplify our generic framework in Sect. 3.5. This is perhaps the most comprehensive approach, with other work concentrating only on one particular aspect of the correlation process, such as the alert fusion [1,2] or the attack thread reconstruction [3]. From a classification point of view, *Cuppens et al.* classify the attack reconstruction approaches into two categories [4]:

1. *Explicit alarm correlation*, which relies on the capabilities of security administrators to express logical and temporal relationships between alerts in order to detect complex multi-step attacks. For instance, *Morin et al.* propose an explicit correlation scheme based on the formalism of the *chronicles* [5].
2. *Implicit alarm correlation*, which is based on employing the machine learning and the data mining techniques to fuse, aggregate, and cluster the alerts for the alert correlation and the intrusion detection purposes. For instance, *Chen et al.* employ the Support Vector Machine (SVM) and the co-occurrence matrix in order to propose a masquerade detection method [6]. In [7], Raftopoulos performs the log correlation using C4.5 decision tree classifiers after analysing the diagnosis of 200 infections that were detected within a large operational network.

One of the shortcomings of the approaches in both categories is that they do not take into account all the available and important information resources such as contextual and vulnerability information. The contextual information has proved to be useful in better identifying specific alerts or in improving the IDS efficiency. *Gagnon et al.*, in [8], have studied the use of target configuration as the context information in order to identify the non-critical alerts. The Workload-aware Intrusion Detection (WIND) proposal by *Sinha et al.* combines the network workload information with the Snort rules to improve Snort's efficiency [9]. Unfortunately, these studies only consider partial contextual information such as target configuration or network traffic and do not allow for the inclusion of other types of contextual concepts.

Ontologies are knowledge representation models that allow the description of the concepts, their attributes, and the inheritance or the association relationships between them. In addition, various types of ontologies have formal description languages that allow for the definition of the complete reasoning logic that are machine-interpretable and solvable. Hence, some researchers have proposed the ontology-based alert correlation approaches for the alert correlation process. capabilities for detecting new types of attacks such as multi-step distributed attacks and various distributed denial of service (DDoS) attacks. The proposed ontologies, however, only include general security concepts and no discussion on how they can be adapted to different contexts. The Intrusion Detection and Diagnosis System (ID2S) proposed by *Coppolino et al.* uses ontologies as well to correlate the detection information at several architectural levels for further intrusion symptom analysis [11].

In summary, while *Valeur et al.* [12] provides a good generic framework for alert correlation into which various other attack reconstruction approaches can be incorporated [3,6,7,13], none of these attacks contrast the alert information with the context. On the other hand, those alert correlation approaches have limited notions of the context that cannot be readily extended and they do not perform attack reconstruction. Finally, the correlation approaches that have employed ontologies have not fully taken the advantage of their expressive power in terms of data modelling and logic reasoning.

Motivated by these shortcomings and in order to provide a common solution encompassing the advantages of all of these approaches, we design and propose henceforth the ONTIDS alert correlation framework that address the data integration problems while attaining the flexibility and extensibility objectives mentioned in Sect. 1.

3   The ONTIDS Alert Correlation Framework

The ONTIDS framework was made context-aware in order to take full advantage of the context information typically available to security analysts have typically access to prioritise alerts, and ontology-based in order to provide a technological solution to the problem of heterogeneous data integration and retrieval.

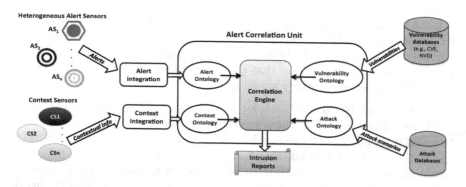

Fig. 1. The ONTIDS ontology-based context-aware alert correlation framework

The ONTIDS framework is depicted in Fig. 1. In its first step, the alerts generated via distributed homogeneous or heterogeneous IDS are collected and transfered into the alert integration component. Also in this step, all the information required for reasoning on these alerts is gathered from three different information resources namely: Context Sensors (CS), common vulnerability databases, and attack databases.

The second step consists of the following two tasks: (*i*) integrating and converting all the alerts generated by the various IDS into a unified format analysable by the alert correlation unit, and (*ii*) integrating all the contextual information received implicitly or explicitly from the various tools implemented in the system.

In the third step, the alert and context ontologies are populated based on the integrated and converted alert and context information. In order to fully automate the alert correlation process, we have designed a group of comprehensive and extensible ontologies, namely alert, context, attack and vulnerability ontologies. The explicit relationships between these ontologies reasoning on the information gathered from various resources, including the (mostly) static attack and vulnerability databases.

The last step consists in correlating the existing information within the ontologies, which is done via the correlation engine using ontology description logic.

3.1 Information Resources

Alert sensors generate alerts based on the suspected malicious behaviours that they observe on the systems they monitor. The most typical and commonly deployed type of sensor are NIDS that generate alerts by examining individual network traffic packets. They can also include host-based IDS that generate alerts based on system or application activity observed on a particular machine. Finally, it can also include other type of non security-related sensors such as application and system logs that are not generating alerts *per se*, but rather system events that the security analyst consider important enough to be correlated with other sources of alert. The difficulty here is that while many NIDS and HIDS will generate IDMEF-compliant alerts by filling generic attributes (e.g. time, severity, etc.), there might some sensor- or log-specific attributes that we might want to correlate on, and that must therefore be integrated also. This is what ontologies are particularly suited for.

Context sensors is a generic term for any information source that can provide contextual information about the systems that are being monitored. The concept of context is purposefully vague to allow analysts to define and use the particular aspects that they think is suitable for monitoring of their systems. This can include different types of information such as configuration (network, host or application), vulnerabilities, user role and profile, location, and even criticality of the corresponding IT asset. Contextual information can be implicitly collected by methods such as vulnerability scanning, network fingerprinting, passive network monitoring tools, or they can be explicitly provided by system administrators through tools such as Configuration Management Systems (CMS), for example.

Known vulnerabilities. At first, we gather information about vulnerabilities from the well-known public databases such as the Common Vulnerabilities and Exposures (CVE) [14] or the NVD. Then, vulnerabilities can be associated to context instances (e.g. hosts, networks, applications) through vulnerability scanning or asset management. Severity information from these databases, in combination with information on asset criticality, can then be used to help prioritise alerts occurring in these contexts.

Attack scenarios and models. Attack information and models can obtained from standardised databases such as the Common Attack Pattern Enumeration and Classification (CAPEC) [15] or expert knowledge. In order to model attacks, any of the existing attack modelling languages such as LAMBDA [13] or STATL [16] could be used. However, it is outside of the scope of this work to implement these formalisms within the ontology description logics that we use.

3.2   Alert and Context Integration

Different types of IDS sensors produce alerts in various formats that might not be natively interpretable by the correlation unit. Hence, it is necessary to pre-process these alert streams and export them in a format that is understandable by the correlation unit. In following good ontological engineering practises, all alert sensor-specific fields should be translated into class attributed at the highest possible class in the taxonomy of alerts, i.e. that where all subclasses contain that type of information (or an equivalent one). The use of standard representations such as IDMEF [17] or the Common Event Expression (CEE) [18] should be encouraged, but not at the detriment of not integrating sensor-specific information that is not standard-compliant; that is what sensor-specific alert subclasses are for. For simplicity of presentation and for illustrative purposes, we use an IDMEF-specific ontology in the rest of this paper.

The context integration component of our framework also integrates all the contextual information in various formats received implicitly or explicitly from various tools implemented in the system. In this component, the contextual information gathered using our designed drivers is converted into a unified format analysable by the other components, i.e. into instances in the context ontology. Once the integration process is complete, the correlation process can start.

3.3   Description of the Ontologies

We chose to use ontologies because they provide a powerful knowledge representation information structure in a unified format that is understandable by both machines and humans. The use of ontologies and ontology description logic enables us to fully automate the correlation process that is typically done manually by security analysts, and this uniformly considering all relevant information, no matter what its original format or source.

In order to integrate the data inputs to the correlation process and allow generic correlation reasoning, independent of specificities of information resources, we have constructed basic ontologies capturing the essence of the concepts of alert, context, vulnerability, and attack. Essentially, they correspond to the following intuitive security facts:

1. Attack scenarios will generate system events that might in turn trigger sensors to *cause* related alerts. Depending on the attack model, an attack scenario might be described as linear sequence of events, or a partial ordering of events with pre- and post-conditions, an attack graph, etc.
2. Alerts *happen in* a context, whether this is an IT asset, network location, application, user, etc. In our case this relationship will be made explicit through information provided by the sensor with the alert (e.g. IP address).
3. Vulnerabilities are always associated to a context, whether to high-level context concepts (e.g. an asset or service type) or to lower-level context subclasses (e.g. particular versions of OS or applications). Conversely, explicit context instances can be linked to specific or generic vulnerabilities, through vulnerability assessment or CMS information.
4. (Most) attack scenarios will require certain vulnerabilities to be present on the systems (context) so that they can *exploited* by that attack.

Figure 2 illustrates these class relationships and some of the subclasses of the basic ontology. These "starter" ontologies are not meant to be the end state of knowledge representation that security analysts would need in using our framework, but rather a starting point or template from which to build on, depending on the kind of sensors, context information or granularity of vulnerabilities and attack modelling desired. We now describe each of these ontologies in more detail.

Alert ontology. All the integrated alerts are transferred into this ontology as its instances. Alert ontology has dependency relationship with the context ontology and an association relationship with the attack ontology, since usually each alert a is typically by a (suspected) attack at in a particular context c. The generic base class *Alert* in Fig. 2 includes generic alert attributes such as source, target, time, and analyser (i.e. sensor). It is important to note that because the concept

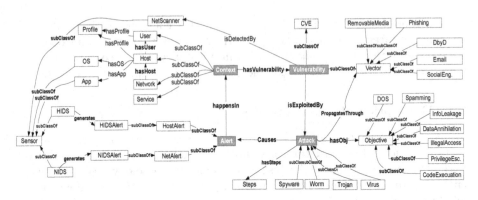

Fig. 2. Class diagram relationship of the designed ontologies

of context is potentially very rich and multifaceted, it is likely that a single alert might have to be linked to multiple context instances from various subclasses (e.g. a user, a network segment, an application), and thus the association between alert and context will be many-to-many at the Context base class level.

Context ontology. The integrated contextual information is transferred into the context ontology. We split contextual information into two categories: (*i*) static context information that rarely changes over time (e.g. network architecture, host/user profiles, and OS type), and (*ii*) dynamic context information that changes continuously over time (e.g. traffic type, system usage, time of day/week). As depicted in Fig. 2, the context ontology includes a Context base class and User, Host, Network and Service subclasses with their corresponding attributes.

Vulnerability ontology. This ontology represents the list of vulnerabilities related to the existing assets in the underlying context. This ontology has a part-whole relationship (composition) with the context ontology, since every vulnerability v is specific to a particular type of system, which is represented as a subclass of Context (typically Host). Thus, v can be associated with all the asset (context) instances $[c_1, \ldots, c_n]$ that are vulnerable to it, by querying the ontology for Host instances whose applications (App) or OS are those associated to that vulnerability. This ontology also has an association relationship with attack ontology, since usually every vulnerability v is exploitable by one or more attacks.

Attack ontology. The attack ontology includes information related to the known attack scenarios, and it includes generic attack attributes such as vectors, objectives, and so on. The Vector class represents the method that is used by an attack to infect computer systems, with subclasses in Fig. 2 including social engineering, phishing and removable media are examples of such methods. The Objective class includes subclasses such as information leakage, remote core execution, spamming and privilege escalation. The attack ontology has dependency relationships with the context ontology, and association relationship with the alert and vulnerability ontologies, since basically every attack at needs a particular context c to proceed, it might need to exploit particular vulnerabilities $[v_1, \ldots, v_n]$, and it results in triggers some alerts $[a_1, \ldots, a_n]$.

3.4   Correlation Engine

In order to implement the correlation logic, we employ Ontology Web Language-Description Logic (OWL-DL) to design and populate an ontology for each of the above four inputs. The use of generic language like OWL-DL provides significant flexibility to the framework by allowing the reuse or adaptation of data queries expressed in that logic to various deployment and security monitoring scenarios, e.g. on-line detection or after-the-fact network forensics analysis.

The correlation process is two-fold and can be viewed as two independent traversals on the core ontology classes:

1. *Context- and vulnerability-based filtering.* Given an alert (or alerts) determine which contexts instances are involved, what are their associated known vulnerabilities, and finally determine which attack scenarios could be exploiting them.
2. *Attack reconstruction.* For each possible attack scenario related to this (or these) alert(s), try to match the sequence of previous alerts with the steps of the attack.

The outcome of this process should hopefully provide the security analyst with a reduced list of high level descriptions of potential ongoing (or completed) attacks that includes few redundancies, non relevant scenarios and false positives.

In order to implement both components of this alert correlation approach we use a set of logic rules expressed in Semantic Web Rule Language (SWRL) and Semantic Query-Enhanced Web Rule Language (SQWRL). While various specific correlation approaches could be implemented within the above generic model, we use certain aspects of the approach described in [12] to illustrate the use of our framework.

3.5   Example Implementation of Valeur *et al.*'s Approach

The alert correlation approach proposed in [12], includes a comprehensive set of steps that covers various aspects of the alert correlation process. In order to show how ONTIDS automatically implement these steps, in the following, we explain the implementation details of some of these steps employing ONTIDS.

Alert fusion. Alert fusion is the process of merging alerts that represent the independent detection of the same malicious event by different IDS. An important condition in order to fuse two or more alerts is that they should be in the same time window. We have defined Rule 1 within the correlation engine in order to perform alert fusion:

Rule 1

ALERT(?a1) ∧ ALERT(?a2) ∧ ANALYSER(?an1) ∧ ANALYSER(?an2) ∧ DetectTime(?dt1) ∧ DetectTime(?dt2)∧
SOURCE(?s1) ∧ SOURCE(?s2) ∧ TARGET(?tar1) ∧ TARGET(?tar2) ∧ CLASSIFIC(?cl1) ∧ CLASSIFIC(?cl2)∧
ASSESSMENT(?as1) ∧ ASSESSMENT(?as2) ∧ stringEqual(?s1,?s2) ∧ stringEqual(?tar1,?tar2)∧
stringEqual(?cl1,?cl2) ∧ stringEqual(?as1,?as2) ∧ subtractTimes(?td,?dt1,?dt2)∧
lessThan(?td,"5s") ⟶ sqwrl:select(?a1)

Alert Verification. Alert verification is the process of recognising and reducing non-relevant alerts which refer to the failed attacks. The major reason of attack failure is the unavailability of the contextual requirements of the attack, i.e. the absence of required vulnerabilities in the attack context. Identifying failed attacks allows the correlation engine to reduce the effects of non-relevant alerts in its decision process. Rules 2 and 3 within the correlation engine of our framework perform alert verification based on the targeted system vulnerabilities:

Rule 2

ALERT(?a) ∧ HOST(?h) ∧ OS(?o) ∧ VULNERABILITY(?v) ∧ CLASSIFICATION(?cl) ∧ REFERENCE(?ref)∧
hasTarget(?a,?h) ∧ hasClassific(?a,?cl) ∧ hasOS(?h,?o) ∧ hasReference(?c,?ref)∧
hasVulnerability(?o,?v) ∧ hasName(?ref,?n1) ∧ hasName(?v,?n2) ∧ stringEqual(?n1,?n2)
⟶ sqwrl:select(?a)

Rule 3

ALERT(?a) ∧ HOST(?h) ∧ APP(?ap) ∧ VULNERABILITY(?v) ∧ CLASSIFICATION(?cl) ∧ REFERENCES(?ref)∧
hasTarget(?a,?h) ∧ hasClassific(?a,?cl) ∧ hasApp(?h,?ap) ∧ hasReference(?c,?ref)∧
hasVulnerability(?ap,?v) ∧ hasName(?ref,?n1) ∧ hasName(?v,?n2) ∧ stringEqual(?n1,?n2)
⟶ sqwrl:select(?a)

Attack thread reconstruction. Thread reconstruction is the process of merging a series of alerts that refer to an attack launched by one attacker against a single target, and is another step in the alert correlation process of [12]. Similarly to the alert fusion process, the alerts should happen in the same time window to be correlated. Rule 4 performs the thread reconstruction process:

Rule 4

ALERT(?a) ∧ HOST(?h1) ∧ HOST(?h2) ∧ TIME(?t1) ∧ TIME(?t2) ∧ hasSource(?a,?h1)
∧ hasTarget(?a,?h2) ∧ hasDetectTime(?a,?dt) ∧ greaterThanOrEqual(?dt,?t1)∧
lessThanOrEqual(?dt,?t2) ⟶ sqwrl:select(?a,?h1,?h2)

In summary, we can see how the first component of our canonical description is implemented by the correlation engine by applying first Rules 1, 2 and 3 to reduce non-relevant alerts. For this purpose, it retrieves required information from the alert, context, and vulnerability ontologies. Next, and for those alerts and scenarios that are relevant attack thread reconstruction is performed by applying Rule 4, where the engine attempts to make a mapping between the filtered alerts and the steps of attacks in the attack ontology. Once it finds any mapping between the two ontologies, it will output the whole attack scenario.

4   Implementation and Evaluation

In order to illustrate and validate our approach, we constructed an example reference implementation using various ontology representation and reasoning tools, and used it to conduct some simple security analysis on the well-known UNB ISCX and DARPA 2000 datasets. the capabilities and flexibility of framework, by describing how it is used in two distinct case studies.

4.1   Reference Implementation

To illustrate the integration of distinct IDS, we have selected the Snort [19] and IBM RealSecure [20] NIDS as our alert sensors. As an alert integration tool, we use Prelude [21], which is an agent-less, universal, Security Information Management System (SIM, a.k.a SIEM).

We use the Protégé ontology editor and knowledge acquisition system to design and implement the ontologies using the Ontology Web Language Description Logic (OWL-DL). We instantiate the above-mentioned ontologies from information coming from the alert integration component, the contextual information gathering sensors such as Nessus [22] and Nmap [23], the CVE vulnerability database, and the designed attack scenarios. and relational databases. We use the DataMaster plug-in [24] in order to transfer data from relational databases and the XML Tab plug-in to transfer data from a XML files.

Finally, we utilise the Pellet plug-in [25] as a reasoner for OWL-DL, the Jess rule engine [26] as SWRL rule compiler, and SQWRL [27] in order to query the ontologies for various purposes.

4.2   Case Study 1: Island-Hopping Attacks

As our first case study, we describe an instance of island-hopping attack scenario described in [12] which is part of the UNB ISCX Intrusion Detection Evaluation Dataset [28]. As shown Fig. 3, in this scenario the attacker employs the Adobe Reader `util.printf()` buffer overflow vulnerability (CVE-2008-2992) to execute arbitrary code with the same privileges as the user running it.

To launch the attack, the attacker creates a malicious PDF file using Metasploit (for example), and embeds a Meterpreter reverse TCP shell on port 5555 inside it. Then, the attacker sends a system upgrade email including the PDF file on behalf of admin@[...] to all the users of the testbed. Through user5, who initiates the first session (alert 1), the attacker starts to scan potential hosts on two subnets 192.168.1.0/24 and 192.168.2.0/24 (alert 2). User12 is identified as running Windows XP SP1 with a vulnerable SMB authentication protocol on port 445 (CVE-2008-4037) (alerts 3 and 4). The attacker exploits this vulnerability to capture user12 (alert 5), and a scan is performed from this user to the server subnet (192.168.5.0/24) (alert 6). This scan identifies a Windows Server 2003 running an internal Web application using MS SQL Server as its backend database with only port 80 opened. This leads to the use of Web application hacking techniques such as SQL injection. Finally, the attacker compromises the

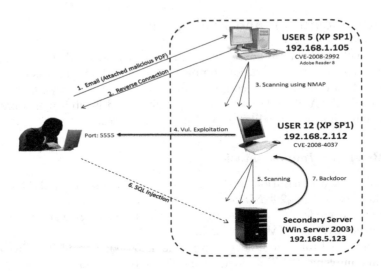

Fig. 3. An instance of island-hopping attack

Table 1. Alerts generated by alert sensors in the island-hopping attack scenario

Alert ID	Name	Sensor	Date	Source	Target	Tag
1	Local exploit	HIDS	6/13/10 16:02:20	192.168.1.105	192.168.1.105	Step 1
2	Scanning	NIDS	6/13/10 16:42:24	192.168.1.105	192.168.1.0/24 192.168.2.0/24	Step 2
3	Windows file sharing	NIDS	6/13/10 17:20:32	192.168.1.105	192.168.2.112	Step 3
4	Windows file sharing	NIDS	6/13/10 17:34:32	192.168.1.105	192.168.2.112	Step 3
5	Local exploit	HIDS	6/13/10 17:50:24	192.168.2.112	192.168.2.112	Step 3
6	Scanning	NIDS	6/13/10 18:02:37	192.168.2.112	192.168.5.0/24	Step 4
7	HTTPWeb	NIDS	6/13/10 18:19:41	192.168.2.112	192.168.5.123	Step 4
8	SQLInjection	AIDS	6/13/10 18:20:19	192.168.5.123	192.168.5.123	Step 5

target system (alerts 7 and 8). Table 1 presents a summary of the alerts, and indicates their corresponding steps.

In order to correlate the alerts generated by alert sensors during the above scenario, first, the alert integration component integrates all received alerts. Then, the integrated alerts are transferred into the alert ontology. Additionally, we manually populate vulnerability and context ontologies based on the published documents related to the UNB ISCX dataset. Therefore, the Adobe Reader util.printf() vulnerability and others that might be present in the IT infrastructure are input into the vulnerability ontology. Contextual information about the existing hosts (IP addresses, open ports, available services, etc.), services and users are also manually input into the context ontology. In this case,

Fig. 4. The island-hopping attack graph detected by the proposed framework

this includes the information about the three compromised hosts (IP addresses 192.168.1.105, 192.168.2.112, and 192.168.5.123), their open ports (i.e. 5555 and 445).

Next, the correlation engine correlates the existing information within the ontologies. For this purpose, we first use the Rules 1, 2 and 3 to eliminate non-relevant alerts. Then, using the following rule we reconstruct the attack scenario.

Rule 5

ATTACK(?at) ∧ hasName(?at,"InsiderAttack1") ∧ ALERT(?a1) ∧ CLASSIFICATION(?cl1) ∧ HOST(?h1)∧

REFERENCE(?ref1) ∧ hasTarget(?a1,?h1) ∧ hasClassific(?a1,?cl1) ∧ hasReference(?cl1,"CVE-2008-2992")

∧ ALERT(?a2) ∧ hasSource(?a2,?h1) ∧ hasName(?a2,"Scanning") ∧ ALERT(?a3) ∧ HOST(?h2)∧

CLASSIFICATION(?cl2) ∧ REFERENCE(?ref2) ∧ hasTarget(?a2,?h2) ∧ hasClassific(?a2,?cl2)∧

hasReference(?cl2,"CVE-2008-4037") ∧ ALERT(?a4) ∧ hasSource(?a4,?h2) ∧ hasName(?a4,"Scanning")∧

ALERT(?a5) ∧ hasSource(?a5,?h2) ∧ hasName(?a5,"SQLInjection")

⟶ sqwrl:select(?a1,?a2,?a3,?a4,?a5,?at)

Rule 5 correlates alert and attack ontologies, and attempts to discover corresponding alerts for each step of the attack. If it finds at least one match regarding each step, the rule will be successful in detecting the whole attack scenario. Figure 4 represents the result of applying Rule 5 to the ontologies, showing that ONTIDS should be able to reconstruct the attack.

4.3   Case Study 2: Recon-Breakin-Escalate Attacks

As the second case study, we evaluate the proposed alert correlation framework using the DARPA 2000 dataset LLDDOS 1.0 scenario [29]. LLDDOS 1.0 is a multi-step scenario corresponding to a Distributed Denial of Service (DDoS) flooding attack. The attack has 5 phases and it takes about three hours to be completed. We again use both the RealSecure and Snort NIDS as base our alerts sensors to detect all the steps of the attack. Snort outputs around 1,211 raw alerts for the LLDDOS 1.0 dataset, but it does not detect the installation phase of the DDoS attack (i.e. phase 4). On the other hand, and as is described in [30], RealSecure outputs 924 raw alerts for the same dataset, corresponding to the 22 alert types shown in Table 2. However, it does not output any alerts related to ICMP pings (i.e. phase 1). Consequently, the combination of Snort and RealSecure can detect all phases of the attack. Nonetheless, just using a combination of both IDS alerts with a simple OR rule will result in a significant number of redundant alerts and false positives, as we will see. With ONTIDS, we expect to have lower redundancy, and fewer non-relevant alerts and false positives.

Table 2. Alert types generated by ISS RealSecure based on the DARPA 2000 dataset

ID	AlertType	ID	AlertType	ID	AlertType
1	*RIPExpire*	9	*Admind*	17	*SSH_Detected*
2	*RIPAdd*	10	*Sadmind_Ping*	18	*Email_Debug*
3	*Email_Ehlo*	11	*Email_Almail_Overflow*	19	*TelnetXdisplay*
4	*TelnetTerminaltype*	12	*HTTP_Java*	20	*TelnetEnvAll*
5	*FTP_User*	13	*Sadmind_Amslverify_Overflow*	21	*Port_Scan*
6	*FTP_Pass*	14	*Mstream_Zombie*	22	*Stream_DoS*
7	*FTP_Syst*	15	*Rsh*		
8	*HTTP_Shells*	16	*HTTP_Cisco_Catalyst_Exec*		

In the second step, Prelude converts all the received alerts into the IDMEF format, and transfers the integrated alerts into the alert ontology as its instances. We manually populate the context and vulnerability ontologies based on the information existing in the published documents related to the DARPA 2000 dataset. Thus, the Solaris sadmind vulnerability (CVE-1999-0977) and others existing vulnerabilities in the underlying network are transferred into the vulnerability ontology. The same is done with contextual information about the existing hosts and users, in this case including the three compromised hosts (IP addresses 172.16.115.20, 172.16.112.50, 172.16.112.10), and their open ports (i.e. telnet port 23) and users (e.g. hacker2).

As before, the correlation engine uses Rules 1–3, to eliminate redundant and non-relevant alerts. Based on our analysis, 32.7 % of all alerts were generated by both Snort and IIS RealSecure. In our case, we report these alerts as a single alert (in order to reduce redundancy) since both IDS agree. Alerts reported by only one IDS are then further analysed by attempting attack reconstruction on the 5 phases of the LLDDOS 1.0 attack scenario, by using the following rule:

Rule 6

```
ATTACK(?at) ∧ hasName(?at,"LLDDOS1") ∧ ALERT(?a1) ∧ ALERT(?a2) ∧ ALERT(?a3) ∧ ALERT(?a4)∧
ALERT(?a5) ∧ ALERT(?a6) ∧ ALERT(?a7) ∧ HOST(?h1) ∧ hasName(?a1,"Scanning") ∧ hasTarget(?a1,?h1)∧
hasService(?h1,"ICMP")∧hasName(?a2,"Sadmind_Ping")∧hasName(?a3,"Sadmind_Amslverify_Overflow")∧
hasName(?a4,"Admind") ∧ hasName(?a4,"Rsh") ∧ hasName(?a4,"MStream_Zombie")∧
hasName(?a4,"StreamDOS") ⟶ sqwrl:select(?a1,?a2,?a3,?a4,?a5,?a6,?a7,?at)
```

Rule 6 correlates alert and attack ontologies, and discovers corresponding alerts for the each step of the attack. If at least one match is found for each step, the rule will be successful in detecting the whole attack scenario. According to this rule, our results indicate that 91.08 % of the alerts were false positives, and only 8.92 % of the alerts were true positives.

Table 3 summarises our results. Since both Snort and ISS RealSecure only detect a few of the 33,787 attack events in Phase 5 (launching DDoS), their total false negative rates are quite high. The recall column consequently reports low values for both sensors and ONTIDS. On the other hand, ONTIDS does considerably well at reducing false positives, in fact reducing it to 0.

Table 3. Experimental results based on the DARPA 2000 dataset

IDS	Redundant alerts (%)	FP	TP	FN	Precision	Recall	F-measure
Snort	0.00	1118	93	33814	0.07	2×10^{-3}	2×10^{-3}
RealSecure	0.00	870	54	33853	0.05	10^{-3}	10^{-3}
ONTIDS	32.7	0	123	33784	1.00	3×10^{-3}	5×10^{-3}

5 Conclusions

In this paper, we introduced ONTIDS an ontology-based automated alert correlation framework to try to benefit from the combined advantages of previous
alert correlation approaches (including context awareness), while providing a
level of flexibility that would allow it to be used in the many different deployment scenarios that security analysts are likely to face.

The main idea behind ONTIDS is to use and leverage a template ontology
containing base classes and some subclasses for the concepts of IT asset context, alert, vulnerability and attack. The correlation engine is then implemented
using logic rules written in Semantic Web Rule Language (SWRL) and Semantic
Query-Enhanced Web Rule Language (SQWRL) based on the OWL description
logic (OWL-DL). The ontologies and correlation rules described here are generic
enough to (i) implement as special cases other existing correlation approaches
such as that of *Valeur et al.*, and, (ii) be applied with minimal changes to different analysis scenarios, such as in the two case studies demonstrated.

We have demonstrated the use of the ONTIDS alert correlation framework in
two quite different case studies involving considerably distinct attack scenarios.
More important than the reduction in false positives (in this somewhat contrived
evaluation scenario), the point of this exercise was to show the level of flexibility
of such an approach. The fact that the same correlation Rules 1–3 are used for
the context-based alert filtering in both scenarios deceptively hides the fact that
the vulnerability and context instances in both cases are quite different as they
come from different sources, and hence have different attributes and properties.
As security analysts start to use ONTIDS, we expect that these ontologies will
naturally expand to include new subclasses capturing the idiosyncrasies of the
systems being monitored, the various types of sensors monitoring them, and
richer and more complex attack models and vulnerabilities.

In conclusion, we hope to continue to evaluate its viability and usefulness
by conducting field studies with data collected from real-world systems and
analysed by real security analysts. On the one hand, this will force us to test the
flexibility of the framework by incorporating richer context and sensor ontologies
(possibly stretchning the limits of abstraction), while also having to express
richer correlation algorithms, possibly based on more sophisticated attack models
and description languates such as LAMBDA or STATL.

Acknowledgements. This research was sponsored in part by the Inter-networked Systems Security Strategic Research Network (ISSNet), funded by Canada's Natural Sciences and Engineering Research Council (NSERC).

References

1. Li-Zhong, G., Hui-bo, J.: A novel intrusion detection scheme for network-attached storage based on multi-source information fusion. In: 2012 Eighth International Conference on Computational Intelligence and Security, pp. 469–473 (2009)
2. Thomas, C., Balakrishnan, N.: Improvement in intrusion detection with advances in sensor fusion. Trans. Inf. For. Sec. **4**(3), 542–551 (2009)
3. Dreger, H., Kreibich, C., Paxson, V., Sommer, R.: Enhancing the accuracy of network-based intrusion detection with host-based context. In: Julisch, K., Kruegel, C. (eds.) DIMVA 2005. LNCS, vol. 3548, pp. 206–221. Springer, Heidelberg (2005)
4. Cuppens, F., Miege, A.: Alert correlation in a cooperative intrusion detection-framework. In: Proceedings of the IEEE Symposium on Security and Privacy, pp. 202–215 (2002)
5. Morin, B., Debar, H.: Correlation of intrusion symptoms: an application of chronicles. In: Vigna, G., Kruegel, C., Jonsson, E. (eds.) RAID 2003. LNCS, vol. 2820, pp. 84–112. Springer, Heidelberg (2003)
6. Chen, L., Aritsugi, M.: An SVM-based masquerade detection method with online update using co-occurrence matrix. In: Büschkes, R., Laskov, P. (eds.) DIMVA 2006. LNCS, vol. 4064, pp. 37–53. Springer, Heidelberg (2006)
7. Raftopoulos, E., Egli, M., Dimitropoulos, X.: Shedding light on log correlation in network forensics analysis. In: Flegel, U., Markatos, E., Robertson, W. (eds.) DIMVA 2013. LNCS, vol. 7591, pp. 232–241. Springer, Heidelberg (2013)
8. Gagnon, F., Massicotte, F., Esfandiari, B.: Using contextual information for ids alarm classification (extended abstract). In: Flegel, U., Bruschi, D. (eds.) DIMVA 2009. LNCS, vol. 5587, pp. 147–156. Springer, Heidelberg (2009)
9. Sinha, S., Jahanian, F., Patel, J.M.: WIND: workload-aware intrusion detection. In: Kruegel, C., Zamboni, D. (eds.) RAID 2006. LNCS, vol. 4219, pp. 290–310. Springer, Heidelberg (2006)
10. Vorobiev, A., Bekmamedova, N.: An ontology-driven approach applied to information security. J. Res. Prac. Inf. Technol. **42**(1), 61 (2010)
11. Coppolino, L., D'Antonio, S., Elia, I., Romano, L.: From intrusion detection to intrusion detection and diagnosis: An ontology-based approach. In: Lee, S., Narasimhan, P. (eds.) SEUS 2009. LNCS, vol. 5860, pp. 192–202. Springer, Heidelberg (2009)
12. Valeur, F., Vigna, G., Kruegel, C., Kemmerer, R.: Comprehensive approach to intrusion detection alert correlation. IEEE Trans. Depend. Secur. Comput. **1**(3), 146–169 (2004)
13. Cuppens, F., Ortalo, R.: LAMBDA: A language to model a database for detection of attacks. In: Debar, H., Mé, L., Wu, S.F. (eds.) RAID 2000. LNCS, vol. 1907, pp. 197–216. Springer, Heidelberg (2000)
14. CVE: Common vulnerabilities exposures (CVE), the key to information sharing. http://cve.mitre.org/
15. CAPEC: Common attack pattern enumeration and classification (capec). http://capec.mitre.org/
16. Eckmann, S.T., Vigna, G., Kemmerer, R.A.: STATL: An attack language for state-based intrusion detection. J. Comput. Secur. **10**(1), 71–103 (2002)

17. Debar, H., Curry, D., Feinstein, B.: The intrusion detection message exchange format (idmef) (2007)
18. Mitre Corporation: A standardized common event expression (CEE) for event interoperability (2013)
19. Roesch, M.: Snort - lightweight intrusion detection for networks. In: Proceedings of the 13th USENIX Conference on System Administration (LISA '99), pp. 229–238. USENIX Association, Berkeley (1999)
20. Corporation, I.: IBM RealSecure. http://www-935.ibm.com/services/us/en/it-services/express-managed-protection-services-for-server.html
21. Zaraska, K.: Prelude ids: current state and development perspectives (2003). http://www.prelude-ids.org/download/misc/pingwinaria/2003/paper.pdf
22. Deraison, R.: The nessus project (2002). http://www.nessus.org
23. Lyon, G.F.: Nmap network scanning: The official Nmap project guide to network discovery and security scanning. Insecure, USA (2009)
24. Nyulas, C., O'Connor, M., Tu, S.: Datamaster–a plug-in for importing schemas and data from relational databases into protege. In: Proceedings of the 10th International Protege Conference (2007)
25. Parsia, B., Sirin, E.: Pellet: An OWL-DL reasoner. In: Third International Semantic Web Conference-Poster, p. 18 (2004)
26. Friedman-Hill, E. et al.: Jess, the rule engine for the java platform (2003)
27. O'Connor, M., Das, A.: SQWRL: a query language for OWL. In: Proceedings of the 6th Workshop on OWL: Experiences and Directions (OWLED2009) (2009)
28. Shiravi, A., Shiravi, H., Tavallaee, M., Ghorbani, A.A.: Toward developing a systematic approach to generate benchmark datasets for intrusion detection. Comput. Secur. **31**(3), 357–374 (2012)
29. MIT Lincoln Laboratory: 2000 DARPA intrusion detection scenario specific data sets (2000)
30. Hu, Y.: TIAA: A toolkit for intrusion alert analysis (2004)

Quantitative Evaluation
of Enforcement Strategies
Position Paper

Vincenzo Ciancia[1], Fabio Martinelli[2], Matteucci Ilaria[2(✉)],
and Charles Morisset[3]

[1] CNR-ISTI, Via Moruzzi 1, 56124 Pisa, Italy
vincenzo.ciancia@isti.cnr.it
[2] CNR-IIT, Via Moruzzi 1, 56124 Pisa, Italy
{fabio.martinelli,matteucci.ilaria}@iit.cnr.it
[3] School of Computing Science, Newcastle University, NE17RU, Newcastle, UK
charles.morisset@ncl.ac.uk

Abstract. A *security enforcement mechanism* runs in parallel with a
system to check and modify its run-time behaviour, so that it satisfies some security policy. For each policy, several enforcement strategies
are possible, usually reflecting trade-offs one has to make to satisfy the
policy. To evaluate them, multiple dimensions, such as security, cost of
implementation, or cost of attack, must be taken into account. We propose a formal framework for the quantification of enforcement strategies,
extending the notion of *controller processes* (mimicking the well-known
edit automata) with weights on transitions, valued in a semiring.

Keywords: Enforcement mechanisms · Quantitative process algebra ·
Semiring

1 Introduction

Security is often regarded as a binary concept, as it usually strictly depends
on satisfaction of a boolean policy. However, in a broader sense, security has
several dimensions e.g., secrecy, anonymity, enforceability, availability, risk, trust.
These interesting features give rise to a multi-dimensional solution space for the
construction of a "secure program". Functional requirements add to the picture
costs, execution times, rates, etc. All these dimensions make it meaningless to
talk about a "secure" program, shifting the focus to the definition of a globally
optimal solution, which easily fails to exist.

The research leading to these results has received funding from the European Union
Seventh Framework Programme (FP7/2007-2013) under grants no 256980 (NES-
SoS) and no 295354 (SESAMO). This work has been also partially supported by
the TENACE PRIN Project (no 20103P34XC) funded by the Italian Ministry of
Education, University and Research.

J.-L. Danger et al. (Eds.): FPS 2013, LNCS 8352, pp. 178–186, 2014.
DOI: 10.1007/978-3-319-05302-8_11, © Springer International Publishing Switzerland 2014

In this work, we consider security as a quantitative, multi-dimensional measure of a system, and investigate possible answers to the question of what it means to enforce a security policy in this new setting. Our main actors will be *controllers* that constrain *targets* to obey to policies, using *enforcement strategies*. The ultimate goal of the proposed research direction is to define *quantitative evaluation of enforcement strategies*, that would provide analysis tools to compare and select different controllers, according to several metrics. Instead of asking if a controller enforces a policy or not, one can ask if a controller is the *optimal* one for a certain combination of metrics. The plethora of dimensions demands for a parametric approach. We address this aspect by adopting *semirings*, that are well-known domains for optimization problems (see e.g., [1]) and permit multi-dimensional valuations by composition.

Summing up, beyond the state of the art (Sect. 2), in this paper we make a distinction between monitors and controllers. Monitors (Sect. 4) associate quantities to an existing system without changing its behaviour. Controllers (Sect. 5) modify the behaviour of a target, using *control actions* for suppressing or inserting possible incorrect actions. In Sect. 6 we propose a formal approach to evaluate and compare controllers in the quantitative, multi-dimensional setting.

2   State of the Art

Runtime enforcement is a well-studied problem [2–4], in particular with security automata [2], designed to prevent bad executions, and edit automata [5], that can suppress, insert or replace observed actions. Concurrent languages (e.g., process algebras) can also model both the target and the controlled system within the same formalism [3,6]. As a prototypical example, we chose the process algebra GPA [7], featuring CSP-style synchronization, with actions weighted over a semiring. We add to it control operators in the style of edit automata, in order to study enforcement strategies from the quantitative standpoint. Compared to the existing literature, our work identifies an abstract approach to quantitative and multi-dimensional aspects of security, by introducing semirings. The quest for a unifying formalism is witnessed by the significant amount of inhomogeneous work in quantitative notions of security and enforcement.

The problem of finding an optimal control strategy is considered in [8] in the context of software monitoring, taking into account rewards and penalties, and can be solved using a Markov Decision Process [9]. Bielova and Massacci propose in [10] a notion of *edit distance* among traces, that extends to an ordering over controllers.

Metrics can be used for evaluating the correctness of a mechanism, such as *More Corrective, Permissiveness, Memory Use,* and *Versatility* [11]. Additionally, mechanisms can be compared with respect to their *cost* [12]. In this work, we follow some intuitive leads from [13] to move from qualitative to quantitative enforcement, and generalise that idea using semirings. We also consider the possibility for a controller not to be correct, i.e., to allow for some violations of the policy. Such a possibility is quantified over traces in [14] for non-safety policies, where a controller cannot be both correct and fully transparent. In [15], the authors use a notion of *lazy* controllers, which only check the security of a system at some points in time, proposing a probabilistic quantification of the expected risk.

3   Quantitative Processes

In a *quantitative process*, observable transitions are labelled with some quantity, denoting a cost or a benefit associated to a step in the behaviour of a system. We use *semirings* to model two fundamental modes of composing observable behaviour, either by combination of different traces, or by sequential composition. As a syntax to describe such behaviour, we adopt GPA from [7]. We first provide the definition of a semiring.

Definition 1. *A semiring* $\mathbb{K} = (K, +, *, \mathbf{0}, \mathbf{1})$ *consists of a set K with two binary operations $+, *$, and two constants $\mathbf{0}, \mathbf{1}$, such that $+$ is associative, with neutral element $\mathbf{0}$; $*$ is associative, with neutral and absorbing elements $\mathbf{1}, \mathbf{0}$; $*$ distributes over $+$.*

Examples of semirings are natural numbers, the positive real numbers, boolean algebras, that may denote, e.g., time, costs, lattices of values. Semirings have a partial order $\sqsubseteq$, such that $k_1 \sqsubseteq k_2$ if, and only if $k_1 + k_2 = k_2$. Intuitively, $\sqsubseteq$ indicates *preference*, that is, $k_1 \sqsubseteq k_2$ can be read as k_2 is "better" than k_1. Sometimes, the $+$ operation is idempotent, and it extends to an operation $\sum_{\{S\}}$ defined over an arbitrary, possibly infinite subset S of K. The well-known C-semirings [1] are of this form. For the sake of simplicity, when needed, we silently assume that this is the case.

The cartesian product of semirings is a semiring; thus, multi-dimensional notions of cost can be modelled. The partial order of values in the product does not prioritize dimensions. Further composite semirings exist, such as the lexicographic semiring, the expectation semiring, etc. When the specific composition operator is not relevant, we shall indicate a composite semiring by $\mathbb{K}_1 \odot \ldots \odot \mathbb{K}_n$.

Process algebras are simple languages with precise mathematical semantics, tailored to exhibit and study specific features of computation. Typically, a *process* P, specfied by some syntax, may non-deterministically execute several *labelled transitions* of the form $P \xrightarrow{a} P'$, where a is an observable effect and P' is a new process. In quantitative process algebras, transitions are labelled by pairs (a, x) where x is a quantity associated to the effect a. We now define *Generalized Process Algebra* (GPA).

Definition 2. *The set $\mathcal{L}$ of agents, or processes, in GPA over a countable set of transition labels Act and a semiring $\mathbb{K}$ is defined by the grammar*

$$A ::= 0 \mid (a, k).A \mid A + A \mid A \|_S A \mid X$$

where $a \in Act$, $k \in K$, $S \subseteq Act$, and X belongs to a countable set of process variables, coming from a system of co-recursive equations of the form $X \triangleq A$. We write GPA[$\mathbb{K}$] for the set of GPA processes labelled with weights in $\mathbb{K}$.

Process 0 describes inaction or termination; $(a, k).A$ performs a with *weight* k and evolves into A; $A+A'$ non-deterministically behaves as either A or A'; $A\|_S A'$ describes the process in which A and A' proceed concurrently and independently on all actions which are not in S, and synchronize over actions in S.

As we are dealing with *run-time* enforcement, we work with *traces*, or paths, of processes. A *path* is a sequence $(a_1, k_1) \cdots (a_n, k_n)$, and we call $\mathcal{T}(A)$ the set of paths rooted in A. Given a path $(a_1, k_1) \cdots (a_n, k_n)$, we define its *label* $l(t) = a_1 \cdots a_n$, and its *run weight* $|t| = k_1 * \ldots * k_n \in K$. Finally, the *valuation* of a process A is given by $[\![A]\!] = \sum_{\{t \in \mathcal{T}(A)\}} |t|$.

4 Quantitative Monitor Operators

A system, hereafter named *target*, does not always come with the quantities we are interested in evaluating, and might even be not labelled at all. Hence, in the most general case, the security designer must provide a *labelling function* $\lambda : \mathsf{GPA}[\mathbb{K}_1] \to \mathsf{GPA}[\mathbb{K}_2]$, such that given any process A labelled in $\mathbb{K}_1$, $\lambda(A)$ represents the process A labelled with a quantity in $\mathbb{K}_2$. A simple example is the function λ_v, which assign any transition with the value $v \in \mathbb{K}_2$, thus erasing any previous quantity.

In practice, a *monitor* often measures a particular aspect, by probing the system and indicating the weight of each operation. In terms of security, a monitor is usually passive, i.e., it does not effectively modify the behaviour of the considered target, and thus does not prevent violation of a security policy. On the other hand, a *controller* is able to modify the behaviour of a target in order to guarantee security requirements. A security monitor and a security controller are often merged into a single entity, responsible both for deciding whether an action would violate the policy and what corrective action should be taken if necessary. We propose to make an explicit distinction between these two processes and to extend the monitoring to measures other than security. In this section we investigate quantitative monitors. Controllers are detailed in Sect. 5.

Intuitively, a monitor measures a quantity not already present in the monitored target. Since the target might be already equipped with some quantities, coming for instance from another monitor, we need to *merge* the quantities from the monitor with those of the target. Given a process A labelled with $\mathbb{K}$, a process A' labelled with $\mathbb{L}$ and a composition operator $\odot$, we write $A \odot A'$ for the merged process, defined as:

$$\frac{A \xrightarrow{a, k} A_1 \quad A' \xrightarrow{a, l} A_1'}{A \odot A' \xrightarrow{a, k \odot l} A_1 \odot A_1'}$$

A merged process can only move on when both of its components can move on with the same action. We are now able to define a monitor, which is a process that can be composed with a target without affecting its behaviour.

Definition 3. *Given a composition operator $\odot$ and a process A, a process M is a monitor for A if and only if $\{l(t) \mid t \in \mathcal{T}(A \odot M)\} = \{l(t) \mid t \in \mathcal{T}(A)\}$.*

Given any process A labelled with $\mathbb{K}_1$, any monitor M for A labelled with $\mathbb{K}_2$ and any composition operator $\odot$, we can define the labelling function $\lambda : \mathsf{GPA}[\mathbb{K}_1] \to \mathsf{GPA}[\mathbb{K}_1 \odot \mathbb{K}_2]$ as $\lambda(A) = A \odot M$.

Example 1. Let us define an energy monitor using $\mathbb{K}_C = \langle \mathbb{R}_0^+, min, +, +\infty, 0 \rangle$ for the alphabet $\Sigma = \{a, b\}$, such that the action a consumes 3 units, and the action b consumes $2n$ units, where n is the number of times b has been performed (i.e., b has an increasing energy cost). Hence, for $n > 0$, we define the monitor:

$$M_n = (a, 3).M_n + (b, 2n).M_{n+1}$$

For instance, the process $A = a.b.b.a.b$ can be monitored with

$$A \odot M_1 = (a, 3).(b, 2).(b, 4).(a, 3).(b, 6)$$

The valuation of the monitored process corresponds to the total energy consumed, i.e., $[\![A \odot M_1]\!] = 18$. Similarly, the monitored process of $B = a + b$ is $B \odot M_1 = (a, 3) + (b, 2)$, and its valuation $[\![B \odot M_1]\!] = 2$, since the valuation returns the best quantity.

Clearly, finer-grained approaches can be used to monitor a security policy. Note that a monitor is only one possible way to build a labeling function λ. Although monitors are expressive enough for the examples, in this paper, we consider more complex labeling functions may also be of interest.

5   Quantitative Control Operators

The role of the monitor is to *observe* the actions from a target, and not to *prevent* a *target* system from performing any. For instance, given a policy P, a monitor can observe the target actions, labelling them with *true* when they obey to the policy P or *false* when they violate P. On the contrary, a *controller* can decide not only to accept but also to change target traces, which result in a *controlled process* $E \triangleright F$, where F denotes the target system, following the semantics in Fig. 1.

Intuitively speaking, each rule corresponds to a different controlling behaviour. The alphabets of E, F, and of the resulting process $E \triangleright F$ are different, as E may perform *control actions* that regulate the actions of F, and $E \triangleright F$ may perform internal actions, denoted by τ, as a consequence of suppression. Let Act be the alphabet of (the GPA describing) F, and let $\{a, \boxminus a.b, \boxminus a\}$, for $a, b \in Act$, be the alphabet of E, respectively denoting *acceptance*, *suppression*, and *insertion*; the alphabet of $E \triangleright F$ is $Act \cup \{\tau\}$.

$$\frac{E \xrightarrow{a,k} E' \quad F \xrightarrow{a,k'} F'}{E \triangleright F \xrightarrow{a,k*k'} E' \triangleright F'} \text{ (A)} \quad \frac{E \xrightarrow{\boxminus a,k} E' \quad F \xrightarrow{a,k'} F'}{E \triangleright F \xrightarrow{\tau,k*k'} E' \triangleright F'} \text{ (S)} \quad \frac{E \xrightarrow{\boxplus a.b,k} E' \quad F \xrightarrow{a,k'} F'}{E \triangleright F \xrightarrow{b,k} E' \triangleright F'} \text{ (I)}$$

Fig. 1. MLTS rules for quantitative control operators.

The *acceptance rule* (A) constrains the controller and the target to perform the same action, in order for it to be observed in the resulting behaviour; the observed weight is the product of those of the controller and the target. Given two processes A and B, the semantics of truncation is equivalent to that of CSP-style parallel composition of A and B, where synchronisation is forced over all actions of the two processes.

The *suppression rule* (S) allows the controller to hide target actions. The target performs the action, but the controlled system does not, and the observed result is a τ action, with the weight given as the product of the suppressing and the target action.

The *insertion rule* (I) describes the capability of correcting some bad behaviour of the target, by inserting another action in its execution trace. The weight of insertion is only the weight provided by the controller; this accounts for the fact that the target does not perform any action, but rather stays in its current state, as in [5].

Interestingly, monitoring a target F inside a controlled system $E \triangleright F$ or monitoring $E \triangleright F$ leads to different valuations. For instance, monitoring F for a policy P will associate with *false* each trace where F tried to violate P, even though the action was corrected by E; on the other hand, monitoring $E \triangleright F$ for P associates each trace with *true* if E correctly enforces P. In other words, the nesting of monitors impacts the valuation of processes, and we therefore introduce the notion of *matching operator* $\bowtie$:

$$E \bowtie F = \lambda_T(\lambda_E(E) \triangleright \lambda_F(F))$$

where λ_E labels the controller, λ_F labels the target and λ_T labels the controlled target.

For instance, we can consider the following evaluation strategies:

$$E \bowtie_D F = \lambda_{true}(E) \triangleright (F \odot M_P) \qquad E \bowtie_P F = (E \triangleright F) \odot M_P$$
$$E \bowtie_C F = (E \odot M_c) \triangleright (F \odot M_1) \qquad E \bowtie_G F = M_P \odot_L (E \bowtie_C F)$$

where M_P stands for the monitor for the policy P, $\bowtie_D$ detects policy violations, even if they are corrected by the controller, $\bowtie_P$ monitors the satisfaction of the policy by the controlled target, $\bowtie_C$ monitors the energy of both the controller and the target, and $\bowtie_G$ defines a lexicographic measure of the cost and the satisfaction of the policy.

6   Ordering Controller Strategies

The matching operator defined provides a simple way to compare controllers, for any considered semiring.

Definition 4. *Given a target F and a matching operator $\bowtie$, a controller E_2 is better than a controller E_1 with respect to F, and in this case, we write $E_1 \sqsubseteq_{\bowtie,F} E_2$, if and only if $[\![E_1 \bowtie F]\!] \sqsubseteq [\![E_2 \bowtie F]\!]$. Furthermore, we write*

$E_1 \sqsubseteq_{\bowtie} E_2$ and say that E_1 is always better than E_2 if and only if $E_1 \sqsubseteq_{\bowtie,F} E_2$, for any target F. Finally, if $E_1 \sqsubseteq_{\bowtie} E_2$ and there exists at least one target F such that $[\![E_1 \bowtie F]\!] \sqsubset [\![E_2 \bowtie F]\!]$, we write $E_1 \sqsubset_{\bowtie} E_2$.

This definition does not directly depend on the semiring used to quantify the controlled target, and it is therefore possible to use the same definition to say that a controller is better than another one with respect to a security monitor, a cost monitor or any other measure. Note that since each individual trace can be represented as a target, $E_1 \sqsubseteq_{\bowtie} E_2$ implies that the valuation of E_1 should be lower than that of E_2 for every possible trace.

Example 2. Let us extend the example described in Sect. 4, such that we have now three actions $\{a, b, c\}$, and a policy P stating that any trace should start with at least one action b. Now, consider the four following controllers:

$$E_1 = a.E_1 + b.E_1 + c.E_1 \qquad E_2 = \boxminus a.E_2 + b.E_1 + c.E_2$$
$$E_3 = \boxminus a.E_3 + b.E_1 + \boxminus c.E_3 \qquad E_4 = \boxplus a.b.E_1 + b.E_1 + \boxplus c.b.E_1$$

Intuitively, E_1 accepts all actions, E_2 suppresses all initial actions a, but accepts c, E_3 suppresses both actions a and c, and E_4 inserts a b before any initial a or c. As soon as an action b is performed, all processes are equivalent to E_1, and accept all actions.

Since E_3 and E_4 are sound, we have $[\![E_3 \bowtie_P F]\!] = [\![E_4 \bowtie_P F]\!] = true$, for any target F. In addition, given any target F such that $[\![E_2 \bowtie_P F]\!] = false$, we also have $[\![E_1 \bowtie_P F]\!] = false$. Since there are also targets F such that $[\![E_2 \bowtie_P F]\!] = true$ and $[\![E_1 \bowtie_P F]\!] = false$, we have $E_1 \sqsubset_{\bowtie_P} E_2 \sqsubset_{\bowtie_P} E_3 \equiv_{\bowtie_P} E_4$, where $\equiv_{\bowtie}$ is the equivalence relation induced by the partial order $\sqsubseteq_{\bowtie}$. In other words, E_3 and E_4 are maximal, and E_1 is strictly worse than E_2.

However, it is worth observing that E_1 is not the worst possible controller. Indeed, E_1 leaves unchanged the correct traces of F, meaning that there exists some targets F such that $[\![E_1 \bowtie_P F]\!] = true$. The worst controller always outputs incorrect traces, even when the target is correct. For instance, we can define the controller $E_0 = \boxplus b.a.E_1 + a.E_0 + c.E_0$, which satisfies $[\![E_0 \bowtie_P F]\!] = false$, for any target F, and therefore $E_0 \sqsubset_{\bowtie_P} E_1$.

In some cases, controllers can be incomparable. In the previous example, the controller that only suppresses bad actions a is incomparable with the one that only suppresses bad actions c. Furthermore, the choice of the controlling operators can have an impact on the overall evaluation. For instance, if one cannot implement the controlling strategy E_3 because the action c is uncontrollable [16], i.e., cannot be suppressed or protected, then a security designer may prefer to choose E_2 over E_1, and over E_0 even if they are incorrect. The controllers E_3 and E_4 are equivalent with respect to $\bowtie_P$, since they are both correct, and, if policy satisfaction is the only criterion, a security designer might choose either. However, other dimensions can easily be included within our framework, with the intuition that the more accurate is the quantification of the controlled system, the more informed is the security designer to choose a controller.

Example 3. In order to compare the previous controllers E_3 and E_4, let us consider the extended cost monitor $M_c = (x, 0).M_c + (\boxminus y, 1).M_c + (\boxplus w.v, 2).M_c$ with the matching operator $\bowtie_G$. First, it is worth observing that since we use the lexicographic ordering, the relations $E_0 \sqsubseteq_{\bowtie_G} E_1 \sqsubseteq_{\bowtie_G} E_2 \sqsubseteq_{\bowtie_G} E_3$ and $E_0 \sqsubseteq_{\bowtie_G} E_1 \sqsubseteq_{\bowtie_G} E_2 \sqsubseteq_{\bowtie_G} E_4$ still hold. However, E_3 and E_4 are no longer equivalent, and as a matter of fact, they become incomparable. Indeed, consider the target $F_1 = a$: we have $[\![E_3 \bowtie_G F_1]\!] = (true, 1)$ and $[\![E_4 \bowtie_G F_1]\!] = (true, 2)$, meaning that $E_4 \sqsubseteq_{\bowtie_G, F_1} E_3$. On the other hand, given the target $F_2 = a.a.a$, we have $[\![E_3 \bowtie_G F_1]\!] = (true, 3)$ and $[\![E_4 \bowtie_G F_1]\!] = (true, 2)$, meaning that $E_3 \sqsubseteq_{\bowtie_G, F_2} E_4$, and therefore that E_3 and E_4 are incomparable.

The previous example illustrates that, in general, there might not be a strictly best strategy. In some cases, it might be possible to define an *optimal* strategy, which is best *in average*. Another possibility is to prioritize one dimension over another (depending on the order of the components in the lexicographic order itself). According to which dimension is prioritized, we are able to classify controllers into categories. For instance, we have a *secure controller*, when the controllers are ordered based on their security or an *economical controller* when the priority is given to the dimension of cost.

7   Discussion – Future Work

Our framework allows a system designer to consider security as yet another dimension to measure. Instead of a binary classification between sound/unsound controllers, we provide a finer-grained ordering, distinguishing between different degrees of soundness.

The valuation of processes is currently done on the best-case scenario. It is not difficult to focus instead on the worst-case scenario, thus following a rather traditional, pessimistic approach to security. In the presence of an inverse to addition in the considered semiring, the two kind of valuations could be mixed. As we saw, some controllers are incomparable over the set of all targets. To improve the situation, one can consider small subsets of possible targets (e.g., typical behaviours, or even single use-cases).

Adding non-deterministic choice to the controller itself always improves security. Clearly, this characteristic is mostly of theoretical importance, but it raises the interesting question whether, given some quantities, there exists a deterministic maximal controller or not. For instance, if we only monitor security, we can build an optimal deterministic controller for any safety property, as described in the literature [5]. However, adding a notion of cost can lead to two incomparable deterministic controllers, which are strictly worse than their non-deterministic composition.

Finally, our notion of a security policy is just a boolean predicate, that could be specified by e.g., automata or logics. Predicates, and formulas specifying them, could also be quantitative by themselves, e.g., employing logics with valuations in a semiring, e.g., [17, 18]. In this paper, we do not yet investigate this aspect of the framework; this is left as future work. In particular, we plan to use quantitative evaluation of security policies, specified by logic formulas, in order to extend previous work on automated verification and synthesis of (qualitative) controllers [19].

References

1. Bistarelli, S.: Semirings for Soft Constraint Solving and Programming. LNCS, vol. 2962. Springer, Heidelberg (2004)
2. Schneider, F.B.: Enforceable security policies. ACM TISSEC **3**(1), 30–50 (2000)
3. Martinelli, F., Matteucci, I.: Through modeling to synthesis of security automata. ENTCS **179**, 31–46 (2007)
4. Khoury, R., Tawbi, N.: Which security policies are enforceable by runtime monitors? a survey. Comput. Sci. Rev. **6**(1), 27–45 (2012)
5. Bauer, L., Ligatti, J., Walker, D.: Edit automata: enforcement mechanisms for run-time security policies. Int. J. Inf. Secur. **4**(1–2), 2–16 (2005)
6. Gay, R., Mantel, H., Sprick, B.: Service automata. In: Barthe, G., Datta, A., Etalle, S. (eds.) FAST 2011. LNCS, vol. 7140, pp. 148–163. Springer, Heidelberg (2012)
7. Buchholz, P., Kemper, P.: Quantifying the dynamic behavior of process algebras. In: de Luca, L., Gilmore, S. (eds.) PAPM-PROBMIV 2001. LNCS, vol. 2165, pp. 184–199. Springer, Heidelberg (2001)
8. Easwaran, A., Kannan, S., Lee, I.: Optimal control of software ensuring safety and functionality. Technical report MS-CIS-05-20, University of Pennsylvania (2005)
9. Martinelli, F., Morisset, C.: Quantitative access control with partially-observable markov decision processes. In: Proceedings of CODASPY '12, pp. 169–180. ACM (2012)
10. Bielova, N., Massacci, F.: Predictability of enforcement. In: Erlingsson, Ú., Wieringa, R., Zannone, N. (eds.) ESSoS 2011. LNCS, vol. 6542, pp. 73–86. Springer, Heidelberg (2011)
11. Khoury, R., Tawbi, N.: Corrective enforcement: a new paradigm of security policy enforcement by monitors. ACM Trans. Inf. Syst. Secur. **15**(2), 10:1–10:27 (2012)
12. Drábik, P., Martinelli, F., Morisset, C.: Cost-aware runtime enforcement of security policies. In: Jøsang, A., Samarati, P., Petrocchi, M. (eds.) STM 2012. LNCS, vol. 7783, pp. 1–16. Springer, Heidelberg (2013)
13. Martinelli, F., Matteucci, I., Morisset, C.: From qualitative to quantitative enforcement of security policy. In: Kotenko, I., Skormin, V. (eds.) MMM-ACNS 2012. LNCS, vol. 7531, pp. 22–35. Springer, Heidelberg (2012)
14. Drábik, P., Martinelli, F., Morisset, C.: A quantitative approach for inexact enforcement of security policies. In: Gollmann, D., Freiling, F.C. (eds.) ISC 2012. LNCS, vol. 7483, pp. 306–321. Springer, Heidelberg (2012)
15. Caravagna, G., Costa, G., Pardini, G.: Lazy security controllers. In: Jøsang, A., Samarati, P., Petrocchi, M. (eds.) STM 2012. LNCS, vol. 7783, pp. 33–48. Springer, Heidelberg (2013)
16. Basin, D., Jugé, V., Klaedtke, F., Zălinescu, E.: Enforceable security policies revisited. In: Degano, P., Guttman, J.D. (eds.) POST 2012. LNCS, vol. 7215, pp. 309–328. Springer, Heidelberg (2012)
17. Lluch-Lafuente, A., Montanari, U.: Quantitative mu-calculus and ctl defined over constraint semirings. TCS **346**(1), 135–160 (2005)
18. Ciancia, V., Ferrari, G.L.: Co-algebraic models for quantitative spatial logics. ENTCS **190**(3), 43–58 (2007)
19. Martinelli, F., Matteucci, I.: A framework for automatic generation of security controller. Softw. Test. Verif. Reliab. **22**(8), 563–582 (2012)

Access Control

Collusion Resistant Inference Control for Cadastral Databases

Firas Al Khalil[✉], Alban Gabillon, and Patrick Capolsini

Université de la Polynésie française, BP 6570, Faa'a Aéroport, French Polynesia
{firas.khalil,alban.gabillon,patrick.capolsini}@upf.pf

Abstract. In this paper we present a novel inference control technique, based on graphs, to control the number of accessible parcels in a cadastral database. Different levels of collusion resistance are introduced as part of the approach. The dynamic aspect of the cadastral application, caused by mutation operations, is handled. We propose a scheme for gradually resetting the inference graph allowing continuous access to the data.

Keywords: Security · Inference control · Database · Collusion

1 Introduction

In the context of collaboration with the French Polynesian computer science service, specifically with the GIS (Geographic Information System) department, we were expected to analyze their requirements in terms of security and propose solutions to secure access to their databases and applications.

In this work we study the cadastral application used to manage French Polynesian real estate: ownership management, land boundaries operations, and other legal processes. The application is accessed through a mapping interface by employees of the service (to deliver official statements about lands to the public upon personal request), geographers, civil law notaries, among other employees from different services. The service intends to make all cadastral information available to the public. Basically, the security policy shall be the following: (1) Users are permitted to see parcel boundaries. (2) Users are permitted to know the owner's name of any random parcel.

However, the security policy includes also the following two prohibitions restricting the scope of the second permission: Pr_1: Users are prohibited to know the complete list of owners in a confined geographic region; Pr_2: Users are prohibited to know the complete list of parcels owned by a single legal entity.

In other words, the owner's name of any random parcel is considered as an unclassified data whereas the complete list of owners in a confined geographic region and the complete list of parcels owned by a single legal entity are both considered as classified data.

In the online cadastral application, users can see region maps through a mapping interface showing parcel boundaries. Users can select any parcel to learn its owner's name. However, as a basic restriction mechanism to enforce

J.-L. Danger et al. (Eds.): FPS 2013, LNCS 8352, pp. 189–208, 2014.
DOI: 10.1007/978-3-319-05302-8_12, © Springer International Publishing Switzerland 2014

prohibitions Pr_1 and Pr_2, it is not possible to issue queries selecting multiple parcels filtered by the owner's name or by region. Users can only query parcels one by one.

The inference problem in databases occurs when sensitive information can be disclosed from non-sensitive data and meta-data [14]. In the context of our cadastral database, users can infer information regarded as sensitive (and therefore violate either Pr_1 or Pr_2) by repeatedly querying (either manually or by using a bot) non-sensitive data. Both Pr_1 and Pr_2 are similar to the phone book problem as presented by Lunt [16] where a user has the right to access some phone numbers but not the entire phone book; she classifies these problems as quantity-based aggregation problems.

In this paper, we propose a dynamic inference control approach based on user query history that evolves with the evolution of the database through time. We also provide different levels of collusion resistance over the complete database or a subset of the database. We show how to use the same approach (with minor modifications) to enforce both Pr_1 and Pr_2.

This paper is organized as follows: In Sect. 2 we present the legislative context behind the security policy. In particular we investigate the reasons motivating prohibitions Pr_1 and Pr_2. Section 3 introduces our approach for Pr_1, step by step, starting from the basic model and scheme, ending with collusion resistance. Afterwards, we discuss necessary modifications that should be introduced to the approach in order to enforce Pr_2 in Sect. 4. Section 5 provides solutions for operations specific to the cadastral application, and the general issue of resetting the scheme over time. Related work is presented in Sect. 6. Finally, we conclude this paper in Sect. 7.

2   Legislative Context

We investigated the state of online cadastral applications, and in this section we will give a couple of examples from different countries reflecting the legal point of view on the publication of parcel ownership information. Afterwards, we explain the French point of view on the subject and the case for French Polynesia motivating this work.

For instance, access to the Spanish [6] cadaster is provided through a mapping interface built with Google Maps . Parcel ownership information is considered sensitive and it is not available to the public. Land owners form a different level of users (more privileged than the public) and they are granted access to all information related to their own properties if they provide a valid X509 certificate associated with their national electronic ID Similarly, the Belgian cadaster is available online for the public where ownership information is considered sensitive, thus prohibited. Authenticated users, using their national electronic ID, can access land ownership through another website.

In Croatia, parcel ownership information is public. Users can access the online website where they can submit a query on any parcel and get a list of information related to the parcel, including land ownership. Queries are submitted by selecting the desired department, office and parcel ID or deed ID. Users are required to solve a CAPTCHA before query submission. Similarly, the state of Montana considers land ownership as public information and they provide the cadaster for online browsing through a mapping interface.

In France, the cadaster is available through a mapping interface, however no information is available to the public (except for land boundaries). This prohibition is due to the CNIL recommendation [1] (La Commission Nationale de l'Informatique et des Libertés, an independent administrative authority whose mission is to ensure that IT is at the service of citizens and does not undermine human identity, rights, private life or individual and public liberties) where it is stated "the diffusion of any identifying information (directly or indirectly) on interactive terminals or public websites entails the risk of using this information for other purposes, including commercial, without the concerned people's consent". The Cada [2] (La Commission d'accès aux documents administratifs, an independent administrative authority responsible for ensuring freedom of access to administrative documents) indicates that "punctual demands" of cadastral excerpts are allowed. Furthermore, cadastral excerpts may contain the name of land owners, but no other identifying information such as the national ID or the address. The frequency of demands and the number of parcels requested should be analyzed to insure that these demands do not infringe the principle of free communication of cadastral documents. However there is no clear definition of "punctual demands" and it is subject to various interpretations, therefore the Cada recommends a restrictive interpretation of the term.

French Polynesia is an overseas country of France, where the recommendations of the CNIL and Cada are applicable. Currently, the "punctuality" of demands issued by citizens is insured by employees of the French Polynesian real estate service when they are physically present at their offices. The work presented in this paper is a requirement of the French Polynesian computer science service expressing their interpretation of the recommendations of both CNIL and Cada in order to provide the same service offered by the real estate service through the internet: a user should have access to the ownership information of any parcel, at random, but s/he is not allowed to exploit the service for commercial (or social,...) ends. This interpretation is the foundation of prohibitions Pr_1 and Pr_2 presented in Sect. 1.

3   Enforcing Pr_1

3.1   Definitions

In this section we show how to solve Pr_1 presented in Sect. 1. First, we need to introduce the following definition:

Definition 1. *[Parcel] The smallest geographical unit considered. A geo-referenced polygon, defining the surface and the boundaries of a piece of land owned by one or many legal entities.*

Let P be the set of parcels in the cadastral database and O the set of owners; o_p denotes the set of owners of a parcel p; $\delta(.,.)$ is a function that returns

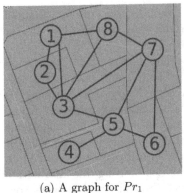

(a) A graph for Pr_1

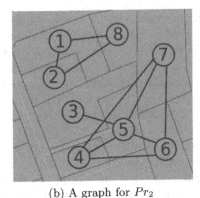

(b) A graph for Pr_2

Fig. 1. Different graphs for the same part of a cadastral database.

the minimal euclidean distance between 2 parcels. We create an inference graph $G(V, E)$: $G(V) = P$, while $G(E)$ is defined as follows: two parcels are neighbors in the inference graph if they touch each other, or if they are separated by a maximal distance τ. Formally $G(E) = \{(p, q) : p, q \in G(V), p \neq q, 0 \leq \delta(p, q) \leq \tau\}$ for a given $\tau \in \mathbb{Z}$. We could select $\tau = 0$, i.e. only parcels touching each other, but parcels which are separated by thin boundaries, like rivers or roads, require a value of τ greater than 0 to be considered as neighbors. Figure 1a shows an inference graph for Pr_1 representing part of the cadastral database, where parcel 1 touches $\{2, 3, 8\}$, parcel 4 touches 5, parcel 7 touches $\{3, 5, 6, 8\}$, etc.

$G(V, E)$ is an undirected unlabeled graph. $N(.)$ and $dist(., .)$ denote the graph's neighborhood and distance functions respectively.

Definition 2. *[Zone] The zone of a parcel p, namely zone$_p$, is the network formed by p itself and all the neighbors $N(p)$ of p.*

Notice that every parcel belongs to its proper zone and to every zone formed by every neighboring parcel.

Section 3.2 introduces the basic model and scheme. Then we define collusion in Sect. 3.3, and we build upon the basic scheme to support different levels of collusion resistance in Sects. 3.4 and 3.5. We discuss the problem of inference from user's a priori knowledge in Sect. 3.6. And finally we investigate whether users can derive sensitive data from a denial of access in Sect. 3.7.

3.2   Model and Scheme

Pr_1 clearly states that "users are prohibited to know the complete list of owners in a confined geographic **region**". The definition of a region is problematic: what is the minimum and maximum number of parcels that could define a region? How can we define limits between two neighboring regions?

We opt to use the narrowest definition of a region, namely a zone as per Definition 2. Preventing users from knowing the complete list of owners in any

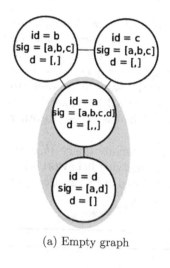

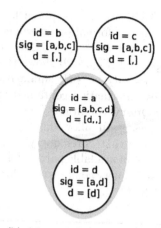

(a) Empty graph

(b) After a successful access to the vertex with $id = d$.

Fig. 2. A graph showing for every node its id, signature and the set of consumed tokens. Highlighted vertices form the zone of the vertex with $id = d$.

zone implies that they cannot learn the complete list of owners in any region of any size and location.

We consider that "isolated" parcels, i.e. parcels that do not have neighbors in the range τ, do not fall within the scope of Pr_1: access to these parcels is granted automatically.

Preventing the full disclosure of any zone is simply preventing the disclosure of the full network. For instance, assume that p has 5 neighbors. The maximal number of parcels that could be disclosed from the zone of p is 5 ($|zone_p| - 1$). We could be more restrictive by preventing the full disclosure of ($|zone_p| - \alpha$), where α is a positive integer, but we will consider $\alpha = 1$ for the sake of simplicity. At the heart of the zone is the parcel, therefore the vertex. Every vertex v holds 3 pieces of information: (1) **id$_v$**: a unique token. (2) **sig$_v$**: the signature of v (set of acceptable tokens). It is the set of **ids** of all parcels in $zone_v$. (3) **d$_v$[][]**: a map associating users (key) with the set of consumed tokens by each one of them (value), initially empty. The set of consumed tokens in d_v is restricted to values from sig_v.

Figure 2a shows an example of an inference graph: the highlighted area represents the zone of the vertex with $id = d$.

Querying a vertex v is allowed if the **PreQuery** condition (line 2) of Algorithm 1 is satisfied. In fact, access to vertex v is allowed if it has been queried (line 8). If it has not been queried before, access is granted if all vertices in $zone_v$ can accept the token id_v (line 10). If the **PreQuery** condition is satisfied, id_v is propagated to all parcels in $zone_v$ (line 4) and the set of owner o_v is returned (line 5).

To illustrate the approach, let us consider the graph of Fig. 2a. A user wants to access information contained in the vertex $id = d$. The **PreQuery** condition is satisfied: $id_d \notin d_d$, $id_d \notin d_a$, and $(|d_a| = 0) < (|sig_a| - 1 = 3)$. Therefore, access is granted. Figure 2b shows the state of the same graph after query execution: $(d_a += id_d) = \{d\}$; similarly, $(d_d += id_d) = \{d\}$. If the same user wants to access information contained in vertex a, s/he will be blocked for violating the **PreQuery** condition: $(|d_d| = 1) > (|sig_d| - 1 = 0)$, whereas access to other vertices is still allowed.

Note that, after querying parcel d, the user can maximally query $\{b, c, d\}$. The set of available parcels for any user depends on his querying behavior: other possible query combinations for the inference graph presented in Fig. 2a are $\{a, c\}$ and $\{a, b\}$.

Algorithm 1 for Pr_1

1: **function** QUERY(A parcel v, A user u)
2:     **if** PreQuery(v, u) **then**
3:         **for all** $z \in zone_v$ **do**
4:             $d_z[u] += id_v$
5:         **return** o_v
6:     **return** $\emptyset$
7: **function** PREQUERY(A parcel v, A user u)
8:     **if** $id_v \in d_v[u]$ **then return** true   ▷ Access granted
9:     **for all** $z \in zone_v$ **do**
10:         **if** $|d_z[u]| \geq |sig_z| - 1$ **then return** false   ▷ Access denied
11:     **return** true   ▷ Access granted

A zone is maximized if the PreQuery condition cannot be satisfied for that zone. A graph is saturated when the PreQuery condition cannot be satisfied by any unqueried zone. A graph is maximally saturated if the set of queried parcels is maximal (highest cardinality). It is possible to find multiple maximal combinations for a given graph. e.g. in Fig. 2a: – the zone of parcel d is maximized if d or a is queried; – the graph is saturated if $\{a, c\}$, $\{a, b\}$, or $\{b, c, d\}$ are queried; – the graph is maximally saturated if the set $\{b, c, d\}$ is queried.

Our model as presented in Sects. 3.1 and 3.2 is basically on how to prevent a user from violating prohibition Pr_1, by repeatedly querying the database. However, there are other potential inference channels that might help the user to violate Pr_1. First, users can collude to break Pr_1. This issue is discussed in Sects. 3.3, 3.4 and 3.5. Second, users can use some external knowledge they possess on the cadaster. This issue is discussed in Sect. 3.6. Finally, users can derive some information from a denial of access. This issue is discussed in Sect. 3.7.

3.3 Collusion Resistance

The Merriam-Webster online dictionary defines collusion as a "secret agreement or cooperation especially for an illegal or deceitful purpose". In our context, the illegal or deceitful purpose is to access a given parcel and all of its neighbors (thus the zone of that parcel). Therefore a collusion happens when x users secretly agree or cooperate to access a given zone.

Definition 3. *[Zone-level collusion] We say that x users collude to compromise a zone of a parcel p if, and only if, the union of consumed tokens by those x users cover the signature of p.*

However, devising a scheme preventing x users from colluding on a single zone will prevent all subsequent users, possibly legitimate, from accessing the parcel.

This level of collusion resistance does not differentiate between accidental and intentional collusions, therefore we refine our definition of collusion resistance in the upcoming sections.

3.4   (x, y)-Collusion Resistance

Algorithm 2 for Pr_1

1: **function** QUERY(A parcel v, A user u)
2:     new[][] = empty map   ▷ Same type as c
3:     **if** PreQuery(v, u, new) **then**
4:         **for all** $z \in zone_v$ **do**
5:             $d_z[u]$ += id_v
6:         AddNewCollusions(c,new)
7:         **return** o_v
8:     **return** $\emptyset$
9: **function** PREQUERY(A parcel v, A user u, A map $new[][]$)
10:     **if** $id_v \in d_v[u]$ **then return** true   ▷ Access granted
11:     **for all** $z \in zone_v$ **do**
12:         **if** $|d_z[u]| \geq |sig_z| - 1$ **then return** false   ▷ Access denied
13:     new = NewCollusions($zone_v$, u)   ▷ Returns a map of old and new potential collusions relative to user u on all parcels of $zone_v$
14:     **for all** $n \in new$ **do**
15:         **if** $|n.value| \geq y - 1$ **then**   ▷ n.value returns the set of signatures that the set of users in n.key are colluding on
16:             **return** false   ▷ Access denied
17:     **return** true   ▷ Access granted

Definition 4. *[MultiZone-level collusion] We say that x users collude to compromise y zones if there is y zone-level collusions between those x users on all y zones. A scheme is (x, y)-collusion resistant if it forbids x or less users to collude on y or more zones.*

For instance, a scheme is (4,7)-collusion resistant if it forbids 2, 3, or 4 users from colluding on 7 parcels or more; 5 or more colluding users will not be detected.

In order to implement (x, y)-collusion resistance in our scheme, we record zone-level collusions with a map c associating a combination of $2, 3, \ldots, x$ users to a combination of $1, 2, \ldots, y - 1$ signatures.

We **modify** Algorithm 1 to support (x, y)-collusion resistance and we get Algorithm 2. Querying a vertex v is allowed if the PreQuery condition (line 3) of Algorithm 2 is satisfied. In fact, access to vertex v is allowed if it has been queried (line 10), and it is denied if there is no vertex in $zone_v$ that can accept the token id_v (line 12). Access is also denied if querying the designated parcel causes additional collusions that, if added to the existing ones, can exceed the $y - 1$ threshold (lines 13 to 16). If the PreQuery condition is satisfied, id_v is propagated to all parcels of $zone_v$ (line 5), new collusions (if there is any) are registered (line 6), and the set of owner o_v is returned (line 7).

Note that if $x = 1$, $(1, y)$-collusion resistance will limit every user on y parcels in the whole graph. If $x > 1$ and $y = 1$, $(x, 1)$-collusion resistance will perform a zone-level collusion resistance.

3.5   (x, y, z)-Collusion Resistance

Definition 5. *[z-Zone] Is defined as a subset of the database where the distance* dist *between any two parcels belonging to the subset is lower than* z *(where* dist *is the graph distance function). Formally, a set* V' *of parcels belong to a z-Zone if, and only if,*

$$v_m, v_n \in V', v_m \neq v_n, 1 \leq dist(v_m, v_n) \leq z \tag{1}$$

The only difference between (x, y)-collusion resistance and (x, y, z)-collusion resistance is the following: **(x,y)**-collusion resistance considers that y collusions can be anywhere in the database, whereas (x, y, z)-collusion resistance considers that y collusions are all within the same subset of the database, namely in the same z-Zone subset.

Collusions should be tracked on geographical subsets, i.e. the number of allowed collusions between x users on a given z-Zone, where any 2 parcels belonging to that z-Zone are separated by $z - 1$ parcels at most, should be less than y.

Definition 6. *[z-Zone-level collusion] We say that* x *users collude to compromise* y *zones belonging to a z-Zone if there is* y *zone-level collusions between those* x *users on all* y *zones. A scheme is* **(x,y,z)**-*collusion resistant if it is* (x, y)-*collusion resistant in that z-Zone.*

The algorithm for (x, y, z)-collusion resistance is the same as the one presented in Algorithm 2, with the following single exception: the NewCollusions method will return a map of old collusions relative to user u falling in the z-Zone of v only, thus removing signatures of parcels that do not belong to the z-Zone from the value field of each entry, in addition to new potential collusions on all parcels of $zone_v$.

It is obvious that the probability of detecting false collusions with (x, y, z)-collusion resistance is lower than the probability of detecting false collusions with (x, y)-collusion resistance, which itself is lower than the probability of detecting false collusions with zone-level collusion resistance only.

Disclosing the values of x, y and z does not compromise the security of the approach. In fact, an attacker might be able to infer the values of x, y, and z by means of trial and error using a known reference set of parcels. For instance, a user might know the owners of parcels in his neighborhood, village, or belonging to a member of his family. By issuing queries on known parcels, this user can derive the values of x, y and z.

3.6   Inference from External Knowledge

Most of the people using the cadastral application do have some external knowledge. Very often, they know the owner's name of some parcels from their neighborhood or their village. Because of this external knowledge, users can break Pr_1 without being detected by the inference control mechanisms. Dealing with external knowledge is theoretically impossible since it is simply impossible to know what a given user knows. However, the security administrator can roughly estimate the average level of users' external knowledge. This estimation can help him to choose the proper α value discussed in Sect. 3.2. An $\alpha = 1$ means the users are assumed to have no external knowledge whereas an $\alpha > 1$ means the users are assumed to have some external knowledge.

3.7   Inference from Denial of Access

In the framework of multilevel database, Sandhu and Jajodia [19] underlined the fact that a denial of access provides the user with the information that the data s/he is trying to access is highly classified. In the context of our application, if a user is denied an access then s/he can conclude that s/he is about to break prohibition Pr_1.

If the user is trying to break Pr_1 then s/he actually does not learn much from the denial of access. From the parcels s/he has accessed before the denial of access, s/he can simply verify that s/he has queried at least one complete zone. If it is not the case, i.e. s/he has not queried a complete zone, then s/he can only deduce that other users have been querying the same region and that the system has detected a potential collusion attack.

4   Enforcing Pr_2

The basic idea for enforcing Pr_2 is to use the scheme we developed for Pr_1 in the previous section by only modifying the graph definition as follows:

We consider an ownership notion of neighborhood. Two parcels are considered neighbors in the inference graph if they belong to the same owner. In such a graph, vertices belonging to the same owner are all interconnected, forming a complete graph. Formally, $G(E) = \{(p,q) : p,q \in G(V), p \neq q, o_p \cap o_q \neq \emptyset\}$. For instance, Fig. 1b shows an inference graph for Pr_2 representing part of the cadastral database (the same part as in Fig. 1a), where parcels $\{1,2,8\}$ are owned by Joe, $\{4,5,6,7\}$ are owned by Elissa, and $\{3,5\}$ are owned by Lucy. Notice that parcel 5 has two owners, namely Elissa and Lucy.

It is clear that a zone, as presented in Definition 2, depends only on the inference graph: for Pr_1, the zone of a parcel $\mathbf{p}$ is $\mathbf{p}$ and the set of parcels touching, or located at a given distance from $\mathbf{p}$; for Pr_2, the zone of a parcel $\mathbf{p}$ is $\mathbf{p}$ and the set of parcels owned by the same legal entity.

However, applying the scheme developed for Pr_1, as is, on the resulting graph does not work for the following reasons: – Within the framework of Pr_2, a user with some external knowledge can deduce from a denial of access that s/he has found a land belonging to the target entity. This issue is discussed in Sect. 4.1; – The definition of z-Zone from Sect. 3.5 is a geographical one best suited for Pr_1, which is a geographical prohibition. A new definition for Pr_2, which is rather a social prohibition than geographical, is presented in Sect. 4.2;

Note that we consider that "isolated" parcels, i.e. a parcel belonging to a single owner who himself does not own other parcels, do not fall within the scope of Pr_2: access to these parcels is granted automatically.

4.1 Inference Channel from Denial of Access and External Knowledge

First of all, we should notice that in order to be successful, an attacker trying to break Pr_2 should already know the approximate location of all the target entity's parcels. Without this external knowledge, the attacker would need to randomly select parcels from the entire database which is of course infeasible.

Nonetheless, we consider it as a probable attack and we shall address it: let us assume that Bob already knows the approximate location of all Alice's parcels. We also assume that after several queries, Bob has identified several parcels belonging to Alice. If Bob is denied access to an additional parcel then he can reasonably deduce that this parcel belongs to Alice. Returning "access denied" can even be seen as worse than returning Alice's name since it informs Bob that he has found the last parcel in Alice's list of parcels.

One possible solution to prevent Bob from deducing that he has found the last parcel in Alice's parcels list is to increase the α value as discussed in Sect. 3.2. In that case, Bob would be denied access to Alice's parcels before finding the last parcel. However, there is no solution to prevent Bob from deducing from a denial of access that he has found a parcel belonging to Alice.

Another possible solution would be to return a cover story instead of denying access. A cover story is a lie introduced in the database in order to hide the existence of a sensitive data [7]. Cover stories have mainly been used in the framework of military multilevel databases [10]. In our cadastral application using a cover story would mean returning a fake owner for a given parcel. This solution is of course unacceptable for an official online public cadastral application where answers to query have a legal value and have therefore to be trusted.

We propose another solution: we deny access to the remaining parcel and all its geographical neighbors. In the same example of Alice and Bob, we deny access for the remaining parcel, namely $\mathbf{p}$, and all parcels of its geographical zone. This way, we increase the confusion for Bob, thus lowering his confidence in the inference by denial of access from $1/1$ (the case where only the remaining parcel is blocked) to $1/n$, where n is the number of geographical neighbors of $\mathbf{p}$. This confidence can even be lowered by increasing the number of blocked parcels by including 2nd degree neighbors, i.e. the geographical neighbors of neighbors of $\mathbf{p}$.

Algorithm 3 for Pr_2

1: **function** QUERY(A parcel v, A user u)   ▷ Same type as c
2:     **if** PreQuery(v, u) **then**
3:         **for all** $z \in zone_v$ **do**
4:             $d_z[u] \mathrel{+}= id_v$
5:         **if** $|d_v[u]| \geq |sig_v| - 1$ **then**
6:             r = GetParcelByID($sig_v - d_v[u]$)   ▷ Returns the remaining unqueried parcel
7:             **for all** $n \in neighbors_r$ **do**
8:                 $d_n[u] \mathrel{+}= di_r$ ▷ Blocking token of the ramining parcel assigned to all geographical neighbors
9:             **return** o_v
10:     **return** $\emptyset$
11: **function** PREQUERY(A parcel v, A user u)
12:     **if** $d_v[u]$ contains a di **then return** false   ▷ Access denied
13:     **if** $id_v \in d_v[u]$ **then return** true   ▷ Access granted
14:     **for all** $z \in zone_v$ **do**
15:         **if** $|d_z[u]| \geq |sig_z| - 1$ **then return** false   ▷ Access denied
16:     **return** true   ▷ Access granted

Considering this, we present a modified version of the model, of Algorithm 1 and of its collusion resistant version, namely Algorithm 2: the only difference is in the way we treat the last parcel in a zone (since we chose to limit access to $|zone_p| - 1$ parcels of any zone, otherwise it would be the last α parcels). (1) In the model, every vertex v should be associated with a "blocking token" or "blocking id", denoted di_v. This token acts as a boolean flag: its presence indicates a denial of access and can only exist in the set of geographical neighbors of v, namely $neighbors_v$. We opted to use this method instead of actually putting a boolean flag in the model for 1 reason: to keep the resetting scheme of Sect. 5.2 simpler. (2) The modification of Algorithm 1 is reflected in Algorithm 3: in the PreQuery condition, if a vertex contains a "blocking token" access is immediately denied (line 12). When the limit $|sig - 1|$ is reached, the geographical neighbors of the remaining parcel are filled with the "blocking token" of the remaining parcel (lines 5 to 8; the remaining parcel is already blocked, i.e if the user wants to query the remaining parcel s/he will fail for not satisfying the PreQuery condition). (3) The modification of Algorithm 2 is reflected in Algorithm 4: in the PreQuery condition, if a vertex contains a "blocking token" access is immediately denied (line 14). When the limit $|sig - 1|$ is reached, the geographical neighbors of the remaining parcel are filled with the "blocking token" of the remaining parcel (lines 6 to 9; the remaining parcel is already blocked for the same reason presented earlier in point 2.).

4.2   (x,y,z)-Collusion Resistance

Algorithm 4 for Pr_2

1: **function** QUERY(A parcel v, A user u)
2:     new[][] = empty map   ▷ Same type as c
3:     **if** PreQuery(v, u, new) **then**
4:         **for all** $z \in zone_v$ **do**
5:             $d_z[u]$ += id_v
6:         **if** $|d_v[u]| \geq |sig_v| - 1$ **then**
7:             r = GetParcelByID($sig_v - d_v[u]$)   ▷ Returns the remaining unqueried parcel
8:             **for all** $n \in neighbors_r$ **do**
9:                 $d_n[u]+ = di_r$ ▷ Blocking token of the ramining parcel assigned to all geographical neighbors
10:         AddNewCollusions(c,new)
11:         **return** o_v
12:     **return** $\emptyset$
13: **function** PREQUERY(A parcel v, A user u, A map $new[][]$)
14:     **if** $d_v[u]$ contains a di **then return** false   ▷ Access denied
15:     **if** $id_v \in d_v[u]$ **then return** true   ▷ Access granted
16:     **for all** $z \in zone_v$ **do**
17:         **if** $|d_z[u]| \geq |sig_z| - 1$ **then return** false   ▷ Access denied
18:     new = NewCollusions($zone_v$, u)   ▷ Returns a map of old and new potential collusions relative to user u on all parcels of $zone_v$
19:     **for all** $n \in new$ **do**
20:         **if** $|n.value| \geq y - 1$ **then**   ▷ n.value returns the set of signatures that the set of users in n.key are colluding on
21:             **return** false   ▷ Access denied
22:     **return** true   ▷ Access granted

For this collusion resistance level, we define a distance function $dist_{social}$ as follows:

$$dist_{social} : V^2 \rightarrow \mathbb{Z} \ . \tag{2}$$

$dist_{social}$ returns the smallest social distance between the owners of 2 parcels according to some social relationship (friend, friend of friend, father, grand-child, etc). This distance function is essential to the definition of a z-Zone in Pr_2: Definition 5 is substituted by Definition 7.

Definition 7. *[z-Zone] Is defined as a subset of the database where the distance $dist_{social}$ between any two parcels belonging to the subset is lower than z . Formally, a set V' of parcels belong to a z-Zone if, and only if,*

$$v_m, v_n \in V', v_m \neq v_n, 1 \leq dist_{social}(v_m, v_n) \leq z \tag{3}$$

In Pr_2 collusions should be tracked on social subsets, i.e. the number of allowed collusions between x users on a given z-Zone, where the owners of any 2 parcels belonging to that z-Zone are separated by z social relationships at most, should be less than y.

The algorithm for (x, y, z)-collusion resistance in Pr_2 is the same as the one presented in Algorithm 4, with the following single exception: the NewCollusions method will return a map of old collusions relative to user u falling in the z-Zone of v only, thus removing signatures of parcels that do not belong to the z-Zone from the value field of each entry, in addition to new potential collusions on all parcels of $zone_v$.

5 Life-Cycle

So far, we have considered a static database, where a graph is built from parcel data. Afterwards, the graph is initialized with tokens, access to the parcels is handled according to described schemes, with the desired collusion resistance level. But in fact, the cadastral application is highly dynamic, and our approach as presented in Sect. 3 falls short in addressing issues raised by the following: (1) Mutation operations (i.e. buy, sell, merge and split), discussed in Sect. 5.1, and (2) Resetting the scheme for continuous access, discussed in Sect. 5.2.

5.1 Mutations

Four cadastral operations (called mutations) are performed daily on the database: – Buy and Sell: a parcel's ownership is transferred from its original owner to a new person, affecting the topology of the graph in Pr_2 only; – Merge and Split: two or more parcels are merged (split) into a single parcel (multiple parcels), affecting the topology of the graph in Pr_1 and Pr_2.

For any operation, existing vertices (and edges, if needed) should be removed and replaced by new ones (with new ids): the ownership information is to be protected and the result of any mutation operations changes this information. Therefore, new vertices that are produced by mutation operations should be considered as new and unqueried. These operations affect the signature of designated parcel(s) and all neighbors, hence its (their) zone and zones of all neighbors.

We developed a passive strategy to remove all traces of old parcels and their access tokens that applies for both Pr_1 and Pr_2 (except for steps related to dis which renders them specific to Pr_2): (1) initially, the querying history of every new parcel is empty, i.e. d is empty for all users; (2) old ids are removed from old neighbors, i.e. removed from the signature sig and the query history d of neighbors of new parcels; old dis of old parcels are removed from the query history of their neighbors; (3) signatures of new parcels' neighbors are modified, i.e. the id of a new parcel is added to the signature of all its neighbors; (4) new parcels inherit access tokens from their neighbors if they were queried, i.e. d of new parcels contains the id of every queried neighbor; new parcels inherit blocking tokens issued by their neighbors; (5) finally, every signature containing an old id is removed from every entry in the collusion map c .

The details of these strategies are omitted due to space limitations. One would be tempted to define an active strategy where new parcels inherit the query state of their parents (parcels they are replacing). While it could be reasonable for buy/sell operations, merge and split operations turn out to be problematic. For instance, if a user queried 1 parcel out of $V' = \{v_1, v_2, v_3\}$ and V' is merged into a new parcel v_4, what should be the state of v_4? Is it fair to consider it as queried? If yes, zones of non-queried parcels from V' and their neighbors would be affected and may add fake collusions to the account of the user. Similarly, if v_4 is split into V', what should be the state of V'. Is it fair to consider all new parcels as queried? If yes, then fake collusions from V' and its neighbors could be added to the account of the user.

5.2   Gradually Resetting the Scheme

A simple analysis of the presented scheme shows that, given enough time, the inference graph becomes saturated, restricting existing users on a set of parcels defined by their own querying behavior. Access rights of new users are influenced by previous users' behavior.

To eliminate this issue, we propose a periodical soft resetting strategy. First of all, we add (to our model) a global timer, ticking every given unit of time. We also define a map e to manage the expiry date of access tokens and collusions. e associates a tuple (u, id) with a non-negative integer. Initially, all entries of e are set to 0.

Timer ticks are separated by a time-span t: the minimum time a user should wait before s/he is granted access to a full zone (given that none of its parcels was the subject of any mutation). On every timer tick, a tuple (u, id) holds one of the following values: **0** : The parcel has never been queried; **1** : The parcel has been queried, but its zone, and the zones of all of its neighbors has never been maximized; **> 1** : The parcel has been queried, and at least one of the zones that id belongs to, has been maximized by u.

If the value is 1, (i) queries executed by the user are legitimate (so far) if there is no collusion on id, or (ii) the user has been waiting for at least t unit of times to access the complete zone. If the value is >1, the user is a probable attacker. A value higher than 2 suggest a persistence from the user to gain full access to a zone of a parcel, therefore s/he should wait for longer time-spans before re-gaining access to the complete zone.

Algorithm 5 for Pr_1

1: **function** QUERY(A parcel v, A user u)
2:     new[][] = empty map   ▷ Same type as c
3:     **if** PreQuery(v, u, new) **then**
4:         **for all** $z \in zone_v$ **do**
5:             $d_z[u]$ += id_v
6:         AddNewCollusions(c,new)
7:         $e(u, id_v) = 1$
8:         **return** o_v
9:     **else**
10:         **if** new is not empty **then**
11:             $e(u, id_v)$ += 1
12:     **return** $\emptyset$
13: **procedure** ONTIMERTICK
14:     **for all** $entry \in e$ **do**
15:         **if** $entry.value = 1$ **then**
16:             v = GetParcelByID($entry.key[1]$)   ▷ entry.key[1] returns the second item in the key tuple, namely parcel id
17:             $d_v[entry.key[0]]$ -= id_v
18:             RemoveCollusions($entry.key[0]$, sig_v)   ▷ entry.key[0] returns the first item in the key tuple, namely the user
19:         **if** $entry.value > 0$ **then** entry.value -= 1

Algorithm 5 shows a modified version of the Query function from Algorithm 2 for Pr_1 adding support for the resetting scheme (the PreQuery function does not change therefore it is not included in this algorithm). If the PreQuery condition for user u on parcel v is met, $e(u, id_v)$ is set to one, marking it for removal after a single timer tick (line 7). If the PreQuery condition was not met because of a collusion attempt (line 10), the user is penalized by postponing the reset of this particular parcel another tick (line 11).

In addition to the modification of the Query function, Algorithm 5 introduces a procedure, OnTimerTick, that is scheduled for execution on every t units of time. This procedure routinely releases access tokens (line 17) and collusion entries (line 18) that already expired, then decreases the expiration date of access tokens (line 19).

Algorithm 6 for Pr_2

1: **function** QUERY(A parcel v, A user u)
2:    new[][] = empty map   ▷ Same type as c
3:    **if** PreQuery(v, u, new) **then**
4:        **for all** $z \in zone_v$ **do**
5:            $d_z[u]$ += id_v
6:        **if** $|d_v[u]| \geq |sig_v| - 1$ **then**
7:            r = GetParcelByID($sig_v - d_v[u]$)   ▷ Returns the remaining unqueried
   parcel
8:            **for all** $n \in neighbors_r$ **do**
9:                $d_n[u] += di_r$
10:            $e(u, di_r) = 1$
11:            AddNewCollusions(c,new)
12:            $e(u, id_v) = 1$
13:            **return** o_v
14:    **else**
15:        **if** $d_v[u]$ contains a di **then**
16:            $blocking$ = GetAllDis($d_v[u]$)
17:            **for all** $b \in blocking$ **do**
18:                $e(u, b)$ += 1
19:        **if** new is not empty **then**
20:            $e(u, id_v)$ += 1
21:    **return** $\emptyset$
22: **procedure** ONTIMERTICK
23:    **for all** $entry \in e$ **do**
24:        **if** $entry.value = 1$ **then**
25:            v = GetParcelByIDorDI($entry.key[1]$)
26:            **if** $d_v[entry.key[0]]$ is an id **then**
27:                $d_v[entry.key[0]]$ $-=$ id_v
28:            **else**
29:                $d_v[entry.key[0]]$ $-=$ di_v
30:            RemoveCollusions($entry.key[0]$, sig_v)
31:        **if** $entry.value > 0$ **then** $entry.value$ $-=$ 1

For Pr_2, 3 additional modifications should be applied: (1) the map e should accept **ids** and **dis** (introduced in Sect. 4.1). (2) Algorithm 5 is modified and this modification is reflected in Algorithm 6. When the limit $|sig - 1|$ is reached, all geographical neighbors of the remaining parcel are filled with the "blocking token" of the remaining parcel (lines 6 to 9; the remaining parcel is already blocked, i.e if the user wants to query the remaining parcel s/he will fail for not satisfying the PreQuery condition), where they are tracked for removal according to the resetting scheme (line 10). If the PreQuery condition was not met because the user is blocked by one or many blocking tokens (line 15), the user is penalized by postponing the reset of already blocked parcels to another tick (lines 16 to 18). If it was not met because of a collusion attempt (line 19), the user is penalized by postponing the reset of this particular parcel to another tick (line 20). (3)

OnTimerTick, that is scheduled for execution on every t unit of times. This procedure releases routinely access tokens (line 27) and collusion entries (line 30) that already expired, then decreases the expiration date of access tokens (line 31).

The choice of t is very important: a small value renders the complete inference control, proposed in this paper, useless; a high value renders the resetting scheme, described in this section, useless too. The value should take into consideration the "normal" behavior of a user when accessing zones, derived from a study of user access patterns on the cadastral database.

6   Related Work

The problem of inference and inference control has been heavily studied in the literature [12]. In the domain of relational databases [14,27], Delugach and Hinke [9] developed a system that takes the database schema and a knowledge source as input, then informs database administrators about potential inference channels. Their approach is based on conceptual graphs for knowledge representation. Cuppens and Gabillon [7,8] proposed a method based on coverstories (lies) for closing the inference channels caused by the integrity constraints of a multilevel database. Chen and Chu [5] created a semantic inference model based on data, schema and semantic information which initiated a semantic inference graph to detect inferences while executing queries. Tolas, Farkas, and Eastman [24] extended their previous work [13] on inference control in the presence of database updates, to guarantee confidentiality and maximize availability; a problem that we tackle in Sect. 5.1. Katos, Vrakas, and Katsaros [15] proposed an approach to reduce inference control to access control, where they consider the probabilistic correlation between attributes in the inference channel. They consider inference control in stochastic channels, while we consider them in deterministic channels.

Concerning data publishing, Yang and Li [26,28] worked on the inference problem in XML documents, showing how users can use common knowledge in conjunction with partially published documents to infer sensitive data. Staddon, Golle and Zimmy [21] showed how data from partial documents, when used with a source of knowledge like the web, can be used to infer hidden information.

Inference is also an issue in micro-data *publishing* (privacy preserving data publishing, or PPDP), where Sweeney [22] shows that 87 % of the population in the U.S. had reported characteristics that likely made them unique based only on 3 quasi-identifiers {5-digit ZIP, gender, date of birth}. Therefore removing directly identifying attributes (e.g. name or SSN) from the micro-data before publishing is not enough. Techniques such as $k-anonymity$ [23], $l-diversity$ [17] and *anatomy* [25] were developed to prevent these types of inference, but they target a problem different from ours: these techniques look for the disassociation of data owners and their data, while we want to publish this association as long as it does not violate the given constraints (Pr_1 or Pr_2).

While PPDP focuses on anonymizing datasets before publishing them for later statistical use (by means of generalization, suppression, etc.), privacy preserving data *mining* (or PPDM) does not transform original data before publishing. In fact, in PPDM, data holders provide a querying interface for interested parties so that they can run mining queries on the original data. Data holders must ensure that the result of such queries do not violate the privacy of data subjects. The main technique used is ϵ-differential privacy [11], that shares a lot of similarities with our approach: limiting (and knowing beforehand) the types of queries permitted to be run on the original data and ensuring collusion resistance [18]. However, the problem that ϵ-differential privacy addresses is different from ours: the goal is to use data for statistical purposes, where personal identifying information is not accessible (like PPDP). In addition, ϵ-differential privacy is usually achieved by adding noise to the resulting queries (unacceptable for our problem).

Another close area of research is controlled query evaluation (CQE) [3,4]. In CQE, user's a priori knowledge is taken into account with the history of submitted queries in order to perform inference control. Refusal and lying are employed as means of restriction and perturbation respectively to protect the confidentiality of classified information. CQE cannot identify colluding users.

The closest approach to ours is the one presented by Staddon [20]. In her paper, Staddon presented a dynamic inference control scheme that does not depend on user query history. This implies fast processing time and ensures a crowd-control property: a strong collusion resistance property that not only prevents c collaborating users (where c is the degree of collusion-resistance) from issuing complementary queries to complete an inference channel. This property also guarantees that "if a large number of users have queried all but one of the objects in an inference channel, then no one will be able to query the remaining object regardless of the level of collusion resistance provided by the scheme". Initially, we tried to adopt this approach to our problem but we faced two issues unsolved in the original paper: (i) objects shared by different channels and (ii) resetting the scheme. Nonetheless, we managed to solve the case of channels sharing multiple objects, but resetting the scheme for continuous inference control turned out to be a major and nontrivial challenge. Furthermore, we failed to justify the crowd-control property that may be suitable in the case of Staddon, but undesirable in ours.

7   Conclusion

In this paper, we presented an approach for inference control in cadastral databases, based on user query history, with different levels of collusion resistance. We then discussed the effects of database updates specific to the cadastral application, namely buy/sell and merge/split operations, and how to deal with these operations in the overall scheme. A gradual re-initialization strategy to allow continuous access to the database is also proposed.

We do realize that achieving inference control efficiently, as proposed, requires an extensive analysis on the target database, and a fine tuning of all the parameters presented in this paper, i.e. x, y and z for (x, y, z)-collusion resistance, and the timespan t for gradual resetting. Tuning these parameters should be done according to the application's requirements: a trade-off between confidentiality of cadastral data and their availability.

This approach can be applied to other types of inference control (geographic or not), by simply modifying the definition of neighborhood (edges) from our definition, to an application-specific one. It is worth noting that we have developed a prototype to simulate inference graphs using eclipse RCP and its zest framework. Sources can be found on Bitbucket (https://bitbucket.org/fearus/rattack/). We are currently researching efficient methods to implement this approach on a real cadastral database. We are also preparing a user access pattern study for the gradual resetting scheme (see Sect. 5.2).

Acknowledgments. The authors wish to thank the following people for fruitful discussions on some legal aspects applying to the cadastral application and for providing them access to a sample cadastral database. – Tania Berthou, Directrice des Affaires Foncières de la Polynésie Française; – Bertrand Malet, Chef de la Division du Cadastre, Direction des Affaires Foncières; – Jean-Louis Garry, Directeur du Service Informatique de la Polynésie Française; – Emmanuel Bouniot, Chef de la Cellule Systèmes d'Informations Géographique du Service Informatique de la Polynésie Française.

References

1. Les guides de la cnil. les collectivités locales. http://www.cnil.fr/fileadmin/documents/Guides_pratiques/CNIL_Guide_CollLocales.pdf (2009)
2. Fiscalité locale et cadastre. http://www.cada.fr/fiscalite-locale-et-cadastre,6090.html. Accessed June 2013
3. Biskup, J., Bonatti, P.: Controlled query evaluation for known policies by combining lying and refusal. Ann. Math. Artif. Intell. **40**(1), 37–62 (2004)
4. Biskup, J., Tadros, C.: Inference-proof view update transactions with minimal refusals. In: Garcia-Alfaro, J., Navarro-Arribas, G., Cuppens-Boulahia, N., de Capitani di Vimercati, S. (eds.) DPM 2011 and SETOP 2011. LNCS, vol. 7122, pp. 104–121. Springer, Heidelberg (2012)
5. Chen, Y., Chu, W.: Protection of database security via collaborative inference detection. In: Chen, H., Yang, C.C. (eds.) Intelligence and Security Informatics, pp. 275–303. Springer, Heidelberg (2008)
6. Conejo, C., Velasco, A.: Cadastral web services in spain. http://www.ec-gis.org/Workshops/13ec-gis/presentations/4_sdi_implementaion_I_Conejo_1.pdf. Accessed June 2013
7. Cuppens, F., Gabillon, A.: Logical foundations of multilevel databases. Data Knowl. Eng. **29**(3), 259–291 (1999)
8. Cuppens, F., Gabillon, A.: Cover story management. Data Knowl. Eng. **37**(2), 177–201 (2001)
9. Delugach, H., Hinke, T.: Wizard: a database inference analysis and detection system. IEEE Trans. Knowl. Data Eng. **8**(1), 56–66 (1996)
10. Denning, D.E., Lunt, T.F., Schell, R.R., Shockley, W.R., Heckman, M.: The seaview security model. In: Proceedings of the 1988 IEEE Symposium on Security and Privacy, 1988, pp. 218–233. IEEE (1988)

11. Dwork, C.: Differential privacy: a survey of results. In: Agrawal, M., Du, D.-Z., Duan, Z., Li, A. (eds.) TAMC 2008. LNCS, vol. 4978, pp. 1–19. Springer, Heidelberg (2008)
12. Farkas, C., Jajodia, S.: The inference problem: a survey. ACM SIGKDD Explor. Newsl. 4(2), 6–11 (2002)
13. Farkas, C., Toland, T.S., Eastman, C.M.: The inference problem and updates in relational databases. In: Proceedings of the Fifteenth Annual Working Conference on Database and Application Security Das'01, pp. 181–194. Kluwer Academic Publishers, Norwell (2002)
14. Jajodia, S., Meadows, C.: Inference problems in multilevel secure database management systems. In: Abrams, M.D., Jajodia, S., Podell, H. (eds.) Information Security: An Integrated Collection of Essays, pp. 570–584. IEEE Computer Society Press, Los Alamitos (1995)
15. Katos, V., Vrakas, D., Katsaros, P.: A framework for access control with inference constraints. In: 2011 IEEE 35th Annual Computer Software and Applications Conference (COMPSAC), pp. 289–297. IEEE (2011)
16. Lunt, T.F.: Aggregation and inference: facts and fallacies. In: Proceedings of the 1989 IEEE Symposium on Security and Privacy, 1989, pp. 102–109. IEEE (1989)
17. Machanavajjhala, A., Kifer, D., Gehrke, J., Venkitasubramaniam, M.: l-diversity: privacy beyond k-anonymity. ACM Trans. Knowl. Discov. Data (TKDD) 1(1), 3 (2007)
18. McSherry, F., Talwar, K.: Mechanism design via differential privacy. In: 48th Annual IEEE Symposium on Foundations of Computer Science, 2007, FOCS'07, pp. 94–103. IEEE (2007)
19. Sandhu, R.S., Jajodia, S.: Polyinstantiation for cover stories. In: Deswarte, Y., Quisquater, J.-J., Eizenberg, G. (eds.) Computer Security - ESORICS 92. LNCS, vol. 648, pp. 305–328. Springer, Heidelberg (1992)
20. Staddon, J.: Dynamic inference control. In: Proceedings of the 8th ACM SIGMOD Workshop on Research Issues in Data Mining and Knowledge Discovery, pp. 94–100. ACM (2003)
21. Staddon, J., Golle, P., Zimny, B.: Web-based inference detection. In: Proceedings of 16th USENIX Security Symposium, pp. 71–86 (2007)
22. Sweeney, L.: Simple Demographics Often Identify People Uniquely. Health (San Francisco), pp. 1–34. Carnegie Mellon University, Pittsburgh (2000)
23. Sweeney, L.: k-anonymity: a model for protecting privacy. Int. J. Uncertain. Fuzziness Knowl.-Based Syst. 10(05), 557–570 (2002)
24. Toland, T., Farkas, C., Eastman, C.: The inference problem: maintaining maximal availability in the presence of database updates. Comput. Secur. 29(1), 88–103 (2010)
25. Xiao, X., Tao, Y.: Anatomy: simple and effective privacy preservation. In: Proceedings of the 32nd International Conference on Very Large Data Bases, pp. 139–150. VLDB Endowment (2006)
26. Yang, X., Li, C.: Secure xml publishing without information leakage in the presence of data inference. In: Proceedings of the Thirtieth International Conference on Very Large Data Bases, vol. 30, pp. 96–107. VLDB Endowment (2004)
27. Yip, R., Levitt, E.: Data level inference detection in database systems. In: Proceedings of the 11th IEEE Computer Security Foundations Workshop, 1998, pp. 179–189. IEEE (1998)
28. Yixiang, D., Tao, P., Minghua, J.: Secure multiple xml documents publishing without information leakage. In: International Conference on Convergence Information Technology, 2007, pp. 2114–2119. IEEE (2007)

Leveraging Ontologies upon a Holistic Privacy-Aware Access Control Model

Eugenia I. Papagiannakopoulou[1]([✉]), Maria N. Koukovini[1],
Georgios V. Lioudakis[1], Nikolaos Dellas[2], Joaquin Garcia-Alfaro[3],
Dimitra I. Kaklamani[1], Iakovos S. Venieris[1], Nora Cuppens-Boulahia[4],
and Frédéric Cuppens[4]

[1] School of Electrical and Computer Engineering,
National Technical University of Athens,
Heroon Polytechniou 9, 15773 Athens, Greece
epapag@icbnet.ntua.gr
[2] SingularLogic S.A., Al. Panagouli & Siniosoglou, 14234 Nea Ionia, Greece
[3] Institut Mines-Telecom, Telecom SudParis, CNRS Samovar UMR 5157,
Evry, France
[4] Institut Mines-Telecom, Telecom Bretagne, CS 17607,
35576 Cesson-Sévigné, France

Abstract. Access control is a crucial concept in both ICT security and privacy, providing for the protection of system resources and personal data. The increasing complexity of nowadays systems has led to a vast family of solutions fostering comprehensive access control models, with the ability to capture a variety of parameters and to incorporate them in the decision making process. However, existing approaches are characterised by limitations regarding expressiveness. We present an approach that aims at overcoming such limitations. It is fully based on ontologies and grounded on a rich in semantics information model. The result is a privacy-aware solution that takes into consideration a variety of aspects and parameters, including attributes, context, dependencies between actions and entities participating therein, as well as separation and binding of duty constraints.

1 Introduction

In order to ensure ICT security and privacy, a given security policy must be defined. A security policy can be seen as a series of rules stating what is permitted and what is not permitted in a system during normal operations. Indeed, the policy must contain the complete set of requirements for the system in terms of security and data protection. This way, access control is the core component of any ICT system in terms of security and privacy protection.

Beyond legacy access control models, such as the well-adopted Role-Based Access Control (RBAC) [36], most of the prominent recent approaches typically propose enhancements of existing security models, and incorporate different criteria to take dynamic decisions. In that respect, access control models have

J.-L. Danger et al. (Eds.): FPS 2013, LNCS 8352, pp. 209–226, 2014.
DOI: 10.1007/978-3-319-05302-8_13, © Springer International Publishing Switzerland 2014

incorporated concepts such as organisation [2], context [9], and attributes [42], among others, whereas, the consideration of features that are specific to privacy protection has resulted in the emergence of the field referred to as Privacy-Aware Access Control (cf. e.g., [3]). In this context, ontologies have also been proposed for the specification of complex access control policies.

This paper presents an access control approach that leverages the full potential of ontologies, in order to enable the specification of very expressive access control rules. The approach is grounded on an innovative access control model, developed in the frame of the FP7 ICT project DEMONS [11], and first presented in [29,30]. It aims at handling security and privacy requirements for distributed processes in a holistic and comprehensive manner. The proposed approach combines various features, including context, attributes, privacy-awareness, Separation and Binding of Duty [5], and a variety of dependencies, and has been successfully applied in the automatic privacy-aware verification and transformation of distributed workflows [23].

The rest of this paper is organised as follows. Section 2 surveys related work. Section 3 presents the Information and Policy models underlying our solution. Sections 4 and 5 present, respectively, the ontological implementation of such models. Section 6 describes an extension providing support for *offline* knowledge extraction. Finally, Sect. 7 concludes the paper.

2   Related Work

The advent of the Semantic Web and the technologies it brings, especially semantic ontologies, have provided access control with new potentials. Therefore, several approaches have leveraged Semantic Web technologies in various ways, seeking expressiveness, formal semantics and reasoning capabilities; as a starting point, the Web Ontology Language (OWL) [39] was used to develop policy languages for the Web, such as Rei and KAoS [41], as well as to provide interoperability while accessing heterogeneous databases, as in [26,28,38].

Since RBAC [36] constitutes the baseline for access control, various approaches targeting its ontological implementation have been proposed. In this context, ontologies are used to represent the main concepts of RBAC —Action, Subject, Object, Role, Permission— as well as role hierarchies and dynamic and static Separation of Duty (SoD) constraints. An important work in this field is presented in [15], where R*OWLBAC* is introduced, proposing two different approaches regarding role representation: the first maps roles to classes and subclasses to which individual subjects can belong, whereas the second represents roles as instances of the generic `Role` class. Similarly, the approach referred to as XACML+OWL [14] combines OWL with XACML [27], with a view to decouple the management of constraints and RBAC hierarchies from the specification and the enforcement of the actual XACML policies. On the other hand, approaches such as [8,18] combine RBAC with the Attribute Based Access control (ABAC) paradigm [42], in order to take into account attributes during the definition of policies and the access control decision.

Apart from XACML+OWL [14], several approaches have leveraged XACML together with ontologies, most of them targeting the expression limitations of the attribute-based paradigm. In this direction, the approach described in [32] proposes an ontology-based inference engine which extends XACML attribute management for simplifying the specification and maintenance of ABAC policies. The work presented in [20] addresses the expressiveness limitations of XACML regarding knowledge representation; it extends it in order to support ontology-based reasoning and rule-based inference, while maintaining the usability of its original features. Likewise, in [34] an XML filter is created for regulating the disclosure of information, according to both the XML document structure and the semantics of its contents; this is achieved by directly integrating a knowledge base, which contains a description of the domain, in an XACML engine.

An important aspect of access control is reflected by the concept of *context*, which generally refers to information describing a specific situation; context includes static and dynamic environmental characteristics, such as temporal, spatial and historical ones. In that respect, there have been proposed various extensions to well established models in order to include contextual constraints, such as the Extended RBAC Profile of XACML, presented in [1]. A prominent approach in this area constitutes the Temporal Semantic Based Access Control (TSBAC) model [33], which enhances the specification of user-defined authorisation rules by constraining time interval and temporal expressions over users' history of accesses, which are stored in a History Base. OrBAC [2,9,31] is rather the most mature approach in this area; it is the first to express all different types of context within a unique homogeneous framework. In particular, OrBAC defines a *Context Ontology* comprised not only of temporal, spatial, and historical context but also of *user-declared* and *application dependent* context; the latter depends on the characteristics that join the subject, the action and the object and can be evaluated by querying the system database, whereas user-declared context allows for modelling contexts that are difficult to be described using environmental conditions.

The complex relations considered in Online Social Networks (OSNs) and the associated applications highlight the need for semantic organisation of the contained knowledge and for semantic access control mechanisms. In this context, the work presented in [12] leverages ontologies for representing relationships with the individuals and the community in order to determine the access restrictions to community resources. Carminati et al. provide in [6] a much richer OWL ontology for modelling various aspects of OSNs, while also proposing *authorisation*, *administration* and *filtering* policies that depend on trust relationships among various users. A more detailed approach is presented in [25], which proposes the Ontology-based Social Network Access Control (OSNAC) model, encompassing two ontologies; the Social Networking systems Ontology (SNO), capturing the information semantics of a social network, and the Access Control Ontology (ACO), which allows for expressing access control rules on the relations among concepts in the SNO.

However, all the approaches described above present limitations as far as *expressiveness* is concerned. In most cases, they focus on and capture a limited number of concepts, constraints and access parameters, missing the necessary expressiveness for the specification of complex provisions and access structures. For instance, only few of these models (e.g., [6,12,25,34]) are privacy-aware, yet they do not provide support for separation and binding of duty constraints, whereas presenting limited, if any, context-awareness. Moreover, the semantic taxonomies created within existing approaches are typically limited to very basic hierarchies (e.g., of roles), with no support for relations beyond *is-a* generalisations, or complex expressions and logical relations thereof. These limitations have been the motivation for the development of a new model, being *holistic* in terms of providing the means for incorporating a manifold of concepts and features, as described in the following sections.

3   Policy-Based Access Control Model

This Section outlines the policy-based access control model, on which the proposed ontological approach has been based. The starting point for this work has been the data protection legislation and related policy-oriented best practice guidelines, which provide, and often codify, the fundamental principles surrounding the provision of privacy-aware services. These typically concern lawfulness of data collection and processing, purpose specification and binding, necessity, adequacy, proportionality and quality of the data processed, minimal use of personal information, application of security measures, special provisions regarding retention and protection of information, enforcement of data subjects rights, coordination with the competent authorities, etc. The elaboration of principles and requirements stemming from the legislation and fair information practices have been the subject of various studies and extensive research (e.g., [16,17,24,37]). Rethought from the point of view of access control, the corresponding principles converge to the following challenges:

Multi-aspect access rights definition: Given the inherent complexity of the notion of privacy and the underlying implications, the associated solutions should incorporate various criteria in access and usage control decisions, rather than just *which user* holding *which role* is performing *which action* on *which object*.

Purpose: The "purpose principle" is essential for privacy awareness, being a core part of data collection and processing lawfulness [13]; a privacy-aware access control framework should provide for purpose specification and binding.

Privacy-aware information flow: Beyond controlling access and usage, a privacy-aware access control model should provide for the specification of acceptable patterns as far as the flow of data is concerned; this implies, for instance, the prevention of some data to be communicated from a system to another, whereas the latter may be *per se* allowed to receive the same data by a third system.

Unlinkability: Along the same line, a privacy-aware access control model should provide support for preventing linkability. Whereas privacy-aware information flow refers to "direct" passing of data among systems, processes or people, the need for unlinkability reflects a generalization towards mutually exclusive availability or processing of data, either explicitly or implicitly.

Separation and Binding of Duty (SoD/BoD): Similarly, SoD and BoD constraints should be possible to be specified and enforced, since they hold an important position among authorization requirements [21], serving, among others, conflicts avoidance and unlinkability.

Complementary actions: In several cases, access to the data should be accompanied by certain actions that should follow the collection and/or processing of information. These are often referred to in the literature as "privacy obligations" ([7,19]) and may concern, for instance, the application of immediate protection measures, the interaction with the data subjects (e.g., in terms of information or request for consent), and the enforcement of data retention provisions.

Context-awareness: It has become apparent that effective security and privacy policies largely depend on contextual parameters ([9,22]). Therefore, a privacy-aware access control framework should incorporate the corresponding aspects, in terms of restrictions over contextual parameters and events, and be enabled to impose different access rights according to the applicable constraints.

Semantics: Vertical to all the above is the need for precise semantics of the underlying concepts; data, actors, actions, context, purposes, among others, should be semantically defined, fostering transparency, accountability and effectiveness in terms of privacy.

The policy-based access control model presented here has been specified according to and achieves to address all the highlighted requirements for privacy awareness in access control.

3.1   Information Model

The day-to-day operation of an organisation involves a variety of entities, like machines, users and data[1]. We consider two representation levels; the *concrete level* refers to well-specified entities, e.g., named humans, while the *abstract level* enables referring to entities by using abstractions, especially their semantic type and attributes. The main concepts considered by the model are presented in Table 1.

At a concrete level, the set of *Users* (U) represents human entities, while this of *Organisations* (Org) describes internal divisions (e.g., departments) or external parties (e.g., sub-contractors). The various machinery comprise the *Machines* (M) set, providing hosting to *Operation Containers* (OpC) that offer *Operation Instances* (OpI). Operation Instances correspond to actual implementations of functionalities, while Operation Containers bundle collections of Operation Instances provided by the same functional unit[2]. Finally, information comprises the set of *Data* (D).

---

[1] Naturally, the information model may vary depending on the application domain; still, several concepts (e.g., organisational roles, operations, data types, etc.) are pervasive and are the focus of the following.

[2] In Web Services terms, Operation Containers correspond to a service *interface*, whereas Operation Instances represent the associated *operations* [40].

All above elements constitute instantiations of their semantic equivalents described at the abstract level. Users are assigned with *Roles* (*R*), Operation Instances provide implementations of *Operations* (*Op*), while data, organisations, machines and operation containers have *types*, reflecting the semantic class they fall under; thus, sets of *Data Types* (*DT*), *Organisation Types* (*OrgT*), *Machine Types* (*MT*) and *Operation Container Types* (*OpCT*) are defined. The semantic model also includes *Context Types* (*ConT*), enabling the definition of contextual parameters, *Attributes* (*Att*), leveraged for describing properties and characteristics of other elements, and *Purposes* (*Pu*) justifying access requests.

All concepts shown in Table 1 comprise graphs of elements characterised by relations; the latter are implemented by predicates defining AND- and OR- hierarchies and enable the inheritance of attributes and rules, as well as the specification of dependencies. For instance, and with respect to the DT graph, three partial order relations are defined: $isA(dt_i, dt_j)$, $lessDetailedThan(dt_i, dt_j)$ and $isPartOf(dt_i, dt_j)$, where $dt_i, dt_j \in DT$, reflecting the particularisation of a concept, the detail level and the inclusion of some data types to another, respectively. Moreover, the model specifies the necessary predicates in order to link concepts from different graphs; for example, the predicate $mayActForPurposes(r, \langle pu \rangle^k)$, where $r \in R$, $\langle pu \rangle^k \subseteq \mathcal{P}(Pu)$, indicates the legitimate purposes $\langle pu \rangle^k$ for which the users assigned with the role r may act.

Table 1. Concepts of the information model

Abstract level	Concrete level	Description	Act	Res
Data Types (*DT*)	Data (*D*)	Data being collected and/or processed, organised according to their semantic types		✓
Roles (*R*)	Users (*U*)	Human users assigned with roles reflecting their responsibilities inside an organisation	✓	✓
Operations (*Op*)	Operation Instances (*OpI*)	Operations reflect all actions that can take place in the context of the system's operation	✓	✓
Operation Container Types (*OpCT*)	Operation Containers (*OpC*)	Components or other functional structures that typically offer a set of operations together	✓	✓
Machine Types (*MT*)	Machines (*M*)	Hardware components hosting operation containers		✓
Organisation Types (*OrgT*)	Organisations (*Org*)	The various domains within which actions are performed		
Context Types (*ConT*)	Context values	Real-time parameters and events		
Purposes (*Pu*)	(No concrete representation)	Purposes for which access to resources is requested		
Attributes (*Att*)	Attribute values	Characteristics further describing members of the other sets		

3.2   Actions

The entities of the Information Model participate in the definition of *Actions* (*Act*), that are the main components of access control rules. An *action* refers to the situation where an *actor* performs an *operation* on a *resource*. Different types of entities may play the role of actors and resources, thus be members of the corresponding *Actors* (*A*) and *Resources* (*Res*) sets, as indicated in Table 1. An action is defined as follows.

Definition 1. An *action* $act_i \in Act$ is a tuple $\langle a_i, op_i, res_i, org \rangle$, such that: $act_i \in A$ is an actor; $op_i \in Op$ is an operation; $res_i \in Res$ is a resource; and *org* $\in Org$ is the organisation within which an action takes place.

An action can be either *atomic* or *composite*, depending on whether the associated operation can be decomposed to more elementary operations or not, following the hierarchical relations in *Op*. Actions are also categorised to *abstract*, *concrete* and *semi-abstract*, depending on whether actors and resources are defined at abstract, concrete or mixed level.

Finally, it should be stressed that the elements of an action can be specified as *enhanced entities* that include, apart from the entity's semantic type, expressions over its attributes and/or sub-concepts, thus refining the concept definition, towards specifying attribute-based constraints and access control rules.

3.3   Access Control Rules

Access control rules are used for defining *permissions*, *prohibitions* and *obligations* over actions and, since actions can be abstract, concrete or semi-abstract, rules are also specified at these three levels. They are defined as follows.

Definition 2. An *access control rule* is a structure:

$$\left. \begin{array}{l} Permission \\ Prohibition \\ Obligation \end{array} \right\} (pu, act, preAct, cont, postAct)$$

where $act \in Act$ is the action that the rule applies to; $pu \in Pu$ is the purpose for which *act* is permitted/prohibited/obliged to be executed; $cont \in \mathcal{P}(ConT)$ is a structure of contextual parameters; $preAct \in Act$ is a structure of actions that should have preceded; $postAct \in Act$ refers to the action(s) that must be executed following the rule enforcement.

An important observation here is that the concept of organisation is not involved in the rules' body, but instead it is specified for each action; although a rule concerns the execution of an action within an organisation, pre- and post-actions may take place within other organisations.

Apart from single actions, pre- and post- actions may also refer to structures of actions. Thus, they may consist of actions interrelated by means of logical

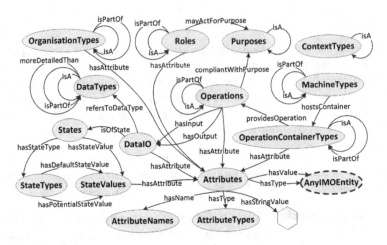

Fig. 1. Information Model Ontology (IMO).

operators ∧ and ∨, including negation, i.e., ¬*preAct*, ¬*postAct*. The term *Skeleton* is used to denote structures of actions following various sequence patterns. In addition, pre-/post-actions may be characterised by *sequence constraints*, putting constraints regarding *when* they are executed with respect to the action that the rule applies to.

4   Information Model Ontology

Figure 1 provides an overview of the Information Model Ontology (IMO). As shown, all abstract concepts described in Sect. 3.1 and summarised in Table 1 comprise classes, characterised by intra- and inter-class relations that are implemented as OWL object properties. The main intra-class properties are isA, isPartOf and moreDetailedThan that, along with their inverses[3], essentially comprise AND- and OR- hierarchies, enabling inheritance, as well as dependencies specification. Inter-class relations describe associations between concepts of different classes, indicating, for instance, the roles that may act for a purpose (mayActForPurpose), or the attributes characterising a concept (hasAttribute).

Individuals of the Attributes class are associated with an identifier (AttributeNames), a type, that can be a usual type (e.g., "Integer") or an IMO entity, and optionally a value, which can be an ontological element, or an arbitrary string, declared using the hasValue and hasStringValue properties, respectively. A valued attribute is considered *immutable*, as opposed to *mutable* attributes, the values of which are free to be determined during execution. Finally, instances of the DataIO class map an operation with its inputs and outputs, indicating the

---

[3] Inverse properties are explicitly defined for all object properties in the ontology, in order to ease navigation from one ontological element to another.

attributes characterising each input/output relation, as well as the associated States, referring to different states of information, such as "anonymised" vs. "identifiable". States are very important for applying access control at large scale, in the context of workflow verification [23].

5 Policy Model Ontology

Figure 2 provides an overview of the Policy Model Ontology (PMO), while its main aspects are described in what follows. Further, Fig. 3 illustrates the ontological representation of an example rule, inspired from guidelines for the health sector [10]: *"For the purpose of medical research and in the context of an ongoing R&D project, a statistician is allowed to perform statistical analysis on identifiable medical records of a patient, if the said patient has provided consent therefor; for accountability reasons, access should be immediately logged".*

5.1 Expressions and Logical Relations

In the direction of achieving rich expressiveness, two useful tools are *expressions* and *logical relations*. The latter allow specifying logical structures of concepts. For instance, a rule may specify different post-actions to be jointly executed (AND), or pre-actions that should precede inclusively (OR) or exclusively (XOR). A logical relation is defined as follows.

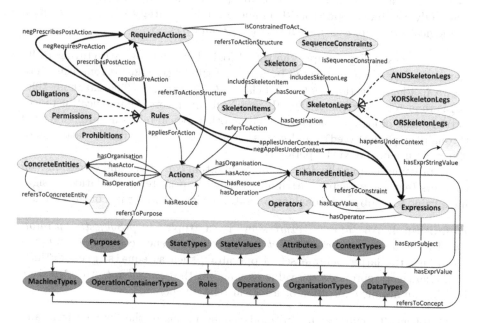

Fig. 2. Policy Model Ontology (PMO).

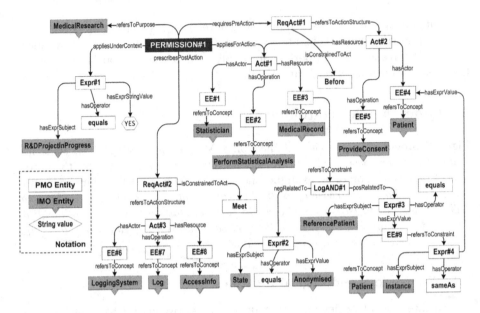

Fig. 3. Example of ontological access control rule.

Definition 3. Let $\mathcal{F}$ be the class of all functions on a set S, such that each $\phi_i(V) \in \mathcal{F}$ is a well-formed formula built up from the n-ary operators AND, OR and XOR, the unary operator NOT, and a set V of variables; a *logical relation* is a logical structure $\phi(S')$, such that $\phi \in \mathcal{F}$ and $S' \subseteq S$.

Thick lines in Fig. 2 imply the use of logical relations for structuring PMO elements; they are implemented by means of the LogicalRelations class (not shown in Fig. 2). Instances of its subclasses ANDRelations, ORRelations, XOR-Relations represent the AND, OR and XOR operators. Ontological instances participating in logical relations, including other logical relations, are referenced through the posRelatedTo and negRelatedTo properties, with the latter modelling the use of the NOT operator.

Expressions enable the definition of contextual conditions and constraints on concepts (e.g., on an actor's attributes); they comprise ternary relations assigning a value to a subject through an operator, or logical structures of such triples.

Definition 4. An *atomic expression* is a tuple ⟨*exprSubject*, *operator*, *exprValue*⟩, such that: *exprSubject* reflects the reference concept; *operator* ∈ *Operators*, the latter being a set of operators, such as equals, greaterThan, etc.; *exprValue* represents the value assigned to the *exprSubject*. An *expression* is either an atomic expression or a logical relation thereof.

Ontologically, expressions are modelled by means of the Expressions and LogicalRelations classes; instances of the former essentially model atomic expressions, whereas the latter provide for structuring composite expressions out of atomic ones. Based on Definition 4, appropriate properties are defined for `Expressions` individuals, indicating the subject (`hasExprSubject`), operator (`hasOperator`) and value (`hasExprValue`). Operators are ontologically defined as individuals of the `Operators` class, while the subject and object of an expression can be individuals of both PMO and IMO. However, an expression value can also be arbitrary, i.e., not an ontologically defined concept; in such case, the `hasExprStringValue` datatype property is used instead of `hasExprValue`, in order to assign a String value.

5.2 Actions and Entities

As stressed in Sect. 3, actions lie at the core of access control rules; not only rules are applied over actions, but they also appoint pre- and post-actions that should (or not) be executed before and after a rule's enforcement. Ontologically, actions are implemented as `Actions` class instances. Following Definition 1, $\langle a_i, op_i, res_i, org \rangle$ is reproduced by means of object properties indicating the actor (`hasActor`), operation (`hasOperation`), resource (`hasResource`) and organisation (`hasOrganisation`) of the action (Fig. 2).

However, the afore-described properties do not point directly to the reference concept, such as a role declared as the actor; instead, the proposed approach makes use of intermediate objects, being instances of the `EnhancedEntities` class. An enhanced entity not only indicates the reference abstract entity described in IMO, but it also defines constraints for this entity, thus enabling the enforcement of attribute-based access control. The corresponding object properties are `refersToConcept` and `refersToConstraint`, with the latter pointing at either an `Expressions` or a `LogicalRelations` instance, whereas the constraints are defined on the attributes of the entity, or its elements, i.e., individuals related (directly or indirectly) through the `isPartOf` object property.

As mentioned in Sect. 3.2, actions may contain elements defined at the concrete level; therefore, the class `ConcreteEntities` is defined for representing such entities, e.g., a specific user, instead of abstract concepts, by means of the `refersToConcreteEntity` datatype property.

Figure 3 illustrates three actions, corresponding to the statistical analysis (`Act#1`), the pre-action of consent provision (`Act#2`), and the post-action of logging (`Act#3`). These involve various enhanced entities, most of which are unconstrained, such as `EE#1` corresponding to the `Statistician` actor, or `EE#2` reflecting the statistical analysis operation. On the other hand, `EE#3` referring to the `MedicalRecord` resource has two constraints, described by expressions `Expr#2` and `Expr#3`, and associated through an AND logical relation (`LogAND#1`). Specifically, `Expr#2` implies identifiable data, through negation over `Anonymised` state, while `Expr#3` is an example of concepts' binding, further elaborated in Sect. 5.5.

Finally, it is important to note that actions themselves may comprise resources of other actions. This is the case with `Act#1`, comprising the resource of `Act#2`, in the sense that the patient must have provided consent for `Act#1` execution.

5.3 Ontological Access Control Rules

Access control rules are implemented in PMO by means of the `Rules` class (Fig. 2); as rules may describe *permissions, prohibitions,* or *obligations,* this is appropriately sub-classed by `Permissions`, `Prohibitions` and `Obligations`. Each rule is described by a `Rules` instance defining its elements, that is, the action it applies for, the pre-/post-actions, the contextual conditions and the underlying purpose.

In this context, `refersToPurpose` property maps a rule with a `Purposes` instance, whereas `appliesUnderContext` and its negative equivalent `negAppliesUnderContext` point at an `Expressions` or `LogicalRelations` (having `Expressions` as leaves) instance, declaring the contextual parameters under which the considered rule applies. For example, the permission of Fig. 3 applies for the purpose of `MedicalResearch`, given that an R&D project is in progress (`R&DProjectInProgress`).

The main action of the rule is an `Actions` instance, directly defined through the `appliesForAction` property. As for pre- and post-actions, they are also `Actions` instances; however, the rule is connected with `RequiredActions` instances that mediate between the rule and the actions, through the `requiresPreAction`, `prescribesPostAction`, and their negative variants. This choice is motivated by two introduced features: first, it enables the description of complex actions structures, referred to as *skeletons* (cf. Sect. 5.4); second, it allows putting constraints regarding *when* a pre-/post-action is executed with respect to the main action of the rule. In this context, the `isConstrainedToAct` property is leveraged for expressing temporal and sequence constraints, expressed by instances of the `SequenceConstraints` class. In the example, the use of `Meet` imposes a strict temporal constraint, prescribing that the end of the main action should coincide with the beginning of the post-action (`Act#3`), whereas `Before` implies a loose sequence constraint, meaning that the pre-action `Act#2` should be executed sometime before the main action.

5.4 Skeletons

In order to enable combination of actions so as to form complex structures thereof, the concept of *skeletons* is introduced. Implemented as instances of the `Skeletons` class, they provide the means for the definition of actions' structures, together with their sequential associations. Skeletons can comprise pre- and post- actions, being referred to by `RequiredActions` instances by means of the `refersToActionStructure` property.

The underlying actions are indicated by instances of the `SkeletonItems` class through the `refersToAction` property, whereas `SkeletonLegs` describe the interaction patterns among them. A skeleton leg is essentially an *edge* connecting two actions; it has an initial and a terminal skeleton item, appointed by `hasSource` and `hasDestination` properties, while it can be subject to contextual conditions, as well as to sequence constraints. The latter are implemented by means of `SequenceConstraints`, describing also whether the leg is *critical* or *non-critical* regarding the potential intervention of other actions between the initial and terminal skeleton items. Finally, for more flexibility in describing whether the implied transition will occur or not, three `SkeletonLegs` subclasses reflect, respectively, AND, OR and XOR associations among an action's outbound legs.

5.5 Separation and Binding of Duty

The high expressiveness of the proposed approach enables the specification of advanced Separation and Binding of Duty (SoD/BoD) constraints. Instead of relying on role-/user- centric constraints, it allows for SoD/BoD application to all elements comprising an action, i.e., the actor, the operation, the resource and the organisation. This is achieved by dependencies among the entities comprising the actions of a rule.

For instance, consider the case of the `MedicalRecord`, being the resource of statistical analysis (`Act#1`) in Fig. 3; it is assumed to contain the `ReferencePatient` field, i.e., `ReferencePatient`$\xrightarrow{\text{isPartOf}}$`MedicalRecord`, indicating the patient it refers to. Since `Patient` is a `Roles` instance, it has to be explicit that it is not *any* patient who has provided consent, but the one being the data subject of the `MedicalRecord`. In that respect, `EE#9` is constrained by `Expr#4`, specifying that the reference patient `instance` should be `sameAs` the patient implied by `EE#4`.

6 Offline Reasoning over Access Control Rules

The core Policy Model Ontology described so far is extended in order to support *Offline Reasoning*, i.e., proactive extraction of knowledge contained in the access control rules. Through the Offline Reasoning procedure, all the required knowledge becomes available already by the request time, thus reducing the number of queries to the ontology and offering performance gains. In other words, all the heavy processing tasks are performed offline and only when the PMO is updated, for instance, when new access control rules are added or existing ones are revoked.

For this purpose, and as illustrated in Fig. 4, two classes have been specified, namely `OfflineReasoningActions` and `OfflineRequiredActions`. The instances contained in the first class represent all the actions permitted to be executed in the context of the system's operation; in that respect, `OfflineReasoningActions` instances are derived by the specified `Permissions` instances. An offline reasoning action refers to the original action being the access action of the considered permission; it is valid under a purpose and some contextual conditions and requires or forbids the presence of other action structures.

Obviously, `OfflineRequiredActions` class reflects the required or forbidden pre- and post-actions complementing the considered permitted access action. As opposed to the `OfflineReasoningActions`, instances of this class are derived not

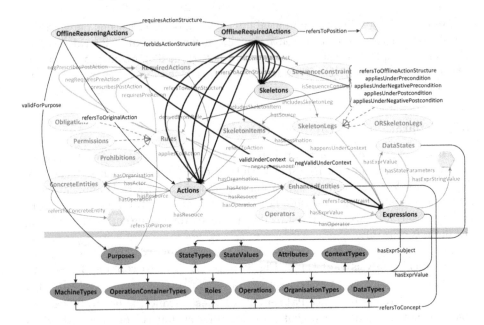

Fig. 4. Offline reasoning in the PMO.

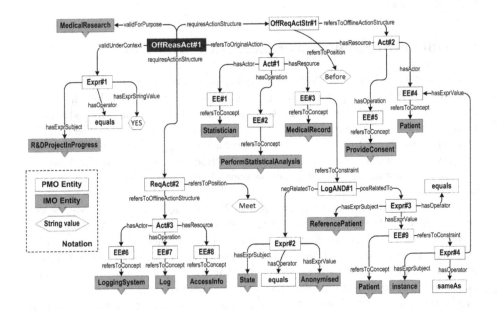

Fig. 5. Example of offline reasoning action.

only from `Permissions`, but from any kind of rules. Essentially, while constructing an offline reasoning action, for each original access action all the permissions, prohibitions and obligations by which this action is referred, either as the main action of the rule or as a pre-/post-action, are gathered. In the case of a permission, the specified pre- and post-actions are directly mapped to offline required actions, with the offline reasoning action referring to the main action of the rule, while in the case of prohibitions and obligations, we search for those where the considered offline reasoning action participates in the pre-action structure of the rule. Interrelations among pre- and post-actions of the found rules prescribe the need to also define pre- and post-conditions on the offline required actions.

Figure 5 shows the offline reasoning action derived from the permission of Fig. 3. A question about the validity of the action ⟨`Statistician`, `PerformStatisticalAnalysis`, `MedicalRecord`⟩ would return the valid purpose `MedicalResearch`, the valid context `Expr#1`, as well as the offline required action structures `OffReqActStr#1` and `OffReqActStr#2`.

7   Conclusion

This paper has presented an innovative policy-based privacy-aware access control model, focusing on its ontological implementation. Due to the high complexity and expressiveness of the base approach, we have chosen to implement it as an OWL ontology; this presents by itself various advantages, including formal and machine interpretable semantics, semantic consistency, inference of knowledge not explicitly contained in the ontologies, as well as direct integration with the DEMONS workflow management system, relying on comprehensive workflows also specified by means of ontologies. In fact, a success story behind the described model has been its use in the context of privacy-aware workflow verification and transformation.

The proposed framework relies on policies that are built on top of a rich information model, implemented as an ontology, while the associated rules are specified over *actions* that reflect operational activities and can be described in different abstraction levels. The major advantage of the approach is its *expressiveness*, combining a manifold of advanced features; these include attributed entities and constraints, context awareness, the specification of complex dependencies among actions and entities, as well as sophisticated SoD and BoD provisions.

Perspectives for future work mainly concern aspects pertaining to the enforcement of the underlying provisions. In particular, a research priority is to combine the proposed model with the Attribute-Based Encryption (ABE) paradigm [4,35], in order to make possible to evaluate access rights by cryptographic means. In this context, the mechanisms for deriving access policies implemented with ABE from the proposed model are under investigation, extending the scope of offline knowledge extraction.

Acknowledgment. The research of M.N. Koukovini is co-financed by the European Union (European Social Fund — ESF) and Greek national funds through the Operational Program "Education and Lifelong Learning" of the National Strategic Reference Framework (NSRF) — Research Funding Program: *Heracleitus II. Investing in knowledge society through the European Social Fund.* This research was also supported by the European Commission, in the frame of the FP7 DEMONS project.

References

1. Abi Haidar, D., Cuppens-Boulahia, N., Cuppens, F., Debar, H.: An extended RBAC profile of XACML. In: Proceedings of the 3rd ACM Workshop on Secure Web Services, SWS '06, pp. 13–22. ACM, New York (2006)
2. Abou-El-Kalam, A., Baida, R.E., Balbiani, P., Benferhat, S., Cuppens, F., Deswarte, Y., Miège, A., Saurel, C., Trouessin, G.: Organization based access control. In: 4th IEEE International Workshop on Policies for Distributed Systems and Networks (Policy'03), lake Come, Italy, June 2003, pp. 120–131 (2013)
3. Antonakopoulou, A., Lioudakis, G.V., Gogoulos, F., Kaklamani, D.I., Venieris, I.S.: Leveraging access control for privacy protection: a survey. In: Yee, G. (ed.) Privacy Protection Measures and Technologies in Business Organizations: Aspects and Standards, pp. 65–94. IGI Global, Hershey (2012)
4. Bethencourt, J., Sahai, A., Waters, B.: Ciphertext-policy attribute-based encryption. In: Proceedings of the 2007 IEEE Symposium on Security and Privacy, SP '07, pp. 321–324. IEEE Computer Society, Washington (2007)
5. Botha, R.A., Eloff, J.H.P.: Separation of duties for access control enforcement in workflow environments. IBM Syst. J. **40**(3), 666–682 (2001)
6. Carminati, B., Ferrari, E., Heatherly, R., Kantarcioglu, M., Thuraisingham, B.: A semantic web based framework for social network access control. In: SACMAT '09: Proceedings of the 14th ACM Symposium on Access Control Models and Technologies, pp. 177–186. ACM (2009)
7. Casassa Mont, M.: Dealing with privacy obligations: important aspects and technical approaches. In: Katsikas, S.K., López, J., Pernul, G. (eds.) TrustBus 2004. LNCS, vol. 3184, pp. 120–131. Springer, Heidelberg (2004)
8. Cruz, I.F., Gjomemo, R., Lin, B., Orsini, M.: A constraint and attribute based security framework for dynamic role assignment in collaborative environments. In: Bertino, E., Joshi, J.B.D. (eds.) CollaborateCom 2008. LNICST, vol. 10, pp. 322–339. Springer, Heidelberg (2009)
9. Cuppens, F., Cuppens-Boulahia, N.: Modeling contextual security policies. Int. J. Inf. Secur. **7**(4), 285–305 (2008)
10. Data Protection Commissioner of Ireland: data protection guidelines on Research in the Health Sector (2007)
11. DEMONS (DEcentralized, cooperative, and privacy-preserving MONitoring for trustworthinesS) EU FP7 project. http://fp7-demons.eu/
12. Elahi, N., Chowdhury, M., Noll, J.: Semantic access control in web based communities. In: ICCGI 2008: Proceedings of the Third International Multi-Conference on Computing in the Global Information Technology, pp. 131–136. IEEE Computer Society, August 2008
13. European Parliament and Council: Directive 95/46/EC of the European Parliament and of the Council of 24 october 1995 on the protection of individuals with regard to the processing of personal data and on the free movement of such data. Official J. Eur. Communities L **281**, 31–50, (1995)

14. Ferrini, R., Bertino, E.: Supporting rbac with xacml+owl. In: SACMAT '09: Proceedings of the 14th ACM Symposium on Access Control Models and Technologies, pp. 145–154. ACM (2009)
15. Finin, T.W., Joshi, A., Kagal, L., Niu, J., Sandhu, R.S., Winsborough, W.H., Thuraisingham, B.M.: R OWLBAC: representing role based access control in OWL. In: SACMAT '08: Proceedings of the 13th ACM Symposium on Access Control Models and Technologies. ACM (2008)
16. Gutwirth, S., De Hert, P., Poullet, Y.: Reinventing Data Protection?. Springer, Berlin (2009)
17. Gutwirth, S., De Hert, P., Poullet, Y.: European Data Protection: Coming of Age. Springer, Berlin (2013)
18. He, Z., Huang, K., Wu, L., Li, H., Lai, H.: Using semantic web techniques to implement access control for web service. In: Zhu, R., Zhang, Y., Liu, B., Liu, C. (eds.) ICICA 2010. CCIS, vol. 105, pp. 258–266. Springer, Heidelberg (2010)
19. Hilty, M., Basin, D., Pretschner, A.: On obligations. In: di Vimercati, S.C., Syverson, P.F., Gollmann, D. (eds.) ESORICS 2005. LNCS, vol. 3679, pp. 98–117. Springer, Heidelberg (2005)
20. Ching Hsu, I.: Extensible access control markup language integrated with semantic web technologies. Inf. Sci. **238**, 33–51 (2013)
21. Joshi, J.B.D., Shafiq, B., Ghafoor, A., Bertino, E.: Dependencies and separation of duty constraints in GTRBAC. In: SACMAT '03: Proceedings of the 8th ACM Symposium on Access Control Models and Technologies. ACM (2003)
22. Kapitsaki, G.M., Lioudakis, G.V., Kaklamani, D.I., Venieris, I.S.: Privacy protection in context-aware web services: challenges and solutions. In: Quan, Z., Sheng, M., Yu, J., Dustdar, S. (eds.) Enabling Context-Aware Web Services: Methods, Architectures, and Technologies, pp. 393–420. Chapman and Hall/CRC, London (2010)
23. Koukovini, M.N., Papagiannakopoulou, E.I., Lioudakis, G.V., Kaklamani, D.I., Venieris, I.S.: A workflow checking approach for inherent privacy awareness in network monitoring. In: Garcia-Alfaro, J., Navarro-Arribas, G., Cuppens-Boulahia, N., de Capitani di Vimercati, S. (eds.) DPM 2011 and SETOP 2011. LNCS, vol. 7122, pp. 295–302. Springer, Heidelberg (2012)
24. Lioudakis, G.V., Gaudino, F., Boschi, E., Bianchi, G., Kaklamani, D.I., Venieris, I.S.: Legislation-aware privacy protection in passive network monitoring. In: Portela, I.M., Cruz-Cunha, M.M. (eds.) Information Communication Technology Law, Protection and Access Rights: Global Approaches and Issues, Chap. 22, pp. 363–383. IGI Global, Hershey (2010)
25. Masoumzadeh, A., Joshi, J.: OSNAC: an ontology-based access control model for social networking systems. In: Proceedings of the 2010 IEEE Second International Conference on Social Computing, SOCIALCOM '10, pp. 751–759. IEEE Computer Society, Washington (2010)
26. Mitra, P., Pan, C.C., Liu, P., Atluri, V.: Privacy-preserving semantic interoperation and access control of heterogeneous databases. In: ASIACCS '06: Proceedings of the 2006 ACM Symposium on Information, Computer and Communications Security, pp. 66–77. ACM (2006)
27. Organization for the Advancement of Structured Information Standards (OASIS): eXtensible Access Control Markup Language (XACML) Version 2.0. http://docs.oasis-open.org/xacml/2.0/access_control-xacml-2.0-core-spec-os.pdf (February 2005), OASIS Standard

28. Pan, C.C., Mitra, P., Liu, P.: Semantic access control for information interoperation. In: SACMAT '06: Proceedings of the 11th ACM Symposium on Access Control Models and Technologies, pp. 237–246. ACM, New York (2006)

29. Papagiannakopoulou, E.I., Koukovini, M.N., Lioudakis, G.V., Garcia-Alfaro, J., Kaklamani, D.I., Venieris, I.S.: A contextual privacy-aware access control model for network monitoring workflows: work in progress. In: Garcia-Alfaro, J., Lafourcade, P. (eds.) FPS 2011. LNCS, vol. 6888, pp. 208–217. Springer, Heidelberg (2012)

30. Papagiannakopoulou, E.I., Koukovini, M.N., Lioudakis, G.V., Garcia-Alfaro, J., Kaklamani, D.I., Venieris, I.S., Cuppens, F., Cuppens-Boulahia, N.: A privacy-aware access control model for distributed network monitoring. Comput. Electr. Eng. 35(5), 1579–1597 (2012)

31. Preda, S., Cuppens, F., Cuppens-Boulahia, N., Garcia-Alfaro, J., Toutain, L.: Dynamic deployment of context-aware access control policies for constrained security devices. J. Syst. Softw. 84, 1144–1159 (2011)

32. Priebe, T., Dobmeier, W., Kamprath, N.: Supporting attribute-based access control with ontologies. In: ARES 2006: Proceedings of the the First International Conference on Availability, Reliability and Security, pp. 465–472. IEEE Computer Society (2006)

33. Ravari, A., Amini, M., Jalili, R., Jafarian, J.: A history based semantic aware access control model using logical time. In: 11th International Conference on Computer and Information Technology, ICCIT 2008, pp. 43–50, December 2008

34. Rota, A., Short, S., Rahaman, M.A.: Xml secure views using semantic access control. In: Proceedings of the 2010 EDBT/ICDT Workshops, EDBT '10, pp. 5:1–5:10. ACM, New York (2010)

35. Sahai, A., Waters, B.: Fuzzy identity-based encryption. In: Cramer, R. (ed.) EUROCRYPT 2005. LNCS, vol. 3494, pp. 457–473. Springer, Heidelberg (2005)

36. Sandhu, R., Coyne, E., Feinstein, H., Youman, C.: Role-based access control models. IEEE Comput. 29(2), 38–47 (1996)

37. Solove, D.J.: A brief history of information privacy law. In: Wolf, C. (ed.) Proskauer on Privacy: A Guide to Privacy and Data Security Law in the Information Age, Chap. 1, pp. 1–46. Practising Law Institute, New York (2006)

38. Sun, Y., Pan, P., Leung, H.-F., Shi, B.: Ontology based hybrid access control for automatic interoperation. In: Xiao, B., Yang, L.T., Ma, J., Muller-Schloer, C., Hua, Y. (eds.) ATC 2007. LNCS, vol. 4610, pp. 323–332. Springer, Heidelberg (2007)

39. The World Wide Web Consortium (W3C): OWL Web Ontology Language Overview, February 2004, W3C Recommendation

40. The World Wide Web Consortium (W3C): Web Services Description Language (WSDL) Version 2.0, June 2007, W3C Standard

41. Tonti, G., Bradshaw, J.M., Jeffers, R., Montanari, R., Suri, N., Uszok, A.: Semantic web languages for policy representation and reasoning: a comparison of KAoS, Rei, and Ponder. In: Fensel, D., Sycara, K., Mylopoulos, J. (eds.) ISWC 2003. LNCS, vol. 2870, pp. 419–437. Springer, Heidelberg (2003)

42. Yuan, E., Tong, J.: Attributed based access control (ABAC) for web services. In: ICWS '05: Proceedings of the IEEE International Conference on Web Services (2005)

Formal Modelling of Content-Based Protection and Release for Access Control in NATO Operations

Alessandro Armando[1,2], Sander Oudkerk[3], Silvio Ranise[2], and Konrad Wrona[4(✉)]

[1] DIBRIS, University of Genoa, Genova, Italy
[2] Security and Trust Unit, FBK-Irst, Trent, Italy
[3] Agent Sierra Consultancy Services, Amsterdam, The Netherlands
[4] NATO Communications and Information Agency, The Hague, The Netherlands
konrad.wrona@ncia.nato.int

Abstract. The successful operation of NATO missions requires the effective and secure sharing of information among coalition partners and external organizations, while avoiding the disclosure of sensitive information to unauthorized users. To resolve the conflict between confidentiality and availability in a dynamic coalition and network environment while being able to dynamically respond to changes in protection requirements and release conditions, NATO is developing a new information sharing infrastructure.

In this paper we present the Content-based Protection and Release (CPR) access control model for the NATO information sharing infrastructure. We define a declarative specification language for CPR based on the first-order logical framework underlying a class of efficient theorem-proving tools, called Satisfiability Modulo Theories solvers, and describe how they can support answering authorization queries. We illustrate the ideas in a use case scenario drawn from the NATO Passive Missile Defence system for simulating the consequences of intercepting missile attacks.

1 Introduction

The successful operation of NATO missions requires the effective and secure sharing of information not only among partners of the coalition, but also with external organizations such as the International Committee of the Red Cross (ICRC). To alleviate the conflict between security and availability, suitable access control mechanisms should be adopted. Information sharing in current NATO operations is hampered by the use of security markings as access control conditions [16]. There are three main problems related to such a usage. First, it is not possible to give access to selected parts of a document since security markings are attached to a document as a whole. Indeed, this is one of the main barriers to obtaining a good trade-off between confidentiality and availability. Second, declassification is complex and time-consuming as it requires

J.-L. Danger et al. (Eds.): FPS 2013, LNCS 8352, pp. 227–244, 2014.
DOI: 10.1007/978-3-319-05302-8_14, © NATO/OTAN 2014

manual modification of the markings associated to resources. Declassification is important for NATO: over-classification of data both hampers information sharing within NATO and results in unnecessary cost due to the enhanced protection measures required for classified data. Third, fuzziness is introduced by the (human) interpretation of the policy that determines security markings. This may lead to documents with similar content being labelled with different security markings by different authors.

To overcome these limitations, NATO is developing a new information sharing infrastructure [26] that bases decisions on the release of information contained in data containers (called *structured* resources) in which units of information (called *atomic* resources) are associated to pairs of the form (*element, content-metadata*). Selecting a suitable granularity of the atomic resources makes it possible to enable fine-grained access control. Being *content-based*, the new NATO infrastructure will require users to assign correct content-metadata to information instead of inferring the correct classification and release conditions based on numerous NATO directives and policies, e.g., [17–19]. This will reduce the possibility of errors being introduced as a result of subjective interpretation of security directives. Although CPR is mainly motivated by NATO use cases, its applicability is wider since large enterprises and organizations experience similar trade-off between availability and confidentiality of sensitive information.

In this paper we define the *Content-based Protection and Release* (*CPR*) model (Sect. 3) for specifying and enforcing access control policies that arise in complex organizations such as NATO [26]. Similarly to Attribute-Based Access Control (ABAC) [13,28], authorization decisions in CPR are based on the properties, called attributes, that may be associated to the entities (such as users and resources) involved in authorization decisions. For example, the identity, military rank and role are typical attributes of users whereas the pairs (*element, content-metadata*) can be modelled as attribute-value pairs associated to resources.

CPR refines ABAC in several respects; one of the most important is that access control policies are decomposed into those specifying *release* conditions and those for *protection* requirements (Sect. 3). Decomposition enables a more efficient implementation of the policies and procedures that are mandated by existing directives within NATO and other international/governmental organizations. These directives prescribe the fulfilment of complex combinations of release conditions and protection requirements. In fact, security officers who are experts in stating conditions on information release are not necessarily experts with respect to defining protection requirements. By separating the two types of policy, a division of responsibilities for the formulation of each policy becomes possible: the protection policy can be formulated by IT security experts with in-depth knowledge of the technical security environment, whereas the release policy can be formulated by experts in the workflow and operational structure of the organization. Another important refinement of CPR with respect to ABAC is the notion of *bridge predicates*, which express relationships among the values of collections of attributes associated to the same set of entities

(Sect. 3.2). For example, NATO security experts can design policies on a set A_1 of content-metadata derived from NATO directives and policies, such as [17–19], facilitating the homogeneous protection of resources with similar content. At the same time, we can think of using available linguistic classification techniques (e.g., [22]) to automatically extract a set A_2 of content-metadata related to the information stored in parts of the documents. It would then be possible to avoid the burden of associating the attribute-value pair in A_1 to the documents if it were possible to define a bridge predicate $B_{1,2}$ relating the values of the attributes in A_1 to those in A_2. Notice how this also allows for separation of concerns: security officers can first design policies focusing on security-relevant attributes and later consider the problem of relating these to the actual content of the documents.

Another contribution of this paper is the definition of the CPR Language, CPRL, which supports the formal specification of CPR policies and authorization queries (Sect. 4). We use the NATO Passive Missile Defence system scenario (described in Sect. 2) to illustrate the various constructs of CPRL.

The framework underlying CPRL is that of Satisfiability Modulo Theories (SMT) [6,24]. CPRL takes advantage of logic-based languages for authorization policies [11] and allows reduction of problems related to answering authorization queries (Sects. 4.1 and 4.2) to theorem-proving problems that can be efficiently tackled by state-of-the-art SMT solvers [6,12].

We also provide an extensive discussion of the motivation and design choices underlying CPR together with a comparison with existing work (Sect. 5).

2   The Passive Missile Defence Scenario

The goal of the NATO Passive Missile Defence (PMD) system is to minimize the effects of missile attacks; to this end, simulations are run in specific geographic areas, taking into account several parameters (e.g., the type of missile and weather conditions). The result of a simulation is a map of the predicted missile impact area, annotated with the consequences of the impact at several locations, hazard areas with risk analysis, the trajectories of the threatening and intercepting missiles, sub-munition locations and descriptions, etc.

Maps generated by the PMD system can be used in NATO missions for crisis-response planning, disaster preparation and rescue, and medical operations, including those that require the coordination of NATO coalition partners with civilian organizations such as the ICRC. The maps can contain different types of graphical objects ranging from threat operating areas to missile trajectories and public information about several zones in the area of the mission. Each graphical object has a different sensitivity level and—in order to realize effective information sharing—it is crucial to be able to disclose each object to only those users who are authorized to see them. For example, a NATO user may see both missile trajectories and public information about the zones of operation, while an ICRC member must not see the former (because he may be able to infer the location from which the intercepting missile was fired) yet should be allowed to access the public information. In addition to release conditions, protection requirements should be enforced

#	from	clr	cat	top
1.a	NATO	Sec	Descr	Toas
1.b	NATO	Sec	Descr	TItds
2	NATO	Res	MCOI	Smal
3	NATO	Pub	PI	Hal
4	*	Pub	PI	*

#	auth	strg	cat	top
1.a	NATO	Enhanced	Descr	Toas
1.b	NATO	Enhanced	Descr	TItds
2	NATO	Basic	MCOI	Smal
3	NATO	NoInfo	MCOI	Hal
4	*	NoInfo	PI	*

Fig. 1. PMD scenario: release conditions (left) and protection requirements (right)

to guarantee that accessed information can be handled with an adequate level of technical and operational support; e.g., data should be downloaded using an SSL protocol and stored in encrypted form on the laptop of the user. The attributes of terminals characterize the technical and operational features of how information is accessed, transmitted, and stored by users.

The user attributes are from and clr. The value of from is the name of the organization to which the user belongs, e.g., NATO or Red_Cross. The value of clr is the user clearance level, i.e. Public, Unclassified, Restricted, Confidential, or Secret. The terminal attributes are auth and strg. The value of auth is the name of the organization managing the terminal (e.g., NATO). The value of strg is the level of strength of the protection mechanisms for data offered by the terminal, i.e. NoInfo, Basic, or Enhanced. The resource attributes are cat and top. The value of cat is the content category associated to the graphical object, namely Descr (description of geographical zones in the area for which the simulation is conducted), MCOI (metrics related to the consequences of the impact between the threatening and intercepting missiles), or PI (public information related to the simulation). The value of top is the content topic, i.e. Toas (threat operating areas), TItds (threat and interceptor trajectory details), Hal (hazard area location), or Smal (sub-munition area location).

Figure 1 shows release conditions and protection requirements in tabular format. For example, the first two lines 1.a and 1.b of the table on the left can be read as follows: NATO employees whose clearance level is Secret can access resources whose content-metadata label cat is equal to Descr and top can be either Toas or TItds. The wild-card '*' stands for an arbitrary value of the attributes. For example, the last row (4) of the table on the right can be read as follows: a terminal managed by any authority with no information about the configuration can handle resources whose content-metadata label cat is PI. Implicit in the table on the left is the fact that a higher clearance level (with respect to the standard decreasing order, i.e. Sec, Conf, Res, Uncl, Pub) subsumes the one explicitly stated. For instance, in the table on the left, a user with clearance Sec may be able to get access to resources by lines 2, 3, and 4 in addition to 1.a and 1.b. Similarly in the table on the right, a higher configuration level (with respect to the decreasing ordering, i.e. Enhanced, Basic, NoInfo) subsumes the one mentioned in the table. For instance, a terminal with configuration level Enhanced may handle resources by lines 2, 3, and 4 in addition to 1.a and 1.b.

Access criteria are derived by 'joining' the two tables in Fig. 1 over the resource attributes `cat` and `top`. For instance, the 'combination' of the first two lines (identified by 1.a) in the two tables says that a `NATO` employee whose clearance level is `Secret` can access resources whose content-metadata label `cat` is equal to `Descr` and `top` is `Toas` via a terminal managed by `NATO` with strength level `Enhanced`.

3   The CPR Model

The most important feature of CPR is the sharp separation between release conditions and protection requirements. The motivation for such a decoupling is to facilitate the separation of policy management roles by reflecting the current procedures used within NATO, and other international and governmental organizations, that support the independent specification of release conditions and protection requirements. In fact, security officers who are experts in stating conditions on information release are not necessarily experts with respect to defining protection requirements To illustrate, consider the situation in which a user wants to access NATO classified information: (*i*) the user is required to connect to a network infrastructure used for processing NATO classified information and (*ii*) the user should prove that he has the right to access the information. For (*i*), the user should be equipped with a device satisfying a number of technical requirements about hardware and software configurations that are precisely defined in NATO technical directives and security settings documents (access to these documents is restricted; they can be obtained via national NATO contact points). Terminal attributes allow for the expression of both hardware and software configurations such as the hardware model, the type of encryption used to locally store data, and the type of connection used to retrieve resources (e.g., SSL) [26]. A protection policy states the requirements for which a terminal—in a given environment—can manipulate the information contained in a resource. For (*ii*), the user should be able to prove that his security-relevant attributes (such as identity, role, or military rank) entitle him to access information with certain attributes (such as identity, compartment, or sensitivity) when the attributes of the environment (such as time of day or some part of the system state) have certain values. A release policy specifies the conditions under which a user is granted access to a resource in a given environment.

3.1   The Core CPR model

The architecture of a Policy Decision Point (PDP) for the (core) CPR model is shown in Fig. 2. It is structured as two (sub-)decision points and a simple logic to combine them. One decision point computes the release decision by considering the user, resource, and environment properties, called *attributes*, together with the release policy. The other one takes the terminal, resource, and environment attributes together with the protection policy and returns the corresponding access decision. If both access decisions are 'grant', the PDP returns 'grant'; otherwise (i.e. if one of the two decisions is 'deny'), it returns 'deny'.

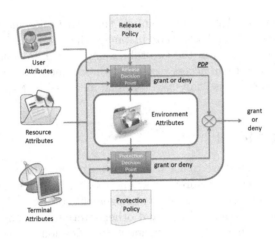

Fig. 2. The architecture of a PDP for the (core) CPR model

Basic entities and attributes. Let U, R, T, and En be infinite sets of users, resources, terminals, and environments, respectively.[1] (It is easy to extend the model to consider actions and their attributes. Here, for the sake of simplicity, we omit this aspect and assume that the only action occurring is reading/viewing information.) Let $\mathcal{E}$ be $\{U, R, T, En\}$, A a finite set of attributes, and $\mathcal{D}$ a collection of sets of attribute values called *domains*. An element of a set E in $\mathcal{E}$ is generically called an *entity*. A set E of entities is associated with a subset A_E of A, called the *attribute signature*. An attribute $a \in A$ ranges over the elements of a domain D_a in $\mathcal{D}$. An *attribute assignment* aa_e associated to an entity e in E is a function mapping the attribute a of the attribute signature A_E to an element of the domain D_a in $\mathcal{D}$.

Predicates on entity attributes. We model release conditions and protection requirements as predicates on the attribute values of the involved entities, i.e. as Boolean functions that map attribute values to true ('grant') or false ('deny'). Let $\mathbf{d}_E = d_{a_1}, \ldots, d_{a_m}$ be a tuple of domain values such that d_{a_i} is in the domain D_{a_i}, a_i is in the attribute signature $A_E = \{a_1, \ldots, a_m\}$, and let there exist an arbitrary (fixed) total order $\sqsubseteq$ over the set A of attributes such that $a_i \sqsubseteq a_{i+1}$ for $i = 1, \ldots, m-1$. A *predicate* $P_{E_1,\ldots,E_n}$ is a Boolean-valued function mapping tuples $(\mathbf{d}_{E_1}, \ldots, \mathbf{d}_{E_n})$ to either true or false. We write $aa_e(A_E)$ to denote the tuple $(aa_e(a_1), \ldots, aa_e(a_n))$ of domain values where aa_e is an attribute assignment, e is an entity in E, and $A_E = \{a_1, \ldots, a_n\}$ is an attribute signature. The attribute assignments $aa_{e_1}, \ldots, aa_{e_n}$ *satisfy* the predicate $P_{E_1,\ldots,E_n}$ if and only if (abbreviated as iff) $P_{E_1,\ldots,E_n}(aa_{e_1}(A_{E_1}), \ldots, aa_{e_n}(A_{E_n}))$ is true, also written as $aa_{e_1}, \ldots, aa_{e_n} \vdash P_{E_1,\ldots,E_n}$.

---

[1] Assuming these sets to be infinite allows us to model any scenario in which users, resources, terminals, and environments are finitely many.

Policies and access control decisions. A *protection policy* is a predicate $P_{R,T,En}$ on the attribute values of resources, terminals, and environments. $P_{R,T,En}$ (r, t, en) is true when the resource r can be accessed with terminal t in the environment *en* and false otherwise. A *release policy* is a predicate $P_{U,R,En}$ on the attribute values of users, resources, and environments. $P_{U,R,En(u,r,en)}$ is true when the user u is entitled to access resource r in the environment *en* and false otherwise. Given a release policy $P_{U,R,En}$ and a protection policy $P_{R,T,En}$, we say that (*1*) a *user u can access resource r in environment en under attribute assignments aa_u, aa_r, and aa_{en} iff aa_u, aa_r, $aa_{en} \vdash P_{U,R,En}$* (see the Release Decision Point in Fig. 2); (*2*) a *terminal t can handle resource r in environment en under attribute assignments aa_r, aa_t, and aa_{en} iff aa_r, aa_t, $aa_{en} \vdash P_{R,T,En}$* (see the Protection Decision Point in Fig. 2); and (*3*) a *user u can access resource r via terminal t in environment en under attribute assignments aa_u, aa_r, aa_t, and aa_{en} iff (3.1) u can access r in en under aa_u, aa_r, and aa_{en} and (3.2) t can handle r in en under aa_r, aa_t, and aa_{en}* (see the conjunction $\otimes$ in Fig. 2).

3.2 An Extension to the Core CPR Model: Bridge Predicates

We present an extension of the core CPR model in which a set E of entities in $\mathcal{E}$ is associated to a collection $\{A_E^1, \ldots, A_E^m\}$ of attribute signatures. The notions of attribute assignment and predicate, previously introduced, can be easily extended to accommodate multiple attribute signatures by assigning each involved set of entities an integer that uniquely identifies the attribute signature among those associated to it. For instance, aa_e^j denotes an attribute assignment associated to an element e in E with respect to the attribute signature A_E^j ($j = 1, \ldots, m$) among those in the collection $\{A_E^1, \ldots, A_E^m\}$. Let $A_E^j = \{a_1, \ldots, a_n\}$ be one of the m attribute signatures associated to the set E of entities ($j = 1, \ldots, m$) and $\mathbf{d}_E^j = d_{a_1}^j, \ldots, d_{a_m}^j$ a tuple of domain values such that $d_{a_i}^j$ is in the domain D_{a_i}; a *bridge* predicate $B_{E^{i_1}, \ldots, E^{i_k}}$ (or simply $B_{i_1, \ldots, i_k}$ when E is clear from the context) is a Boolean-valued function on tuples $(\mathbf{d}_E^1, \ldots, \mathbf{d}_E^n)$ where $A_E^{i_1}, \ldots, A_E^{i_k}$ are k attribute signatures among those in $\{A_E^1, \ldots, A_E^m\}$ that are (semantically) related.

Considering several attribute signatures associated to the same set of entities related by bridge predicates can be useful in several situations. For instance, consider the problem of migrating actual authorization policies about NATO documents based on security markings—which can grant or deny access to whole documents only—to CPR policies that allow for accessing selected portions. Migration can be achieved by exploiting linguistic classification techniques guided by terminologies (along the lines of, e.g., [22]) to automatically infer a collection A_R^1 of content-metadata associated to portions of documents (e.g., paragraphs and sections). It would then be possible to apply classification techniques developed in Formal Concept Analysis [25] to automatically synthesize bridge predicates $B_{1,2}$ between the inferred content-metadata in A_R^1 and a collection A_R^2 of security-relevant attributes identified by security experts. At this point, the experts can use A_R^2 to express the desired release policy $P_{U,R^2,En}$ on selected parts of the documents. Defining $P_{U,R^2,En}$ is likely to take a substantial amount of time. For availability, it is essential to find a simpler way to mediate access to the documents. This is possible, for example, by synthesizing an alternative bridge predicate $B'_{1,0}$ that associates the content metadata in A_R^1 with the (standard) NATO security markings in A_R^0, namely Top Secret, Secret, Confidential, Restricted, and Unclassified. This would allow for the re-use of the available (and well-known in NATO [21]) authorization policy $P_{U,R^0,En}$ involving security markings to handle the migration to CPR policies as follows: a user u can access resource r in environment en under attribute assignments aa_u, aa_r^1, and aa_{en} iff either (i) there exists a tuple $\mathbf{s}$ of values for the security-sensitive attributes in A_R^2 such that $(aa_r^1(A_R^1), \mathbf{s}) \in B_{1,2}$ and $P_{U,R^2,En}(aa_u(A_U), \mathbf{s}, aa_{en}(En))$ is true, or (ii) there exists a tuple $\mathbf{m}$ of security markings such that $(aa_u^1(A_R^1), \mathbf{m}) \in B'_{1,0}$ and $P_{U,R^0,En}(aa_u(A_U), \mathbf{m}, aa_{en}(A_{En}))$ is true. According to the above definition, if clause (i) holds it is possible to apply a release policy based on the security-sensitive attributes in A_R^2; otherwise it is possible to resort to a release policy based on traditional security markings, see clause (ii). Use of bridge predicates supports coexistence of systems relying on both $P_{U,R^2,En}$ and $P_{U,R^0,En}$, at the price of reduced granularity in access, since security markings apply to whole documents whereas the security-sensitive attributes in A_R^2 apply to paragraphs or sections.

4   CPRL: A Language for the Core CPR Model

We base CPRL on the theory of Satisfiability Modulo Theories (SMT) solvers [6, 24] whereby theories are used to model the algebraic structure of types.

Basic framework. We assume the availability of a set of primitive types, including Integers ($\mathbb{Z}$) and Booleans ($\mathbb{B}$). We also assume the possibility of defining enumerated types and records. For instance, the enumerated types for the PMD scenario (described in Sect. 2) are the following: $\mathtt{Clr} := \{\mathtt{Pub}, \mathtt{Uncl}, \mathtt{Res}, \mathtt{Conf}, \mathtt{Sec}\}$, $\mathtt{Level} := \{\mathtt{NoInfo}, \mathtt{Basic}, \mathtt{Enhanced}\}$, $\mathtt{Categ} := \{\mathtt{Descr}, \mathtt{MCOI}, \mathtt{PI}\}$, and $\mathtt{Topic} := \{\mathtt{Toas}, \mathtt{TItds}, \mathtt{Hal}, \mathtt{Smal}\}$, where the symbol ':=' introduces an abbreviation (left) for an expression (right). The values of $\mathtt{Clr}$ are the clearance levels, those of $\mathtt{Level}$ are the strengths of the terminals, those of $\mathtt{Categ}$ are the content categories of the objects in the maps, and those of $\mathtt{Topic}$ are the content types of the objects. The record types of the entities in the PMD scenario are: $\mathtt{User} := [\mathtt{from} : \mathtt{Org}, \mathtt{clr} : \mathtt{Clr}]$, $\mathtt{Terminal} := [\mathtt{auth} : \mathtt{Org}, \mathtt{strg} : \mathtt{Level}]$, and $\mathtt{Resource} := [\mathtt{cat} : \mathtt{Categ}, \mathtt{top} : \mathtt{Topic}]$, where the record fields correspond to the attributes with the same name in Sect. 2. If r is a record type expression, then $r.f$ denotes the value of the field f in r.

Attribute assignment expressions. Let e be a variable of type $\mathtt{User}$, $\mathtt{Resource}$, $\mathtt{Terminal}$, or $\mathtt{Environment}$; an *attribute assignment expression* is a quantifier-free formula $\alpha(e)$ in which e is the only variable that occurs. An attribute assignment expression $\alpha(e)$ denotes the set $[\![\alpha(e)]\!]$ of elements whose attribute values satisfy (in the logical sense) $\alpha(e)$. In other words, $\alpha(e)$ identifies the set of attribute assignments that map the attributes of e to values satisfying α.

For instance, in the PMD scenario consider the following attribute assignment expressions for users and terminals:

$$\text{UN.from} = \text{NATO} \wedge \text{UN.clr} = \text{Sec} \tag{1}$$

$$\text{TN.auth} = \text{NATO} \wedge (\text{TN.strg} = \text{Enhanced} \vee \text{TN.strg} = \text{Basic}) \tag{2}$$

where UN is a variable of type User and TN is a variable of type Terminal. The former identifies a set containing just one attribute assignment that maps from to NATO and clr to Sec. The latter identifies the set containing two attribute assignments that map auth to NATO and strg to either Basic or Enhanced.

CPRL expressions. A *predicate expression over types* $t_1, \ldots, t_n$ is a quantifier-free formula $\gamma(e_1, \ldots, e_n)$ containing (at most) the variables $e_1, \ldots, e_n$ of types $t_1, \ldots, t_n$, respectively. A predicate expression $\gamma(e_1, \ldots, e_n)$ denotes the set $[\![\gamma]\!]$ of tuples of n elements whose attribute values satisfy the formula π. A *release policy expression* is a predicate expression over User, Resource, and Environment. A *protection policy expression* is a predicate expression over Resource, Terminal, and Environment.

To express release and protection policies in the PMD scenario, we introduce attribute assignment expressions over User to describe groups of users whose clearance level is higher than or equal to a given value. For instance, the group he_Res of users whose clearance level is higher than or equal to Restricted can be described by the following attribute assignment expression over User:

$$\text{he\_Res}(u) := (u.\text{clr} = \text{Res} \vee u.\text{clr} = \text{Conf} \vee u.\text{clr} = \text{Sec})$$

where u is a variable of type User.

For instance, he_Res(UN) stands for UN.clr = Res $\vee$ UN.clr = Conf $\vee$ UN.clr = Sec, which is indeed satisfied by the set $[\![(1)]\!]$ of attribute assignments. This implies that UN belongs to the group of users whose clearance level is higher than or equal to Res. It is easy to see that

$$\forall u : \text{User}, u.\text{clr} = \text{Sec} \Rightarrow \text{he\_Res}(u) \tag{3}$$

holds, where $\Rightarrow$ denotes logical implication. In other words, the (increasing) order over clearance levels is modelled in CPRL by logical implication.

To see how he_Res is helpful in writing release policies, consider line 2 of the table on the left of Fig. 1, i.e. NATO employees with clearance Res or higher can access resources whose content-metadata label cat is MCOI and top is Smal. This can be expressed by the following release policy expression:

$$\text{rp\_2}(u, r) := (u.\text{from} = \text{NATO} \wedge \text{he\_Res}(u) \wedge r.\text{cat} = \text{MCOI} \wedge r.\text{top} = \text{Smal}),$$

where u is a variable of type User and r a variable of type Resource.

Now, recall the attribute assignment expression (1) and consider the following question: can the user UN access an object Obj_2 such that

$$\text{Obj\_2.cat} = \text{MCOI} \wedge \text{Obj\_2.top} = \text{Hal} \; ? \tag{4}$$

The answer can be found by evaluating the truth value of rp_2(UN, Obj_2). For this, consider the part of rp_2(UN, Obj_2) that applies to UN, namely UN.from = NATO ∧ he_Res(UN), that is satisfied by the set $[\![(1)]\!]$ of attribute assignments; notice that he_Res(UN) is implied by UN.clr = Sec and (3). Then, consider the part of rp_2(UN, Obj_2) that applies to Obj_2, namely Obj_2.cat = MCOI ∧ Obj_2.top = Smal: although Obj_2.cat = MCOI is satisfied by $[\![(4)]\!]$, this is not the case for Obj_2.top = Smal because Smal ≠ Hal and Obj_2.top = Hal is in (4). Thus, rp_2(UN, Obj_2) is false and UN cannot access Obj_2; i.e. the answer to the question above is no.

The protection policies for the PMD scenario can be specified in a similar way; they are omitted for lack of space.

4.1   Answering Authorization Queries in CPRL

An *authorization query expression* is a quantifier-free formula of the form

$$\alpha_U(u) \wedge \alpha_R(r) \wedge \alpha_T(t) \wedge \alpha_{En}(en) \wedge \rho(u, r, en) \wedge \pi(r, t, en) \tag{5}$$

where u, r, t, and en are variables of type User, Resource, Terminal, and Environment, respectively, α_U, α_R, α_T, and α_{En} are attribute assignment expressions over User, Resource, Terminal, and Environment, respectively, ρ is a release policy expression, and π is a protection policy expression. The satisfiability of (5) will be denoted as $[\![\alpha_U]\!], [\![\alpha_R]\!], [\![\alpha_T]\!], [\![\alpha_{En}]\!] \vdash [\![\rho \wedge \pi]\!]$. The intuition underlying this notation is the following: when (5) is satisfiable, the entities u, r, t, and en satisfy—in the sense of Sect. 3—both ρ and π under some attribute assignments aa_u in $[\![\alpha_U]\!]$, aa_r in $[\![\alpha_R]\!]$, aa_t in $[\![\alpha_T]\!]$ and aa_{en} in $[\![\alpha_{En}]\!]$, i.e. $aa_u, aa_r, aa_t, aa_{en} \vdash [\![\rho \wedge \pi]\!]$. When $[\![\alpha_U]\!], [\![\alpha_R]\!], [\![\alpha_T]\!], [\![\alpha_{En}]\!] \vdash [\![\rho \wedge \pi]\!]$, we say that the answer to the authorization query expression (5) is 'permit,' otherwise, it is 'deny.' Thus, CPRL supports the specification of positive authorizations only. While negative authorizations can be useful to specify exceptions (see, e.g., [11]), their interplay with positive authorizations may give rise to conflicts, i.e. situations for which an access query is permitted by a positive authorization and denied by a negative authorization. To avoid this kind of problems, in this paper, we have chosen to consider positive authorizations only and leave to future work the development of extensions of CPRL capable of supporting negative authorizations.

Let P and Π be (possibly empty) finite sets of release and protection policy expressions, respectively, the authorization query expression (5) is satisfied by P and Π iff there exists $\rho \in P$ and $\pi \in \Pi$ such that $[\![\alpha_U]\!], [\![\alpha_R]\!], [\![\alpha_T]\!], [\![\alpha_{En}]\!] \vdash [\![\rho \wedge \pi]\!]$. When P or Π is empty, any authorization query expression is unsatisfiable because it is obviously impossible to find a release or a protection policy (depending on which of the sets P or Π is empty) satisfying the query.

Intuitively, the capability of answering an authorization query α_E allows for establishing that some entities in the (large) set $[\![\alpha_E]\!]$ satisfy certain conditions, expressed as the attribute assignment expression α_E. For instance, since the attribute assignment expression $\alpha_U(u) := (u.\text{from} = \text{NATO})$ identifies the group of all NATO employees, the capability of answering an authorization query of the form (5) in which this α_U occurs allows us to establish if there exists a NATO employee able to access certain resources in some environment, regardless of his rank and clearance. In this way, policy designers can check that the release and protection policies grant or deny access to users (with certain profiles) to some given resources. In the PMD scenario, for example, one may wish to check that a NATO user may see objects whose content-metadata labels are MCOI (metrics related to the consequences of the impact between the threatening and intercepting missiles) and PI (public information) while an ICRC member is granted access to objects labelled PI but should not see those with MCOI, to prevent him from being able to infer details about missile trajectories.

We now give conditions under which it is possible to automatically answer authorization queries.

Theorem 1. *Let $\{T_j\}_{j \in J}$ be the collection of theories formalizing the types of attributes of users, resources, terminals, and environments (for J some finite index set). If checking the satisfiability of quantifier-free formulae in T_j is decidable for each $j \in J$, then answering authorization queries of the form (5) is decidable. Furthermore, if satisfiability checking in T_j is in NP (for each $j \in J$), then answering authorization queries is also in NP.*

Proof (Sketch). The problem of answering authorization queries reduces to checking the satisfiability of the quantifier-free formulae of the form (5) (observe that (5) is a quantifier-free formula because, by definition, all its parts are quantifier-free) in the theory obtained by combining the theories for records for users, resources, terminals, and environments with the theories for the fields in the collection $\{T_j\}_{j \in J}$. This is a well-studied problem in SMT solving: the theorem follows from the main result in [23]. ☐

Modern SMT solvers have been shown to be quite effective in handling a wide range of instances of satisfiability problems in NP (see, e.g., [12]). Our experience in using the SMT solver Yices [27] on the PMD scenario was that answering authorization queries is almost instantaneous on a standard laptop.

4.2 Computing Permitted Views by Max-SMT Solving

Computing yes-or-no answers to authorization queries is not always enough to provide an optimal permitted view to structured resources. For example, in the PMD scenario, it is necessary to compute permitted views of a map that depend on the user and terminal used to access it. In other words, the content of a map generated by the PMD system must be filtered to produce views in which, for instance, the trajectories of the threatening and intercepting missiles are included for a NATO user equipped with a NATO terminal. A member of ICRC coordinating a rescue operation can, instead, see the map annotated with the consequences of impact in hazard areas and their location, but the missile trajectories are omitted. The problem of computing answers to multiple authorization queries pertaining to the parts of the same (structured) resource can be reduced to an optimization problem for which some SMT solvers (e.g., Yices) offer support.

The *problem of computing permitted views* in CPRL can be stated as follows (from an authorization perspective): given a release policy expression ρ, a protection policy expression π, attribute expressions α_U, α_T, α_{En} over User, Terminal, Environment, respectively, and a finite set AER of attribute assignment expressions over Resource, find the largest possible subset AER' of AER such that $\alpha_R \in AER'$ iff $[\![\alpha_U]\!], [\![\alpha_R]\!], [\![\alpha_T]\!], [\![\alpha_{En}]\!] \vdash [\![\rho \wedge \pi]\!]$.

By Theorem 1 it is possible to automatically compute permitted views.

Theorem 2. *Let $\{T_j\}_{j \in J}$ be the collection of theories formalizing the types of attributes of users, resources, terminals, and environments (for J some finite index set). If checking the satisfiability of quantifier-free formulae in T_j is decidable for each $j \in J$, then the problem of computing permitted views is decidable.*

Proof. The proof is constructive. Given a release policy expression ρ, a protection policy expression π, attribute expressions α_U, α_T, α_{En} over User, Terminal, Environment, respectively, and a finite set AER of attribute assignment expressions over Resource, we describe an algorithm capable of returning the largest subsets AER' of AER whose elements α_R are such that $[\![\alpha_U]\!], [\![\alpha_R]\!], [\![\alpha_T]\!], [\![\alpha_{En}]\!] \vdash [\![\rho \wedge \pi]\!]$.

For each subset AER' of AER, consider the following 'associated' formula: $\bigwedge_{\alpha_R \in AER'} (\alpha_U \wedge \alpha_R \wedge \alpha_T \wedge \alpha_{En} \wedge \rho \wedge \pi)$. Notice that each conjunct in this formula is of the form (5), i.e. it is an authorization query expression. By Theorem 1, it is possible to check the satisfiability of each conjunct of this formula and thus also of the formula. After considering all subsets of AER, the procedure simply returns the largest subsets (if any) whose associated formula is satisfiable.

To conclude the proof, it is sufficient to notice that the procedure terminates because there are only finitely many subsets of AER. $\square$

The goal is to design efficient ways to solve instances of the problem of computing permitted views by avoiding the enumeration of all possible subsets of attribute assignment expressions for resources, as is suggested by the proof of Theorem 2. Fortunately, it is possible to reduce this problem to an optimization problem, called a Max-SMT (MSMT) problem (see, e.g., [2]), whose solution is supported by some state-of-the-art SMT solvers.

The Max-SMT problem. We say that a formula is *soft* when it may or may not be satisfiable and that it is *hard* when it must be satisfiable. Given a theory T and two sets H and S of hard and soft formulae, respectively, the Max-SMT problem consists of finding a subset S' of S such that the conjunction of the formulae in H and the cardinality of the set $S \setminus S'$ is minimal. I.e., a solution to a Max-SMT problem must satisfy all hard formulae and minimize the number of unsatisfied soft formulae.

Reduction. Let PV be an instance of the problem of computing permitted views: ρ is a release policy expression, π is a protection policy expression, α_U, α_T,

α_{En} are attribute expressions over User, Terminal, Environment, respectively, and AER is a finite set of attribute assignment expressions over Resource. We reduce PV to the following instance of the Max-SMT problem: $\mathcal{T}$ is the theory obtained by combining the theories for the records User, Resource, Terminal, and Environment with the theories for their fields, $S_{MSMT} := AER$ is the set of soft formulae, and $H_{MSMT} := \{\alpha_U \wedge \alpha_T \wedge \alpha_{En} \wedge \rho \wedge \pi\}$ is the set of hard formulae. It is easy to see that a solution S'_{MSMT} of MSMT is also a solution of PV, i.e. $AER'_{PV} = S'_{MSMT}$, and the solution is such that, for each $\alpha_R \in AER'_{PV}$, $[\![\alpha_U]\!], [\![\alpha_R]\!], [\![\alpha_T]\!], [\![\alpha_{En}]\!] \vdash [\![\rho \wedge \pi]\!]$. In other words, the reduction is correct.

It is possible to support a simple form of risk-based[2] access control by using a variant of the Max-SMT problem, called the weighted Max-SMT problem. In addition to the sets H and S of hard and soft formulae, respectively, we consider a function w that assigns weights to each element in S. The solution to a weighted Max-SMT problem must then satisfy all hard formulae in H and minimize the weights of the unsatisfied soft formulae in S. We can then define a risk-based version of the problem of computing permitted views by defining a weight function w that associates the advantage (as opposed to risk) of disclosing the information in the resources identified by the attribute assignment expressions in AER to each soft formula in S. The solution to this problem will be a subset of AER that minimizes the cumulative advantage associated to the attribute assignment expressions that are not satisfied, thereby minimizing the risk of disclosing those pieces of information. Indeed, there are a number of ways of explicitly defining the function w depending on the scenario to be considered. For example, in the PMD scenario, w may assign the value of showing an object in the map according to user location and time; e.g., the value increases as the user gets closer to a certain hazard area or to the actual time of the foreseen impact of an intercepting missile.

Similarly to what has already been observed for answering authorization queries, our experience in using the (weighted) Max-SMT solving capabilities of Yices [27] in the PMD scenario was that computing permitted views takes at most 1 second on a standard laptop.

We conclude this section by observing that it is easy to extend CPRL to include bridge predicates. We do not do this here for lack of space.

5 Discussion and Related Work

The main goal of CPR is the seamless integration of access control in the NATO information sharing infrastructure [26]. Two design decisions are key to achieving this goal. First, CPR assumes that resources are labelled with content-metadata carrying sufficient information about their content to allow access decisions to be made. Thus, the type of a resource is not required to be known to the PDP of CPR (Fig. 2) but can be delegated to another module

---

[2] In CPR, the risk measures the severity of disclosing a piece of information contained in a resource combined with the likelihood that a user and a terminal maliciously or inadvertently leak it.

in the NATO infrastructure. An implementation of this idea as a refinement of the XACML (eXtensible Access Control Markup Language) architecture [20] is described in [4].

Relationship with other content-based authorization models. Existing content-based authorization models [1] base their access decisions on the 'concepts' related to resources (e.g., books in digital libraries). Concepts are extracted from resources and thus their type (e.g., textual documents) must be known to access control systems. An advantage of this approach is the possibility to capture the semantic relationships among the concepts (e.g., hierarchies) and to specify authorization conditions involving such relationships. This can be useful in the context of the NATO infrastructure. To see why, consider the PMD scenario: while it may be legitimate to disclose the position of a few soldiers in a certain area, disclosure should be avoided when their number is one hundred or more, since (untrusted) users may infer that a military operation is likely to occur in that area. We can extend the CPR model to take into account this kind of semantic relationship (among content-metadata) by generalizing attribute assignment expressions and permitting the occurrence of more than one variable of type Resource. Such expressions can, for instance, encode constraints on the type (e.g., soldier) and number (few or many) of objects on a map. It is then straightforward to adapt the reduction to a Max-SMT problem as described in Sect. 4.2 to also consider this kind of predicate expression. We leave the investigation of this interesting issue as future work.

The other main design decision underlying CPR that facilitates its integration in the NATO information sharing infrastructure is the sharp separation between release and protection policies. This enables a more efficient implementation of the policies and procedures that are mandated by existing directives within NATO and other international/governmental organizations. It also promotes an effective division of responsibilities for the formulation of each policy: experts with in-depth knowledge of technical security environments for protection requirements and experts with in-depth knowledge of organization workflows and operational structure for release conditions. To support the natural and modular specification of release and protection policies, CPR introduces the notion of terminal, encapsulating the properties of the device and connection used for accessing information. By using terminals and protection policies (as a complement to release policies), CPR naturally supports the specification of authorizations based on devices. These are gaining more and more importance in large enterprise organizations because of the widespread use of corporate or even personal (with bring-your-own-device policies, see, e.g., [15]) mobile devices to access work-related information. Thus, the applicability of CPR extends beyond NATO to large enterprise or governmental organizations, seeking a good trade-off between confidentiality and availability of information.

Relationship with classical authorization models. The separate specification of release conditions and protection policies is one of the main refinement of CPR with respect to ABAC. In the latter, the properties of terminals are seen as part of the environment [28] thus making the specifications of protection requirements more difficult to read and maintain. Another important refinement of CPR with respect to ABAC is the notion of bridge predicate (Sect. 3.2), which encodes relationships among different collections of attributes associated to a given set of entities. Use of bridge predicates allows decomposition of policy specifications by allowing security officers to focus on security-relevant attributes of the resources in isolation and later relate these to the content-metadata of resources.

Since it is a refinement of ABAC, CPR inherits its expressive power. As observed in [13], ABAC can express and extend the three classical models (namely discretionary, mandatory, and role-based; see, e.g., [11] for an overview) as well as others that mix mandatory and discretionary features (such as Bell-La Padula [7]). Thus, CPR also allows policies inspired by these classical models to be expressed and combined.

Relationship with XACML. As sketched in [4], release conditions and protection policies can be translated into XACML [20]. This allows for re-using available XACML engines to implement the PDP for the CPR model (Fig. 2). The crucial difference between an authorization query in CPRL (Sect. 4.1) and one in XACML is that the former corresponds to a (large) set of the latter. This is because a query in CPRL is defined in terms of attribute assignment expressions, which identify (large) sets of attribute assignments for the involved entities. Thus, the technique for answering authorization queries based on SMT solvers (Theorem 1) enables the handling of more general questions than does the technique based on XACML engines. The situation is similar to comparing standard and symbolic execution of programs [14]. Instead of executing a program on a set of sample inputs, a program can be 'symbolically' executed for a set of classes of inputs so that a single symbolic execution result may be equivalent to a large number of normal test cases. Similarly, instead of answering an authorization query with respect to a single user, resource, terminal, and environment, the technique in Sect. 4.1 can answer a (large) set of authorization queries by using attribute assignment expressions for groups of users, resources, terminals, and environments (specified by attribute assignment expressions). Using this technique, policy designers can check the consequences of their policies against (large) sets of attribute assignments, thereby gaining a deeper understanding of their policies and facilitating the reconciliation between what they intend to authorize and what the policies actually authorize.

Relationship with SMT solvers techniques. It is recognized that policy designers can be assisted in their tasks by tools capable of automatically solving policy analysis problems. CPRL permits the re-use of results and techniques from the SMT field once policy analysis problems are reduced to SMT problems (this is similar in spirit to the work in [3,5]). This is possible for several policy analysis problems. An interesting example is checking the observational equivalence of two policies (see, e.g., [8]), which amounts to establishing whether or not it is always the case that the policies return the same answer for any authorization request. In CPRL, the problem can be stated as follows: given release policy ρ_i

and protection policy π_i expressions for $i = 1, 2$, the *observational equivalence problem* amounts to checking whether or not for every user u, resource r, terminal t, and environment en, the formula

$$(\rho_1(u, r, en) \wedge \pi_1(r, t, en)) \Leftrightarrow (\rho_2(u, r, en) \wedge \pi_2(r, t, en)) \tag{6}$$

holds, where $\Leftrightarrow$ denotes logical equivalence. By Theorem 1 it is possible to automatically solve this problem.

Theorem 3. *Let $\{T_j\}_{j \in J}$ be the collection of theories formalizing the types of attributes of users, resources, terminals, and environments (for J some finite index set). If checking the satisfiability of quantifier-free formulae in T_j is decidable for each $j \in J$, then the observational equivalence problem is also decidable.*

Proof. The key argument is similar to that in the proof of Theorem 1. By refutation, the fact that (6) holds is equivalent to the unsatisfiability of its negation, or equivalently to the unsatisfiability of the negation of (6), which is indeed a quantifier-free formula whose satisfiability is decidable by Theorem 1. □

Relationship with Datalog-based access control models. Compare Theorem 3 with the undecidability result in [8] for the same problem when policies are expressed in Datalog (see, e.g., [9]). In the past, Datalog was widely used as the semantic foundation of access control languages because the algorithms for answering authorization queries are polynomially complex. Polynomial complexity was achieved by requiring the formulae of Datalog to contain only constant and predicate symbols, and admitting only restricted forms of negation and disjunction. In contrast, CPRL permits arbitrary Boolean combinations (i.e. unrestricted negation and disjunction) in policy expressions together with the use of function symbols. However, while recursion is available in Datalog, this is not the case in CPRL. It is the presence of recursion that makes the observational equivalence problem undecidable for policies expressed in Datalog [8]. At the same time, the absence of recursion together with the results of Theorem 1 make observational equivalence decidable in CPRL (Theorem 3). To date, our experience has been that recursion is not needed for expressing release and protection policies arising in typical NATO scenarios.

CPR and structural metadata. So far, in the CPR model, values of resource attributes have been used for representing content-metadata. Another possibility is to use resource attributes to represent the design and specification of data structures (structural metadata). For instance, it would be interesting to investigate to what extent it is possible to encode the sophisticated access control model for XML documents and schema proposed in [10]. In future work, we envisage extending CPRL with theories that would allow the representation of structural relationships such as those in XML schemas and documents.

References

1. Adam, N.R., Atluri, V., Bertino, E., Ferrari, E.: A content-based authorization model for digital libraries. IEEE Trans. Knowl. Data Eng. **14**(2), 296–315 (2002)
2. Ansótegui, C., Bofill, M., Palahí, M., Suy, J., Villaret, M.: Satisfiability modulo theories: an efficient approach for the resource-constrained project scheduling problem. In: SARA, AAAI (2011)
3. Arkoudas, K., Loeb, S., Chadha, R., Chiang, J., Whittaker, K.: Automated policy analysis. In: 2012 IEEE International Symposium on Policy, July 2012, pp. 1–8 (2012)
4. Armando, A., Grasso, M., Oudkerk, S., Ranise, S., Wrona, K.: Content-based information protection and release in NATO operations. In: SACMAT, ACM (2013)
5. Armando, A., Ranise, S.: Automated and efficient analysis of role-based access control with attributes. In: Cuppens-Boulahia, N., Cuppens, F., Garcia-Alfaro, J. (eds.) DBSec 2012. LNCS, vol. 7371, pp. 25–40. Springer, Heidelberg (2012)
6. Beckert, B., Hoare, C.A.R., Hähnle, R., Smith, R., Green, D.R., Ranise, S., Tinelli, C., Ball, T., Rajamani, S.K.: Intelligent systems and formal methods in software engineering. IEEE Int. Syst. **21**(6), 71–81 (2006)
7. Bell, D.E., La Padula, L.J.: Secure computer systems: mathematical foundations. Technical report MTR-2547, MITRE Corporation, Bedford (1973)
8. Bertino, E., Catania, B., Ferrari, E., Perlasca, P.: A logical framework for reasoning about access control models. ACM TISSEC **6**(1), 71–127 (2003)
9. Ceri, S., Gottlob, G., Tanca, L.: What you always wanted to know about datalog (and never dared to ask). IEEE TKDE **1**(1), 146–166 (1989)
10. Damiani, E., De Capitani di Vimercati, S., Paraboschi, S., Samarati, P.: A fine-grained access control system for XML documents. TISSEC **5**(2), 169–202 (2002)
11. De Capitani di Vimercati, S., Foresti, S., Jajodia, S., Samarati, P.: Access control policies and languages. Int. J. Comput. Sci. Eng. **3**(2), 94–102 (2007)
12. De Moura, L., Bjørner, N.: Satisfiability modulo theories: introduction and applications. CACM **54**, 69–77 (2011)
13. Jin, X., Krishnan, R., Sandhu, R.: A unified attribute-based access control model covering DAC, MAC and RBAC. In: Cuppens-Boulahia, N., Cuppens, F., Garcia-Alfaro, J. (eds.) DBSec 2012. LNCS, vol. 7371, pp. 41–55. Springer, Heidelberg (2012)
14. King, J.C.: Symbolic execution and program testing. CACM **19**(7), 385–394 (1976)
15. Casassa Mont, M., Balacheff, B.: On device-based identity management in enterprises. Technical report HPL-2007-53, Helwett-Packard Laboratories (2007)
16. Nato HQ C3 Staff. Directive on the marking of NATO information (2011)
17. NATO Security Committee. Primary directive on INFOSEC. Number AC/35-D/2004-REV2 (2010)
18. North Atlantic Council. Security within the North Atlantic Treaty Organization. Number C-M(2002) 49 (2002)
19. North Atlantic Council. Primary directive on information management. Number C-M(2008) 0113(INV) (2008)
20. OASIS. eXtensible Access Control Markup Language (XACML) version 3.0. (2010)
21. Oudkerk, S., Bryant, I., Eggen, A., Haakseth, R.: A proposal for an XML confidentiality label syntax and binding of metadata to data objects. In: NATO RTO Symposium on Information, Assurance and Cyber Defence (2010)
22. Prediger, S.: Logical scaling in formal concept analysis. In: Delugach, H.S., Keeler, M.A., Searle, L., Lukose, D., Sowa, J.F. (eds.) ICCS 1997. LNCS (LNAI), vol. 1257, pp. 332–341. Springer, Heidelberg (1997)

23. Ranise, S., Ringeissen, C., Zarba, C.G.: Combining data structures with nonstably infinite theories using many-sorted logic. In: Gramlich, B. (ed.) FroCos 2005. LNCS (LNAI), vol. 3717, pp. 48–64. Springer, Heidelberg (2005)
24. Ranise, S., Tinelli, C.: The SMT-LIB standard: version 1.2. http://www.smt-lib. org (2006)
25. Wille, R.: Restructuring lattice theory: an approach based on hierarchies of concepts. In: Rival, I. (ed.) Ordered Sets, pp. 445–470. Reidel, Dordrecht (1982)
26. Wrona, K., Hallingstad, G.: Controlled information sharing in NATO operations. In: IEEE Military Communications Conference (MILCOM) (2011)
27. Yices. http://yices.csl.sri.com (2013)
28. Yuan, E., Jin, T.: Attribute-based access control (ABAC) for web services. In: IEEE International Conference on Web Services, pp. 561–569 (2005)

Cipher Attacks

Computational Soundness of Symbolic Blind Signatures under Active Attacker

Hideki Sakurada[✉]

NTT Communication Science Laboratories, NTT Corporation, Kanagawa, Japan
sakurada.hideki@lab.ntt.co.jp

Abstract. Blind signature schemes enable users to obtain signatures on texts without revealing the texts to signers. They are often used to provide anonymity in protocols such as electronic cash and voting protocols. To confirm the security of such a voting scheme, Kremer and Ryan employ a symbolic model for protocols that use blind signatures. However, the soundness of this model with respect to the computational model in which security of blind signatures is defined is yet to be explored. In this paper, we discuss certain difficulties involved in establishing the computational soundness of their symbolic model, propose an alternative symbolic model, and show its computational soundness.

1 Introduction

Blind signature schemes (e.g. [5]) enable users to obtain signatures without revealing the texts to signers. They are used to provide anonymity and privacy in protocols such as electronic cash protocols [5] and voting schemes such as FOO [10]. The security of blind signature schemes is computationally formalized as unforgeability [17] and blindness properties [12].

To confirm the security of the FOO voting scheme, Kremer and Ryan [15] employ a symbolic model for blind signatures and commitments. To enable automatic verification, messages are modeled as terms consisting of symbols that represent cryptographic primitives such as encryption and signature, and operations on messages are restricted to a number of rules in a symbolic model. Since such a symbolic model is a simplification of the computational model, computational soundness is required [1,2,6–8,11,13,14]: security in the symbolic model implies that in the computational model. However, the computational soundness of a symbolic model with blind signatures has not been established. Although computational soundness results for symbolic models with digital signatures [2,8,11] and ring signatures [13] exist, these results cannot be immediately applied to blind signatures because, differently from other signature schemes, a blind signature scheme is an interactive protocol between a user and a signer, and whose security is defined in terms of the number of interactions.

This paper first presents a few difficulties as regards establishing the computational soundness of Kremer and Ryan's symbolic model under standard security assumptions on blind signatures. We then propose an alternative symbolic

J.-L. Danger et al. (Eds.): FPS 2013, LNCS 8352, pp. 247–263, 2014.
DOI: 10.1007/978-3-319-05302-8_15, © Springer International Publishing Switzerland 2014

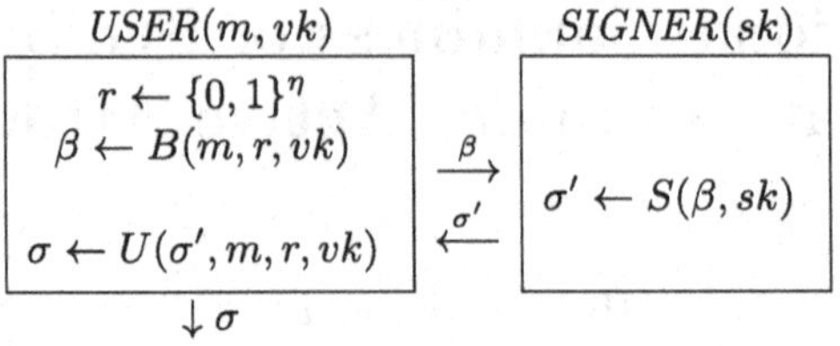

$$USER(m, vk) \qquad\qquad SIGNER(sk)$$

Fig. 1. Two-move blind signature scheme

model and prove its computational soundness for safety properties assuming a
secure blind signature scheme.

2 Blind Signatures

In this paper, we focus on two-move deterministic blind signature schemes
because, for example, a three-move scheme requires a symbolic model different from that required by a two-move scheme. A two-move deterministic blind
signature scheme $\mathcal{BS}$ consists of five algorithms G, B, S, U, and V. The key-
generation algorithm G generates a signing key sk and a verification key vk on
input a security parameter 1^η. As shown in Fig. 1, a user of this scheme has a
text m as well as vk and encrypts ("blinds") m into a bitstring $\beta = B(m, r, vk)$
by using the blinding algorithm B, where r is the randomness for blinding. Then
he asks the signer to compute $\sigma' = S(\beta, sk)$ by using the signing algorithm S
and computes a signature $\sigma = U(\sigma', m, r, vk)$ by using the unblinding algorithm.
The signature σ is verified as $V(\sigma, m, vk) = 1$ by a third party using the verification algorithm. Here we assume that S is a deterministic algorithm, and that the
signatures are deterministic: $V(\sigma_0, m, vk) = V(\sigma_1, m, vk) = 1$ implies $\sigma_0 = \sigma_1$.

Blind signatures are used, for example, in electronic cash protocols [5]. In
such a protocol, a customer obtains a fresh coin by interacting as a user with a
bank who runs the signing algorithm. The merchant receives coins in payment
and forwards them to the bank. The bank verifies the signature and that the
coins have not been used before and gives the merchant real money. In this
protocol, A (malicious) customer should not be able to obtain more coins than
those signed by the bank. For privacy, a (malicious) bank should not be able
to know the customer who used the coin. These are guaranteed if the scheme is
secure, i.e. satisfies the unforgeability and blindness properties defined below.

The FDH-RSA blind signature scheme [3,5] and the blind GDH signature
scheme [4] satisfies all assumptions introduced in this section. These schemes are
shown to be secure in the random oracle model.

The unforgeability property [17] guarantees that no malicious user can obtain
$\ell+1$ signatures by interacting with ℓ instances of the signer. Formally, we consider
the following experiment $\mathsf{ExptU}^{\mathcal{A},\mathcal{BS}}(\eta)$:

$$\mathsf{ExptU}^{\mathcal{A},\mathcal{BS}}(\eta) = \left[\begin{array}{l} (sk, vk) \leftarrow G(1^\eta); \\ (m_1, \sigma_1), \ldots, (m_n, \sigma_n) \leftarrow \mathcal{A}^{\mathcal{O}_{S_{sk}}}, \end{array} \right.$$

where $\mathcal{O}_{S_{sk}}$ is the signing oracle that replies with $S(m, sk)$ for each query m. The attacker $\mathcal{A}$ interacts with the oracle and outputs a number of mutually distinct texts $m_1, \ldots, m_n$ and their signatures $\sigma_1, \ldots, \sigma_n$. A scheme $\mathcal{BS}$ has the unforgeability property if and only if the following probability is negligible with η:

$$\Pr[\mathsf{ExptU}^{\mathcal{A},\mathcal{BS}}(\eta) : V(m_i, \sigma_i, vk) = 1 \text{ for all } i, \text{ and } n > \ell]$$

where ℓ is the number of queries received by the oracle.

The blindness property [12] guarantees that no malicious signer can know the text m by interacting with the user. Formally, we consider the following experiment $\mathsf{ExptB}_b^{\mathcal{A},\mathcal{BS}}(\eta)$:

$$\mathsf{ExptB}_b^{\mathcal{A},\mathcal{BS}}(\eta) = \begin{bmatrix} (sk, vk) \leftarrow G(1^\eta); \\ (m_0, m_1, t) \leftarrow \mathcal{A}(sk); \\ \tilde{b} \leftarrow \mathcal{A}^{Challenger(vk, m_0, m_1)}(sk, t). \end{bmatrix}$$

In this experiment, the attacker generates a pair (m_0, m_1) of bitstrings, interacts with the challenger, and outputs a guess $\tilde{b}$ for the bit b. The challenger simulates two instances $USER(vk, m_b)$ and $USER(vk, m_{1-b})$ of $USER$ for the attacker, depending on the bit b. The signatures are sent to the attacker only if both users succeed in obtaining them. They are sent as a tuple (σ_0, σ_1) consisting of signatures σ_0 and σ_1 on m_0 and m_1, respectively. A scheme $\mathcal{BS}$ has the blindness property if and only if for any probabilistic polynomial-time attacker $\mathcal{A}$, the following difference is negligible with respect to η

$$|\Pr[\mathsf{ExptB}_0^{\mathcal{A},\mathcal{BS}}(\eta) : \tilde{b} = 1] - \Pr[\mathsf{ExptB}_1^{\mathcal{A},\mathcal{BS}}(\eta) : \tilde{b} = 1.]|$$

3   Symbolic Blind Signatures

In this section, we see the ability of the symbolic attacker defined by Kremer and Ryan and a few examples that show gaps between this model and the computational assumptions on blind signatures.

In a symbolic model, messages are represented by terms consisting of symbols that represent operations such as concatenation and encryption. Attackers are only allowed to perform operations on messages defined by the rules of the symbolic model. Such rules should reflect computational attackers' ability so that symbolic analysis can capture all computationally possible attacks.

In Kremer and Ryan's symbolic model for blind signatures, a signature on a text u signed by an agent a is represented by a term $\mathsf{sign}(u, a)$. It is obtained by unblinding a term $\mathsf{blindsign}(\mathsf{blind}(u, r, a), a)$ by using the randomness r, where $\mathsf{blindsign}(\mathsf{blind}(u, r, a), a)$ represents the output of the signing algorithm on input $\mathsf{blind}(u, r, a)$, which represents the output of the blinding algorithm on text u. This operation is defined as the following derivation rule, which is equivalent to the equational rule they actually use:

$$\frac{H \vdash \mathsf{blindsign}(\mathsf{blind}(u, r, a), a), u, r}{H \vdash \mathsf{sign}(u, a).}$$

Table 1. Non-committing query

1. $\mathcal{A} \to O : \beta_1$
2. $P \to \mathcal{A} : n_1, n_2$
3. $O \to \mathcal{A} : S(\beta_1, sk)$
4. $\mathcal{A} \to O : \beta_2$
5. $O \to \mathcal{A} : S(\beta_2, sk)$
6. $\mathcal{A} \to P : \sigma_{n_1}, \sigma_{n_2}.$

Table 2. Modification of signing query

1. $P \to \mathcal{A} : \beta = B(m, r, vk)$
2. $\mathcal{A} \to O : \beta' \ (\neq \beta)$
3. $O \to \mathcal{A} : S(\beta', sk)$
4. $\mathcal{A} \to P : \sigma'$
5. $P \to \mathcal{A} : \sigma_m.$

This rule means that if terms $\mathsf{blindsign}(\mathsf{blind}(u, r, a), a)$, u, and r are computable from a set H of terms, then the term $\mathsf{sign}(u, a)$ is computable from H. This model has no rule that enables the attacker to make a term of the form $\mathsf{blindsign}(v, a)$ without corrupting the agent a. Although their model is simple and suitable for symbolic analysis, it does not capture certain computational attacks, a few of which are given as examples below.

Example 1. In the computational execution shown in Table 1, the attacker $\mathcal{A}$ interacts with an uncorrupted agent O that executes the signing algorithm twice. An agent P sends two fresh nonces n_1 and n_2 after the attacker has sent the first message β_1 to O. After interacting with O and P, the attacker outputs valid signatures σ_{n_1} and σ_{n_2} on these nonces. Since this attacker obtains two signatures by sending two queries to the signing oracle, this execution does not (obviously) violate the unforgeability property. On the other hand, this execution is impossible in the symbolic model because to obtain signatures on n_1 and n_2, the symbolic attacker must send either $\mathsf{blind}(n_1, r, O)$ or $\mathsf{blind}(n_2, r, O)$ as the first message but knows neither n_1 nor n_2, since they have not yet been generated.

Example 2. In the computational execution in Table 2, the uncorrupted agents P and O execute the machines *USER* and *SIGNER* of a blind signature scheme. Agent P successfully outputs a signature on a bitstring m although the attacker alters messages between agents P and O. In the symbolic model, agent P who sends $\mathsf{blind}(u, r, O)$ can obtain a signature $\mathsf{sign}(u, O)$ only if he receives the term $\mathsf{blindsign}(\mathsf{blind}(u, r, O), O)$. If the attacker alters $\mathsf{blind}(u, r, O)$ with a distinct term v, the agent O sends a term $\mathsf{blindsign}(v, O)$ instead of the term $\mathsf{blindsign}(\mathsf{blind}(u, r, O), O)$. Since no rule enables the attacker to obtain the term $\mathsf{blindsign}(\mathsf{blind}(u, r, O), O)$, this execution is impossible in the symbolic model.

These examples shows that their symbolic model does not capture all computationally possible attacks and thus may not guarantee computational security. This is caused by the restriction of the symbolic model: the signature $\mathsf{sign}(u, a)$ is computed only from a term $\mathsf{blindsign}(\mathsf{blind}(u, r, a), a)$ for some r, and the term $\mathsf{blindsign}(\mathsf{blind}(u, r, a), a)$ is computed only by agent a unless agent a is corrupted.

To relax the restriction, we add rules that enable the attacker to make a "fake" blinded term $\mathsf{fakeblind}(r^{adv(j)}, a)$ and to make a signature $\mathsf{sign}(u, a)$ from the term u and the term $\mathsf{blindsign}(\mathsf{fakeblind}(r^{adv(j)}, a), a)$. This extension makes the execution in Table 1 possible in the symbolic model, as shown in

Table 3. Non-committing query

1. $\mathcal{A} \rightarrow O$: fakeblind(r_1, O)
2. $P \rightarrow \mathcal{A}$: n_1, n_2
3. $O \rightarrow \mathcal{A}$: blindsign(fakeblind$(r_1, O), O)$
4. $\mathcal{A} \rightarrow O$: blind(n_2, r_2, O)
5. $O \rightarrow \mathcal{A}$: blindsign(blind$(n_2, r_2, O), O)$
6. $\mathcal{A} \rightarrow P$: sign$(n_1, O),$ sign(n_2, O)

Table 4. Modification of signing query

1. $P \rightarrow \mathcal{A}$: blind(u, r, O)
2. $\mathcal{A} \rightarrow O$: fakeblind(r_1, O)
3. $O \rightarrow \mathcal{A}$: blindsign(fakeblind$(r_1, O), O)$
4. $\mathcal{A} \rightarrow P$: blindsign(blind$(u, r, O), O)$
5. $P \rightarrow \mathcal{A}$: sign(u, O)

Table 3, where $r_1 = r^{adv(1)}$ and $r_2 = r^{adv(2)}$. Additionally, we add another rule that enables the attacker to make a term blindsign(blind$(u, r, a), a)$ from terms blind(u, r, a) and blindsign(fakeblind$(r^{adv(j)}, a), a)$. This rule makes the execution in Table 2 possible, as shown in Table 4. If we allow the attacker to use a term blindsign(fakeblind$(r^{adv(j)}, a), a)$ multiple times with such rules, the attacker can make any number of signatures from this term and is far stronger than any computational attacker. We therefore restrict the use of blindsign(fakeblind$(r^{adv(j)}, a), a)$ to at most once, by introducing a partial function F. This partial function is arbitrary but fixed throughout an execution. The attacker can make only a term $F($blindsign(fakeblind$(r^{adv(j)}, a), a))$ from blindsign(fakeblind$(r^{adv(j)}, a), a)$ with the above rules. We formalize our extensions as the last two derivation rules in Table 5, where C is a set of corrupted agents. We introduce this set for concise presentation of the proofs shown later. A judgement $F, H \vdash_C u_1, \ldots, u_n$ means that the symbolic attacker who corrupts the agents in set C can construct terms $u_1, \ldots, u_n$ from terms in a set H. Terms will be formally defined in the next section.

4   Protocol Language and Models

By adapting the framework described in [8,16], we define our protocol syntax and the computational and symbolic models. The main differences between our syntax and models and those in [8] are as follows:

- Our syntax allows operators *Blind*, *Bsign*, and *Sign* for blind signatures, while encryption and signatures are omitted for brevity. We also adapt their definition of executable protocols.
- Our computational model has a pattern-matching algorithm for bitstrings output by the blind signature scheme.
- Our symbolic model incorporates the attacker's derivation rules for blind signatures presented in Sect. 3

Protocol syntax. A k-party protocol $\Pi = \Pi_1, \ldots, \Pi_k$ is a sequence of roles. A role $\Pi_i = \Pi_i^1, \cdots, \Pi_i^n$ is a sequence of pairs $\Pi_i^p = (l_i^p, r_i^p)$ consisting of patterns l_i^p and r_i^p defined below. Intuitively, an honest party receives a message that matches the pattern l_i^p and sends a message constructed according to the pattern r_i^p. A pattern is an element of the algebra generated from a set X of sorted variables and the following operators with arities:

$$\langle \_, \_ \rangle : \text{Term} \times \text{Term} \to \text{Pair} \qquad Blind : \text{Term} \times \text{Random} \times \text{ID} \to \text{Blinded}$$
$$Bsign : \text{Term} \times \text{ID} \to \text{Bsigned} \qquad Sign : \text{Term} \times \text{ID} \to \text{Sig}.$$

The sorts ID, Pair, and Nonce are for the identities of parties, pairs, and nonces, respectively. The sort Random is for the random seeds used in the blinding and unblinding algorithms. The sorts Blinded, Bsigned, Sig are for outputs of the blinding, signing, and unblinding algorithms, respectively. The sort Term is the supersort of these sorts except for Random. It does not include Random because the random seeds are used only in the blinding and unblinding algorithms and are not used as texts.

The set of variables of a sort s is denoted by X_s. We fix the sets X_{ID}, X_{Nonce}, and X_{Random} as $X_{\text{ID}} = \{A_1, \ldots, A_k\}$, $X_{\text{Nonce}} = \bigcup_i X_{\text{Nonce}}(A_i)$, and $X_{\text{Random}} = \bigcup_i X_{\text{Random}}(A_i)$ where $X_{\text{Nonce}}(A_i) = \{N_{A_i}^j \mid j \in \mathbf{N}\}$ and $X_{\text{Random}}(A_i) = \{R_{A_i}^j \mid j \in \mathbf{N}\}$. The set of variables is denoted by X.

Table 5. Symbolic deduction rules

$$\frac{u \in H}{F, H \vdash_C u} \qquad \frac{a \in C}{F, H \vdash_C n^{a,j,s}} \qquad \frac{F, H \vdash_C \langle u_1, u_2 \rangle \quad i \in \{1,2\}}{F, H \vdash_C u_i} \qquad \frac{F, H \vdash_C u_1, u_2}{F, H \vdash_C \langle u_1, u_2 \rangle}$$

$$\frac{F, H \vdash_C u \quad r \in R_C}{F, H \vdash_C \text{blind}(u, r, a)} \qquad \frac{F, H \vdash_C \text{blind}(u, r, a) \quad r \in R_C}{F, H \vdash_C u}$$

$$\frac{}{F, H \vdash_C \text{fakeblind}(r^{adv(j)}, a), \ n^{adv(j)}, \ a}$$

$$\frac{F, H \vdash_C u \quad a \in C}{F, H \vdash_C \text{blindsign}(u, a)} \qquad \frac{F, H \vdash_C \text{blindsign}(u, a)}{F, H \vdash_C u}$$

$$\frac{F, H \vdash_C \text{blindsign}(\text{blind}(u, r, a), a) \quad r \in R_C}{F, H \vdash_C \text{sign}(u, a)} \qquad \frac{F, H \vdash_C \text{sign}(u, a)}{F, H \vdash_C u}$$

$$\frac{F, H \vdash_C \text{blindsign}(\text{fakeblind}(r^{adv(j)}, a), a), u \quad F(\text{blindsign}(\text{fakeblind}(r^{adv(j)}, a), a)) = \text{sign}(u, a)}{F, H \vdash_C \text{sign}(u, a)}$$

$$\frac{F, H \vdash_C \text{blindsign}(\text{fakeblind}(r^{adv(j)}, a), a), \text{blind}(u, r, a) \quad F(\text{blindsign}(\text{fakeblind}(r^{adv(j)}, a), a)) = \text{blindsign}(\text{blind}(u, r, a), a)}{F, H \vdash_C \text{blindsign}(\text{blind}(u, r, a), a)}$$

where $R_C = \{r^{adv(j)}, r^{a,j,s} \mid a \in C, j \in \mathbf{N}, s \in \mathbf{N}\}$.

Not all the protocols described in this syntax are executable because (1) agents can use a variable X only after receiving and generating its value, (2) agents can sign on messages only with their signing key, and (3) the blindness property requires that random seeds for blinding and unblinding are not used elsewhere. We consider only executable protocols formally defined in [19].

Computational model. In the computational model, messages are bitstrings. For each sort s except for the supersort Term, we consider a set $\mathcal{C}^\eta.s$ of bitstrings whose lengths are bounded by a polynomial of the security parameter η. We assume that these sets are mutually disjoint, for example, by adding tags to their elements. We denote by $\mathcal{C}^\eta$ the union $\bigcup_s \mathcal{C}^\eta.s$ of these sets. We assume that the set $\mathcal{C}^\eta.$Nonce is sufficiently large, i.e. $1/|\mathcal{C}^\eta.$Nonce$|$ is negligible with respect to η. For blind signatures, we assume that $\mathcal{C}^\eta.$Random contains the set of random seeds used in the blinding algorithm.

We use assignments to store values of variables. An assignment ξ is a partial function from X to $\mathcal{C}^\eta$ that respects sorts, i.e. $\xi(\mathsf{X}.s) \subseteq \mathcal{C}^\eta.s$ for any sort s. From a pattern T and an assignment ξ, a bitstring $T\xi$ is recursively defined as follows if all variables occurring in T are defined in ξ:

$$X\xi = \xi(X)$$
$$\langle T_1, T_2 \rangle \xi = \langle T_1\xi, T_2\xi \rangle$$
$$Blind(T, X, A_i)\xi = B(T\xi, \xi(X), vk_{\xi(A_i)})$$
$$Bsign(T, A_i)\xi = S(T\xi, sk_{\xi(A_i)})$$
$$Sign(T, A_i)\xi = U(S(B(T\xi, r, vk_{\xi(A_i)}), sk_{\xi(A_i)}), r, vk_{\xi(A_i)})$$

where $\langle \_, \_ \rangle$ on the right-hand side of an equation is the constructor of a tuple, B, S, and U are the blinding, signing, and unblinding algorithms of a blind signature scheme, respectively, r is an arbitrary bitstring that can be used with the blinding algorithm, and $vk_{\xi(A_i)}$ and $sk_{\xi(A_i)}$ are the verification and signing keys, respectively. These keys are generated in an execution, which is explained later. We fix the bitstring r before an execution of a protocol. Note that since we assume that the blind signature scheme is deterministic, $Sign(T, A_i)\xi$ does not depend on the bitstring r. To avoid ambiguity, we assume that signers' IDs are attached to the outputs of the algorithms B, S, and U and that the texts of the signatures are attached to the outputs of the unblinding algorithm U.

We model computational executions of a protocol Π as interactions between a probabilistic polynomial-time attacker $\mathcal{A}$ and a simulator $\mathcal{M}$ of honest agents. The simulator $\mathcal{M}$ has a state (Sid, g) where Sid is a set of session identifiers, and g is the partial function defined below. A session identifier is a triplet $(s, i, (a_1, \ldots, a_k))$ where s is a unique number for each session identifier, i is the index of the role Π_i executed in this session, and $(a_1, \ldots, a_k)$ is the sequence of the names of the agents involved in this session. The function g maps a session identifier sid $= (s, i, (a_1, \ldots, a_k))$ to a local state (ξ, i, p) consisting of an assignment ξ, the index i of the role Π_i, and a program counter p. The assignment ξ has the values of the variables occurring in the role Π_i. The program counter p keeps track of the next step to be executed in this session.

The simulator transits according to queries from the attacker as follows:

- Only once in the initial state, it accepts a query $\mathbf{corrupt}(a_1, \ldots, a_\ell)$, which allows the attacker to corrupt agents $a_1, \ldots, a_\ell$. It replies with signing and verification keys $(sk_i, vk_i) \leftarrow G(1^\eta)$ for each agents $a_1, \ldots, a_\ell$ generated by the key-generation algorithm G and stays in the initial state:

$$(\mathsf{Sld}, g) \stackrel{\mathbf{corrupt}(a_1, \ldots, a_\ell)}{\longrightarrow} (\mathsf{Sld}, g).$$

- On receiving a query $\mathbf{new}(i, a_1, \ldots, a_k)$, it starts a new session of the ith role Π_i that involves agents $a_1, \ldots, a_k$. It transits as follows:

$$(\mathsf{Sld}, g) \stackrel{\mathbf{new}(i, a_1, \ldots, a_k)}{\longrightarrow} (\mathsf{Sld} \cup \{\mathsf{sid}\}, g \cup \{\mathsf{sid} \mapsto (\xi, i, 1)\})$$

where $\mathsf{sid} = (|\mathsf{Sld}| + 1, i, (a_1, \ldots, a_k))$ is a new session identifier, $(\xi, i, 1)$ is its local state defined as follows for $j \in \mathbf{N}$:

$$\begin{cases} \xi(A_j) = a_j \\ \xi(N_{A_i}^j) = n(a_i, j, |\mathsf{Sld}| + 1) \leftarrow \mathcal{C}^\eta.\mathsf{Nonce} \\ \xi(R_{A_i}^j) = r(a_i, j, |\mathsf{Sld}| + 1) \leftarrow \mathcal{C}^\eta.\mathsf{Random}. \end{cases}$$

Then, the simulator generates signing and verification keys $(sk_q, vk_q) \leftarrow G(1^\eta)$ for each $q = 1, \ldots, k$, if they have not been generated, and gives the verification keys $vk_1, \ldots, vk_k$ to the attacker. Since the attacker can simulate corrupted agents, we assume that the attacker does not send $\mathbf{new}(i, a_1, \ldots, a_k)$ if a_i is corrupted.

- On receiving a query $\mathbf{send}(\mathsf{sid}, m)$ at a state (Sld, g), the simulator tries to match the bitstring m with the pattern l_i^p that the session sid expects to receive. Formally, it tries to find an extension ξ' of ξ such that $m = l_i^p \xi'$, where $(\xi, i, p) = g(\mathsf{sid})$ and (l_i^p, r_i^p) is the pth element of Π_i. If the matching succeeds, it transits as follows:

$$(\mathsf{Sld}, g) \stackrel{\mathbf{send}(\mathsf{sid}, m)}{\longrightarrow} (\mathsf{Sld}, g|_{dom(g) \setminus \{\mathsf{sid}\}} \cup \{\mathsf{sid} \mapsto (\xi', i, p+1)\})$$

by sending the bitstring $r_i^p \xi'$ to the attacker. The matching algorithm recursively parses the bitstring m according to the pattern l_i^p using the assignment ξ. For example, if $l_i^p = \langle T_0, T_1 \rangle$, it splits m as a pair $\langle m', m'' \rangle$ and matches m' and m'' with T_0 and T_1, respectively. If the pattern is $Bsign(Blind(T, R, A), A)$, the parsing succeeds if the bitstring can be unblinded into a signature on $T\xi$ by using the randomness $\xi(R)$ and the verification key of $\xi(A)$. The algorithm is formally defined in [19].

For randomness $r_\mathcal{A}$ and $r_\mathcal{M}$ of the attacker $\mathcal{A}$ and the simulator $\mathcal{M}$ of the protocol, respectively, a computational trace $\mathrm{Exec}^c_{\eta, r_\mathcal{A}, r_\mathcal{M}}(\mathcal{A}, \Pi)$ is the sequence of transitions of $\mathcal{M}$ that starts with the initial state $(\emptyset, \emptyset)$. It is often regarded as a random variable on $r_\mathcal{M}$ and $r_\mathcal{A}$ and denoted by $\mathrm{Exec}^c_\eta(\mathcal{A}, \Pi)$.

In this paper, we consider safety properties of security protocols. A computational security (safety) criterion of a protocol is defined as a set P_c of computational traces. We say that a protocol Π satisfies a security criterion P_c, which we write as $\Pi \models P_c$, if and only if the following probability is overwhelming for any probabilistic polynomial-time attacker $\mathcal{A}$:

$$\Pr[tr_c \leftarrow \mathrm{Exec}_\eta^c(\Pi, \mathcal{A}) : tr_c \in P_c.]$$

Symbolic model In the symbolic model, messages are terms defined by the following grammar:

$$u ::= a \mid n^{a,j,s} \mid n^{adv(j)} \mid \langle u_1, u_2 \rangle \mid \mathsf{blind}(u, r, a) \mid$$
$$\mathsf{fakeblind}(r^{adv(j)}, a) \mid \mathsf{blindsign}(u, a) \mid \mathsf{sign}(u, a)$$
$$r ::= r^{a,j,s} \mid r^{adv(j)}.$$

The term a is the name of an agent. It is sometimes regarded as a bitstring in $\mathcal{C}^\eta.\mathrm{ID}$, by abuse of notation. The terms $n^{a,j,s}$ and $n^{adv(j)}$ are nonces generated by an agent and the attacker, respectively. The term $\langle u_1, u_2 \rangle$ is a pair of terms u_1 and u_2. The terms $\mathsf{blind}(u, r, a)$, $\mathsf{blindsign}(u, a)$, and $\mathsf{sign}(u, a)$ represent the outputs of the blinding, signing, unblinding algorithm, respectively. Randomness r is either $r^{a,j,s}$ or $r^{adv(j)}$, which are generated by an agent or the attacker, respectively. The term $\mathsf{fakeblind}(r^{adv(j)}, a)$ is a "fake" blinded message as explained in the previous section. With these notations, we assume that the signing key of each agent is implicitly given to the agent and kept secret unless the agent is corrupted. We also assume that the verification keys are published.

We model symbolic executions of a protocol Π as state transition systems. Each system is associated with a partial function F. The systems are similar to the simulator in the computational model although terms are used instead of bitstrings and the attacker's knowledge is also contained in a state of the system.

A state of a system is a triplet (SId, f, H) consisting of a set SId of session ids, a function f, and a set H of terms. The function f maps each session id $\mathsf{sid} \in \mathsf{SId}$ to a local state (ζ, i, p) of the session consisting of an assignment ζ, an index i, and a program counter p. The set H contains the messages that have been sent to the attacker. An assignment ζ is a partial function from X into the set of terms. From a pattern T and an assignment ζ, the term $T\zeta$ substitutes terms for variables in T according to the assignment ζ.

The system has the following transitions:

- At the beginning of the execution, the attacker may send a query **corrupt**$(a_1, \ldots, a_\ell)$. Then, we associate the set $C = \{a_1, \ldots, a_\ell\}$ with this execution.
- The attacker may send a query **new**$(i, a_1, \ldots, a_k)$. In this case the simulator starts a new session of the ith role Π_i involving agents $a_1, \ldots, a_k$. The simulator transits as follows:

$$(\mathsf{SId}, f, H) \overset{\mathbf{new}(i, a_1, \ldots, a_k)}{\longrightarrow} (\mathsf{SId} \cup \{\mathsf{sid}\}, f \cup \{\mathsf{sid} \mapsto (\zeta, i, 1)\}, H)$$

where sid $= (|\mathsf{Sld}| + 1, i, (a_1, \ldots, a_k))$ is a new session identifier and $(\zeta, i, 1)$ is its local state defined by $\zeta(A_j) = a_j$, $\zeta(N^j_{A_i}) = n^{a_i, j, s}$, $\zeta(R^j_{A_i}) = r^{a_i, j, s}$, and $s = |\mathsf{Sld}| + 1$ for $j \in \mathbf{N}$.

- The attacker may send a query **send**(sid, u) to the system, which is in a state (Sld, f, H), if $F, H \vdash_C u$ is derived from the rules in Table 5, where F is the partial function associated to the system. The system lets $(\zeta, i, p) = f(sid)$ and transits as follows if the message u matches the pattern l^p_i under the assignment ζ, i.e., there is an extension of ζ' of ζ such that $u = l^p_i \zeta'$:

$$(\mathsf{Sld}, f, H) \overset{\mathbf{new}(sid, m)}{\to} (\mathsf{Sld}, f|_{dom(g) \backslash \{sid\}} \cup \{sid \mapsto (\zeta', i, p+1)\}, H \cup \{r^p_i \zeta'\}).$$

A symbolic trace of a system is a sequence of transitions that starts with the initial state $(\emptyset, \emptyset, \emptyset)$. The set of symbolic traces of the system associated with a partial function F is denoted by $\mathrm{Exec}^s(\Pi, F)$. The set of symbolic traces of a protocol Π is denoted by $\mathrm{Exec}^s(\Pi) = \bigcup_F \mathrm{Exec}^s(\Pi, F)$, where F is taken over the sets of partial functions from terms to terms.

A symbolic security (safety) criterion of a protocol is defined as a set P_s. We say that a protocol Π satisfies a security criterion P_s, which we write as $\Pi \models P_s$, if and only if $\mathrm{Exec}^s(\Pi) \subseteq P_s$ holds. Since the set $\mathrm{Exec}^s(\Pi)$ is prefix-closed, $\mathrm{Exec}^s(\Pi) \subseteq P_s$ if and only if $\mathrm{Exec}^s(\Pi) \subseteq P'_s$ for the largest prefix-closed subset $P'_s \subseteq P_s$. We therefore deal with only prefix-closed P_s, which implies that we consider only safety properties.

5   Computational Soundness

The goal of this paper is to prove computational soundness of symbolic verification: if a protocol is secure in the symbolic model, it is also secure in the computational model. To state and prove this formally, we first relate the two models. More precisely, we define a relation $\prec$ between symbolic traces and computational traces as follows:

$$tr_s \prec tr_c \overset{\triangle}{\Leftrightarrow} tr_s = c(tr_c) \text{ for some mapping } c,$$

where c is a mapping from bitstrings into terms and $c(tr_c)$ replaces each bitstring m occurring in tr_c with the term $c(m)$. Formally, $c(tr_c)$ is the symbolic trace obtained from tr_c by replacing each label **send**(sid, m) with **send**$(sid, c(m))$ and each global state (Sld, g) with (Sld, f, H), where f is defined by $f(sid) = (c \circ \xi, i, p)$ for any sid with $(\xi, i, p) = g(sid)$ and $H = c(S)$ is the image of the set S of bitstrings sent to the attacker until this state.

To prove the soundness, we will show that almost all computational executions have their symbolic counterparts that comply with the attacker's rule. We will show a mapping lemma for our models formally.

Lemma 1 (Mapping Lemma). *Let $\mathcal{BS}$ be a secure blind signature scheme. Let Π be an arbitrary executable k-party protocol and $\mathcal{A}$ be an arbitrary probabilistic* *polynomial-time attacker. Then, the following probability is overwhelming with respect to the security parameter η*

$$\Pr[tr_c \leftarrow \mathrm{Exec}_\eta^c(\mathcal{A}, \Pi) : \exists tr_s \in \mathrm{Exec}^s(\Pi).\ tr_s \prec tr_c],$$

where the probability is taken over the coin-flipping of the attacker $\mathcal{A}$ and the simulator of the protocol Π.

Using this lemma, we prove the soundness theorem as follows. Since our goal is to analyze computational security through symbolic analysis, for a computational criterion P_c, we must consider a symbolic criterion P_s that is "not weaker" than P_c, i.e. for any symbolic trace $tr_s \in P_s$, any computational trace tr_c with $tr_s \prec tr_c$ satisfies $tr_c \in P_c$. Since we are considering only prefix-closed P_s, this implies that P_c must be also prefix-closed.

Theorem 1 (Soundness theorem). *Let $\mathcal{BS}$ be a secure blind signature scheme. Let Π be an arbitrary executable k-party protocol and P_c and P_s be their symbolic and computational security criteria, respectively, such that for all tr_s and tr_c, $tr_s \in P_s$ and $tr_s \prec tr_c$ imply $tr_c \in P_c$. Then, $\Pi \models P_s$ implies $\Pi \models P_c$.*

Proof. Assuming that $\mathrm{Exec}^s(\Pi) \subseteq P_s$, we show that $\Pr[tr_c \leftarrow \mathrm{Exec}_\eta^c(\Pi, \mathcal{A}) : tr_c \in P_c]$ is overwhelming with respect to the security parameter η. From the assumption on the criteria, it is sufficient to show that $\Pr[tr_c \leftarrow \mathrm{Exec}_\eta^c(\Pi, \mathcal{A}) : \exists tr_s \in P_s.\ tr_s \prec tr_c]$ is overwhelming. This follows from $\mathrm{Exec}^s(\Pi) \subseteq P_s$ and the mapping lemma. □

We prove the mapping lemma by using a sufficient condition for deducibility $H, F \vdash_C u$ given in the lemma shown below. The condition is formulated by using a subterm relation $\sqsubseteq_C$, which is the least reflexive and transitive relation satisfying

$$u_i \sqsubseteq_C \langle u_1, u_2 \rangle \qquad\qquad u \sqsubseteq_C \mathsf{blindsign}(u, a)$$

$$u \sqsubseteq_C \mathsf{blind}(u, r, a) \qquad\qquad u \sqsubseteq_C \mathsf{sign}(u, a)$$

for any terms u, u_1, and u_2, and for any name a, $r \in R_C$, and $i \in \{1, 2\}$, where $R_C = \{r^{adv}(j), r^{a,j,s} \mid a \in C, j, s \in \mathbf{N}\}$. We denote $u \sqsubseteq_C H$ if and only if $u \sqsubseteq_C v$ for some $v \in H$. It is easy to see that $u \sqsubseteq_C H$ implies $H, F \vdash u$ for any F.

Lemma 2. *Let H be a set of terms and u be a term. Let C be a set of (corrupted) agents and F be a partial function on terms. Then, for any term u, $F, H \vdash_C u$ if both of the following conditions hold:*

(i) *For any term $u' \sqsubseteq_C u$ that is either an honest nonce $n^{a,j,s}$ or a blinded message $\mathsf{blind}(u_0, r^{a,j,s}, a')$ with $a \notin C$, it holds that $u' \sqsubseteq_C H$, and*

(ii) *For any term $u' \sqsubseteq_C u$ that is either a signature term $\mathsf{sign}(u_0, a)$ or a signed blinded term $\mathsf{blindsign}(\mathsf{blind}(u_0, r, a'), a)$ with $a \notin C$, if $u' \not\sqsubseteq_C H$, then both $\mathsf{blindsign}(\mathsf{fakeblind}(r^{adv(j')}, a), a) \sqsubseteq_C H$ and $u' = F(\mathsf{blindsign}(\mathsf{fakeblind}(r^{adv(j')}, a), a))$ hold for some randomness $r^{adv(j')}$ of the attacker.*

This lemma is easily shown by the induction on the structure of u and by using the rules in Table 5.

Proof of Lemma 1 The proof proceeds as follows. (1) From a computational trace tr_c, we construct a (pseudo) symbolic trace tr_s by parsing bitstrings sent by the attacker in tr_c. (2) We show that with an overwhelming probability, the (pseudo) symbolic trace tr_s is in $\mathrm{Exec}^s(\Pi)$.

(1) From a computational trace tr_c, we construct a (pseudo) symbolic trace tr_s by using a parsing algorithm. This algorithm parses bitstrings while updating a partial injection c from bitstrings into terms. When a bitstring m is input, it returns the term $c(m)$ if $c(m)$ is defined. Otherwise, it recursively parses m into a term u as follows and extends the partial function c with $m \mapsto u$:

- Case m is of sort Nonce. It returns a fresh nonce term $n^{adv(j)}$.
- Case m is of sort ID. It returns a name term for m.
- Case m is of sort Pair. It parses the components m_1 and m_2 of the pair m, respectively, into terms u_1 and u_2 and returns $\langle u_1, u_2 \rangle$.
- Case m is of sort Blinded. It extracts the name a of the signer from m and returns $\mathsf{fakeblind}(r^{adv(j)}, a)$, where $r^{adv(j)}$ is a fresh randomness term of the attacker.
- Case m is of sort Sig. It extracts the text m_0 and the agent name a, of the signature, and checks whether $V(m, m_0, vk_a) = 1$ where vk_a is user a's verification key. If the verification succeeds, it parses m_0 into a term u_0 and returns $\mathsf{sign}(u_0, a)$. Otherwise it returns a fresh nonce term $n^{adv(j)}$.
- Case m is of sort Bsigned. It first extracts the signer's name a from m. If the bitstring is unblinded by some uncorrupted party a' with some text m_0 and randomness $r(a', j, s)$ in tr_c, then it parses m_0 into a term u_0 and returns term $\mathsf{blindsign}(\mathsf{blind}(u_0, r^{a', j, s}, a), a)$. Otherwise, if the bitstring is computed by the honest party a using the signing algorithm with an input m_0, then it parses m_0 into a term u_0 and returns term $\mathsf{blindsign}(u_0, a)$. Otherwise it returns a fresh nonce term $n^{adv(j)}$.

Using the above parsing algorithm, we construct a partial function c from bitstrings to terms as follows. We first let the partial mapping c contain (only) the pairs: $a \mapsto a$ for any agent a, where the first and second elements are a bitstring and a term, respectively, and $n(a, j, s) \mapsto n^{a, j, s}$ as well as $r(a, j, s) \mapsto r^{a, j, s}$ for any agent a and any j and s. Then, for each transition of the form

$$(\mathsf{SId}, f) \xrightarrow{\mathsf{send}(\mathsf{sid}, m)} (\mathsf{SId}, f')$$

in tr_c, we update c by running the parsing algorithm on the bitstring m sent by the attacker and then update c as follows according to how the reply m' to the message m is computed. Recall that m' is computed as $m' = r_i^p \xi'$ using r_i^p and ξ' defined by $f'(\mathsf{sid}) = (\xi', i, p + 1)$ and $(l_i^p, r_i^p) = \Pi_i^p$. We extend c with $m' \mapsto r_i^p(c \circ \xi')$. Note that since each variable $X \in dom(\xi')$ is bound either in a prior step or in this step by the matching algorithm, the parsing algorithm has also seen the bitstring $\xi'(X)$, thus $\xi'(X) \in dom(c)$.

(2) We show that the symbolic trace $tr_s = c(tr_c)$ is in the set $\text{Exec}^s(\Pi)$. It is sufficient to show that with an overwhelming probability, there is a partial function F such that $F, H \vdash u$ for any **send** transition

$$(\mathsf{Sld}, f, H) \overset{\mathbf{send}(\mathsf{sid}, u)}{\to} (\mathsf{Sld}, f', H')$$

in tr_s. With Lemma 2, it is sufficient to check the two conditions (i) and (ii) instead of the deducibility $F, H \vdash u$.

(2-i) To derive contradiction, assume that condition (i) does not hold with a non-negligible probability. Then, both $u' \sqsubseteq_C u$ and $u' \not\sqsubseteq_c H$ for a term u' that is either a nonce or a blinded message computed by an uncorrupted party, where C is the set of parties corrupted in tr_c. Let m and m' be the bitstrings that are parsed into u and u', respectively. Then, m' is a nonce or a blinded message generated by an uncorrupted party, which are not computable by the attacker. Since $u' \sqsubseteq_C u$, the bitstring m' is easily computed by parsing m. Thus the attacker must have received some information on m'. Since $u' \not\sqsubseteq_C H$, the attacker must break the blinding algorithm to extract the information from the received messages. This contradicts the blindness property.

More formally, we use the following polynomial-time machines $\mathcal{B}_1$ and $\mathcal{B}_1'$.

- $\mathcal{B}_1$ is a machine that simulates the simulator $\mathcal{M}$ and the attacker $\mathcal{A}$ of the protocol, parses the computational trace tr_c into a symbolic trace tr_s, checks whether the condition (i) holds for tr_s, and outputs 1 if it holds.
- $\mathcal{B}_1'$ is a machine that is identical to $\mathcal{B}_1$ except that (1) each time it uses the blinding algorithm B for uncorrupted parties, it blinds a fresh random bitstring $n \leftarrow \{0,1\}^\eta$ instead of the input m, and (2) when it unblinds a bitstring into a signature on this plaintext m, it first unblinds the bitstring into a signature σ_n on the random bitstring n and, if it succeeds, uses a signature $\sigma_m = U(S(B(m, r, vk), sk), m, r, vk)$ on m instead of σ_n.

It is easy to see that both machines runs in polynomial time. Then, what we want to show is that the probability $\Pr[\mathcal{B}_1 = 1]$ is overwhelming. The probability $\Pr[\mathcal{B}_1' = 1]$ is overwhelming because the bitstrings to be blinded, which may be computed from m', are replaced by random bitstrings. These probabilities are shown to be negligibly close by using the blindness property and a hybrid argument. Thus $\Pr[\mathcal{B}_1 = 1]$ is overwhelming.

(2-ii) Similar to condition (i), we consider two polynomial-time machines $\mathcal{B}_2$ and $\mathcal{B}_2'$ that are identical to $\mathcal{B}_1$ and $\mathcal{B}_1'$, respectively, except that they check condition (ii) instead of condition (i). The probabilities $\Pr[\mathcal{B}_2 = 1]$ and $\Pr[\mathcal{B}_2' = 1]$ are shown to be by using the blindness property and a hybrid argument. Thus it is sufficient to show that $\Pr[\mathcal{B}_2']$ is overwhelming.

To show this, we paraphrase condition (ii) by introducing the two sets $BF_{a,i}$ and $BS_{a,i}$ for each index i and each agent $a \notin C$:

- $BF_{a,i}$ is the set of terms u of the form $\mathsf{blindsign}(\mathsf{fakeblind}(r^{adv(j)}, a), a)$ such that $u \sqsubseteq_C H$ where (Sld, f, H) is the ith state of tr_s.

– $BS_{a,i}$ is the set of terms u' having either of the forms $\mathsf{blindsign}(\mathsf{blind}(u_0, r, a), a)$ with an honest party's randomness r and $\mathsf{sign}(u_0, a)$ such that $u' \sqsubseteq_C u$ and $u' \not\sqsubseteq_C H$ for some **send** transition before the ith state of the following form:

$$(\mathsf{SId}, f, H) \overset{\mathbf{send}(\mathsf{sid}, u)}{\to} (\mathsf{SId}, f', H').$$

Then, condition (ii) holds if there is a partial function F such that $F(BF_{a,i}) \supseteq BS_{a,i}$ for all $a \notin C$ and index i. By construction, we have $BF_{a,i} \subseteq BF_{a,i+1}$ and $BS_{a,i} \subseteq BS_{a,i+1}$ for all i and a. Then, it is easy to see that such an F exists if the inequality $|BF_{a,i}| \geq |BS_{a,i}|$ holds for all i and $a \notin C$.

To show that this inequality holds for all i and $a \notin C$ with an overwhelming probability, it is sufficient to show that conditional probability $\Pr[|BF_{a,i}| \geq |BS_{a,i}| \mid a \notin C.]$ is overwhelming for any agent a and $i \in \mathbf{N}$.

To show this by using the unforgeability property, we modify the machine $\mathcal{B}_2'$ so that it uses the signing oracle $\mathcal{O}_{S_{sk}}$ instead of the signing algorithm for agent a. Without loss of generality, we can assume that no bitstring is sent more than once to the signing oracle, for example by assuming that each query and the replies are stored on a table. Let $\mathcal{Q}$ be the set of queries sent to this oracle. Let $\mathcal{S}$ be the set consisting of the signatures used in tr_c and those obtained by unblinding bitstrings used in tr_c. Then, the unforgeability property implies $|\mathcal{Q}| \geq |\mathcal{S}|$ with an overwhelming probability. To show $|BF_{a,i}| \geq |BS_{a,i}|$, it is sufficient to show that there are sets $\mathcal{Q}_\mathcal{A}$ and $\mathcal{S}_\mathcal{A}$ that satisfy inequalities $|BF_{a,i}| \geq |\mathcal{Q}_\mathcal{A}| \geq |\mathcal{S}_\mathcal{A}| \geq |BS_{a,i}|$.

Let $\mathcal{Q}_\mathcal{A} \subseteq \mathcal{Q}$ be the set of queries issued by the attacker. Then, the replies to the queries in $\mathcal{Q}_\mathcal{A}$ are parsed into mutually distinct terms of the forms $\mathsf{blindsign}(\mathsf{fakeblind}(r^{adv(j)}, a), a)$ in the set $BF_{a,i}$. Thus we have $|BF_{a,i}| \geq |\mathcal{Q}_\mathcal{A}|$.

Let $\mathcal{S}_\mathcal{A} \subseteq \mathcal{S}$ be the set consisting of signatures computed by the attacker and signatures obtained by unblinding bitstrings computed by the attacker. Then, the set $\mathcal{S}_\mathcal{A}$ contains the signatures that are parsed into terms in $BS_{a,i}$ of the form $\mathsf{sign}(u_0, a)$ and those obtained by unblinding bitstrings that are parsed into terms in $BS_{a,i}$ of the form $\mathsf{blindsign}(\mathsf{blind}(u_0, r, a), a)$. Thus, the inequality $|\mathcal{S}_\mathcal{A}| \geq |BS_{a,i}|$ holds if the latter signatures are mutually distinct and distinct from the former signatures. This is true, except with negligible probability of coincidence of random bitstrings, because we are considering the simulator $\mathcal{B}_2'$, which blinds fresh random bitstrings each time it uses the blinding algorithm and never sends them over the network.

With $|\mathcal{Q}| \geq |\mathcal{S}|$, the inequality $|\mathcal{Q}_\mathcal{A}| \geq |\mathcal{S}_\mathcal{A}|$ follows from another inequality $|\mathcal{Q} \setminus \mathcal{Q}_\mathcal{A}| \leq |\mathcal{S} \setminus \mathcal{S}_\mathcal{A}|$. We will divide the set $\mathcal{Q} \setminus \mathcal{Q}_\mathcal{A}$ into two mutually disjoint sets $\mathcal{Q}_B$ and $\mathcal{Q}_S$ and introduce two subsets $\mathcal{S}_B$ and $\mathcal{S}_S$ of the set $\mathcal{S}$. For such sets, the inequality $|\mathcal{Q} \setminus \mathcal{Q}_\mathcal{A}| \leq |\mathcal{S} \setminus \mathcal{S}_\mathcal{A}|$ follows from the inequalities $|\mathcal{Q}_B| \leq |\mathcal{S}_B|$ and $|\mathcal{Q}_S| \leq |\mathcal{S}_S|$ if the sets $\mathcal{S}_B$, $\mathcal{S}_S$, and $\mathcal{S}_\mathcal{A}$ are mutually disjoint. Let $\mathcal{Q}_B$ and $\mathcal{Q}_S$ be the sets of queries made by the simulator to compute bitstrings for patterns of the forms $Bsign(Blind(\_, \_, \_), \_)$ and $Sign(\_, \_)$, respectively. Let $\mathcal{S}_B$ and $\mathcal{S}_S$ be the set of signatures obtained by unblinding replies to queries in $\mathcal{Q}_B$ and $\mathcal{Q}_S$, respectively. Since we are considering the simulator $\mathcal{B}_2'$, each query in $\mathcal{Q}_B$ is computed by blinding a fresh random bitstring, thus we have $\mathcal{S}_B \cap (\mathcal{S}_\mathcal{A} \cup \mathcal{S}_S) = \emptyset$

and $|Q_B| \leq |S_B|$ except with negligible probability of coincidence. We also have $|Q_S| \leq |S_S|$ except with negligible probability of coincidence, as we compute the bitstring from a pattern of the form $Sign(\_,\_)$ by using a fixed randomness bitstring.

Without loss of generality, we can assume that the simulator $\mathcal{B}'_2$ makes signatures without sending a query to the signing oracle whenever possible. More specifically, we assume that

- the simulator $\mathcal{B}'_2$ reuses signatures that are sent over the network whenever possible and does not send a query to make such signatures, and
- the simulator $\mathcal{B}'_2$ does not make a query to compute the first arguments of the algorithm B, which are replaced with fresh random bitstrings.

Note that the former assumption is allowed since we are considering deterministic blind signature scheme. Otherwise the attacker can detect signature reuse.

Using these assumptions, we show that sets S_S and S_A are disjoint as follows. For any signature σ, we have two cases:

- If σ is sent by the attacker before it is computed by any honest party, then it follows from the first assumption above that the simulator does not make a query to make σ but reuses σ, thus we have $\sigma \notin S_S$.
- If σ is computed by an honest party before it is sent by the attacker, the signature term $\mathsf{sign}(u, a)$ obtained by parsing σ occurs in H of a state (Sld, f, H) that before the attacker sends $\mathsf{sign}(u, a)$. It follows from the second assumption above that there is such a state that satisfies $\mathsf{sign}(u, a) \sqsubseteq_C H$ because otherwise the signature is computed only to construct a first argument of the algorithm B and is actually not computed by $\mathcal{B}'_2$ as we have assumed. Thus we have $\mathsf{sign}(u, a) \notin BS_{a,i}$ by definition of $BS_{a,i}$, thus $\sigma \notin S_A$. $\qquad\square$

6   Discussion of the Symbolic Attacker's Ability

To establish computational soundness, we have given our symbolic attacker more computational power than the symbolic model of Kremer and Ryan. Some may wonder whether our symbolic attacker is too strong and that even computationally secure protocols will not be secure under this attacker. We will make a few observations showing that this is not true at least for some protocols and security properties.

As indicated by the examples in Sect. 3, there are two main differences between our symbolic model and that of Kremer et al. The first is that our symbolic attacker is not required to know the message u of a signature $\mathsf{sign}(u, a)$ when he sends a query $\mathsf{fakeblind}(r, a)$ to make this signature while their symbolic attacker is required to know u when he sends a query $\mathsf{blind}(u, r, a)$. For protocols that accept only signatures $\mathsf{sign}(u, a)$ on messages u that the attacker can know before sending $\mathsf{fakeblind}(r, a)$, e.g. messages consisting of constants, this actually does not strengthen the attacker because the attacker may use $\mathsf{blind}(u, r, a)$ and unblind $\mathsf{blindsign}(\mathsf{blind}(u, r, a), a)$ as honest parties do, instead of using $\mathsf{fakeblind}(r, a)$ and the rules involving $\mathsf{fakeblind}$.

The second is that our symbolic attacker can alter a query $\mathsf{blind}(u, r, a)$ with $\mathsf{fakeblind}(r', a)$ and the reply $\mathsf{blindsign}(\mathsf{fakeblind}(r', a), a)$ with $\mathsf{blindsign}(\mathsf{blind}(u, r, a), a)$, which can be unblinded by an honest party who makes the message $\mathsf{blind}(u, r, a)$. The honest party can output the signature $\mathsf{sign}(u, a)$ even if the attacker does not alter the messages. Thus, as long as considering safety properties that are not dependent on the exact messages sent as queries and their replies, the difference does not affect the security properties.

We believe that these observations can be formalized and generalized to some extent, although this is beyond the scope of this paper. Such a theorem might allow us to use an existing automatic analysis tool for computationally sound analysis and justify analysis based on a previous symbolic model.

7   Conclusion

In this paper, we describe a few difficulties involved in establishing the computational soundness of Kremer and Ryan's symbolic model under standard security assumptions on blind signatures. We then propose an alternative symbolic model and prove its computational soundness assuming a secure blind signature scheme.

In addition to the papers we have cited, there is a large body of work on symbolic analysis techniques and their computational soundness. Owing to space limitations, we mention only a few expected extensions.

Our symbolic model has only blind signatures as primitives and allow a rather restricted class of protocols. To analyze practical protocols, it must be extended with other primitives and a larger class of protocols, and the soundness must be proved again for the extended symbolic model, although some parts of our results can be used in the symbolic model and the proof. A general framework of Backes et al. [2] and Cortier and Warinschi's results [9] on composable computational soundness might be helpful to do this.

Our symbolic model and soundness result deal with security properties that are defined as predicates on a protocol execution trace such as weak secrecy and authentication. Such trace-based properties include protection against double spending in e-cash protocols [5] and eligibility of voting protocols [15]. On the other hand, since blind signatures are used for protecting privacy and anonymity, it is desirable to extend our results to equivalence properties such as observational equivalence as in [6,7]. The "trace mapping" technique, which we adapt to blind signatures, is also used in all soundness results for equivalence properties, to the best of our knowledge. We therefore believe that our results also serve as a first step toward the soundness for equivalence properties.

References

1. Abadi, M., Rogaway, P.: Reconciling two views of cryptography (the computational soundness of formal encryption). J. Cryptology 15(2), 103–127 (2002)
2. Backes, M., Hofheinz, D., Unruh, D.: CoSP: a general framework for computational soundness proofs. In: Al-Shaer, E., Jha, S., Keromytis, A.D. (eds.) ACM Conference on Computer and Communications Security. pp. 66–78. ACM (2009)

3. Bellare, M., Namprempre, C., Pointcheval, D., Semanko, M.: The one-more-RSA-inversion problems and the security of chaum's blind signature scheme. J. Cryptology **16**(3), 185–215 (2003)
4. Boldyreva, A.: Threshold signatures, multisignatures and blind signatures based on the gap-diffie-hellman-group signature scheme. In: Desmedt, Y. (ed.) PKC 2003. LNCS, vol. 2567, pp. 31–46. Springer, Heidelberg (2003)
5. Chaum, D.: Blind signatures for untraceable payments. In: Chaum, D., Rivest, R.L., Sherman, A.T. (eds.) CRYPTO, pp. 199–203. Plenum Press, New York (1982)
6. Comon-Lundh, H., Cortier, V.: Computational soundness of observational equivalence. In: Proceedings of the 15th ACM Conference on Computer and Communications Security, CCS'08, pp. 109–118. ACM, New York (2008)
7. Comon-Lundh, H., Hagiya, M., Kawamoto, Y., Sakurada, H.: Computational soundness of indistinguishability properties without computable parsing. In: Ryan, M.D., Smyth, B., Wang, G. (eds.) ISPEC 2012. LNCS, vol. 7232, pp. 63–79. Springer, Heidelberg (2012)
8. Cortier, V., Warinschi, B.: Computationally sound, automated proofs for security protocols. In: Sagiv [18], pp. 157–171
9. Cortier, V., Warinschi, B.: A composable computational soundness notion. In: Chen, Y., Danezis, G., Shmatikov, V. (eds.) ACM Conference on Computer and Communications Security. pp. 63–74. ACM (2011)
10. Fujioka, A., Okamoto, T., Ohta, K.: A practical secret voting scheme for large scale elections. In: Seberry, J., Zheng, Y. (eds.) ASIACRYPT 1992. LNCS, vol. 718, pp. 244–251. Springer, Heidelberg (1993)
11. Janvier, R., Lakhnech, Y., Mazaré, L.: Completing the picture: soundness of formal encryption in the presence of active adversaries. In: Sagiv [18], pp. 172–185
12. Juels, A., Luby, M., Ostrovsky, R.: Security of blind digital signatures. In: Kaliski Jr, B.S. (ed.) CRYPTO 1997. LNCS, vol. 1294, pp. 150–164. Springer, Heidelberg (1997)
13. Kawamoto, Y., Sakurada, H., Hagiya, M.: Computationally sound symbolic anonymity of a ring signature. In: Proceedings of Joint Workshop on Foundations of Computer Security, Automated Reasoning for Security Protocol Analysis and Issues in the Theory of, Security (FCS-ARSPA-WITS'08), June 2008, pp. 161–175 (2008)
14. Kawamoto, Y., Sakurada, H., Hagiya, M.: Computationally sound formalization of rerandomizable RCCA secure encryption. In: Cortier, V., Kirchner, C., Okada, M., Sakurada, H. (eds.) Formal to practical security. LNCS, vol. 5458, pp. 158–180. Springer, Heidelberg (2009)
15. Kremer, S., Ryan, M.D.: Analysis of an electronic voting protocol in the applied pi-calculus. In: Sagiv [18], pp. 186–200
16. Micciancio, D., Warinschi, B.: Soundness of formal encryption in the presence of active adversaries. In: Naor, M. (ed.) TCC 2004. LNCS, vol. 2951, pp. 133–151. Springer, Heidelberg (2004)
17. Pointcheval, D., Stern, J.: Security arguments for digital signatures and blind signatures. J. Cryptology **13**, 361–396 (2000)
18. Sagiv, S. (ed.): ESOP 2005. LNCS, vol. 3444. Springer, Heidelberg (2005)
19. Sakurada, H.: Computational soundness of symbolic blind signatures under active attacker (in preparation)

Improved Davies-Murphy's Attack
on DES Revisited

Yi Lu[1]([✉]) and Yvo Desmedt[2,3]

[1] National Engineering Research Center of Fundamental Software,
Institute of Software, Chinese Academy of Sciences, Beijing, China
luyi666@gmail.com
[2] The University of Texas at Dallas, Richardson, TX, USA
[3] University College London, London, UK

Abstract. DES is a famous 64-bit block cipher with balanced Feistel structure. It consists of 16 rounds. The key has 56 bits and the round key has 48 bits. Two major cryptanalysis techniques (namely, linear cryptanalysis and differential cryptanalysis) were notably developed and successfully applied to the full 16-round DES in the early 1990's. Davies-Murphy's attack can be seen as a special linear attack, which was developed before invention of linear cryptanalysis. It was improved by Biham and Biryukov and most recently by Jacques and Muller. In this paper, we revisit the recent improved Davies-Murphy's attack by Jacques and Muller from an algorithmic point of view. Based on Matsui's algorithm 2, we give an improved attack algorithm. Our improved attack algorithm works in time (2^{41}) with memory (2^{33}). In contrast, Jacques-Muller's attack takes time (2^{43}) and memory (2^{35}). It seems that our results of the time and memory complexities are optimal, due to the use of Walsh transform. Meanwhile, we generalize and further improve the results of the improved Matsui's algorithm 2 for the case that the subkeys are XORed into the round function.

Keywords: DES · Block cipher · Davies-Murphy's attack · Linear cryptanalysis · Matsui's algorithm 2 · Walsh transform

1 Introduction

DES is one of the most famous block ciphers [13]. It has been studied for 30 years and is still undergoing the progress of advanced cryptanalysis research today. Of the two major cryptanalysis techniques are linear cryptanalysis and differential

Y. Lu—Supported by the National Science and Technology Major Project under Grant No. 2012ZX01039-004, and the National Natural Science Foundation of China under Grant No. 61170072. Part of this work done while funded by British Telecommunications under Grant No. ML858284/CT506918.

Y. Desmedt—Part of this work was done while funded by EPSRC EP/C538285/1 and by BT, as BT Chair of Information Security.

J.-L. Danger et al. (Eds.): FPS 2013, LNCS 8352, pp. 264–271, 2014.
DOI: 10.1007/978-3-319-05302-8_16, © Springer International Publishing Switzerland 2014

cryptanalysis. They both proved to be successful to the full 16-round DES [2,12]. Besides, another new cryptanalysis technique (i.e. algebraic attacks) has emerged since the last decade, which works on 6 rounds of DES [5].

Davies-Murphy's attack [6] can be seen as a special linear attack, which was developed in the 1980's before invention of linear cryptanalysis (cf. [4]). It was improved by Biham and Biryukov [1] and most recently by Jacques and Muller [9]. For review on Davies-Murphy's attacks we refer to [9], and we refer to [4] for strengthening DES against Davies-Murphy's attacks.

In this paper, we revisit the improved Davies-Murphy's attack [9] from an algorithmic point of view. Based on Matsui's algorithm 2 [3,7], we give an improved attack algorithm. In summary, our improved attack algorithm works in time (2^{41}) with memory (2^{33}). In contrast, the attack [9] takes time (2^{43}) and memory (2^{35}). Due to the use of Walsh transform[1], it seems that our results of the time and memory complexities are optimal. Meanwhile, our results generalize and improve the results of the improved Matsui's algorithm 2 in [3,7] for the case that the subkeys are XORed into the round function.

2   Related Works

In Fig. 1, we let 32-bit L_0, R_0 be the left and right half of the plaintext. Let L_{16}, R_{16} be the left and right half of the ciphertext. Similarly, L_i, R_i denote the left and right half of DES output at Round i. As convention, the initial and final permutation of DES is ignored. The 48-bit subkey used for Round i is denoted by K_i (omitted in Fig. 1). Due to lack of space, we omit the detailed description on DES (cf. [13]).

Let $\alpha = 0xa100c21$ in hexadecimal representation[2]. Let the 32-bit A_i be the output of DES round function f at Round i. Define the bias (also called imbalance [8]) of a binary random variable X by $|\Pr(X = 0) - \Pr(X = 1)|$. Recall due to Davies and Murphy [6], the bit $\alpha \cdot A_1 \oplus \beta \cdot K_1 = \alpha \cdot (L_0 \oplus L_1) \oplus \beta \cdot K_1$ has bias $2^{-3.4}$, with the subkey's mask[3] $\beta = 0xf0$. As DES consists of 16 rounds, this one-round characteristics is iterated 8 times in the original Davies-Murphy's attack [6]. That makes a total bias $2^{-3.4 \times 8} = 2^{-27.2}$ by Piling-up Lemma [12]. Later, Biham and Biryukov [1] proposed to use the technique of partial decryption to work with 15-round DES instead. Thus, the one-round characteristics is iterated 7 times. It makes an enlarged total bias of $2^{-3.4 \times 7} = 2^{-23.8}$. Recently, with the trick of chosen-plaintext strategy, Jacques and Muller [9] showed that partial decryption actually allows to work with further reduced 13-round DES. It thus makes the increased bias of $2^{-3.4 \times 6} = 2^{-20.4}$.

---

[1] Note that Walsh transform and Fourier transform have been useful tools to aid linear cryptanalysis, e.g., [10,11].

[2] Throughout the paper, we always let bit 0 be the least significant bit.

[3] The subkey's mask β corresponds to the highest 2 bits of the subkey's 6-bit input to S-box S8 and the lowest 2 bits of the subkey's 6-bit input to S-box S7.

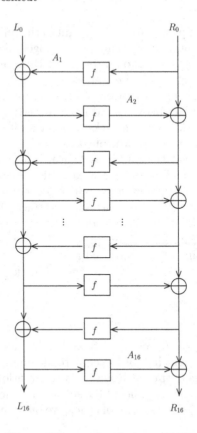

Fig. 1. The untwisted view of DES

3   Our Improved Algorithm for Jacques-Muller's Core Attack

As $\alpha \cdot A_i$ equals the XOR of the four output bits of S-box S7 and the output bit 0,2,3 of S-box S8, let the Boolean function $g(\ell_{16} \oplus k_{16})$ compute the bit $\alpha \cdot A_{16}$. Here, the 12-bit ℓ_{16}, k_{16} denote inputs to S-box $S7, S8$ at Round 16. And ℓ_{16} is obtained by bit expansion from 10 bits of L_{16}.

On the other hand, we let the 24-bit r_0, k_1 denote inputs to S-boxes $S5-S8$ at Round 1. And r_0 is obtained by bit expansion from 18 bits of R_0. Let the 12-bit ℓ_0, k_2 denote inputs to both S-boxes $S7, S8$ at Round 2. And ℓ_0 is obtained by bit expansion from 10 bits of L_0. We let the Boolean function

$$h_{k_1, k_2}(\ell_0, r_0) = h(\ell_0 \oplus k_2 \oplus h'(r_0 \oplus k_1)) \qquad (1)$$

compute the bit $\alpha \cdot A_2$. Here, $h'(r_0 \oplus k_1)$ maps 12 bits to 12 bits, 5 bits of which can be determined[4] from k_1, r_0 and we define this function by $h''(r_0 \oplus k_1)$. Further,

---

[4] Because they are bit expansion from 4 bits of $S5-S8$ outputs (i.e., output bit 1 of S5, output bit 2 of S6, output bit 3 of S7, output bit 2 of S8) at Round 1.

the trick of chosen-plaintext strategy [9] allows to have that the remaining 7 bits of the 12-bit output of $h'(r_0 \oplus k_1)$ are *always* fixed, which was considered an intermediate variable of 7 bits (denoted by x herein[5]) in [9]. For our convenience, we let

$$h'(r_0 \oplus k_1) = P(h''(r_0 \oplus k_1)\|x), \tag{2}$$

where $\|$ denotes string concatenation and P is the bit permutation function.

Given the plaintext and ciphertext pair $(L_0, R_0, L_{16}, R_{16})$ (and we use the superscript i to denote each sample), define[6] the binary function

$$F_{k_1,k_2,k_{16}}^x(L_0, L_{16}, R_0, R_{16}) = (-1)^{\alpha \cdot (R_0 \oplus R_{16}) \oplus g(\ell_{16} \oplus k_{16}) \oplus h_{k_1,k_2}(\ell_0,r_0)}. \tag{3}$$

Clearly, with the correct x, k_1, k_2, k_{16}, the right-hand side of (3) is equal to $(-1)^{\alpha \cdot (A_4 \oplus A_6 \oplus A_8 \oplus A_{10} \oplus A_{12} \oplus A_{14})}$. Jacques-Muller's core attack idea [9] is shown in Algorithm 1, which aims at partial key-recovery of x, k_1, k_2, k_{16}. As direct computation of Algorithm 1 is impractical, [9] proposed techniques to decompose into several steps: at each step, by guessing a few key bits, some intermediate information can be derived which allows to get rid of the old precomputation table. The optimization techniques [9, Sect. 3.4] solves Algorithm 1 with total time $O(2^{43})$ and the table size $O(2^{35})$. It is worth noting that if x, k_1, k_2, k_{16} (of $7 + 24 + 12 + 12 = 55$ bits in total) *were* linearly independent, we can apply the improved Matsui's algorithm 2 in [7, Sect. 4] to solve Algorithm 1 with time $O(3 \times 55 \times 2^{55})$ and memory $O(2^{55})$.

Algorithm 1. The core partial key-recovery idea of Jacques-Muller's attack [9]

    for all x, k_1, k_2, k_{16} **do**
        $u_{k_1,k_2,k_{16}}^x \leftarrow 0$
        compute $u_{k_1,k_2,k_{16}}^x = \sum_i F_{k_1,k_2,k_{16}}^x(L_0^i, L_{16}^i, R_0^i, R_{16}^i)$, with F defined in (3)
    end for
    output the largest $u_{k_1,k_2,k_{16}}^x$ with x, k_1, k_2, k_{16}

Nonetheless, from the description of DES [13], x, k_1, k_2, k_{16} are *not* linearly independent and [7] is not applicable. Inspired by the improved Matsui's algorithm 2 [3,7], based on the use of Walsh transform, we now give another algorithm for Jacques-Muller's core attack [9] in order to compute Algorithm 1 with reduced time and memory.

First, we define two sets $E_0 = \{i : \alpha \cdot (R_0^i \oplus R_{16}^i) = 0\}$ and $E_1 = \{i : \alpha \cdot (R_0^i \oplus R_{16}^i) = 1\}$. So, we have $E_0 \bigcup E_1 = \{i\}$. For the set $E = E_0$, we let $G_1(\ell \oplus k_{16}) = (-1)^{g(\ell \oplus k_{16})}$ and $G_2(\ell) = \sum_{i \in E} \mathbf{1}_{\ell_{16}=\ell}$, where $\mathbf{1}$ is the indicator function. Meanwhile, by (1), (2), we know the XOR (denoted by v) of x and 7 bits out of k_2 becomes a new key material. And the linear transformation

---

[5] Note that the 7-bit x actually is bit expansion from 6 unknown bits.
[6] Note that $k_1, k_2, k_{16}, \ell_0, r_0, \ell_{16}$ simply is the bit selection function of $K_1, K_2, K_{16}, L_0, R_0, L_{16}$ with reduced bit length respectively.

(denoted by 12-bit k_2') of x, k_2 consists of the remaining 5 bits of k_2 and the 7-bit v, which allows to rewrite the right-hand side of (1) as $\mathcal{H}(\ell_0 \oplus k_2', r_0 \oplus k_1) = h(\ell_0 \oplus k_2' \oplus P(h''(r_0 \oplus k_1)\|\mathbf{0}))$, where $\mathbf{0}$ is the all zero vector of 7 bits. Let $H_1(\ell_0 \oplus k_2', r_0 \oplus k_1) = (-1)^{\mathcal{H}(\ell_0 \oplus k_2', r_0 \oplus k_1)}$, $H_2(b, c) = \sum_{i \in E} 1_{\ell_0 = b, r_0 = c}$. We compute

$$
\mu^{<E_0>}_{k_1, k_2', k_{16}} = \sum_{\ell, b, c} G_1(\ell \oplus k_{16}) \times G_2(\ell) \times H_1(b \oplus k_2', c \oplus k_1) \times H_2(b, c)
$$

$$
= (G_1 \otimes G_2(k_{16})) \cdot (H_1 \otimes H_2(k_2', k_1))
$$

Here, $\otimes$ denotes convolution. Next, for the other set $E = E_1$, we repeat above computation to obtain $\mu^{E_1}_{k_1, k_2', k_{16}}$. We can easily check that we have

$$
u^x_{k_1, k_2, k_{16}} = \mu^{<E_0>}_{k_1, k_2', k_{16}} - \mu^{<E_1>}_{k_1, k_2', k_{16}}. \tag{4}
$$

As x, k_2 are combined into k_2' as aforementioned, we denote $u^x_{k_1, k_2, k_{16}}$ by $u'_{k_1, k_2', k_{16}}$ from now on.

We now discuss how to find the largest u' with corresponding k_1, k_2', k_{16}. First, we consider the simplified case when k_1, k_2', k_{16} (of total $24 + 12 + 12 = 48$ bits) are linearly independent. For each set of E_0, E_1, computing[7] and storing the tables of $G_1 \otimes G_2$ and $H_1 \otimes H_2$ needs time $O(3 \times 12 \times 2^{12}), O(3 \times 36 \times 2^{36})$ respectively. Then, for all 48-bit k_1, k_2', k_{16}, computing $u'_{k_1, k_2', k_{16}}$ by (4) and finding the largest needs time $O(2^{48})$. The overall time cost is $O(2^{48})$ and the memory cost is dominated by $O(2 \times 2^{36})$ in order to store two tables of $H_1 \otimes H_2$. In comparison, using the results of [7], we would need more time $O(3 \times 48 \times 2^{48})$ and higher memory $O(2^{48})$.

By DES key schedule [13], the 24-bit k_1 and 12-bit k_2' makes a total of 33 bits rather than $24 + 12 = 36$ bits; k_1, k_2', k_{16} makes a total of 35 bits rather than 48 bits. Thus, we propose to proceed as follows. For each set of E_0, E_1, computing and storing the table of $G_1 \otimes G_2$ needs same time $O(3 \times 12 \times 2^{12})$ as before, as only k_{16} is involved. With regards to $H_1 \otimes H_2$ for k_1, k_2', we do not need to get the complete table of results for all 36 bits. We are only interested in the results over $GF(2)^{33}$. We use the techniques of linear transformation below to solve our problem with time $O(3 \times 33 \times 2^{33})$ and memory $O(2^{33})$, for each set of E_0, E_1.

Useful Techniques on Walsh Transforms: For a real function F over $GF(2)^L$, recall that the Walsh transform of F is defined as $\hat{F}(x) = \sum_{x'} (-1)^{x \cdot x'} F(x')$, for all $x \in GF(2)^L$. Note that the order of the bit position does not affect the results of Walsh transforms. That is, we denote x by $x_0, x_1, \ldots, x_{L-2}, x_{L-1}$, and given a fixed bit permutation p over $\{0, 1, 2, \ldots, L - 1\}$, we let $y = x_{p(0)}, x_{p(1)}, \ldots, x_{p(L-2)}, x_{p(L-1)}$ (which is a special bijection of x). We define another real function $F'(y) = F(x)$ for all $y \in GF(2)^L$. It is easy to see $\hat{F}(x) = \hat{F}'(y)$ for all $x \in GF(2)^L$. In the case of DES, we have $L = 36$. Denote our target real function by F with the input $x = x_0, x_1, \ldots, x_{34}, x_{35}$. Due to the dependency of the key bits in DES, we can use the above property

---

[7] Note that convolution can be computed by three times of Fast Walsh Transforms.

to arrange the bit order of the input (without affecting the results of Walsh transforms) from the bit permutation p over $\{0, 1, 2, \ldots, 35\}$ such that the three redundant bit positions are placed at bit $33, 34, 35$. This way, we're interested in the results over all 33-bit $y_0, y_1, \ldots, y_{34}, y_{35}$ only with $y_{33} = y_{34} = y_{35} = 0$, where $y = y_0, y_1, \ldots, y_{34}, y_{35} = x_{p(0)}, x_{p(1)}, \ldots, x_{p(34)}, x_{p(35)}$ and $F'(y) = F(x)$ for all $y \in GF(2)^{36}$. Now, we let $f(a) = \sum_{y:a=(y \gg 3)} F'(y)$ for all $a \in GF(2)^{33}$, where $\gg$ denotes the (non-cyclic) bit shift (to the right) operation. We now show that $\hat{f}(a) = \hat{F}'(a \ll 3)$ for all 33-bit a, where $\ll$ denotes the (non-cyclic) bit shift (to the left) operation. To prove this, we check that we have

$$\hat{f}(a) = \sum_{a' \in GF(2)^{33}} (-1)^{a \cdot a'} \sum_{y' \in GF(2)^{36}:(y' \gg 3)=a'} F'(y')$$

$$= \sum_{a' \in GF(2)^{33}} \sum_{y' \in GF(2)^{36}:(y' \gg 3)=a'} (-1)^{a \cdot (y' \gg 3)} F'(y')$$

As $(a \ll 3) \cdot y' \equiv a \cdot (y' \gg 3)$ holds for all 33-bit a and 36-bit y', we finally have $\hat{f}(a) = \sum_{y' \in GF(2)^{36}} (-1)^{(a \ll 3) \cdot y'} F'(y')$, which completes our proof. Consequently, we have shown that computing $\hat{f}(a)$ for all 33-bit a is equivalent to computing $\hat{F}'(y)$ for all 33-bit $y_0, y_1, \ldots, y_{32}$ (with $y_{33} = y_{34} = y_{35} = 0$). This can be done with time $O(33 \times 2^{33})$ and memory $O(2^{33})$.

After that, to find the largest u', an exhaustive search for all 35-bit k_1, k_2', k_{16} will do with time $O(2^{35})$. We give our algorithm of the partial key-recovery attack in Algorithm 2. The total memory cost is dominated by $O(2^{33})$ for computing and storing $H_1 \otimes H_2$, and the time is dominated by $O(2 \times 3 \times 33 \times 2^{33})$ to compute $H_1 \otimes H_2$ for two sets E_0, E_1, i.e., $O(2^{40.6})$. Consequently, our results improve the Jacques-Muller's Attack [9] which needs time $O(2^{43})$ and memory $O(2^{35})$.

Algorithm 2. Our improved algorithm for Jacques-Muller's core partial key-recovery attack [9]

---

   for each set of E_0, E_1 **do**
      compute and store $G_1 \otimes G_2$ and $H_1 \otimes H_2$
   end for
   for all k_1, k_2', k_{16} **do**
      compute $u'_{k_1, k_2', k_{16}}$ by (4)
   end for
   output the largest u' with k_1, k_2', k_{16}

Note that this partial-key recovery attack recovers k_1, k_2', k_{16}, which contain 28 bits of the 56-bit key and the 7-bit v. Then the 7-bit x can be deduced from v and the recovered key. When the data amount is not sufficiently large and the correct key is not ranked No.1, it is clear that our attack algorithm can obtain the top n candidates with same time complexity. After that, as discussed in [9], for each of n candidates, the remaining $56 - 28 = 28$ bits of the key (containing only $28 - 7 = 21$ unknown bits due to recovery of the 7-bit x) can be found by exhaustive search using one pair of plaintext and ciphertext. Finally, for the suggested complete attack [9] which recovers the key with chosen plaintexts $O(2^{45})$, time $O(2^{43})$ and memory $O(2^{35})$, our algorithm works in time $O(2^{41})$ with memory $O(2^{33})$ given the same amount of data.

4   Further Discussions

Following our attack algorithm (Algorithm 2), we see that our results actually generalize and improve the recent improved Matsui's algorithm 2 in [3,7] when the subkeys are XORed into the round function (e.g., DES). When the subkeys used for partial decryption are linearly independent of total ℓ bits, our results show that the time complexity is $\max(2^{\ell}, 3\ell_1 \cdot 2^{\ell_1}, 3\ell_2 \cdot 2^{\ell_2})$, where ℓ_1, ℓ_2 denotes the total key bits to decrypt top down and bottom up respectively, and $\ell = \ell_1 + \ell_2$. We have the memory cost $\max(2^{\ell_1}, 2^{\ell_2})$. Note that the results of [3,7] would need time $O(3\ell \cdot 2^{\ell})$ and memory $O(2^{\ell})$, regardless of the values of ℓ_1, ℓ_2. As another example, for the attack on 22-round block cipher SMS4 [7, Sect. 4.2] with time cost $2^{115.9}$ and memory 2^{112}, here we have $\ell_1 = \ell_2 = 56, \ell = 112$. Accordingly, our results would need improved time $\max(2^{112}, 3 \times 56 \times 2^{56}) = 2^{112}$ computations, i.e., $2^{112}/22 = 2^{107.5}$ 22-round computations with greatly decreased memory $O(2^{56})$.

When the subkeys used for partial decryption are linearly dependent as we have studied above, [3,7] did not consider this case. Let the subkeys involved consist of ℓ independent bits, and ℓ_1, ℓ_2 denotes the independent key bits to decrypt top down and bottom up respectively. Note that $\ell = \ell_1 + \ell_2$ or $\ell \neq \ell_1 + \ell_2$ could be possible now. We then have exactly the same results as above, which has been demonstrated to improve the Jacques-Muller's attack algorithm with $\ell = 35, \ell_1 = 33, \ell_2 = 12$.

5   Conclusion

In this paper, we revisit the improved Davies-Murphy's attack [9] on DES from an algorithmic point of view. Our improved attack algorithm works in time (2^{41}) with memory (2^{33}). In contrast, the attack [9] takes time (2^{43}) and memory (2^{35}). Further, it seems that our results of the time and memory complexities are optimal, due to the use of Walsh transform. Meanwhile, our results generalize and improve the recent improved Matsui's algorithm 2 in [3,7] for the case that the subkeys are XORed into the round function.

References

1. Biham, E., Biryukov, A.: An improvement of Davies' attack on DES. In: De Santis, A. (ed.) EUROCRYPT 1994. LNCS, vol. 950, pp. 461–467. Springer, Heidelberg (1995)

2. Biham, E., Shamir, A.: Differential cryptanalysis of the full 16-round DES. In: Brickell, E.F. (ed.) CRYPTO 1992. LNCS, vol. 740, pp. 487–496. Springer, Heidelberg (1993)
3. Collard, B., Standaert, F.-X., Quisquater, J.-J.: Improving the time complexity of Matsui's linear cryptanalysis. In: Nam, K.-H., Rhee, G. (eds.) ICISC 2007. LNCS, vol. 4817, pp. 77–88. Springer, Heidelberg (2007)
4. Courtois, N.T., Castagnos, G., Goubin, L.: What do DES S-boxes say to each other?, IACR eprint. http://eprint.iacr.org/2003/184 (2003)
5. Courtois, N.T., Bard, G.V.: Algebraic cryptanalysis of the data encryption standard, IACR eprint. http://eprint.iacr.org/2006/402 (2006)
6. Davies, D., Murphy, S.: Pairs and triplets of DES S-Boxes. J. Cryptol. 8(1), 1–25 (1995)
7. Etrog, J., Robshaw, M.J.B.: The cryptanalysis of reduced-round SMS4. In: Avanzi, R.M., Keliher, L., Sica, F. (eds.) SAC 2008. LNCS, vol. 5381, pp. 51–65. Springer, Heidelberg (2009)
8. Harpes, C., Massey, J.L.: Partitioning cryptanalysis. In: Biham, E. (ed.) FSE 1997. LNCS, vol. 1267, pp. 13–27. Springer, Heidelberg (1997)
9. Kunz-Jacques, S., Muller, F.: New improvements of Davies-Murphy cryptanalysis. In: Roy, B. (ed.) ASIACRYPT 2005. LNCS, vol. 3788, pp. 425–442. Springer, Heidelberg (2005)
10. Lu, Y., Desmedt, Y.: Bias analysis of a certain problem with applications to E0 and Shannon cipher. In: Rhee, K.-H., Nyang, D. (eds.) ICISC 2010. LNCS, vol. 6829, pp. 16–28. Springer, Heidelberg (2011)
11. Lu, Y., Wang, H., Ling, S.: Cryptanalysis of Rabbit. In: Wu, T.-C., Lei, C.-L., Rijmen, V., Lee, D.-T. (eds.) ISC 2008. LNCS, vol. 5222, pp. 204–214. Springer, Heidelberg (2008)
12. Matsui, M.: Linear cryptanalysis method for DES cipher. In: Helleseth, T. (ed.) EUROCRYPT 1993. LNCS, vol. 765, pp. 386–397. Springer, Heidelberg (1994)
13. Menezes, A.J., van Oorschot, P.C., Vanstone, S.A.: Handbook of Applied Cryptography. CRC Press, Boca Raton (1996)

Yet Another Fault-Based Leakage
in Non-uniform Faulty Ciphertexts

Yang Li[1]([✉]), Yu-ichi Hayashi[2], Arisa Matsubara[1], Naofumi Homma[2],
Takafumi Aoki[2], Kazuo Ohta[1], and Kazuo Sakiyama[1]

[1] The University of Electro-Communications, Chofu-Shi, Japan
[2] Tohoku University, Sendai, Japan
{liyang,matsubara,kazuo.ohta,sakiyama}@uec.ac.jp,
yu-ichi@m.tohoku.ac.jp, homma@aoki.ecei.tohoku.ac.jp,
aoki@ecei.tohoku.ac.jp

Abstract. This paper discusses the information leakage that comes
from the non-uniform distribution of the faulty calculation results for
hardware AES implementations under setup-time violations. For the
setup-time violation, it is more difficult to predict the faulty value than
the introduced difference itself. Therefore, the faulty calculation results
have been always paired with the fault-free calculations as the information leakage. However, the faulty calculation results under statistical
analyses can directly leak the secret. This leakage is mainly caused by
the circuit structure rather than the transition differences for variant
input data. Generally, this work explains the mechanism of the non-
uniform distribution of faulty calculation results. For the widely used
composite field based AES S-box, we explain and demonstrate that the
probability of the emergence of a particular faulty value is much higher
than other values. We use the key recovery method proposed by Fuhr *et
al.*, and show the successful key recovery using only the faulty calculation results. In addition, against the attack target that encrypts random
plaintexts, we extend the attack in case the faults are injected remotely
using electromagnetic interference without any injection timing trigger.

Keywords: Fault analysis · Non-uniform mapping · Setup-time
violation

1 Introduction

Fault attacks are very powerful to extract the secret information from cryptographic devices. There are many previous works to demonstrate it, including
differential fault analysis (DFA), safe-error attack (SEA), fault sensitivity analysis (FSA), fault behavior analysis (FBA) and so on [1–5]. These attacks can be
achieved by setup-time violations, where the clock period is shortened using
illegal clock/power supply so that there is no enough timing for appropriate signal propagations. Note that most of these fault analyses share a common attack

J.-L. Danger et al. (Eds.): FPS 2013, LNCS 8352, pp. 272–287, 2014.
DOI: 10.1007/978-3-319-05302-8_17, © Springer International Publishing Switzerland 2014

requirement, i.e. the same calculation has to be repeated at least twice. For DFA and FBA, the faulty calculation results make sense as the leakage only if they are paired with fault-free calculation results. For SEA and FSA, the distinguish of a faulty calculation needs the comparison with the fault-free one. In practice, repeating the same calculation multiple times is not natural as user behavior since the calculation results are always the same. Therefore, without any access of calculation inputs, it is not practically feasible to apply a fault attack based on setup time violations.

In [6], Fuhr et al. showed that non-uniform distribution of faulty value can leads to key recovery of AES without the necessity of knowing fault-free calculation results. In this work, we refer this type of attack as *non-uniform faulty value analysis* (NU-FVA). This paper follows their work about fault attacks with faulty ciphertexts only, and demonstrates the practical NU-FVA using setup-time violations. We first explain the basic mechanism of the non-uniform faulty mapping, which is a combined result of the non-uniform fault sensitivity and the non-uniform faulty value. Then, we take a 128-bit AES implementation based on a composite-field S-box as a case study. We demonstrate and verify the non-uniform faulty mapping of the S-box by practical experiments, in which the emergence probability of a particular faulty value is much higher than others. Lastly we consider the discussed vulnerability is suitable to challenge a remote fault analysis, where the injections are remotely performed without any trigger for timing or any control over the processed data.

The rest of this paper is organized as follows. In Sect. 2, we briefly review the previous fault analyses. In Sect. 3, we explain the basic mechanism of the non-uniform faulty ciphertexts. In Sect. 4, we take AES-comp as a case study to analyze the non-uniform calculation result of its S-box calculation. In Sect. 5, we apply the key recovery method from [6] and show the successful key recovery of NU-FVA. In Sect. 6, we show an extended NU-FVA that is trigger free and uses remote fault injections. Section 7 concludes this paper.

2 Previous Fault Analysis

For the simplicity, the review of previous fault analyses is focused on the setup-time violation against the encryption of hardware AES implementations. Setup-time violation occurs when the clock period is shorter than the calculation time, which can be achieved by manipulating the clock signal, the power supply or the temperature. Compared to permanent fault injections or laser-based fault injections, relatively the setup-time violation has a lower cost and leaves less attack evidence but lacks fault injection accuracy. Recent results show that the setup-time violation can also be performed remotely using electromagnetic interference [7].

Biham and Shamir proposed the concept of *differential fault analysis* in 1997 [1]. In the DFA attack, pairs of ciphertexts from the same calculation (i.e. the same plaintext and secret key) is required. Yen and Joye proposed *safe error attack* (SEA) in 2000 [3]. In 2007, *differential behavioral analysis* (DBA) [4] was proposed as a combination of the differential power analysis (DPA) attack [2] and SEA. By introducing the concept of fault injection intensity, *fault sensitivity analysis* (FSA) was proposed in 2010 [8]. The FSA attack was combined with a correlation collision distinguisher and successfully breaks 42 ASIC AES cores [5]. The similar idea also appeared in [9]. In [5], the faulty ciphertexts are used to break two AES cores with masking countermeasures. This attack was generalized and summarized in [10] as the *fault behavior analysis* (FBA). Generally, all the mentioned fault analyses require repeating the same calculation at least twice to observe the difference between fault-free and faulty calculations. In [6], several key recovery methods against AES using non-uniform faulty value models were proposed. The fault models assumed in [6] is similar to the one demonstrated and explained in this paper. More detailed comparison between this work and previous work will be given in Sect. 5.

3   Non-uniform of Faulty Ciphertexts

3.1   Basic Mechanism of Faulty Ciphertexts

In Fig. 1, we show the general structure of the hardware implementation that we target in this paper. The implementation in Fig. 1 is a 128-bit data path AES, which has 16 S-box calculations in parallel and takes 1 clock cycle for each round calculation. As shown in Fig. 1, focusing on an S-box, we denote the S-box input in the previous cycle, the S-box input and S-box output in the current cycle by x_p, x and y, respectively. The signal transitions for the S-box calculation are illustrated in Fig. 2, where the S-box mapping is denoted as $S(.)$.

Let t be the time after the start of a clock cycle. When t is small enough, $y = S(x_p)$, since the S-box output is still the calculation result in the previous clock cycle. When t is near the period of a clock cycle, $y = S(x)$, since the calculation with the S-box input x should be completed. Between the states of $S(x_p)$ and $S(x)$, signal y is not stable and has many intermediate values.

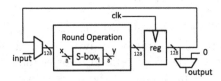

Fig. 1. S-box calculation in a hardware implementation.

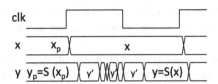

Fig. 2. Signal transitions for hardware S-box calculation.

Table 1. Comparison between fault-free S-box and faulty S-box with random inputs.

Fault-free S-box	Faulty S-box
$y = S(x)$	$y' = S'_F(x_p, x)$
8-bit to 8-bit	16-bit to 8-bit
Independent of F and x_p	Dependent on F and x_p
Uniformly distributed output	Non-uniformly distributed output

We denote these intermediate values by y', and the value of y' depends on x_p, x and t.

In a fault-free environment, all the calculations in one clock cycle can finish appropriately. When the S-box input x follows a uniform distribution, e.g. in case of random plaintexts, the S-box output y follows a uniform distribution as well. In a faulty environment, where a setup time violation tends to occur, the computational faults can be triggered for some S-box calculations. We compare the fault-free S-box mapping $S(.)$ and the faulty S-box mapping $S'_F(.)$ as shown in Table 1.

In Table 1, for a faulty S-box mapping, the output y' depends on not only x but also x_p and F, where F denotes the *fault injection intensity* describing how much the faulty environment is different from a reference fault-free working environment. For example, for clock glitches, the shorter of the period of the glitch clock cycle, the stronger the fault injection intensity is. In FSA, the F that corresponds to the threshold between fault-free and faulty calculations is the used leakage. For a fixed F, $S'_F(.)$ is a 16-bit to 8-bit mapping, which is more complicated than the fault-free one. Generally, it is almost impossible to ensure the faulty S-box mapping $S'_F(.)$ being a uniform mapping for every possible F, while a non-uniform faulty S-box is not secure. The faulty S-box mapping is not usually in the scope of circuit design, while it is available for an fault attacker.

3.2   Reasons for Non-uniform Distribution of Faulty Ciphertexts

The detailed faulty mapping depends on the S-box implementation method. Generally, the non-uniform mapping of faulty S-box calculations is caused by *non-uniform fault sensitivity* and *non-uniform faulty value*.

Non-uniform Fault Sensitivity. The first reason of non-uniform faulty S-box mapping comes from the non-uniform fault sensitivity. The combinational circuit for S-box requires different amount of time to finish the calculations with different inputs. The length of a clock cycle restricts the maximum amount of calculation time. When the period of a clock cycle is shorter than the critical path delay, the calculation cannot finish appropriately, therefore some faulty result is stored by registers.

For some weak fault injections, only a part of the calculations become faulty ones, while the other calculations follow the original deterministic mapping.

The faulty calculations leads to some incorrect values, so that the completeness of the original uniform mapping is broken. In other words, the variation of the fault sensitivities for different input data can cause a non-uniform faulty value distribution. Actually, we expect the vulnerability against the FSA attack can be extended to the vulnerability of the non-uniformly mapping.

Non-uniform Faulty Value. Another reason for non-uniform S-box output is that the incorrect calculation results can hardly have a perfectly uniform distribution. The faulty values of an S-box calculation is not in the scope of the S-box design. Although the mapping of the faulty values is largely implementation dependent, the faulty S-box mapping could be a non-uniform mapping for certain fault injection setups. In Sect. 4, we show a detailed example of the causal relationship between an S-box implementation method and the non-uniform faulty value for the well-known composite-field based S-box implementation.

3.3   An Example of Non-uniform Faulty S-box Mapping

We show an imagination example just to illustrate the concept of non-uniform mapping for an S-box. Consider a 3-bit S-box that has a mapping as shown in the left of Fig. 3, we assume 0x05 → 0x04 and 0x00 → 0x01 have the maximum and the minimum delay timings, respectively.

As shown in the middle of Fig. 3, for a weak fault injection intensity, only the 0x05→0x04 is affected to become a faulty mapping. For the S-box input x of 0x05, the output is different from 0x04. Then for a uniformly distributed set of S-box inputs, the S-box output distribution is non-uniformly distributed since there is no occurrence of 0x04.

As shown in the right of Fig. 3, for a strong fault injection intensity, except 0x00 → 0x01 all the other calculations become incorrect. Then, except the correct mappings of 0x00 → 0x01, we except that some faulty calculations get 0x01 as output as well. Consequently, for uniformly distributed S-box inputs, the S-box outputs become non-uniform and have more occurrence of 0x01 than normal. The more faulty calculation that gets 0x01 as output, the easier for attackers to exploit the vulnerability.

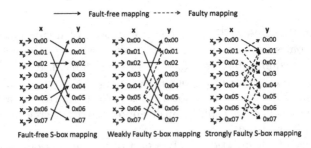

Fig. 3. A simple example to illustrate the non-uniform mapping.

4 Non-uniform Faulty Ciphertext Distribution for AES-comp

To show an example in practice, we take a composite-field based AES S-box (AES-comp), which is a well-known and widely used compact S-box realization, as a case study to verify its non-uniform faulty mapping. Our analysis and experiments are based on the AES-comp implemented on SASEBO, whose detail is written in [11] and its HDL code is available in [12]. The AES S-box is a uniform mapping that is constructed by combining the multiplicative inverse over $GF(2^8)$ and an invertible affine transformation. For 0x00 S-box input, which has no inverse in the mathematical definition, its multiplicative inverse is set to be 0 and the consequent S-box output is 99 in decimal or 0x63 in hexadecimal.

In Fig. 4, AES-comp S-box takes 3 steps for the multiplicative inverse calculation in $GF(2^8)$. We follow [11,13] to briefly explain it. In the first step, the S-box input $x \in GF(2^8)$ is mapped to a new composite field by an isomorphism function so that $x = a_0 + \beta a_1$ where β follows a primitive polynomial form of $\beta^2 + \beta + \lambda = 0$, and $a_0, a_1, \lambda \in GF(2^4)$. In the second step, the multiplicative inverse of (a_0, a_1), (b_0, b_1) is computed, where $b_0, b_1 \in GF(2^4)$. In the last step, the inverse $x^{-1} \in GF(2^8)$ is obtained by a re-map of (b_0, b_1) since $x^{-1} = b_0 + \beta b_1$.

Step 2, i.e. the multiplicative inverse of (a_0, a_1), is the computational heaviest one and the composite field for the multiplicative inverse computation can be selected to reduce the implementation cost. In step 2, $b_0, b_1 \in GF(2^4)$ is calculated as $b_0 = (a_0 + a_1)\Delta^{-1}$ and $b_1 = a_1\Delta^{-1}$, where $\Delta = a_0(a_0 + a_1) + \lambda a_1^2$. Hereafter, we show this kind of structure leads to a leakage of faulty value that the emergence probability of a particular value is much higher than other values.

Non-uniformity Caused by Implementation Structure. This section shows an observation for AES-comp S-box, where its implementation structure causes a more frequently occurring faulty S-box output. As shown in the top-right of Fig. 4, a calculation schematic is shown for the multiplicative inverse

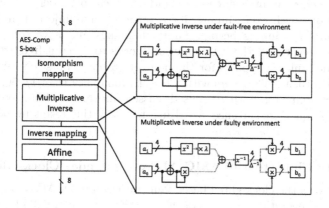

Fig. 4. Mechanism of non-uniform faulty mapping for AES-comp.

part of AES-comp S-box (step 2). For the multiplicative inverse, when $\Delta^{-1} = 0$, $(b_0, b_1) = ((a_0 + a_1)\Delta^{-1}, a_1\Delta^{-1}) = (0, 0)$. When $(b_0, b_1) = (0, 0)$, the S-box output follows a bijection mapping and become 0x63, which corresponds to fault-free S-box input 0x00. For an S-box that has a uniformly distributed input and in a fault-free environment, it is easy to know $\Pr[\Delta^{-1} = 0] = \Pr[(b_0, b_1) = (0, 0)] = 1/256$. The probability of $\Pr[\Delta^{-1} = 0] = 1/256$ is relatively low considering that Δ^{-1} is a 4-bit value. And when $\Delta^{-1} = 0$, the S-box output become 0x63 regardless of the values of a_1 and a_0.

From the schematic of the multiplicative inverse, we see that the critical path delay of the calculation of Δ^{-1} is much longer than a_1 and $a_0 + a_1$. In other words, the correct result Δ^{-1} takes a longer time to be calculated. When the S-box is in a faulty environment, e.g. under a clock glitch, the calculation result of Δ^{-1} is easier to be affected to become a faulty one. The faulty values of Δ^{-1} do not hold the meaning of the original calculation and become some non-sense values. Consider Δ^{-1} being a 4-bit intermediate calculation result, we believe the faulty values of Δ^{-1} are tend to have a larger probability than 1/256 to be 0. The practical distribution depends on the fault injection setup and the implementation details such as place and route. Following a rough assumption that the faulty value of Δ^{-1} is a 4-bit random value in $GF(2^4)$, we have $\Pr[\Delta^{-1} = 0] = \Pr[(b_0, b_1) = (0, 0)] = 1/2^4$ in a faulty environment. Thus, 0x63 occurs in the faulty S-box output with probability of $1/2^4$, which is 16 times larger than that of the fault-free environment.

Non-uniformity Caused by Fault Sensitivity. There is another reason that causes more occurrences of 0x63 in the faulty S-box output for AES-comp, which is the zero-value property. When AES-comp S-box input is zero, the power consumption and the critical path delay tends to be significantly lower or shorter than those for other input values [5,14]. The reason is that the multiplication with zero input consumes much less power and shorter critical path delay. This non-uniform fault sensitivity makes AES-comp a suitable implementation for a case study of NU-FVA.

Since the 0x00 input has a much shorter critical path delay than those of the calculations with other inputs, for a range of fault injection intensity, all the other non-zero inputs become faulty mappings and have some faulty S-box outputs except that the 0x00 input still leads to its fault-free 0x63 output. Assume some faulty mappings for the non-zero S-box inputs have 0x63 as the faulty output, then 0x63 occurs with a larger probability than 1/256.

For AES-comp, for both reasons discussed above, the S-box output 0x63 has a more frequent occurrence. We'd like to verify this result by both device experiments and simulations.

4.1   Faulty Ciphertext of ASIC AES-comp Under Clock-Glitch

We first perform the clock glitch based fault injection to an AES-comp on ASIC to verify the expectation of the frequently emerged value of 0x63 for the faulty S-box output.

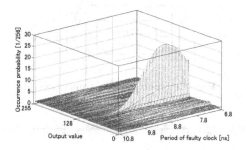

Fig. 5. Clock-glitch based faulty outputs for AES-comp under various fault injection intensities.

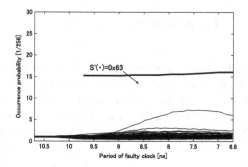

Fig. 6. Evolution of occurrences against cycle period for all output values.

The target is set to the AES-comp implementation on the custom LSI of type-R Side-channel Attack Standard Evaluation Board (SASEBO-R). SASEBO-R has a cryptographic ASIC using TSMC 130-nm CMOS library and a Xilinx VirtexTM-II Pro FPGA device xc2vp30. We setup a clock glitch based fault injection environment that is similar to the one used in [8]. Only one clock cycle for the final AES round is a clock glitch, which has an especially short clock period in order to trigger the setup time violation. The glitch period for the final AES round is fully controllable and only the calculation of the final AES round is working in a faulty environment.

We measured the faulty S-box output distribution for 5000 random plaintexts for several fault injection intensities. With the voltage of the power supply for the ASIC core being reduced to 0.85 V, we tested 71 different clock glitches between 10.8 to 6.8 ns. For each fault injection intensity setting, the random plaintexts are encrypted and the calculation results are collected. Also to keep the consistency, the used 5000 plaintexts are kept the same for all the fault injection intensities.

After that, with the known key, we combined all the outputs for 16 S-box calculations into one set of data and make a 3-dimensional figure as Fig. 5. In Fig. 5, the x-axis is for the period of faulty cycle, and the y-axis and z-axis correspond to the histogram figure for the S-box outputs. In Fig. 5, we can

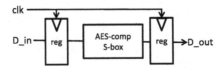

Fig. 7. Circuit used in simulation.

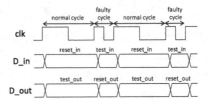

Fig. 8. Logic used in simulation.

clearly see an especially frequently occurring value, which corresponds to the 0x63 S-box output. To show it more clearly, for 256 S-box output values, we plot the evolution for their occurrences against the clock cycle periods in Fig. 6. As shown in Fig. 6, we can see that the peak of the 0x63 occurrence probability is $8029/(5000 \cdot 16) \approx 25.7/256$, which is about 25.7 times of that in fault-free case.

4.2 Faulty Ciphertext of AES-comp Under Dynamic Delay Simulation

In order to verify the non-uniform faulty mapping more clearly, we perform the simulation based on the HDL code of AES-comp. Take simulation can help us to survey the evolution of the distribution for all the possible input patterns and all fault injection intensities with less time (Fig. 7).

To obtain the output information under certain calculation time, the dynamic timing analysis is performed based on the Xinlix, ModelSim-SE, and a netlist of ASIC implementation of AES-comp. We built a gate module for each gate component in the ASIC netlist to perform the simulation. In other words, our simulation is performed based on the ASIC netlist, but with the FPGA-based delay information. The accuracy requirement of the absolute delay information for each gate is not important since we only care about the statistical result of the simulation. For the verification of the frequent occurrence of 0x63, we believe the relative delay information between gates are accurate enough for our simulation purpose.

For each setting of a fault injection intensity (period of faulty cycle), we collect the S-box outputs for $256 \cdot 256 = 65536$ S-box calculations. These 65536 calculations corresponds to all the combinations of the reset value x_p and the set value x. In this simulation, x_p acts as the S-box input in the second to last AES round, and the x acts as the S-box input in the final round. As shown in Fig. 8, the S-box calculations are given the reset value and the test value as the inputs

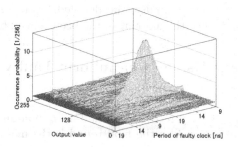

Fig. 9. Simulated faulty outputs for AES-comp under various fault injection intensities.

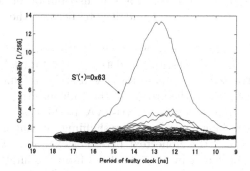

Fig. 10. Evolution of occurrences against cycle period for all output values.

alternatively. The calculations using the reset values are provided with fault-free clock cycles and the ones using the test values are provided with faulty clock cycles. This is to simulate the situation that the fault injections are targeted at the final AES round. For each fault injection intensity, the 65536 S-box outputs are used to make a histogram of the occurrence probabilities.

We collect the distribution histograms for the cycle periods from 19 to 9 ns with the interval of 0.1 ns. Using these 100 histograms, we make a 3-dimension figure of Fig. 9 to show the evolution of distributions against the fault injection intensity. In Fig. 9, the x-axis is for the period of faulty cycle, and the y-axis and z-axis correspond to the histogram figure for the occurrence probabilities. As shown in Fig. 9, between 14 to 9 ns there is a peak curve corresponding to the frequently occurring output, 0x63.

To show it more clearly, for 256 output values, we plot the evolution for their occurrence probabilities against the clock cycle periods in Fig. 10. The largest number of occurrence of 0x63 is 3415 times at about 12.8 ns. The corresponding occurrence probability is $3415/65536 \approx 13.3/256$, which is 13.3 times of that for the fault-free case.

Both the practical experiment and the simulation show the consistency with the analysis of AES-comp. Interestingly, although the general structure of

AES-comp leads to the vulnerability, the detailed layout and gate delay difference can largely influence the amount of the occurrence probability of 0x63.

5   Key Recovery Using Non-uniform Faulty S-box Mapping

This section discusses the key recovery method using non-uniform faulty value. For AES encryption, we consider the final round is the most convenient round to exploit the leakage from the non-uniform faulty mapping for the S-box. The final AES round performs $C = S(x) \oplus K_{10}$ for each byte, where C, x and K_{10} are a ciphertext byte, a byte of the final round input and a final round key byte, respectively. This is to say, the non-uniform distribution of the S-box output is shuffled according to the final round key to become the distribution of a ciphertext byte.

We divide the key recovery into two cases. For the first case, we assume that the attackers know the implementation detail of the target S-box, then some model can be constructed to estimate the distribution of faulty S-box outputs. Also we expect the models or the profiles of the fault sensitivity data can also be converted to the distribution model for NU-FVA. In this case, the key recovery is straightforward by checking which key guess shuffling can match the distributions for the S-box output and the ciphertext byte. For example, for AES-comp, the frequent occurrence of 0x63 can be understood from the implementation detail as shown in Sect. 4. Thus, the correct key K_{10} is the difference between the most occurring value for the faulty ciphertext byte and 0x63. Note that this key recovery method has been covered in the Sect. III-B of [6] as the key recovery method for the fault injected at the 9th round.

In the second case, we assume the implementation details of the S-box is unknown to attackers. The non-uniform faulty S-box mapping still leaks the information, however, the attackers do not know the correct model to directly recover the key value. The technique called the collision-based distinguisher used in [15] becomes useful here. With a guess of the difference between two key bytes, the output distributions for two ciphertext bytes are compared after one of them is shuffled. When the key difference is correct, the faulty output distributions are compared when the S-box inputs are the same. Therefore it is expected that the correct key byte difference leads to the largest correlation between two ciphertext byte distributions. We refer the detail of this collision-based distinguisher to Sect. 4 of [15]. In conclusion, as long as the ciphertext distribution is deterministically non-uniform, the key recovery of NU-FVA is theoretically possible.

Comparison with [6]. Fuhr *et al.* discussed the key recovery methods based on the assumptions of the probabilistic stuck-at fault model [6]. The fault models of [6] is equivalent to this paper from the view point of the key recovery, but different from the view point of fault injection mechanism. In [6], the AES round result is assumed to be byte-wise biased and each bit of the faulty value has more

0 outputs. Their paper has a more general discussion of the key recovery for the fault model been applied to different AES rounds.

Compared with the work of [6], this paper focuses on exploiting the mechanism and practical demonstration of the non-uniform of faulty value under setup-time violations. We show that the setup-time violation can lead to a probabilistic stuck-at fault for certain implementation, such as AES-comp. In this work, our analyses show that the faulty S-box output is the one that can be biased under setup-time violation rather than the AES round output. Note that a byte-wise biased S-box output distribution will be distorted in the MixColumns calculation. Our work is the first one showing that the setup-time violations can be related to a stuck-at fault. An application of the key recovery method from [6] to extend our practical attack experiment is considered as future work.

Comparison with Other Fault Analyses. As also mentioned in [6], the largest unique features for NU-FVA are no requirement of fault-free calculation result, and the key recovery for calculations with random inputs. In FDTC 2012, Ronan Lashermes et al. showed an DFA attack on AES based on the entropy of the error distribution [16]. Similar to NU-FVA, this attack is based on the statistical analysis of multiple fault injection results for the key recovery. However, this attack belongs to DFA and the value of error needs a pair of the same calculations to be calculated.

The FBA in second contribution of [5,10] also looks similar to the NU-FVA attack. The attack concept behind FBA attack is checking the similarity of the fault behavior when the input and the fault injection intensity are the same. The important fact of FBA is keeping calculating the same plaintext for the fault injections in order to get the similarity for the same input pattern. NU-FVA extends the similar leakage and takes the attack to another level, where NU-FVA do not care the behavior for a single input pattern, but the statistical feature of the set of the random input patterns. Different from FBA, the key recovery for NU-FVA does not require the fault-free result and repeated calculation input.

6 NU-FVA with Trigger Free Remote Fault Injection

This section discusses how the NU-FVA can be extended for a remotely performed fault attack. In our experiment, setup-time violations are injected based on remotely performed EM interference, where no trigger signal is employed, and each plaintext is encrypted only once. For each obtained ciphertext, it can be a fault-free one, or a faulty one with the fault being injected at any AES round operation or the interface. In this case, previous fault analysis cannot work, and only the ciphertexts corresponding to the fault injections at the final AES round are useful for the NU-FVA key recovery. The rest of ciphertexts are all noise for the key recovery. The best assumption is that noise are uniformly distributed. Theoretically, a non-uniform distribution stays non-uniform after overlapping a uniform distribution. In practice, the key recovery is dependent on the share of useful ciphertexts.

Experiment Setup. The experiment setup follows the intentional electromagnetic interference (IEMI) fault injection showed in [7,17,18]. As shown in Fig. 11, the cryptographic module is mounted on a common device, i.e., a PCB board, equipped with a twisted-pair power cable. In general, IEMI is an overt threat that usually causes permanent damage when applied to electronic devices [19]. However, in this experiment, we cause transient setup-time violations in the cryptographic module without damaging the hardware. We employ an injection probe in order to transmit a sinusoidal wave through a power cable. When the injection probe is applied to a cable attached to the target device, an arbitrary sinusoidal wave can be generated in the cable by utilizing the principle of mutual inductance between the cable and the injection probe.

We employ SASEBO-G as the test device [20] as shown in Fig. 11. An AES-comp circuit supporting 128-bit key length is implemented in FPGA1 as described in [12]. The circuit uses a loop architecture, where a single encryption operation takes 10 clock cycles for the ten cryptographic rounds and one additional clock cycle for data I/O. The clock frequency and the supply voltage on SASEBO-G are 24 MHz and 3.3 V, respectively. The fault injections are performed for approximately 160,000 random plaintexts, and the faulty outputs (i.e., cipher-texts) are stored in a PC. Sinusoidal waves are generated by a signal generator (MG3641A), after which they are amplified by using an amplifier (ZHL-2-12). Finally, the sinusoidal waves are introduced via an injection probe (FCC F-140) into a power cable attached to SASEBO-G. As shown in Fig. 11, the injection probe is located 60 cm away from SASEBO-G. Figure 12 shows the transfer function from the injection probe to the observation points of FPGA1. In this experiment, we selected a specific frequency band between 160 and 180 MHz at steps of 10 MHz and injected sinusoidal waves with voltage between 124 to 140 dBμV at steps of 2 dBμV. The ranges of frequency and voltage were easily generated with off-the-shelf equipment.

From a practical point of view, attackers would increase the injection level gradually and scan a frequency band while monitoring the output for any faults, which makes it rather simple to identify an injection level and a frequency which is effective for fault injection.

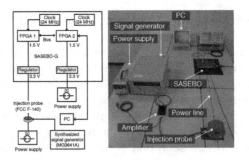

Fig. 11. Experimental setup.

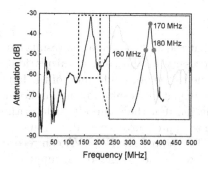

Fig. 12. Transfer function.

Table 2. Trigger-free NU-FVA attack result using all ciphertexts.

Byte #:	0	1	2	3	4	5	6	7	8	9	10	11	12	13	14	15
# of 0x63⊕K:	619	659	638	657	649	681	606	660	633	719	584	648	601	746	633	706
Rank of 0x63⊕K:	132	14	56	21	39	1	184	17	76	1	236	35	203	1	77	3

Table 3. Trigger-free NU-FVA attack result using faulty ciphertexts only.

Byte #:	0	1	2	3	4	5	6	7	8	9	10	11	12	13	14	15
# of 0x63⊕K:	199	207	147	205	190	232	160	195	190	222	164	198	163	264	193	240
Rank of 0x63⊕K:	1	1	227	1	6	1	156	5	6	1	119	4	123	1	4	1

Attack Result. In our experiments, the SASEBO-G is kept on encrypting random plaintexts while the fault injections are conducted remotely. A direct key recovery result with all 158667 obtained ciphertexts is shown in Table 2, in which 3 key bytes can be correctly identified. To understand the meaning of this result correctly, we find that among all 158667 obtained ciphertexts, only 41847 (26.4 %) ones are affected to become faulty values. Since no trigger signal is used, we consider the ciphertexts corresponding to final-round fault injection is less than one tenth of the faulty ones, i.e. 4184. In other words, even though the noise data is about 40 times of the useful data, there is still 3 key bytes can be recovered.

In fact, our experiment restricts the power of the EM interference to keep the device safe, which causes about 75 % fault-free ciphertexts. For a real attacker, the fault injection can be performed with a larger intensity to increase the number of fault ciphertexts. Also, it is possible that the attacker can access the decryption process to identify the correctness of ciphertexts. Therefore, as a reference, we show the key recovery result using only the 41847 faulty ciphertexts in Table 3. As shown in Table 3, in total there are 12 key bytes have their rank of 0x63 ⊕K higher than 10, and 7 of them can be identified. Considering the tough setting of the attack environment, we believe the obtained attack result is noticeable.

7   Conclusion

This paper presented that the faulty calculation results can leak the secret information without the necessity of the correct calculation results in pair under setup-time violation. Due to the non-uniformity of the faulty value and the fault sensitivity, the faulty calculation results are not uniformly distributed, which leaks the secret information. For the composite field arithmetic AES S-box, the faulty S-box output shows an occurrence peak of value 0x63, which enables an easy key recovery. We also showed the NU-FVA can recover the key in a remote fault injection scenario, where no trigger or no input control is available. The future work includes verifying the same vulnerability for other S-box implementations such as table based S-box and the implementations with countermeasures.

Acknowledgement. The authors would like to thank the anonymous reviewers of FPS 2013 for their insightful comments. This research was partially supported by SPACES project and Strategic International Cooperative Program (Joint Research Type), Japan Science and Technology Agency.

References

1. Biham, E., Shamir, A.: Differential fault analysis of secret key cryptosystems. In: Kaliski Jr, B.S. (ed.) CRYPTO 1997. LNCS, vol. 1294, pp. 513–525. Springer, Heidelberg (1997)
2. Piret, G., Quisquater, J.-J.: A differential fault attack technique against SPN structures, with application to the AES and KHAZAD. In: Walter, C.D., Koç, Ç.K., Paar, C. (eds.) CHES 2003. LNCS, vol. 2779, pp. 77–88. Springer, Heidelberg (2003)
3. Yen, S.-M., Joye, M.: Checking before output may not be enough against fault-based cryptanalysis. IEEE Trans. Comput. **49**(9), 967–970 (2000)
4. Robisson, B., Manet, P.: Differential behavioral analysis. In: Paillier, P., Verbauwhede, I. (eds.) CHES 2007. LNCS, vol. 4727, pp. 413–426. Springer, Heidelberg (2007)
5. Moradi, A., Mischke, O., Paar, C., Li, Y., Ohta, K., Sakiyama, K.: On the power of fault sensitivity analysis and collision side-channel attacks in a combined setting. In: Preneel, B., Takagi, T. (eds.) CHES 2011. LNCS, vol. 6917, pp. 292–311. Springer, Heidelberg (2011)
6. Fuhr, T., Jaulmes, E., Lomne, V., Thillard, A.: Fault attacks on AES with faulty ciphertexts only. In: FDTC 2013, pp. 108–118. IEEE (2013)
7. Hayashi, Y., Homma, N., Mizuki, T., Aoki, T., Sone, H.: Transient IEMI threats for cryptographic devices. IEEE Trans. Electromagn. Compat. **55**, 140–148 (2013)
8. Li, Y., Sakiyama, K., Gomisawa, S., Fukunaga, T., Takahashi, J., Ohta, K.: Fault sensitivity analysis. In: Mangard, S., Standaert, F.-X. (eds.) CHES 2010. LNCS, vol. 6225, pp. 320–334. Springer, Heidelberg (2010)
9. Li, Y., Ohta, K., Sakiyama, K.: New fault-based side-channel attack using fault sensitivity. IEEE Trans. Inf. Forensics Secur. **7**(1), 88–97 (2012)
10. Li, Y., Ohta, K., Sakiyama, K.: A new type of fault-based attack: fault behavior analysis. IEICE Trans. **96–A**, 177–184 (2013)

11. Satoh, A., Morioka, S., Takano, K., Munetoh, S.: A compact Rijndael hardware architecture with S-Box optimization. In: Boyd, C. (ed.) ASIACRYPT 2001. LNCS, vol. 2248, p. 239. Springer, Heidelberg (2001)
12. Cryptographic Hardware Project SASEBO. http://www.aoki.ecei.tohoku.ac.jp/crypto/
13. Rudra, A., Dubey, P.K., Jutla, C.S., Kumar, V., Rao, J.R., Rohatgi, P.: Efficient Rijndael encryption implementation with composite field arithmetic. In: Koç, Ç.K., Naccache, D., Paar, C. (eds.) CHES 2001. LNCS, vol. 2162, pp. 171–184. Springer, Heidelberg (2001)
14. Mangard, S., Oswald, E., Popp, T.: Power Analysis Attacks - Revealing the Secrets of Smart Cards. Springer, Heidelberg (2007)
15. Moradi, A., Mischke, O., Eisenbarth, T.: Correlation-enhanced power analysis collision attack. In: Mangard, S., Standaert, F.-X. (eds.) CHES 2010. LNCS, vol. 6225, pp. 125–139. Springer, Heidelberg (2010)
16. Lashermes, R., Reymond, G., Dutertre, J.-M., Fournier, J., Robisson, B., Tria, A.: A DFA on AES based on the entropy of error distributions. In: Bertoni, G., Gierlichs, B. (eds.) FDTC, pp. 34–43. IEEE (2012)
17. Hayashi, Y., Gomisawa, S., Li, Y., Homma, N., Sakiyama, K., Aoki, T., Ohta, K.: Intentional electromagnetic interference for fault analysis on AES block cipher IC. In: 2011 8th Workshop on Electromagnetic Compatibility of Integrated Circuits (EMC Compo), pp. 235–240, November 2011
18. Hayashi, Y., Homma, N., Sugawara, T., Mizuki, T., Aoki, T., Sone, H.: Non-invasive trigger-free fault injection method based on intentional electromagnetic interference. In: Non-Invasive Attack Testing Workshop (NIAT) (2011)
19. Radasky, W.A., Baum, C.E., Wik, M.W.: Introduction to the special issue on high-power electromagnetics (HPEM) and intentional electromagnetic interference (IEMI). IEEE Trans. Electromagn. Compat. **46**, 314–321 (2004)
20. Research Center for Information Security (RCIS). Side-channel Attack Standard Evaluation Board (SASEBO). http://www.rcis.aist.go.jp/special/SASEBO/CryptoLSI-en.html

Ad-hoc and Sensor Networks

A Hierarchical Anti-Counterfeit Mechanism: Securing the Supply Chain Using RFIDs

Zeeshan Bilal[(✉)] and Keith Martin

Information Security Group, Royal Holloway, University of London,
Egham, Surrey TW20 0EX, UK
Zeeshan.Bilal.2010@live.rhul.ac.uk, Keith.Martin@rhul.ac.uk

Abstract. Counterfeiting is a very serious threat to supply chain management systems. RFID systems are widely used to automate and speed up the process of remotely identifying products, however these systems are vulnerable to counterfeiting. In this paper, we propose a hierarchical anti-counterfeiting mechanism which uses a layered approach to identify dishonest middle parties involved in both counterfeiting and processing stolen/missing items. Our layered approach, which is designed for EPC Class-1 Gen-2 standard compliant tags, offers scalability and is suitable for different sizes of groups of tagged items.

Keywords: RFID security · EPC Class-1 Gen-2 standard · Counterfeiting · Supply chain management systems

1 Introduction

Radio Frequency Identification (RFID) systems are extensively used in many applications. In this paper, we discuss their deployment in supply chain management, where an RFID system is capable of identifying products throughout the supply chain process [1]. Such systems have three main components: (1) a *server* (usually centralized), (2) *readers* (from tens to hundreds, depending on the application), and (3) *tags* (potentially millions). A tagged object starts its journey in a large group from manufacturer to customer [2]. During this journey, the object may be read by readers located from the manufacturing company through to retail stores.

RFID technology has replaced barcode mainly because items can be individually identified without line-of-sight requirements [3]. Although RFID systems face similar challenges to those faced by barcode technologies, such as cloning and impersonation, RFID systems have the advantage that they are capable of providing identification as well as authentication. However, counterfeiting, caused by cloning and impersonation attacks, has been a problem for some RFID systems [3]. The counterfeiting of products is one of the most serious threats to modern commerce according to estimates by the Counterfeiting Intelligence Bureau (CIB) of the International Chamber of Commerce (ICC),

J.-L. Danger et al. (Eds.): FPS 2013, LNCS 8352, pp. 291–305, 2014.
DOI: 10.1007/978-3-319-05302-8_18, © Springer International Publishing Switzerland 2014

which claims that counterfeit goods account for up to 7 % of world trade [4]. To address counterfeiting, RFID researchers have designed many schemes which trade-off between cost, security, and performance, however existing approaches all have significant drawbacks which we outline in Sect. 2.

Since a tag will respond to every query sent by any compatible reader, if no authentication mechanism is employed, an adversary can query a genuine tag and learn the sensitive information associated with the tag's identifier which can then be used to make counterfeit tags. When using authentication, a tag will respond to every query sent by a compatible reader that has been authenticated as legitimate. However, the adversary can still eavesdrop the tag's identifier and then copy this information to a counterfeit tag. So there is a need for *secure identification with authentication* in which case a tag will securely provide its information in response to every query sent by a compatible reader that has been authenticated as legitimate. Although an adversary cannot learn the sensitive information, if this information is static then it can be copied or replayed by counterfeit tags to impersonate genuine tags. Finally the adversary can collude with legitimate but dishonest middle parties to gain benefits.

Considering these threats and capabilities of the adversary, we now propose an anti-counterfeiting mechanism for EPC Class-1 Gen 2 standard [5] compliant tags (*EPC tags*). Our mechanism uses three layers of verification. It is based on the use of shared secrets to generate dynamic verification codes which change in each transaction and can be used to verify groups of tags, as well as individual tags. Our scheme not only provides protection against counterfeiting but also identifies dishonest middle parties. Additionally, it can detect any missing or stolen items and is sufficiently scalable to be applicable to the complete lifecycle of a tagged object within a supply chain management system.

2   Existing Work

There are several existing approaches to managing RFID counterfeiting (see [6,7]). We briefly review some schemes and identify their drawbacks.

2.1   Unique Serial Numbers

Several proposals [8,9] use unique serial numbers to identify products. These numbers are compared against a database to check legitimacy and highlight any missing items. However, this technique is detection only and does not prevent counterfeiting since the serial number is transmitted in the clear and any adversary can eavesdrop the serial number in order to clone or impersonate it. If a genuine tag is removed and a counterfeit tag is impersonated as genuine, this scheme cannot detect it.

A number of proposed schemes [8,10,11] include a *track and trace* method where a counterfeit or missing item can be tracked down and traced back anywhere in the process. This is done using the complete trail of the exchanges of

cloned tag updated by each shipping and receiving record. However, this approach is time consuming and creates bottlenecks if multiple clones are detected
at the same time as each cloned tag is individually checked using its complete
shipping record from the database. Another drawback of this approach is that a
genuine but dishonest retailer can copy a genuine tag and attach this copy to a
counterfeit product. They can then sell the counterfeit to a customer, who verifies it to be legitimate using track and trace process, not updated by the retailer
or the middle parties [10]. Since this process needs an update by each middle
party, therefore it is vulnerable to both intentional and unintentional errors [6].

2.2 Cryptographic Anti-Counterfeit Mechanisms

Cryptographic mechanisms can be used to tackle counterfeits. The basic idea is
to base authentication on a secret value possessed by each tag, which is then
disclosed to the verifier as a proof of authenticity in a challenge-response protocol [12]. This approach may be based on symmetric cryptography or asymmetric
cryptography.

If symmetric cryptography is used [13–16], the secret is already known to
the verifier who matches it with the secret value received from the tag. To avoid
a single point of failure, each tag is given a unique secret key, hence there will
potentially be millions of such keys. One approach to establishing all these keys
is to distribute all keys to each reader in the form of a local database. However if
a reader is compromised then this approach results in the breaking of the whole
system. A preferred approach is to store all the keys in an online database which
each reader can access. However, this results in extensive communication and
computational overheads [17], even higher than the track and trace approach. In
addition, the reader needs to be trusted by the supplier since the reader stores
or accesses the secret values of the tags in this system.

In contrast, asymmetric cryptography can be used [17–19] to distribute keys.
However, this still requires each tag to have a unique secret key and involves
considerable computational overheads. Although researchers have proposed some
lightweight public key cryptographic systems, it is still unclear whether such
schemes can be deployed in the resource-constrained low-cost RFID systems in
supply chain management.

2.3 Unclonable RFID Tags

Physical Unclonable Functions (PUFs) are tamper-proof, unclonable items of
hardware which produce a unique signature, given an input. In [20] an offline
authentication scheme based on physically printed challenge-response pairs from
a certain PUF was proposed for tag authentication. However, the printout has
to be physically read and cannot easily be automated. Further, it is relatively
easy to program a cloned tag to give responses to particular challenges instead
of using a PUF. These issues were addressed in another PUF-based scheme [21],
but tracking of a tag is possible in this scheme as the PUF identifier is unique
and does not change. Moreover, it is infeasible to maintain a large number of

challenge-response pairs for one tag, potentially resulting in the few challenge-response entries being eavesdropped and the cloning of the tag.

2.4 Built-in Passwords

Juels has suggested a solution based on the tag's built-in passwords to counter the threat of cloning [22]. The idea is to use the existing *Kill* and *Access* password PINs to perform mutual authentication in order to avoid cloning. The reader sends a set of apparently random values except that one is the correct password PIN. The tag in response has to send the position of the correct PIN to get its legitimacy verified. However, legitimate but dishonest readers can store the complete set of PINs with a tag's responses to clone the tag. Even if the reader is honest, the challenge set of PINs and responses can be eavesdropped. Juels also noted that this scheme is not secure against a simple three-step attack [22] based on skimming a tag identifier, interacting with the reader to obtain the challenge set of PINs, and then using these to obtain the correct PIN.

3   A Hierarchical Anti-Counterfeiting Mechanism

We now propose a new approach to prevent counterfeiting in supply chain processes where tags travel in groups. Our mechanism is based on a hierarchical model which involves three layers of verification. The three layers can be considered to range from low to high complexity with respect to trade-offs between cost, performance and level of security. If an upper layer verification fails, verification drops down to the next layer. We design new first and second layers, and then use the track and trace approach [8] for the third layer.

3.1   Goals

Our mechanism is designed to achieve the following goals:

1. **Anti-Cloning.** Protection against copying the data from a genuine tag attached to a legitimate product and cloning it onto another tag attached to a counterfeit (see Sect. 2.1).
2. **Anti-Spoofing.** Protection against replay (impersonation) attacks (see Sects. 2.3 and 2.4).
3. **Anti-Theft.** Detection of stolen or missing items.
4. **Scalability.** Ability to operate efficiently when tags are in large groups as well as when a tag is attached to a single item.
5. **Compatibility.** Compatible with EPC Class-1,Gen-2 standard tags.
6. **Efficient Key Management.** Supportable using an efficient key management scheme (see Sect. 2.2).
7. **Good Throughput.** Avoidance of bottlenecks which degrade the overall supply chain system throughput (see Sect. 2.2).

3.2   The Layered Approach

The three hierarchical layers used for the legitimacy verification of a product
(see Fig. 1) are:

1. **Group Verification (GV) Layer.** For most of their journey in the supply
   chain products travel in groups (based on their type, specification, manufacturer and lot number, etc.) Our first layer verifies a complete group. In this
   layer the reader does not need continuous access to a central repository for
   verifying each tag because the complete group is read first and then verified
   as a whole.
2. **Product Verification (PV) Layer.** If *GV* layer verification fails, product
   verification is initiated using an individual tag's verification code. This lowers
   the performance and throughput since the reader has to access the database
   multiple times. Since the server verifies the legitimacy of a single product,
   the additional computational overheads are acceptable since the server is
   anticipated to be powerful. The *PV* layer identifies individual products that
   are either counterfeit or missing, their values and complete specifications.
3. **Track and Trace (TT) Layer.** After the *PV* layer has identified counterfeit or missing products, track and trace is initiated using the complete
   shipping/receiving record of the product. This gathers important information
   that includes the location of the anomaly and the type of anomaly (dishonest
   reader, counterfeit tag, or missing tag).

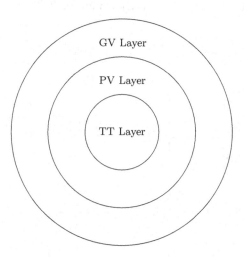

Fig. 1. Hierarchical verification model.

Each layer of hierarchical verification detects anomalies in the supply chain
in the following order:

1. **GV Anomaly Detection.** *GV* mainly fails if the reader is not legitimate, a counterfeit is detected, or a tag is completely missing. When *GV* fails, this will generate an alarm in the server. The server will record the location and details of the reader where the alarm is raised. The server then switches to the *PV* layer.
2. **PV Anomaly Detection.** *PV* identifies the exact cause of *GV* failure. It highlights the exact tagged product which is either counterfeit or missing. The server makes a corresponding entry.
3. **TT Anomaly Detection.** *TT* is carried out as a last step which recovers the complete shipping/receiving record of the tag that was identified in *PV* anomaly detection. This further shows whether more clones exist in the supply chain, or whether the original product is completely missing. The server records the details of anomalies.

3.3   Hierarchical Anti-Counterfeiting Mechanism

We now explain the detailed operation of our hierarchical anti-counterfeiting mechanism. The notation used is summarized in Table 1.

Key Distribution Phase. In this phase, the supplier who is responsible for shipping the tagged items in groups (or stand alone as explained in Sect. 3.1) to different geographic locations holds a database with shared secrets. This database is securely connected to a supplier's or Trusted Third Party's (TTP) server S. The supplier distributes the keys as shown in Fig. 2. There are n tags grouped

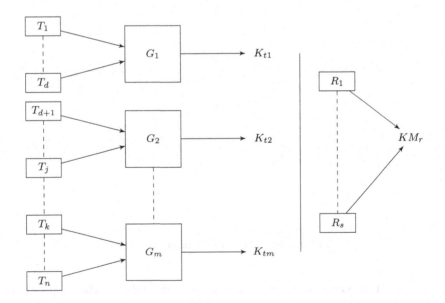

Fig. 2. Key distribution phase.

Table 1. Notation

Notation	Description
S	The server holding the database with shared secrets
G_j	The group consisting of many tags with identifier j
HVT_i	The tag employing HV mechanism with identifier i
ID_i	Tag's (with index i) secret, static and unique identity such as EPC
R_h	The reader with identifier h scanning groups of tags
K_{tj}	The group secret key embedded in every tag belonging to group G_j
KM_r	The master key given to every reader in supply chain system
KDF	A key derivation function agreed between the server and all readers
KS_{hj}	The session key derived from master key KM_r by the reader R_h using KDF, currently scanning group G_j
$rand_j$	Random number generated by server to be sent as challenge for a particular group G_j or tag HVT_j verification
TVC_i	A tag verification code used to verify the legitimacy of a tag HVT_i
RVC_h	A reader verification code used to verify the legitimacy of a reader R_h
GVC_j	A group verification code used to verify the legitimacy of a group G_j of tags
$EGVC_j$	An encrypted version of group verification code GVC_j
$T_{timeout}$	The maximum time after a server S sends $rand_j$ to the reader and acquires GVC_j or TVC_j
L	Length of the secret keys and static identity
$F : K \times X \to Y$	A lightweight secure PRF such as Hummingbird-2 [23] designed for EPC Class-1 Gen-2 compliant tags
$E : K \times X \to X$	A secure PRP such as AES defined over (K, X)
$X \oplus Y$	Exclusive-OR of two values X and Y

in m groups depending on their type, specification, application, date of manufacture, lot number, date of expiry and geographic location, etc. Since, $n \gg m$, it is easy to distribute a total of m keys to n tags (the same key for each tag belonging to one group). The number of readers that scan these groups is denoted by s. The supplier distributes one master key KM_r to each reader.

Group Verification Phase. After the key distribution phase is complete, and the supplier makes corresponding entries in the database, the groups of tagged items are shipped to their respective locations. When a group reaches a particular reader in the supply chain process, the GV phase is initiated. The protocol is shown in Fig. 3 and is as follows:

1. The reader R_h initiates an EPC Class-1 Gen-2 UHF protocol.
2. The tag HVT_i (whose slot-counter is zero, see [5]) responds showing that it is an HV tag belonging to group G_j.
3. The reader sends this group identifier G_j and its own identifier R_h to server S.

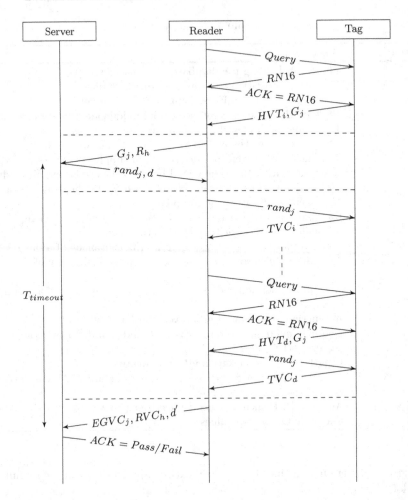

Fig. 3. Group verification protocol.

4. The server S generates a random nonce $rand_j$ and sends it to the reader R_h along with the total number of tags d in group G_j.
5. The reader R_h then forwards $rand_j$ to each tag.
6. Each tag computes its verification code and sends it to reader R_h. Tag HVT_i belonging to group G_j computes its TVC_i as follows:

$$TVC_i = ID_i \oplus F(K_{tj}, rand_j). \tag{1}$$

7. The reader R_h computes a GVC by XOR-ing with the previous TVC every time it receives a new TVC, until all d tags have responded:

$$GVC_j = TVC_i \oplus ... \oplus TVC_d. \tag{2}$$

8. The reader R_h computes a session key as:

$$KS_{hj} = KDF(KM_r, R_h, G_j). \tag{3}$$

9. The reader R_h encrypts $rand_j$ to compute RVC_h and GVC_j using KS_{hj}, and sends it as $EGVC_j$ along with the total number of tags d' that it read within time $T_{timeout}$ to the server S. RVC_h and $EGVC_j$ are computed as follows:

$$RVC_h = E(KS_{hj}, rand_j). \tag{4}$$

$$EGVC_j = E(KS_{hj}, GVC_j). \tag{5}$$

10. The server first checks the legitimacy of reader R_h by decrypting RVC_h. The server S next checks that reader R_h has read all the tags from the value of d' (to determine any missing/dummy tags). The server S finally decrypts the $EGVC_j$ sent by reader R_h to check whether GVC_j is correct:

    if $D(KS_{hj}, RVC_h) == rand_j$ **then**

        R_h is legitimate;

        Check;

        if $d' == d$ **then**

            All tags have been read;

            Check;

            if $D(KS_{hj}, EGVC_j) == GVC_j$ **then**

                G_j is successfully authenticated;

                Send $ACK = Pass$ to R_h;

            end if

        else

            GV has failed;

            Send $ACK = Fail$ to R_h;

        end if

    else

        R_h is not legitimate;

        Abandon the protocol;

    end if

If the final $ACK = Pass$, this shows that group G_j has passed the GV phase successfully. A corresponding entry is made in the database for the group G_j scanned by reader R_h, which also helps in future transactions with this particular reader in terms of trust level. The construction of the GV layer is as shown in the example given in Fig. 4, where the group G_1 consisting of four tags is being scanned by the reader R_5.

Product Verification Phase. When $ACK = Fail$ is sent to reader R_h, this shows that the GV layer has not verified the authenticity of the group. In this case the PV phase is initiated as shown in Fig. 5.

1. The reader R_h sends the tag identifiers $HVTs$ to the server.
2. The server S generates a random challenge $rand$ for each tag.
3. The reader R_h forwards this challenge to the corresponding tag, receives the TVC and forwards it back to the server S.

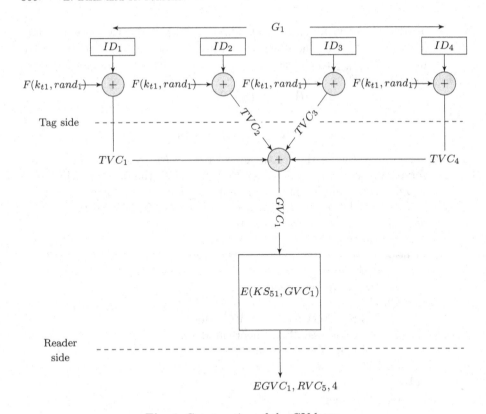

Fig. 4. Construction of the GV layer.

4. The server S verifies the legitimacy of an individual tag as follows:
   if $TVC_i == ID_i \oplus F(K_{tj}, rand_i)$ **then**
       Tag with identifier HVT_i is a genuine tag;
   else
       Tag with identifier HVT_i is a counterfeit tag;
   end if
5. At the end of this protocol, the server S is able to identify the counterfeit tags as well as missing/dummy tags.

Track and Trace Phase. In the EPC Global Network Class-1, Gen-2 standard, the unique and secret identifier ID (the EPC) is used to track and trace the tag's movement throughout the supply chain. We give an example in Fig. 6 to explain the TT phase. Suppose that a particular item travels in a group through three different companies (Company 1, 2 and 3) before reaching its retailer. The server S maintains its receiving and shipping record at each company. The entry $ID_5, t_1, 1$ shows that the item with tag identifier ID_5 was received at time t_1 by Company 1. A track and trace operation results in one of the following:

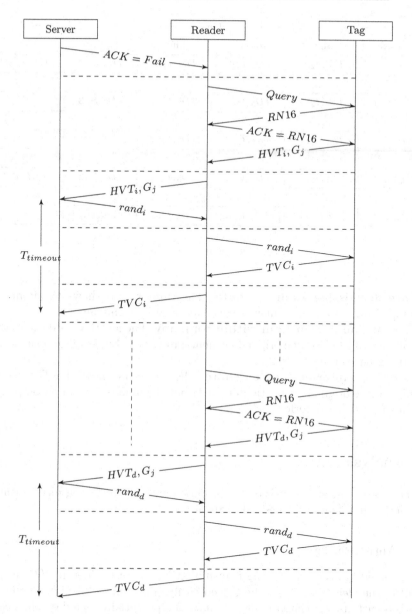

Fig. 5. Product verification protocol.

- **Case 1: No anomaly.** The first record in Fig. 6 shows an ideal case where a particular item ID_5 is successfully shipped to the retailer.
- **Case 2: Missing item within company.** The second record is that Company 3 received the item at t_5 but never shipped it to the retailer.

Time

Receive	Ship	Receive	Ship	Receive	Ship
$ID_5, t_1, 1$	$ID_5, t_2, 1$	$ID_5, t_3, 2$	$ID_5, t_4, 2$	$ID_5, t_5, 3$	$ID_5, t_6, 3$

$ID_5, t_1, 1$	$ID_5, t_2, 1$	$ID_5, t_3, 2$	$ID_5, t_4, 2$	$ID_5, t_5, 3$	

$ID_5, t_1, 1$	$ID_5, t_2, 1$	$ID_5, t_3, 2$	$ID_5, t_4, 2$		

$ID_5, t_1, 1$	$ID_5, t_2, 1$	$ID_5, t_3, 2$	$ID_5, t_4, 2$	$ID_5, t_5, 3$	$rand, t_6, 3$

$ID_5, t_1, 1$	$ID_5, t_2, 1$	$ID_5, t_3, 2$	$ID_5, t_4, 2$	$rand, t_5, 3$	

Fig. 6. Track and trace example.

- **Case 3: Missing item en-route.** The third record shows the item was shipped by Company 2 but was never received by Company 3.
- **Case 4: Counterfeit item within company.** The fourth record shows that Company 3 received the original authentic item at t_5 but shipped a suspected counterfeit to the retailer.
- **Case 5: Counterfeit item en-route.** The last record shows that Company 2 shipped the original authentic item at t_4 but the item received by Company 3 is a suspected counterfeit.

4   Analysis

We now carry out an analysis of our proposed anti-counterfeiting mechanism as to whether it achieves the desired goals of Sect. 3.1.

4.1   Anti-Cloning

As discussed in Sect. 2.1, if a tag transmits its static secret identity ID such as EPC in the clear then it can be copied easily. This unique identity of the tag is linked with its associated information, which potentially includes value, composition and other useful supplier-related data. In the proposed mechanism the tag hides this secret static identity in its verification code. The tag thus transmits its verification code which appears to be random data. Thus an adversary cannot make a copy of the secret static identity from a genuine tag. However the adversary can copy the public identifier HVT of a tag to a counterfeit tag, but this counterfeit tag will not be able to reproduce the correct verification code and thus will fail the legitimacy verification.

4.2 Anti-Spoofing

As discussed in Sects. 2.3 and 2.4, static secret identities can be replayed by a counterfeit tag to spoof as genuine. In the proposed mechanism the secret information, transmitted for verification, changes in every transaction because of the use of a fresh random nonce generated by the server. An adversary can thus not replay this secret information during a later transaction because of the use of a new nonce.

4.3 Anti-Theft

The proposed mechanism employs a layered approach in order to detect stolen/missing products. As described in Sect. 3.2, this approach can be used to identify the exact cause and location of any anomaly since the final Track and Trace layer provides the complete shipping and receiving record of the identified stolen/missing item. After tracing the root cause of the anomaly, suitable processes can be undertaken to hold the responsible parties accountable. Appropriate countermeasures can then be applied in order to prevent this anomaly from occurring again.

We note that a smart adversary can prevent this detection by relaying the genuine verification code from a stolen/missing item which is not physically present in the vicinity of the scan range. To counter such an adversary, we have employed a time-out clock within our scheme. The server pre-computes this time, depending on the number of tags involved in the scheme. The server then expects the reader to answer back within that specified time. If the reader delays its response, this is an indication of a potential relay attack. The server can thus ask the respective reader for a physical check for the completeness of this group and makes a corresponding entry for this anomaly in its database.

4.4 Scalability

In supply chain environments, tags travel most part of their journey in groups. These groups can be large, medium or even consisting of a single item depending on their size, value, and application. Sometime these groups change in their sizes en-route from manufacturer to end-users. Our proposed group verification layer can verify any group irrespective of its size and, during the product verification layer, the legitimacy of a single tagged item is checked. Therefore, our scheme scales well through from large groups, to medium and small groups, and even to stand-alone items.

4.5 Compatibility

The proposed mechanism uses the standard UHF Air Interface Protocol as specified in [5]. If a tag is not employing hierarchical verification, it can be read as per the existing standard.

4.6   Efficient Key Management

The proposed mechanism avoids some of the scalability problems of using symmetric cryptography by providing all tags belonging to a specific group with a unique key. Since the number of groups is much smaller than the number of tags, it is comparatively easy to manage the keys in the database. Additionally, all readers involved in the supply chain management system are only given one master key. By reducing the overall number of keys in the system, the key management is considerably more efficient than schemes with a unique key for each tag as mentioned in [17].

4.7   Good Throughput

The layered approach is partly designed to reduce the likelihood of potential bottlenecks arising from readers having to stay online during authentication and verification, and regularly interact with the database. By first deploying relatively lightweight group-level checks we avoid bottlenecks in the top layer of the hierarchical verification process. Overall performance decreases in the lower layers, but these are only activated if anomalies are detected during the group-level checking. In this way a reasonable throughput can be expected of the system.

5   Conclusion

We have proposed a hierarchical anti-counterfeiting mechanism using three layers of verification to determine the legitimacy of a tagged item. The mechanism is designed for EPC Class-1 Gen-2 tags used in supply chain management where counterfeiting present a very serious threat. This threat is countered using dynamic verification codes generated using symmetric cryptography. Our model detects the stolen/missing items, provides efficient key management, avoids bottlenecks and is scalable to the complete lifecycle of tags in the supply chain. This approach also potentially lends itself to deployment in schemes based on other standards.

References

1. Lee, Y., Cheng, F., Leung, Y.T.: Exploring the impact of RFID on supply chain dynamics. In: Simulation Conference, December 2004, vol. 2, pp. 1145–1152. IEEE (2004)
2. Juels, A., Pappu, R., Parno, B.: Unidirectional key distribution across time and space with applications to RFID security. In: Proceedings of the 17th USENIX Security Symposium, July–August 2008, pp. 75–90 (2008)
3. Juels, A.: RFID security and privacy: a research survey. IEEE J. Sel. Areas Commun. 24(2), 381–394 (2006)
4. Avery, P., Cerri, F., Fayle, L.H., Olsen, K., Scorpeci, D., Stryzowski, P.: The economic impact of counterfeiting and piracy. Organisation for Economic Co-operation and Development (OECD) (2008)

5. Standards, G.E.: EPC Radio-Frequency Identity Protocols Class-1 Generation-2 UHF RFID Protocol for Communications at 860 MHz-960 MHz. In: Specification for RFID Air Interface (2008)
6. Lehtonen, M., Staake, T., Michahelles, F., Fleisch, E.: From identification to authentication - a review of RFID product authentication techniques. In: Cole, P.H., Ranasinghe, D.C. (eds.) Networked RFID Systems and Lightweight Cryptography, pp. 169–187. Springer, Heidelberg (2008)
7. Saarinen, M.-J.O., Engels, D.: A do-it-all-cipher for RFID: design requirements (extended abstract). Cryptology ePrint Archive, Report 2012/317. IACR (2012)
8. Koh, R., Schuster, E.W., Chackrabarti, I., Bellman, A.: Securing the pharmaceutical supply chain. White Paper, Auto-ID Labs, Massachusetts Institute of Technology (2003)
9. Takaragi, K., Usami, M., Imura, R., Itsuki, R., Satoh, T.: An ultra small individual recognition security chip. IEEE Micro 21(6), 43–49 (2001)
10. Staake, T., Thiesse, F., Fleisch, E.: Extending the EPC network: the potential of RFID in anti-counterfeiting. In: Proceedings of the 2005 ACM Symposium on Applied Computing, ser. SAC '05, vol. 6, pp. 1607–1612. ACM (2005)
11. Pearson, J.: Securing the pharmaceutical supply chain with RFID and Public-key Infrastructure (PKI) technologies. Texas Instruments White Paper, June 2005
12. Vajda, I., Buttyán, L.: Lightweight authentication protocols for low-cost RFID tags. In: Second Workshop on Security in Ubiquitous Computing, ser. Ubicomp 2003 (2003)
13. Feldhofer, M., Dominikus, S., Wolkerstorfer, J.: Strong authentication for RFID systems using the AES algorithm. In: Joye, M., Quisquater, J.-J. (eds.) CHES 2004. LNCS, vol. 3156, pp. 357–370. Springer, Heidelberg (2004)
14. Feldhofer, M., Aigner, M., Dominikus, S.: An application of RFID tags using secure symmetric authentication. In: International Workshop on Security, Privacy and Trust in Pervasive and Ubiquitous Computing, pp. 43–49 (2005)
15. Dominikus, S., Oswald, E., Feldhofer, M.: Symmetric authentication for RFID systems in practice. In: The Ecrypt Workshop on RFID and Lightweight Crypto, July 2005
16. Poschmann, A., Leander, G., Schramm, K., Paar, C.: A family of light-weight block ciphers based on DES suited for RFID applications. In: Workshop on RFID Security. LNCS (2006)
17. Arbit, A., Oren, Y., Wool, A.: Toward practical public key anti-counterfeiting for low-cost EPC tags. In: International IEEE Conference on RFID (2011)
18. Batina, L., Guajardo, J., Kerins, T., Mentens, N., Tuyls, P., Verbauwhede, I.: An elliptic curve processor suitable for RFID-tags. In: IACR (2006)
19. Martínez, S., Valls, M., Roig, C., Miret, J.M., Giné, F.: A secure elliptic curve-based RFID protocol. J. Comput. Sci. Technol. 24(2), 309–318 (2009)
20. Tuyls, P., Batina, L.: RFID-tags for anti-counterfeiting. In: Pointcheval, D. (ed.) CT-RSA 2006. LNCS, vol. 3860, pp. 115–131. Springer, Heidelberg (2006)
21. Lee, Y.-S., Kim, T.-Y., Lee, H.J.: Mutual authentication protocol for enhanced RFID security and anti-counterfeiting. In: 26th International Conference on Advanced Information Networking and Applications Workshops, 2012, pp. 558–563 (2012)
22. Juels, A.: Strengthening EPC tags against cloning. RSA Laboratories, March 2005
23. Engels, D., Saarinen, M.-J., Schweitzer, P., Smith, E.M.: The Hummingbird-2 lightweight authenticated encryption algorithm. In: Juels, A., Paar, C. (eds.) RFIDSec 2011. LNCS, vol. 7055, pp. 19–31. Springer, Heidelberg (2012)

A More Realistic Model for Verifying Route Validity in Ad-Hoc Networks

Ali Kassem$^{(\boxtimes)}$, Pascal Lafourcade, and Yassine Lakhnech

Verimag, Grenoble University, Gières, France
{ali.kassem,pascal.lafourcade,yassine.lakhnech}@imag.fr

Abstract. Many cryptographic protocols aim at ensuring the *route validity* in ad-hoc networks, i.e. the established route representing an exists path in the network . However, flaws have been found in some protocols that are claimed secure (e.g. the attack on SRP applied to DSR). Some formal models and reduction proofs have been proposed to give more guarantees when verifying route validity and facilitate verification process. The existing approaches assume the cooperative attacker model. In this paper, we consider the non-cooperative attacker model, and we show that verifying the route validity under the non-cooperative model requires to verify only five topologies, each containing four nodes, and to consider only three malicious (compromised) nodes. Furthermore, we prove that a protocol is secure for any topology under the non-cooperative model, if and only if, it is secure for any topology under the cooperative model.

Keywords: Routing protocols · Non-cooperative attacker · Route validity · Reduction proof

1 Introduction

Wireless ad-hoc networks have no existing infrastructure. This enables them to play more and more important role in extending the coverage of traditional wireless infrastructure (e.g. cellular networks, wireless LAN, etc.). These networks have no central administration control, and thus the presence of dynamic and adaptive routing protocols is necessary for them to work properly. Routing protocols aim to establish a route between distant nodes, enabling wireless nodes to communicate with the nodes that are outside their transmission range. Attacking routing protocol may disable the whole network operation. For example, forcing two nodes to believe in an invalid route (a path that is not in the network) will prevent them from communicating with each other. Several routing protocols [PH02,HPJ05,SDL+02] have been proposed to provide more guarantees on the resulting routes for ad-hoc networks. However, they may be still subject to attacks. For example, a flaw has been discovered on the Secure Routing Protocol SRP [PH02] when it applied to Dynamic Source Routing protocol DSR [JMB01], allowing an attacker to modify the route, which makes the source node accept an

J.-L. Danger et al. (Eds.): FPS 2013, LNCS 8352, pp. 306–322, 2014.
DOI: 10.1007/978-3-319-05302-8_19, © Springer International Publishing Switzerland 2014

invalid one [BV04]. Another attack was found on the Ariadne protocol [HPJ05] in the same paper. This shows that designing secure routing protocol is a difficult and error-prone task. An NP-decision procedure has been proposed by M. Arnaud *et al.* [ACD10] for analysing routing protocols looking for attacks on route validity in case of a fixed topology. However, the existence of an attack strongly depends on the network topology, i.e. how nodes are connected and where malicious nodes are located. This results in an infinite number of topologies to verify, which is not tractable. Indeed, in contrast to classical Dolev-Yao attacker [DY83] that controls all the communications, an attacker for routing protocols has to situate somewhere in the network. It can control only a finite number of nodes (typically one or two), and thus it can listen to the communication of its neighbours but it is not possible to listen beyond the neighbouring nodes. Cortier *et al.* [CDD12] proposed a reduction proof when looking for route validity property under the *cooperative attacker model*, i.e. a model that allows distant malicious nodes to communicate using out-of-band resources, and thus to share their knowledge.

In fact, due to their minimal configuration and quick deployment ad-hoc networks are suitable for emergency situations like natural disasters or military conflicts where no infrastructure is available. So, usually it is difficult to have common channels between malicious nodes. As an example, consider the case of ad-hoc sensors that are thrown from a plane into the enemy field during a battle. Also, in-band-communications between malicious nodes are unfeasible in some cases where nodes have low power capabilities (e.g. sensor networks). Moreover, it is well-known that the presence of several colluding malicious nodes often yields straightforward attacks [cHPJ06,LPM+05].

Contributions: We consider route validity property under the *non-cooperative* attacker model, where malicious nodes work independently, i.e. they have no ability to share their knowledge. We use the CBS♯ [NH06] calculus to model routing protocol, and the transition rules introduced in [ACD10] to model the communications between nodes, after updating them to handle the behaviour of the non-cooperative malicious nodes instead of the cooperative ones.

Then, we revisit the work presented by Cortier *et al.* in [CDD12], where they show that when looking for attacks on route validity under the cooperative model it is enough to check only five particular small topologies. We show that the same result is also valid in case the of non-cooperative model: first, we show that if there is an attack on a routing protocol in a certain topology under the non-cooperative model, then there is an attack on this protocol in a smaller topology obtained from the original one by a simple reduction. Then, we show that applying the reduction procedure to any topology leads to (at most) five small topologies. The resulting topologies are the same ones obtained in [CDD12] under the cooperative model.

Finally, we prove that a protocol is secure under the cooperative model in any topology, if and only if, it is secure under the non-cooperative model in any topology. The latter result does not hold when we consider only one fixed topology.

Related work: The non-cooperative model is already used in [ACRT11] to analyse the web-service applications looking for attacks that exploit XML format. Verifying route validity under this model is equivalent to satisfiability of general constraints where knowledge monotonicity does not hold. The satisfiability of such kind of constraints has been proven to be NP-complete [Maz05, ACRT11]. However, verifying routing protocols requires considering an infinite number of topologies as we mentioned before.

To the best of our knowledge, the first approach proposing a reduction result in the context of routing protocols is [ABY11]. In this paper, the authors have shown how to reduce the number of network topologies that need to be considered, taking advantage of the symmetries. However, the total number of networks is still large, for example, 5698 networks need to be considered when the number of nodes is six.

Our work follows the spirit of [CDD12] where it has been shown that only five topologies need to be considered when looking for attacks on properties such as route validity under the cooperative model. Our work differs by considering the non-cooperative model which is a weaker one. We show that the problem of checking if a certain protocol is secure for any topology is equivalent under the two models. However, in a fixed topology we may find a protocol that is secure under the non-cooperative model, but not under the cooperative one. Actually, considering a powerful attacker model by giving malicious nodes the ability to share their knowledge may introduce some false positive attacks in the sense that we may found some attacks that can not be to mounted in practice. Also, we should note that studying protocol security under the non-cooperative model requires strictly less executions to be considered.

Outline: We introduce notations and attacker capabilities in Sect. 2. Then in Sect. 3, we show how to model routing protocols by process calculus, and we define the security property. In Sect. 4, we present our reduction proof and show that only five topologies are sufficient. Finally, before concluding, we make a comparison between the cooperative and non-cooperative models in Sect. 5.

2   Preliminaries

To model messages we consider an arbitrary term algebra and deduction system.

2.1   Messages

We use *terms* to represent messages and *function symbols* to represent cryptographic primitives such as encryption and hash function. We consider a *signature* $(\Sigma, \mathbb{S})$ made of a set of sorts $\mathbb{S}$ and a set of function symbols Σ with *arities*, $ar(\cdot) : \Sigma \mapsto \mathbb{N}$. The set of function symbols of arity n is denoted by Σ_n. For a function symbol $f \in \Sigma_n$ we have that $f : s_1 \times \cdots \times s_n \mapsto s$ with $s, s_1, \ldots, s_n \in \mathbb{S}$. We consider a countable set of variables $\mathbb{X}$. For a set $X \subseteq \mathbb{X}$, we define a set of terms $\mathbb{T}(\Sigma, X)$ to be the smallest set containing Σ_0 and X, such that for a function symbol $g \in \Sigma_n$: if $t_1, \ldots, t_n \in \mathbb{T}(\Sigma, X)$ then $g(t_1, \ldots, t_n) \in \mathbb{T}(\Sigma, X)$. In the case that $X = \emptyset$, we simply write $\mathbb{T}(\Sigma)$, this is the set of ground terms.

We assume two special sorts: the sort Agent that only contains agent's names and variables, and the sort Term that subsumes all other sorts so that any term is of the sort Term. As an example, a typical signature for representing the primitives used in SRP [PH02] protocol is the signature $(\Sigma_{SRP}, \mathbb{S}_{SRP})$ defined by $\mathbb{S}_{SRP} = \{\mathsf{Agent}, \mathsf{List}, \mathsf{Term}\}$ and $\Sigma_{SRP} = \{hmac.(\cdot), \langle \cdot, \cdot \rangle, \ :: \ , [], req, rep\}$, where req and rep are unitary constants identify the request and response phases respectively, $[]$ represents an empty list and other symbols are defined as follows:

$$\langle \cdot, \cdot \rangle \ : \mathsf{Term} \times \mathsf{Term} \to \mathsf{Term} \quad :: \ : \mathsf{Agent} \times \mathsf{List} \to \mathsf{List}$$
$$hmac.(\cdot) \ : \mathsf{Term} \times \mathsf{Term} \to \mathsf{Term}$$

The symbol $hmac.(\cdot)$ takes two terms and computes the message authentication code MAC of the first term with the second one as a key. The operator $\langle \cdot, \cdot \rangle$ produces a concatenation of two terms, and the operator $::$ is the list constructor. We write $<t_1, t_2, t_3>$ for the term $\langle \langle t_1, t_2 \rangle, t_3 \rangle$, and $[t_1, t_2, t_3]$ for $(([] :: t_1) :: t_2) :: t_3$.

Substitutions and unifications: A *substitution* σ is a mapping from $\mathbb{X}$ to $\mathbb{T}(\Sigma, \mathbb{X})$ with the domain $dom(\sigma) = \{x \in \mathbb{X} \mid \sigma(x) \neq x\}$. We consider only *well-sorted substitutions*, that is substitution for which x and $\sigma(x)$ have the same sort. We extend σ to a homomorphism on functions, processes and terms as expected. We say that the two terms t and s are *unifiable* if there exists a substitution θ, called *unifier*, such that $\theta(t) = \theta(s)$. We define the *most general unifier* (for short *mgu*) of two terms t and s to be a unifier, denoted $mgu(t, s)$, such that for any unifier θ of t and s there exists a substitution σ with $\theta = \sigma \circ mgu(t, s)$ where $\circ$ is a composition of two mappings. We write $mgu(t, s) = \perp$ when t and s are not unifiable.

2.2   Attacker Capabilities

We consider a non-cooperative model where there are multiple independent attackers that have no ability to share knowledge between each other. The ability of each attacker is modelled by a deduction relation $\vdash$. Such a relation is defined through an inference system, i.e. a finite set of rules of the form $\frac{t_1 \cdots t_n}{t}$, where $t, t_1, \ldots, t_n \in \mathbb{T}(\Sigma, \mathbb{X})$. A term t is *deducible* from a set of terms I, denoted by $I \vdash t$, if there exists a proof tree with a root labelled by t and leaves labelled by $t' \in I$ and every intermediate node is an instance of one of the rules of the inference system. We can associate to the SRP signature $(\Sigma_{SRP}, \mathbb{S}_{SRP})$, the following inference system:

$$\frac{t_1 \quad t_2}{\langle t_1, t_2 \rangle} \qquad \frac{\langle t_1, t_2 \rangle}{t_i} \ i \in \{1, 2\} \qquad \frac{l_1 \quad l_2}{l_1 :: l_2} \qquad \frac{l_1 :: l_2}{l_i} \ i \in \{1, 2\} \qquad \frac{t_1 \quad t_2}{hmac_{t_2}(t_1)}$$

The terms t_1 and t_2 are of sort Term, l_1 is of sort List, whereas l_2 is of sort Agent. The system gives the attacker an ability to concatenate terms, build lists, as well as to retrieve their components. The last inference rule models the fact that the attacker can also compute a MAC provided he knows the corresponding key.

3   Modelling Routing Protocols

3.1   Process Calculus

The intended behaviour of each node in the network can be modelled by a process defined using the grammar given in Fig. 1. We use the CBS♯ calculus introduced in [NH06]. We parameterized them by a set **P** of predicates to represent the checks performed by the agents, and a set $\mathcal{F}$ of functions over terms to represent the computations performed by the agents. The set of functions $\mathcal{F}$ contains functions that are more complex than basic cryptographic primitives represented by Σ, for example a function $f : (x, y, z) \mapsto hmac_z(\langle x, y \rangle)$ which takes three terms, concatenates the first two and then computes the MAC over them with the third term. They can also be used to model operations on lists, for example we can define a function that take a list and return its reverse.

The process $out(f(t_1, \ldots, t_n)).P$ first computes the term $t = f(t_1, \ldots, t_n)$, emits t, and then behaves like P. The reception process $in(t).P$ expects a message m matching the pattern t and then behaves like $\sigma(P)$ where $\sigma = mgu(m, t)$. The process $if \ \Phi \ then \ P$ tests whether Φ is true, if Φ is true it then behaves like P. Two processes P and Q running in parallel represented by the process $P|Q$. The replication process $!P$ denotes an infinite number of copies of P, all running in parallel. The process $new \ m.P$ creates a fresh name m and then behaves like P. Sometimes, for the sake of clarity we omit the null process. We assume that the predicates $p \in \mathbf{P}$ are given together with their semantics that may depend on the underlying graph G. We consider two kinds of predicates: a set $\mathbf{P_I}$ of predicates whose semantics is independent of the graph and a set $\mathbf{P_D}$ of predicates whose

$$
\begin{array}{lll}
P, Q ::= & & \text{Processes} \\
\quad 0 & & \text{null process.} \\
\quad out(f(t_1, \ldots, t_n)).P & & \text{emission} \\
\quad in(t).P & & \text{reception} \\
\quad if \ \Phi \ then \ P & & \text{conditional} \\
\quad P|Q & & \text{parallel composition.} \\
\quad !P & & \text{replication} \\
\quad new \ m.P & & \text{fresh name generation}
\end{array}
$$

where $t, t_1, \ldots, t_n$ are terms, m is a name, $f \in \mathcal{F}$ and Φ is a formula:

$$
\begin{array}{lll}
\Phi, \Phi_1, \Phi_2 ::= & & \text{Formula} \\
\quad p(t'_1, \ldots, t'_n) & & p \in \mathbf{P}, \ t'_1, \ldots, t'_n \text{ are terms} \\
\quad \Phi_1 \wedge \Phi_2 & & \text{conjunction}
\end{array}
$$

Fig. 1. Process grammar

semantics is dependent on the graph. For a graph dependent formula Φ and a graph G, we write $[\![\Phi]\!]_G = true$ (resp. *false*) to denote that Φ is *true* (resp. *false*) in G. For example, we can use the predicates $\mathbf{P_{SRP}} = \mathbf{P_I} \cup \mathbf{P_D}$ for SRP, with $\mathbf{P_I} = \{\mathsf{checksrc}, \mathsf{checkdest}\}$ and $\mathbf{P_D} = \{\mathsf{check}, \mathsf{checkl}\}$. The purpose of the $\mathbf{P_I}$ predicates is to model some checks that are performed by the source when it receives the route. The semantics of these predicates is defined as follows:

- $\mathsf{checksrc}(S, l) = true$ if and only if l is of sort List and its first element is S,
- $\mathsf{checkdest}(D, l) = true$ if and only if l is of sort List and its last element is D.

The predicates $\mathsf{checksrc}(S, l)$ and $\mathsf{checkdest}(D, l)$ are used by the source process to verify that the first and last nodes of the established route are the source and destination of the route discovery respectively.

While, the purpose of the $\mathbf{P_D}$ predicates is to model neighbourhood checks. Given a graph $G = (V, E)$, their semantics is defined as follows:

- $[\![\mathsf{check}(A, B)]\!]_G = true$ if and only if $(A, B) \in E$ or $(B, A) \in E$,
- $[\![\mathsf{checkl}(C, l)]\!]_G = true$ if and only if C appears in l and for any l' subterm of l we have $(A, C) \in E$ if $l' = l_1 :: A :: C$ and $(C, B) \in E$ if $l' = l_1 :: C :: B$.

The aim of the predicate $[\![\mathsf{check}(A, B)]\!]_G$ is to check if A and B are neighbours in G, while the aim of the predicate $[\![\mathsf{checkl}(C, l)]\!]_G$ is to check if the node C appears in l between two neighbours in G. We assume that each nodes knows its neighbours in the network, this can be achieved by running a certain neighbour discovery protocol in advance.

We write $fv(P)$ for the set of *free variables* that occur in P, i.e. the set of variables that are not in the scope of an input. We consider ground processes, i.e. processes P such that $fv(P) = \emptyset$, and parameterized processes, denoted $P(x_1, \ldots, x_n)$ where $x_1, \ldots, x_n$ are variables of sort Agent, and such that $fv(P) \subseteq \{x_1, \ldots, x_n\}$. A routing role is a parameterized process that does not contain any name of sort Agent. A routing protocol is then simply a set of routing roles.

The secure routing protocol SRP applied on DSR, already modelled in [CDD12] using these process calculus. Here we give only the source process as an example. Considering the signature $(\Sigma_{SRP}, \mathbb{S}_{SRP})$ and the predicates $\mathbf{P_{SRP}}$ introduced before, and the set $\mathcal{F}_{SRP}$ of functions over terms that only contains the identity function (omitted for sake of clarity), the process played by the source x_S initiating the search of a route towards a destination x_D is given as follows:

$$P_{src}(x_S, x_D) = \mathsf{new}\ id.out(u_1).in(u_2).\mathsf{if}\ \Phi_S\ \mathsf{then}\ 0$$

where id is a constant identifies the request, x_S, x_D are variables of sort Agent, and x_L is a variable of sort List and

$$u_1 = \langle req, x_S, x_D, id, [] :: x_S, hmac_{k_{x_S x_D}}(\langle req, x_S, x_D, id \rangle) \rangle$$
$$u_2 = \langle req, x_D, x_S, id, x_L, hmac_{k_{x_S x_D}}(\langle req, x_D, x_S, id, x_L \rangle) \rangle$$
$$\Phi_S = \mathsf{checkl}(x_S, x_L) \wedge \mathsf{checksrc}(x_S, x_L) \wedge \mathsf{checkdest}(x_D, x_L)$$

3.2   Configuration and Topology

Each process is located at a specified node of the network. Unlike the classical Dolev-Yao model [DY83], the attacker does not control the entire network but can only interact with its neighbours. More specifically, we assume that the *topology* of the network is represented by a tuple $T = (G, \mathcal{M}, S, D)$ where:

- $G = (V, E)$ is an undirected graph with $V \subseteq \{A \in \Sigma_0 \mid A$ of sort Agent$\}$, where an edge in the graph models the fact that two agents are neighbours. We only consider graphs such that $\{(A, A) | A \in V\} \subseteq E$ which means that an agent can receive a message sent by himself;
- $\mathcal{M} = \{M_i\}_{i=1}^{i=k}$ is a set of nodes that are controlled by k attackers we have in the network, where each attacker controls only one node. Note that $\mathcal{M} \subseteq V$. These nodes that are in $\mathcal{M}$ are called malicious whereas nodes not in $\mathcal{M}$ are called honest;
- S and D are two honest nodes that represent respectively the source and the destination for which we analyse the security of the routing protocol.

Note that malicious nodes cannot communicate using out-of-band resources or hidden channels.

A *configuration* of the network is a pair $(\mathcal{P}, \mathcal{I})$ where:

- $\mathcal{P}$ is a multiset of expressions of the form $\lfloor P \rfloor_A$ that represents the process P executed by the agent $A \in V$. We write $\lfloor P \rfloor_A \cup \mathcal{P}$ instead of $\{\lfloor P \rfloor_A\} \cup \mathcal{P}$;
- We assume an independent knowledge for each attacker as we define the set of sets of terms $\mathcal{I} = \{I_i\}_{i=1}^{i=k}$, where the set I_i represents the messages seen by the malicious node $M_i \in \mathcal{M}$ as well as its initial knowledge.

A possible topology $T_0 = (G_0, \mathcal{M}_0, S, D)$ is modelled in Fig. 2, where M_1 and M_2 are malicious nodes (colored in black), i.e. $\mathcal{M}_0 = \{M_1, M_2\}$ while A is an extra honest node (colored in white). To refer to the source and destination we use $\rightarrow\!\bigcirc$ and $\bigcirc\!\rightarrow$ respectively. A typical initial configuration for the SRP protocol is

$$K = (\lfloor P_{src}(S, D) \rfloor_S \mid \lfloor P_{req}(A) \rfloor_A \mid \lfloor P_{rep}(A) \rfloor_A \mid \lfloor P_{dest}(D) \rfloor_D; \mathcal{I})$$

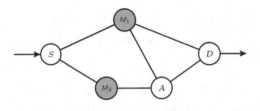

Fig. 2. Topology T_0

COMM $(\{\lfloor in(t'_j).P_j \rfloor_{A_j} \mid mgu(t, t'_j) \neq \bot, (A, A_j) \in E\}$
$\cup \lfloor out(f(t_1, \ldots, t_n).P \rfloor_A \cup \mathcal{P}; \mathcal{I}) \rightarrow_\mathcal{T} (\lfloor P_j \sigma_j \rfloor_{A_j} \cup \lfloor P \rfloor_A \cup \mathcal{P}; \mathcal{I}'),$
where $\sigma_j = mgu(t, t'_j)$ with $t = f(t_1, \ldots, t_n)$, and for $i \in \{1, \ldots, k\}$, if $(A, M_i) \in E$, then $I'_i = I_i \cup \{t\}$, else $I'_i = I_i$.

IN $(\lfloor in(t').P \rfloor_A \cup \mathcal{P}; \mathcal{I}) \rightarrow_\mathcal{T} (\lfloor P\sigma \rfloor_A \cup \mathcal{P}; \mathcal{I}'),$ if $(A, M_j) \in E, I_j \vdash t$ & $M_j \in \mathcal{M}$
    where $\sigma = mgu(t, t')$, and if $(M_j, M_i) \in E$ $I'_i = I_i \cup \{t\}$, else $I'_i = I_i$.

IF-THEN $(\lfloor \text{if } \Phi \text{ then } P \rfloor_A \cup \mathcal{P}; \mathcal{I}) \rightarrow_\mathcal{T} (\lfloor P \rfloor_A \cup \mathcal{P}; \mathcal{I}),$ if $[\![\Phi]\!]_G = 1$.

PAR $(\lfloor P_1 | P_2 \rfloor_A \cup \mathcal{P}; \mathcal{I}) \rightarrow_\mathcal{T} (\lfloor P_1 \rfloor_A \cup \lfloor P_2 \rfloor_A \cup \mathcal{P}; \mathcal{I})$

REPL $(\lfloor !P \rfloor_A \cup \mathcal{P}; \mathcal{I}) \rightarrow_\mathcal{T} (\lfloor P \rfloor_A \cup \lfloor !P \rfloor_A \cup \mathcal{P}; \mathcal{I})$

NEW $(\lfloor new\ m.P \rfloor_A \cup \mathcal{P}; \mathcal{I}) \rightarrow_\mathcal{T} (\lfloor P\{m \mapsto m' \rfloor_A \cup \mathcal{P}; \mathcal{I}),$
    where m' is a fresh name.

Fig. 3. Transition system.

3.3 Execution Model

The communication system is formally defined by the rules of Fig. 3. These rules are parameterized by the underlying topology $\mathcal{T} = (G, \mathcal{M}, S, D)$ with $G = (V, E)$. They are quite similar to the ones used in [ACD10, CDD12] with the difference that we use an independent attackers knowledge, and we assume that the message sent by a certain malicious node can be captured by its malicious neighbours due to broadcast nature of the communications in wireless add-hoc networks, this modelled in the rule IN. The COMM rule allows nodes to communicate provided they are directly connected in the underlying graph. The exchanged message is added to the knowledge I_i of the malicious node M_i if the agent emitting the message is a direct neighbour of M_i, this reflects the fact that a malicious node can listen to the communications of its neighbours. The IN rule allows a malicious node M_i to send any message it can deduce from its knowledge I_i to one of its neighbours, and like in COMM rule this message captured by neighbour malicious nodes. The rule IF-THEN states that the node A executes the process P only if the formula Φ is true. PAR rule says that parallel processes are equivalent to parallel nodes running these processes. The replication process $!P$ expanded using the rule REPL. The last rule NEW says that nodes can use fresh names of their choice when required. The relation $\rightarrow_\mathcal{T}^*$ is the reflexive and transitive closure of $\rightarrow_\mathcal{T}$.

3.4 Security Property

We consider the route validity property. We say that a protocol satisfies route validity property and thus secure if it results in a *valid route*. In the follows, we define what is the valid route and what is the attack on a routing protocol.

Definition 1 (Valid route). *Let $T = (G, \mathcal{M}, S, D)$ be a topology with $G = (V, E)$, we say that a list $l = [A_1, \ldots, A_n]$ of agent names is an valid route in T if and only if for any $i \in \{1, \ldots, n-1\}$ $(A_i, A_{i+1}) \in E$ or $A_i, A_{i+1} \in \mathcal{M}$.*

We do not consider the case of wormhole attack where we have two successive non-neighbour malicious nodes.

After successfully executing a routing protocol, the source node stores the resulting received route. We assume that processes representing instances of routing protocols contain a process that has a special action of the form $out(end(l))$ which output the flag $end(l)$ at the end. The list l represent the established route so that we can check if the established route is valid. Checking whether a routing protocol ensures the validity of accepted route can be defined as a reachability property.

The attack on the configuration of a routing protocol can be modelled by the following definition.

Definition 2 (Attack on a configuration for a routing protocol). *Let $T = (G, \mathcal{M}, S, D)$ be a topology and K be a configuration. We say that K admits an attack in T if $K \rightarrow_T^* (\lfloor out(end(l)).P \rfloor_A \cup \mathcal{P}; \mathcal{I})$ for some A, P, $\mathcal{P}$, $\mathcal{I}$, and some term l that is not a valid route in T.*

The valid configuration for a routing protocol should satisfy this definition.

Definition 3 (Valid configuration). *Let $T = (G, \mathcal{M}, S, D)$ be a topology with $G = (V, E)$, and $\mathcal{I}$ be a set of sets representing the initial knowledge of the attackers. A configuration $K = (\mathcal{P}, \mathcal{I})$ is valid for the routing protocol $\mathcal{P}_{routing}$ and the routing role P_0 with respect to T if*

- *$\mathcal{P} = \lfloor P_0(S, D) \rfloor_S \uplus \mathcal{P}'$ and for every $\lfloor P' \rfloor_{A_1} \in \mathcal{P}'$ there exist $P(x_1, \ldots, x_n) \in \mathcal{P}_{routing}$, and $A_2, \ldots, A_n \in V$ such that $P' = P(A_1, \ldots, A_n)$.*
- *the only process containing a special action of the form $out(end(l))$ is $P_0(S, D)$ witnessing the storage of a route by the source node S.*

The first condition says that we only consider configurations that are made up using $P_0(S, D)$ and roles of the protocol, and the agent who executes the process is located at the right place. Moreover, we check whether the security property holds when the source and the destination are honest. The second condition ensures that the process witnessing the route is the process $P_0(S, D)$. Below we define the attack on a routing protocol $\mathcal{P}_{routing}$.

Definition 4 (Attack on $\mathcal{P}_{routing}$). *We say that there is an attack on the routing protocol $\mathcal{P}_{routing}$ and the routing role P_0 given an initial knowledge $\mathcal{I}$ if there exist a topology $T = (G, \mathcal{M}, S, D)$ and a configuration K that is valid for $\mathcal{P}_{routing}$ and P_0 with respect to T, such that K admits an attack in T.*

4   Reduction Procedure

We show that if there is an attack on route validity in a given topology then there is an attack in a smaller topology obtained by doing some reduction in the initial one. Our reduction procedure consists of two main steps:

1. Adding edges to the graph yielding a quasi-complete topology.
2. Merging nodes that have the same nature (honest or malicious) and same neighbours.

Finally in Sect. 4.3, we consider an arbitrary topology and apply our procedure on it. We end up with five particular topologies that contain at most three malicious nodes such that if there exists a network topology admitting an attack then there is an attack on one of these five topologies.

4.1   From an Arbitrary Topology to a Quasi-Complete One

Projecting nodes and reducing the size of the graph require that the nodes to be merged have the same nature and same neighbours. In order to ensure that most of the nodes have the same neighbours we first add edges to the graph. Actually, we add all edges except one. We show that the attack is preserved when we add these edges.

Definition 5 (Quasi-completion [CDD12]). *Let* $T = (G, \mathcal{M}, S, D)$ *be a topology with* $G = (V, E)$, *and A, B be two nodes in V that are not both malicious and such that* $(A, B) \notin E$. *The quasi-completion of* T *with respect to* (A, B) *is a topology* $T^+ = (G^+, \mathcal{M}, S, D)$ *such that* $G^+ = (V, E^+)$ *with* $E^+ = V \times V \smallsetminus \{(A, B), (B, A)\}$.

For example, a possible quasi-completion T_0^+ of the topology T_0 of Fig. 2 is the one with respect to the pair (S, D) given below. As we see the graph is almost highly connected, the only missing edge is (S, D).

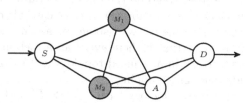

Definition 6 (Completion-friendly [CDD12]). *A predicate p is completion-friendly if* $[\![p(t_1, \ldots, t_n)]\!]_G = true$ *implies that* $[\![p(t_1, \ldots, t_n)]\!]_{G^+} = true$ *for any ground terms* $t_1, \ldots, t_n$ *and any quasi-completion* $T^+ = (G^+, \mathcal{M}, S, D)$ *of* $T = (G, \mathcal{M}, S, D)$. *We say that a routing protocol (resp. a configuration) is completion-friendly if the predicates* $\mathbf{P_D}$, *i.e. the predicates that are dependent of the graph are completion-friendly.*

Predicates have to be completion-friendly so that their values are preserved when adding some edges to the graph.

Lemma 1 (Quasi-completion). *Let* T *be a topology,* K_0 *be a configuration that is completion-friendly. If there is an attack on* K_0 *in* T, *then we can find two non-neighbour nodes* $B, C \in V$ *that are not both malicious and a topology* T^+ *quasi-completion of* T *with respect to* (B, C), *such that there exists an attack on* K_0 *in* T^+.

Proof. We give the sketch of the proof, full proof is available in the technical report [KLL13].

Let $\mathcal{T} = (G, \mathcal{M}, S, D)$ be a topology with $G = (V, E)$ and K_0 be a configuration that is completion-friendly. If there is an attack on K_0 in $\mathcal{T}$ then, by the definition of the attack, there exist A, P, $\mathcal{P}$, $\mathcal{I}$ and $l_0 = [A_1, \ldots, A_n]$, such that $K_0 \rightarrow^*_{\mathcal{T}} (\lfloor out(end(l_0)).P \rfloor_A \cup \mathcal{P}; \mathcal{I}) = K$ and l_0 is not a valid route in $\mathcal{T}$, i.e. there exists $1 \leq a \leq n$ such that $(A_a, A_{a+1}) \notin E$ and $(A_a \notin \mathcal{M}$ or $A_{a+1} \notin \mathcal{M})$. Consider the quasi-completion $\mathcal{T}^+ = (G^+, \mathcal{M}, S, D)$ of $\mathcal{T}$ with respect to $(B, C) = (A_a, A_{a+1})$. The edge (A_a, A_{a+1}) is missing in $\mathcal{T}^+$, thus l_0 is not a valid route in $\mathcal{T}^+$.

We show by induction on the length r of a derivation $K_0 \rightarrow^r_{\mathcal{T}} K_r$ that K_r is completion-friendly and that $K_0 \rightarrow^r_{\mathcal{T}^+} K_r$. This will allow us to obtain that $K_0 \rightarrow^*_{\mathcal{T}^+} (\lfloor out(end(l_0)).P \rfloor_A \cup \mathcal{P}; \mathcal{I})$, and thus we conclude that K_0 admits an attack in $\mathcal{T}^+$. We distinguish cases according to the rule involved in the step $K_{r-1} \rightarrow_{\mathcal{T}} K_r$. In the case of the rule IF-THEN since K_{r-1} is completion-friendly and $[\![\Phi]\!]_G = true$ then $[\![\Phi]\!]_{G^+} = true$, it follows that we can apply the rule IF-THEN on K_{r-1} in $\mathcal{T}^+$, and thus we get that $K_{r-1} \rightarrow_{\mathcal{T}^+} K_r$. For rules COMM and IN we can easily conclude since $E \subseteq E^+$, and for other rules it is straightforward as they do not depend on the underlying graph. □

4.2   Reducing the Size of the Topology

In this step, we merge nodes that have the same nature and same neighbours. The initial knowledge of malicious nodes are joined when they merged. In fact, sometimes one malicious node could do the job of several malicious nodes if we give it the required initial knowledge, for instance the case where we have a chain of malicious nodes. Also, in some cases existence or absence of some malicious nodes has no effect. We show that if there exists an attack in a given topology $\mathcal{T}$ then there exists an attack in a reduced topology $\rho(\mathcal{T})$ (some times written $\mathcal{T}\rho$) where ρ is a node renaming mapping.

Let $\mathcal{T} = (G, \mathcal{M}, S, D)$ be a topology with $G = (V, E)$ and E a reflexive and symmetric relation, and let ρ be a renaming on the agent names (not necessarily a one-to-one mapping). We say that the renaming $\rho : V \mapsto V$

- *preserves honesty* of $\mathcal{T}$ if $A, \rho(A) \in \mathcal{M}$ or $A, \rho(A) \notin \mathcal{M}$ for every $A \in V$.
- *preserves neighbourhood* of $\mathcal{T}$ if $\rho(A) = \rho(B)$ implies that $\{A' \in V \mid (A, A') \in E\} = \{B' \in V \mid (B, B') \in E\}$.

Given a term t, we denote by $t\rho$ the term obtained by applying the renaming ρ on t. This notation is extended to set of terms, configurations, graphs, and topologies. In particular, given a graph $G = (V, E)$, we denote $G\rho$ the graph $(V\rho, E')$ such that $E' = \{(\rho(A), \rho(B)) \mid (A, B) \in E\}$. Note that when we apply a renaming ρ to a configuration $K = (\mathcal{P}, \mathcal{I})$ then the knowledge $I_i \in \mathcal{I}$ of $M_i \in \mathcal{M}$ is joined with the knowledge $I_{i'}$ of $M_i\rho = M_{i'}$ and the I_i is removed from $\mathcal{I}$.

Consider the quasi-completion $\mathcal{T}_0^+$ we seen before, a possible renaming ρ_0 that preserves neighbourhood and honesty and that allows us to reduce the size of the graph is defined by: $\rho_0(S) = S, \rho_0(A) = A, \rho_0(M_1) = \rho_0(M_2) = M_1, \rho_0(D) = D$. The resulting topology $\mathcal{T}_0^+ \rho_0$ is given as follows:

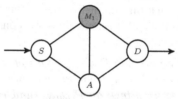

Here, the two malicious nodes M_1 and M_2 are merged in M_1 then the knowledge I_2 corresponding to M_2 should be pooled with I_1 that of M_1. For instance, assume that we have initially $I_1 = \{M_1, S, D\}$, $I_2 = \{M_2, S, A\}$ and $\mathcal{I} = \{I_1, I_2\}$ then after merging we have that $I_1 \rho_0 = \{M_1, S, D, A\}$ and $\mathcal{I} \rho_0 = \{I_1 \rho_0\}$.

Note that ρ_0 does not preserve neighbourhood of the topology $\mathcal{T}_0$, this emphasises the importance of the completion step in order to make a safe merging.

Definition 7 (Projection-friendly [CDD12]). *A predicate p is projection-friendly if $[\![p(t_1, \ldots, t_n)]\!]_G = true$ implies $[\![p(t_1 \rho, \ldots, t_n \rho)]\!]_{G\rho} = true$ for any ground terms $t_1, \ldots, t_n$ and any renaming ρ that preserves neighbourhood and honesty. A function f over terms is projection-friendly if $f(t_1 \rho, \ldots, t_n \rho)) = f(t_1, \ldots, t_n)\rho$ for any ground terms $t_1, \ldots, t_n$ and any renaming ρ that preserves neighbourhood and honesty. We say that a routing protocol (resp. a configuration) is projection-friendly if the predicates $\mathbf{P_I} \cup \mathbf{P_D}$ and the functions in $\mathcal{F}$ are projection-friendly.*

Lemma 2 (Reducing). *Let $\mathcal{T}$ be a topology, K_0 be a configuration that is projection-friendly, and ρ be a renaming that preserves neighbourhood and honesty. If there is an attack on K_0 in $\mathcal{T}$, then there exists an attack on K_0' in $\mathcal{T}'$ where K_0' and $\mathcal{T}'$ are obtained by applying ρ on K_0 and $\mathcal{T}$ respectively.*

Proof. We give the sketch of the proof, full proof is available in the technical report [KLL13].

Let $\mathcal{T} = (G, \mathcal{M}, S, D)$ be a topology with $G = (V, E)$ and K_0 be a configuration that is projection-friendly. If there is an attack on K_0 in $\mathcal{T}$ then, by the definition of the attack, there exist $A, P, \mathcal{P}, \mathcal{I}$ and $l_0 = [A_1, \ldots, A_n]$, such that $K_0 \rightarrow_{\mathcal{T}}^* K = (\lfloor out(end(l_0)).P \rfloor_A \cup \mathcal{P}; \mathcal{I})$ and l_0 is not a valid route in $\mathcal{T}$. Let $K_0' = K_0 \rho$ and $\mathcal{T}' = \mathcal{T}\rho$, we show:

1. by induction on the length r of a derivation $K_0 \rightarrow_{\mathcal{T}}^r K_r$ that K_r is projection-friendly and $K_0' \rightarrow_{\mathcal{T}'}^r K_r'$ with $K_r' = K_r \rho$. We reason on case analysis according to the rule involved in the step $K_{r-1} \rightarrow_{\mathcal{T}} K_r$. This allow us to obtain that $K_0' \rightarrow_{\mathcal{T}'}^* K'$ with $K' = K\rho$.
2. $l_0 \rho = [A_1 \rho, \ldots, A_n \rho]$ is not a valid route in $\mathcal{T}'$. We show that if $B \notin \mathcal{M}$ then $B\rho \notin \mathcal{M}\rho$, and if $(B_1, B_2) \notin E$ then $(B_1 \rho, B_2 \rho) \notin E\rho$. Thus, as there exists $1 \leq a \leq n$ such that $(A_a, A_{a+1}) \notin E$ and $(A_a \notin \mathcal{M}$ or $A_{a+1} \notin \mathcal{M})$ since l_0 is not an admissible path in $\mathcal{T}$, we deduce that $(A_a \rho, A_{a+1} \rho) \notin E\rho$ and $(A_a \rho \notin \mathcal{M}\rho$ or $A_{a+1} \rho \notin \mathcal{M}\rho)$. Hence, $l_0 \rho$ is not a valid route in $\mathcal{T}'$.

Therefore, we can conclude.   □

4.3   Five Topologies Are Sufficient

We show that for a protocol $\mathcal{P}_{routing}$ there is an attack on an arbitrary topology if and only if there is an attack on one of five particular topologies. Our result holds for an unbounded number of sessions since we consider arbitrarily many instances of the roles occurring in $\mathcal{P}_{routing}$.

Theorem 1 (Five topologies). *Let $\mathcal{P}_{routing}$ be a routing protocol and P_0 be a routing role which are both completion-friendly and projection-friendly and $\mathcal{I}$ be a set of knowledge. There is an attack on $\mathcal{P}_{routing}$ and P_0 given the knowledge $\mathcal{I}$ for some $\mathcal{T}$, if and only if, there is an attack on $\mathcal{P}_{routing}$ and P_0 given the knowledge $\mathcal{I}$ for one of five particular topologies $\mathcal{T}_1, \mathcal{T}_2, \mathcal{T}_3, \mathcal{T}_4$ and $\mathcal{T}_5$.*

Proof. If there is an attack on $\mathcal{P}_{routing}$ and P_0 given $\mathcal{I}$ for one of the five particular topologies, we easily conclude that there is an attack on $\mathcal{P}_{routing}$ and P_0 given $\mathcal{I}$ for some topology $\mathcal{T}$. We consider now the other implication. Let $\mathcal{T} = (G, \mathcal{M}, S, D)$ be a topology with $G = (V, E)$, $\mathcal{I}$ be a set of knowledge and $K = (\mathcal{P}, \mathcal{I})$ be a valid configuration for $\mathcal{P}_{routing}$ and P_0 with respect to $\mathcal{T}$, such that there is an attack on K in $\mathcal{T}$. Without lost of generality, we assume that V contains at least three distinct honest nodes and three distinct malicious nodes. Note that otherwise, it is easy to add some nodes in the topology $\mathcal{T}$ and still preserving the existence of an attack.

First, it is easy to see that K is completion-friendly as $\mathcal{P}_{routing}$ and P_0 are both completion-friendly. Thanks to the Lemma 1, we deduce that there exists two non-neighbour nodes $B, C \in V$ that are not both malicious and a topology $\mathcal{T}^+ = (G, \mathcal{M}, S, D)$, a quasi-completion of $\mathcal{T}$ with respect to (B, C), such that there is an attack on K in $\mathcal{T}^+$. As $\mathcal{T}^+$ is a quasi-completion of $\mathcal{T}$ with respect to a pair (B, C), then the neighbours of B in G^+ denoted $N_{G^+}(B) = V \smallsetminus \{C\}$, $N_{G^+}(C) = V \smallsetminus \{B\}$, and $N_{G^+}(W) = V$ for any $W \in V \smallsetminus \{B, C\}$. Since we have assumed that V contains at least three distinct nodes that are not in $\mathcal{M}$ and three distinct nodes in $\mathcal{M}$, we deduce that $V \smallsetminus \{B, C\}$ contains at least an honest node let us say A and a malicious one let us say M. Let ρ be a renaming on the agent names such that for any $W \in V \smallsetminus \{B, C\}$, $\rho(W) = A$ if $W \notin \mathcal{M}$ and $\rho(W) = M$ else. Clearly, we have that ρ preserves honesty and neighbourhood. Thanks to Lemma 2, we deduce that there is an attack on $K' = K\rho$ in $\mathcal{T}' = (G\rho, \mathcal{M}\rho, S\rho, D\rho) = \mathcal{T}^+\rho$.

The topology $\mathcal{T}'$ has four nodes: one honest, one malicious and two nodes B, C. We distinguish cases depending in the nature of the nodes B and C:

1. B honest and C malicious (the reverse is the same due to symmetry). In this case $\mathcal{T}'$ has two honest nodes, thus according to the position of the source and destination we have the following four possibilities:

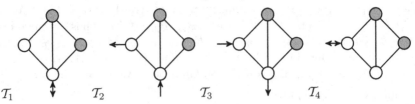

Note that the topology T_4 can obtained only if the source and destination are the same in the original topology.

2. Both are honest. So T' has three honest nodes in this case. Depending on the position of the source and destination we have nine possibilities, but due to symmetry four of them can be eliminated. This results in only five topologies:

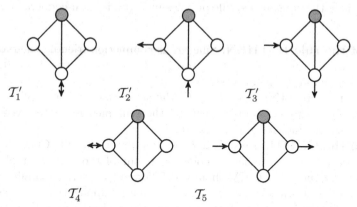

Again the topologies T_1', T_2', T_3' and T_4' are subsumed by T_1, T_2, T_3 and T_4 respectively, since if there is an attack in T_i' for $i \in \{1, 2, 3, 4\}$, then this attack can be mounted in T_i where an honest node is now malicious.

So T' is one of the five topologies T_1, T_2, T_3, T_4 and T_5. Now, since $P_{routing}$ and P_0 do not contain any names, Definition 3 is satisfied and thus $K' = (\mathcal{P}\rho, \mathcal{I}\rho)$ is a valid configuration with respect to T'.   □

5   Comparison between the Two Models

We show the equivalence of cooperative model and non-cooperative one when considering all possible topologies. First, if we have a topology T that a protocol admits an attack under the cooperative model, we show how to obtain a topology T' from such T that this protocol admits an attack on it under the non-cooperative model. Then, we present the equivalence theorem.

Lemma 3 (Preservation of the attack). *Let K be a configuration that is completion friendly. If there exists a topology T such that the configuration K admits an attack in T under the cooperative model then there exists a topology T' to be obtained from T such that K admits an attack in T' under the non-cooperative model.*

Proof. Let $T = (G, \mathcal{M}, S, D)$ be a topology with $G = (V, E)$ and K be a configuration that is completion friendly. Suppose that there is an attack on K in T then, by the definition of the attack, there exist A, P, $\mathcal{P}$, $\mathcal{I}$ and $l_0 = [A_1, \ldots, A_n]$ such that $K \rightarrow_T^* (\lfloor out(end(l_0)).P \rfloor_A \cup \mathcal{P}; \mathcal{I})$ and l_0 is not a valid route in T.

Let $T' = (G', \mathcal{M}, S, D)$ be a topology such that $G' = (V, E')$ with $E' = E \cup (\mathcal{M} \times \mathcal{M})$. Since l_0 is inadmissible in T, it is also inadmissible in T' according to the definition. To deduce that there is an attack on K in T' we show that $K \to_{T'}^*$ ($\lfloor out(end(l_0)) \rfloor . P \rfloor_A \cup \mathcal{P}; \mathcal{I}$). Note that we assume the same initial knowledge for all attackers, if its not the case we can reach this state by applying successively the COMM rule a certain number of times as all malicious nodes are connected in T'. For each rule involved in the transition $K_r \to_T K_{r+1}$ under the cooperative model we show the equivalence rule or rules in T' under non-cooperative model to have $K_r \to_{T'}^* K_{r+1}$

- **Case of the rule IF-THEN:** Since K is completion friendly then any formula ϕ that is true for T, its true also for T'. Thus, the rule IF-THEN can also be applied in T' in this case.
- **Case of the rule IN:** Since $E \subseteq E'$ the same rule can be applied and as all malicious nodes are connected in T' the sent message is received by all attackers so the knowledge remains equal.
- **Case of the COMM:** Since $E \subseteq E'$ we can apply the rule COMM, but in case where we have a malicious node neighbour of the node that plays the role of sender the rule COMM should be followed by a certain number (equal to the number of other malicious nodes) of rule IN application. The last step is to share in an indirect way the message received by one of the malicious nodes as it is a neighbour of the sender.
- **Case of the rules PAR, REPL, and NEW:** These rules do not depend on the underlying graph. So same rules can be applied in T'. □

Theorem 2 (Equivalence). *Let $\mathcal{P}_{routing}$ be a routing protocol and P_0 be a routing role and $\mathcal{I}$ be a set of knowledge. We have that $\mathcal{P}_{routing}$ and P_0 given the knowledge $\mathcal{I}$ are secure for any T in the cooperative model, if and only if, $\mathcal{P}_{routing}$ and P_0 given the knowledge $\mathcal{I}$ are secure for any T in the non-cooperative model.*

Proof. First direction: in non-cooperative model the malicious nodes have weaker abilities. So, if there is no attack on $\mathcal{P}_{routing}$ and P_0 given $\mathcal{I}$ in cooperative model then there is no attack on $\mathcal{P}_{routing}$ and P_0 in the non-cooperative model.

Second direction: Suppose that there is no attack on $\mathcal{P}_{routing}$ and P_0 given $\mathcal{I}$ for any topology in the non-cooperative model. Assume that there exists a topology T such that there is an attack on $\mathcal{P}_{routing}$ and P_0 given $\mathcal{I}$ in T for cooperative model, then by the definition of the attack there are a configuration K that is valid for $\mathcal{P}_{routing}$ and P_0 such that there is an attack on K in T under cooperative model. Then, by Lemma 3, there is a topology T' obtained from T such that there is an attack in it on the configuration K for the non-cooperative model and thus an attack on $\mathcal{P}_{routing}$ and P_0 given $\mathcal{I}$ in T' which leads to a contradiction. □

Considering one fix topology T this equivalence do not hold anymore as we can find an attack on a protocol in T under the cooperative model, while this protocol is secure in T under the non-cooperative model. This due to the fact that under the cooperative model we give the malicious nodes a powerful capabilities that are not exists in reality, this leads to a false positive attacks that can not be mounted in practice. Having a fixed known topology one could prefer to verify the used protocol under the non-cooperative model which gives a more realistic security level.

6 Conclusion

We consider the non-cooperative attacker model where there are multiple attackers working independently, so that no one share any of its knowledge with the others. We give a reduction proof: when looking for attacks on route validity in presence of multiple independent attackers if there is an attack in a certain topology then there is an attack in a smaller one. Then, we show that there is an attack on an arbitrary topology if and only if there is an attack on one of five particular topologies, each of them having only four nodes. This result facilities verification of routing protocols as we have to check only five small topologies. Finally, we show that a protocol is secure in any topology under the cooperative model if and only if it is secure for any topology under the non-cooperative model.

For future work, it could be interesting to develop a tool that able to solve multiple attackers constraints, so that we can reason on the five topologies one by one in order to verify ad-hoc network routing protocols.

References

[ABY11] Andel, T.R., Back, G., Yasinsac, A.: Automating the security analysis process of secure ad hoc routing protocols. Simul. Model. Pract. Theor. **19**(9), 2032–2049 (2011)

[ACD10] Arnaud, M., Cortier, V., Delaune, S.: Modeling and verifying ad hoc routing protocols. In: CSF, pp. 59–74. IEEE Computer Society (2010)

[ACRT11] Avanesov, T., Chevalier, Y., Rusinowitch, M., Turuani, M.: Satisfiability of general intruder constraints with and without a set constructor. CoRR abs/1103.0220 (2011)

[BV04] Buttyn, L., Vajda, I.: Towards provable security for ad hoc routing protocols. In: Proceedings of the ACM Workshop on Security in Ad Hoc and Sensor Networks (SASN), pp. 94–105. ACM Press (2004)

[CDD12] Cortier, V., Degrieck, J., Delaune, S.: Analysing routing protocols: four nodes topologies are sufficient. In: Degano, P., Guttman, J.D. (eds.) POST 2012. LNCS, vol. 7215, pp. 30–50. Springer, Heidelberg (2012)

[cHPJ06] Hu, Y.C., Perrig, A., Johnson, D.B.: Wormhole attacks in wireless networks. IEEE J. Sel. Areas Commun. **24**, 370–380 (2006)

[DY83] Dolev, D., Yao, A.C.: On the security of public key protocols. IEEE Trans. Inf. Theor. **29**(2), 198–207 (1983)

[HPJ05] Hu, Y.C., Perrig, A., Johnson, D.B.: Aariadne: a secure on-demand routing protocol for ad hoc networks. Wireless Netw. **11**(1–2), 21–38 (2005)

[JMB01] Johnson, D.B., Maltz, D.A., Broch, J.: Dsr: the dynamic source routing protocol for multi-hop wireless ad hoc networks. In: Perkins, C.E. (ed.) Ad Hoc Networking, Chapter 5, pp. 139–172. Addison-Wesley, Boston (2001)

[KLL13] Kassem, A., Lafourcade, P., Lakhnech, Y.: A more realistic model for verifying route validity in ad-hoc networks. Technical report TR-2013-10, Verimag, September 2013. http://www-verimag.imag.fr/TR/TR-2013-10.pdf

[LPM+05] Lazos, L., Poovendran, R., Meadows, C., Syverson, P., Chang, L.W.: Preventing wormhole attacks on wireless ad hoc networks: a graph theoretic approach. In: IEEE Wireless Communications and Networking Conference WCNC, pp. 1193–1199 (2005)

[Maz05] Mazaré, L.: Satisfiability of dolev-yao constraints. Electr. Notes Theor. Comput. Sci. **125**(1), 109–124 (2005)

[NH06] Nanz, S., Hankin, C.: A framework for security analysis of mobile wireless networks. Theoret. Comput. Sci. **367**, 203–227 (2006)

[PH02] Papadimitratos, P., Haas, Z.: Secure routing for mobile ad hoc networks. In: SCS Communication Networks and Distributed Systems Modeling and Simulation Conference (CNDS 2002) (2002)

[SDL+02] Sanzgiri, K., Dahill, B., Levine, B.N., Shields, C., Belding-Royer, E.M.: A secure routing protocol for ad hoc networks. In: ICNP, pp. 78–89. IEEE Computer Society (2002)

On the Security of a Privacy-Preserving Key Management Scheme for Location Based Services in VANETs

Bao Liu[1], Lei Zhang[1]([⊠]), and Josep Domingo-Ferrer[2]

[1] Shanghai Key Laboratory of Trustworthy Computing, Software Engineering
Institute, East China Normal University, Shanghai, China
[2] UNESCO Chair in Data Privacy, Department of Computer Engineering
and Mathematics, Universitat Rovira i Virgili, Tarragona, Catalonia
baoliu@ecnu.cn, leizhang@sei.ecnu.edu.cn, josep.domingo@urv.cat

Abstract. Location based services (LBSs) are promising value-added
services in vehicular *ad hoc* networks (VANETs), which can yield substantial economic profits. To extensively deploy LBSs in VANETs, it
is essential to establish an efficient privacy-preserving key management
scheme. In this paper, we point out a privacy weakness in a recent key
management scheme based on group signatures for LBSs in VANETs;
then we propose a secure and privacy-enhanced version. In our scheme,
roadside units (RSUs) act as group managers. Vehicles are distributed
into groups maintained by these RSUs. If a vehicle's member key is compromised, one just needs to update the group public key corresponding
to its group manager. With this method, the member revocation and privacy leakage problems in schemes based on group signatures are solved
effectively. As a result, a vehicle may enjoy LBSs efficiently without sur-
rendering its privacy.

Keywords: Security · Vehicle privacy · Vehicular *ad hoc* networks ·
Location based services · Key management

1 Introduction

As the society is paying more and more attention to the road safety and efficiency, vehicular *ad hoc* networks (VANETs) are becoming a hot research spot.
Based on the vehicle-to-vehicle (V2V), vehicle-to-roadside (V2R) and roadside-
to-vehicle (R2V) communications in VANETs, vehicles can communicate with
each other and the nearby RSUs to share information about the current traffic
conditions (e.g., traffic jams, accidents, icy roads, flooded roads, closed roads,
etc). With these mechanisms, VANETs are expected to improve road safety and
traffic efficiency. In the near future, VANETs are expected to serve as a general
platform for the development of any vehicle centered application [9].

In addition to the safety applications, value-added applications are envisioned
to offer various entertaining services to drivers and passengers, e.g., internet

J.-L. Danger et al. (Eds.): FPS 2013, LNCS 8352, pp. 323–335, 2014.
DOI: 10.1007/978-3-319-05302-8_20, © Springer International Publishing Switzerland 2014

access, navigation, social media, payTV, etc. Obviously, value-added applications promise substantial business opportunities. Location based service (LBS) is one type of promising and important value-added applications. To deploy LBSs in VANETs, one must deal with security issues (e.g., identity authentication, data integrity) and privacy issues (e.g., protection of the user's identity and/or location). Further, since LBSs are only intended for authenticated vehicles, we also have to consider confidentiality. A substantial body of studies has been devoted to security, privacy and confidentiality issues in VANETs (e.g., [4,8–10,17–19]). However, only a few of them (e.g., [8,9]) concern the key management for LBSs, which is crucial for efficient confidential communications in LBS sessions.

In [9], a dynamic privacy-preserving key management scheme was designed for location based services in VANETs. In this scheme, a privacy-preserving authentication (PPA) scheme, which is derived from the verifier-local group signature scheme in [2], is proposed for a vehicle to securely obtain a session key from a service provider without violating its privacy. We note that member revocation is usually a crucial problem in group signature based schemes. In [9], all the vehicles (members) are in a single group (which may contain numerous vehicles) maintained by a trusted authority (TA). It is reasonable to assume that a vehicle's member key may be leaked. Therefore, we need to consider the member revocation problem.

1.1 Contribution and Plan of This Paper

In this paper, we first point out a privacy weakness in the key management scheme for location based services in [9]. Although the PPA scheme can be used to protect the privacy of a vehicle, if a vehicle's member key is leaked, its privacy may be under threat. This is because when the member key of a vehicle is revoked, the revocation token of the vehicle should be added to the revocation list maintained by the TA. Based on the revocation token, a service provider can link all the requests of the revoked vehicle, which results in undesirable vehicle profiling. Therefore, it is reasonable to consider vehicle privacy even after revocation.

Secondly, we propose a secure and privacy enhanced version. In our scheme, TA never acts as the group manager. Instead, RSUs work as group managers to manage the groups. Before joining an LBS session, a vehicle has to request a member key from an RSU at first. The TA is only used to authenticate a vehicle and to detect whether a vehicle has already obtained a member key from an RSU. In this way, the vehicles are enrolled into various groups maintained by the RSUs. To solve the member revocation problem, instead of using revocation lists, we assume the RSUs can update their public keys. Once a vehicle is revoked, its corresponding group manager (RSU) has to update the group public key. We note that the number of vehicles enrolled by a single RSU may not be large and the vehicles in this group who are in an LBS session are limited. The public key update mechanism influences the efficiency of the whole system only slightly. Further, batch verification mechanism is used to improve the efficiency of the scheme.

The rest of this paper is organized as follows. Section 2 introduces the system architecture and the security requirements. In Sect. 3, we show some technical preliminaries utilized in our scheme. Section 4 reviews the key management scheme in [9] and points out a weakness in it. In Sect. 5, we propose a privacy enhanced version. Section 6 evaluates the proposed scheme. Section 7 concludes this paper.

2   Background

In this section, we illustrate the system architecture and the security requirements for LBSs in VANETs.

2.1   System Architecture

Figure 1 shows the system architecture in [9] and in this paper. It consists of a trusted authority (TA), roadside units (RSUs), service providers (SPs) and vehicles.

◇ **TA**: It is a trusted third party who generates public parameters for the whole system. All entities in the system must register with TA to get their own private and public keys. TA is also employed to keep and manage the real identity of each vehicle.

◇ **SP**: Service providers that provide LBSs, such as establishing an exclusive network for the vehicles from the same corporation or building a social network for the vehicles with the same destination based on their location.

◇ **RSU**: The road-side units are deployed along the roadside, and they are always equipped with some processing units and sensors. In our scheme, RSUs are used to maintain groups and transfer messages between vehicles and TA/SPs.

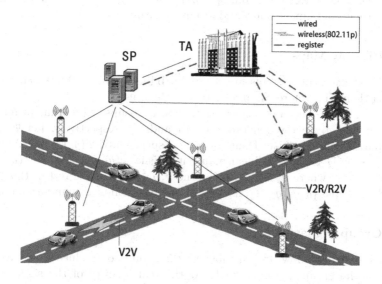

Fig. 1. System architecture

◇ **Vehicle:** Vehicles are the customers of LBSs and they are all equipped with on-board units (OBUs). With OBUs, vehicles are able to communicate with the other entities.

2.2 Security Requirements

In this section, we illustrate the security requirements for LBSs in VANETs.

- **Message Confidentiality.** An LBS request may contain sensitive information. Therefore, message confidentiality is required. This means that only the vehicle and the RSU/SP should see the information exchanged between the vehicle and the RSU/SP. In addition, a vehicle should not be able to obtain the services provided by the SP before it joins the session or after it departs from the session. This also implies the *forward secrecy* and the *backward secrecy* properties defined in [9].
- **Vehicle Authentication.** The SP wants to ensure that the LBS is only provided to its subscribers. In addition, the SP should be able to detect whether the vehicle is double-registering to the same session, in order to avoid some attacks (e.g., the Sybil attack [6]).
- **Vehicle Privacy.** Except the message generator and TA, it must be computationally hard for any entity to decide whether two different messages are generated by the same vehicle. For LBSs to gain wide social acceptance, it is essential to protect the privacy of vehicles.

3 Technique Preliminaries

In this section, we explicate some preliminaries served as bases in our scheme. Mainly, they are bilinear maps and group signatures.

3.1 Bilinear Maps

Many efficient cryptosystems are based on bilinear maps. Our scheme is also built on them. Therefore, we briefly review them here.

Let $\mathbb{G}_1$, $\mathbb{G}_2$, $\mathbb{G}_T$ be three multiplicative cycle groups of the same prime order q. Let g_1 and g_2 be the generators of $\mathbb{G}_1$ and $\mathbb{G}_2$, respectively. Let Ψ denote a computable isomorphism from $\mathbb{G}_2$ to $\mathbb{G}_1$, specifically, $\Psi(g_2) = g_1$. A map $e: \mathbb{G}_1 \times \mathbb{G}_2 \longrightarrow \mathbb{G}_T$ is called bilinear map if it satisfies $e(g_1, g_2) \neq 1$ and $e(u^a, v^b) = e(u, v)^{ab} \in \mathbb{G}_T$, where $u \in \mathbb{G}_1$, $v \in \mathbb{G}_2$ and $a, b \in \mathbb{Z}_q^*$. In the rest of this paper, we call the tuple $\{q, g_1, g_2, \mathbb{G}_1, \mathbb{G}_2, \mathbb{G}_T, e\}$ the basic bilinear map parameters.

3.2 Group Signatures

Group signatures allow any member of the group to produce a signature on behalf of the group. No one can know the real identity of the signer except the group manager, who issues member keys for the members. Furthermore, it is computational hard for anyone but the manager to distinguish whether two signatures are issued by the same signer.

Member revocation is a crucial problem in group signature based schemes. That is, if a member leaves the group or its group member key is leaked, the problem is how to exclude this member from the group. Verifier-local revocation (VLR) group signatures are designed to alleviate this member revocation problem. In a VLR group signature scheme, each member has a revocation token. If a member is revoked, the group manager just needs to publish its revocation token. The other members are able to distinguish the revoked member based on the revocation token.

4   Privacy Weakness of a Key Management Scheme

In this section, we first review the key management scheme in [9] at high level and then point out a privacy weakness of the scheme.

4.1   High Level Description

There are four stages in the key management scheme in [9]: system initialization, LBS settings, vehicle joining and vehicle departure. We outline these stages as follows.

In the first stage, TA generates the system master key and the public parameters of the system. It also extracts a private key for each SP. Furthermore, TA also acts as a group manager of a group signature scheme who issues member keys for the vehicles in the system.

During the second stage, each SP initializes the parameters for the LBS sessions. The SP also generates a series of keys (e.g., the session master key, the session key, the combine keys and the encryption keys), beacon messages and a dummy user set. The session key, the combine keys and the encryption keys are derived from the session master key. The session key will be distributed to the authenticated vehicle, and the combine keys and the encryption keys will be used to update the session key in the last stage. The beacon message is broadcasted periodically via RSUs to inform the vehicles of the service. The dummy user set will be used to help a vehicle to update the session key when it cannot connect to the SP.

In the third stage, if a vehicle wants to join an LBS session, it first verifies the beacon message broadcasted by the corresponding SP. If the beacon message is valid, the vehicle will request to join the session with a privacy-preserving authentication (PPA) scheme, which is derived from the verifier-local group signature scheme in [2]. By the PPA scheme, the SP can authenticate vehicles without leaking their private information and is able to check the vehicle's double registration [9]. If a vehicle is authenticated as valid, the SP generates a unique pseudonym and the private key corresponding to the pseudonym for the vehicle, which will be used for the session key update. Finally, the SP sends pseudonym, private key, session key and combine key to the vehicle through a secure channel. With the session key, the session members are able to access the LBS.

The last stage is vehicle departure. A vehicle may leave the session. Therefore, it is reasonable for the SP to update the session key to avoid the vehicle accessing the service after its departure. To do this, when a vehicle leaves the LBS session, a key update message is generated by the SP and broadcasted via RSUs to the session members. In the case that a vehicle can connect to the SP through one hop or multi-hop communication via an RSU, then the vehicle can get the new session key from the SP directly; otherwise, the vehicle derives the new session key by a dynamic threshold update algorithm [5], which takes as input pseudonym, private key, current session key, encryption key, combine key, and dummy user set.

4.2   The Weakness

In the above scheme, the PPA scheme (which is essentially a verifier-local group signature scheme) is adopted to secure the system. However, as mentioned in Sect. 3.2, the group manager needs to publish the revocation token of a revoked vehicle. This leads to a new problem. If a revocation token is published, the signatures related to this revocation token can be linked. Therefore, if a vehicle in the system is revoked, its privacy may be violated. Furthermore, the efficiency of the system declines as the scale of the revocation list grows.

5   Privacy Enhanced Key Management Scheme

In this section, we propose a privacy-enhanced scheme. To simplify the description, we first define some notations in Table 1.

5.1   The Scheme

As the scheme in [9], our scheme also has four stages: system initialization, LBS settings, vehicle joining and vehicle departure.

[System Initialization]

The first stage is similar to that of [9]. In this stage, TA generates its master key and the public parameters. It also generates private keys for SPs. Unlike in [9], TA does not issue group member keys for vehicles, but leaves this task to the RSUs. For a vehicle, it only issues a secret, which is used to authenticate the vehicle. In addition, each RSU in our system has a private-public key pair and a certificate issued by TA.

Let the system master key be $\gamma \in \mathbb{Z}_q^*$, the public parameters PUB= $(q, g_1, g_2, u_1, u_2, \mathbb{G}_1, \mathbb{G}_2, \mathbb{G}_T, e, E_K(\cdot)/D_K(\cdot), H, H_0, H_1, H_2, l)$,   where $\{q, g_1, g_2, \mathbb{G}_1, \mathbb{G}_2, \mathbb{G}_T, e\}$ is a tuple of basic bilinear map parameters, $H : \{0,1\}^* \longrightarrow \mathbb{Z}_q^*$, $H_0 : \{0,1\}^* \longrightarrow \mathbb{G}_2{}^2$, $H_1 : \mathbb{G}_T \longrightarrow \{0,1\}^l$, $H_2 : \{0,1\}^* \longrightarrow \mathbb{G}_2$ are cryptographic hash functions, $u_1 = g_1{}^\gamma$, $u_2 = g_2{}^\gamma$, $E_K(\cdot)/D_K(\cdot)$ represents a symmetric key

Table 1. Description of notation

NOTATION	Description
TA:	The trusted authority
V:	A vehicle
R:	An RSU or its corresponding group
SP:	An LBS service provider
T_t:	A time stamp
$\|$:	Message concatenation operation
ID:	The identity of an entity
PUB:	The public parameters
SK:	The secret key
PK:	The public key
mk:	The group member key
CRL:	The certificate revocation list maintained by TA
RL:	The record list maintained by TA
ML:	The member list maintained by TA
$E_K(\cdot)/D_K(\cdot)$:	A symmetric encryption/decryption scheme

encryption/decryption scheme and l is the length of the key used in the encryption/decryption scheme. For an RSU R_j, TA selects $\zeta_j \in \mathbb{Z}_q^*$ as its private key and it computes $PK_{R_j} = g_2{}^{\zeta_j}$ as its public key. Finally, TA issues a certificate Cer_{R_j} of the form $\{ID_{R_j}, PK_{R_j}, T, Sig_{R_j}\}$ [11] for R_j, where ID_{R_j} is the unique identity of R_j, T is the certificate lifetime, Sig_{R_j} is TA's signature on (ID_{R_j}, PK_{R_j}, T). Each RSU broadcasts its certificate periodically in its communication range. For an SP, TA computes $SK_{SP} = g_1^{\frac{1}{\gamma+H(ID_{SP})}}$ as SP's private key, where ID_{SP} is the identity of the SP. For a vehicle V_k, TA randomly selects $x_k \in \{0,1\}^\ell$ as V_k's secret which will be used to authenticate a vehicle, where ℓ is a security parameter.

TA also manages three lists: certificate revocation list (CRL), member list (ML) and record list (RL). The CRL contains the information of the revoked certificates of RSUs. ML has the form (ID_{V_k}, x_k), where ID_{V_k} is the real identity of V_k. RL will be defined in the third stage.

[LBS Settings]
This stage is the same as that of the scheme in [9]. The SP generates the initial session key, a dummy user set and a series of session related keys, which contains the session master key, the combine keys, the encryption keys. In addition, SP also constructs and broadcasts the LBS session beacon message in this stage.

[Vehicle Joining]
In the stage of vehicle joining, if a vehicle V_k wants to join an LBS session, it must join a group maintained by an RSU at first. When a vehicle V_k receives the beacon message of its interested LBS, it first verifies the LBS beacon message. The verification procedure is the same as that of the scheme in [9]. If V_k is not

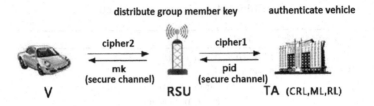

Fig. 2. Group-Join

a member of any group maintained by an RSU or its member key has expired, V_k registers to its nearby RSU R_j using the Group-Join protocol below. Figure 2 illustrates the basic idea.

Group-Join Protocol

1. V_k verifies the certificate Cer_{R_j} of R_j. If it is valid, V_k extracts the public key PK_{R_j} and the identity ID_{R_j} of R_j from Cer_{R_j}, sets $M_1 = (T_t \parallel x_k)$, randomly selects $s \in \mathbb{Z}_q^*$, computes $C_1 = g_1^s$, $K_1 = H_1(e(u_1^s, u_2))$, $C_2 = E_{K_1}(M_1)$, sets $cipher1 = (C_1 \parallel C_2)$, chooses $f \in \mathbb{Z}_q^*$ at random, sets $M_2 = (T_t \parallel ID_{R_j} \parallel cipher1 \parallel'' join'')$, computes $C_3 = g_1^f$, $K_2 = H_1(e(u_1^f, PK_{R_j}))$, $C_4 = E_{K_2}(M_2)$, sets $cipher2 = (C_3 \parallel C_4)$, sends $cipher2$ to R_j, where T_t is a timestamp.
2. When R_j receives $cipher2$, it computes $K_2 = H_1(e(C_3, u_2^{\zeta_j}))$, computes $M_2 = D_{K_2}(C_4) = (T_t \parallel ID_{R_j} \parallel cipher1 \parallel'' join'')$. If T_t and ID_{R_j} are valid, R_j forwards $cipher1$ to TA.
3. When TA receives $cipher1$ from R_j, it computes $K_1 = H_1(e(C_1, u_2^\gamma))$, $M_1 = D_{K_1}(C_2) = (T_t \parallel x_k)$. If T_t is valid, it does the following:
   - If x_k does not exist in a tuple (ID_{V_k}, x_k) on ML, TA replies with 0, which means that V_k is not a registered vehicle.
   - Else if there exists a tuple $(ID_{V_k}, ID_{R_*}, pid_*)$ on RL, it means V_k is already a member of the group maintained by R_*. TA replies with 1, which means that V_k's member key is still valid.
   - Else, TA generates a pseudonym pid_i for V_k, replies with pid_i to R_j.
4. If R_j receives 1 or 0 from TA, it aborts; otherwise, it randomly selects $\eta_i \in \mathbb{Z}_q^*$, computes $\theta_i = g_1^{\frac{1}{\zeta_j + \eta_i}}$, sets $mk_i = (\eta_i, \theta_i)$ as the group member key, adds the tuple (mk_i, pid_i) to its group member list, computes $cipher3 = E_{K_2}(mk_i)$, sends $cipher3$ to V_k.
5. When V_k receives $cipher3$ from R_j, it computes $D_{K_2}(cipher3)$ to extract the member key.
6. Finally, if the protocol is successfully terminated, $(ID_{V_k}, ID_{R_j}, pid_i)$ is added to RL.

In the above Group-Join protocol, only when x_k is valid and the identity of the vehicle corresponding to x_k is not recorded in RL, TA generates a pseudonym for V_k. By this mechanism, a vehicle cannot register with two groups maintained by two different RSUs. In other words, each vehicle cannot obtain more than one group member key. Therefore, similar to [9], the double-registration can be detected using the PPA scheme.

After getting mk_i from R_j, V_k can join any LBS session via a nearby RSU R_i using the PPA scheme as [9]. The communication model is shown in Fig. 3, where "request" represents the message sent by a vehicle to the SP for joining a session and "reply" represents all the keys that the SP distributed to the vehicle. The basic procedure is illustrated in following Session-Join Protocol. We note that the only difference between our idea and that in [9] is that the group manager of V_k is no longer the TA but R_j. Therefore, V_k also needs to send the certificate of its group manager R_j to R_i. R_i has to check the validity of the certificate when it performs the PPA scheme.

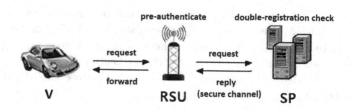

Fig. 3. Session-Join

Session-Join Protocol

1. V_k generates a joining session request as follows:
   (a) Computes $(\hat{u}, \hat{v}) = H_0(PUB, sid)$, $u = \psi(\hat{u})$, $v = \psi(\hat{v})$, randomly selects $\alpha \in Z_q^*$, sets $\delta = \eta_i \cdot \alpha$, $T_1 = u^\alpha$, $T_2 = \theta_i \cdot v^\alpha$.
   (b) Generates $R_1 = u^{r_\alpha}$, $R_2 = e(T_2, g_2)^{r_x} \cdot e(v, PK_{R_j})^{-r_\alpha} \cdot e(v, g_2)^{-r_\delta}$ and $R_3 = T_1^{r_x} \cdot u^{-r_\delta}$, computes $h = H(PUB, sid, ID_{R_j}, T_t \parallel g_e^x \parallel g_e^y, T_1, T_2, R_1, R_2, R_3)$, where $r_\alpha, r_x, r_\delta, y$ are randomly selected from Z_q^*, $g_e = e(g_1, g_2)$, g_e^x is obtained from the beacon message broadcasted by the SP via RSUs.
   (c) Computes $s_\alpha = r_\alpha + h \cdot \alpha$, $s_x = r_x + h \cdot \eta_i$, $s_\delta = r_\delta + h \cdot \delta$, sets the request as $Req = (ID_{R_j}, T_t \parallel g_e^x \parallel g_e^y, T_1, T_2, h, s_\alpha, s_x, s_\delta)$, sends Req to its nearby RSU R_i.
2. When R_i receives Req from V_k, it pre-authenticates the request as follows:
   (a) Extracts ID_{R_j} from the request, checks the validity of its corresponding certificate Cer_{R_j} and T_t in the request,
   (b) If both of them are valid, computes $R'_1 = \frac{u^{s_\alpha}}{T_1^h}$, $R'_2 = e(T_2, g_2)^{s_x} \cdot e(v, PK_{R_j})^{-s_\alpha} \cdot e(v, g_2)^{-s_\delta} \cdot (e(T_2, PK_{R_j})/e(g_1, g_2))^h$ and $R'_3 = T_1^{s_x} \cdot u^{-s_\delta}$, checks whether the following equation holds:

$$h = H(PUB, sid, ID_{R_j}, T_t \| g_e^x \| g_e^y, T_1, T_2, R'_1, R'_2, R'_3).$$

   (c) If the equation holds, forwards the request to the SP.

3. While receiving the request from R_i, the SP does the double-registration check at first. If the request is legal, it then builds a secure communication channel with V_k. The detailed steps comes as follows:

   (a) SP extracts (T_1, T_2) from the request, checks whether the equation

$$e(T_2, \hat{u})e(T_1, \hat{v}^{-1}) = e(T_2^i, \hat{u})e(T_1^i, \hat{v}^{-1})$$

   holds for $(T_1^i, T_2^i) \in \mathrm{T} = \{(T_1^1, T_2^1), \cdots, (T_1^m, T_2^m)\}$, where m represents the number of registered vehicles.

   (b) If none of the above equations holds, SP adds (T_1, T_2) to T, computes the encryption key $(g_e^y)^x$, generates pseudonym, private key, session key and combine key, encrypts all the keys with $(g_e^y)^x$, and sends the encrypted message to V_k.

In the above Session-Join Protocol, an SP may receive amounts of requests at the same time. If it performs the double-registration check individually, then it will be quite time consuming due to the expensive bilinear map operation. We therefore put forward an efficient batch verification algorithm to improve the performance. Assume there are N requests. We phrase the nth request as $Req_n = (ID_{R_j}, T_{n,t}||g_e^x||g_e^{y_n}, T_{n,1}, T_{n,2}, h_n, s_{n,\alpha}, s_{n,x}, s_{n,\delta})$, where $n \in (1, N)$. The SP does the batch verification as follows:

1. For $1 \leq n \leq N$, extracts the $(T_{n,1}, T_{n,2})$ part from each request Req_n, selects random width-ω non-adjacent forms (ω-NAFS [3]) $\delta_1, ..., \delta_N$.
2. For each (T_1^i, T_2^i) in T, $1 \leq i \leq m$, checks whether the following equation holds:

$$e(\prod_{n=1}^{N} T_{n,2}^{\delta_n}, \hat{u})e(\prod_{n=1}^{N} T_{n,1}^{\delta_n}, \hat{v}^{-1}) = e(\prod_{n=1}^{N} (T_2^i)^{\delta_n}, \hat{u})e(\prod_{n=1}^{N} (T_1^i)^{\delta_n}, \hat{v}^{-1}).$$

3. If none of the above equations holds, replies the keys as that of the Session-Join Protocol. Otherwise, one may employ the recursive divide-and-conquer approach in [7] to exclude the illegal request(s).

[Vehicle Departure]

In the last stage, similar to that of the scheme in [9], if any session member V_k departs from the session, the SP needs to update the session key. This procedure is the same as that in [9]. In addition, the group member key of a vehicle V_k may be leaked. In [9], if the member key of a vehicle is compromised, TA has to publish the revocation token of the vehicle. As discussed in Sect. 3.2, the privacy of the vehicle is violated and the efficiency of the system declines. In our system, we propose a new method to solve the member revocation problem. When a vehicle V_k's member key is compromised, V_k has to send a revocation request to TA. Suppose V_k is a member of the group maintained by R_j. When TA receives this request, TA adds Cer_{R_j} to CRL and it deletes all the records of the form $(*, ID_{R_j}, *)$ in RL. R_j will generate a new private-public pair and receive a new certificate issued by TA. Note that, since we distribute the vehicles to many groups maintained by RSUs, the number of group members in the group maintained by R_j will not be large. We also note that, by our setting, the SP has to periodically check the CRL. Once the SP finds that the certificate of an RSU corresponding to its session member(s) is revoked, it excludes all this/these session member(s) and updates the session key instantly.

6 Evaluation

In this section, we evaluate the proposed key management scheme. Firstly, we show that our scheme meets all the security requirements defined in Sect. 2.2. Then, we evaluate the performance of the proposed scheme.

6.1 Security Analysis

The key management scheme in [9] is shown to satisfy message confidentiality, vehicle authentication and vehicle privacy as defined in Sect. 2.2. Our scheme is based on the scheme in [9]. The main difference between our key management scheme and that in [9] is that our scheme also considers the privacy of a vehicle when it is revoked. This is realized by distributing the vehicles into the groups maintained by RSUs and updating the public key of an RSU when its member is revoked. We only need to consider the security of our Group-Join Protocol. In the Group-Join protocol, the symmetric key encryption/decryption scheme is employed to guarantee the secrecy of the massages. Hence, confidentiality is satisfied. Further, in the protocol, a vehicle may obtain a member key if it is authenticated by TA. Except TA, no entity can learn the real identity of a vehicle. Hence, vehicle authentication and vehicle privacy are achieved.

6.2 Performance Evaluation

The main differences between our scheme and that in [9] are the group joining and session joining protocols, in which the latter mainly dominates the efficiency of the whole scheme. We thus compare the performance of session joining protocol in our scheme with that in [9].

The most time consuming operation in the scheme is the bilinear map operation. Let τ_m denote the time to compute a bilinear map. We select a non-supersingular curve with an embedded degree $k = 6$ and run the computation on an Intel i5-2430M 2.4-GHz machine[1], τ_m is 2.17 ms.

In our proposed scheme, a vehicle has to join an RSU maintained group first and then join the session. For a single vehicle, the total time cost of this whole joining procedure is similar to that of [9]. However, under the condition that many vehicles request to join a session at the same time, our scheme will be more efficient. Assume there are N vehicles request to join a session at the same time. In the best case, i.e., all the requests are legal, our scheme only takes

---

[1] The operation system is Ubuntu 12.04 and exploiting the Miracl library [1].

$2(m + 1)\tau_m$ to do the double-registration check, while the scheme in [9] takes $2N(m + 1)\tau_m$, where m represents the number of registered vehicles. According to [7], even if up to 15 % requests are invalid, the performance of our scheme is better than the individual check.

7 Conclusion

We pointed out a privacy weakness of a recent key management scheme for LBSs in VANETs and proposed a privacy enhanced one. In our scheme, each vehicle can join a group maintained by an RSU without leaking its privacy. Furthermore, each vehicle can be authenticated without leaking its privacy when it joins an LBS session. We also proposed a novel method to solve the member revocation problem in group signature based systems. By our method, even if a vehicle's group member key is compromised, its privacy still can be protected.

Acknowledgments and Disclaimer. Thanks goes to Chuanyan Hu and Ya Gao for the proofreading. This work was supported in part by the NSF of China under grants 61202465, 61021004, 11061130539, 91118008 and 61103222; EU FP7 under projects "DwB" and "Inter-Trust"; the Spanish Government under projects TIN2011-27076-C03-01 and CONSOLIDER INGENIO 2010 "ARES" CSD2007-0004; the Government of Catalonia under grant SGR2009-1135; the Shanghai NSF under grant no. 12ZR1443500; the Shanghai Chen Guang Program (12CG24); the Fundamental Research Funds for the Central Universities of China; the Open Project of Shanghai Key Laboratory of Trustworthy Computing (no. 07dz22304201101). J. Domingo-Ferrer was supported in part as an ICREA-Acadèmia researcher by the Government of Catalonia.

References

1. Multiprecision integer and rational arithmetic C/C++ library (MIRACL). http://www.shamus.ie/
2. Boneh, D., Shacham, H.: Group signatures with verifier-local revocation. In: 11th ACM Conference on Computer Communications Security-CCS 2004, pp. 168–177 (2004)
3. Cheon, J.H., Yi, J.H.: Fast batch verification of multiple signatures. In: Okamoto, T., Wang, X. (eds.) PKC 2007. LNCS, vol. 4450, pp. 442–457. Springer, Heidelberg (2007)
4. Chim, T.W., Yiu, S.M., Hui, L.C.K., Li, V.O.K.: Security and privacy issues for inter-vehicle communications in VANETs. In: Procedings of 6th Annual IEEE Communications Society Conference on SECON Workshops, pp. 1–3 (2009)
5. Delerablée, C., Pointcheval, D.: Dynamic threshold public-key encryption. In: Wagner, D. (ed.) CRYPTO 2008. LNCS, vol. 5157, pp. 317–334. Springer, Heidelberg (2008)
6. Douceur, J.R.: The Sybil attack. In: Druschel, P., Kaashoek, M.F., Rowstron, A. (eds.) IPTPS 2002. LNCS, vol. 2429, pp. 251–260. Springer, Heidelberg (2002)

7. Ferrara, A.L., Green, M., Hohenberger, S., Pedersen, M.Ø.: Practical short signature batch verification. In: Fischlin, M. (ed.) CT-RSA 2009. LNCS, vol. 5473, pp. 309–324. Springer, Heidelberg (2009)
8. Huang, J.-L., Yeh, L.-Y., Chien, H.-Y.: ABAKA: an anonymous batch authenticated and key agreement scheme for value-added services in vehicular ad hoc networks. IEEE Trans. Veh. Technol. 60(1), 248–262 (2011)
9. Lu, R., Lin, X., Liang, X., Shen, X.: A dynamic privacy-preserving key management scheme for location based services in VANETs. IEEE Trans. Intell. Transp. Syst. 13(1), 127–139 (2012)
10. Mahajan, S., Jindal, A.: Security and privacy in VANET to reduce authentication overhead for rapid roaming networks. Int. J. Comput. Appl. 1(20), 21–25 (2010)
11. Papadimitratos, P., Buttyan, L., Hubaux, J., Kargl, F., Kung, A., Raya, M.: Architecture for secure and private vehicular communications. In: 7th International Conference on Intelligent Transportation Systems-ITS 2007, pp. 1–6 (2007)
12. Raya, M., Aziz, A., Hubaux, J.: Efficient secure aggregation in VANETs. In: Proceedings of the 3rd International Workshop on Vehicular, Ad Hoc NetWorks 2006, pp. 67–75 (2006)
13. Raya, M., Hubaux, J.: The security of vehicular ad hoc networks. In: 3rd ACM Workshop on Security of Ad Hoc and Sensor Networks-SASN 2005, pp. 11–21 (2005)
14. Wu, Q., Domingo-Ferrer, J., González-Nicolás, U.: Balanced trustworthiness, safety and privacy in vehicle-to-vehicle communications. IEEE Trans. Veh. Technol. 59(2), 559–573 (2010)
15. Wu, Q., Qin, B., Zhang, L., Domingo-Ferrer, J., Farràs, O.: Bridging broadcast encryption and group key agreement. In: Lee, D.H., Wang, X. (eds.) ASIACRYPT 2011. LNCS, vol. 7073, pp. 143–160. Springer, Heidelberg (2011)
16. Zhang, C., Lu, R., Lin, X., Ho, P.-H., Shen, X.: An efficient identity-based batch verification scheme for vehicular sensor networks. In: 27th Conference on Computer Communications, pp. 246–250 (2008)
17. Zhang, L., Wu, Q., Qin, B., Domingo-Ferrer, J.: Practical privacy for value-added applications in vehicular Ad Hoc networks. In: Xiang, Y., Pathan, M., Tao, X., Wang, H. (eds.) IDCS 2012. LNCS, vol. 7646, pp. 43–56. Springer, Heidelberg (2012)
18. Zhang, L., Wu, Q., Qin, B., Domingo-Ferrer, J.: APPA: aggregate privacy-preserving authentication in vehicular Ad Hoc networks. In: Lai, X., Zhou, J., Li, H. (eds.) ISC 2011. LNCS, vol. 7001, pp. 293–308. Springer, Heidelberg (2011)
19. Zhang, L., Wu, Q., Solanas, A., Domingo-Ferrer, J.: A scalable robust authentication protocol for secure vehicular communications. IEEE Trans. Veh. Technol. 59(4), 1606–1617 (2010)

Resilience

Resilience

CheR: Cheating Resilience in the Cloud via Smart Resource Allocation

Di Pietro Roberto[1,2], Flavio Lombardi[1], Fabio Martinelli[2],
and Daniele Sgandurra[2(✉)]

[1] Department of Mathematics and Physics, University Roma Tre,
Largo S. Leonardo Murialdo, 00146 Rome, Italy
{dipietro,lombardi}@mat.uniroma3.it
[2] Institute for Informatics and Telematics,
National Research Council of Italy, Pisa, Italy
{fabio.martinelli,daniele.sgandurra}@iit.cnr.it

Abstract. Cloud computing offers unprecedented ways to split and offload the workload of parallel algorithms to remote computing nodes. However, such remote parties can potentially misbehave, for instance by providing fake computation results in order to save resources. In turn, these erroneous partial results can affect the timeliness and correctness of the overall outcome of the algorithm. The widely successful cloud approach increases the economic feasibility of leveraging computational redundancy to enforce some degree of assurance about the results. However, naïve solutions that dumbly replicate the same computation over several sets of nodes are not cost-efficient.

In this paper, we provide several contributions as for the distribution of workload over (heterogeneous) cloud nodes. In particular, we first formalize the problem of computing a parallel function over a set of nodes; later, we introduce *CheR* (for Cheating Resilience), a novel approach based upon modelling the assignment of input elements to cloud nodes as a linear integer programming problem aimed at minimizing cost while being resilient against misbehaving nodes. Further, we describe the *CheR* approach in different scenarios and highlight the novelty with respect to other state-of-the-art solutions. Finally, we present and discuss some experimental results showing the viability and quality of our proposal.

1 Introduction

The Internet has paved the way to large scale distributed computing. The trend towards outsourced computing is culminated with the *Computing-as-a-Service* model, presently offered at different layers by cloud providers. In particular, the trend towards rendering application software available as-a-service (SaaS) on the cloud is increasingly successful for a number of reasons, in particular tied to licensing and management costs. As an example Matlab on cloud [1], Mathematica on Amazon [2], and in general High Performance Computing as-a-Service [3,4], allow system administrators to avoid the setup and management costs due to the creation and software configuration of computing nodes.

J.-L. Danger et al. (Eds.): FPS 2013, LNCS 8352, pp. 339–352, 2014.
DOI: 10.1007/978-3-319-05302-8_21, © Springer International Publishing Switzerland 2014

The problem of providing some forms of assurance over outsourced computation is not novel, and several efforts have been devoted to enforce some sort of control over the correctness and on the timeliness of returned results. The naïve solution that simply replicates the same computation on different sets of nodes is not satisfactory. The novelty of the problem when contextualized in the cloud scenario is that it is now economically feasible to dynamically rent a large number of computing resources (possibly from heterogeneous sources) at the same time. As such, the chances of large rational coalitions of adversary or malicious cloud servers are low—but not negligible. In fact, in the approach presented in this work, we assume that at most k, over the total n nodes that host computation, are rational adversaries [5] that aim to minimize their resource consumption as well as the chances of being detected. We also assume that $(n - k)$ cloud servers are non-malicious and well-behaving. That is to say, that they compute the correct result in the least possible time.

This paper contributes to solve the above issues by devising an effective and reliable solution to enforce distributed computing in the cloud. In particular, we introduce and discuss *CheR*, a novel approach based upon a linear integer programming model [6]. *CheR* assumes a rational adversary whose goal is to reduce its computing effort. The goal of the proposed approach is to enable efficient reliable computation of parallel functions of a large number m of elements over n nodes by minimizing the cost of selected cloud resources and keeping the computing time below a given usage threshold. Furthermore, and more importantly, we want to ensure that the output of the distributed computation is correct, within a reasonable confidence interval, even when cheating nodes are present. Hence, some form of computation redundancy and supervision of the collected results is required. We assume that cheaters are rational, i.e. the node can choose to return a fake result in order to reduce resource consumption. A cheater node can return fake results for the entire computation or it can cheat only on a subset of the input data set.

The contribution of this paper is multi-fold, and includes: (i) describing *CheR*, a novel approach leveraging linear programming for distributing the workload over a large number of computing nodes (see Sect. 3); (ii) showing how the proposed system guarantees that the result of the distributed computations is not affected (within a given threshold) by misbehaving nodes (see Sect. 3); (iii) describing how the proposed approach can be deployed on various cloud scenarios also representative of real-world clouds such as Amazon EC2 (see Sect. 4.1); (iv) evaluating the proposed approach that achieves cost-effective workload distribution guaranteeing min-cost and timeliness of results (see Sect. 4). The paper is organized as follows. Section 2 introduces a use case where the proposed framework can be leveraged. Section 3 models the problem as a linear integer programming problem. Section 4 gives implementation details and provides a first set of results by discussing some real use-case examples and by validating the results through simulations. Section 5 discusses relevant related works. Finally, Sect. 6 draws conclusions and introduces some hints for future extensions.

2   A Use Case

In this Section, a simple use case is described to clarify the main problem. Suppose a system administrator is required to rent some cloud resources to perform a computationally-intensive and embarrassingly parallel task over a large data set. Two main possible scenarios exist: in the first one, the system administrator has to ensure that the computation ends reliably within a given timeframe and she is willing to spend as little as possible. In the second scenario, she has a fixed maximum budget and she has to reliably compute the function by minimizing the required time. That is, having a fixed maximum budget, we aim to obtain the best possible performance, given the reliability requirements. In the first scenario, the system administrator is willing both to have guarantees that the *computation is correct* and to *minimize the cost* involved with renting cloud computing resources. In the following, we will specifically consider the first scenario, leaving the second one as further work.

Hence, a system administrator has to compute a function, over a large input vector, using a set of nodes chosen from available cloud nodes, some of which may be cheaters. From the administrator's point of view it is interesting to know what is the amount of cloud resources required to satisfy the above-mentioned requirements, i.e. correctness and cost-efficiency. In the following, the adversary is modeled by assuming a standard/average (low) percentage of cheaters, such as 5 % of the total number of nodes. This assumption is realistic as shown in [7]. As a general problem, nodes are required to compute an embarrassingly parallel function f over an input vector of length m, i.e. the output is itself a vector of length m where the jth element is $f(j)$. At present, the most cost-effective computing resources are found in the cloud. Hence, in our model we assume that there are n cloud nodes (indicated as *nodes*, or *VMs*, from now on) where each node n_i (VM_i) can compute a subset (possibly overlapping) of the input vector.

The main goal here is to guarantee *reliability, timeliness, cost-effectiveness* and *correctness* of the computed results. We model the adversary as a *static* cheater P, i.e. a node that always fakes its computations with a given probability. In our model we assume guaranteed message delivery and no network cheating or lost messages. For simplicity, but without loss of generality, we also assume zero communication overhead (as in other related works e.g. [8,9]).

3   Problem Modeling

We generalize the use case discussed in the previous section, by assuming that a system administrator has to to compute a function f on a large vector X of length m. To this end, the manger has to send X to a cloud, which contains n cloud nodes (VMs), where each node VM_i has an associated unitary cost per operation c_i and the time to perform an unitary operation is t_i[1]. Given that we assume some of the nodes are cheaters, where the percentage of cheaters (*CheaterRate*) is $\frac{k}{n}$,

---

[1] We assume that the application of f has the same cost and complexity for each input.

Table 1. Cost and time vectors

VM_1	VM_2	VM_3	VM_4	VM_5
c_1	c_2	c_3	c_4	c_5
t_1	t_2	t_3	t_4	t_5

Table 2. Matrix assignment of the example

	x_1	x_2	x_3	x_4	x_5	x_6	x_7
VM_1	1	0	1	0	0	1	0
VM_2	0	1	0	1	1	0	1
VM_3	1	0	0	1	0	0	1
VM_4	0	1	0	1	1	0	1
VM_5	0	1	1	0	1	1	0

where k is the number of cheaters, the system administrator has to send multiple (possibly overlapping) subsets of X to the nodes to be confident that the output is correct, i.e. most of the results for the same input is correct. The confidence threshold, chosen by the system administrator to be reasonably ensured that the results are correct, is $DetConf$. The goal of the system administrator is to minimize the total cost of the operations, given a maximum time of computation T_{max} and given the fact that he/she wants all the results to be correct with an error less than $DetConf$. As an example, if $DetConf$ is equal to 0.01, we require that at most 1 % of fake results are considered correct, i.e. they are not detected by the administrator as wrong results.

As an example, suppose we have five VMs. The cost and time vectors will store c_i and t_i for all nodes VM_i, as shown in Table 1. To better model the scenario we use a matrix $M^{n \times m}$, where $M_{i,j}$ means that the node n_i receives the element x_j to be computed on the function f. Indexes of the rows are coupled with the nodes, where $1 \leq i \leq n$, and indexes of the columns are associated with the elements of the vector, where $1 \leq j \leq m$. If we extend this example, by supposing that we have 7 elements, then we can model the assignment of workpiece x_j to node n_i on an $n \times m$ matrix as depicted in Table 2[2].

The associated *total cost* C_i of the operations performed by the ith node on the subset of the input received is:

$$C_i = \sum_{j=1}^{m} c_i \cdot M_{i,j} = c_i \cdot \sum_{j=1}^{m} M_{i,j} \tag{1}$$

Analogously, the *total time* T_i of the ith node to perform the operations on the received elements is:

$$T_i = \sum_{j=1}^{m} t_i \cdot M_{i,j} = t_i \cdot \sum_{j=1}^{m} M_{i,j} \tag{2}$$

---

[2] The ordering of the performed operations does not take actual time into consideration.

By taking into consideration the constraints imposed by the system administrator (as discussed in Sect. 2), i.e. costs-effectiveness and timeless of the results, we can formulate the problem as an integer linear program, where the goal is to minimize the cost of the assignment of all the elements to the nodes, i.e.:

$$\text{Minimize} \sum_{i=1}^{n} \sum_{j=1}^{m} c_i \cdot M_{i,j} \tag{3}$$

Subject to the following time constraints:

$$\sum_{j=1}^{m} t_i \cdot M_{i,j} \leq T_{max} \quad \forall i \tag{4}$$

This value is a parameter of the model chosen by the system administrator so that results are returned in a timely fashion. As an example, the system administrator may set T_{max} in such a way that the slowest node (which is usually the cheapest one as well) cannot process more than a fraction of the input elements. Hence, each node can only process a predefined number of elements, according to its performance, so as to not exceed T_{max}. Hence, the previous equation can be rewritten as:

$$\sum_{j=1}^{m} M_{i,j} \leq Max(i) \quad \forall i \tag{5}$$

where $Max(i)$ is the maximum number of elements that the node i can process, considering its speed (time t_i to process each element) and T_{max}. Furthermore, in the model we have to consider that each input element can also be processed by a cheater node. To this end, we introduce the following equation:

$$\sum_{i=1}^{n} M_{i,j} \geq Repl(j) \quad \forall j \tag{6}$$

where $Repl(j)$ is the number of elements that has to be replicated for each input element j according to the confidence level $DetConf$. By replicating the computation, the chances of wrong results due to cheater nodes, are lower. Hence, the system administrator can verify that all results are correct within the given confidence level. $Repl(j)$ is an a-priori value that is computed out of $DetConf$ as follows: the number of requested replicas is computed using the hypergeometric distribution by considering that at least half of the replicated elements are given to, and processed by, cheater nodes. In this case, if at least half of the results are computed by cheaters, the system administrator would consider as correct their result. This is a conservative approach against a worst-case scenario were (i) all the cheaters cheat on their input and (ii) they return the same result.

Finally, in the model we have to consider the binary condition variables that are used to decide which of the input elements are given to which nodes:

$$\text{Binary } M_{i,j} \quad \forall i, j \tag{7}$$

Table 3. LP model

$$\text{Minimize} \sum_{i=1}^{n} \sum_{j=1}^{m} c_i \cdot M_{i,j}$$

$$\text{Subject to} \sum_{j=1}^{m} M_{ij} \leq Max(i) \quad , 1 \leq i \leq n$$

$$\sum_{i=1}^{n} M_{ij} \geq Repl(j) \quad , 1 \leq j \leq m$$

$$\text{Binary } M_{i,j} \quad , 1 \leq i \leq n, 1 \leq j \leq m$$

All previous conditions and goals are summarized in Table 3. Once this LP model is solved, if a solution exists, an optimal assignment of input elements to cloud nodes is returned that satisfies all the system administrator-imposed requirements.

4   CheR: Implementation and Results

Starting from the above-described model, we have implemented *CheR* and validated it through a large number of simulations. In the current prototype, *CheR* is composed of a meta-program that creates linear programming problems in Cplex syntax using a range of different parameters as input. To solve such LP problems, *CheR* exploits a state-of-the-art solver such as GLPK [10]. In the following, we show and discuss some real-world examples to validate the proposed approach.

To study the behavior of the system with respect to scenario changes, the *CheR* meta-program takes as input the following parameters:

- the number of nodes n;
- the number of input elements m;
- the confidence level $DetConf$;
- the features of available nodes, such as time t_i required to process a single element and costs c_i;
- the time constraints for the termination of the reliable distributed computation (T_{max}): since every node has a corresponding cost, this means that every node n_i can process at most $Max(i)$ elements.

CheR firstly computes the number of required replicas to satisfy the given confidence level, and then it outputs the LP model that is later fed to the LP solver.

It is worth noticing that *CheR* can make use of a central node collecting the results of all the nodes. Such node can compare the various response values that are obtained by the processing nodes over the input. As such, if different results are given for the same input, a warning on a possible cheating node is raised. In the *CheR* approach, the central collector can also discover a cheater by calculating a *divergence index* for each node counting how many times such node has given responses that were different from other ones on the same input, i.e. what is the percentage of results in which the cheater was in minority.

4.1   The Cloud Case

In this section, we introduce costs and time that are roughly representative of Amazon AWS [11], so that we can find a realistic solution for actual cloud service performance and associated costs. In order to model an Amazon-like cloud, 5 different node typologies (*VMt* stands for VM Type) are considered, ranging from Medium to XXXLarge according to the cost (which has been normalized) and time vectors of Table 4.

In our tests, the number of nodes n is set to 100, where there are 20 nodes for each of the 5 typologies, there are 5 static cheaters P, i.e. 5 % of the total nodes and 1,000 input elements m are considered. Finally, the confidence level $DetConf$ is set to 0.01: considering the number of nodes, this level results in 3 replicas for each element. We have depicted four scenarios, where T_{max} is set so that nodes can process at most the number of elements shown in Table 5. These four scenarios depict four different alternatives: the first one targeted at extreme cost savings; the second one with moderate balance requirements, with the bottom part (more costly, faster resources) is less used; the third scenario where tight time constraints are in place but where we also aim to cost containment; the fourth scenario, with extremely tight time constraints.

As regards the values chosen for the T_{max} time in experiments E1 to E4, the rationale is that we aimed at modeling real world time and budget constraints for an administrator. We have considered such limitations and put them in relation with standard computing capability of available VM instances. As regards experiment E1, T_{max} is set such that the result is obtained in less than 250 units of time; this implies that a slow VM will not be able to process more than 250

Table 4. Cost and time vectors of the cloud case

Node Type	VMt_1	VMt_2	VMt_3	VMt_4	VMt_5
Cost	48	99	249	500	1000
Speed	1000	500	250	100	50

Table 5. Maximum number of processed elements for experiments E1-E4

Experiment	VMt_1	VMt_2	VMt_3	VMt_4	VMt_5
E1	250	300	350	400	500
E2	100	150	200	250	300
E3	25	50	100	150	200
E4	12	16	25	50	50

chunks. The same holds for the other experiments. It is worth noticing that the value of the T_{max} parameter is important in our model. This is chosen so that the allowed time is dependant on the administrator's requirements. In fact, in the kind of problems that we have analyzed, the global execution time is predictable given the computing capability of the heterogeneous nodes. As a matter of fact, we assume that the total cost is the real quantity to minimize. So the problem is to guarantee execution termination in a given time by efficiently using resources in order to minimize cost while remaining within a given timeframe. As such, the rationale behind the choice of the T_{max} value is as follows: T_{max} is set so that the slowest node can process at most a small fraction of the input elements. Otherwise one node could serially process all the items and the other obvious solution would be to minimize time only by assigning all chunks to the fastest nodes. These are borderline solutions that often are not realistic. Our approach is realistic and better fits the cloud model/approach.

The results of the matrix assignments are shown in Fig. 1. In every sub-figure, cheaper nodes are located at the top of the figure whereas increasingly more costly nodes follow towards the bottom; conversely, slowest nodes are located at the top of sub-figures whereas increasingly faster towards the bottom (results will be discussed in Sect. 4.3). Tests were performed on a computer featuring an

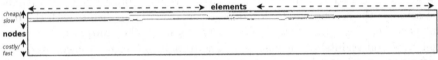

(a) Bitmap representing an actual assignment of elements (x-axis) to nodes (y-axis) for experiment/scenario E1 targeted at cost savings.

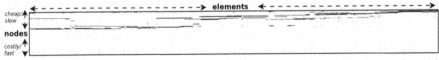

(b) Bitmap representing an actual assignment of elements (x-axis) to nodes (y-axis) for experiment/scenario E2 targeted at moderate cost savings.

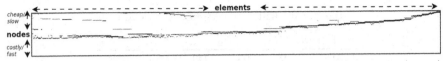

(c) Bitmap representing an actual assignment of elements (x-axis) to nodes (y-axis) for experiment/scenario E3 targeted at moderate time constraints.

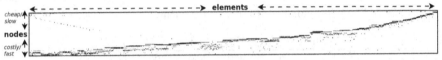

(d) Bitmap representing an actual assignment of elements (x-axis) to nodes (y-axis) for experiment/scenario E4 targeted at extremely tight time constraints.

Fig. 1. Amazon-like matrix assignment

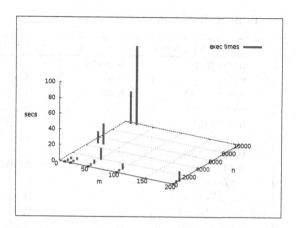

Fig. 2. Execution time of the GLPK LP solver software

Intel Core i5 CPU 750 @2.67 GHz, 4 cores, 4 GB of memory. We have performed several further tests to compute time and memory required by GLPK on different values of n and m. Figure 2 show the plotting of these values. Both the execution time and memory requirements are $O(n \times m)^3$. This is interesting as it shows the proposed approach can scale well to larger scenarios.

4.2   Validation Tests

We have run several simulation tests that exploit the assignment matrix of E4. Such tests were aimed at discovering whether there was any wrong result that would be erroneously considered as correct by the collector. For each test, each experiment was repeated 10, 000 times by randomly choosing the set of k cheaters. In the end, for each test, we counted (i) the number of results that are wrong (ii) the number of tests that contain at least one wrong results. In each of these tests, we select a cheating probability for each static cheater P, i.e. how often a cheater returns a fake result. As a consequence, if a cheater returns wrong results more often, it will be easier to detect it. Conversely, if a smaller number of wrong results is returned, then it can be detected with more difficulty.

The number of performed simulated experiments for each test is 10, 000; the total number of processed input elements (with replicas) throughout all the experiments is 10, 000, 000. Table 6 reports the results of the validations tests. The acronyms used in the Table are:

P cheating probability of static cheaters: how often a cheater cheats;
FNT percentage of false negative tests: ratio of failed tests without centralized control (at least one wrong results in an experiment);
FNE percentage of false negative elements: ratio of wrong results without centralized control (in all the experiments);

---

[3] Given that the complexity of the LP model is the same.

Table 6. Results of the Validation tests

P	FNT (%)	FNE (%) (Avg)	FNTC (%)	FNEC (%) (Avg)
1	0.236	0.006 (6.1)	0.00375	0.0025 (2.445)
0,9	0.223	0.0045 (4.5)	0.022	0.0012 (1.17)
0.8	0.228	0.0038 (3.8)	0.0075	3.393E-4 (0.34)
0.75	0.226	0.0036 (3.45)	0.0047	2.144E-4 (0.21)
0.66	0.208	0.0025 (2.5)	0.0011	5.14E-5 (0.05)
0.6	0.2	0.0021 (2.1)	6.0E-4	1.267E-5 (0.0127)
0.5	0.19	0.0015 (1.5)	0	0 (0)
0.4	0.17	9.436E-4 (0.94)	0	0 (0)
0.33	0.16	6.573E-4 (0.66)	0	0 (0)
0.3	0.16	5.358E-4 (0.54)	0	0 (0)
0.25	0.14	3.77E-4 (0.38)	0	0 (0)
0.2	0.12	2.5E-4 (0.25)	0	0 (0)
0.1	0.05	6.14E-5 (0.06)	0	0 (0)

FNTC percentage of false negative tests (centralized scenario): ratio of failed tests with centralized control (at least one wrong results in an experiment).
FNEC percentage of false negative elements (centralized scenario): ratio of wrong results with centralized control (in all the experiments).

4.3   Discussion

It is interesting to analyze the outcome of these first *CheR* tests. The workload distribution over the available computing nodes in different conditions is depicted in Fig. 1(a, b, c, d). The trend of the workload distribution with respect to shifting timing requirements is quite clear. As the maximum allowed execution time is compressed, the workload, including the replicated computations, seamlessly shifts towards the bottom lines, representing the more costly but faster nodes. Actually, this behavior is quite intuitive, but for large sizes of the problem matchmaking is nontrivial and as such an automated approach, such as the one presented in this paper, is needed. Is it worth noticing that, even in the more tight time-constrained test, from the figure it is evident that the function mapping input elements to nodes strives to pair elements to less-costly nodes as soon as the time constraints have been satisfied.

5   Related Work

The problem of guaranteed/verifiable outsourced computation is not novel, and various efforts have been devoted to obtaining some form of control or guarantee over the correctness [9] and on the timely availability of the results [12] of such outsourced computing. The novelty is that the cloud scenario renders now economically feasible to dynamically rent a large number of computing resources from heterogeneous sources at the same time. This is different than having many parallel processors on a single system as in that case they would be much less heterogeneous as regards performance, cost and behavior. This way the chances that a rational adversary or malicious cloud server coalitions can alter and or corrupt the final result without the user noticing it become very low. If the system administrator were able to fully control cloud VMs and ensure the integrity of the entire software stacks [13], rational or malicious behavior would not be possible, but set-up and management of cloud services would be more costly. Conversely, in this paper we consider more realistic scenarios where the system administrator is not willing/cannot explicitly deal with bare VM configuration but uses pre-configured SaaS services.

Golle [8] discusses the motivations of cheating by untrusted computing resources. He proposes security schemes that protect against this threat by discouraging cheating convenience. Golle also introduces a scheme that allows computing resources to prove they have done most of the work they were assigned with high probability. Das Sarma and Holzer [14] study the verification problem in distributed networks via a distributed algorithm. They give almost tight time lower bounds for distributed verification algorithms for many fundamental problems such as connectivity, spanning connected subgraph, and $s - t$ cut verification. Cheon et al. [15] study redundant work distribution techniques to exclude malicious participants. They aim at reducing work completion time by leveraging the characteristics of works and dynamic resources. They suggest a regional matchmaking technique to redistribute works to resources. In our paper we also make distinctions regarding speed and cost of available resources. Costa et al. [16] present a MapReduce algorithm that tolerate crash faults that uses twice the resources of the original Hadoop. In the SaaS model, clients get access virtual machines without having a direct access to the underlying hardware. Therefore, they cannot verify whether the provider gives the negotiated amount of resources or only a part of it. In particular, the assigned share of CPU time can be easily forged by the provider. The client could use a normal benchmark to verify the performance of the provided virtual machine but, since the Cloud provider owns the underlying infrastructure, the provider could also tamper with the benchmark execution. To detect this tampering, [17] proposes using proof-of-work functions and [18] to introduce a tamper-resistant benchmark to assess the performances of virtual machine instances. Proof-of-work functions are challenge response systems, where it is simple to generate a challenge and verify the result while solving the challenge is compute intensive. *CloudProof* [19] is a secure storage system for Cloud that allows customers to detect, among the others, violations of integrity and to prove the occurrence of these violations to a third party. Furthermore, also the Cloud provider can disprove false accusations made by clients. The proofs are based upon attestations, which are signed messaged that bind the requests made by the clients and the cloud itself to a certain state of the data. As regards Byzantine Fault Tolerance (BFT), some relevant work is due to Alvisi et al. [20], leveraging service replicas that optimistically process the request and reply immediately to the client. This model relies on the client to detect inconsistencies and correct them. This is the only similarity to our approach. However, work by Alvisi does not feature a proper cost model and does not consider cloud nodes and scenarios that are the main objectives of present work. Xin et al. [21] proposes using the remote attestation mechanism in Trusted Computing for cloud user's verification need. In this paper, a property-based remote attestation method is designed through an attestation proxy, and users can validate the security property of the actual computing platform in the virtual cloud computing environment. *HOPE* [22] is a check-pointing and roll-back recovery system for providing fault tolerance message-passing distributed systems. HOPE aims at scalability using an interesting group-based Hybrid Optimistic check-pointing and selective Pessimistic mEssage logging (HOPE) protocol. A system for compositional verification of asynchronous objects is proposed in [23]. Beimel et al. [24] study 1/p-secure protocols in the multi-party setting for general functionalities. They construct 1/p-secure protocols that are resilient against any number of corrupt parties provided that the number of parties is constant and the size of the range of the functionality is at most polynomial (in the security parameter n). They also show that when the number of parties is super-constant, 1/p-secure protocols are not possible when the size of the domain is polynomial. Parno et al. introduce Pinocchio [25] a crypto-based system for efficient verification of remote computation. Pinocchio uses quadratic programs [26] for encoding computations and produces small-sized proof independently from the size of the computation.

Our approach is novel with respect to such state-of-the-art solutions. First of all, it combines LP with distributed on-the-fly/real-time resource allocation. Secondly, advanced real-world-like scenarios are considered. Finally, test results are analyzed in-depth and commented to show the viability of the proposed approach.

6   Conclusion

In this paper, we have addressed the vexed issue of enforcing integrity of distributed computations in the novel context of cloud computing. In particular, we have proposed *CheR*, a novel model for reliable execution of workload over a large number of heterogeneous (in cost and capabilities) computing nodes, where some of them can cheat according to a few identified models. *CheR* helps system administrators that are assessing whether and how to distribute computation over an heterogeneous cloud, to reason about the possible scenarios, available approaches, and their convenience and feasibility. *CheR* provides probabilistic assurance that the result of the distributed computations is not affected by misbehaving nodes, and that the incurred cost (as well as completion time) is minimized. Experimental evidence based on a real-world cloud provider such as Amazon shows the quality and viability of our proposal. Further work will be devoted to develop resilience approaches against smart cheaters.

Acknowledgements. This work has been partially supported by the TENACE PRIN Project (n.20103P34XC) funded by the Italian Ministry of Education, University and Research.

The research leading to these results has received funding from the EU Seventh Framework Programme (FP7/2007-2013) under grant n. 256980 (NESSoS), n. 257930 (Aniketos), and EIT ICT Labs activity 13083.

References

1. Cornell-University: Red cloud with MATLAB. http://www.cac.cornell.edu/wiki/index.php?title=Red_Cloud_with_MATLAB
2. Nimbis: Cloud services for mathematica. https://www.nimbisservices.com/marketplace/wolfram-research/mathematica-clouds
3. D'Angelo, G.: Parallel and distributed simulation from many cores to the public cloud. In: 2011 International Conference on High Performance Computing and Simulation (HPCS), pp. 14–23 (2011)
4. Church, P., Wong, A., Brock, M., Goscinski, A.: Toward exposing and accessing HPC applications in a SaaS cloud. In: Proceedings of the 2012 IEEE 19th International Conference on Web Services, ICWS '12, pp. 692–699. IEEE Computer Society, Washington, DC (2012)
5. Groce, A., Katz, J., Thiruvengadam, A., Zikas, V.: Byzantine agreement with a rational adversary. In: Czumaj, A., Mehlhorn, K., Pitts, A., Wattenhofer, R. (eds.) ICALP 2012, Part II. LNCS, vol. 7392, pp. 561–572. Springer, Heidelberg (2012)
6. Mahdavi-Amiri, N., Nasseri, S.H.: Duality results and a dual simplex method for linear programming problems with trapezoidal fuzzy variables. Fuzzy Sets Syst. **158**(17), 1961–1978 (2007)
7. Martins, F.S., Andrade, R.M., dos Santos, A.L., Schulze, B., de Souza, J.N.: Detecting misbehaving units on computational grids. Concurr. Comput.: Pract. Exper. **22**(3), 329–342 (2010)
8. Golle, P., Mironov, I.: Uncheatable distributed computations. In: Naccache, D. (ed.) CT-RSA 2001. LNCS, vol. 2020, pp. 425–440. Springer, Heidelberg (2001)
9. Gennaro, R., Gentry, C., Parno, B.: Non-interactive verifiable computing: outsourcing computation to untrusted workers. In: Rabin, T. (ed.) CRYPTO 2010. LNCS, vol. 6223, pp. 465–482. Springer, Heidelberg (2010)
10. Makhorin, A.O.: GLPK GNU Linear Programming Kit. http://www.gnu.org/software/glpk/glpk.html
11. Amazon: Amazon web services. http://aws.amazon.com
12. Moser, H.: Towards a real-time distributed computing model. Theor. Comput. Sci. **410**(6–7), 629–659 (2009)
13. Lombardi, F., Di Pietro, R., Soriente, C.: CReW: cloud resilience for Windows guests through monitored virtualization. In: Proceedings of the 2010 29th IEEE Symposium on Reliable Distributed Systems, SRDS '10, pp. 338–342. IEEE Computer Society, Washington, DC (2010)
14. Das Sarma, A., Holzer, S., Kor, L., Korman, A., Nanongkai, D., Pandurangan, G., Peleg, D., Wattenhofer, R.: Distributed verification and hardness of distributed approximation. In: Proceedings of the 43rd Annual ACM Symposium on Theory of Computing, STOC '11, pp. 363–372. ACM, New York (2011)
15. Cheon, E., Kim, M., Kuk, S., Kim, H.S.: A regional matchmaking technique for improving efficiency in volunteer computing environment. In: Proceedings of the 1st ACIS/JNU International Conference on Computers, Networks, Systems and Industrial Engineering, CNSI '11, pp. 285–289. IEEE Computer Society, Washington, DC (2011)

16. Costa, P., Pasin, M., Bessani, A.N., Correia, M.: Byzantine fault-tolerant mapreduce: faults are not just crashes. In: Proceedings of the 2011 IEEE Third International Conference on Cloud Computing Technology and Science, CLOUDCOM '11, pp. 32–39. IEEE Computer Society, Washington, DC (2011)

17. Koeppe, F., Schneider, J.: Do you get what you pay for? using proof-of-work functions to verify performance assertions in the cloud. In: 2010 IEEE Second International Conference on Cloud Computing Technology and Science (CloudCom), pp. 687–692, 30 November 2010-3 December 2010

18. Dwork, C., Naor, M.: Pricing via processing or combatting junk mail. In: Brickell, E.F. (ed.) CRYPTO 1992. LNCS, vol. 740, pp. 139–147. Springer, Heidelberg (1993)

19. Popa, R.A., Lorch, J.R., Molnar, D., Wang, H.J., Zhuang, L.: Enabling security in cloud storage slas with cloudproof. In: Proceedings of the 2011 USENIX Conference on USENIX Annual Technical Conference, USENIXATC'11, p. 31. USENIX Association, Berkeley (2011)

20. Kotla, R., Alvisi, L., Dahlin, M., Clement, A., Wong, E.: Zyzzyva: speculative byzantine fault tolerance. ACM Trans. Comput. Syst. 27(4), 7:1–7:39 (2010)

21. Xin, S., Zhao, Y., Li, Y.: Property-based remote attestation oriented to cloud computing. In: Proceedings of the 7th International Conference on Computational Intelligence and Security, CIS '11, pp. 1028–1032. IEEE Computer Society, Washington, DC (2011)

22. Luo, Y., Manivannan, D.: Hope: a hybrid optimistic checkpointing and selective pessimistic message logging protocol for large scale distributed systems. Future Gener. Comput. Syst. 28(8), 1217–1235 (2012)

23. Ahrendt, W., Dylla, M.: A system for compositional verification of asynchronous objects. Sci. Comput. Program. 77(12), 1289–1309 (2012)

24. Beimel, A., Lindell, Y., Omri, E., Orlov, I.: 1/p-secure multiparty computation without honest majority and the best of both worlds. In: Rogaway, P. (ed.) CRYPTO 2011. LNCS, vol. 6841, pp. 277–296. Springer, Heidelberg (2011)

25. Parno, B., Gentry, C., Howell, J., Raykova, M.: Pinocchio: nearly practical verifiable computation. In: Proceedings of the 34th IEEE Symposium on Security and Privacy (2013)

26. Groenwold, A.A.: Positive definite separable quadratic programs for non-convex problems. Struct. Multidiscip. Optim. 46(6), 795–802 (2012)

Evaluation of Software-Oriented Block Ciphers on Smartphones

Lukas Malina[1]([envelope]), Vlastimil Clupek[1], Zdenek Martinasek[1], Jan Hajny[1], Kimio Oguchi[2], and Vaclav Zeman[1]

[1] Department of Telecommunications, Brno University of Technology,
Technicka 12, Brno, Czech Republic
{malina,clupek,martinasek,hajny,zeman}@feec.vutbr.cz
http://crypto.utko.feec.vutbr.cz
[2] Faculty of Science and Technology, Seikei University, 3-3-1 Kichijoji-Kitamachi,
Musashino, Tokyo, Japan
oguchi@st.seikei.ac.jp

Abstract. The main purpose of block ciphers is to ensure data confidentiality, integrity and robustness against security attacks. Nevertheless, several ciphers also try to be efficient in encryption and decryption phases, have a small energy consumption and/or small memory footprint. These ciphers are usually optimized for certain software or hardware platforms. In this work, we analyze lightweight and classic block ciphers. Further, we implement an application which employs 20 current software-oriented block ciphers and benchmark them on a smartphone. The experimental results and the performance evaluation of ciphers are presented. Moreover, we compare the performance of two forms of implementation by native JAVA cryptography APIs and by an external cryptography provider. In addition, we measure the current consumption of the selected block ciphers on a smartphone.

Keywords: Block cipher · Efficiency · Encryption · JAVA · Lightweight cryptography

1 Introduction

Encryption plays an essential role in many security applications and systems. Nowadays, the real time applications (such as secure voice calling, video calling, remote control applications, real time warning messages in vehicular networks, ...) have to secure data with a minimal computational overhead and provide a minimal delay to ensure the quality of services. The ciphers providing efficient data encryption can be called lightweight ciphers. Lightweight cryptography algorithms and ciphers are also important for energy, memory and computationally restricted devices. Lightweight ciphers can be hardware-oriented or software-oriented. Usually, the hardware-oriented lightweight ciphers are implemented in assemblers and are optimized for concrete devices and nodes. On the

J.-L. Danger et al. (Eds.): FPS 2013, LNCS 8352, pp. 353–368, 2014.
DOI: 10.1007/978-3-319-05302-8_22, © Springer International Publishing Switzerland 2014

other hand, the software-oriented lightweight ciphers are optimized for concrete software platforms and operate with 16/32 bit sized data blocks and do not use substitution tables.

In some heterogeneous communication systems, where many types of devices exist, it is hard to optimize a cipher to every single type of device individually. Due to frequent software upgrades in these systems with various devices, the lightweight cryptography implementation needs to be machine-independent, and applicable to major software platforms such as the android platform, .NET, JAVA etc. These systems use various communication technologies (GSM, 3G, WiFi, Wimax etc.) to connect with hundreds of types of nodes, such as mobile phones, smartphones and tablets. To secure the connection between nodes against eavesdroppers, this communication has to be encrypted by an appropriate symmetric cipher on the application layer. In many systems such as Many to one Networks (MANET) and Vehicular ad hoc Networks (VANET), the cipher must be highly efficient in the decryption phase as one node decrypts sessions from other nodes in real time. On the other hand, in some WEB and cloud services, many sessions are encrypted to many nodes. Thus, the efficient encryption is needed. Nevertheless, the encryption and decryption phases of symmetric block ciphers usually take equal or similar time. In this paper, we deal with the performance of block ciphers, their features and security issues. Besides classic ciphers such as AES, TDES, IDEA, Serpent or TWOFISH, we also analyze the lightweight ciphers like Present, Hight, KATAN, TEA, XTEA etc. In this paper, we aim to software-oriented ciphers which are machine-independent and we outline their performance by our experimental implementation which runs on the Android platform. Further, we provide the comparison of cipher performance implemented by native JAVA APIs and by external library API, and we measure the current consumption of the selected block ciphers on a smartphone.

2 Related Work

There are various studies in the literature aimed to lightweight cryptography and symmetric ciphers. In this paper, we focus on block ciphers.

2.1 Hardware-Oriented Block Ciphers

The works [1–4] deal with the performance comparison of block ciphers on 8-bit microcontrollers. The papers [5,6] add the investigation of lightweight block ciphers in terms of energy efficiency. In [4], the authors investigate 12 lightweight and standard block ciphers, namely AES, DESXL, HIGHT, IDEA, KASUMI, KATAN, KLEIN, mCrypton, NOEKEON, PRESENT, SEA and TEA. All of these algorithms are implemented on an 8-bit platform, more precisely on ATMEL's AVR 8-RISC microcontroller ATtiny45. The implemented ciphers are written in assembly and individually optimized to minimize data-memory use and the code size. The authors evaluate algorithms' performance as well as their energy consumption. The results show that AES offers excellent trade-off between energy consumption and efficiency measured as the cycle counts of encryption or decryption. The lightweight ciphers as HIGHT, NOEKEON, SEA or KATAN have better memory footprint (stored $\leq$ 500 Bytes in ROM) than other lightweight ciphers. Nevertheless, the authors do not consider the security issues of tested algorithms and countermeasures against physical attacks.

2.2 Software-Oriented Block Ciphers

While many of related works deal with the investigation of lightweight ciphers in terms of energy efficiency on 8-bit microcontrollers, there are only few studies such as [7,8] dealing with lightweight block ciphers implemented in machine-independent languages. The paper [7] investigates the performance of block ciphers implemented in JAVA as machine-independent codes. Nevertheless, the authors investigate only 3 algorithms, namely AES, DES and IDEA. The work [8] investigates the optimization of block ciphers in the Android platform by using the Native Development Kit (NDK) that uses native code (e.g. C, C++). The results show that the ciphers implemented by NDK are remarkably faster than ciphers implemented in JAVA, especially for messages with length $\geq$ 1024 bytes. Nevertheless, the authors test only 3 ciphers (SEED, AES and Triple DES). The work [9] investigates the general performance and energy optimization for the Android platforms. This work shows that the latest versions of Android platforms have improved the performance of JAVA code. Since the performance of native codes written by NDK is better than the performance of JAVA codes on Android 2.3 and older versions, JAVA and native codes show similar performance on the recent Android versions (4.x.x).

2.3 Our Contribution

In our paper, we analyze the basic properties of 28 block ciphers, their security issues and possible attacks stated in related works. We aim to block ciphers which can be implemented by using a machine-independent language, e.g. JAVA. We implement by JAVA the application tester of 20 software-oriented block ciphers on the Android platform used by many computationally restricted devices which are connected to heterogeneous systems. By our Android implementation, we enhance the prior performance evaluation in related work [7] of only 3 ciphers to 20 ciphers. Moreover, we investigate and compare two forms of the implementation of selected ciphers. The first form of the implementation uses native JAVA cryptography APIs. The second form of the implementation is based on an external cryptography provider. In addition, we analyze the current consumption of the block ciphers (AES, DES and TDES) on an android device.

3 Analysis of Block Ciphers

In our analysis, we primarily aim to block ciphers. We investigate this range of block ciphers: AES [37], Blowfish [38], Camellia [39], CAST5 [40], CAST6

Table 1. The basic properties of block ciphers

Cipher	Block Size [bit]	Key Size [bit]	Rounds [#]	S-box [#]	Platform orientation	Significant Known Attacks	Security Overall
AES	128	128, 192, 256	10, 12, 14	1	SW, HW	Biclique attack on 14 R with KS = 192 b (2^{80} PCP, time enc. $2^{189.74}$) [10]	Secure
Blowfish	64	32 ÷ 448	16	4	SW	Reflection attack on 16 R with KS = 320 b (2^{34} KP, time enc. $2^{313.3}$) [11]	Secure
Camellia	128	128, 192, 256	18, 24, 24	4	SW, HW	HO-MitM on 16 R with KS = 256 b (2^{126} CP, time enc. 2^{252}) [12]	Secure
CAST5	64	40 ÷ 128	12, 16	8	SW	Differential attack on 5 R with KS = 256 b (2^{17} CP, time enc. 2^{25}) [13]	Secure
CAST6	128	128, 160, 192, 224, 256	48	4	SW	Differential attack on 24 R with KS = 256 b (2^{24} CP, time enc. 2^{244}) [14]	Secure
Clefia	128	128, 192, 256	18, 22, 26	2	HW, SW	Improbable differential attack on 15 R with KS = 256 b ($2^{127.4}$ CP, time enc. $2^{247.49}$) [15]	Secure
DES	64	56	16	8	HW	Linear attack (2^{43} PCP, time enc. 2^{39}) [16]	Insecure
DESede (3DES)	64	168, 112, 56	48	24	HW	RK attack on 2 / 3 keys (2^{32} KP and 2^{32} RK-KC, time enc. 2^{88}) [17]	Insecure
DESL, DESX, DESXL	64	56, 184, 184	16	1, 8, 1	HW	Slide attack on DESX ($2^{32.5}$ KP, time enc. $2^{87.5}$) [18]	Insecure
GOST	64	256	32	1	HW	2DMITM attack (2^{64} PCP, time enc. 2^{192}) [19]	Insecure
Hight	64	128	32	0	HW	Biclique attack (2^{48} PCP, time enc. $2^{126.4}$) [20]	Relative secure
IDEA	64	128	8.5	0	SW	Narrow-Biclique attack (2^{59} CP, time enc. $2^{125.97}$) [21]	Relative secure
KASUMI	64	128	8	2	HW, SW	Sandwich attack (2^{26} PCP, time enc. 2^{32}) [22]	Insecure
KATAN (KTAN-TAN)	32, 48, 64	80	0	0	HW	MitM attack for KS = 64 b (4 CC, time enc. $2^{74.4}$) [23]	Relative secure
KLEIN	64	64, 80, 96	12, 16, 20	16	HW, SW	Truncated differential attack on 8 R with KS = 80 b ($2^{34.3}$ CP, time enc. $2^{77.5}$) [24]	Secure
mCrypton	64	64, 96, 128	12	4	HW, SW	RK rectangle attack on 8 R with KS = 128 b (2^{46} CP, time enc. 2^{46}) [25]	Secure
Noekeon	128	128	16	1	HW, SW	Cube attack (2^{10} CP, time enc. 2^{68}) [26]	Insecure
Present	64	80, 128	31	1	HW	Independent-Biclique attack with KS = 128 b (2^{44} CP, time enc. $2^{127.37}$) [27]	Secure
RC2	64	8 ÷ 128	18	0	SW	RK (2^{34} CP) [28]	Insecure
RC5	32, 64, 128	0 ÷ 2040	0 ÷ 255	0	SW, HW	Differential attack on 16 R (2^{61} CP) [29]	Secure
RC6	128	128, 192, 256	20	0	SW, HW	Multiple Linear attack on 18 R with KS = 256 b ($2^{127.42}$ KP, time enc. $2^{193.43}$) [30]	Secure
Rijndael	128, 160, 192, 224, 256	128, 160, 192, 224, 256	10, 12, 14	1	SW, HW	Improving integral attack on 9 R with KS = 256 b (2^{119} CP, time enc. 2^{204}) [31]	Secure
SEA	Variable	Variable	Variable	2	SW	-	Secure
SEED	128	128, 192, 256	16, 20, 24	2	SW, HW	Differential attack on 8 R with KS = 128 b (2^{125} CP, time enc. 2^{122}) [32]	Secure
Serpent	128	128, 192, 256	32	8	SW, HW	Multidimensional linear attack on 12 R with KS = 128 b (2^{116} KP, time enc. $2^{237.5}$) [33]	Secure
Skipjack	64	80	32	1	SW, HW	Slide attack ($2^{32.5}$ known texts, time enc. 2^{44}) [34]	Insecure
TEA	64	128	32	0	SW	RK attack (2^{23} CP, time enc. 2^{32}) [35]	Insecure
Twofish	128	128, 192, 256	16	8	SW, HW	Saturation attack on 8 R with KS = 256 b (2^{127} CP, time enc. 2^{253}) [35]	Secure
XTEA	64	128	64	0	SW, HW	3-Sub. MitM on 28 R (2^{37} CP, time enc. $2^{120.38}$) [36]	Secure

[41], Clefia [42], DES [43], DESL [44], GOST 28147-89 [45], Hight [46], IDEA [47], KASUMI [48], KATAN [49], KLEIN [50], mCrypton [51], Noekeon [52], PRESENT [53], RC2 [54], RC5 [55], RC6 [56], SEA [57], SEED [58], Serpent [59], Skipjack [60], TEA [61], Twofish [62] and XTEA [63]. Table 1 sums up the basic properties of the block ciphers. The block size of ciphers is usually 64 and 128 bits. There are ciphers such as KATAN, RC5 or SEA which offer variable sizes of blocks. This feature is appropriate in scenarios with a limited communication overhead. According to common security recommendations, almost all ciphers support $\geq$ 80b key size. Majority of the block ciphers employ a Substitution-box (S-box). Nevertheless, the block ciphers Hight, IDEA, KATAN, RC2, RC5, RC6, TEA and XTEA do not use any S-box but employ modular operations, shifts and eXclusive ORs (XOR)s. Ciphers without an S-box usually have smaller code size than the ciphers with the S-box. This is useful in memory restricted nodes such as wireless sensors. Ciphers can be designed as software-oriented, hardware-oriented or both. The software oriented ciphers are widely spread in web services, cloud services and heterogeneous networks where a lot of various types of nodes can be found, such as in the security solution [64]. Hardware-oriented ciphers are usually implemented in systems such as sensor networks, RFID tags etc. In these systems, only few of types of nodes are and it is easy to optimize the codes. Besides ciphers' design and performance, the fast establishment of secret keys and the subkeys is also important. This feature is referred to as key agility. Key agility considers both the computation of subkeys and the ability of their switching. Nodes, which work as gateways, have to decrypt several sessions encrypted by different keys. The fast recomputing of the keys also impacts on the throughput of communication via these nodes.

Table 1 also shows known attacks on the ciphers that have been confirmed in literature. In Table 1, the attacks and abbreviations are denoted as follows: R - Rounds, KS - Key Size, CC - Chosen Ciphertexts, CP - Chosen Plaintexts, KP - Known Plaintexts, RK - Related-Key, PCP - Plaintext-Ciphertext Pairs, HO-MitM - Higher-Order Meet-in-the-Middle, RK-KC - Related-Key Known Cipher-texts, SaC MitM-BD - Splice and Cut Meet-in-the-Middle Biryukov-Demirci attack. The most common attacks are brute force attacks and related-key attacks. According to this survey, we evaluate the security of every cipher. In the security overall, we evaluate the block ciphers as secure, relative secure and insecure based on the feasibility of known attacks. The known attacks on ciphers marked as 'secure' are still computationally infeasible. Secure ciphers such as AES, CAST6 etc. are usually recommended to apply. Relatively secure ciphers such as TDES and KATAN are recommended under certain conditions (using higher key size etc.). Insecure ciphers like obsolete DES, IDEA or TEA are not recommended to be applied because the known attacks on these insecure ciphers are nowadays computationally feasible.

4   Experimental Implementation

To investigate the performance of software-oriented block ciphers, we have implemented 20 ciphers using JAVA which is a machine-independent language.

Since Clefia, HIGHT, DESXL, KATAN, mCrypton, PRESENT and SEA are designed as hardware-oriented ciphers, we omit them in our experimental software implementation. We focus on android devices and make our android application called Cipher Tester.

4.1 Our Application

Our application called Cipher Tester employs the repackage of Bouncy Castle (BC) library[1] for Android called Spongy Castle. The Spongy Castle (SC) library[2] is a cut-down version of BC which provides these following block ciphers: AES, Blowfish, Camellia, CAST5, DES, TDES, GOST28147, IDEA, NOEKEON, RC2, RC532, RC564, RC6, Rijndael, SEED, Serpent, Skipjack, TEA, Twofish and XTEA in various modes supported. In our application, we use also a secure random generator to generate symmetric keys. Further, we use JAVA cryptography API to compare the performance of Spongy Castle (SC) provider with native JAVA algorithms of AES, DES and Triple DES. Our 6 MB-sized application runs on every android device with Android OS v2.2 or higher.

4.2 Experimental Results

We have measured the software-oriented block ciphers using our android implementation (Cipher Tester) on the Android device (Samsung Galaxy S i9000, CPU 1 GHz Cortex-A9, 512 MB RAM, OS Android v2.3). Table 2 sums up the performance measurement of 20 block ciphers. To normalize measurement, we have set 128-bit key size for all ciphers which provide this size and we have used the electronic codebook (ECB) mode. The length of message/ciphertext is denoted as l. On the input of every cipher, we have put the short 64-bit message and 512-bit message. We have measured every phase (Initialization, Encryption and Decryption) atomically. The measurement of every cipher has been performed 2500x and mean values have been outlined. To obtain the relevant results and minimize the impact of 3G signal processing, we have switched the smartphone into the flight mode that cut down the 3G connection. Moreover, we have switched off all unnecessary applications that are running on background.

In Fig. 1, the performance measurement of 128-bit block sized ciphers is depicted for a 512-bit message. The most efficient cipher from all compared ciphers is Camellia. The encryption and decryption operations of Camellia take about 110 μs. The second most efficient cipher is AES which achieves the performance of encryption and decryption under 150 μs. Figure 2 depicts the performance of 64-bit block sized ciphers with a 512-bit message on the input. The most efficient cipher from all compared ciphers is TEA. The encryption and decryption of TEA take about 60 μs. Also, XTEA achieves good performance, 64 μs for encryption and 67 μs for decryption. We omit 64-bit block sized Blowfish and 128-bit block sized Twofish ciphers because of their inefficiency ($\geq$ 1 ms) to improve graph resolution in Figs. 1 and 2.

---

[1] http://www.bouncycastle.org/specifications.html
[2] http://rtyley.github.com/spongycastle/

Table 2. Performance of software-oriented block ciphers

Cipher	Key size (used) bit	Block Size	Initialization μs	Encryption $l = 64$ b μs	$l = 512$ b μs	Decryption $l = 64$ b μs	$l = 512$ b μs
AES	0 .. 256 (128)	128 bit	242	128	140	141	151
Blowfish	0 .. 448 (128)	64 bit	272	1404	1406	1368	1380
Camellia	128, 192, 256	128 bit	217	85	110	65	111
CAST5	0 .. 128(128)	64 bit	215	129	186	115	174
CAST6	0 .. 256(128)	128 bit	290	111	195	136	184
DES	64	64 bit	214	150	164	139	166
DESede	128, 192	64 bit	200	257	349	242	366
GOST28147	256	64 bit	209	58	115	59	147
IDEA	128 (128)	64 bit	215	88	127	111	173
Noekeon	128(128)	128 bit	213	72	231	80	213
RC2	0 .. 1024 (128)	64 bit	183	102	123	115	157
RC5	0 .. 128 (128)	64 bit	215	86	106	85	128
RC6	0 .. 256 (128)	128 bit	257	104	155	93	167
Rijndael	0 .. 256 (128)	128 bit	220	293	531	258	680
SEED	(128)	128 bit	208	87	189	89	196
Serpent	(128), 192, 256	128 bit	207	115	249	119	275
Skipjack	0 .. 128 (128)	64 bit	193	67	164	84	118
TEA	(128)	64 bit	214	36	60	49	62
Twofish	(128), 192, 256	128 bit	669	1148	1183	1566	1580
XTEA	128 (128)	64 bit	228	41	64	45	67

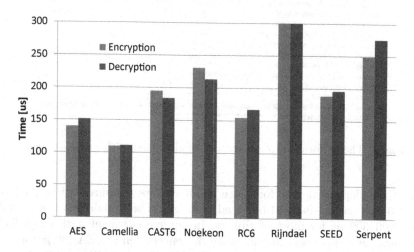

Fig. 1. The performance measurement of 128 bit block sized ciphers

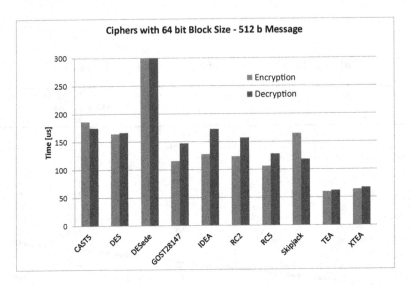

Fig. 2. The performance measurement of 64 bit block sized ciphers

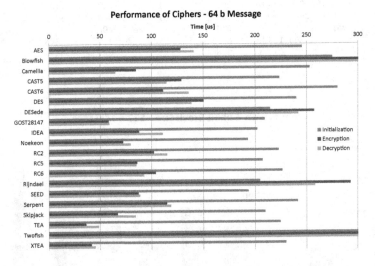

Fig. 3. The performance measurement of all ciphers with 64-bit messages

Figure 3 depicts the performance of all ciphers measured with x-axis cut out of 0–300 μs for small 64-bit sized messages. The initialization phase takes about 200–300 μs for most of ciphers. In our measurement with small 64-bit sized messages, the most efficient cipher for encryption is TEA (36 μs) and the most efficient cipher for decryption is XTEA (45 μs). GOST 28147, Noekeon and Skipjack have also good performance with measured times between 50–75 μs. The performance of all ciphers with 512 bit sized messages is depicted in Fig. 4. TEA, XTEA and Camellia have better performance than other ciphers.

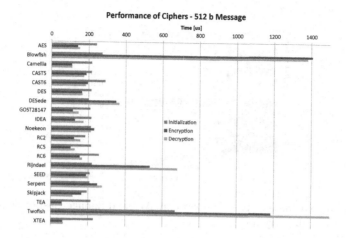

Fig. 4. The performance measurement of all ciphers with 512-bit messages

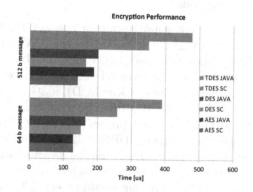

Fig. 5. The comparison of JAVA cryptography API and Sponge Castle (SC) provider for chosen ciphers in encryption

On the other hand, Blowfish and Twofish seem quite inefficient. Widely used AES has average performance characteristics from the range of tested ciphers and is approx. 3 times slower than XTEA but offers very high key agility than the rest of the tested ciphers.

Furthermore, we compare the implementation by native JAVA Cryptography APIs and by the Sponge Castle (SC) provider for three block ciphers: AES, DES and TDES. Figure 5 shows the comparison of encryption performance and the decryption performance of these ciphers are depicted in Fig. 6. For most cases, the implementation of these ciphers by SC provider is usually more efficient than implementation using the JAVA cryptography API. Especially, TDES algorithm implemented by SC overcomes the implementation by native JAVA cryptography APIs. AES implemented by SC provider has slightly better performance than AES implemented by native APIs. For the encryption of a 512-bit sized message, AES implemented by native APIs requires approx. 34 % more time.

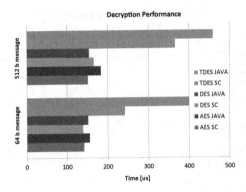

Fig. 6. The comparison of JAVA cryptography API and Sponge Castle (SC) Provider for chosen ciphers in decryption

4.3   Consumption Analysis

We have measured the current consumption of the well-known block ciphers AES, DESede (TDES) and DES implemented by the JAVA cryptography API on the Android device (Samsung Nexus S i9023, CPU 1 GHz Cortex-A9, 512 MB RAM, OS Android v2.3). To get the most relevant results, we have switched off the display (4.0 inches 480×800 Super Clear LCD), a 3G connection and other applications. The battery has been substituted by a power source. The consumption has been measured by the current probe Tektronix CT-6 which has been connected to the oscilloscope Tektronix DPO 4032. Our workstation is depicted in Fig. 7. We have used the same approach for the measurement as in [65]. The current consumptions of these ciphers are depicted in Figs. 8, 9 and 10. The message has the length 614442 B in our measurement. The total current consumption of the ciphers strongly depends on the total encryption time. Table 3 sums up the measured results. The current consumptions normalized for 1 h of the measured ciphers are almost the same on the smartphone.

Moreover, we have compared the current consumption of the device before and after the encryption algorithm, see Fig. 11. According to these measurement results, the ciphers have not a significant impact on the current consumption unlike the display or the GSM module have.

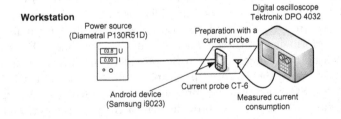

Fig. 7. Our workstation

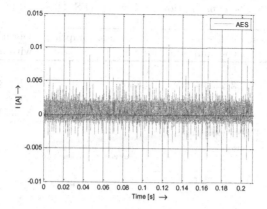

Fig. 8. Current consumption of AES

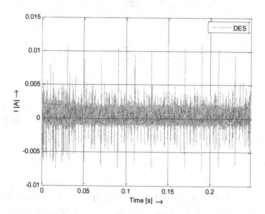

Fig. 9. Current consumption of DES

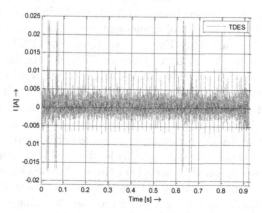

Fig. 10. Current consumption of TDES

Table 3. The consumption analysis of AES, DES and DESede

Cipher	Encryption time	Current consumption	Current consumption for 1 h	Duration of encryption with a 2.1 Ah battery
-	[s]	[A]	[A]	[h]
AES	0.21164	3.4454e-005	0.58605	3.5833
DES	0.24808	3.956e-005	0.57406	3.6581
DESede	0.925	0.00014615	0.56879	3.6920

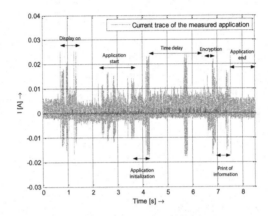

Fig. 11. The current trace of the measured application

5   Conclusions

There are a lot of block ciphers which are designed to provide various features and performance characteristics. We have analyzed 28 and implemented 20 block ciphers. In our study, we have focused on cipher performance. This paper presents the performance evaluation of software-oriented block ciphers implemented by using machine independent language JAVA on the Android platform. According to the results of our experimental implementation, the most efficient software-oriented block ciphers are Tiny Encryption Algorithm (TEA) and TEA's successor XTEA. Due to the security issues of TEA, XTEA should be the first option in communication systems like VANETs, Cloud services etc. where the efficiency of encryption and decryption phases is crucial. XTEA is more than 3 times efficient than widely used AES. On the other hand, AES has a very high key agility. According to our comparison of two implementation forms, AES based on native JAVA cryptography APIs requires approx. 34 % more time than AES implemented by the Sponge Castle library. The current consumptions of block ciphers depend on the encryption times of these ciphers. Nevertheless, these current consumptions are lower than the current consumptions of displays or 3G modules on android devices. Our future plans are aimed on the investigation of hardware-oriented block ciphers and their performance. We would like to confront the properties and measured performance of hardware-oriented ciphers with software-oriented block ciphers.

Acknowledgments. This research work is funded by project SIX CZ.1.05/2.1.00/03.0072; the Technology Agency of the Czech Republic projects TA02011260 and TA03010818; the Ministry of Industry and Trade of the Czech Republic project FR-TI4/647.

References

1. Rinne, S., Eisenbarth, T., Paar, C.: Performance analysis of contemporary light-weight block ciphers on 8-bit microcontrollers. In: ECRYPT Workshop SPEED-Software Performance Enhancement for Encryption and Decryption booklet, Cite-seer, pp. 33–43 (2007)
2. Eisenbarth, T., Kumar, S.: A survey of lightweight-cryptography implementations. Des. Test Comput., IEEE **24**(6), 522–533 (2007)
3. Çakiroglu, M.: Software implementation and performance comparison of popular block ciphers on 8-bit low-cost microcontroller. Int. J. Phys. Sci. **5**(9), 1338–1343 (2010)
4. Eisenbarth, T., et al.: Compact implementation and performance evaluation of block ciphers in ATtiny devices. In: Mitrokotsa, A., Vaudenay, S. (eds.) AFRICACRYPT 2012. LNCS, vol. 7374, pp. 172–187. Springer, Heidelberg (2012)
5. Wu, W., Zhang, L.: LBlock: a lightweight block cipher. In: Lopez, J., Tsudik, G. (eds.) ACNS 2011. LNCS, vol. 6715, pp. 327–344. Springer, Heidelberg (2011)
6. Kerckhof, S., Durvaux, F., Hocquet, C., Bol, D., Standaert, F.-X.: Towards green cryptography: a comparison of lightweight ciphers from the energy viewpoint. In: Prouff, E., Schaumont, P. (eds.) CHES 2012. LNCS, vol. 7428, pp. 390–407. Springer, Heidelberg (2012)
7. Weis, R., Lucks, S.: The performance of modern block ciphers in JAVA. In: Schneier, B., Quisquater, J.-J. (eds.) CARDIS 1998. LNCS, vol. 1820, pp. 125–133. Springer, Heidelberg (2000)
8. Paik, J.H., Seo, S.C., Kim, Y., Lee, H.J., Jung, H.C., Lee, D.H.: An efficient implementation of block cipher in android platform. In: 2011 5th FTRA International Conference on Multimedia and Ubiquitous Engineering (MUE), pp. 173–176. IEEE (2011)
9. Lewerentz, A., Lindvall, J., Fogelström, N.D.: Performance and energy optimization for the android platform (2012)
10. Bogdanov, A., Khovratovich, D., Rechberger, C.: Biclique cryptanalysis of the full AES. In: Lee, D.H., Wang, X. (eds.) ASIACRYPT 2011. LNCS, vol. 7073, pp. 344–371. Springer, Heidelberg (2011)
11. Kara, O., Manap, C.: A new class of weak keys for blowfish. In: Biryukov, A. (ed.) FSE 2007. LNCS, vol. 4593, pp. 167–180. Springer, Heidelberg (2007)
12. Lu, J., Wei, Y., Kim, J., Pasalic, E.: The higher-order meet-in-the-middle attack and its application to the camellia block cipher. In: Part at the First Asian Work-shop on Symmetric Key Cryptography (ASK 2011), August 2011. https://sites.google.com/site/jiqiang.
13. Moriai, S., Shimoyama, T., Kaneko, T.: Higher order differential attack of a CAST cipher. In: Vaudenay, S. (ed.) FSE 1998. LNCS, vol. 1372, pp. 17–31. Springer, Heidelberg (1998)

14. Pestunov, A.: Differential cryptanalysis of 24-round cast-256. In: IEEE Region 8 International Conference on Computational Technologies in Electrical and Electronics Engineering, SIBIRCON 2008, pp. 46–49. IEEE (2008)

15. Tezcan, C.: The improbable differential attack: cryptanalysis of reduced round CLEFIA. In: Gong, G., Gupta, K.C. (eds.) INDOCRYPT 2010. LNCS, vol. 6498, pp. 197–209. Springer, Heidelberg (2010)

16. Junod, P.: On the complexity of matsui's attack. In: Vaudenay, S., Youssef, A.M. (eds.) SAC 2001. LNCS, vol. 2259, pp. 199–211. Springer, Heidelberg (2001)

17. Phan, R.-W.: Related-Key attacks on triple-DES and DESX variants. In: Okamoto, T. (ed.) CT-RSA 2004. LNCS, vol. 2964, pp. 15–24. Springer, Heidelberg (2004)

18. Biryukov, A., Wagner, D.: Advanced slide attacks. In: Preneel, B. (ed.) EURO-CRYPT 2000. LNCS, vol. 1807, pp. 589–606. Springer, Heidelberg (2000)

19. Dinur, I., Dunkelman, O., Shamir, A.: Improved attacks on full GOST. In: Canteaut, A. (ed.) FSE 2012. LNCS, vol. 7549, pp. 9–28. Springer, Heidelberg (2012)

20. Hong, D., Koo, B., Kwon, D.: Biclique attack on the full HIGHT. In: Kim, H. (ed.) ICISC 2011. LNCS, vol. 7259, pp. 365–374. Springer, Heidelberg (2012)

21. Khovratovich, D., Leurent, G., Rechberger, C.: Narrow-bicliques: cryptanalysis of full IDEA. In: Pointcheval, D., Johansson, T. (eds.) EUROCRYPT 2012. LNCS, vol. 7237, pp. 392–410. Springer, Heidelberg (2012)

22. Dunkelman, O., Keller, N., Shamir, A.: A practical-time related-key attack on the KASUMI cryptosystem used in GSM and 3G telephony. In: Rabin, T. (ed.) CRYPTO 2010. LNCS, vol. 6223, pp. 393–410. Springer, Heidelberg (2010)

23. Wei, L., Rechberger, C., Guo, J., Wu, H., Wang, H., Ling, S.: Improved meet-in-the-middle cryptanalysis of KTANTAN (Poster). In: Parampalli, U., Hawkes, P. (eds.) ACISP 2011. LNCS, vol. 6812, pp. 433–438. Springer, Heidelberg (2011)

24. Yu, X., Wu, W., Li, Y., Zhang, L.: Cryptanalysis of reduced-round KLEIN block cipher. In: Wu, C.-K., Yung, M., Lin, D. (eds.) Inscrypt 2011. LNCS, vol. 7537, pp. 237–250. Springer, Heidelberg (2012)

25. Park, J.: Security analysis of mcrypton proper to low-cost ubiquitous computing devices and applications. Int. J. Commun. Syst. **22**(8), 959–969 (2009)

26. Abdul-Latip, S.F., Reyhanitabar, M.R., Susilo, W., Seberry, J.: On the security of NOEKEON against side channel cube attacks. In: Kwak, J., Deng, R.H., Won, Y., Wang, G. (eds.) ISPEC 2010. LNCS, vol. 6047, pp. 45–55. Springer, Heidelberg (2010)

27. Abed, F., Forler, C., List, E., Lucks, S., Wenzel, J.: Biclique cryptanalysis of the present and led lightweight ciphers. Technical report, Cryptology ePrint Archive, Report 2012/591 (2012)

28. Kelsey, J., Schneier, B., Wagner, D.: Related-key cryptanalysis of 3-WAY, Biham-DES, CAST, DES-X, NewDES, RC2, and TEA. In: Han, Y., Quing, S. (eds.) ICICS 1997. LNCS, vol. 1334, pp. 233–246. Springer, Heidelberg (1997)

29. Kaliski, B., Yin, Y.: On the security of the rc5 encryption algorithm. Technical report, RSA Laboratories Technical Report TR-602. To appear (1998)

30. Shimoyama, T., Takenaka, M., Koshiba, T.: Multiple linear cryptanalysis of a reduced round RC6. In: Daemen, J., Rijmen, V. (eds.) FSE 2002. LNCS, vol. 2365, p. 76. Springer, Heidelberg (2002)

31. Galice, S., Minier, M.: Improving integral attacks against rijndael-256 Up to 9 rounds. In: Vaudenay, S. (ed.) AFRICACRYPT 2008. LNCS, vol. 5023, pp. 1–15. Springer, Heidelberg (2008)

32. Sung, J.: Differential cryptanalysis of eight-round seed. Inf. Process. Lett. **111**(10), 474–478 (2011)

33. Nguyen, P.H., Wu, H., Wang, H.: Improving the algorithm 2 in multidimensional linear cryptanalysis. In: Parampalli, U., Hawkes, P. (eds.) ACISP 2011. LNCS, vol. 6812, pp. 61–74. Springer, Heidelberg (2011)

34. Chung-Wei Phan, R.: Cryptanalysis of full skipjack block cipher. Electron. Lett. **38**(2), 69–71 (2002)

35. Lucks, S.: The saturation attack - A bait for twofish. In: Matsui, M. (ed.) FSE 2001. LNCS, vol. 2355, pp. 1–15. Springer, Heidelberg (2002)

36. Sasaki, Y., Wang, L., Sakai, Y., Sakiyama, K., Ohta, K.: Three-subset meet-in-the-middle attack on reduced XTEA. In: Mitrokotsa, A., Vaudenay, S. (eds.) AFRICACRYPT 2012. LNCS, vol. 7374, pp. 138–154. Springer, Heidelberg (2012)

37. Daemen, J., Rijmen, V.: The Design of Rijndael: AES-the Advanced Encryption Standard. Springer, Heidelberg (2002)

38. Schneier, B.: Description of a new variable-length key, 64-bit block cipher (Blowfish). In: Anderson, R. (ed.) FSE 1993. LNCS, vol. 809, pp. 191–204. Springer, Heidelberg (1994)

39. Aoki, K., Ichikawa, T., Kanda, M., Matsui, M., Moriai, S., Nakajima, J., Tokita, T.: Specification of camellia-a 128-bit block cipher (2000)

40. Adams, C.: The cast-128 encryption algorithm (1997)

41. Gilchrist, J., Adams, C.: The cast-256 encryption algorithm (1999)

42. Shirai, T., Shibutani, K., Akishita, T., Moriai, S., Iwata, T.: The 128-Bit blockcipher CLEFIA (extended abstract). In: Biryukov, A. (ed.) FSE 2007. LNCS, vol. 4593, pp. 181–195. Springer, Heidelberg (2007)

43. Smid, M., Branstad, D.: Data encryption standard: past and future. Proc. IEEE **76**(5), 550–559 (1988)

44. Leander, G., Paar, C., Poschmann, A., Schramm, K.: New lightweight DES variants. In: Biryukov, A. (ed.) FSE 2007. LNCS, vol. 4593, pp. 196–210. Springer, Heidelberg (2007)

45. Courtois, N.: Security evaluation of gost 28147–89 in view of international standardisation. Cryptologia **36**(1), 2–13 (2012)

46. Hong, D., et al.: HIGHT: a new block cipher suitable for low-resource device. In: Goubin, L., Matsui, M. (eds.) CHES 2006. LNCS, vol. 4249, pp. 46–59. Springer, Heidelberg (2006)

47. Lai, X., Massey, J.L.: A proposal for a new block encryption standard. In: Damgård, I.B. (ed.) EUROCRYPT 1990. LNCS, vol. 473, pp. 389–404. Springer, Heidelberg (1991)

48. Specification of the 3gpp confidentiality and integrity algorithms, document 2: Kasumi specification (release 10) (2011)

49. Cannire, C., Dunkelman, O., Kneevi, M.: Katan and ktantan a family of small and efficient hardware-oriented block ciphers. In: Clavier, C., Gaj, K. (eds.) CHES 2009. LNCS, vol. 5747, pp. 272–288. Springer, Heidelberg (2009)

50. Gong, Z., Nikova, S., Law, Y.W.: KLEIN: a new family of lightweight block ciphers. In: Juels, A., Paar, C. (eds.) RFIDSec 2011. LNCS, vol. 7055, pp. 1–18. Springer, Heidelberg (2012)

51. Lim, C.H., Korkishko, T.: mCrypton - a lightweight block cipher for security of low-cost RFID tags and sensors. In: Song, J.-S., Kwon, T., Yung, M. (eds.) WISA 2005. LNCS, vol. 3786, pp. 243–258. Springer, Heidelberg (2006)

52. Daemen, J., Peeters, M., Van Assche, G., Rijmen, V.: Nessie proposal: Noekeon. In: First Open NESSIE Workshop (2000)

53. Bogdanov, A., Knudsen, L., Leander, G., Paar, C., Poschmann, A., Robshaw, M., Seurin, Y., Vikkelsoe, C.: Present: an ultra-light weight block cipher. In: Paillier,

P., Verbauwhede, I. (eds.) CHES 2007. LNCS, vol. 4727, pp. 450–466. Springer, Heidelberg (2007)

54. Knudsen, L.R., Rijmen, V., Rivest, R.L., Robshaw, M.: On the design and security of RC2. In: Vaudenay, S. (ed.) FSE 1998. LNCS, vol. 1372, pp. 206–221. Springer, Heidelberg (1998)

55. Rivest, R.: The rc5 encryption algorithm. In: Preneel, B. (ed.) FSE 1994. LNCS, vol. 1008, pp. 86–96. Springer, Heidelberg (1995)

56. Contini, S., Rivest, R., Robshaw, M., Yin, Y.: The security of the rc6 tm block cipher. v1. 0. http://www.rsa.com/rsalabs/aes/security.pdf (1998)

57. Standaert, F.-X., Piret, G., Gershenfeld, N., Quisquater, J.-J.: SEA: a scalable encryption algorithm for small embedded applications. In: Domingo-Ferrer, J., Posegga, J., Schreckling, D. (eds.) CARDIS 2006. LNCS, vol. 3928, pp. 222–236. Springer, Heidelberg (2006)

58. Lee, J., Park, J., Lee, S., Kim, J.: The seed encryption algorithm. SEED (2005)

59. Anderson, R., Biham, E., Knudsen, L.: Serpent: A proposal for the advanced encryption standard. NIST AES Proposal (1998)

60. Biham, E., Biryukov, A., Shamir, A.: Cryptanalysis of skipjack reduced to 31 rounds using impossible differentials. In: Stern, J. (ed.) EUROCRYPT 1999. LNCS, vol. 1592, pp. 12–13. Springer, Heidelberg (1999)

61. Wheeler, D.J., Needham, R.M.: TEA, a tiny encryption algorithm. In: Preneel, B. (ed.) Fast Software Encryption. LNCS, vol. 1008, pp. 363–366. Springer, Heidelberg (1995)

62. Schneier, B., Kelsey, J., Whiting, D., Wagner, D., Hall, C., Ferguson, N.: Twofish: a 128-bit block cipher. NIST AES Proposal 15 (1998)

63. Ko, Y., Hong, S.H., Lee, W.I., Lee, S.-J., Kang, J.-S.: Related key differential attacks on 27 rounds of XTEA and full-round GOST. In: Roy, B., Meier, W. (eds.) FSE 2004. LNCS, vol. 3017, pp. 299–316. Springer, Heidelberg (2004)

64. Malina, L., Hajny, J.: Privacy-preserving framework for geosocial applications. Secur. Commun. Netw. **2013**(8), 1–16 (2013)

65. Martinasek, Z., Zeman, V.: Innovative method of the power analysis. Radioengineering **22**(2), 587 (2013)

Don't Push It: Breaking iButton Security

Christian Brandt and Michael Kasper[✉]

Fraunhofer Institute for Secure Information Technology (FhG-SIT),
Rheinstrasse 75, 64295 Darmstadt, Germany
{christian.brandt,michael.kasper}@sit.fraunhofer.de

Abstract. Maxims iButtons are small portable (steel) tokens that can be attached to objects (e.g., keys, fobs) and are deployed in various applications from access control to devices and buildings to asset management and electronic cash. So far, the security and privacy aspects of iButtons have been widely unexplored. The so-called Secure iButtons are advocated for security critical applications for e.g., micropayment, authentication or feature activation.

In this paper we present for the first time a detailed security analysis of the Secure iButtons DS1963S. Although no technical details are publicly available, Secure iButtons have a variety of physical and cryptographic built-in measures to protect against physical tampering as well as unauthorized access to cryptographic material. We developed methods to bypass all these protection mechanisms of the manufacturer. We present a differential fault attack and implementation attack on the SHA-1-enabled iButton (DS1963S chip). Beside the emulation and impersonation, our attacks succeed in extracting the secret keys stored in the iButton. Our methods allow an infinite rollback to the initial state, which is crucial when targeting micropayment systems based on iButtons. We also demonstrate our attacks on Maxims reference platform of a micropayment system. Our best attack requires a minimal financial invest and take less than ten minutes, including target preparation, while the pure attack on all eight 64-bit keys is completed in a few seconds.

1 Introduction

While there is a large body of literature on the security of smartcards and/or contactless tokens such as RFID [20,22,23,27], car and garage transponders [21,25,28] and other embedded security chips such as [24], *iButtons* have been mostly unexplored by the research community. iButtons are micro-chips produced as a small stainless steel can, commonly embedded on special key-fobs (see Fig. 2a). They are used in a wide range of technical services and products. For security critical applications the so-called *Secure iButton* [7–9] are advocated as a real alternative to Magnet Stripe Cards, Smart Cards, and Proximity or Contactless Cards. Typical application scenarios are physical access control (e.g., door lock systems [1,3,4,14]), anti-theft and intrusion protection mechanism (e.g., for protection of train ticket machines [2]), feature activation (e.g., Supermicro' raid controller [15], [16]), electronic cash and tickets (e.g., Akbil micropayment system

J.-L. Danger et al. (Eds.): FPS 2013, LNCS 8352, pp. 369–387, 2014.
DOI: 10.1007/978-3-319-05302-8_23, © Springer International Publishing Switzerland 2014

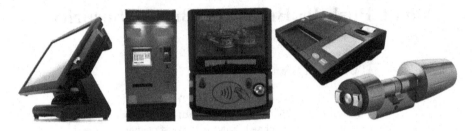

Fig. 1. Application Scenarios and SCUs: [2, 11, 12, 14, 19] (left-to-right)

of the Istanbul metropolitan transportation [19, 29]), cashier systems ([11, 17]), and voting machines ([12]) (Fig. 1).

We point out that these few examples are only the tip of an iceberg and indicate a much wider range of security sensitive applications in the field (including also non-crypto iButtons used for security issues). Most of these systems would be seriously affected when the security of iButtons fails.

1.1 Secure iButton Device Family

There are different device models of Secure iButtons. The DS1963S token is the most advanced iButton product on the market for security applications, and hence the subject of our investigation. It is an high-end model, embedded in a stainless steel container with 704 bytes memory equipped with an internal lithium cell power source. The other two devices DS1961S [7] use EEPROMs instead of volatile memory and allow deployment without a lithium cell. The DS2432 [10] is essentially similar to DS1961S devices, but enclosed in a chip-scale small outline package.

Secure iButtons have sophisticated physical tamper protection and a cryptographic engine for authentication purpose. In the following, we use the term Secure iButton to refer to the DS1963S iButton model. Secure iButtons have a proprietary onboard 512-bit SHA-1 MAC engine with overall eight 64-bit secret

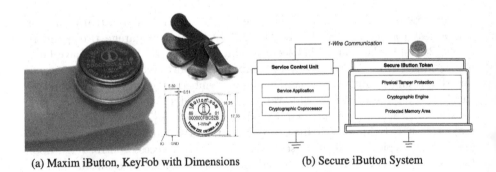

(a) Maxim iButton, KeyFob with Dimensions   (b) Secure iButton System

Fig. 2. iButton hardware architecture

keys using a challenge response procedure for authentication. Those tokens have several integrated physical tamper-protection and access control mechanisms and countermeasures to prevent the secret key extraction and/or the misuse of these devices, although relevant data sheets as well as all other important implementation details are not publicly available.

1.2 Our Contribution

We performed a detailed analysis of Secure iButtons with the focus on the SHA-1-enabled DS1963S device model. We have developed a set of fault- and implementation attacks that overcome various sophisticated physical tamper protection and logical countermeasures allowing a full exposure of these tokens. More concretely, we succeeded in (i) circumventing the physical tamper-protection and self-destruction mechanisms attached to the electrical circuits, (ii) overwriting the protected memory with fault-injected data, (iii) extracting the secret keys, and finally (iv) impersonating and emulating the token in application scenarios such as micro-payments.

As we will elaborate in details, for our analysis, we had to tackle several technical challenging problems to be able to fully reverse engineer this small security token. We stress that our methods are not limited to iButtons and can also be applied to other similar embedded devices. Our most efficient attack requires a small one-time monetary cost of approx. US$350. The complete attack takes less than ten minutes, including target preparation, while the pure attack on all (eight) 64-bit secret keys is completed in a few seconds.

2 Background

Similar to complementary technologies, like NFC/RFID tags, magnet stripes, and smart cards, the Maxim iButtons, also known as *Dallas Keys*, exist in different flavours with special functionality, e.g., real-time clocks (DS1904) [5], autonomous temperature and humidity loggers with password protection (e.g., DS1923) [6], password-protected memories (DS1977) [9], and the so-called *Secure iButtons* for security-critical applications with high security requirements.[1]

A Secure iButton system consists of a Service Control Unit (SCU), as service provider, and an iButton as client token. Communicating with an iButton requires a simple touch of the iButton to a SCU. Both parties communicate by the 1-Wire protocol standard [13]. In the following, we will give a brief introduction to the corresponding components and the underlying technology as far as it is required to understand our attack methods. Figure 2b illustrates a typical system architecture.

---

[1] iButtons were originally invented in the year 1989 by Dallas Semiconductor Corp. After Maxim has been acquired by Maxim Integrated Products in 2001, the token continued under the brand name *iButton*.

1-Wire Device Communication. The 1-wire communication is similar to a *I2C* serial communication[2]. An iButton system requires only one electrical signal and an additional ground. Hence it allows a data transfer over a single wire. The protocol layers are detailed in the technical specification of the manufacturer [26]. The power is supplied over the signal line with 3 or 5 Volts. The low-level signal is at 0V. In order to guarantee a sufficient power supply of the internal circuit, an iButton is always on the high level when idle. The bus master initiates and controls all 1-Wire communications.

For our attack, we only need a set of low level functions on the Transport Layer. These commands allow to perform memory operations, and initiate procedures where the cryptographic SHA-1 engine is involved. See Appendix A for a list of important functions.

Security Architecture and Protection Mechanisms. As mentioned in the previous section, Secure iButtons are high-end tokens for security sensitive services and authentication purposes. In order to prevent modifications of sensitive data records, iButtons have a set of protection mechanisms. The tokens have physical tamper-protection, rugged, and able to perform the cryptographic hash operation within given time constraints.

Physical Tamper Protection and Zeroization. The manufacturer has employed a set of sophisticated barriers for an attacker. In order to prevent modifications of sensitive data records, an internal lithium cell powers the volatile memory inside the iButton. Opening the steel container forces a disconnection from the power source. If an adversary attempts to penetrate the steel container, the chip will clear its memory data. Specific intrusions that typically result in zeroization of the volatile-memory are: (1) opening the steel container with disconnection from the internal power source, and (2) micro-probing of the chip.

Cryptographic Engine. Secure iButtons have an integrated cryptographic engine with the ability to perform cryptographic hash-based message authentication, where the hash input message is combined with a secret key. Therefore, Secure iButtons have a slightly modified 512-bit hardware implementation[3] of the Secure Hash Algorithm (SHA-1) for (H)MAC generation and a read-protected memory area for eight 64-bit secret keys.

Internals of iButton Memory Archtiecture. Secure iButtons have 512 bytes of volatile SRAM memory. The memory comprises of 22 memory pages each having a size of 32 bytes. Figure 3 shows the memory and special registers.

---

[2] A master devices initiates and controls the communication with at least one slave device. The communication channel establishes a half-duplex bidirectional serial channel.

[3] FIPS 180-1 adds a final constant multi-block SHA-1 computations for each block. Since the iButton protocol only compute one block, the final FIPS 180 constants was removed for performance issues. The SCU can opt-in the constant when FIPA 180-1 conformance is required.

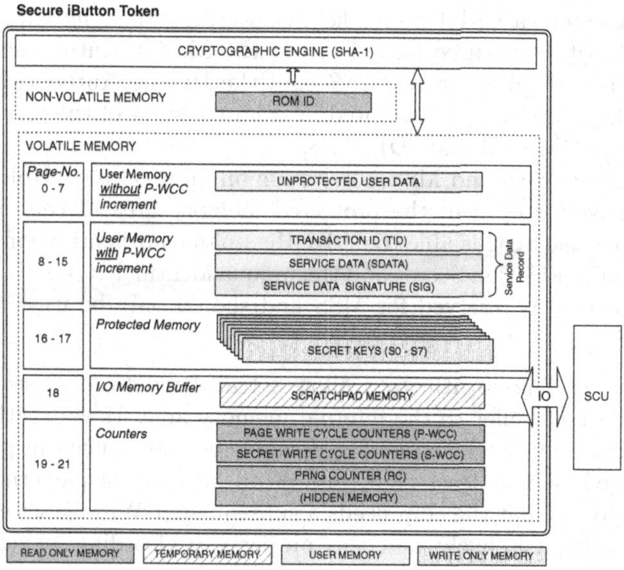

Secure iButton Token

Fig. 3. Secure iButton memory layout

The memory is segmented as follows: Pages 0 to 15 is the user data memory. The user memory of an iButton is neither read nor write protected. The memory pages 16 and 17, which store the secrets, are read protected and memory page 19 to page 21 are write protected.

In particular, this memory serves as storage for the Service Data Record (SDR), which consists of the Service Data $SDATA$ (e.g., the e-Cash balance), the Service Data Signature SIG and the transaction identifier TID.

All iButton devices contain a 64-bit unique number ROM-ID for identification. This number is enrolled and fixed permanently within the manufacturing process (factory laser-burned)[4]. It cannot be easily re-programmed or altered without physical reversing and reconstruction of burned bit lanes of the memory (e.g., with physical attacks).

Eight read-only 32-bit Page Write Cycle Counters (P-WCC) and eight 32-bit Secret Write Cycle Counter (S-WCC) are used for integrity protection. These counter are incremented with each write access to the service data (Page 8-15), and the secret keys, respectively. The counters cannot be changed from outside. It is used for detection of write processes and integrity violations of the service data.

Protected Memory and Secret Keys. The Secret Keys $S0$ to $S7$ resides in the protected memory area of an iButton device. Each protected memory

---

[4] Appendix E shows the silicon layer and the content of the reverse-engineered ROM-ID and gives information about the memory structure.

area is able to store a 64-bit secret key. Concerning their intended use, these secrets are classified in three logical types: the Master Authentication Secret MAS, the Master Signing Secret MSS, and the Unique Authentication Secret UAS. These keys are MACs, generated by a host system of the service provider by UAS = SHA-1(MAS||ROM-ID), cf. [8].

Note, that the MAS and MSS only reside on all service control units, while UAS is exclusively stored in the protected memory area of the unique client token. However, the SCU is able to derive the unique authentication secret from the Master Authentication Secret and the unique identifier ROM-ID of the iButton client. Secret 0 is reserved for MSS and should only be used by a master signing secret.

Memory Copying Process. iButtons allow a transfer data, e.g., secret keys $S0$ to $S7$ from the I/O buffer to the internal memory area. How exactly the copying process internally works is neither documented nor known in public. However, it is noted that at least eight bits of an alternating pattern need to be read. The reason is that the chip needs a subsequent 1-Wire Reset command to respond correctly. It is likely that this property is also directly related to the copying process. In general, to start a memory copy process, a combination of the WriteScratchpad, the ReadScratchpad, and the CopyScratchpad functions are used [26].

The WriteScratchpad command writes an authorization data, which consists of two bytes address register and the payload data (TA1, TA2, Data). The ReadScratchpad command reads an authorization data, which consists of three bytes of the address registers (TA1, TA2, E/S), respectively. Afterward a CopyScratchpad command is performed. When this process has been done correctly with no transmission errors, the authorization accepted flag is set and the copy process starts. During the copying process, the master reads continuously binary values 1_2 (base-2 binary notation), after completion of copying an alternating 10_2 pattern. According to the datasheet the copying process does not take longer than 30 μs.

Atomicity of Protected Memory Access. The cryptographic engine and the SRAM memory are powered by an internal lithium cell. This construction has the advantage, that functions are still working correctly, even if the token is removed from the contact point or the external power supply collapses.

With the internal battery, the atomicity is guaranteed and security critical functions, like memory transactions are processed safely. This has two reasons. First, once executed, a memory copying process from the scratchpad the protected memory areas are carried out completely in a single step. If the CopyScratchpad function is used to overwrite an existing secret key with a new secret from the I/O memory buffer, the target memory page will be overwritten at once. Secondly, specifying a target memory address that only contains a part of the 64-bit secrets, will lead to a full copying process of the complete secret. These two properties should guarantee that it is not possible to overwrite only a smaller part of protected memory.

3   Adversary Model and Attack Goal

The main attack objective is to exploit the iButton security architecture in order to get full access to the secret keys $S0$ to $S7$. In particular, the attack is able to extract a Unique Authentication Secret (UAS) on a user token, as well as a Master Authentication Secret (MAS) or Master Signing Secret (MSS) stored in a SCU coprocessor token. Having access to these secrets, the integrity of arbitrary service data and authentication are compromised.

We emphasize, that the attack does not target the cryptographic SHA-1 engine, and the cryptographic algorithm itself is not affected. Our method targets to attack the memory copying process from the scratchpad to the protected memory area where the secret keys are stored. It aims on interrupting the atomic copy process when writing new secret keys to that protected area. More precisely, we inject faults at certain time instances of the memory copying process that destruct the atomicity of the copying process. As a result, we achieve that copying is aborted, and thus the secret keys are not completely overwritten. Finally, with the gathered results from a small set of faulty MAC operations, we are able to reconstruct the complete original secrets.

Since, additional security properties, like the Write Cycle Counter or the physical ROM-ID, are hard to tamper a subordinate goal is to build an iButton emulator using the extracted secret keys, which allows impersonation and cloning.

4   Security Analysis of Secure iButtons

We break the cryptographic implementation by a differential fault attack where an adversary tamper security sensitive operations. For this, we firstly need unconditional access to the internal circuit without any information loss of the internal volatile memory. Hence, the attack must circumvent the tamper protection mechanisms. Secondly, we need to perform a differential fault attack on the authentication process to produce partially overwritten secrets. The following section gives a detailed description of the attack phases.

4.1   Tamper Protection Mechanisms

One major security feature of iButtons is its tamper protection. Opening the iButton typically results in a complete loss of all data of the whole SRAM memory, including the secret keys.

We have anatomized multiple iButtons. For this purpose, we have opened the devices with different approaches, in order to completely extract all components of a token. Figure 4 shows an exploded view of the individual pieces.

The iButton have an outer shell (Fig. 4a-C) and an inner cup (Fig. 4a-A) dividing the internal components of an iButton token on two major groups of parts. The first group consists of the leaf springs or microswitches (Fig. 4a-E) and (Fig. 4a-G), the lithium cell (Fig. 4a-F) and a plastic bracket (Fig. 4a-B),

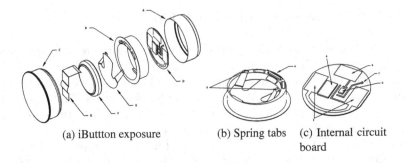

(a) iButtton exposure   (b) Spring tabs   (c) Internal circuit
                                                      board

Fig. 4. iButton hardware architecture

which fixes the lithium cell. The second module is assembled on a printed circuit board with distinct contact surfaces (Fig. 4a-D).

Figure 4b shows the same structure from the top side. The contact points (Fig. 4b-A) and (Fig. 4b-B) are both spring tabs, sticking out of the holder and press the corresponding contact pads on the board. Thus, this produces a reliable electrical connection. Figure 4c shows the printed circuit board of the token. The tab of the spring connects the contact area to ground (GND) (Fig. 4a-B). While pressing the two lugs of the leaf spring on VBAT, the two lugs are connected by a conductor track pad (Fig. 4a-E). The board is placed loosely in the inner cup of the iButton can and is only fixed by the three spring tabs under contact pressure. On the board are two integrated circuits (Fig. 4c-A) and (Fig. 4c-D) connected via bonding wires with the surrounding conductors protected by an epoxy shield. The three pads (Fig. 4c-B) and (Fig. 4c-E) are fully exposed. The 1-wire data line is passed through a via (Fig. 4c-C) on the opposite side. A data loss is reasoned by a disconnection of the spring contacts that are ejected in an attempt to open the iButton.

4.2   Breaking the Tamper Protection

Now we show that it is possible to decapsulate the device and to circumvent the protection mechanisms. For this we have investigated several methods to bypass the tamper protection, like physical extraction with exploiting data remanence properties of low-temperature cooled iButtons, etc. Our preferred method aims the separation of the internal circuit board from the internal lithium cell and the connection to an external voltage source. As a result, we have complete control over the internal chip, which enables escalated implementation attacks. It is a five-step process, which has strictly to be done without any power loss of the internal chip and SRAM during this separation:

Step 1 - Removal of the Cover Plate. At the beginning of the extraction process, the cover plate has to be removed. Thus, the token is mounted on the placement apparatus, directed with the data area of contact to the top, cf. Fig. 11 in Appendix C. We use an end mill cutter to drill a small hole into the top (Fig. 5a).

Fig. 5. Secure iButton exposed

The cutter is lowered slowly. Thereunder, the circuit board becomes visible. The red arrow in Fig. 5a on the left points on this marker. Next, a part of the top cover is removed with a cone mill. The radius is selected in such a way, that an outer rim still remains, which covers the circuit board in the edge region. This ring is necessary in order to keep the board in place without a connection loss to the internal power supply. The copper-coated underside of the board becomes visible on the inner side (Fig. 5b).

Step 2 - Milling of the Circuit Board. The visible underside of the circuit board is part of the data signal line, which is directly contacted with the top cover to the iButton outer shell for 1-wire communication (Fig. 4a-A). In this step, we carefully remove the copper layer of the outer/visible side of the circuit board by grinding. Despite the thinness of the board, this process leads to only a negligible loss of stability. The removal of the copper layer has the result that the plate of the circuit board becomes transparent and the circuit board traces and semiconductors are visible (Fig. 5c).

Step 3 - Perforation of the Circuit Board. After this step, the positions of the traces are directly visible. Thus, it is possible to perform a targeted drilling to get access to the inner circuit. Because of a high risk of shortcuts and instability of the circuit board this drilling is not anywhere safely possible. We have chosen an approach that mills directly into the Vcc data pad and beside the GND pad area. The two arrows in Fig. 5c point to these drill holes.

Step 4 - Providing an External Backup Battery. Next, we attach an external backup power supply to the internal circuit. This process requires to solder two wires through the relatively small openings onto the inner Pads of the board. Figure 5d shows the connected wires. The voltage of the lithium cell can now be measured at the end of the wires. After attaching an external source for the internal power supply to the wires, we are able to extract the inner circuit board from the internal battery without any data loss.

Step 5 - Extraction of the Chip. In a final step, the inner circuit board is extracted from the iButton body. After the overlaying rim has been removed, the board is now completely separated without an interruption of the internal power supply.

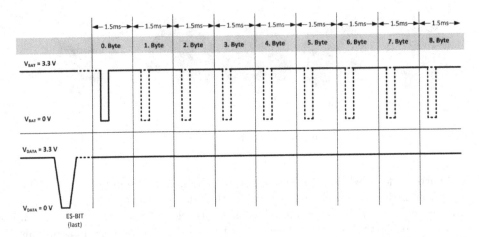

Fig. 6. Fault injection timing procedure

4.3 Differential Fault Attack

After preparation, we are at the point at which the actual fault attacks on the internal secret keys begin. The attack consists of two phases. In the first phase, a series of faults are injected for each SHA-1 MAC computation. During this phase, we obtain information, which are finally evaluated in the second phase. At the end of this evaluation, all secrets $S0 - S7$ are known.

Fault Injection on SHA-1 MAC Computation. The differential fault attack targets the implementation of the cryptographic SHA-1 MAC operation. As a reminder, even if the memory of an iButton is read protected, it allows writing arbitrary data to that memory area and perform a regular MAC computation. Our goal is to perform a set of MAC operations with *partially known secret keys*. We generate these partially known secrets by interrupting the atomic copy of a new (known) secret from the scratchpad to the protected memory area, where the (unknown) secret value resides. Therefore, we inject faults by a power-glitching and controlled disturbance of the power voltage supply. In principle, from a technical point of view, the fault injection works as follows: we have three connections: GND, a 1-Wire data line and the internal connector of the lithium cell. The core of the glitching-attack is to switch the input source of the lithium cell from 3 V to 0 V level. We wait a certain time interval and then pull up the power level back to 3 V. Figure 6 illustrates this fault injection timing procedure.

Since the copy process happens in a period of a few μs, and this process must be interrupted deliberately, a precise timing is necessary. In order to meet this requirement, a micro-controller with 16 MHz clock frequency is used. It acts as both, a bus master as well as a controller of the connected backup lithium cell that glitches the internal power supply of the iButton chip. The voltage of the entire system is selected to 3.3 V, so that it corresponds approximately to the voltage of the internal lithium cell.

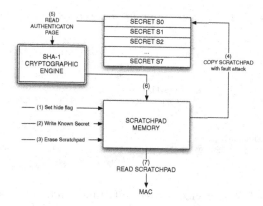

Fig. 7. Fault attack procedure - method 1 (basic attack)

Description of the Attack Procedure. Figure 7 illustrates the process of the basic attack procedure. In order to perform a partial write operation, a known first secret is written in the scratchpad. The procedure begins with the `EraseScratchpad` command. It is used to clear the Hide flag and set the scratchpad to be accessible from the outside (Step 1).

Manual Hide Flagging. An explicit command for setting the Hide flag does not exist. The only known regular method is to remove and reconnect the iButton from the interface. Since this method is neither comfortable, fast, nor error resistant, we prefer another solution. Namely, we also can stimulate the reconnect by a little trick. Since we have full control over the internal power supply, from Sect. 4.2, we are able to lower the internal power supply for about 5 ms to 0 V. This also led to manually setting the Hide flag. As a results, we gain access to the protected memory.

With the `WriteScratchpad` command, we set the known secret key (64-bit zero vector) and write that 64-bit value into the scratchpad buffer (Step 2). Optionally, the `ReadScratchpad` command could be used to verify that the data was written correctly to the scratchpad. Now, we have to set the Hide flag (Step 3) which restricts the write access to the scratchpad buffer.

Copy Scratchpad with Triggered Fault Attack. We pass the target address of the specific protect memory areas, holding the unknown secret key. In this step, finally, we perform the copy function and transmit the previously read three bytes TA1, TA2, E/S, but with one exception: the last bit of the byte E/S is not transmitted immediately. This is important, because the preparation is almost finished, however, the token remains in a trigger-able state. It is crucial that the last bit of the E/S address register value is not transferred. This bit is transmitted by a separate function. With the rising edge of this bit of the copy operation is initiated (Step 4). Therefore, we transfer the last bit manually. After a predetermined time, the internal power supply for a period of 1 ms is lowered to 0 V and the copy process is canceled. When the internal supply voltage is restored,

Table 1. Fault propagation for a a secret key (example)

Partial Secret	Protected Memory	Message Authentication Code	Fault Position
XXXXXXXXXXXXXXXX	F6464F60FAFD145E	D2B1CBD3E23018E3B62531BE26977B6DFE9FDD6D	--
00XXXXXXXXXXXXXX	00464F60FAFD145E	FAD034522EBA8DD39CA375B25B8528E6A5AFC4E8	1. byte
0000XXXXXXXXXXXX	00004F60FAFD145E	C326B7E383910C8358587565DBEC3089894D7EC1	2. byte
000000XXXXXXXXXX	00000060FAFD145E	8B7857FECCCB341BD02BCE873331D7C4C7E4DE94	3. byte
00000000XXXXXXXX	00000000FAFD145E	7A69F499F70FAF800DC2EBCB5551E4D7ECF20A33	4. byte
0000000000XXXXXX	0000000000FD145E	D6415345516D59EC09832921E302BD59BF32E217	5. byte
000000000000XXXX	000000000000145E	4DA1D04EE1C35AF9421EBDCF0954DFB2EB92C64A	6. byte
00000000000000XX	0000000000000005E	16BD50B5B80F66151D240BE7D5B3383D2D3183C8	7. byte
0000000000000000	0000000000000000	0E402A5305246851B055BBDC81D3AA2863AAE859	8. byte

a reset is performed. The device is then fully functional and is able to calculate operations based on the (possibly partially modified) secret key bytes in the protected memory area. We compute a MAC by the `ReadAuthenticatedPage` command (Step 5). The command writes the results into the scratchpad memory (Step 6). Finally, we read out the MAC and store the value for further evaluation (Step 7).

Fault Injection Process and Fault Propagation. At the beginning of the fault propagation process on the secret keys, we initiate a copying process and immediately perform a power-glitch on the circuit directly after 0 ms delay. It is clear that no bytes have been overwritten. We compute a MAC, which is based on the completely unknown secret. In the second iteration, we wait a little longer until we inject a power-glitch and re-calculate a MAC again. Probably, after a few iterations, we overwrite the first byte of the secret key, cf. Figure 6.

It takes a few iterations to overwrite the second byte, and so on, until the last byte of the secret key byte is set. To gain meaningful information from such an attack, a MAC is calculated between each fault injection. Some of the iterations might compute the same MAC. Nevertheless, this attack design makes the procedure more robust. Using predetermined timings might result in a higher error rate, since temperature changes and manufacturing variations might alter the timing properties. Finally, the above procedure is applied for all eight secret keys $S0 - S7$. The computation of the MAC operation is enforced, and all computed data resulting of these operations are stored. With the information obtained from the fault attack, we are now able to determine the unknown original secrets with minimal computational effort. After filtering, we obtain a list of secret entries with exactly nine different MACs (see Table 1).

Table 1 gives an example for a successful fault propagation for all eight secret key bytes. This example shows the fault propagation, the register values in the protected memory area (partially overwritten secret key), and the corresponding MAC operation for all eight secret key bytes and a pristine computation using the original secret key (target).

Reconstruction for all eight Secret Keys. The original unknown secret key is calculated by reverse and stepwise-testing of all MAC candidates for each faulty entry. For each entry, we compute the corresponding MACs for all possible 2^8 secret key bytes and compare the results with the stored MAC values gathered from the previous attack round. A matching pair indicates that a correct secret key byte is found. This process is repeated until the complete secret key is extracted. Appendix B shows an example for all extracted secrets $S0 - S7$.

Optimized Attack with Automatically Generated Secrets. Due to an attack or other processing it might happen that one or few bits of the memory changes unintentionally. Now we present an alternative method which allows an attack even when such a bit flip or even a deletion of the memory has occurred. This procedure has the benefit, that it works with a defective iButton, which has been reinitialized after a complete power loss for a longer period. The method does not aim at the fault attack directly, but it optimizes the preparation phase of our attack. Moreover, the method does not need to set the Hide flag manually, which makes this method much more performant and robust. As detailed in Sect. 4.3, the basic method uses partially known secrets (64-bit zero vector). However, that basic method has some drawbacks due to manual hide flagging. The more the chip is cooled, the better the data remanence. But on the other hand, the difficulty increases to set the Hide flag. Moreover, a manual hide flagging costs most of the attack time.

Our advanced method is based on automated generated secrets. The cryptographic engine calculates those secrets itself. The initialization values are based on seeds. Actually, this functionality is envisaged for usage for distributed key generation. The manufacturer calls this special type of cryptographic keys *partial secrets*. It is quite adjuvant for an attacker that this function also sets the Hide flag and optimize the attack performance drastically. The complete fault attack needs only one second per unknown secret, that is about eight seconds for all eight secret keys.

As a precondition, no computations based on the ROM-ID have to be performed on the iButton token. This, for example, excludes a call of the

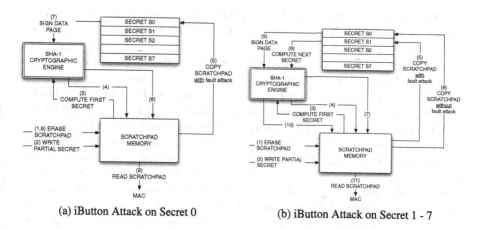

(a) iButton Attack on Secret 0   (b) iButton Attack on Secret 1 - 7

Fig. 8. iButton fault attack procedure - method 2 (optimized attack)

ReadAuthenticatedPage command. However, there is an alternative low level function, namely SignDataPage. This is the only function that calculates a readable MAC without using the ROM-ID. The SignDataPage function computes the signature and sends the result to the scratchpad.

Because this feature is designed for signing purposes with the MSS, it works exclusively on secret $S0$. Therefore, only the first of the eight secret keys is extractable with this method. See Fig. 8a for the attack procedure. We use another trick to attack the other seven secret keys. After each attack cycle, we generate a new secret using the ComputeNextSecret command. This new secret key is based on the target secret. ComputeNextSecret also does not affect the memory. The key is written to the scratchpad, from where we are able to copy it to the memory region of any other secret.

Next we copy this secret key to the storage area of secret $S0$ (which already has been previously extracted successfully). Since it is now placed in the memory region of secret $S0$, we can perform a signing procedure with the method described above. However the operation is based on the target secrets $S1 - S7$. Since it is a concatenation of several SHA-1 functions, we have generated a data path. The concept is based on the principle of a modified rainbow table attack. Figure 8b illustrates the required steps for an attack on secrets $S1 - S7$. As a consequence, the secret key computation must also recalculate this path. The time required for the resolution of all secret keys is still negligible.

5   iButton Emulator for Security Evaluation

Since the ROM-ID is unique, and the Write Cycle Counter is not resettable by our attack, we can not use this token for mounting a replay attack anymore. Both, the ROM-ID and WCCs are relevant in all SHA-1 operations used by an authentication protocol. The counter is automatically incremented by the device, and therefore, is detectable by the authentication protocol.

FPGA-based iButton Emulator. We decided to realize a dedicated FPGA-based iButton emulator. With this approach, we have all the freedom, e.g., to set ROM-ID arbitrarily and the Write Cycle Counter can be modified easily. The protocol sequence has some points that make a software emulation (using a micro-controller) extremely difficult. The whole process needs to happen very quickly, only the small temporal gaps between two-bit I/Os are available for software emulation. The problem drastically increases when the system uses the so-called 'overdrive mode'. Here, the timings are at least 10-times faster.

It is based only on the data sheet and not on any evidence or data that have been obtained from the reverse engineering. The emulator is designed in a way, that has an optimal performance while not need a large and expensive FPGA.

Our implementation provides some additional features: We added special functionality of specific 1-Wire commands that are neither in the original design nor in another one-wire chip. The first feature is that the read memory command allows to read the protected memory areas and does not lead to 0xFF as expected for origin iButton. Second, we added two new functions to the iButton

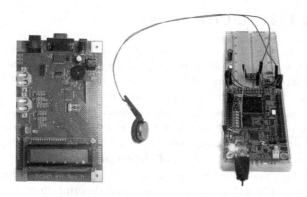

Fig. 9. Maxim DSECASH reference architecture and FPGA iButton emulator

implementation, namely the *Write Memory* and *Write ROM* command. The Write Memory feature gives unrestricted and random byte-write access to the entire SRAM of the emulator, while the Write ROM command allows changing the ROM-ID.

DSECASH Micropayment Reference Architecture. The FPGA-based attack platform is shown in Fig. 9. It was tested on Maxims DSECASH eCash evaluation system [18]. The evaluation kit consists of an eCash evaluation board, a 1-Wire bus master for the PC, some iButtons and various accessories. The eCash Board is a fully functional payment system and proposed as a reference architecture for micropayment applications by the manufacturer. We emphasize, that the iButton emulator works perfectly with the original, absolutely unchanged DSECASH reference design. Assuming that micropayment systems, such as the Akbil metropolitan transportation system [19] or ticketing machines [2], have a similar architecture, our attack should be easily adaptable to the specific application settings.

6   Conclusion

The security analysis presented in this paper clearly show the vulnerability of the Secure iButton DS1963S model. We presented a differential fault attack on the SHA-1-enabled iButton, including the circumvention of the tamper protection mechanisms. We were able to break the most important requirement of iButtons, namely to guarantee integrity and confidentiality of the secrets UAS, MSS and MAS. Our methods allow a key extraction and an infinite rollback to the initial state. We demonstrated the feasibility of the attack on a micropayment reference system. The corresponding research is transferable to other real-world products and give essential feedback to the manufacturers and security researchers by pinpointing on critical security weaknesses and vulnerabilities. Our proposed methods are not restricted to iButtons and can also be applied to other similar embedded devices.

A   Attack Related Commands

For our attack, we need a set of relevant 1-wire low-level commands. Those commands are Read Scratchpad, Write Scratpad, Copy Scratchpad, Erase Scratchpad, Read Authenticated Page, Compute First Secret and Compute Next Secret.

Furthermore, the cryptographic engine has seven SHA-1 command functions, namely the Compute First Secret, Compute Next Secret command for generation of new secrets, SignDataPage for signing and Validate Dat aPagefor HMAC verification. Furthermore, the engine offers a set of function to perform random generator operations and generation of challenges. Finally, the command Read Authenticated Page combines a read operation with a CRC and generation of the corresponding HMAC result. For a detailed description of the commands, we refer the interested reader to the iButton standard [8] and [26].

B   Resolved Secrets S0-S7 (Example)

The following table give an example for resolved secret $S0$ - $S7$ (Fig. 10).

```
$ time ./fa_resolve_key attack.log

SECRET 0: F6464F60FAFD145E  [1108]  (VALID)
SECRET 1: ACDDAF04A550363A  [ 929]  (VALID)
SECRET 2: 79C0ED28C4053F46  [ 924]  (VALID)
SECRET 3: 568CCD45CE6CB6F3  [1239]  (VALID)
SECRET 4: B5EDF140D8938E9F  [1387]  (VALID)
SECRET 5: DE7C444EEDBE6B52  [1108]  (VALID)
SECRET 6: AB99710A33BFE5FF  [1173]  (VALID)
SECRET 7: CF26940A68C6F52E  [ 996]  (VALID)

DONE

real    0m0.015s
user    0m0.016s
sys     0m0.000s
```

Fig. 10. Resolved secrets S0-S7 from an iButton DS1963S device

C   Tamper Protection Milling Aparatus with iButton

Fig. 11. Milling apparatus with iButton

D   Akbil Micropayment System for Electronic Ticketing

The Akbil system [29] is an integrated micropayment for electronic tickets used for fare payment in public transport of Istanbul, Turkey. The system is currently being phased out, but still in use. Figure 12 shows a SCU access control gate to the metropolitan transportation system.

Fig. 12. Akbil SCU access control gate (left) and Ticketing Machine (right)

E   ROM-ID Reverse Engineering

The figure shows the reverse engineered ROM-ID of a Secure iButton. The ROM-ID layout is reconstructed by the following drawing. Purple spots indicate a laser burned bit lane, representing a set bit value.

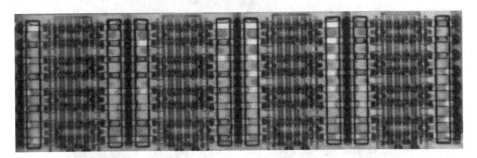

References

1. Aci touchaccess - an intelligent lock. http://acisecurity.com/product_sheets/touchaccess.pdf (Product information) Accessed 28 October 2012
2. Almex ticketing station. http://www.hoeft-wessel.com/uploads/media/almex-station-e_01.pdf (Product information) Accessed 28 October 2012
3. Corby 4300 sa datachip. http://www.corby.com/Sub_Products/product.php?wbprodpage_id=4300 (Product information) Accessed 28 October 2012
4. Cs ikey. http://www.cstech.biz/product_brochure/Brochure%20-%20iKey.pdf (Product information) Accessed 28 October 2012
5. Ds1904 rtc ibutton. http://www.maximintegrated.com/datasheet/index.mvp/id/2817/t/al (Datasheet) Accessed 28 October 2012
6. Ds1923 hygrochron temperature/humidity logger ibutton with 8kb datalog memory. http://www.maximintegrated.com/datasheet/index.mvp/id/4379/t/al (Datasheet) Accessed 28 October 2012
7. Ds1961s 1kb protected eeprom ibutton with sha-1 engine. http://www.maximintegrated.com/datasheet/index.mvp/id/3557 (Datasheet) Accessed 28 October 2012
8. Ds1963s sha ibutton. http://www.maximintegrated.com/datasheet/index.mvp/id/2822/t/al (Datasheet) Accessed 28 October 2012
9. Ds1977 password-protected 32kb eeprom ibutton. http://www.maximintegrated.com/datasheet/index.mvp/id/3951/t/al (Datasheet) Accessed 28 October 2012
10. Ds2432 1kb protected 1-wire eeprom with sha-1 engine. http://www.maximintegrated.com/datasheet/index.mvp/id/2914/t/al (Datasheet) Accessed 28 October 2012
11. Ebn pos systems. http://www.ebn-pos.com/products/all-in-one-pos-terminal.php Accessed 29 October 2012
12. Imagecast precinct voting machine. http://www.dominionvoting.com/products Accessed 29 October 2012
13. Overview of 1-wire technology and its use. http://pdfserv.maximintegrated.com/en/an/AN1796.pdf (Tutorial 1796) Accessed 28 October 2012

14. Schlage mr-1967 electronic interconnected lockset. http://consumer.schlage.com/
    Service-Support/Documents/MR-1967_Electrtonic_Interconnected_Lockset.pdf
    (Product information) Accessed 28 October 2012

15. Super micro computer, ibutton aoc-ibutton68. http://www.supermicro.nl/
    products/accessories/addon/aoc-ibutton68.cfm (Product information) Accessed
    28 October 2012

16. Super micro computer, raid controller. http://www.supermicro.nl/products/
    accessories/addon/AOC-USAS-H4iR.cfm (Product information) Accessed 28
    October 2012

17. Vectron pos colortouch. http://www.vectron.de/products/poscolortouch/index.
    php?l=en Accessed 29 October 2012

18. Dsecash ecash evaluation kit. http://datasheets.maximintegrated.com/en/ds/
    DSECASH.pdf (2002) (Datasheet) Accessed 28 October 2012

19. Belim leading technology. http://www.belbim.com.tr/en/Pages/Homepage.aspx
    (2010) Accessed 28 October 2012

20. Courtois, N., O'Neil, S., Quisquater, J.J.. In: Samarati, P., Yung, M., Martinelli,
    F., Ardagna, C.A. (eds.) ISC, pp. 167–176

21. Eisenbarth, T., Kasper, T., Moradi, A., Paar, C., Salmasizadeh, M., Shalmani,
    M.T.M.: On the power of power analysis in the real world: a complete break of
    the Keeloq code hopping scheme. In: Wagner, D. (ed.) CRYPTO 2008. LNCS, vol.
    5157, pp. 203–220. Springer, Heidelberg (2008)

22. Garcia, F.D., Gans, G.D.K., Muijrers, R., Rossum, P.V., Verdult, R., Schreur,
    R.W., Jacobs, B.: Dismantling mifare classic

23. Garcia, F.D., de Koning Gans, G., Verdult, R.: Exposing iclass key diversification.
    In: Brumley, D., Zalewski, M. (eds.) WOOT, pp. 128–136. USENIX Association.
    http://dblp.uni-trier.de/db/conf/uss/woot201

24. Garcia, F.D., van Rossum, P., Verdult, R., Wichers Schreur, R.: Dismantling
    securememory, cryptomemory and cryptorf. In: Proceedings of the 17th ACM Con-
    ference on Computer and Communications Security, CCS '10, pp. 250–259. ACM,
    New York (2010). http://doi.acm.org/10.1145/1866307.1866336

25. Indesteege, S., Keller, N., Dunkelman, O., Biham, E., Preneel, B.: A practical
    attack on KeeLoq. In: Smart, N.P. (ed.) EUROCRYPT 2008. LNCS, vol. 4965, pp.
    1–18. Springer, Heidelberg (2008)

26. Linke, B.: Book of ibutton(r) standards. http://pdfserv.maximintegrated.com/en/
    an/AN937.pdf (2002) (Application Note 937) Accessed 28 October 2012

27. Nohl, K., Evans, D., Starbug, S., Plötz, H.: Reverse-engineering a cryptographic
    rfid tag. In: Proceedings of the 17th Conference on Security Symposium, SS'08,
    pp. 185–193. USENIX Association, Berkeley (2008). http://dl.acm.org/citation.
    cfm?id=1496711.1496724

28. Verdult, R., Garcia, F.D., Balasch, J.: Gone in 360 seconds: Hijacking with hitag2.
    In: USENIX Security Symposium, pp. 237–252. USENIX Association, August 2012

29. Wikipedia: Akbil (smart ticket). http://en.wikipedia.org/wiki/Akbil_(smart_
    ticket) (2013) accessed 01 July 2013

Intrusion Detection

Discovering Flaws in IDS Through Analysis of Their Inputs

Raphaël Jamet[(✉)] and Pascal Lafourcade

Verimag, CNRS, Université Grenoble 1, Gières, France
jamet.raphael@gmail.com

Abstract. To secure Wireless Ad-hoc Networks (WANET) against malicious behaviors, three components are needed: prevention, detection, and response. In this paper, we focus on Intrusion Detection Systems (IDS) for WANET. We classify the different inputs used by the decision process of these IDS, according to their level of cooperation, and the source of their data. We then propose a decision aid which allows automated discovery of attacks for IDS, according to the inputs used. Finally we apply our framework to discover weaknesses in two existing IDS.

Keywords: Wireless ad-hoc networks · Formal methods · Intrusion detection systems · Security

1 Introduction

Wireless Ad-hoc Networks (WANET) are networks built from several devices, which use multi-hops radio communications to form a mesh network. For instance, such networks can be used to provide low-cost internet in developing countries [1], or to spread messages and make calls in a smartphone-equipped group of people when the infrastructure is unavailable [14]. Wireless Sensor Networks (WSN) are a subset of these networks. They are built from a large quantity of inexpensive motes, which have little computing power and wireless communication abilities, in order to generate data covering a large area. These motes form an ad-hoc network, usually centered around a base station, also called a *sink*.

Due to their intrinsic properties and their applications, these networks are vulnerable to attackers. In order to guarantee the security of ad-hoc wireless networks, several complementary layers of protection are needed. First, *intrusion prevention methods* strive towards blocking eventual attacks. Since these systems are seldom infallible, *intrusion detection* should also be used, to ensure that an attacker bypassing the prevention layer will be noticed. The last level is the *intrusion response system*, whose goal is to mitigate the effect that detected attackers have on the network.

By consequence, intrusion detection systems (IDS) are critical for the security of WANET. Network-based IDS are often evaluated against a few attack scenarios based on specific intruder node behavior. We argue that such an analysis can

J.-L. Danger et al. (Eds.): FPS 2013, LNCS 8352, pp. 391–407, 2014.
DOI: 10.1007/978-3-319-05302-8_24, © Springer International Publishing Switzerland 2014

be dangerous, as they do not specify how the intruder node became part of the network, what is the attacker achieving with that attack, nor what exactly the IDS is trying to prevent. This lack of precision can lead to undiscovered flaws in the network. It is therefore important to formulate the properties that they try to achieve in a clear way, to define the intruder model, to model the protocols and to state the network assumptions, in a formal framework. Then, we can use formal methods, in order to systematically find the flaws in an IDS. A similar process has been done in the last years in cryptographic protocol analysis [3], and our goal is to provide the first components to enable the use of such methods in the context of IDS.

Contributions: Our contribution is threefold: (i) We survey different inputs that an IDS decision process can use. We base our analysis on two axis: the degree of cooperation, and what is being monitored. We also give examples of mechanisms from existing IDS to illustrate our classification. (ii) We develop a formal model to evaluate such systems, based on *anomalies*, which are the results of attacker behavior. We propose some deduction rules (around 40) expressing how the combination of certain anomalies allows an attacker to build more complex attacks. These rules model the logical steps needed for constructing a specific attack. Then, depending on inputs used by an IDS, we determine whether an attacker can mount an attack without being detected. We also provide a prototype of our formal framework. (iii) Using that prototype, we analyze two IDS from the literature, [9, 21]. We show that it is not possible to fool the first IDS in presence of restricted intruders. However, by relaxing some of the hypothesis, we discover some weaknesses in the IDS. For the second IDS, we found undetected attacks using intruder nodes with directional antennas. Finally, we propose some modifications for these IDS in order to prevent these attacks. Overall, using our approach, it is easy to compare the inputs of an IDS to others from the literature, and to find its flaws and possible improvements.

Related work: Intrusion detection systems are usually classified with two main characteristics, which evolved from the seminal work in [10]. The first characteristic expresses what is being observed, and contains two categories: *host-based IDS* monitor their node only, while *network-based IDS* search for signs of malicious activity in the network. The second characteristic is based on the method used to detect intrusions. We do not consider this second aspect. Our classification can be seen as a refinement of the first category. Instead of having two broad categories, we separate the different inputs that an IDS uses and we determine the cooperation level and the sources of the data being monitored.

In [16], the authors provide a specification-based IDS for the AODV routing protocol, based on an extended finite state automaton for modeling the protocol. In their paper, attacks cause various *anomalous basic events*, which are defined as the segments of a routing process that do not follow the routing specification. These events are then classified in two categories: those that can be detected directly, and those that require statistical analysis. They also give a correspondence between some classical attacker models and the related anomalous basic events. Finally, they propose an IDS which is built to detect all of the anomalous basic events they identified. Our work is different from theirs in two ways. First of all, instead of building an IDS specifically for AODV, we focus on the evaluation of any IDS for a wireless ad-hoc network. To achieve this, we built a model which is not protocol dependent and adjustable depending on the assumptions. The second important difference is our concept of anomaly. It is based on their anomalous events, but instead of isolating them, we add a model of their dependencies. This allows us to describe attacks taking into account the whole process, instead of just taking the end results of the attack into account.

Outline: In Sect. 2, we provide our classification of IDS inputs and illustrate it through examples. In Sect. 3, we formally define our model, which we apply on two existing IDS using our prototype in Sect. 4.

2 Decision Process Inputs

IDS build their decision process over a multitude of *inputs* that we classify along two axis. The first one is made of three categories, that express the level of cooperation needed to use an input:

a. **Local** inputs are accessible by a node, without help from their neighbors.
b. Inputs requiring **k-neighborhood-wide cooperation**.
c. Inputs requiring **global cooperation**.

The other axis corresponds to how the IDS collect their inputs. We identified five categories. The first category is independent on the network, then the next categories depend on the protocols.

1. **Offline** inputs, which can be created even if the node is not part of a network.
2. **Topological** inputs, related to the positions of the nodes.
3. **Radio** inputs, linked to the medium access control protocol.
4. **Routing** inputs, related to the routing protocol directly or indirectly.
5. Inputs extracted from the application **data**, as opposed to all the previous categories which analyze how the nodes and the network behave.

Using the second axis, we now describe and illustrate with references each of those inputs according the level of involvement or cooperation needed to use an input, followed by a summary of this classification.

2.1 Offline Inputs

Offline inputs do not depend on the network: the object of their monitoring is internal to a node.

(*a*) The first family of offline inputs we identified are **local**: host-based IDS (with for instance [30]). This family of IDS are looking for a partial compromise of the node running the detection, for instance through viruses or vulnerable applications. (*b*) To allow compromise detection by third-party nodes, we need **neighborhood cooperation**. In [31], the authors proposed a scheme where free memory in nodes is pre-loaded with random noise, the knowledge of which is shared among the node's neighbors. They make the hypothesis that a compromised node would have deleted some of that noise to include its rogue algorithms. Therefore, to detect whether a suspected node has been compromised, its neighbors can collaboratively query it to check the integrity of its random noise. (c) Finally, **global** offline inputs would examine something independent of the network on a network-wide scale, which would not add anything significantly more useful than local or neighborhood-scale analysis, which explains the absence of such systems in the literature.

2.2   Inputs Based on the Network Topology

This category contains mechanisms that use distances, or neighborhoods.

(a) First, this analysis can be **local** to a node. For instance, in the IDS described in [9], nodes have a list of verified neighbors, so that messages coming from unverified neighbors trigger alerts. In [11, 20, 21], nodes remember the strength of the signal received for the last transmissions from each neighbor. The signal strength is related to distance: if an intruder node impersonates some honest node, then the receiver may notice the change of received signal strength. In [24], instead of using previous measurements of signal strength to detect anomalies, the expected value is deduced from distance data.

(b) The IDS described in [25] requires **neighborhood-wide cooperation** to measure distances between nodes in a static network, which allows to detect unexpected changes in localization that are characteristic of a node being manipulated. A similar neighborhood-wide effort can identify Sybil intruders (single nodes that use multiple identities) through signal strength, as described in [11]. By computing the ratios of the signal strength of different nodes, the authors show that it is feasible to triangulate the position of other nodes, allowing detection of nodes that share the same exact position who may be Sybil intruders.

(c) Finally, such an analysis can be done from a **global** point of view. In [12], the authors argue that under some hypothesis on the underlying network, it is feasible to detect wormholes (two distant intruder nodes, linked with a special communication channel) using only topological data. In [7], the authors propose a mechanism to detect nodes sharing identities in the network. It is a global algorithm which reports a suspect node's identity and location to a specific third-party node, using the suspect identity. Then, if that third-party node receives several reports containing different locations for a single identity, an alert is raised.

2.3   Inputs from the Medium Access Control (MAC) Protocol

This category contains all the inputs which use data originating from the wireless transmission medium.

(a) This category is well-suited to **local** analysis, but increasing the cooperation will not significantly improve these techniques. By looking at indicators in the MAC such as collision rate or the number of retransmissions requests, a node may be able to tell if there are degradations of the radio medium, whether they are environmental or caused by an attacker. In all of [4,9,22,26], there is a part of the intrusion detection being done based on the collision rate. This mechanism is close to the definition of specification-based IDS, which detects whether a node respects the protocol they should run. Another approach based on the radio layer is to use characteristic features of the radio emitters to identify them. This technique is called *fingerprinting* [5,15], and would allow detection of some Sybil attackers and impersonation-based attacks.

2.4   Data Based on the Routing Layer and Traffic

This category is based on the analysis of the way messages are routed through the network. Some of the IDS mechanisms we present here are tied to a specific routing protocol, which allows them to monitor the protocol compliance of suspected nodes at the cost of genericity. On the other hand, some of them are built upon generic properties that are common to most routing protocols, such as immediate packet retransmission or each node using only one public identity.

(*a*) A **local** input common to several IDS is that the nodes monitor the variations in the volume of incoming traffic. Then, if there are significant differences when comparing to some reference measure, the node will raise an alert. We observe several variants such as separating traffic streams per message type [8], per neighbor [9], or depending on the messages source and destination [19]. Some IDS also monitor the intervals between reception of messages of different types [8]. Finally, instead of looking at the traffic flow, the authors of [4] suggest observing the data types which are expected on each route. Another category of local inputs require using promiscuous listening, so that a monitor node can observe its neighbor's behavior. By designing an IDS more specific to the routing protocol, it becomes possible to detect deviations from the routing protocol, using an analysis that can span from simple rules or features to a complete specification-based monitoring. Both [9] and [26] propose some IDS which uses promiscuous listening. The IDS in [27,29] monitor the routing process of neighboring nodes using finite state machines, respectively built for AODV[1] and OLSR[2]. Another specification-based IDS built on top of an extended finite state machine for AODV is described in [16]. These examples are still local to a node.

(*b*) By extending to a **neighborhood-wide** effort, specification-based IDS can be more efficient and accurate. For instance, in [28], the authors present DEMEM, a specification-based IDS with new messages overlayed on the routing protocol. These messages allow nodes to verify the claims of their neighbors, to detect more attacks on the routing protocol.

(*c*) Finally, the **global** scale inputs can be illustrated with Lipad [2]. This IDS does traffic analysis in a centralized way, which allows to locate precisely where the anomaly occurred.

---

[1] Advanced On-Demand Distance Vector, a routing protocol described in [23].
[2] Open Link-State Routing, another routing protocol [6].

2.5   Inputs Based on the Application Data

The last category concerns all the inputs which use the application data, and assumptions about it.

(a) A good illustration of **local** application data analysis can be found in [18]. This IDS is designed for general-purpose networks, and operates by statistical analysis of the application data being transmitted in the captured packets, with a different model for each application. (b) Using **neighborhood** collaboration, the authors of [13] present an IDS based on analyzing the data delivered to the application using hidden Markov models. Such a data analysis allows them to detect altered data, depending on what is being monitored. This example is on a global scale, but the idea of application data modeling can also be applied with a lower cooperation level. For instance, in a network monitoring earthquakes, neighborhood-scale cooperation makes sense to detect falsified data insertion. On the other hand, if the network measures are purely local (such as motion sensors in a building), global-scale analysis may not be useful. We only found [13] to illustrate such an analysis for WANET in the literature. We conjecture that this is because this technique is strongly tied to the application.

2.6   Summary

Our classification allows us to categorize the various inputs a network-based IDS uses in its decision process. In Fig. 1, we recapitulate our classification, and we provide a list of the different inputs we identified from existing IDS, plus the categories in which they belong. Note that the same IDS can use different inputs, and will therefore be in several different categories. We also include a few mechanisms built to detect specific intruders such as [7,11], as they are compatible with our definition of IDS input.

We denote by a 'X' the categories which do not bring any new significant information when compared to the lower cooperation levels. Since the MAC protocol is by essence local to a link, nodes have little interest in relying on the declarations of distant nodes to detect intruders. A similar situation appears for global offline inputs. We also denote with a '?' the categories of data analysis where we did not find any example, but we think this combination can be relevant to detect malicious nodes.

Data source	Offline	Topology	Radio	Routing	Data
Local	[31]	[9, 11, 21, 22, 25]	[4, 5, 9, 15, 23, 27]	[4, 8, 9, 16, 19] [27, 28, 30]	[18]
Neighborhood	[32]	[11, 26]	X	[29]	[13]
Global	X	[7, 12]	X	[2]	?

Fig. 1. Classification of IDS data sources

3   Automating Vulnerabilities Discovery

We now introduce our model that finds whether an attacker can reach a certain goal without its actions being noticed by an IDS. This is done through modelization of the different steps necessary to mount an attack. We call those steps *anomalies*. We model the IDS using the different inputs to its detection process, which gives us a set of anomalies that could cause detection of the attack. If an attacker can reach its target, without using any of the steps monitored by the IDS, then this attack will be undetected. We start by giving some definitions then we present different components of our model: facts, anomalies and our attack detection mechanism.

3.1   Definitions

An *identity* is the different items a node needs to join and operate legitimately in the network. For example, in a network where nodes only use their hardware identifier to identify themselves and where there are no other forms of security, the identity is composed of that identifier only (which is trivial to copy or create). Alternatively, the identity can be a combination of various things such as frequency hopping schedules, pre-shared cryptographic material, or a radio which has the right fingerprints.

An *associated* node is a node who is able to use an identity. If this node is an intruder node, the identity is said to be *compromised*. Finally, *valid* messages are messages whose data would be delivered to the application if they reach their destination. Moreover, the wireless network is composed of honest nodes. These nodes generate data messages, which are then routed to one or several destinations, in order to be delivered to the application. These nodes all possess an identity. Also, the attacker can deploy several *intruder nodes*, which are attacker-controlled nodes. These also have memory, computing power, and wireless communication capabilities using an omnidirectional antenna unless otherwise specified. To denote the logical transitions between the attack steps, we use inference rules and axioms.

Definition 1 (Axioms and Rules). *Given $T_1, \ldots, T_n$, a rule (R) concluding C is denoted by $(R)\dfrac{T_1 \quad \cdots \quad T_n}{C}$. An axiom is a rule without any conditions. Such an axiom named (A) concluding C is denoted by $(A)\dfrac{}{C}$.*

3.2   Facts and Relationships

We now describe formally our model, beginning with the notion of facts. A fact is an assumption about the network, the protocols used or the attacker.

Definition 2 (Facts). *Assumptions about the network, protocols and attackers are called facts. They are represented by keywords in italic. We denote the set of all facts $\mathbf{F}$.*

We now detail all facts contained in $\mathbf{F}$, ordered by category. A fact holds if the topology, attacker or protocol described has the associated property.

• The first category contains facts related to the attacker. *CompromisableNodes*: An attacker is able to take full control of legitimate nodes, and recover their identity and knowledge. *TxPowAdjust*: Intruder nodes are able to adjust their radio transmission power. *DirAntenna*: Intruder nodes are equipped with directional antennas. *CanImpersonate*: The attacker is able to impersonate honest nodes (but this does not assume anything about validity).

• The second category contains the facts related to the protocols in use in the network. *SimpleValidity*: An attacker can alter or create a message and keep it valid. *ValidityCheckedEachHop*: An attacker cannot alter a given message in a way that keeps it valid, and originating from an uncompromised node. Validity of a message is checked at each hop. *NoConfidentiality*: Any passive listener is able to recover the contents of messages. *HopConfidentiality*: Nodes outside of the message route cannot recover the contents of a message. *EndToEndConfidentiality*: Only the source and destination(s) of a message can recover its contents. *OpenNetwork*: Nodes have access to new identities at will. Thus, any node can associate, regardless of initial knowledge or pre-existing relationships.

Some of these facts are related. We define that a fact F_1 is more restrictive for an attacker than F_2 when any possible attack when F_1 holds is also possible when F_2 holds.

Definition 3 (Factual relationships $\mathcal{F}$). *If a fact $F_1 \in \mathbf{F}$ is more restrictive for an attacker than a fact $F_2 \in \mathbf{F}$, we express that relation using the following rule named (FR): $(FR)\dfrac{F_2}{F_1}$. We denote by $\mathcal{F}$ the set of rules (F-Conf1),(F-Conf2) and (F-VC1).*

We now describe the contents of $\mathcal{F}$. Having validity checks at each hop blocks any invalid message before it gets retransmitted by an honest node, which only limits what messages an attacker can usefully send. Therefore, the fact *ValidityChecksAtEachHop* is more restrictive for an attacker than *SimpleValidity*.

$$(\text{F-}VC1)\frac{SimpleValidity}{ValidityChecksAtEachHop}$$

Regarding the confidentiality-related facts, the relationship is similar. *HopConfidentiality* strictly restricts attacker knowledge when compared to *NoConfidentiality*, as it only prevents listeners outside of the route from being able to read the data. Therefore, *HopConfidentiality* is more restrictive for an attacker than *NoConfidentiality*.

$$(\text{F-}Conf1)\frac{NoConfidentiality}{HopConfidentiality}$$

If an attack is possible when considering the *EndToEndConfidentiality* fact, then removing the confidentiality aspect for intermediate nodes does not change that possibility, as it merely adds more possibilities for the intruder. Therefore, we say that *EndToEndConfidentiality* is more restrictive for an attacker than *HopConfidentiality*, and the rule, named (F-Conf2), is written as follows:

$$(F\text{-}Conf2)\frac{HopConfidentiality}{EndToEndConfidentiality}$$

The set of facts we want to use for the analysis is denoted $\mathbf{F}_I \subseteq \mathcal{F}$. Using this set of facts, we build a set of axioms, named the selected hypothesis.

Definition 4 (Selected hypothesis $Hyp(\mathcal{H}, \mathbf{F}_I)$). *Let $\mathcal{H}$ be the set of all possible axioms deducing a fact from $\mathbf{F}$, and let $\mathbf{F}_I$ be a subset of $\mathbf{F}$ we want to assume for the verification. The set of selected hypothesis is a set of axioms, denoted by $Hyp(\mathcal{H}, \mathbf{F}_I)$, and defined by:*

$$Hyp(\mathcal{H}, \mathbf{F}_I) = \left\{ (AF)\frac{}{F} \middle| F \in \mathbf{F}_I \right\}$$

3.3 Anomalies

Anomalies are components used to describe the different steps in an attack, which are linked together using rules. We first define them, then we present the contents of **A**, separated in categories.

Definition 5 (Anomalies). *Anomalies are the results of the attacker's behavior. We denote the set of all anomalies **A**.*

- The following anomalies are related to impersonation.

  - *OmniImpersonation*: An intruder node transmits packets as if they were emitted by an honest neighbor, but the message can be received by any neighbor, and the received signal strength may differ from the one from legitimate transmissions.
  - *DirImpersonation*: An intruder node transmits packets in a directed fashion, such that only the attacker and the receiver know the transmission happened. The signal strength of this transmission may however be different from what is expected from the impersonated node.
  - *TxPowImpersonation*: An intruder node impersonates an honest node, while adjusting its transmission power so that the signal strength at the receiver corresponds to the signal strength which would be expected from the impersonated node.
  - *DirTxPowImpersonation*: An intruder node transmits packets in a directed fashion, such that only the attacker and the receiver know the transmission happened. Furthermore, the intruder adjusted its transmission power so that the signal strength at the receiver corresponds to the signal strength which would be expected from the impersonated node.
  - *Impersonation*: The attacker can communicate with any node, as if the communication happened from an honest neighbor. This anomaly is a generic version of the previous ones.

- The next category are anomalies related to node compromise and identities.

  - *VirusCompromise*: The attacker compromises some part of a node, whose identity is now compromised. The attacker is also able to control this node.
  - *TotalCompromise*: The attacker takes full control of a node, whose identity is now compromised.
  - *AttackerAssociated*: The attacker uses intruder nodes which are associated.
  - *RoutingMisbehavior*: Intruder nodes deviate from the routing protocol.

- Finally, the last category of anomalies are related to the application data.

  - *ApplicationDataAltered*: The attacker alters the data which is delivered to the application, either by adding, altering or subtracting data.
  - *Snooping*: The attacker reads some of the application data going through the network.
  - *Alteration*: The attacker alters data in messages.
  - *ValidAlteration*: The attacker alters data in messages, while keeping them both valid and appearing to be from an emitter whose identity is uncompromised.
  - *ImmediateAlteration*: An intruder node is able to alter the data in a message it received.
  - *NeighborVisibleAlteration*: An intruder node alters the data in a message it received, in a way that can be overheard by neighbors.
  - *NeighborVisibleValidAlteration*: An intruder node alters the data in a message it received, while keeping them both valid and appearing to be from an emitter whose identity is uncompromised, in a way that can be overheard by neighbors.
  - *ImmediateValidAlteration*: An intruder node is able to alter the data in a message it received, while keeping it both valid and appearing to be from an emitter whose identity is uncompromised.
  - *NeighborVisibleSuppression*: The attacker drops data messages, which prevents them from being delivered to their destinations. This action can be overheard by the node's neighbors.
  - *Suppression*: The attacker drops data messages at some point in the network, which prevents them from being delivered to their destinations.
  - *ImmediateSuppression*: An intruder node is able to drop valid data-bearing messages.
  - *Insertion*: The attacker creates valid data messages.
  - *NeighVisibleInsertion*: An intruder node creates valid data messages, which may be overheard by neighbors.
  - *ImmediateInsertion*: An intruder node can create valid data messages.

Anomalies follow a logical progression, with certain anomalies and facts being prerequisites to other anomalies. To model these dependancies, we use rules.

We denote by $\mathcal{R}$ the set of all our rules. The set $\mathcal{R}$ contains 39 rules, given in Fig. 2. Due to space constraints, their justifications are available in our technical report [17], Sect. 6. We now explain how those anomalies and rules are used to search for undetected attack.

Name	Prerequisite(s)	Conclusion
CompV	*CompromisableNodes*	*VirusCompromise*
CompT	*CompromisableNodes*	*TotalCompromise*
VAssoc	*VirusCompromise*	*AttackerAssociated*
TAssoc	*TotalCompromise*	*AttackerAssociated*
Open	*OpenNetwork*	*AttackerAssociated*
Misbehave	*AttackerAssociated*	*RoutingMisbehavior*
OmnI	*CanImpersonate*	*OmniImpersonation*
DirI	*DirAntenna ∧ CanImpersonate*	*DirImpersonation*
PowI	*TxPowAdjust ∧ CanImpersonate*	*TxPowImpersonation*
DirPowI	*TxPowAdjust ∧ DirAntenna ∧ CanImpersonate*	*DirTxPowImpersonation*
OtoI	*OmniImpersonation*	*Impersonation*
DtoI	*DirImpersonation*	*Impersonation*
TtoI	*TxPowImpersonation*	*Impersonation*
DTtoI	*DirTxPowImpersonation*	*Impersonation*
IStoS	*ImmediateSuppression*	*NeighVisibleSuppression*
DirIStoS	*ImmediateSuppression ∧ DirAntenna*	*Suppression*
IIntoNVIn	*ImmediateInsertion*	*NeighVisibleInsertion*
AssoIns	*AttackerAssociated*	*ImmediateInsertion*
ImpInser	*Impersonation ∧ SimpleValidity*	*ImmediateInsertion*
IAlt	*AttackerAssociated ∧ RoutingMisbehavior*	*ImmediateAlteration*
VIAlt	*ImmediateAlteration ∧ SimpleValidity*	*ImmediateValidAlteration*
VIaltIAlt	*ImmediateValidAlteration*	*ImmediateAlteration*
ValtAlt	*ValidAlteration*	*Alteration*
NVIaltAlt	*ImmediateAlteration*	*NeighVisibleAlteration*
NVIValtVAlt	*ImmediateValidAlteration*	*NeighVisibleValidAlteration*
NVIaltAlt	*ImmediateAlteration ∧ DirAntenna*	*Alteration*
NVIValtVAlt	*ImmediateValidAlteration ∧ DirAntenna*	*ValidAlteration*
AssoISup	*AttackerAssociated ∧ RoutingMisbehavior*	*ImmediateSuppression*
InSupAlt	*ImmediateSuppression ∧ ImmediateInsertion*	*ImmediateAlteration*
S	*NeighVisibleSuppression*	*Suppression*
DirIIntoIn	*ImmediateInsertion ∧ DirAntenna*	*Insertion*
NVIntoIn	*NeighVisibleInsertion*	*Insertion*
IaltAlt	*NeighVisibleAlteration*	*Alteration*
IValtVAlt	*NeighVisibleValidAlteration*	*ValidAlteration*
SApp	*Suppression*	*ApplicationDataAltered*
AApp	*ValidAlteration*	*ApplicationDataAltered*
IApp	*Insertion*	*ApplicationDataAltered*
HopSnoop	*AttackerAssociated ∧ HopConfidentiality*	*Snooping*
ConfSnoop	*NoConfidentiality*	*Snooping*

Fig. 2. List of all the rules

3.4   Attack Detection

An IDS has a certain number of inputs, each of these noticing a certain number of anomalies. To know if an IDS is adequate to prevent an attacker from reaching a given goal, we need to check if there is a way to reach a target anomaly from accepted facts, in a way that do not use any of the anomalies covered by the set of this IDS's inputs. To model this, given an IDS, we remove all the rules going to anomalies detected by that IDS, leaving only anomalies which do not trigger detection.

Definition 6 (IDS). *We denote the anomalies monitored by an IDS by* $\mathbf{A}_I \subseteq$ $\mathbf{A}$. *We define the set of rules* $IDS(\mathcal{R}, \mathbf{A}_I)$ *which is the allowed set of rules for the attacker given the base rules. This set is defined as:*

$$IDS(\mathcal{R}, \mathbf{A}_I) = \left\{ (R)\frac{T_0 \quad \cdots \quad T_n}{A} \in \mathcal{R} \;\middle|\; A \notin \mathbf{A}_I \wedge \forall i, T_i \notin \mathbf{A}_I \right\}$$

To build $\mathbf{A}_I$, one should examine which are the inputs the IDS uses, and for each of them, which are the anomalies that may be detected by such an input. For instance, message addition or substraction can be detected by traffic analysis. Then, the set $IDS(\mathcal{R}, \mathbf{A}_I)$ is used to build the set of rules which will be used by the analysis.

Definition 7 (Setting). *The set of rules obtained by the union of selected hypothesis, the rules allowed given a specific IDS, and factual relationships is called a setting. We denote it by :* $\mathcal{S} = IDS(\mathcal{R}, \mathbf{A}_I) \cup Hyp(\mathcal{H}, \mathbf{F}_I) \cup \mathcal{F}$

Once the setting is determined, we can search for undetected attacks, by looking at which anomalies are reachable using the rules.

Definition 8 (Undetected attack). *Let* $\mathcal{S}$ *be a setting describing an IDS together with assumptions about the network, protocol and attacker. Let* $G \in \mathcal{A}$ *be an anomaly. We say that there exists an attack resulting in* G *which can not be detected by the IDS described in* $\mathcal{S}$ *if* G *is reachable using* $\mathcal{S}$.

To summarize, in our model, an attack is a chain of anomalies, linked together by rules. Starting from facts, the attacker mounts his attack using only the rules in the setting (*i.e.* the rules that allow him to stay undetected). Each of those rules allow him to progress to further anomalies. Therefore, analyzing whether the attacker can reach a certain anomaly in a specific setting allows us to know whether an undetected attack is possible against that IDS. Also, we focus only on attacks which change the data to the application, impersonations, and node compromise. All considerations linked to the performances and availability of the network are not captured by our model, and constitute a natural future extension of this work.

We built a prototype which automatically goes through all the reachable anomalies, given an IDS and facts. It is available online, along with instructions on how to use it, at the following url: http://www-verimag.imag.fr/~rjamet/IDS/. The examples in the next section were analyzed using that tool, and the analysis took less than a second for each of them on a regular laptop.

4   Modeling Existing IDS

We now use the inputs and the intruder model previously described to evaluate two existing IDS, [21] and [9], and show the weaknesses and the possible improvements we discovered. All the outputs of the tool are available in our technical report [17] Sect. 7.

4.1   A Real-Time Node-Based Traffic Anomaly Detection Algorithm

In [21], Ilker Onat and Ali Miri present an anomaly-based IDS based on two inputs, received signal strength, and packet arrival rates. They make several hypothesis: the routing protocol is based on a tree (such as GBR), nodes are static and can uniquely identify neighbors, all nodes use the same hardware and software, and all nodes use constant transmission power. Our model does not take into account movement of nodes, and assumes that neighbors can be identified. Thus, the only assumption we need to transpose is the constant transmission power. This is modeled by not adding $TxPowAdjust$ to the hypothesis set.

We now build the set $\mathbf{A}_I$ of anomalies the IDS can detect. The first input used by this IDS is a packet arrival rate analysis. This input is able to discover any attacker that stops or inserts more messages than expected from an honest node. The corresponding anomalies in our model are $Suppression$ and $Insertion$. Each node running this IDS also observe the received signal strength, which will detect the anomalies $OmniImpersonation$ and $DirImpersonation$. We therefore have our set of anomalies $\mathbf{A}_I = \{Suppression, Insertion, OmniImpersonation, DirImpersonation\}$.

The next step is to set the attacker's goal. In their paper, the authors address node impersonation, and resource depletion by excessive generation of traffic. As the latter is not covered by our model, we will focus on impersonation first, and then consider a more general anomaly, $ApplicationDataAltered$.

In order to find if an attacker in our model is able to impersonate honest nodes, we need to choose the facts modeling the attacker. The IDS supposes that attackers have the ability to impersonate honest nodes (fact $CanImpersonate$), and we also suppose that they have directional antennas (fact $DirAntenna$) as no assumptions were made about this in the paper. We therefore set $\mathbf{F}_I = \{CanImpersonate, DirAntenna\}$.

From the facts and the IDS description, we compute the set of rules $\mathcal{S}$, and search for a way to reach $Impersonation$ using $\mathcal{S}$. We see that in this case, the tool cannot apply any rules, and so our system did not find weaknesses on this aspect of the IDS.

However, the assumption that the attacker cannot modify its intruder nodes's transmission power is strong, as such hardware is readily available. If we relax that assumption by removing $TxPowAdjust$ from $\mathbf{F}_I$, we find that the attacker can now reach $Impersonation$ by doing an impersonation with adjusted transmission power, effectively bypassing the IDS input. To prevent this, the IDS would need a way of detecting this behavior.

We can also consider other intruder goals. For instance, we wonder if an attacker would be able to alter the data going to the application (*Application-DataAltered*). Let us assume that nodes can be compromised by an attacker (fact *CompromisableNodes*), and that validity is easy to fake for the attacker (fact *SimpleValidity*). As we assumed that nodes can be compromised, and there are no protections against this in the IDS, the intruder can take control of some nodes, and make them alter the data they retransmit. As we assumed that an attacker can fake the validity of a message, the results of that alteration is valid, thus the altered data will get delivered without any alert.

This attack path uses the fact that traffic flow analysis does not protects against message alterations. To prevent this, the IDS would need countermeasures preventing message alterations, such as choosing the right protocols to have integrity and authenticity of the messages, or using more IDS inputs such as the ones used by [9]. The other way to prevent this attack would be to prevent the compromise of nodes, either through specific inputs (see for instance [31] or [25]).

4.2   Decentralized Intrusion Detection

In [9], the authors propose an IDS for WSNs based on promiscuous listening. The network contains monitoring nodes, which observe their neighbor's behavior. If their neighbors break one of a series of rules, an alert is raised. To avoid confusion with the rules from our model, we will call the rules from this IDS *behavior rules*. They are the following: A node must receive messages regularly (the interval rule), neighbors must retransmit packets quickly (the delay rule), without altering them, nor repeating them. Also, transmissions must come from a sensible distance, and there must not be too many collisions.

We first build the set of monitored anomalies $\mathbf{A}_I$. The interval rule detects *Suppression* and *Insertion*, as both addition or suppression of messages alters downstream traffic flows. The integrity rule detects *NeighVisibleAlteration* and *NeighVisibleValidAlteration*, as they are based on promiscuous monitoring. The delay rule detects *NeighVisibleSuppression*. The last three behavior rules are not considered in our model, as we do not model any sort of distance measurements for the range rule, nor availability-related anomalies regarding the collision rule. We therefore have our set of anomalies $\mathbf{A}_I = \{$*Suppression, Insertion, NeighVisibleAlteration, NeighVisibleValidAlteration, NeighVisibleSuppression*$\}$.

There are no specific hypothesis about the nodes in the paper. Regarding facts, we include *CompromisableNodes* to allow the attacker to compromise nodes. We also add *DirAntenna* to model the attacker's access to advanced hardware. Regarding the protocols, we add *EndToEndConfidentiality* to model a protocol ensuring that the data stays confidential, and *SimpleValidity* to be able to find an attack. Thus, we have $\mathbf{F}_I = \{$*CompromisableNodes, DirAntenna, EndToEndConfidentiality, SimpleValidity*$\}$. For the intruder goal, we select *ApplicationDataAltered* as it encompasses most of what this IDS aims to prevent. The tool's output shows that there is an undetected attack.

Similarly to the previous IDS, this attack stems from the assumption that the attacker can compromise honest nodes, as there are no countermeasures regarding these anomalies. With an associated intruder node, the attacker can therefore modify the data being routed, as we assumed intruder nodes can alter data while keeping packets valid. However, the IDS makes honest nodes monitor their neighbors for such a behavior. This is where we use the directional antennas: with these, the intruder node is able to send the altered packet to its destination, while sending the initial version of that packet to the monitors. This way, the attacker can alter data, while appearing to satisfy the behavior rules triggering the intrusion detection. Then, that altered packet will be forwarded to its destination and delivered, effectively altering application data, which is the goal we set.

The straightforward way to prevent this specific attack in our model is to use a protocol that guarantees the validity of the transmitted message. Indeed, when removing the *SimpleValidity* fact, our tool was not able to find an undetected attack. Alternatively, one may try to prevent any association of the intruder, through for instance tamper-resistant nodes and secure software. This way, attackers will not be able to alter the traffic going through the network, and this would also prevent an attacker from reaching *ApplicationDataAltered* in our model.

5   Conclusion

We presented a characterization and modeling of the different data sources used in network-based intrusion detection systems, focusing on wireless ad-hoc networks. We found that a lot of IDS from the literature base their decisions on a small set of distinct inputs, which we have listed in this paper. We then used those inputs to build a decision aid in order to help IDS designers to locate some of the weak points of their algorithms, depending on the protocols used in their network.

In the future, we would like to further refine that model and take into account various families of protocols, especially when looking at the low levels of the protocol stack, such as the medium access protocols. Also, we would like to extend our model to include availability attacks.

References

1. Adeyeye, M., Gardner-Stephen, P.: The village telco project: a reliable and practical wireless mesh telephony infrastructure. EURASIP J. Wirel. Commun. Network. **2011**(1), 1–11 (2011)
2. Anjum, F., Talpade, R.: Lipad: lightweight packet drop detection for ad hoc networks. In: Vehicular Technology Conference VTC2004-Fall, vol. 2, pp. 1233–1237. IEEE (2004)
3. Basin, D., Cremers, C., Meadows, C.: Model checking security protocols. In: Clarke, E., Henzinger, T., Veith, H. (eds.) Handbook of Model Checking. Springer, Heidelberg (2011)
4. Bhuse, V., Gupta, A.: Anomaly intrusion detection in wireless sensor networks. J. High Speed Networks **15**(1), 33–51 (2006)

5. Rasmussen, K.B., Capkun, S.: Implications of radio fingerprinting on the security of sensor networks. In: SecureComm 2007, pp. 331–340. IEEE (2007)
6. Clausen, T., Jacquet, P.: Optimized link state routing protocol (OLSR). RFC 3626 (Experimental), October 2003
7. Conti, M., Di Pietro, R., Mancini, L.V., Mei, A.: A randomized, efficient, and distributed protocol for the detection of node replication attacks in wireless sensor networks. In: Proceedings of the 8th ACM MobiHoc, pp. 80–89. ACM (2007)
8. Cucurull, J., Asplund, M., Nadjm-Tehrani, S.: Anomaly detection and mitigation for disaster area networks. In: Jha, S., Sommer, R., Kreibich, C. (eds.) RAID 2010. LNCS, vol. 6307, pp. 339–359. Springer, Heidelberg (2010)
9. da Silva, A.P.R., Martins, M.H., Rocha, B.P., Loureiro, A.A., Ruiz, L.B., Wong, H.C.: Decentralized intrusion detection in wireless sensor networks. In: Q2SWinet'05, pp. 16–23. ACM (2005)
10. Debar, H., Dacier, M., Wespi, A.: Towards a taxonomy of intrusion-detection systems. Comput. Networks 31(8), 805–822 (1999)
11. Demirbas, M., Song, Y.: An rssi-based scheme for sybil attack detection in wireless sensor networks. In: WoWMoM'06, pp. 564–570. IEEE Computer Society (2006)
12. Dong, D., Li, M., Liu, Y., Li, X.-Y., Liao, X.: Topological detection on wormholes in wireless ad hoc and sensor networks. IEEE/ACM ToN'11 Trans. Network. 19(6), 1787–1796 (2011)
13. Doumit, S.S., Agrawal, D.P.: Self-organized criticality and stochastic learning based intrusion detection system for wireless sensor networks. In: MILCOM'03, vol. 1, pp. 609–614. IEEE (2003)
14. Gardner-Stephen, P., Palaniswamy, S.: Serval mesh software-wifi multi model management. In: ACWR'11, pp. 71–77. ACM (2011)
15. Hall, J., Barbeau, M., Kranakis, E.: Enhancing intrusion detection in wireless networks using radio frequency fingerprinting. In: CIIT'04, pp. 201–206. IASTED (2004)
16. Huang, Y., Lee, W.: Attack analysis and detection for ad hoc routing protocols. In: Jonsson, E., Valdes, A., Almgren, M. (eds.) RAID 2004. LNCS, vol. 3224, pp. 125–145. Springer, Heidelberg (2004)
17. Jamet, R., Lafourcade, P.: Discovering flaws in IDS through analysis of their inputs. Technical report, Verimag Research report, http://www-verimag.imag.fr/TR/TR-2013-9.pdf, (2013)
18. Krügel, C., Toth, T., Kirda, E.: Service specific anomaly detection for network intrusion detection. In: SAC'02, pp. 201–208. ACM (2002)
19. Liu, Y., Li, Y., Man, H.: Short paper: a distributed cross-layer intrusion detection system for ad hoc networks. In: SecureComm 2005, pp. 418–420. IEEE (2005)
20. Onat, I., Miri, A.: An intrusion detection system for wireless sensor networks. In: WiMob'2005, vol. 3, pp. 253–259. IEEE (2005)
21. Onat, I., Miri, A.: A real-time node-based traffic anomaly detection algorithm for wireless sensor networks. In: Systems Communications, 2005, pp. 422–427. IEEE (2005)
22. Parker, J., Patwardhan, A., Joshi, A.: Cross-layer analysis for detecting wireless misbehavior. In: CCNC 2006, pp. 6–9. IEEE (2006)
23. Perkins, C., Belding-Royer, E., Das, S.: Ad hoc On-Demand Distance Vector (AODV) Routing. RFC 3561, July 2003
24. Pires, W.R. Jr, de Paula Figueiredo, T.H., Wong, H.C., Loureiro, A.A., Malicious node detection in wireless sensor networks. In: IPDPS'04, p. 24. IEEE (2004)
25. Song, H., Xie, L., Zhu, S., Cao, G.: Sensor node compromise detection: the location perspective. In: IWCMC'07, pp. 242–247. ACM (2007)

26. Thamilarasu, G., Balasubramanian, A., Mishra, S., Sridhar, R.: A cross-layer based intrusion detection approach for wireless ad hoc networks. In: MASS'05, pp. 7–11. IEEE (2005)
27. Tseng, C., Song, T., Balasubramanyam, P., Ko, C., Levitt, K.: A specification-based intrusion detection model for OLSR. In: RAID'06, pp. 330–350. Springer 2006
28. Tseng, C.H., Wang, S.-H., Ko, C., Levitt, K.N.: DEMEM: distributed evidence-driven message exchange intrusion detection model for MANET. In: Zamboni, D., Kruegel, C. (eds.) RAID 2006. LNCS, vol. 4219, pp. 249–271. Springer, Heidelberg (2006)
29. Tseng, C.-Y., Balasubramanyam, P., Ko, C., Limprasittiporn, R., Rowe, J., Levitt, K.: A specification-based intrusion detection system for AODV. In: SASN'03, pp. 125–134. ACM (2003)
30. Wagner, D., Soto, P.: Mimicry attacks on host-based intrusion detection systems. In: *ACM CCS'2002*, pp. 255–264. ACM (2002)
31. Yang, Y., Wang, X., Zhu, S., Cao, G.: Distributed software-based attestation for node compromise detection in sensor networks. In: SRDS 2007, pp. 219–230. IEEE (2007)

On the Reverse Engineering
of the Citadel Botnet

Ashkan Rahimian$^{(\boxtimes)}$, Raha Ziarati, Stere Preda, and Mourad Debbabi

National Cyber-Forensics and Training Alliance CANADA,
Concordia University Montreal, Quebec H3G 1M8, Canada
a_rahimi@encs.concordia.ca

Abstract. Citadel is an advanced information stealing malware that targets financial information. This malware poses a real threat against the confidentiality and integrity of personal and business data. Recently, a joint operation has been conducted by FBI and Microsoft Digital Crimes Unit in order to take down Citadel command-and-control servers. The operation caused some disruption in the botnet but has not stopped it completely. Due to the complex structure and advanced anti-reverse engineering techniques, the Citadel malware analysis process is challenging and time-consuming. This allows cyber criminals to carry on with their attacks while the analysis is still in progress. In this paper, we present the results of the Citadel reverse engineering and provide additional insights into the functionality, inner workings, and open source components of the malware. In order to accelerate the reverse engineering process, we propose a clone-based analysis methodology. Citadel is an offspring of a previously analyzed malware called Zeus. Thus, using the former as a reference, we can measure and quantify the similarities and differences of the new variant. Two types of code analysis techniques are provided in the methodology namely assembly to source code matching, and binary clone detection. The methodology can help reduce the number of functions that should be analyzed manually. The analysis results prove that the approach is promising in Citadel malware analysis. Furthermore, the same approach is applicable to similar malware analysis scenarios.

Keywords: Reverse Engineering · Malware Analysis · Clone Analysis

1 Introduction

One of the offspring of Zeus malware that has been making headlines in recent months *(March 2013 - July 2013)* is called Citadel. Cyber criminals behind the Citadel malware have stolen more than 500 million dollars from online bank accounts [15]. Zeus was a prolific information stealing Trojan that has been around since 2007. In 2011, its source code was leaked on the internet and became available to the underground community. Since then, several malware have been developed based on the Zeus source code. Citadel has been employed by botnet

J.-L. Danger et al. (Eds.): FPS 2013, LNCS 8352, pp. 408–425, 2014.
DOI: 10.1007/978-3-319-05302-8_25, © Springer International Publishing Switzerland 2014

operators to steal banking credentials and personal information [10,17]. In addition, Citadel has features that extend beyond targeting financial institutions. Spying capabilities such as video capture is an example of such features that literally enables cyber criminals to collect anything from a victim's machine. The malware also acts as ransomware and scareware in order to extort money from victims. Reverse engineering is often considered as the primary step taken to gain an in-depth understanding of a piece of malware. However, it is a challenging and time-consuming process, which requires a great deal of manual intervention.

The major objectives of this paper are to reverse engineer the Citadel malware and gain more insights into its structure and functionality. In particular, the objectives can be summarized as follows:

1. Quantify the similarities and differences between Citadel and Zeus malware.
2. Get additional insights into online open source components used in Citadel.
3. Accelerate the reverse engineering process of similar malware variants.

To enhance and speed up the process, a new approach termed as clone-based analysis is employed in this study. Indeed, this paper illustrates the usefulness of the proposed approach in the analysis of new variants of a malware family. In this scenario, a preceding malware P is supposed to be analyzed and understood. If a variant V uses portions of the P code, the approach will highlight the shared portions. Consequently, disregarding the clones could reduce the analysis time. In a more general case where P is not known in advance, the approach can still provide insights into the components of V, in comparison to other sources.

The main contributions of this paper are three folds. First, a detailed reverse engineering analysis of the Citadel malware is presented and its functionality is described. Second, a new methodology for reverse engineering malware is proposed. This methodology significantly decreases malware analysts' efforts and reduces the analysis time. Third, the similarity between the Citadel malware and the Zeus malware is precisely quantified. Also, additional insights are provided into the open-source components used in the Citadel malware.

This case study has been chosen for a number of reasons. First, Citadel and Zeus are real threats against confidentiality, integrity and availability of information systems. Cyber criminals are constantly enhancing their tools for gaining access to personal and financial data. The profitability of such crimeware tools in the underground market depends on the timeliness and support for new vulnerabilities. Therefore, malicious developers often reuse all or parts of existing components during their incremental development process. As a result, it is quite probable that they leave fingerprints of previously analyzed malcode on the new releases. Clone-based analysis comes in handy in such situations due to its potential for producing quick results. Integrating a clone-based analysis in the reverse engineering process will significantly reduce the overall analysis time. The second benefit of this case study is that it allows us to leverage our developed tools such as *RE-Source* [7] and *RE-Clone* [8] in reverse engineering sophisticated malware. The lessons learned during the analysis would bring new opportunities for future extensions of our tools. Third, the analysis provides us with practical solutions for mitigating future threats in a timely fashion. Once the analysis is performed on Zeus and Citadel, new Zeus-based malware variants with shared components can be analyzed faster.

The reminder of this paper is organized as follows. Section 2, is dedicated to explaining our methodology in studying the malware. Section 3 details the dynamic analysis and explains the debugging process and memory forensic approaches. The main features of the Citadel malware are also described in this section. Section 4 presents the static analysis and the steps led to the actual de-obfuscated code. Section 5 presents the clone-based analysis. The threat mitigation is briefly presented in Sect. 6 and the conclusion is drawn in Sect. 8.

2   Methodology

Static and dynamic analysis are commonly used in studying malware [1,5]. Static analysis focuses on malware code for inspecting its structure and functionality without execution. In contrast, dynamic analysis deals with behavior monitoring during the malware execution. In general, the process of malware reverse engineering is a combination of these two approaches, which is time-consuming and costly. The success of these approaches are tightly coupled with the functionalities of the tools and skills of the reverse engineer [3,4].

To enhance and accelerate the process in analyzing the Citadel malware another dimension is considered in our study as shown in Fig. 1. This new dimension is called clone-based analysis. In few words, the clone-based analysis identifies the pieces of code in Citadel malware that are originated from other malware and open-source applications. This step is performed automatically by leveraging the tools that are designed and developed in our security lab [7,8]. There are two main advantages in considering this extra dimension into the static analysis. First, to avoid dealing with low-level assembly code in situations where the corresponding high-level code is available. Second, to prevent reverse engineering parts of the malware that has already been analyzed. This approach is very promising, especially in scenarios similar to Citadel that shares a significant portion of code with a previously reverse engineered malware like Zeus [6]. The process of assembly to source

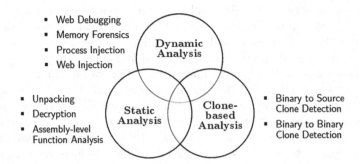

Fig. 1. The overlap in reverse engineering methodologies

code matching is performed using the *RE-Source* framework [7]. Also, the binary clone matching is carried out using *RE-Clone* [8].

The proposed methodology is composed of three processes. Each process comprises several steps. We will elaborate each step in the following sections.

1. *Static Analysis Process*
    - The disassembly is reviewed for finding obfuscated segments, decoder stubs, and embedded file images. The feasibility of static data decryption is assessed. It might be necessary to switch to dynamic analysis for code and data decryption.
    - A suitable circumvention strategy is adopted for bypassing the anti-static protection of the malware. Having a de-obfuscated/decrypted disassembly is a prerequisite for the clone-based analysis process.
    - Control flow analysis and data flow analysis are applied to gain an understanding of the crypto algorithms and encoding/decoding functionality.
2. *Dynamic Analysis Process*
    - A debugging environment is set to execute the binary, attach the debugger, set the breakpoints, control the unpacking, dump the process memory, generate an executable image, and save the process to file. The dumping process is repeated according to the analysis scenario.
    - System calls are monitored, malware activities are logged, network traffic is captured, downloaded files are backed up, and the communication protocol is observed. Also, the interesting artifacts are extracted.
3. *Clone-based Analysis Process*
    - Using the unpacked and de-obfuscated disassembly, a search is performed for standard and open-source components by applying the assembly to source-code matching technique of *RE-Source* [7]. The data matching technique encompasses two threads of *online* and *offline* analysis. This step is repeated for all process memory dumps and the set of matched projects are stored as *online* analysis results.
    - An *offline* analysis is performed for assigning the functionality tags according to API call classification in *RE-Source*. Function labels are updated, the proportion of assembly functions in each functionality group is calculated, and the functionality tags are reviewed based on the scenario.
    - Using the unpacked and de-obfuscated disassembly, a binary clone matching is done against the previously analyzed malware binaries in *RE-Clone*. Then, the occurrences of *inexact* and *exact* clones are recorded.
    - The outputs of assembly to source-code matching and binary clone matching are combined for quantifying the similarities and difference of malware variants. The results draw a high-level picture of the code.
    - The clones are selectively used to guide the static and dynamic analyses. In order to speed up the process, the clones are removed and the analysis focus is shifted to the original (non-clone) functions.

According to Fig. 1, three connected processes are defined in the proposed methodology. In the Citadel case study, the dynamic analysis track focuses on web debugging, memory forensics, process injection and web injects. An important aspect in this process is the observation of malware's behavior in response to controlled inputs. On the other hand, the static analysis process focuses on assembly-level functions. De-obfuscation could occur in the overlapping area of these two methods. Unpacking and decryption are relevant examples that fall in this area. It is assumed that a database of previously analyzed code is available during the analysis. Code search engines provide an interface to online open source code repositories. Likewise, an offline code repository is maintained for storing the malware assembly code and the results of previous analysis sessions. One advantage of the clone-based analysis is that it can guide the dynamic and static steps. In other words, it highlights the important directions that the other two processes should follow by eliminating code clones, recognizing library functions, and providing additional comments. Therefore, the analysis focus is shifted to non-clone parts of the payload, resulting in a shorter analysis timeline.

3   Dynamic Analysis

The purpose of the dynamic analysis process is to execute the malware and monitor its behavior in a controlled environment. Many tools and techniques are available for debugging malware [2,3]. Sandboxing is a common technique in dynamic analysis and it is used for running untrusted code in a virtual setting. However, modern malware are well-equipped with anti-virtual machine protection against popular tools such as *Oracle VirtualBox* and *VMWare Workstation*. The malware can easily sense whether it is running on a virtual machine by checking certain artifacts in memory or on disk. As a result, the malware might change its normal behavior by taking an alternative execution path for hindering the analysis. Malware can even go one step further and try to exploit the virtual machine vulnerabilities in order to gain access to the host operating system. Thus, successful dynamic analysis may require caution and pre-processing steps. Debugging Citadel is challenging due to the built-in anti-debugging and injection capabilities but the protection can be circumvented by choosing the right strategy. As it will be discussed in Sect. 5, *RE-Source* can provide informative tags such as ADB, PSJ or AVM for functions that potentially contain anti-debugging, process injection, or anti-virtual machine functionality. Upon the first execution, Citadel begins the infection process based on an embedded attack configuration.

3.1   Debugging and Memory Forensics

After setting up the analysis environment and infecting it with the malware, the bot execution can be monitored and controlled using a scriptable debugger [18,19]. Several techniques are available for hiding the debugger process from the bot and gaining more control over the debugger [2]. A web debugger or a network protocol analyzer is used for monitoring the HTTP network communications of the malware. Citadel encrypts the command-and-control (C&C) network traffic with RC4. Therefore, the crypto keys are required to intercept the commands, and view the stolen data. One way to find the keys is through debugging and setting hardware breakpoints on functions that precede network communication.

As it will be discussed in Sect. 5, such network-related functionality can be identified through the NET, WNT and CRY tags assigned in the offline analysis. Upon successful installation, the bot checks for Internet connectivity and tries to connect to embedded C&C addresses in order to announce its availability. The bot sends requests such as POST /carfca/basket.php HTTP/1.1 or POST /carfca/file.php HTTP/1.1 to the server. The server then replies and sends the encrypted config file to the bot. One major difference between Zeus and Citadel is in the way they handle the transmission of the configuration file. It was possible to find the location of Zeus config file and download it with minimal effort. Whereas in Citadel, it is more difficult to obtain the config file during the analysis. Citadel uses dynamic APIs and it decrypts strings in memory during the execution. This can be considered as an extra layer of protection that prevents the config file from being detected easily. Figure 2 shows one of the decrypted links to a Citadel C&C server which hosts the encrypted "sport.doc" config file. During the debug, the bot allocates memory for new segments and overwrites the memory space with decrypted code and data. The zero values in Fig. 2 show the bytes that are yet to be overwritten by data. Blocking the malware's access to the requested C&C and modifying its timing mechanism will force the malware to enumerate the list of alternative embedded C&C servers.

Several tools and plug-ins are available for dumping memory, reconstructing import tables, and fixing PE headers. OllyDump and ImpRec are examples of such tools for unpacking Citadel [1,3]. Volatility [20] was the most versatile and straightforward tool for memory forensics that was used in this project. It automatically builds the import tables and generates the executable versions of the unpacked binary. Volatility was utilized for creating executable process dumps and retrieving decrypted strings from memory. Table 1 lists the utilized tools,

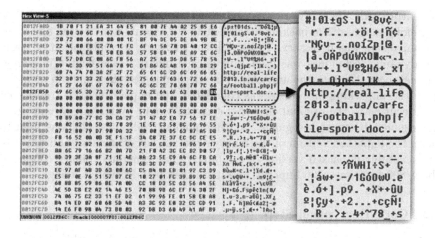

Fig. 2. Decoded Citadel config file name and location

Table 1. Unpacking stages of Citadel binary

	IDA Pro	PE Unpack	PE Explorer	OllyDump	ImpREC	x86 EMU	Volatility
Detected Functions	13	155	162	160	161	160	796
Extracted Strings	337	3	3805	120	67	6628	917
Function Imports	11	16	107	-	107	107	386
Executable Dump	Yes	Yes	Yes	No	No	No	Yes

and shows the number of detected functions, extracted strings, and identified function imports during different stages of the unpacking process.

4   Static Analysis

In this section, we describe the main steps taken during the static analysis of the Citadel. The static malware analysis process normally starts by disassembling the malware binary. However, the initial disassembled code may not draw a complete picture of the original code due to different layers of obfuscation. Disassembling the Citadel malware using *IDA Pro* [19] results in a packed binary containing merely 13 functions, 11 imports, and 337 strings. The binary was compressed, encrypted, and employed anti-reverse engineering techniques. Therefore, our static analysis started by de-obfuscating the malware. According to the first process of the proposed methodology, static and dynamic techniques should be interleaved for advancing the analysis.

4.1   Unpacking Step

Not surprisingly, the malware was packed with a non-standard packing scheme. Therefore, automatic unpacking tools such as *UPX* could not be used and manual unpacking was necessary. To unpack the malware, a combination of static and dynamic techniques was used. The packed binary was executed in *Immunity debugger* [18] until the unpacking stub decompressed the binary in memory. Once the unpacking procedure was completed, the unpacking stub transferred the execution to the original entry point of the binary by making a jump from one segment to another segment. At this moment, *Volatility* [20] was used to dump the unpacked version of the binary's process out of memory and generate an executable unpacked version of the binary. The generated binary contained about 800 functions, 386 imports, and more than 900 decrypted strings.

4.2   Code Decryption Step

The unpacking allowed the static analysis to be resumed. After this step, there were still some encrypted portions in the binary code. One of the interesting

---

Algorithm 1: String Decryption Procedure

```
/*Python command for decrypting the embedded strings        */
for j in range length do
    ⌊ UNPACKED_DATA = join(char(PACKED_DATA[j]) ^ j ^ key)
```

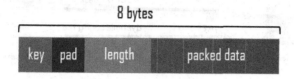

8 bytes

| key | pad | length | packed data |

Fig. 3. Structure of the encrypted data

points was located at the address of 0x0040336 in our sample. An in-depth examination of the function, which cross-referenced this portion revealed the structure of encrypted data and the decryption mechanism. As shown in Fig. 3, the structure size is 8 bytes and it consists of 4 chunks. Also, the key for string decryption is embedded in the binary file. Algorithm 1, presents the decryption procedure used for decrypting the data. It helped us recover more than 300 strings and 45 C&C commands from the packed data in the binary.

4.3   Crypto Algorithms

Receiving an RC4 encrypted configuration file from a C&C server in response to a plain GET request, and reusing of nonrandom values for encrypted messages were two main weaknesses of the Zeus malware. To overcome these weaknesses, significant improvements have been taken place concerning crypto algorithms in Citadel. As shown in Fig. 4, Citadel C&C server requires a specially crafted RC4-encrypted POST message to send the configuration file. In addition, in order to provide better security, the configuration file is encrypted using AES. The Citadel authors have used a composition of different ciphers as shown in Figs. 5 and 6. The RC4 encryption (Fig. 5) starts by an customized encoding (obfuscation) mechanism known as *Visual Encrypt (VE)*.

The input to the algorithm is an encoded buffer. The *VE* code is provided in Algorithm 2. This function was used in Zeus for crypto purposes as well. After the XOR operation, the non-standard RC4 initialization routine generates a

---

Algorithm 2: Visual Encrypt Algorithm

```
void Crypt::VisualEncrypt(void *buffer, DWORD size) {
    for (DWORD i = 1; i ¡ size; i++) do
        ⌊ ((LPBYTE)buffer)[i] ^ = ((LPBYTE)buffer)[i − 1];
}
```

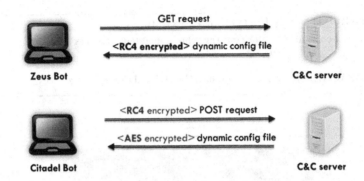

Fig. 4. Communication messages for retrieving the configuration file

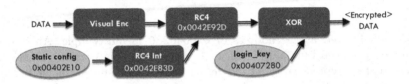

Fig. 5. Citadel RC4 Encryption process

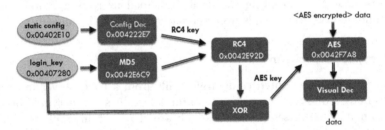

Fig. 6. Citadel AES Decryption process

0x100 bytes key based on the static configuration data embedded in the binary. The output of the routine is a new RC4 key that is used in RC4 encryption function along with the customized XOR-ed data. Finally, performing an XOR on the RC4 output and the login key embedded in the binary, results in the RC4 encrypted data. Given *login_key=lkey* and *VE=encode*, the functionality can be stated as: $out = lkey$ XOR $RC4_{rkey}(encode(in))$. Therefore, $out=Enc(in)$.

The AES decryption is depicted in Fig. 6. The configuration decryption routine takes the embedded static configuration data as input, and outputs the RC4 key. The MD5 hashed login key and the embedded RC4 key are fed to the RC4 routine. Next, the AES key is generated by performing an XOR on the output of the RC4 routine, and the login key. This key is used by the AES decryption function. Finally, the *Visual Decrypt (VD)* function (Algorithm 3) takes the result of the AES routine and decodes the decrypted data. The process can be formulated as: $AES_{key} = MD5(lkey)$ XOR $RC4_{rkey}$. Given *VD=decode*, the

Algorithm 3: Visual Decrypt Algorithm

```
void Crypt::VisualDecrypt(void *buffer, DWORD size) {
if  size ¿ 0 then
    for  (DWORD i = size − 1; i ¿ 0; i−−) do
        ((LPBYTE)buffer)[i] ^= ((LPBYTE)buffer)[i − 1];
}
```

output can be stated as: $out = decode(\text{AES}_{\text{AES\_key}}(in))$. The weakest point in the crypto process is that it is based on static config data, which shows that the authors lack competency in security algorithms and cipher composition.

5   Clone-based Analysis

The third process of the proposed methodology focuses on clone-based analysis, which can be applied for complementing the process of reverse engineering. Particularly, it could be helpful in reducing the required time for the static analysis phase. In this context, two techniques are taken into account for quantifying the similarities between Citadel and Zeus samples. The first approach uses *RE-Source* in order to reveal the open-source building blocks of the malware. The second approach utilizes *RE-Clone* for binary code matching. The major steps in the clone-based methodology can be enumerated as follows: (1) identification of standard algorithms and open-source library code in the malware disassembly, (2) assigning meaningful labels to assembly-level functions based on API classification, (3) commenting the assembly code based on a predefined dictionary of malware functions, (4) applying a window-based search and comparison mechanism for finding the pre-analyzed code components.

5.1   Assembly to Open-Source Code Matching

The *RE-Source* framework [7] has been used for extracting assembly-level features from Citadel. This framework examines assembly functions in two phases of online and offline in order to find source files that share features with the disassembly. The key steps of the framework are: (1) extraction of interesting features, (2) feature-based query encoding, (3) query refinement for online code search engines, (4) request/response processing, (5) data extraction and parsing, (6) reporting results and updating comments, (7) feature-based offline analysis. Different features are considered for online and offline analysis. During the online analysis phase, *RE-Source* revealed the correlation between function-level features of Citadel and several open-source projects. The video capture capability of the malware was unleashed through the links to source files such as: *MHRecordContol.h, stopRecord.c, trackerRecorder.h, signalRecorder.h, waitRecord.c*, etc. (Fig. 10, Appendix A.1). This observation was further supported

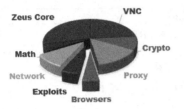

Sample Matched Project Names
Zeus Core, libcurl, HttpTrailer, Chromium, VNC, prsocket, Metasploit framework, ZipCrypto, emulate, crc32hash, KernelEx, OpenJDK6, image-uploader, Free Download Manager, netlink, DemuxFS, Mozilla Firefox, TrackRecoder, Anon Proxy Server, Scilab, Psiphon3, Socket Redirection

Fig. 7. Matched features with open-source projects

by occurrences of strings such as *"_startRecord16"* during the dynamic API de-obfuscation. Moreover, a "`video_start`" C&C command was also found in this process. Even though screen capture is a common feature in modern malware, live video capture capability is a new feature, which is only seen in complex and progressive samples. It should be noted that the online analysis results of *RE-Source* that suggested video-related capability were the outcome of an approximate code matching process. Although the matching process was not perfect, it was accurate enough to reveal the functionality context in this case. Similarly, *RE-Source* had commented the code with references to other open-source projects such as the ones listed in Fig. 7. The number of matched projects in each category determines the size of each pie slice. Many Zeus-based malware variants have appeared online since the release of Zeus source code in 2011. Having access to Zeus source code enabled us to match Citadel binary against Zeus source code. The pie chart in Fig. 7 shows the general categories of open-source projects that are used in Citadel. Apart from the detached slices, Citadel and Zeus share a considerable amount of code related to the core, VNC, crypto, and proxy functionality. However, the differences can be summarized in network communication code, new exploits and browser-specific code for web injects.

5.2   Offline Analysis and Functionality Tags

RE-Source can also be used for tagging assembly functions based on API calls and classifying functions according to their potential functionality. When applied to the unpacked version of Citadel, 652 functionality tags were detected by the offline analyzer. A function is assigned several tags if it contains more than one system call. Accurate functionality tags could convey meaningful hints to the reverse engineer during the static analysis phase. In conjunction with the code and data cross-referencing, functionality tags can enrich the disassembly by highlighting the final system calls in a multi-level function call hierarchy. Since system calls serve as interaction points with the operating system, having a high-level view of them could draw a more organized view of the code.

Functionality tags are not limited to simple system calls merely for file processing or registry modifications. They can be composed of several operations related to common malware behavior. New patterns can be defined for highlighting common malicious code in downloaders, launchers, reverse shells, remote calls and keyloggers based on the combination of several simple system operations.

Table 2. Functionality tags for offline analysis

TAG	Functionality	TAG	Functionality	TAG	Functionality
ADB	Anti-debugging	REG	Registry update	CER	Certificates
PSJ	Process injection	DIR	Directory	OSI	OS Information
DLJ	DLL injection	MTX	Mutex	SRC	Search
DRJ	Direct injection	PIP	Pipe	VIR	Virtual memory
HKJ	Hook injection	HTP	HTTP, Web	CRT	Critical section
ACJ	APC injection	URL	URI links	MOD	Modification
AUJ	APC userspace	ENP	Enumeration	SRV	Service
AKJ	APC kernerlspace	HAS	Hashing	LCH	Launcher
WNT	Win networking	CRY	Cryptography	AVM	Anti-VM
NET	Low-level socks	FIL	File processing	CSH	Cache

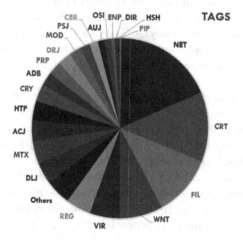

Fig. 8. Functionality tags assigned by offline analysis

In this context, process memory modification and code injection points are of great interest to the reverse engineer. *RE-Source* includes tagging categories such as *process injection, launcher, DLL injection, process replacement, hook injection, APC injection* and *resource segment manipulation* in the offline analysis. Table 2 lists some of the available functionality tags in the prototype. A practical application of functionality tags is in disassembly comparison/synchronization of two malware variants. Instead of comparing the files by address, the code can be analyzed offline and the generated tags can be used as association criteria/sync points. In this process, the functions are sorted based on the assigned tags and the ones with similar tags are analyzed side by side. This technique was specifically helpful in synchronizing the disassembly of Citadel versus Zeus. Figure 8 depicts the detected functionality tags. The pie chart sectors are proportional to the number of assembly functions categorized under the same functionality group. The NET tag was assigned to 60 functions related to low-level socks.

Table 3. RE-Source analysis results

	Assembly Functions	Functionality tags	Malware API	Tagged Functions	Source URLs	Matched Projects	Imported Functions	Unicode Strings
Citadel 1.3.5.1	788	652	173	318	293	81	386	917
Zeus 2.1.0.1	565	461	149	250	185	56	350	955

Also, 41 functions were tagged with CRT (critical section objects) for mutual exclusion synchronization. Similarly, 36 FIL tags were assigned to file manipulating functions. The other tags such as crypto, hashing, search and code injection were also identified during the analysis. The CRY (crypto) and HSH (hashing) tags provided an easy way of disassembly synchronization between Citadel and Zeus as the slight differences between the assembly files had no effect on the overall functionality group.

Translated into quantifiable terms, Table 3 shows the output of *RE-Source* for Citadel vs. Zeus comparison. The numbers are reported in accordance with occurrence of certain features such as the number of assembly functions, API and functionality tags, common API in malware, number of matched opens source components, imported function calls, and Unicode strings. The results imply that the framework has been successful in revealing the internal components of the malware. The final outcome of assembly to source code matching is a list of source files along side the description from the malware dictionary. These information provide valuable insights into the potential functionality of the malicious code and facilitate the analysis.

5.3 Binary Clone Analysis

The malware analysis process can be accelerated by identifying and removing the previously analyzed code fragments. The aim of binary clone analysis is to compare the assembly file of a new binary sample with a repository of analyzed code. The result of this analysis is a set of matched *clones*. In this context, we rely on the *RE-Clone* binary clone detector tool [8] that implements an improved version of the clone detector framework proposed in [9]. *RE-Clone* considers the same problem definition, that is the *exact* and *inexact* clone detection, as stated in [9]. Exact clones share the same assembly features, i.e., mnemonics, operands and registers. The only difference is in memory addresses. Inexact clones can be regarded as equal up to a certain level of abstraction, which means the number of common features must be greater than a certain threshold. The analysis parameters such as search window size, normalization level and detection algorithm play a significant role on the analysis results. These parameters are set according to each analysis scenario. After marking the detected code fragments as clones,

Fig. 9. Code analysis after clone elimination

Table 4. Binary clone detection results

Malware Bot.exe	Functions	Window Size	Exact Clones	Inexact Clones
Citadel 1.3.5.1	788	15	526	1876
Zeus 2.1.0.1	565			

the analysis focus is shifted to non-analyzed and new code segments. The core components of the Zeus malware has been thoroughly studied in [6]. Also, the source and binary files are available online. Therefore, a new Zeus variant can be compared against the existing files in order to measure the similarity and detect the potential exact and inexact clones. This analysis is also applicable to finding the additional functions of the new malware variant. Table 4 shows the results of the binary clone matching process. The samples share 526 exact binary clones with a window size of 15 instructions. In other words, almost %93 of Zeus assembly code also appears in Citadel. These clones form approximately %67 of the Citadel binary. This analysis highlights the remaining %33 of the Citadel assembly to be analyzed. Thus, a significant amount of time is saved by disregarding the clones. *RE-Clone* shows the address of each clone in the disassembly. Furthermore, the remaining functions can be examined in *RE-Source* before the manual analysis process is begun by the reverse engineer. This approach is depicted in Fig 9. The 1876 inexact clones reported by the tool include multiple combinations of regions that also contain the exact clones.

An interesting example of crypt-related clones is the detection of an inexact clone in the RC4 function that is used for encrypting the C&C network traffic. There are a few extra assembly instructions in the Citadel version of the RC4 function. This clone was found with a threshold of 0.8 and a two-combination inexact clone search method. In this approach, each two-combination of features are considered as a cluster. If more than %80 of regions appear in the same clusters, then they are treated as inexact clones.

6   Threat Mitigation by Sinkholing

In June 2013, Microsoft Digital Crimes Unit reported on an operation known as *Operation b54*, in collaboration with FBI to shut down Citadel C&C servers [14]. As a result of this operation, 1400 Citadel botnets around the world were interrupted and redirected to sinkhole servers controlled by Microsoft. A comprehensive list of the domain names is available in [16]. Although, the operation has significantly disrupted Citadel botnets and has reduced the threat levels, it has also affected the honeypot systems that were used for identifying and locating the malware creators and distributors. Even though the threat counter-measurement has been successful, cyber criminals can still operate by infecting new machines and controlling their bots using alternative servers.

7   Related Work

AnhLab [11], presented a comprehensive static analysis of Citadel malware. To the authors' knowledge, this report is the most complete analysis on Citadel malware which has been released so far. The process of infection, the structure of the malware binary, and malware's main functionalities and features are explained in details in this technical report. The report gives valuable insights on the malware and its capabilities, however, the methodology and steps that were taken for reaching the outcomes were not discussed. Also, although it is mentioned in the report that Citadel is remarkably similar to Zeus, the precise quantification of their similarity is not provided. Only approximate resemblance percentages is given without any details. To compare our analysis to this work, we provided a new methodology for reverse engineering malware by adopting clone-based analysis. Following our methodology, we concisely explained the steps we took in reverse engineering Citadel and insights that we obtained through our study.

SophosLabs [12], provided a brief report on Citadel malware. The major enhancements occurred in Citadel comparing to Zeus is explained in high-level and very briefly in this report. No explanation was provided about the process of reverse engineering the malware and how the authors gained those insights. Indeed, this report gave a decent overview about the Citadel malware without digging into the details. CERT Polska [13], also provided a technical report on Citadel malware. Similar to the previously mentioned report, this report was high-level and goes through the main features of Citadel without providing details. The reports mainly provided statistics focusing on the impact of the malware and its geographical distribution. The statistics were gathered based on the traffic to the sinkhole server after the domain had been taken down.

By leveraging the tools developed in our security lab, we quantified the similarity between Zeus and Citadel malware. These results could be further refined by integrating other existing techniques designed to automate malware analysis. For instance, our binary clone detector could be extended with a CFG-like dimension. For this purpose, we could benefit from the model proposed in [21] which aims to identify the common code fragments between two executable files and analyze the CFG subgraphs containing these fragments.

8   Conclusion

The Citadel malware targets confidential data and financial transactions. It is an emergent threat against the online privacy and security. Citadel reverse engineering is challenging as it is equipped with anti-reverse engineering techniques for hindering the malware analysis process. As the number of incidents entailing new malware attacks are increasing, agile approaches are required for obtaining the analysis results in a timely fashion. The malware reverse engineering process consists of two major stages of static and dynamic analysis. This process can be accelerated and enhanced by adding a new dimension for clone analysis. Instead of initiating the process from the scratch, a quick clone-based analysis can easily highlight the similarities and differences between two samples of the same family. The analysis focus is then shifted to the differing sections. We have presented a methodology along with the tools and techniques for analyzing the Citadel malware. Also, we have compared Citadel with its predecessor, Zeus. The similarities have been quantified as the result of two code matching techniques namely assembly to source, and binary code matching. The same methodology can be applied to other malware samples for providing insights into the potential malware functionality. The results of the malware analysis process can be added to a local code repository and used as a reference for measuring the similarities between future samples. They can also be used for improving the accuracy of the results. Overall, the successful completion of our objectives has led to underline best practices for supporting real-world malware analysis scenarios.

Acknowledgments. The authors would like to thank ESET Canada for their collaboration and acknowledge the support of Mr. Pierre-Marc Bureau and the guidance provided by Mr. Marc-Etienne Leveille on de-obfuscation.

A   Appendix

A.1   Example of Source Code Clones

See Fig. 10

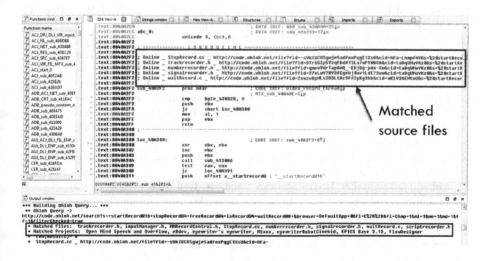

Fig. 10. The output of RE-Source pointing to video capture source code

References

1. Sikorski, M., Honig, A.: Practical Malware Analysis, The Hands-On Guide to Dissecting Malicious Software. No Starch Press, San Francisco (2012)
2. Seitz, J.: Gray Hat Python: Python Programming for Hackers and Reverse Engineers. No Starch Press, San Francisco (2009)
3. Malware Forensics Field Guide for Windows Systems: Digital Forensics Field Guides. Waltham: Syngress (2012)
4. Eagle, C.: The IDA Pro book : The Unofficial Guide to the World's Most Popular Disassembler. No Starch Press, San Francisco (2011)
5. Singh, A.: Identifying Malicious Code Through Reverse Engineering (Advances in Information Security). Springer, New York (2009)
6. Binsalleeh, H., Ormerod, T., Boukhtouta, A., Sinha, P., Youssef, A., Debbabi, M., Wang, L.: On the analysis of the zeus botnet crimeware toolkit. In: International Conference on Privacy Security and Trust (PST), Ottawa (2010)
7. Rahimian, A., Charland, P., Preda, S., Debbabi, M.: RESource: a framework for online matching of assembly with open source code. In: Garcia-Alfaro, J., Cuppens, F., Cuppens-Boulahia, N., Miri, A., Tawbi, N. (eds.) FPS 2012. LNCS, vol. 7743, pp. 211–226. Springer, Heidelberg (2013)
8. Charland, P., Fung, B.C.M., Farhadi, M. R.: Clone search for malicious code correlation. In: ATO RTO Symposium on Information Assurance and Cyber Defense (IST-111), Koblenz (2012)
9. Saebjornsen, A., Willcock, J., Panas, T., Quinlan, D., Su, Z.: Detecting code clones in binary executables. In: International Symposium on Software Testing and Analysis (ISSTA), Chicago (2009)
10. Sherstobitoff, R.: Inside the World of the Citadel Trojan. McAfee (2013)
11. AnhLab ASEC: Malware Analysis: Citadel. http://seifreed.es/docs/Citadel%20Troja%20Report_eng.pdf (December 2012). Accessed May 2013
12. Wyke, J.: The Citadel Crimeware Kit - Under the Microscope. http://nakedsecurity.sophos.com/2012/12/05/the-citadel-crimeware-kit-under-the-microscope/ (December 2012). Accessed May 2013
13. CERT Polska: Takedown of the plitfi Citadel botnet. www.cert.pl/PDF/Report_Citadel_plitfi_EN.pdf (April 2013). Accessed May 2013
14. Microsoft Digital Crimes Unit: Microsoft, financial services and others join forces to combat massive cybercrime ring. http://www.microsoft.com/en-us/news/Press/2013/Jun13/06-05DCUPR.aspx (June 2013). Accessed June 2013
15. Vincent, J.: $500 million botnet Citadel attacked by Microsoft and the FBI: Joint operation identified more than 1000 botnets, but operations continue. http://www.independent.co.uk/life-style/gadgets-and-tech/news/500-million-botnet-citadel-attacked-by-microsoft-and-the-fbi-8647594.html (June 2013). Accessed June 2013
16. List of Domain Names by Registry (Citadel). http://botnetlegalnotice.com/citadel/files/Compl_App_A.pdf (June 2013)
17. Milletary, J.: Citadel Trojan Malware Analysis. Dell SecureWorks (2012)
18. Immunity Debugger: The Best of Both Worlds, Immunity. http://www.immunityinc.com/products-immdbg.shtml (2013)
19. IDA Pro: Multi-processor Disassembler and Debugger, Hex-Rays. https://www.hex-rays.com/products/ida/debugger/index.shtml (2013)

20. The Volatility Framework: Volatile Memory (RAM) Artifact Extraction Utility Framework, Volatile Systems. https://www.volatilesystems.com/default/volatility (2013)
21. Bonfante, G., Marion, J., Sabatier, F., Thierry, A.: Code Synchronization by morphological analysis. In: International Conference on Malicious and Unwanted Software (MALWARE), Washington (2012)

The Carna Botnet Through the Lens
of a Network Telescope

Erwan Le Malécot$^{(\boxtimes)}$ and Daisuke Inoue

National Institute of Information and Communications Technology (NICT),
4-2-1 Nukui-Kitamachi, Koganei, Tokyo 184-8795, Japan
{lemalecot,dai}@nict.go.jp

Abstract. Earlier this year (2013), a massive dataset advertised as containing the result of a year-long exhaustive scan of the entire IPv4 address space was anonymously released into the wild under the rather provocative "Internet Census 2012" designation. While the subject matter of that dataset was in itself controversial, it was made even more so by the fact that its covert instigator also claimed to have temporarily assembled a 420 thousand nodes strong botnet from presumably unsecured embedded devices so as to perform the scan (aka the "Carna" botnet). In this paper, we relate our attempt to confirm the validity of that intriguing story based on the forensic analysis of the network traffic captured by our network telescope for the corresponding period of time (i.e. April 2012 to December 2012), share some of the observations that we made doing so and further discuss the potential repercussions of the creation and disclosure of such dataset.

Keywords: Internet · Reconnaissance · Network monitoring · Security · Traffic analysis · Ethics

1 Introduction

On March 2013, an anonymous researcher discreetly released a massive dataset for download, claiming it to be the product of a year-long effort of repeatedly and methodically scanning the entire IPv4 address space through an extensive mix of probing techniques [1]. That dataset totals 9TB of raw records purportedly collected over a period spanning from April 2012 to December 2012 and, if genuine, provides a rare peek into the composition and dynamics of the (publicly reachable) Internet. It, however, comes with a catch: in the notes attached to the release and a longer paper detailing its "back-story" [2], the same researcher readily admits to having built a 420 thousand nodes strong botnet (that he baptized "Carna") from inadequately protected embedded devices in order to perform his study. That peculiar aspect obviously raises some questions regarding the ethics of exploring/exploiting the resulting dataset for research purposes. Still, as operators of a relatively large network telescope monitoring unsolicited

J.-L. Danger et al. (Eds.): FPS 2013, LNCS 8352, pp. 426–441, 2014.
DOI: 10.1007/978-3-319-05302-8_26, © Springer International Publishing Switzerland 2014

traffic being sent over the Internet to unused space, it is rather difficult to turn a blind eye on it.

In this paper, we mainly report on a number of interesting observations that we were able to make regarding the Carna botnet and its modus operandi through the combined analysis of the published dataset and of actual traffic data captured by the sensors making up our network telescope. The main take-away is that the Carna dataset is most probably authentic with the anonymous researcher providing a fairly candid description of the way he proceeded to collect the data it incorporates, notably on the subject of the tools he used. In particular, we observed a significant amount of probing traffic in our captured data that specifically matched features advertised in the Carna paper (or that could be easily inferred from it). We also briefly examine the latent ramifications of the Carna release, trying to gauge its impact from various perspectives.

The remainder of this paper is organized as follows. In Sect. 2, we introduce the background of our study, providing more detailed information regarding the nature of our network telescope and the contents of the Carna dataset. In Sect. 3, we further reflect on our motivation(s) for performing that study in light of such background. In Sect. 4, we present the results of the rather extensive analysis that we conducted of the Carna dataset. In Sect. 5, we discuss those results and certain additional aspects linked to the study of the Carna botnet (e.g. ethical concerns). Finally, in Sect. 6, we conclude on our work.

2   Background and Definitions

2.1   Darknets (Related Work)

The way the Internet was initially designed makes it so that any connected host can freely and effortlessly send traffic directed to any IP address (cf. notion of end-to-end connectivity). It has certainly proved to be instrumental in the rapid growth of the Internet but has also led to a situation where IP(v4) addresses are now continuously targeted by a fair amount of unsolicited traffic, ranging from benign artifacts resulting from misconfiguration to malicious scanning activity and infection attempts [3,4]. A rather simple way to single out that unsolicited traffic for study is by monitoring unused address space. A continuous portion of address space dedicated to that usage is then commonly called a "darknet" [5], and, while definitions vary in the academic literature, we use the term "network telescope" to designate a collection of darknets operated by a common entity.

The network telescope that we operate presently amounts to approximately 210 thousand unused IPv4 addresses spread over the networks of a number of partner organizations (located in Japan and abroad). Those unused addresses form darknets ranging in size from a few addresses to whole /16 subnets (i.e. blocks of IPv4 addresses sharing the same first 16 bits). It is also useful to introduce the notion of "greynet" which is a subnet of a given size that is composed of a mixture of used and unused IP addresses (i.e. not entirely "dark"). Obviously, a greynet can be broken down into a collection of smaller darknets yet it makes administration easier to consider them as a whole. For this study, we mainly relied on the data captured by two of our largest sensors, a /16 darknet (aka S0) and a /16 greynet (aka S1). We also made use of the data captured by another /16 greynet (aka S2) for validation purposes but did not incorporate it in the presented results. The reason is that while the makeup of sensor S1 (i.e. the size of its dark sections and their positioning) was kept relatively stable over the course of the Carna "incident", for sensor S2 it varied heavily making it difficult to extract clean statistics. Regarding the data itself, we passively capture all the incoming traffic to the unused IP addresses "leased" to us, traffic that is then saved and stored in the pcap format pending further investigation (cf. packet header information plus its payload when applicable).

It is to be noted that there exist several other comparable public efforts to monitor Internet activity through the use of large-scale darknets/greynets (and probably many more unadvertised ones). The most prominent example is the long-standing "UCSD Network Telescope" project overseen by the Cooperative Association for Internet Data Analysis (CAIDA) which, according to published documentation, consists in the monitoring of a lightly populated /8 network segment [6,7]. Although it no longer appears to be active, another work of significance is the "Internet Motion Sensor" put together by researchers from the University of Michigan [8]. It consisted in a highly distributed and fairly large network telescope with a twist in that it selectively responded to some traffic in order to elicit further interactions from remote hosts (in contrast with our totally passive approach). Finally, we should mention the enduring efforts of the Team Cymru group [9] and of the Arbor Networks corporation (apparently a spin-off from the research having been conducted at the University of Michigan [10]).

2.2   Carna Dataset

The Carna dataset was originally released by its creator in a highly compressed form (using the cutting edge zpaq tool [11]) and distributed through the BitTorrent peer-to-peer protocol. The 568 GB bundle includes some metadata, the content of the website put online by the anonymous researcher to publicize his work and, of course, the "output" of his probing activity. The main logs are first organized into folders each standing for a type of probing (e.g. /data/icmp_ping/) and then subdivided into files each standing for a particular /8 network segment (e.g. /data/icmp_ping/1.zpaq). Predictably missing from the logs are the segments officially reserved for private networks (i.e. 10.0.0.0/8, 172.16.0.0/12 and 192.168.0.0/16) and other specific usages (i.e. 127.0.0.0/8, 224.0.0.0/4 and 240.0.0.0/4). That organization makes the dataset rather straightforward to explore and manipulate, the only hurdle being the time and resources it takes to uncompress desired files (cf. up to several hours for a single log file).

Regarding the probing activity itself, the anonymous researcher indicates that he relied on slightly modified versions of "off-the-shelf" open source software, namely: the fping and nmap tools, and some simple wrapping code around the libevent library. Arming the Carna botnet with these tools and enlisting the traceroute utility sometimes found on subverted devices, he eventually performed the following scans (cf. reusing his nomenclature [2]):

- ICMP Ping (fping): consists in sending an ICMP echo request packet to a target IP address; receiving a response indicates that the corresponding host is "up and running".
- Reverse DNS (libevent): queries the DNS infrastructure for the domain name associated with a target IP address.
- Hostprobes (nmap): consists in sending a predetermined "cocktail" of packets to a target IP address to test if it is in use (cf. slightly more sophisticated "Ping scanning").
- Syncscans (nmap): consists in sending a TCP SYN packet to a target port (i.e. trying to open a connection to that port) to assess its status [12,13].
- Serviceprobes (nmap): consists in sending more specialized traffic (i.e. including payloads) to an open TCP/UDP port in an attempt to deduce the service running on it [14].
- TCP IP Fingerprints & IP ID Sequence (nmap): consists in sending a controlled series of packets to a target IP address in an attempt to guess the Operating System (OS) the corresponding host is running (cf. exploiting some discriminating features of the triggered responses [15]).
- Traceroute (traceroute): reveals the network path leading to a target IP address by modulating the Time-To-Live (TTL) value of packets sent to it (eliciting diagnostic messages from intermediate routers).

With the exception of the somehow indirect "Reverse DNS" variant, all those scanning techniques are bound to have left a trace into the traffic logs of our network telescope if employed against one of its dark pieces. We will return to that point in Sect. 4 when detailing the results of our forensic study.

2.3 Botnets

Before going further, we should also briefly discuss botnets [16] and how the Carna botnet fits into that genus. A botnet can be defined as a collection of network-connected devices collaboratively acting under the command of a single entity or so-called "botmaster". Nowadays, botnets are for the most part assembled illegally by compromising vulnerable devices and then leveraged to perform malicious activity (i.e. DDoS attacks, spamming/phishing campaigns, click fraud, etc.) giving the term a rather negative connotation. When trying to characterize/classify such illegal botnets, the main criteria usually considered are their mode of recruitment and their organizing architecture.

Starting with the first criterion, the "traditional" way for malicious botmasters to acquire new bots is by exploiting a remote vulnerability in the software running on targeted devices to covertly install their own controlling software on them (i.e. through the network). The Carna botnet was allegedly constructed employing another basic method: by trying a number of "trivial" username/password combinations against the Telnet remote login service occasionally found running on connected devices for management purposes and, in case of success, simply installing the bot software via that channel. In that aspect, it is reminiscent of the "Chuck Norris" botnet that made the news in early

2010 [17], and of the even earlier "Psyb0t" worm. Indeed, those two pieces of malware also propagated by brute-forcing Telnet credentials, albeit trying a much larger number of combinations against their targets (mainly routers).

Regarding the infrastructure sustaining the Carna botnet, the anonymous researcher touts it as "C&C less" meaning that, contrary to classic botnets, the nodes of his botnet are not required to "call back home" to a central location to receive instructions: exploiting the fact that by construction all of his bots are reachable from the Internet, the botmaster instead directly connects to them to push his commands. While the Carna paper is rather scarce in details, it appears to be roughly based on a 2-tier architecture with an upper layer of "servent" nodes (i.e. serving both as server and client) composed of the most powerful compromised devices and a lower layer of client nodes solely in charge of performing scans (cf. it somehow resemble the hybrid architecture proposed by Wang et al. although heavily simplified by removing the peer-to-peer component of the upper layer [18]). Each client node is then apparently instructed to report and upload the result of its activity to a given set of servent nodes to be later retrieved by the botmaster. In practice, such strategy also has the intended benefit of shielding the botmaster from takedown as he can be kept mobile.

Although we could not directly observe interactions between nodes with our setup, some of the traffic that hit our network telescope was indeed consistent with that depiction (cf. in particular Sect. 4.5).

3   Motivation

As mentioned earlier on, the Carna story initially attracted our attention for the rather close relationship it shared with our passive Internet traffic monitoring project. At first, our principal motivations for retrieving and examining the Carna dataset were (1) to determine its accuracy (i.e. was the published data correct and, if so, to which point?) and, more interestingly, (2) to verify the truthfulness of the corresponding allegations (i.e. were scans really performed to produce the data?). Indeed, given the anonymous nature of the source, there was a non-negligible chance for the whole thing to be no more than an elaborate hoax. What's more, while any system administrator could compare the actual layout of his network with the information contained in the Carna dataset and partially respond to (1), with our network telescope we were among the few people with access to data that could address (2). We quickly confirmed that the darknets constituting our network telescope were in fact being correctly reported as unresponsive IP address space in the logs of the Carna dataset. A preliminary look at our traffic logs then revealed noticeable spikes in the number of unique IP addresses sending certain types of "conventional" scanning probes for the time periods when the Carna botnet was reportedly active (cf. Sect. 4.3).

All in all, it sent a rather strong signal that the Carna story was actually real and that its instigator had done what he claimed to have had done. As a consequence, we decided to spend some more time investigating that matter. In particular, we wanted to verify if, given the information provided in the dataset and the corresponding paper, it was possible to accurately identify and extract the probes sent by the Carna bots from the surrounding "noise" in our logs. Success would enable us to gain further insight into the way the scans were coordinated and performed, which in turn could provide us with some clues about the structure of the Carna botnet and its global behavior. To tell the truth, although the anonymous researcher offered a rather comprehensive overview of his modus operandi, we were left slightly unsatisfied by the lack of details regarding certain practical aspects. The next section summarizes our findings.

4 Analysis

4.1 Preliminary Remarks

In a way, we ended up conducting a rather conventional "botnet case study" from the traffic logs captured by our network telescope, with the unusual difference that this time we were also provided with partial information regarding what to look for and what to expect. Such conditions manifestly simplify our forensic work but they also lead to some complications inherent to the use of darknets. Indeed, the value of darknets (and other network-based sensors such as honeypots/honeynets [19]) lies to a certain degree in their locations being kept confidential so as to prevent attackers from targeting them with pollution, or from simply avoiding them. Clearly, the public disclosure of detailed information about the traffic received by a darknet increases the risk for it to be uncovered by an investigative person, more so if it was specifically targeted with dedicated uncloaking probes [20]. With its open release and presumably wide distribution, the Carna dataset basically magnifies the "problem" allowing anyone to mine the data for revealing signs. Therefore, it makes it somehow challenging to communicate results without accidentally giving away "too much". In this paper, we tried to strike a fair balance between the amount of disclosure and concealment steps taken to protect our network telescope.

Another delicate issue is the assortment of ethical questions surrounding the Carna dataset, and in particular, touching upon its exploration. We will discuss those questions further in Sect. 5.2 but, from the outset, we should call attention to the fact that by respect for such concerns we restricted ourselves to the examination of the parts of the dataset matching the IP address space covered by our network telescope for this initial study.[1]

4.2 Basic Strategy

The Carna dataset provides the following pieces of information for each scanning probe that is reported: the IP address targeted by the probe, a timestamp dating the probe, and some text describing (or encoding) the outcome of the scan.

---

[1] To be entirely correct, we also briefly peeked into the data concerning a series of arbitrary selected unrelated subnets in order to roughly confirm the "universality" of some of the observations that we made based on our restricted dataset.

At first glance, it seems to be more than enough to accurately (and automatically) identify matching traffic in our logs. However, the timestamp information happens to be quite problematic. For one thing, it is relatively coarse with values ostensibly adjusted to coincide with a time resolution of 15 min (i.e. the interval between two consecutive timestamps is, as far as we looked, always a multiple of 15 min). And slightly more troublesome, there are no indications in the Carna paper as to what that timestamp information actually refers to: it may be the time the scanning probe was sent, the time a conclusion was reached about the status of the targeted address/port, the time the data was collected by one of the servent nodes, etc. All things considered, only the destination IP address comes across as being truly reliable for matching purposes.

The traffic reaching our network telescope is eventually collected/organized by sensor and archived as daily binary dumps. Considering the above description, we first relied on the following crude strategy: (1) pick up a sample of successive scanning records (cf. ordering by timestamp and filtering by subnet) from the Carna dataset, (2) for each record, use the timestamp to select the "closest" daily dump from our archive and extract from it the traffic having for destination the stated IP address (and matching the protocol presumably used for the probes when applicable), (3) extract all the source IP addresses responsible for that traffic, (4) manually inspect the traffic sent by those sources during the same time frame (i.e. one day period). Surprisingly, it often yielded a fairly small number of sources and by repeating that procedure a few times, we were usually able to single out sources surfacing multiple times and/or sending traffic sharing very similar characteristics (i.e. very likely to belong to the Carna botnet). The review of those characteristics then enabled us to develop signatures that we later used to automatically seek potential Carna bots...

4.3   Host Probes

We decided to start our investigation of the Carna dataset by concentrating on the so-called "hostprobe" scans for we suspected that their verbosity would make them fairly easy to pick up from the logs of our network telescope (cf. reliance on multiple distinct packets). In particular, the anonymous researcher provides the following description in the Carna paper:

> "Before doing a sync scan Nmap did hostprobes to determine if the host was alive. The Nmap hostprobe sends an ICMP echo request, a TCP SYN packet to port 443, a TCP ACK packet to port 80, and an ICMP timestamp request."

Making use of the previously introduced "searching strategy", we eventually located hosts sending traffic to our sensors that matched that particular sequence of packets at dates/times compatible with the information contained in the Carna dataset. However, we also noticed that in most occasions, the components making up the probes were duplicated. That is, the sources that we identified as being part of the Carna botnet were instead relying on the sequence: 2 ICMP echo requests, 2 TCP SYN packets to port 443, etc. Further inspection showed that those "doublets" were not the product of retransmission mechanisms but rather intentional, which is actually consistent with the default behavior of the stock nmap tool (at least in its recent iterations). We then proceeded with the extraction of the number of hostprobes being sent daily to our network telescope along with the number of unique sources/hosts responsible for sending those (cf. we searched our traffic logs for the complete "doubled" sequence of packets ignoring incomplete ones). Figure 1 represents that information for sensor S0 (cf. top graph of each pair) and sensor S1 (cf. bottom graphs). Additionally, we displayed through greyed areas on the graphs the "official" periods of hostprobe scanning activity of the Carna botnet as derived from the "data.tsv" global summary file distributed with the Carna bundle.

From that figure, we can first observe that both sensors were/are almost continuously sprinkled with hostprobe-like probes, meaning that the nmap tool is likely used by a number of different entities to sporadically scan the Internet (cf. some trouble prevented sensor S0 from collecting traffic between April 28 and May 16 explaining the wide gap observed for that period). However, the main point is that it shows significant surges in the number of unique scanning sources targeting our sensors for many of the days flagged as "Carna active". Although not entirely conclusive, it gives further credence to the physical reality of the Carna botnet.

4.4 ICMP Ping

We then considered the slightly more challenging case of the "ICMP ping" probes. What makes them less accommodating is the sheer amount of such probes being sent to our network telescope (e.g. hundreds of thousands per day for sensor S0). To draw a parallel with the precedent case, here is how the anonymous researcher describes the ICMP ping probes in the Carna paper:

> "A modified version of fping was used to send ICMP ping requests to every IP address. We did fast scans where we probed the IPv4 address space within a day, as well as a long term scan where the IP address space was probed for 6 weeks on a rate of approximately one scan of the complete IPv4 address space every few days."

That description already provides a number of useful clues that could be exploited for the identification of traffic generated by the Carna botnet (cf. the usage of a customized tool and the reference to two different scanning patterns). However, we later found a much more revealing criteria "hidden" within the Carna dataset itself. For illustration purposes, Fig. 2 reproduces an excerpt of the logs provided for the ICMP ping probes, albeit with rows reordered differently (i.e. numerical sort on the timestamp column). The important point to notice is that successive IP addresses occasionally happen to be separated by the same numerical difference (cf. 11229 in that particular case). Separately, the anonymous researcher indicates in the Carna paper that scanning instructions

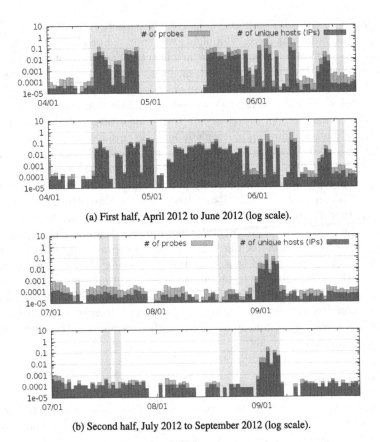

(a) First half, April 2012 to June 2012 (log scale).

(b) Second half, July 2012 to September 2012 (log scale).

Fig. 1. Daily count of the number of hostprobes received by sensor S0 (cf. top) and sensor S1 (cf. bottom), and of the number of unique sending hosts (both normalized to the sizes of the sensors).

sent to bots included a "step width" that was then exploited by them to generate their lists of targets. Could those two aspects somehow (not) be related?

Again making use of the basic strategy introduced in Sect. 4.2, but this time armed with the aforementioned observations, we thus went hunting for potential "Carna traffic" in the logs of our network telescope (filtered to only include ICMP echo request packets for this task). Before long, we came across a number of sources sending traffic mirroring the pattern depicted on Fig. 3 (aka P1), that is to say, sequentially sending a single probing packet to a series of targets, then repeating the exact same scenario two more times at rapid intervals. Interestingly, the targeted IP addresses were consistently separated by a common step (cf. "$(C - B) = (B - A)$" for Fig. 3), step that was also often found being reused by multiple sources active during the same time interval.

A more detailed inspection of the packets sent by sources matching scanning pattern P1 revealed that those packets actually shared distinctive values for

1.1.33.44	1333493100	unreachable
1.1.77.9	1333493100	unreachable
1.1.120.230	1333493100	unreachable
1.1.164.195	1333493100	unreachable
1.1.208.160	1333493100	alive, 42508

Fig. 2. Head of the file "/data/icmp_ping/1", sorted first by timestamp and then by IP address.

```
00:00:00.000 IP (tos 0x0, ttl 43, id 0, offset 0, flags [DF], proto ICMP (1),
        length 84) #.#.#.# > A: ICMP echo request, id #, seq #, length 64
00:00:00.025 IP #.#.#.# > B: ICMP echo request, id #, seq #, length 64
00:00:00.037 IP #.#.#.# > C: ICMP echo request, id #, seq #, length 64
00:00:24.253 IP #.#.#.# > A: ICMP echo request, id #, seq #, length 64
00:00:00.031 IP #.#.#.# > B: ICMP echo request, id #, seq #, length 64
00:00:00.031 IP #.#.#.# > C: ICMP echo request, id #, seq #, length 64
00:00:24.146 IP #.#.#.# > A: ICMP echo request, id #, seq #, length 64
00:00:00.033 IP #.#.#.# > B: ICMP echo request, id #, seq #, length 64
00:00:00.036 IP #.#.#.# > C: ICMP echo request, id #, seq #, length 64
```

Fig. 3. ICMP ping probes, (rapid) interleaved scanning pattern (cf. heavily sanitized and reformatted version of the output produced by the "tcpdump" tool for one of the instances of that pattern). The time information indicates the delta between consecutive packets (cf. "-ttt" option).

certain fields at the IP protocol level. In particular, they all had the "Don't Fragment" (DF) flag on, the "Identification" field set to 0 and a total packet length of 84 bytes, which translated into the Berkeley Packet Filter (BPF) syntax produces the following signature: $ip[2:2]=84$ and $ip[4:2]=0$ and $ip[6]=64$ and $icmp[0]=8$. The use of that signature in combination with information from the Carna dataset led us to the discovery of sources following a slightly different scanning pattern (aka P2) as illustrated in Fig. 4. That second pattern then consisted in the sending of 3 ICMP echo request packets in rapid succession to each targeted IP address with a pause of several minutes before jumping to the next target. And, at the difference of pattern P1, the list of successive targets did not follow a regular progression (cf. no discernible step).

Finally, to estimate the accuracy of the previously introduced packet signature, we extracted all traffic matching it from the logs of sensor S0 and computed the daily count of the number of unique {source IP, destination IP} pairs reported in that traffic (aka C1). In parallel, we also produced the daily count of ICMP ping probes sent by the Carna botnet to the corresponding address range based on the logs of the Carna dataset (aka C2). When plotted, the graphs for count C1 and count C2 ended up being eerily similar except for a few data points. In order to highlight similitudes/divergences, we then drew the quotient between both counts (cf. $C1/C2$, no value when C2 is null) and their normalized difference (cf. $(C1 - C2)/2^{16}$). The resulting graph is represented on Fig. 5. In similar fashion to Fig. 1, we also greyed out purported periods of activity of the Carna botnet, only this time we relied directly on C2 to do so.

```
00:00:00.000 IP (tos 0x0, ttl 45, id 0, offset 0, flags [DF], proto ICMP (1),
     length 84) #.#.#.# > A: ICMP echo request, id #, seq #, length 64
00:00:23.831 IP #.#.#.# > A: ICMP echo request, id #, seq #, length 64
00:00:23.676 IP #.#.#.# > A: ICMP echo request, id #, seq #, length 64
00:08:36.538 IP #.#.#.# > B: ICMP echo request, id #, seq #, length 64
00:00:23.985 IP #.#.#.# > B: ICMP echo request, id #, seq #, length 64
00:00:23.960 IP #.#.#.# > B: ICMP echo request, id #, seq #, length 64
00:08:38.317 IP #.#.#.# > C: ICMP echo request, id #, seq #, length 64
00:00:23.911 IP #.#.#.# > C: ICMP echo request, id #, seq #, length 64
00:00:23.836 IP #.#.#.# > C: ICMP echo request, id #, seq #, length 64
```

Fig. 4. ICMP ping probes, (slow) sequential scanning pattern.

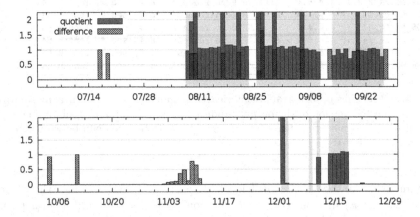

Fig. 5. Comparison between the amount of "Carna-like" ICMP ping probes received by sensor S0 (cf. as estimated from a generic packet signature) and the "actual" amount of such probes as reported by the Carna dataset.

A careful review of Fig. 5 brings to light a few interesting elements. First of all, the figure shows a number of isolated daily spikes between July and October that amount to approximately the size of our sensor (cf. normalized difference). A quick look at the corresponding traffic told us that those spikes were caused by scans most probably unrelated to the Carna botnet: we found them to be originating from hosts clustered in the same subnet and employing a very different strategy. However, the conspicuous "bump" in early November proved to be much more intriguing as the corresponding traffic actually showed the same characteristics as the one being sent by "confirmed" Carna bots (cf. patterns P1 and P2). It then suggests that the anonymous researcher might have conducted a few additional scanning campaigns with the Carna botnet that he then decided to leave out from his final account (i.e. the Carna dataset). To conclude, we may say that the packet signature allowed us to successfully catch most of the Carna traffic for this type of probe but not without generating a few false positives.

4.5 Service Probes

We also rapidly investigated the so-called "serviceprobe" scans and we can report that, as for the other probes that we detailed earlier on, we ended up finding matching traffic in the logs of our network telescope. As a matter of fact, those scans produced rather distinctive traffic patterns that were quite easy to pinpoint when looking at the daily distribution of targeted TCP/UDP ports from our darknets. In particular, we could observe TCP/UDP port numbers becoming, one after the other (and one at a time), the target of large pools of remote hosts. Plus, the "port progression" of that massive distributed scan turned out to be following the sequence given in the Carna paper, that is first concentrating on port 1, then 3, 7, 9, 13, etc. More interestingly, further inspection of some of the sources involved in those serviceprobe scans and notably the tracking of their activity over a longer span revealed that they also occasionally sent connection attempts to both TCP port 23 and TCP port 210. The traffic to port 23 (i.e. Telnet protocol) can easily be explained by the corresponding bots trying to propagate and that behavior is actually explicitly referenced in the Carna paper. As for port 210, the anonymous researcher makes no direct mention to that particular number but from the information that he provides about the operation of the Carna botnet, we can presume that it corresponds to the entry point used to remotely control the bots after their subversion.

5 Discussion

5.1 Results

While the study that we carried out is far from being completely exhaustive in terms of scope (cf. we omitted some of the scanning variants), it certainly shows that the Carna botnet was without doubt completely real and that there is some truth in the Carna dataset (cf. at least in the parts that we checked). Of course, there is also the fact that our network telescope only covers a relatively small portion of the entire IP address space. However, its distributed nature and relative anonymity gives us some confidence that we were not specifically targeted with some decoys and that our results are rather representative. It is also to be noted that the anonymous researcher does not appear to have particularly cared about making its scanning activity stealthy and rather seems to have focused on the simplicity aspect. It is especially apparent in that our darknets were still targeted by serviceprobes regardless of the fact that other types of scans (e.g. syncscans) were already indicating that it was most probably useless (i.e. no feedback loop to minimize the traffic sent by the botnet).

5.2 Ethical Questions

Research in computer security is by essence tightly ingrained with ethical questions as evidenced by the distinction being made between white hat and black hat hackers. And it is often difficult to draw a clean line between what constitutes appropriate/legitimate behavior and what does not [21,22]. In the case of the Carna story, the creation of a large-scale botnet from vulnerable devices to further ones means is obviously illegal but the anonymous researcher indicates that he attempted to be as unobtrusive as possible in doing so and, if trusting him with his words, did not exploit the resulting Carna botnet to conduct overtly malicious activity. In a way, it seems that the whole feat was more about proving a point – that there were/are many weakly protected devices connected to the Internet that might be exploited by evil-intentioned people for bad – than causing some harm, making the anonymous researcher something of a grey hat hacker. In any case, if it is not really our role to judge the conduct of the anonymous researcher (especially as little is known about his background and motivations), we are still left with the tricky issue of how to handle the Carna dataset.

First, there is the fundamental question of the rightfulness of retrieving that dataset for perusal. As indicated at the beginning of this paper, the anonymous researcher specifically released the Carna dataset publicly and further took some steps to facilitate its distribution ensuring a relatively widespread availability. That fact combined with the fact that it seemingly touched upon our network telescope project and could have nontrivial repercussions on the monitoring results that we derived from it (i.e. if proven real) led us to decide that it would be unwise to disregard that bundle of data. Moreover, based on the digest accompanying the release, it was also fair to assume that the contents of the Carna dataset could have important security implications for legitimate Internet users. Eventually, we reached the conclusion that the merits of investigating that matter further were outbalancing the risks incurred and proceeded with our study. In a way, it is not completely different from the conscientious choice made by numerous security researchers to capture and dissect malware samples so as to gain an edge on attackers and devise more effective countermeasures (and is similarly equivocal...).

Then, there are the questions surrounding the ensuing usage that is made of the Carna dataset. Indeed, that dataset constitutes an unprecedented amount of highly detailed and curated "intelligence" about the Internet, and the various subnets composing it. It then makes it possible to get a fairly good picture of the constitution of a target subnet, up to the kind of servers it hosts and the public services they provide (cf. the information produced by the "reverse DNS" and "serviceprobe" scans), picture which could then be exploited by malicious individuals fomenting an attack against that particular subnet. Extrapolating a little bit, it should even be possible to directly pinpoint vulnerable hosts provided that they displayed a signature distinct enough (e.g. a particular combination of open ports). Consequently, mining the Carna dataset as a whole for research purposes implies to first work out an appropriate disclosure policy to manage such sensitive discoveries. In order to stay clear of those "complications" for this initial paper on the subject, we decided to ignore parts of the Carna dataset that were not directly related to the ranges of IP addresses falling under our supervision, thus limiting potential impact on third-parties.

Nevertheless, one side effect of our study is that we eventually recovered the IP addresses of a significant number of devices that were at one point part of the Carna botnet and therefore vulnerable to the unsophisticated Telnet brute-force attack. It is quite difficult to estimate the current status of those devices (i.e. if they are still vulnerable or not, or even still active at all) from our passive stance and therefore we plan to keep those IP addresses confidential until we can find an ethically acceptable (and practical) way to deal with the situation.

5.3 Impact

In the previous section we mentioned that the Carna dataset could be exploited by malicious individuals to mount targeted attacks against designated networks. However, considering the vast amount of scanning traffic reaching our network telescope everyday, we can assume that determined attackers would probably find a way to get their hands on such information regardless. Furthermore, it also suggests that a number of entities are independently gathering data similar to the one included in the Carna dataset for their own private consumption (or even to selectively share it with peers as illustrated by the specialized "Shodan" search engine [23]). In that context, we believe that the real novelty/impact of the Carna story is that, to our knowledge, it constitutes the first time that such data is being circulated completely uncensored in the open (and in such quantity). It undeniably lowers the barrier of entry for people interested in the structure and composition of the Internet, may it be for malicious purposes as predominantly discussed thus far, or for benevolent ones. And we surely hope that, now that the cat is out of the bag, the Carna dataset will end up being used to do more good than evil (cf. the potential for progress is certainly more apparent there).

6 Conclusion

In this paper, we gave a comprehensive account of a preliminary study that we conducted about the Carna botnet (and associated dataset) based on the insight provided by the network traffic captured through our distributed network telescope. We eventually managed to find traces in our logs strongly suggesting that the Carna botnet was real and giving credence to the information disclosed by its alleged anonymous operator, notably regarding the modus operandi that he employed to effectively scan the entire IPv4 address space by means of that resource. Furthermore, we systematically managed to characterize the traffic being sent by nodes of the Carna botnet for several types of scanning activity. Each time, the characteristics that we discovered were consistent with the general description provided in the Carna paper for that particular scan, further comforting our initial assumptions. While certainly partial, our investigation ultimately convinced us of the authenticity of the Carna story. Finally, we also offered our thoughts regarding the validity of the results that we obtained, discussed ethical issues surrounding the study of the Carna dataset, and briefly considered its eventual impact on the status quo.

As for future work, we first plan to further extract and label all the traffic associated with the Carna botnet from the logs of our network telescope as we believe it could be used in the evaluation of data mining algorithms developed for automated botnet detection. It would also enable us to study global trends in the distribution of scanning hosts across our darknet sensors. Then, at the beginning of the Carna paper, the anonymous researcher alludes to a preparatory phase where he deployed his scanning tools to a limited number of subverted devices in order to test their effectiveness. Accordingly, we intend to investigate the traffic captured by our network telescope during the months preceding the official "outbreak" of the Carna botnet to see if we can uncover signs of that preparatory phase. It may also prove interesting to give a look at the data for later months (i.e. after the end of the period reported in the Carna dataset).

Acknowledgments. The authors would like to thank Jumpei Shimamura for his valuable comments and suggestions, and for the curating of some of the data used in this paper. Given the slightly controversial nature of this work, we should also stress that it was the subject of careful evaluation within our institution before publication.

References

1. Internet Census 2012: Port Scanning /0 using Insecure Embedded Devices - Carna Botnet (Release). http://seclists.org/fulldisclosure/2013/Mar/166 (2013)
2. Internet Census 2012: Port Scanning /0 Using Insecure Embedded Devices - Carna Botnet (Paper). http://internetcensus2012.bitbucket.org/ (2013)
3. Pang, R., Yegneswaran, V., Barford, P., Paxson, V., Peterson, L.: Characteristics of internet background radiation. In: Proceedings of the 4th ACM SIGCOMM Conference on Internet Measurement (IMC'04), New York, NY, USA, pp. 27–40. ACM (2004)
4. Wustrow, E., Karir, M., Bailey, M., Jahanian, F., Huston, G.: Internet background radiation revisited. In: Proceedings of the 10th ACM SIGCOMM Conference on Internet Measurement (IMC'10), New York, NY, USA, pp. 62–74. ACM (2010)
5. Bailey, M., Cooke, E., Jahanian, F., Myrick, A., Sinha, S.: Practical darknet measurement. In: Proceedings of the 40th Annual Conference on Information Sciences and Systems (CISS'06), Washington, DC, USA, pp. 1496–1501. IEEE Computer Society (2006)
6. Moore, D., Shannon, C., Voelker, G., Savage, S.: Network telescopes: technical report. Technical report, Cooperative Association for Internet Data Analysis (CAIDA) (July 2004)
7. CAIDA: The UCSD Network Telescope. http://www.caida.org/projects/network_telescope/ (2012)
8. Bailey, M., Cooke, E., Jahanian, F., Nazario, J., Watson, D.: The internet motion sensor: a distributed blackhole monitoring system. In: Proceedings of the 12th Annual Network and Distributed System Security Symposium (NDSS'05), pp. 167–179. The Internet Society (2005)
9. Team Cymru: The Darknet Project. https://www.team-cymru.org/Services/darknets.html (2013)
10. Arbor Networks: ATLAS Dashboard. http://atlas.arbor.net/ (2013)

11. Mahoney, M.: Zpaq. http://mattmahoney.net/dc/zpaq.html (2009)
12. de Vivo, M., Carrasco, E., Isern, G., de Vivo, G.O.: A review of port scanning techniques. SIGCOMM Comput. Commun. Rev. **29**(2), 41–48 (1999)
13. Le Malécot, E.: MitiBox: camouflage and deception for network scan mitigation. In: Proceedings of the 4th USENIX Workshop on Hot Topics in Security (HotSec'09), Berkeley, CA, USA, pp. 4:1–4:6. USENIX Association (2009)
14. Lyon, G.F.: Nmap Network Scanning: The Official Nmap Project Guide to Network Discovery and Security Scanning. Insecure, USA (2009)
15. Greenwald, L.G., Thomas, T.J.: Toward undetected operating system fingerprinting. In: Proceedings of the 1st USENIX Workshop on Offensive Technologies (WOOT'07), Berkeley, CA, USA, pp. 6:1–6:10. USENIX Association (2007)
16. Cooke, E., Jahanian, F., McPherson, D.: The zombie roundup: understanding, detecting, and disrupting botnets. In: Proceedings of the Steps to Reducing Unwanted Traffic on the Internet Workshop (SRUTI'05), Berkeley, CA, USA, pp. 39–44. USENIX Association (2005)
17. Čeleda, P., Krejčí, R., Vykopal, J., Drašar, M.: Embedded malware - an analysis of the Chuck Norris botnet. In: Proceedings of the 2010 European Conference on Computer Network, Defense (EC2ND), pp. 3–10 (2010)
18. Wang, P., Sparks, S., Zou, C.C.: An advanced hybrid peer-to-peer botnet. In: Proceedings of the 1st Workshop on Hot Topics in Understanding Botnets (Hot-Bots'07), Berkeley, CA, USA, pp. 2:1–2:9. USENIX Association (2007)
19. Provos, N.: A virtual honeypot framework. In: Proceedings of the 13th USENIX Security Symposium (SSYM'04), Berkeley, CA, USA, pp. 1:1–1:14. USENIX Association (2004)
20. Shinoda, Y., Ikai, K., Itoh, M.: Vulnerabilities of passive internet threat monitors. In: Proceedings of the 14th USENIX Security Symposium (SSYM'05), Berkeley, CA, USA, pp. 209–224. USENIX Association (2005)
21. Burstein, A.J.: Conducting cybersecurity research legally and ethically. In: Proceedings of the 1st Usenix Workshop on Large-Scale Exploits and Emergent Threats (LEET'08), Berkeley, CA, USA, pp. 8:1–8:8. USENIX Association (2008)
22. Bailey, M., Dittrich, D., Kenneally, E., Maughan, D.: The Menlo report. IEEE Secur. Priv. **10**(2), 71–75 (2012)
23. Matherly, J.: Shodan – Computer Search Engine. http://www.shodanhq.com/ (2009)

Author Index